A-Z LEEDS

CONTENTS

Key to Map Pages	2-3
Large Scale City Centre	4-5
Map Pages	6-59

Index to Streets, Towns,
Villages, Hospitals etc. and
selected Places of Interest — 60-112

REFERENCE

Motorway	**M1**
A Road	**A62**
B Road	**B6126**
Dual Carriageway	
One-way Street Traffic flow on A Roads is also indicated by a heavy line on the driver's left.	
Under Construction Road Opening dates are correct at the time of publication.	
Proposed Road	
Restricted Access	
Pedestrianized Road	
Leeds City Centre Loop Junction Numbers are shown on Large Scale Pages only	(1)
Track / Footpath	
Residential Walkway	
Railway	Station / Level Crossing / Heritage Sta. / Tunnel
Built-up Area	ALMA ST.
Local Authority Boundary	
Posttown Boundary	
Postcode Boundary (within Posttown)	
Map Continuation	**31** Large Scale City Centre **4**

Airport	✈
Car Park (selected)	P
Church or Chapel	†
Cycleway (selected)	⚲
Fire Station	■
Hospital	H
House Numbers (A & B Roads only)	13 / 8
Information Centre	ℹ
National Grid Reference	⁴30
Park & Ride	King Lane P+🚌
Police Station	▲
Post Office	★
Safety Camera with Speed Limit Fixed cameras and long term road works cameras Symbols do not indicate camera direction	(40)
Toilet: without facilities for the Disabled with facilities for the Disabled	▽ ▼
Educational Establishment	▢
Hospital or Healthcare Building	▢
Industrial Building	▢
Leisure or Recreational Facility	▢
Place of Interest	▢
Public Building	▢
Shopping Centre or Market	▢
Other Selected Buildings	▢

SCALE

Map Pages 6-59	1:15,840		Map Pages 4-5	1:7,920

Map Pages 6-59   1:15,840
0   ¼   ½ Mile
0   250   500   750 Metres
4 inches (10.16cm) to 1 mile   6.31cm to 1km

Map Pages 4-5   1:7,920
0   ⅛   ¼ Mile
0   100   200   300   400 Metres
8 inches (20.32cm) to 1 mile   12.63cm to 1km

Copyright of Geographers' A-Z Map Company Limited

Fairfield Road, Borough Green, Sevenoaks, Kent TN15 8PP
Telephone: 01732 781000 (Enquiries & Trade Sales)
01732 783422 (Retail Sales)
www.a-zmaps.co.uk
Copyright © Geographers' A-Z Map Co. Ltd.

Edition 4 2011

Ordnance
Survey® This prod
Ordnance
of Her Ma
© Crown Copyright 2010. /

Safety camera information
Speed Camera Location D:

D0273437

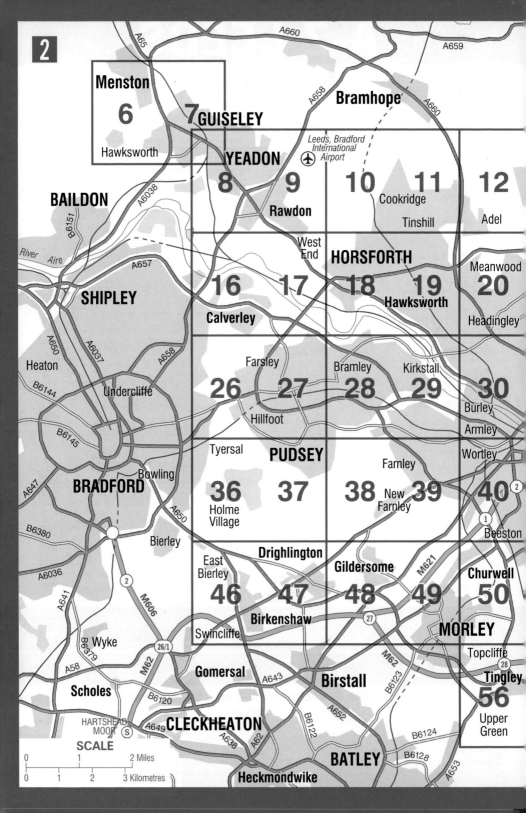

Menston
6
7
GUISELEY
Hawksworth
YEADON
Bramhope
Leeds, Bradford International Airport
8
9
10
11
12
BAILDON
Rawdon
Cookridge
Tinshill
Adel
River Aire
West End
HORSFORTH
Meanwood
SHIPLEY
16
17
18
19
20
Hawksworth
Calverley
Headingley
Heaton
Farsley
Bramley
Kirkstall
Undercliffe
26
27
28
29
30
Burley
Hillfoot
Armley
Tyersal
PUDSEY
Wortley
Farnley
Bowling
BRADFORD
36
37
38
39
40
Holme Village
New Farnley
Beeston
Bierley
East Bierley
Drighlington
Gildersome
Churwell
46
47
48
49
50
Birkenshaw
MORLEY
Swincliffe
Topcliffe
Wyke
Gomersal
Birstall
Tingley
Scholes
56
Upper Green
HARTSHEAD MOOR
CLECKHEATON
BATLEY
Heckmondwike
A660
A65
A659
A658
A6038
B6151
A657
A650
A6037
B6144
B6145
A647
B6380
A6036
A641
M606
M621
M62
B6379
A58
B6120
A649
A638
A62
A643
A652
B6122
B6123
B6124
B6128
A653
26/1
27
28
SCALE
0
1
2 Miles
0
1
2
3 Kilometres

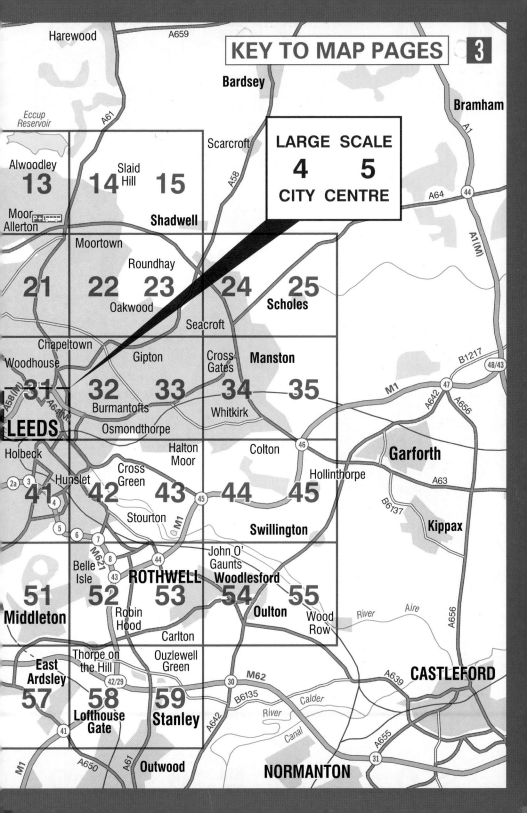
KEY TO MAP PAGES
3
Harewood
A659
Bardsey
Bramham
Eccup Reservoir
A61
LARGE SCALE
4 5
CITY CENTRE
Scarcroft
A58
A1
A64
44
A1(M)
Alwoodley
13
14
Slaid Hill
15
Moor Allerton
Shadwell
Moortown
Roundhay
21
22
23
24
25
Oakwood
Scholes
Seacroft
Chapeltown
Gipton
Cross Gates
Manston
B1217
48/43
Woodhouse
31
32
33
34
35
M1
47
A642
A656
A58(M)
A64(M)
Burmantofts
Whitkirk
LEEDS
Osmondthorpe
46
Holbeck
Halton Moor
Colton
Garforth
Cross Green
Hunslet
Hollinthorpe
A63
2a
3
41
42
43
44
45
4
45
B6137
Stourton
M1
Kippax
5
6
7
Swillington
M621
8
44
John O' Gaunts
Belle Isle
43
ROTHWELL
Woodlesford
51
52
53
54
55
Middleton
Robin Hood
Oulton
Wood Row
River
Aire
A656
Carlton
Thorpe on the Hill
Ouzlewell Green
East Ardsley
42/29
30
M62
A639
CASTLEFORD
57
58
59
B6135
Calder
River
Lofthouse Gate
Stanley
A642
Canal
A655
41
31
M1
A650
A61
Outwood
NORMANTON

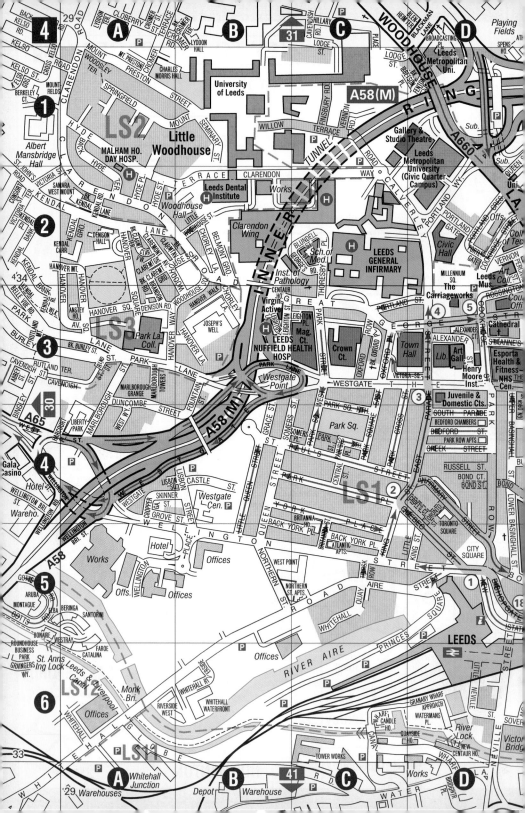

4
A
B
C
D
31
1
2
3
4
5
6
29
34
30
33
41
LS2
LS3
LS1
LS12
LS11
Little Woodhouse
University of Leeds
Leeds Metropolitan Uni.
Lyddon Hall
Charles Morris Hall
Albert Mansbridge Hall
Malham Ho. Day Hosp.
Leeds Dental Institute
Woodhouse Hall
Denison Hall
Clarendon Wing
Works
Sch. of Med.
Inst. of Pathology
Leeds General Infirmary
Gallery & Studio Theatre
Leeds Metropolitan University (Civic Quarter Campus)
Civic Hall
Millennium Sq.
The Carriageworks
Leeds Mus.
Art Coll.
Cathedral
Town Hall
Lib.
Art Gall.
Henry Moore Inst.
Esporta Health & Fitness
NHS Cen.
Juvenile & Domestic Cts.
Crown Ct.
Mag. Ct.
Leeds Nuffield Health Hosp.
Virgin Active
Park La. Coll.
Joseph's Well
Westgate Point
Park Sq.
Westgate Cen.
Hotel
Offices
Offs.
Gala Casino
Wareho.
City Square
Leeds
River Aire
Leeds & Liverpool Canal
St. Anns Ing Lock
Monk Bri.
Roundhouse Business Park
Riverside West
Whitehall Waterfront
Tower Works
Granary Wharf
River Lock
New Centaur Ho.
Candle Ho.
Quayside Ho.
Whitehall Junction
Warehouses
Depot
Warehouse
Playing Fields
Victoria Bridge
Woodhouse Lane
Clarendon Road
Inner Ring Road
A58(M)
A660
A65
A58
Park Lane
Westgate
Wellington Street
Great George Street
Park Row
Boar Lane
Aire Street
Whitehall Road
Globe Road
Water Lane
Neville Street
Calverley Street
Park Place
York Place
King Street
Infirmary Street
Quebec St.
Bishopgate
East Parade
The Headrow
South Parade
Bedford St.
Greek Street
Russell St.
Bond St.
Wellington Bri. St.
Duncombe Street
Kendal Lane
Hyde Terrace
Burley Rd.
Cavendish St.
Marlborough Towers
Marlborough Grange
Hanover Square
Woodhouse Square
Clarendon Way
Willow Terrace
Mount Preston Street
Princes Square
Whitehall Quay
Northern St.
Queen Street
Little Queen Street

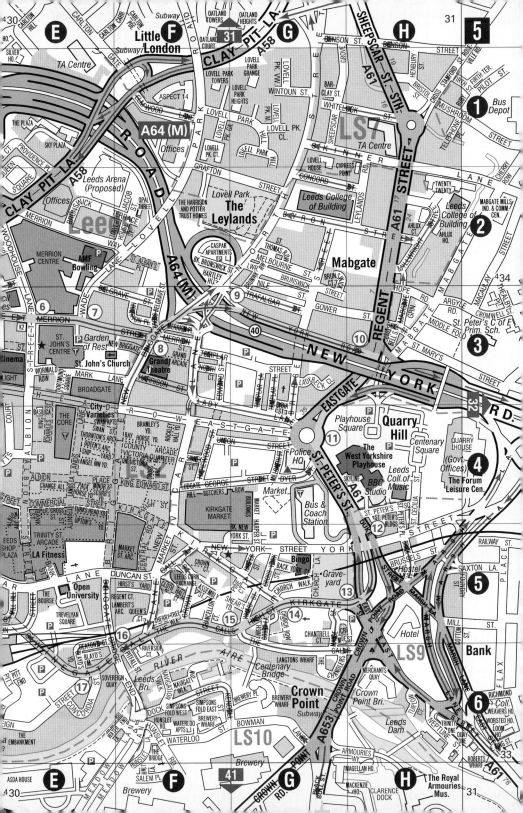

Little London
The Leylands
Mabgate
Quarry Hill
Crown Point
Bank
LS7
LS2
LS9
LS10
Merrion Centre
St. John's Centre
Kirkgate Market
The West Yorkshire Playhouse
Leeds College of Building
The Royal Armouries Mus.

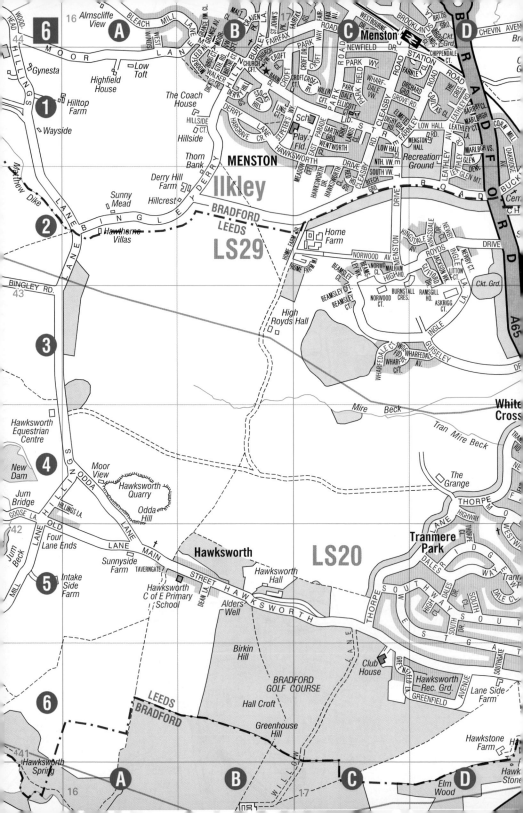
A
B
C
D
1
2
3
4
5
6
16
17
44
43
42
41
Menston
MENSTON
Ilkley
BRADFORD
LEEDS
LS29
LS20
Hawksworth
Tranmere Park
White Cross
A65
Almscliffe View
Gynesta
Highfield House
Low Toft
Hilltop Farm
Wayside
The Coach House
Hillside
Thorn Bank
Derry Hill Farm
Sunny Mead
Hillcrest
Hawthorne Villas
Home Farm
High Royds Hall
Recreation Ground
Sch.
Play. Fld.
Lib.
Ckt. Grd.
Mire Beck
Tran Mire Beck
Matthew Dike
The Grange
Hawksworth Equestrian Centre
New Dam
Jum Bridge
Jum Beck
Moor View
Hawksworth Quarry
Odda Hill
Four Lane Ends
Sunnyside Farm
Intake Side Farm
TAVERNGATE
Hawksworth C of E Primary School
Hawksworth Hall
Alders Well
Birkin Hill
BRADFORD GOLF COURSE
Hall Croft
Greenhouse Hill
Club House
Hawksworth Rec. Grd.
Lane Side Farm
Hawkstone Farm
Hawksworth Spring
Elm Wood
MOOR LANE
BLEACH MILL LANE
BINGLEY LANE
BINGLEY RD.
DERRY LANE
DERRY HILL
BRADFORD ROAD
HAWKSWORTH LANE
HAWKSWORTH DRIVE
MAIN STREET
HAWKSWORTH LANE
HILLINGS LANE
ODDA LANE
GOOSE LA.
OLD LANE
MILL LANE
WILLOW LANE
STATION ROAD
CLEASBY ROAD
PARK ROAD
FAIRFAX ROAD
BURLEY LA.
CHEVIN AVENUE
BROOKLANDS LA.
NEWFIELD DR.
WESTBOURNE DR.
MENSTON DRIVE
ROYDS DRIVE
NORWOOD AV.
GUISELEY DR.
INGLE LA.
THORPE LANE
THORPE
GREENFIELD AVENUE
GREENFIELD LA.
SOUTHGATE
SOUTH WAY
WEST GATE
RIDGE WAY
HIGHWAY
LOW HALL
LEATHLEY AV.
BUCK

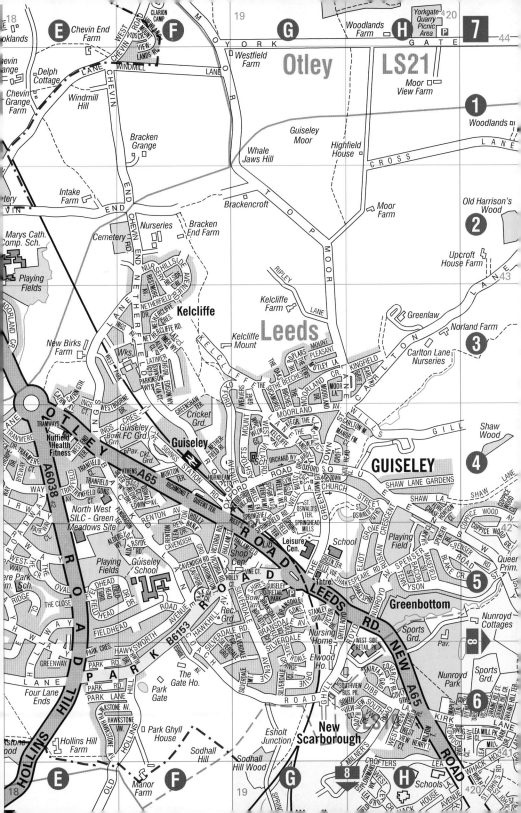
7
Otley
LS21
Leeds
GUISELEY
Kelcliffe
Guiseley
Greenbottom
New Scarborough
Chevin End Farm
Woodlands Farm
Yorkgate Quarry Picnic Area
Westfield Farm
Moor View Farm
Woodlands
Guiseley Moor
Highfield House
Whale Jaws Hill
Bracken Grange
Windmill Hill
Delph Cottage
Chevin Grange Farm
Intake Farm
Brackencroft
Moor Farm
Old Harrison's Wood
Nurseries
Bracken End Farm
Cemetery
Marys Cath. Comp. Sch.
Playing Fields
Upcroft House Farm
Kelcliffe Farm
Greenlaw
Norland Farm
Kelcliffe Mount
Carlton Lane Nurseries
New Birks Farm
Shaw Wood
Nuffield Health Fitness
Guiseley FC Grd.
Cricket Grd.
North West SILC - Green Meadows Site
Guiseley School
Leisure Cen.
School
Playing Field
Shop Cen.
Guiseley Retail Park
Rec. Grd.
Nursing Home
Elwood Ho.
West Side Retail Pk.
Sports Grd.
Nunroyd Cottages
Nunroyd Park
Four Lane Ends
The Gate Ho.
Park Gate
Park Ghyll House
Hollins Hill Farm
Sodhall Hill
Sodhall Hill Wood
Esholt Junction
Manor Farm
Schools
YORK GATE
MOOR ROAD
TOP MOOR
CROSS LANE
CARLTON LANE
OTLEY ROAD
A65
A6038
HOLLINS HILL
LEEDS ROAD
NEW ROAD
PARK ROAD
B6153
GHYLL ROAD
ESHOLT AV.
AVENUE ROAD
KIRK LANE
SHAW LANE
OXFORD ROAD
CHEVIN END
WINDMILL LANE
WEST CHEVIN ROAD
NETHERFIELD LANE
KELCLIFFE LANE
MOORLAND AV.
TOWN ST.
STREET

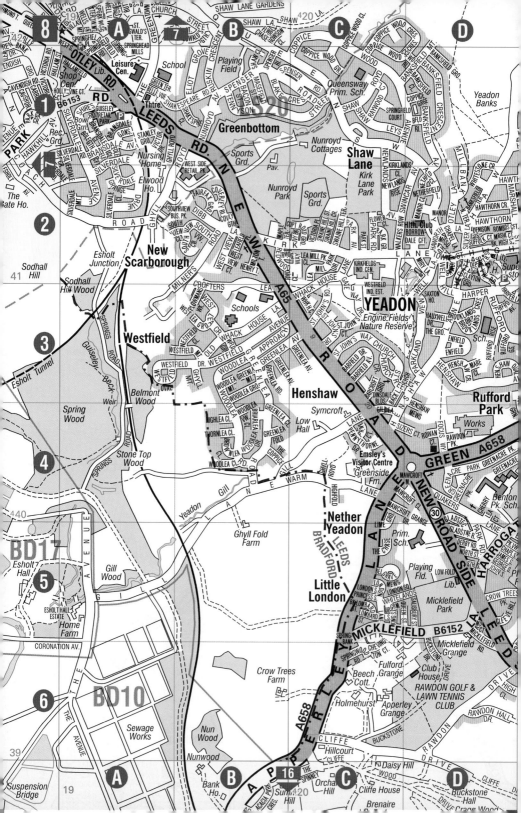
A
B
C
D
1
2
3
4
5
6
7
16
LS20
BD17
BD10
OTLEY RD.
LEEDS RD.
NEW ROAD
A65
A658
B6153
B6152
GREEN A658
MICKLEFIELD
Greenbottom
Shaw Lane
Kirk Lane Park
Nunroyd Park
Nunroyd Cottages
Sports Grd.
Playing Field
School
Leisure Cen.
Lib.
Shop Cen.
Thtre.
Queensway Prim. Sch.
Yeadon Banks
YEADON
Engine Fields Nature Reserve
New Scarborough
Esholt Junction
Sodhall Hill
Sodhall Hill Wood
Westfield
Schools
Henshaw
Symcroft
Low Hall
Emsley's Visitor Centre
Greenside Fm.
Rufford Park
Works
Esholt Tunnel
Guiseley Beck
Weir
Belmont Wood
Spring Wood
Stone Top Wood
Yeadon Gill
WARM LANE
Ghyll Fold Farm
Nether Yeadon
LEEDS
BRADFORD
Little London
Esholt Hall
ESHOLT HALL ESTATE
Home Farm
Gill Wood
CORONATION AV.
Sewage Works
Nun Wood
Nunwood
Bank Ho.
Suspension Bridge
Crow Trees Farm
Beech Cott.
Fulford Grange
Holmehurst
Apperley Grange
Club House
RAWDON GOLF & LAWN TENNIS CLUB
Micklefield Park
Micklefield Grange
Playing Fld.
Prim. Sch.
Hillcourt
Daisy Hill
Cliffe House
Brenaire
Buckstone Hall
Orchard Hill
Summer Hill
Nursing Home
Elwood Ho.
The Gate Ho.
Rec. Grd.
Bowl. Grn.
WEST SIDE RETAIL PK.
SOUTHVIEW BUS. PK.
KIRKFIELDS IND. CEN.
WESTFIELD IND. EST.
Hlth. Club
Benton Pk. Sch.
HARROGATE
Sch.
Pav.

LEEDS BRADFORD
INTERNATIONAL AIRPORT
Leeds
LS19
LS18
YEADON TARN
HORSFORTH
GOLF COURSE
RAWDON
Larkfield
Low Green
Lane
Ends
Yeadon
Moor
Rawdon
Common
Plane
Tree Hill
Billing
Hill
Terminal
Building
Hangars
Yorkshire
Aeroplane
Club
Cold
Harbour Farm
Coney Lodge
Farm
Coney Lodge
Bridge
YEADON AIRPORT
IND. EST.
Headlands
Hotel
Yeadon
Haw
Yeadon
Cemetery
Maria
Regina
Convent
Damfield
Farm
Novia
Farm
Tarnfield
Leeds Sailing
& Activity
Cen.
Bayton
House
Club
House
Westbrook
Farm
Whetstone
Farm
Yarnbury
RUFC
The
Croft
Layton Croft
Layton
Ghyll
Layton
Hall
Jubilee
Hall
Rawdon St. Peter's
C of E
Primary Sch.
Larkfield
Dam
Rawdon
Hall
Rawdon
Hall Farm
Rawdon
Carrs
Horn Hill
Springfield
Cottage
Hill Top
A658
A65
B6152
HARROGATE ROAD
VICTORIA AVENUE
WHITEHOUSE LANE
LAYTON ROAD
LAYTON AVENUE
TOWN STREET
LANE END
WEST END LANE
BROWNBERRIE LA.
YEADON MOOR RD.
10
17

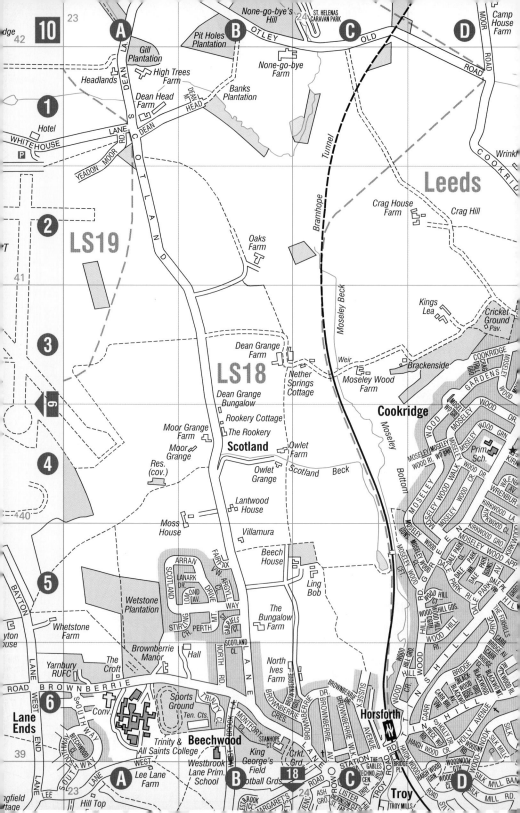

Gill Plantation
Headlands
High Trees Farm
Dean Head Farm
Banks Plantation
Pit Holes Plantation
None-go-bye's Hill
ST. HELENAS CARAVAN PARK
None-go-bye Farm
OTLEY OLD ROAD
Camp House Farm
MOOR ROAD
Hotel
WHITEHOUSE LANE
DEAN LA.
DEAN HEAD
YEADON MOOR RD.
SCOTLAND
LS19
LS18
Leeds
Bramhope Tunnel
Crag House Farm
Crag Hill
Oaks Farm
Moseley Beck
Kings Lea
Cricket Ground
Pav.
Dean Grange Farm
Nether Springs Cottage
Weir
Moseley Wood Farm
Brackenside
Cookridge
Dean Grange Bungalow
Rookery Cottage
The Rookery
Moor Grange Farm
Moor Grange
Scotland
Owlet Farm
Owlet Grange
Scotland Beck
Res. (cov.)
Moseley Bottom
Prim. Sch.
Lantwood House
Moss House
Villamura
Beech House
Ling Bob
Wetstone Plantation
The Bungalow Farm
Whetstone Farm
Brownberrie Manor
Hall
The Croft
Yarnbury RUFC
North Ives Farm
BROWNBERRIE ROAD
Lane Ends
Conv.
Sports Ground
Ten. Cts.
Trinity & All Saints College
Beechwood
Westbrook Lane Prim. School
King George's Field
Football Grds
Crkt. Grd.
Lee Lane Farm
Hill Top
Horsforth
Troy
TROY MILLS
BROWNBERRIE LANE
STATION ROAD
TROY ROAD
COOKRIDGE
MOSELEY WOOD
TINSHILL
HOLLY AVENUE
WOODNOOK
SILK MILL
18
9

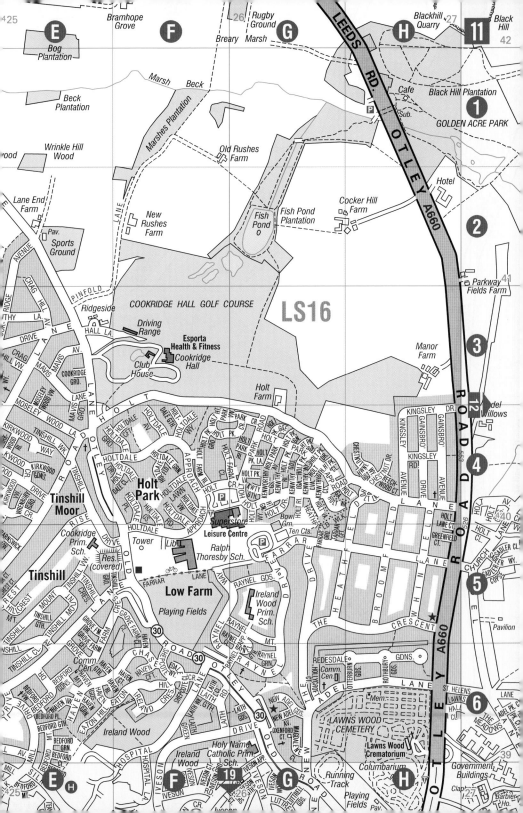
11
E
F
G
H
1
2
3
4
5
6
12
19
Bramhope Grove
Rugby Ground
Breary Marsh
Blackhill Quarry
Black Hill
Bog Plantation
Marsh Beck
Beck Plantation
Marshes Plantation
Cafe
Black Hill Plantation
GOLDEN ACRE PARK
LEEDS RD.
OTLEY A660
Wrinkle Hill Wood
Old Rushes Farm
Hotel
Lane End Farm
New Rushes Farm
Fish Pond
Fish Pond Plantation
Cocker Hill Farm
Sports Ground
Parkway Fields Farm
COOKRIDGE HALL GOLF COURSE
LS16
Ridgeside
Driving Range
Esporta Health & Fitness
Cookridge Hall
Club House
Manor Farm
Holt Farm
Adel Willows
Holt Park
Tinshill Moor
Superstore
Leisure Centre
Tower
Lib.
Ralph Thoresby Sch.
Cookridge Prim. Sch.
Res. (covered)
Tinshill
Low Farm
Playing Fields
Ireland Wood Prim. Sch.
Bowl Grn.
Ten Cts.
Pavilion
Comm. Cen.
Ireland Wood
Holy Name Catholic Prim. Sch.
LAWNS WOOD CEMETERY
Lawns Wood Crematorium
Columbarium
Running Track
Playing Fields
Government Buildings
OTLEY ROAD
HOLT ROAD
FARRAR LANE
ADEL LANE
OTLEY ROAD A660

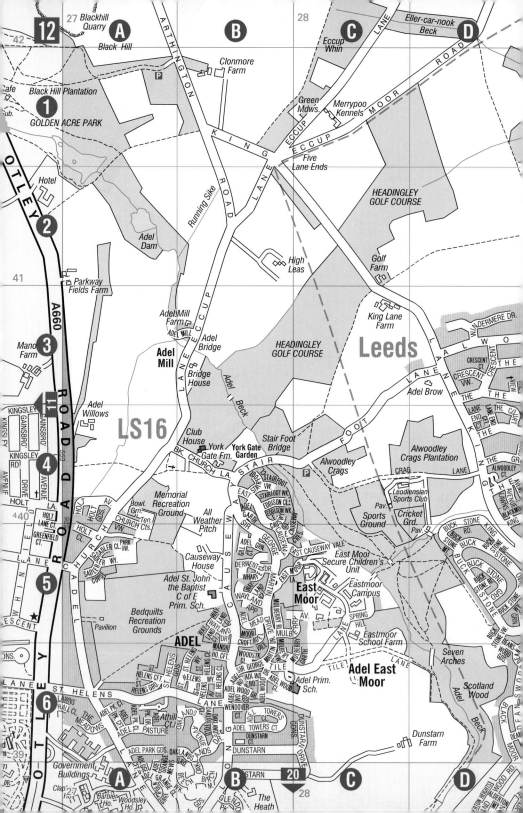

12
Blackhill Quarry
Black Hill
Clonmore Farm
Eccup Whin
Eller-car-nook Beck
Black Hill Plantation
GOLDEN ACRE PARK
Green Mdws.
Merrypoo Kennels
ECCUP MOOR ROAD
ARTHINGTON
KING LANE
Five Lane Ends
Hotel
OTLEY ROAD
Running Sike
HEADINGLEY GOLF COURSE
Adel Dam
High Leas
Golf Farm
Parkway Fields Farm
A660
Adel Mill Farm
King Lane Farm
Adel Bridge
Adel Mill
Leeds
Manor Farm
Bridge House
Adel Beck
Adel Brow
Adel Willows
LS16
Club House
York Gate Fm.
York Gate Garden
Stair Foot Bridge
Alwoodley Crags Plantation
Alwoodley Crags
Memorial Recreation Ground
All Weather Pitch
Leodiensian Sports Club
Sports Ground
Cricket Grd.
East Moor Secure Children's Unit
Causeway House
Adel St. John the Baptist C of E Prim. Sch.
East Moor
Eastmoor Campus
Bedquilts Recreation Grounds
Pavilion
Eastmoor School Farm
ADEL
Seven Arches
Adel East Moor
Adel Prim. Sch.
Scotland Wood
Dunstarn Farm
Government Buildings
The Heath
20

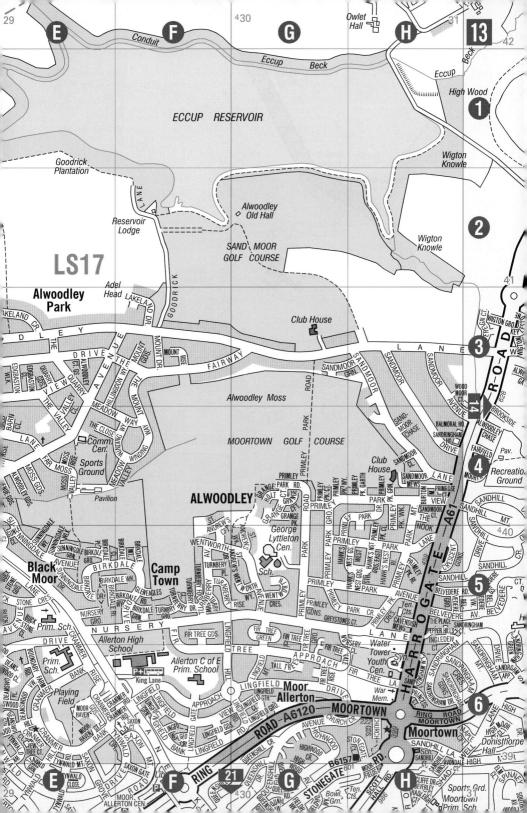
13
ECCUP RESERVOIR
Eccup Beck
Conduit
Owlet Hall
High Wood
Wigton Knowle
Goodrick Plantation
Reservoir Lodge
Alwoodley Old Hall
SAND MOOR GOLF COURSE
LS17
Adel Head
Alwoodley Park
Club House
Alwoodley Moss
MOORTOWN GOLF COURSE
ALWOODLEY
George Lyttleton Cen.
Sports Ground
Pavilion
Black Moor
Camp Town
Allerton High School
Allerton C of E Prim. School
King Lane
Playing Field
Moor Allerton
MOORTOWN
RING ROAD A6120
HARROGATE A61
Moortown
Recreation Ground
Donisthorpe Hall
Water Tower
Youth Cen.
Sports Grd.
Moortown Prim. Sch.
B6157
STONEGATE
SCOTT HALL RD.
21
14
430
31
29
42
41
440
39

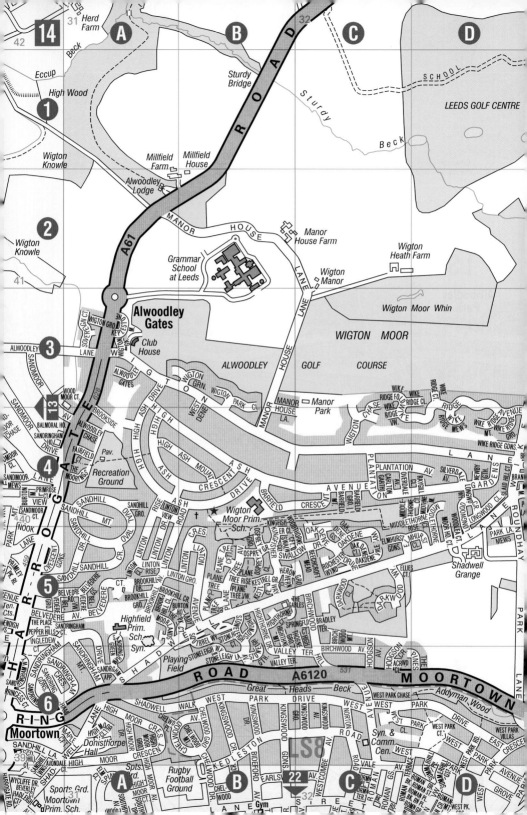
Herd Farm
Eccup Beck
High Wood
Wigton Knowle
Sturdy Bridge
Sturdy Beck
SCHOOL
LEEDS GOLF CENTRE
ROAD
A61
Millfield Farm
Millfield House
Alwoodley Lodge
MANOR HOUSE
Manor House Farm
Grammar School at Leeds
Wigton Heath Farm
Wigton Manor
Wigton Moor Whin
Alwoodley Gates
Club House
WIGTON MOOR
ALWOODLEY GOLF COURSE
ALWOODLEY LANE
WIGTON LANE
MANOR HOUSE LANE
Manor Park
HIGH ASH DRIVE
HIGH ASH AVENUE
Recreation Ground
Wigton Moor Prim. Sch.
PLANTATION AV.
PLANTATION GARDENS
Shadwell Grange
Highfield Prim. Sch.
Syn.
Playing Field
SHADWELL LANE
HARROGATE ROAD
A6120
RING ROAD MOORTOWN
Great Heads Beck
Addyman Wood
Moortown
Donisthorpe Hall
Syn. & Comm. Cen.
LS8
Rugby Football Ground
Sports Grd.
Moortown Prim. Sch.
Spts. Grd.
Gym
ROUNDHAY PARK LANE
13
22

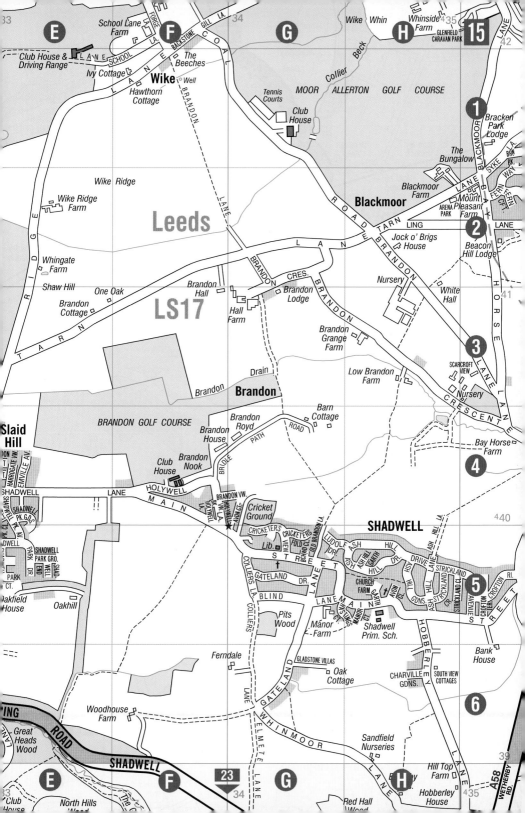

School Lane Farm
Club House & Driving Range
The Beeches
Ivy Cottage
Wike
Well
Hawthorn Cottage
Wike Whin
Whinside Farm
GLENFIELD CARAVAN PARK
Collier Beck
MOOR ALLERTON GOLF COURSE
Tennis Courts
Club House
Bracken Park Lodge
The Bungalow
Blackmoor Farm
Blackmoor
Mount Pleasant Farm
ARENA PARK
Wike Ridge
Wike Ridge Farm
Leeds
Jock o' Brigs House
Beacon Hill Lodge
Whingate Farm
Shaw Hill
One Oak
Brandon Cottage
Brandon Hall
Hall Farm
Brandon Lodge
LS17
Nursery
White Hall
Brandon Grange Farm
Low Brandon Farm
SCARCROFT VIEW
Nursery
Brandon Drain
Brandon
Barn Cottage
BRANDON GOLF COURSE
Brandon Royd
Brandon House
Bay Horse Farm
Slaid Hill
Club House
Brandon Nook
Cricket Ground
SHADWELL
Lib.
CHURCH FARM
Oakfield House
Oakhill
Pits Wood
Manor Farm
Shadwell Prim. Sch.
Bank House
Ferndale
GLADSTONE VILLAS
Oak Cottage
CHARVILLE GDNS.
SOUTH VIEW COTTAGES
Woodhouse Farm
Great Heads Wood
Sandfield Nurseries
Hill Top Farm
Hobberley House
North Hills Wood
Red Hall Wood
SHADWELL
A58 WETHERBY RD.
23

16
A
B
C
D
1
2
3
4
5
6
8
26
420
39
38
37
19
Sewage Works
Nun Wood
Nunwood
Bank Ho.
Hill
Buckstone
Cliffe
Rawdon
Daisy Hill
Cliffe House
Buckstone Hall
Cragg Wood
Orchard Hill
Summer Hill
The Spinney
Acacia Park Dr.
Acacia Farm
Brenaire Park
Cragg Ter.
Underwood Ho.
Lisieux
St. Joseph
Briaden
Holly Lodge
Woodlands Drive
Underwood Drive
Bronte House School
Oaklands
Acacia Park Ter.
Fairway
Lodge
Cawood
Walk Hill Farm
Suspension Bridge
Apperley Viaduct
Walk Hill Bridge
The Avenue
River Aire
Little Park
Woodlands Cl.
Playing Fields
Woodhouse Bridge
Woodhouse Grove School
Apperley Junction
Tennis Courts
Pav.
Leeds and Liverpool Canal
Bradford
BD10
Works
Dobson Locks
Sports Grd.
Elm Tree Fm.
Apperley Bri.
Milman Bri. (Swing)
Apperley Road
Apperley Lane
A658
Sports Ground
Shaw Ho.
Apperley Bridge
Apperley Gdns.
Laburnum Pl.
Whitfield Mill
Waters Wk.
Navigation Dr.
Water Front M.
The Quay
The Moorings
Slingsby Cl.
Tenterfield
Tenterfields Ho.
Overland Cr.
The Knoll
Strafford Wy.
Meadow
Derry
Warehouse
Spts. Gd.
Calverley Cutting
Calverley Wood
Thornhill Drive
Carr Beck
West Wood
Champion House
Stockhill Road
Stockhill Fold
Cavalier
Roundhead Fold
Prim. Sch.
Hosp.
Tenterfields
New Line
A657
Carr Bottom Road
Bateson St.
Ashgrove
Elder St.
Superstore
Greengates
Mill
Holybrook Av.
Jamie Ct.
Swim. Pool
Romanby Shaw
Holybrook Cen.
Roundwood Road
Rimswell
Redcar
Rokeby Gdns.
Reighton Croft
Ryton Dale
Sch.
Eccleshill Park
NHS Treatment Cen.
Eccleshill Community Hosp.
Harrogate Road
Rec. Grd.
Stanhope Rein
Low Rein
Ravenscliffe
Ranelagh Avenue
Norbury
Roundwood Glen
The Oval
Com. Cen.
Bradford
Leeds
Eleanor Drive
Clara Drive
Calverley Carr Farm
Carr Road
Crowther Avenue
Ravenscliffe Rd.
Fraser Rd.
Calverley
Carr Hills
Carr Hill Av.
Carr Hill Rd.
Victoria Rd.
Victoria Park
Salisbury St.
Lydgate St.
Lydgate Pl.
The Knoll
Pearson St.
St. Wilfrid's St.
South Lodge
Wood Lane
Calverley Prim.
Chapel St.
Thornhill St.
W. End Rd.
Portman S.
Blackett S.
Town Wells
Rushton
Clarke
Chestnut Gro.
Capel St.
Brookleigh
Shell Lane
Foxholes La.
Lane
Parkwood Rd.
Park Wood Gdns.
Hollin Pk.
Carr Lane
Upper Carr Lane
Reservoir Ct.
Works
Holly Park Mills
Woodhall Ct.
Woodhall Road
Bill Wood
Round Hill
Round Wood
Woodhall Hills Golf Course
Pudsey
LS28
Red Beck
Crossfield Farm
Crossfield House
Hazelbrook
Fagley
Damon Av.
Hazel Cro.

17
Low Green
Rawdon Hall Farm
Layton Ghyll
Layton Hall
Horn Hill
LEEDS ROAD
RAWDON ROAD
Rawdon Carrs
Works
Springfield Cottage
Lee Lane
Hill Top Farm
Stock Hill
LS19
New York Cottages
Springfield Farm
Larchwood
Woodlands Farm
High Knott Wood
Red Beck House
West End
West End Prim. Sch.
Well Royd Wood
Cragg Wood
Snaith-rend Wood
Woodleigh Hall Farm
Rawdon Crematorium
Kittycroyd
Leeds
Wood Nook
Wellroyd
LS18
HORSFORTH
HORSFORTH HALL PARK
Works
Woodbottom Farm
Redbeck Cottages
Daisybank
Woodbottom
The Meadow
Low Fold
Lodge Wood
Wood Bottom
South Field
Low Hall Farm
Low Hall
Burke Wood
Glenburn
Lodge Farm
Lodge Bridge (Swing)
Sough Wood
Horsforth Cemetery
Mudge Bank Wood
Works
Sports Grd.
Park Lane College (Horsforth Campus)
BROADWAY
A6120
A65
Calverley House Farm
Leeds and Liverpool Canal
Swaine Wood
Weir
Calverley La.
Navigation Ct.
River Aire
Owl Bridge (Swing)
Horsforth Newlaith Jun. Sch.
LS13
Calverley Bridge
HORSFORTH NEW RD.
RODLEY A657
The Grange
Chalybeate Well
Rodley Bri.
Rodley Fold Farm
Bagley Beck
Rec. Grd.
FARSLEY
LANE
TOWN STREET
Ckt. Grd.
Thorne Dene
Wood Hill
Red Beck
CALVERLEY LANE
B6156
RING ROAD
Normington House
Rodley
Works
The Green
Bagley
Coal Hill
Rodley Recreation Grd.
Warehouses
Woodlands Hall Farm
27
9
18

18
Beechwood
Trinity & All Saints College
Westbrook Lane Prim. School
King George's Field Football Grds.
Crkt. Grd.
10
Horsforth
Lane Ends
Lee Lane Farm
Hill Top Farm
Stock Hill
Troy
Troy Mills
Old Mill Beck
Depot
Hunger Hills
Horsforth School
Playing Fields
LS18
West End Prim. Sch.
Day Centre
Lib.
Prim. Sch.
Sch.
HORSFORTH
HORSFORTH HALL PARK
Cricket Ground
Pav.
Youth Cen.
Rec. Ground
Low Fold
A6120
BROADWAY
Rec. Grd.
Leeds
NEW ROAD SIDE
A65
A6120
17
Horsforth Cemetery
Park La. College
Little Hawksworth Wood
Hawksworth
Cow Beck Bridge
The Outwood
Swaine Wood
Horsforth Newlaithes Jun. Sch.
Newlay Bri. (Footbridge)
RIVER AIRE
Newlay
Thornton Wood
Newlay Locks
Leeds & Liverpool Canal
Bagley Beck
Fallwood Marina
Airedale Cliff
BRAMLEY FALL
Sewage Works
Ckt. Grd.
Whitecote House
LS13
Playing Fields
Whitecote
LEEDS AND B6157
Weir
Ross Mill Bri. (Swing)
Rossett Bus. Pk.
28
TOWN A657 ST.

Ireland Wood
Lawnswood
LS16
West Park
Weetwood
Beckett Park
Sandford
Hawksworth Wood
LS5
LS6
RING RD. HORSFORTH A6120 RING ROAD WEST PARK
OTLEY ROAD A660
OTLEY RD.
Lawns Wood Cemetery
Lawns Wood Crematorium
Columbarium
Bodington Hall (University of Leeds)
University Athletics Ground
Weetwood Police HQ
Lawnswood School
Village Hotel & Leisure Club
Abbey Grange C of E High Sch.
St. Chad's C of E Prim. Sch.
West Park Centre
Community Centre
Leeds Metropolitan University (Headingley Beckett Park Campus)
Queen's Wood
Spring Wood
Clayton Wood
Woodside Quarry
Park Lane College (Hawksworth Centre)
Old Mill Bridge
Recreation Ground
Crooked Acres
Rugby Football Grd.
Kirkstall Abbey (rems.)
Kirkstall Lock
Abbey Gardens
Toads Hole Wood
Forge Locks
Batcliffe Wood
Headingley
A65
RIVER AIRE
BECKETT PARK
11
19
20
29

20
A
B
C
D
12
19
30
27
28
39
38
37
36
47
Dunstarn Farm
DUNSTARN LANE
ADEL TOWERS CT.
ADEL PARK GDS.
ADEL PASTURE
Government Buildings
Clapham Ho.
Barbier Ho.
Woodsley Ho.
Grant Ho.
Mortain Ho.
Vaughan Ho.
Seton Ho.
Hey Ho.
Bodington Hall (University of Leeds)
Pavilion
The Heath
Leeds
Bywater Farm
Cricket Ground
Subway
OTLEY ROAD
A660
WEETWOOD RING ROAD
ADEL RING ROAD
RING ROAD
A6120
MEANWOOD
University Athletics Ground
Hope Pastures
Weetwood Grove
Valley Farm
PARKSIDE
Meanwood Grove
Moorlands School
LS16
FOXHILL CRESCENT
Weetwood
Weir
Nurseries
Tennis Courts
Rugby Ground
Football Ground
University Athletics Grounds
Hotel
Pav.
Weetwood
Play-ground
Putting Green
Ten. Cts.
The Hollies
Meanwood
Cricket Ground
Rec. Grd.
Hill Top
Weetwood House
Oxley Hall (Uni. of Leeds)
Bardon Grange
Bardon Hall
Village Hotel & Leisure Club
Water Treatment Works
Weetwood Lane Farm
Sports Ground
Recreation Ground
Tennis Court
Prim. Sch.
Richmond House Sch.
Sports Ground
Hollin Ho.
LS6
MEANWOOD
STONEGATE ROAD
TONGUE LANE
Far Headingley
Prim. Sch.
Spts. Cen.
Leeds Metropolitan University (Headingley Beckett Pk. Campus)
Ten. Cts.
Ckt. Gd.
Church Wood
Beckett Park
Cin.
B6157 MONK BRIDGE RD.
SHAW LA.
GROVE
HEADINGLEY
B6159
STAINBECK LANE
Rugby Grd.
Tennis Courts
BECKETT PARK
ST. CHAD'S DRIVE
BECKETT'S PARK CRESCENT
ST. ANNE'S ROAD
ARNDALE CENTRE
HOSPICE
Sch.
LUPTON FLATS
NEW MOON APTS.
Batcliffe Wood
Meanwood Beck
Batty's Wood
Mt. St. Joseph
Headingley Castle
Hostel
Hinsley Hall
JAMES BAILLIE PARK
Bowl. Grn.
Lib.
Cin.
Headingley Hill
B6157 NTH. LANE
Yorkshire Co. Cricket Club
Headingley

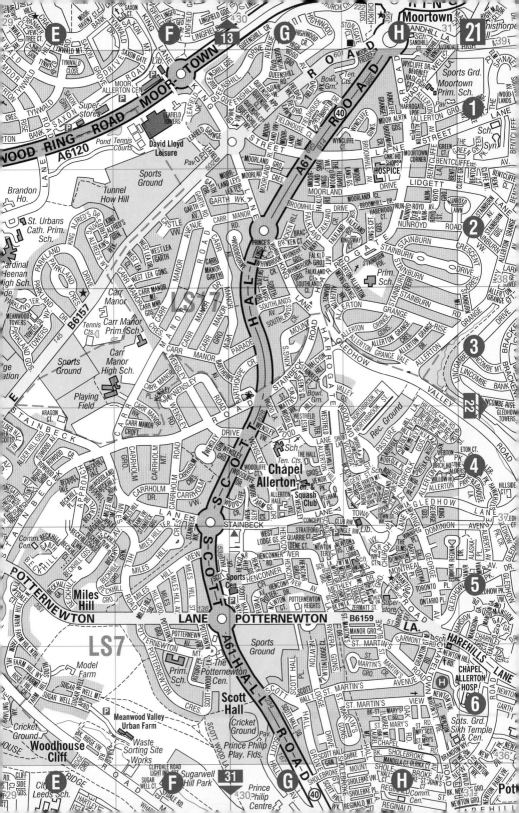
21
Moortown
13
22
31
E
F
G
H
1
2
3
4
5
6
RING ROAD MOORTOWN
A6120
HARROGATE ROAD
A61
KING LANE
David Lloyd Leisure
Sports Ground
Tunnel How Hill
Brandon Ho.
St. Urbans Cath. Prim. Sch.
Cardinal Heenan High Sch.
B6157
Carr Manor
Carr Manor Prim. Sch.
Carr Manor High Sch.
Playing Field
LS17
MOORLAND DRIVE
NUNROYD ROAD
STAINBURN CRESCENT
ALLERTON GRANGE
GLEDHOW VALLEY ROAD
HOSPICE
Moortown Prim. Sch.
Sports Grd.
STREET LANE
HARROGATE ROAD
STAINBECK LANE
SCOTT HALL ROAD
Chapel Allerton
Ten. & Squash Club
Rec. Ground
GLEDHOW LANE
Miles Hill
POTTERNEWTON LANE
B6159
LS7
Sports Ground
Scott Hall
Cricket Ground
Prince Philip Play. Flds.
Model Farm
Meanwood Valley Urban Farm
Waste Sorting Site Works
Woodhouse Cliff
City of Leeds Sch.
Sugarwell Hill Park
Prince Philip Centre
CHAPEL ALLERTON HOSP.
HAREHILLS LANE
Spts. Grd.
Sikh Temple & Cen.
Super-store
Comm. Cen.
Prim. Sch.
The Potternewton Cen.
Sports Cen.
Comm. Cen.
430
436

22
A
B
C
D
14
1
2
3
4
5
6
21
32
LS17
LS7
LS8
Leeds
ROUNDHAY
Park Villas
Lidgett Park
Gledhow
Potternewton
Gipton Wood
Donisthorpe Hall
Rugby Football Ground
Sports Grd.
Moortown Prim. Sch.
Allerton Grange School
Moor Allerton Hall Prim. Sch.
Playing Fields
Comm. Cen.
Tropical World
Canal Gdns.
The Arboretum Lawn
Fox Wood
Sports Ground
SOLDIERS
FIELD
Cricket Grd.
Bowling Green
Gledhow Prim. Sch.
LEEDS SPIRE HOSP.
Bracken Hills Wood
Roundhay School Tech. Coll.
Kerr Mackie Prim. Sch.
Gledhow Beck
Weirs
The Lake
Gledhow Valley Woods
Yorkshire Amateurs FC
Superstores
Gipton Wood
CHAPEL ALLERTON HOSP.
Spts. Grd.
Sikh Temple & Cen.
Prim. Sch.
POTTERNEWTON PARK
HAREHILLS
B6159
STREET LANE
LIDGETT PARK AVENUE
PRINCES AVENUE
GLEDHOW LANE
GLEDHOW VALLEY ROAD
ROUNDHAY ROAD
OLD PARK ROAD
HAREHILLS LANE
EASTERLY ROAD

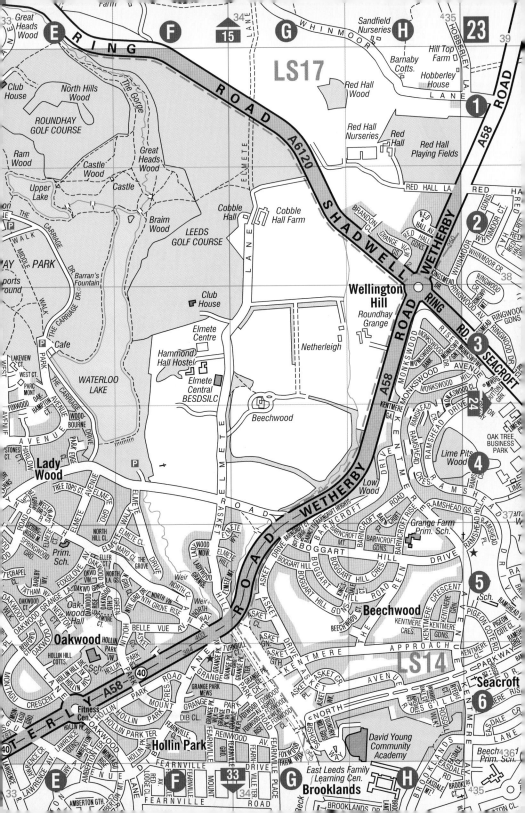
23
LS17
LS14
RING ROAD
A6120
SHADWELL
WETHERBY ROAD
A58
RING RD. SEACROFT
Great Heads Wood
Club House
North Hills Wood
ROUNDHAY GOLF COURSE
Ram Wood
Castle Wood
Castle
Upper Lake
Braim Wood
The Gorge
LEEDS GOLF COURSE
Cobble Hall
Cobble Hall Farm
ELMETE LANE
Club House
Elmete Centre
Hammond Hall Hostel
Elmete Central BESDSILC
Beechwood
Netherleigh
Wellington Hill
Roundhay Grange
Red Hall Wood
Red Hall Nurseries
Red Hall
Red Hall Playing Fields
RED HALL LA.
Sandfield Nurseries
WHINMOOR LANE
Barnaby Cotts.
Hill Top Farm
Hobberley House
HOBBERLEY LA.
Cafe
WATERLOO LAKE
Barran's Fountain
THE CARRIAGE DR.
PARK
Lady Wood
Low Wood
Grange Farm Prim. Sch.
Beechwood
Lime Pits Wood
OAK TREE BUSINESS PARK
Oakwood
Oak-wood Hall
Hollin Park
Fitness Cen.
David Young Community Academy
East Leeds Family Learning Cen.
Brooklands
Seacroft
Beech Prim. Sch.
ELMETE ROAD
BOGGART HILL DRIVE
KENTMERE APPROACH
KENTMERE AVENUE
MONKSWOOD AVENUE
RAMSHEAD DRIVE
FEARNVILLE ROAD
15
24
33

24
A
B
C
D
1
2
3
4
5
6
435
36
39
38
37
436
Hill Top Farm
Hobberley House
HOBBERLEY LA.
WHINMOOR LANE
WELLINGTON HILL
WETHERBY ROAD
A58
S17
Red Hall Playing Fields
RED HALL LA.
RED HALL LANE
SKELTONS LANE
COAL ROAD
Intake Farm
Intake Grange
The Grove
INTAKE LA.
Field Head
Bramley Grange Farm
Bramley Grange College
Skelton Hall Farm
BRAMLEY GDS.
LS14
RED HALL AV.
RED HALL GDNS.
RING ROAD
KINGSMEAD DR.
RINGWOOD AV.
RINGWOOD DR.
RINGWOOD GDNS.
WHINMOOR CT.
WHINMOOR WAY
WHINMOOR GARDENS
RED HALL CRESCENT
RED HALL DRIVE
RED HALL CHASE
RED HALL CROFT
RED HALL VALE
RED HALL APP.
Prim. Sch.
GREEN LA.
Play. Field
Comm. Cen.
Sch.
Lib.
NABURN APPROACH
NABURN RD.
NABURN PL.
NABURN WLK.
NABURN DR.
NABURN CL.
NABURN FOLD
NABURN VW.
WESTWINN GTH.
WESTWINN VW.
ELM CFT.
HAZEL AV.
MAPLE WY.
WAY
HAWTHORNE RI.
HORNBEAM
ACORN DR.
CHERRY RISE
BIRCHFIELDS
BIRCHFIELDS AV.
BIRCHFIELDS GARTH
BIRCHFIELDS CL.
Grimes Dike
WHINMOOR
Whinmoor
SHERBURN ROAD
WHITE LAITHE RD.
HATHAWAY DR.
HAWTHORN PK.
SEACROFT IND. EST.
Works
VICTORIA RD.
THE COURTYARDS
VICTORIA IND. PARK
SEACROFT INDUSTRIAL ESTATE
Warehouses
White Laith Prim. Sch.
WHINMOOR WAY
BAILDON RD.
BAILDON CHASE
BAILDON GN.
BAILDON PTH.
BAILDON DR.
Willow Garth Farm
Morwick Farm
YORK ROAD
A64
50
MONKSWOOD
MONKSWOOD BANK
MONKSWOOD HILL
MONKSWOOD AVENUE
MONKSWOOD DRIVE
DUTTON WAY
DUTTON GRN.
BLUEBELL CT.
23
RAMSHEAD CR.
Lime Pits Wood
RAMSHEAD CRES.
RAMSHEAD HILL
RAMSHEAD CL.
OAK TREE BUSINESS PARK
LIMEWOOD CT.
LIMEWOOD APP.
LIMEWOOD ROAD
SEACROFT IND. EST.
A6120
SEACROFT
Ramshead Wood
Training Cen.
RAMSHEAD APPROACH
KENTMERE
RAMSHEAD GS.
Grange Fm. Prim. Sch.
DRIVE
Our Lady Catholic Prim. Sch.
EASTDEAN BANK
EASTDEAN DRIVE
EASTDEAN RISE
EASTDEAN GROVE
EASTDEAN GRANGE
RAMSHEAD HEIGHTS
RAMSHEAD VW.
RAMSHEAD GRO.
PIGEON COTE RD.
PIGEON COTE CL.
KENTMERE CRES.
KENTMERE GRN.
KENTMERE GDNS.
KENTMERE AVENUE
KENTMERE APPROACH
KENTMERE CL.
KENTMERE RISE
PARKWAY
BAILEY'S HILL
BAILEY'S LANE
BAILEY TOWERS
ROSGILL
ROSGILL WLK.
NORTH PARKWAY
Seacroft
SEACROFT CR.
SEACROFT GA.
SEACROFT AV.
SEACROFT CRES.
QUEENSVIEW
Superstore
HEBDEN WLK.
HEBDEN CHASE
HEBDEN PL.
Mill Green
MILL GREEN RD.
MILL GREEN GDNS.
MILL GREEN CL.
MILL GREEN VW.
HANSBY GRA.
HANSBY BNK.
HANSBY GA.
HANSBY AVENUE
HANSBY DRIVE
SEACROFT RING ROAD
EASDALE CRES.
EASDALE RD.
EASDALE MT.
BROOKLANDS
BROOKLANDS AVENUE
BROOKLANDS TOWERS
Library
The Green
THE GREEN
Beechwood Prim. Sch.
REDMIRE VW.
REDMIRE CT.
COURTENAYS
ST. JAMES APP.
YORK RD.
34
SLEDMERE LA.
SLEDMERE PL.
Grimes Dyke Prim. Sch.
STANKS LANE NORTH
STANKS DRIVE
STANKS AVENUE
SHERBURN APP.
FARNDALE
WHINMOOR WAY
LANGBAR GN.
LANGBAR GTH.
LANGBAR APP.
LANGBAR GRO.
LANGBAR CL.
Lib.
BRAYTON GRO.
BRAYTON GRANGE
BRAYTON APP.
BRAYTON GRN.
ASH TREE GRO.
ASH TREE BANK
ASH TREE CL.
ASH TREE APP.
PENNWELL GARTH
PENNWELL GATE
Swarcliffe Prim. Sch.
SWARCLIFFE AVENUE
SWARCLIFFE RD.
SWARCLIFFE BANK
SWARCLIFFE APP.
Swarcliffe
Stanks
EASTWOOD
THE LARCHES

SAW WOOD
Yorksfield Plantation
Flying Horse Farm
Saw Wood House
Miry Carr Farm
Holly Croft
SANDHILL VS.
LITTLEMOOR LA.
MIRYCARR LANE
Thorner Lane Farm
THORNER LANE
YORK ROAD
A64
Leeds
Whinmoor Grange
Woodhouse Farm
Whinmoor Nook Farm
Whinmoor Nook Wood
STOCKHELD LA.
NOOK RD.
NOOK ROAD
MORWICK TER.
Home Farm
Rake Beck
SCHOLES LANE or STATION ROAD
Arthursdale
Stockheld Grange Farm
THE AVENUE
THE APPROACH
NOOK GS.
ARTHURSDALE DR.
ARTHURSDALE CL.
ARTHURSDALE GRANGE
Glebe Farm
MORTEC PARK
Morwick Hall
Rake Hill
Rakehill Farm
RAKEHILL ROAD
Springfield Farm
Rake Bridge
Playing Fields
LS15
MILTON DRIVE
BELLE VUE
GREEN CT.
STATION GDS.
LYNDHURST CL.
LYNDHURST CRES.
LYNDHURST RD.
LYNNFIELD GDS.
LYNDHURST VW.
ELMETE AV.
ELMETE CFT.
MORWICK GRO.
Scholes Prim. Sch.
Liby.
OAKLEA RD.
BELLE VUE AVENUE
BELLE VUE EST.
GRANGE CT.
BELLE VUE RD.
SCHOLES
Limekiln Hill
Green Lodge Farm
MAIN STREET
SCHOLES LODGE LA.
LANE
Scholes Park
LEEDS ROAD
TAYLOR LANE
Carr Head
Honesty Farm
Lwr. Barnbow Fm.
BARNBOW LANE
Barnbow Carr
Up. Barnbow Fm.
BOG LANE
Carr Beck
WOOD
AINSLEY M.
AINSLEY VW.
AINSLEY CT.
Beck
PENNWELL
DRIVE
E F G H
1 2 3 4 5 6
37 38 39
436

35

26
16
36
A
B
C
D
1
2
3
4
5
6
Ravenscliffe
WOODHALL HILLS GOLF COURSE
Ravenscliffe Wood
Round Wood
Low Rein
Crossfield Farm
Crossfield House
Lees Farm
Hawthorn Glen Farm
Craven Farm
Priesthorpe
Priesthorpe Farm
Club House
Top Farm
Woodhall Hills
Woodhall Plantation
Greatwood Farm
Throstles Nest Farm
Cherry Tree Farm
Lower Fagley
Upper Fagley
BD10
BD2
BD3
BD4
Club House
CALVERLEY GOLF COURSE
Comm. Play. Cen.
Fld.
Woodhall Farm
Play. Fld.
Woodhall Grange
Priesthorpe School
Woodhall Park
Offices
Woodhall
Sports Grd.
Pav.
Tennis Courts
Sports Ground
Playing Field
Thornbury Barracks
TA Cen.
Fagley
Works
Bradford
Bakery
Rec. Grd.
Superstore
WOODHALL RETAIL PARK
Playing Field
Works
Hillfoot
Tunnel
Pudsey Bolton Royd Prim. Sch.
Odeon Cin.
Esporta Health & Fitness Club
GALLAGHER LEISURE PARK
MID POINT BUS. PARK
Spts. Grd.
Club Ho.
Ckt. Grd.
Lib.
Bus Depot
Wks.
Thornbury
Prim. Sch.
Laisterdyke Business & Enterprise Coll.
Reservoir (covered)
Delph End
Tyersal Beck
PHOENIX PARK GOLF COURSE
Ducketts Crossing
Wild Grove
Wild Grove Farm
Wild Grove House
Mill
Nirvana Farm
CITY LINK IND. PARK
Grove View Farm
Community
Laisterdyke
A647
B6381
B6154
ROAD
BRADFORD
LEEDS
RING
WOODHALL
PRIESTHORPE
GALLOWAY
WATERLOO
Res.
Hazelbra
Priesthorpe
Farsley Farfield Prim.

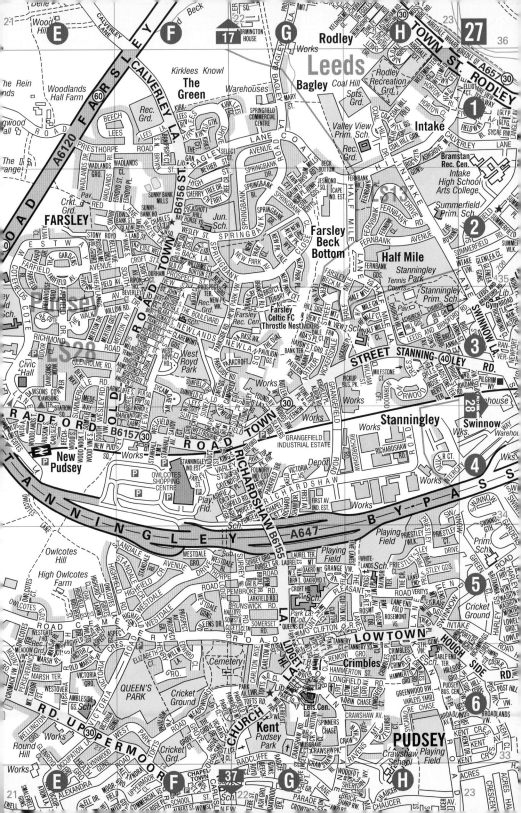

27
17
28
37
E
F
G
H
1
2
3
4
5
6
21
22
23
36
33
34
Rodley
Leeds
Bagley
Coal Hill
The Green
Kirklees Knowl
Woodlands Hall Farm
FARSLEY
Farsley Beck Bottom
Half Mile
Intake
Stanningley
Swinnow
New Pudsey
Pudsey
PUDSEY
Kent
Crimbles
Owlcotes Hill
High Owlcotes Farm
Round Hill
LS13
LS28
A6120
A657
A647
B6156
B6157
B6155
FARSLEY ROAD
CALVERLEY LA.
TOWN ST. RODLEY
STANNINGLEY BY-PASS
STANNINGLEY RD.
STREET
OLD ROAD TOWN
RICHARDSHAW LA.
RADFORD ROAD
UPPERMOOR RD.
LOWTOWN
CHURCH LA.
LIDGET HL.
HOUGH SIDE RD.
SWINNOW LA.
SPRINGBANK
BAGLEY LANE
COAL HILL LA.
PRIESTHORPE ROAD
WESTWAY
CEMETERY ROAD
Rodley Recreation Grd.
Valley View Prim. Sch.
Bramstan Rec. Cen.
Intake High School Arts College
Summerfield Prim. Sch.
Stanningley Park
Stanningley Prim. Sch.
Farsley Celtic FC (Throstle Nest)
Farsley Rec. Cen.
West Royd Park
Civic Hall
OWLCOTES SHOPPING CENTRE
GRANGEFIELD INDUSTRIAL ESTATE
SPRINGFIELD COMMERCIAL CENTRE
PICKUP BUS. PK.
QUEEN'S PARK
Cemetery
Cricket Ground
Pudsey Park
Crawshaw School
Park La. Coll.
Lets.Cen.
NORMINGTON HOUSE
Works
Warehouses

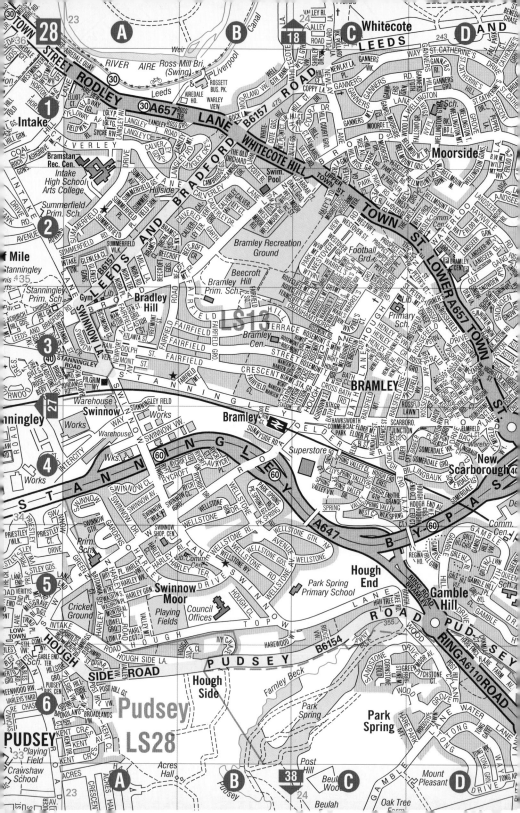
A
B
C
D
1
2
3
4
5
6
18
27
38
Whitecote
Intake
Bramstan Rec. Cen.
Intake High School Arts College
Summerfield Prim. Sch.
Hillside
Stanningley Prim. Sch.
Bradley Hill
Bramley Recreation Ground
Beecroft Hill
Bramley Prim. Sch.
Football Grd
Moorside
Swim. Pool
LS13
Bramley Cen.
BRAMLEY
Primary Sch.
Bramley
Swinnow
Works
Warehouse
Superstore
New Scarborough
Swinnow Moor
Swinnow Shop. Cen.
Park Spring Primary School
Hough End
Gamble Hill
Council Offices
Playing Fields
Cricket Ground
Hough Side
Pudsey
LS28
PUDSEY
Playing Field
Crawshaw School
Acres Hall
Park Spring
Farnley Beck
Post Hill
Beulah Wood
Mount Pleasant
Oak Tree
RIVER AIRE
Ross Mill Bri. (Swing)
Leeds & Liverpool Canal
Weir
ROSSETT BUS. PK.
TOWN STREET RODLEY LANE A657
WHITECOTE HILL
TOWN ST. LOWER TOWN ST. A657
BRADFORD ROAD B6157
LEEDS AND BRADFORD ROAD
LEEDS ROAD B6157
STANNINGLEY ROAD
STANNINGLEY BY-PASS A647
RING ROAD BRAMLEY
RING ROAD A6110
PUDSEY ROAD B6154
HOUGH SIDE ROAD
SWINNOW ROAD
BROAD LANE
INTAKE LANE
CALVERLEY LANE
FAIRFIELD
ROSEMONT
WELLSTONE
HARLEY
HOUGH LANE
ELDER ROAD
BROAD LANE
TONG ROAD
GAMBLE LANE

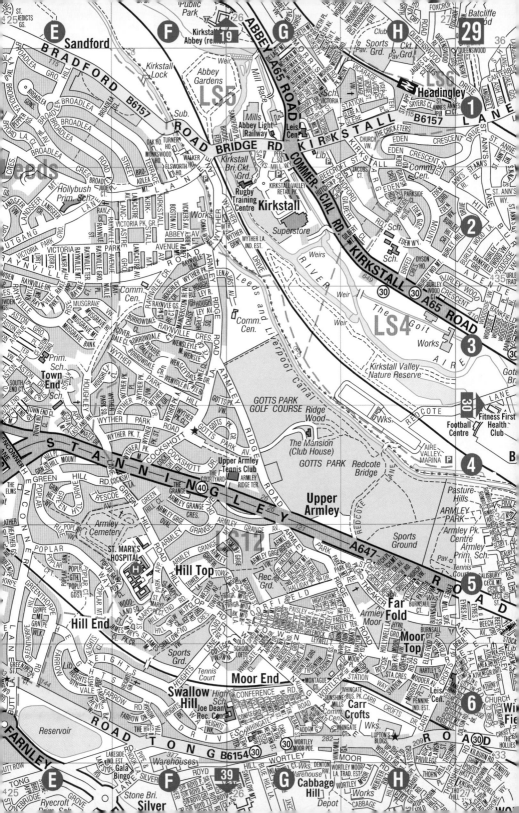

29
E
F
G
H
E
F
G
H
1
2
3
4
5
6
19
39
30
Sandford
Leeds
Kirkstall
Headingley
Upper Armley
Hill Top
Hill End
Town End
Far Fold
Moor Top
Armley Moor
Moor End
Swallow Hill
Carr Crofts
Cabbage Hill
Pasture Hills
Ryecroft
Silver
LS5
LS4
LS6
LS12
BRADFORD ROAD B6157
BRIDGE RD.
KIRKSTALL LANE B6157
ABBEY ROAD A65
COMMERCIAL RD.
KIRKSTALL ROAD A65
STANNINGLEY ROAD A647
ARMLEY RIDGE ROAD
TONG ROAD B6154
FARNLEY
WORTLEY
Kirkstall Abbey (remains)
Public Park
Abbey Gardens
Kirkstall Lock
Mill Race
Abbey Light Railway
Kirkstall Bri. Ckt. Grd.
Rugby Training Centre
Superstore
KIRKSTALL VALLEY RETAIL PK.
Hollybush Prim. Sch.
RIVER AIRE
The Goit
Kirkstall Valley Nature Reserve
Leeds and Liverpool Canal
GOTTS PARK GOLF COURSE
Ridge Wood
The Mansion (Club House)
GOTTS PARK
Redcote Bridge
AIRE VALLEY MARINA
Football Centre
Fitness First Health Club
Upper Armley Tennis Club
Armley Cemetery
ST. MARY'S HOSPITAL
ARMLEY PARK
Armley Pk. Centre
Armley Prim. Sch.
Sports Ground
Reservoir
Joe Dean Rec. Cen.
Warehouses
Gala Bingo
Stone Bri.

A
B
C
D
1
2
3
4
5
6
20
28
27
36
35
34
33
29
40
Headingley
Headingley Hill
Mt. St. Joseph
Hinsley Hall
Hyde Pk.
LS6
LS4
LS3
LS12
Yorkshire Co. Cricket Club (Headingley)
Leeds Rhinos RLFC & Leeds Carnegie RUFC
Burley Pk.
Burley Rec. Ground
Burley
Armley
Armley Rec. Grd.
Armley Pk. Centre
Armley Prim. Sch.
ARMLEY PARK
Armley Mills Leeds Ind. Mus.
Armley Junc.
Moor Top
Wiring Field
New Wortley
New Wortley Cemetery
HMP LEEDS
Castleton Prim. Sch.
Leeds & Liverpool Canal
RIVER AIRE
Gott's Bri.
Refuse Destructor
Football Centre
Fitness First Health Club
Virgin Active
Cinema
Bowl. Alley
Radio Station
The Leeds Studio
Gala Casino
The Roundhouse
Oddy's Locks
Spring Gardens Lock
Pasture Hills
Sports Ground
Batty's Wood
Batcliffe Wood
KIRKSTALL
KIRKSTALL ROAD
HEADINGLEY LANE
A660
A65
A647
B6157
B6154
STANNINGLEY R.
ARMLEY ROAD
CANAL ST.
TONG ROAD
6154 ROAD
BURLEY ROAD
CARDIGAN ROAD
VICTORIA ROAD
HYDE PARK ROAD
WOODSLEY ROAD
VIADUCT ROAD
WELLINGTON ROAD
REDCOTE LANE
CARDIGAN LANE
ST. MICHAEL'S LANE
AIRE VALLEY MARINA

31
E
F
G
H
21
Woodhouse Cliff
City of Leeds Sch.
Waste Sorting Site Works
Urban Farm
Sugarwell Hill Park
Prince Philip Centre
Prince Philip Fields
Buslingthorpe
SCOTT HALL RD.
A61
SHEEPSCAR ST.
LS7
Chapeltown
HAREHILLS AV.
1
2
3
4
5
6
Woodhouse Carr
WOODHOUSE
Sports Grd.
MELVILLE RD.
CAMBRIDGE RD.
Bagby Flds.
Comm. Cen.
Leodis Residences
Northwest Bus. Pk.
BARRACK RD.
A58
Sheepscar
Thomas Danby Coll.
Little London
St. George's Fields
Woodhouse
LS2
A660
BLENHEIM WK.
WOODHOUSE LANE
University of Leeds
4
A58(M)
RING
5
A64(M)
The Leylands
Mabgate
Little Woodhouse
CLARENDON WAY
INNER
LEEDS GENERAL INFIRMARY
Dental Inst.
Civic Hall
CLAY PIT LA.
AMF Bowl
Merrion Centre
NEW YORK RD.
REGENT ST.
Leeds T.H.
City Varieties
County Arc.
Victoria Q.
Kirkgate Mkt.
Playhouse
Quarry Hill
Leisure Cen.
Police HQ
Bus & Coach Sta.
LS1
LEEDS
WELLINGTON
A58(M)
Leeds Shop Plaza
RIVER AIRE
PRINCES SQUARE
LEEDS
STATION
Canal Wharf
Granary Wharf
Monk Bri.
Crown Point Bri.
Centenary Bri.
Merchants Quay
Leeds Dam
Bank
Marsh
Crown Point
CROWN POINT ROAD
A653
41
Brewery
Whitehall Junction Warehouses
Victoria
Mus.
32
4
5
E
F
G
H
29
31
430
435
33
34
36

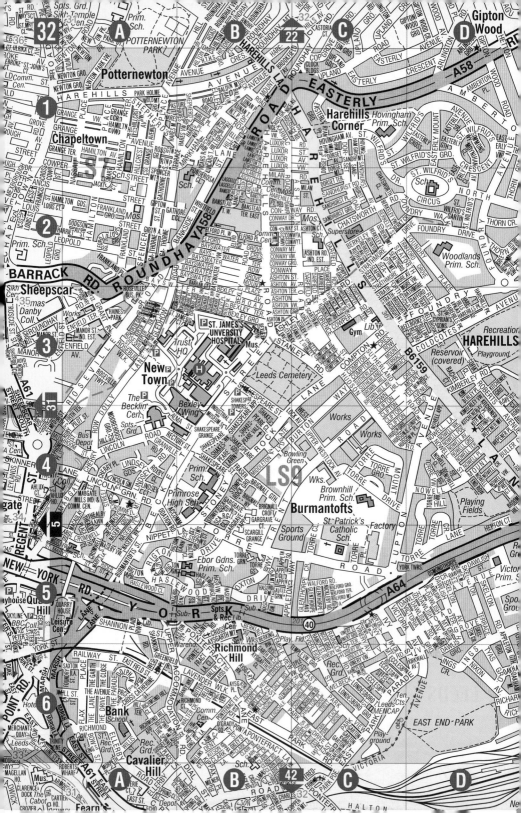

32
A
B
C
D
22
42
1
2
3
4
5
6
Potternewton
POTTERNEWTON PARK
Chapeltown
Gipton Wood
Harehills Corner
Hovingham Prim. Sch.
HAREHILLS
Sheepscar
New Town
ST. JAMES'S UNIVERSITY HOSPITAL
Bexley Wing
Trust HQ
Mus.
The Becklin Cen.
Leeds Cemetery
LS9
Burmantofts
Brownhill Prim. Sch.
St. Patrick's Catholic Sch.
Sports Ground
Factory
Woodlands Prim. Sch.
Recreation
Playground
Reservoir (covered)
Playing Fields
Primrose High Sch.
Prim. Sch.
Ebor Gdns. Prim. Sch.
Richmond Hill
Bank
School
Cavalier Hill
Quarry Hill
Leisure Cen.
EAST END PARK
Leeds MENCAP
Play-ground
Superstore
Gym
Works
Bowling Green
Thomas Danby Coll.
ROUNDHAY ROAD
A58
EASTERLY ROAD
HAREHILLS LANE
HAREHILLS AVENUE
BARRACK RD.
ROUNDHAY ROAD A58
YORK RD.
A64
A61
B6159
BECKETT STREET
STANLEY RD.
COMPTON RD.
TORRE ROAD
LUPTON AVENUE
FOUNDRY DRIVE
ST. WILFRID'S CIRCUS
EAST PARK RD.
PONTEFRACT LANE
MARSH LANE
REGENT ST.
NEW YORK RD.
Mabgate Mills Ind. & Comm. Cen.

33
E
F
G
H
23
34
35
36
David Young Community Academy
East Leeds Family Learning Cen.
Brooklands
Fearnville
Leeds
Oakwood Pupil Support Centre
All Weather Pitch
Fearnville Sports Centre
Recreation Ground
Gipton
Wyke Beck
Parkway Towers
Seacroft Gardens
Comm. Cen.
St. Nicholas Catholic Prim. Sch.
LS14
The Oval
Killingbeck RC Cemetery
Superstore
Killingbeck Retail Park
Tennis Courts
Bowling Greens
Harehills Cemetery
War Meml.
Killingbeck
Acorn Bus. Pk.
Seacroft Hospital
Newsam Unit
Playing Fields
Playing Field
York Road
A64
40
Selby Road
B6159
Halton Deans
Sports Ground
LS15
Tennis Courts
Bowling Green
Halton
Corpus Christi Catholic Coll.
Corpus Christi Catholic Sch.
Recreation Ground
Osmondthorpe
Meadowfield Prim. Sch.
Leisure Cen.
Halton Moor
Club House
Rec. Grd.
43
1
2
3
4
5
6
Fearnville Road
Fearnville Drive
Foundry Lane
Coldcotes Circus
Coldcotes Drive
Wykebeck Valley Rd.
Gipton Approach
Rookwood Avenue
Wykebeck Avenue
South Parkway
Brooklands Lane
Amberton Road
Oakwood Lane
Halton Moor Road
Temple Newsam Road
Sherbrooke Avenue
Neville Road
Osmondthorpe Lane

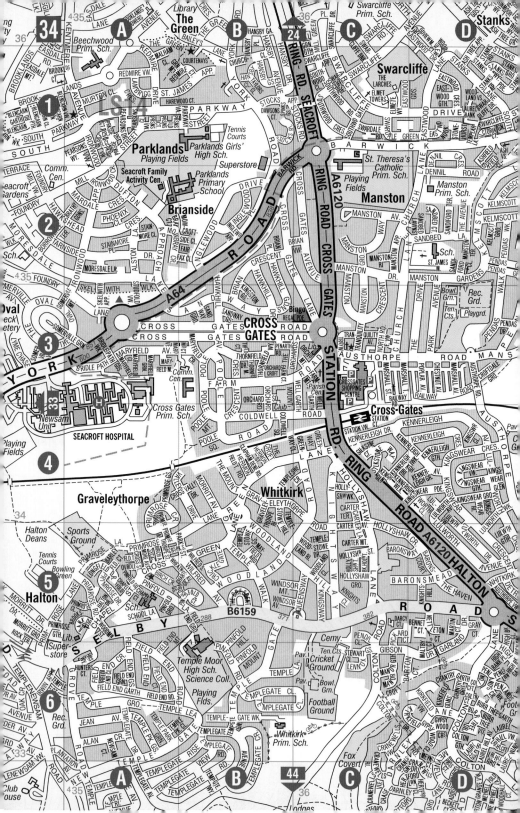
34
24
33
44
A
B
C
D
1
2
3
4
5
6
LS14
The Green
Library
Stanks
Swarcliffe
Swarcliffe Prim. Sch.
Beechwood Prim. Sch.
Parklands
Playing Fields
Parklands Girls' High Sch.
Tennis Courts
Superstore
Seacroft Family Activity Cen.
Parklands Primary School
Brianside
Comm. Cen.
Seacroft Gardens
St. Theresa's Catholic Prim. Sch.
Playing Fields
Manston
Manston Prim. Sch.
CROSS GATES
Bingo
Cross-Gates
CROSSGATES SHOPPING CENTRE
Parish Cen.
Cross Gates Prim. Sch.
Newsam Unit
SEACROFT HOSPITAL
Playing Fields
Graveleythorpe
Whitkirk
Halton Deans
Sports Ground
Tennis Courts
Bowling Green
Halton
Super-store
Temple Moor High Sch. Science Coll.
Playing Flds.
Cemy.
Cricket Ground
Football Ground
Whitkirk Prim. Sch.
Fox Covert
Rec. Grd.
Playgrd.
Bowl. Grn.
Ten. Cts.
Club House
RING RD. SEACROFT
RING ROAD CROSS GATES
A6120
A64
YORK ROAD
STATION RD.
RING ROAD A6120 HALTON
B6159
SELBY ROAD
BARWICK ROAD
CROSS GATES ROAD
AUSTHORPE ROAD
SOUTH PARKWAY
PARKWAY
SANDWAY
COLDWELL ROAD
TEMPLE NEWSAM
TEMPLEGATE
WOODLAND
KINGSWEAR CRES.
MANSTON DR.
PENDAS WAY
KELMSCOTT
COLTON

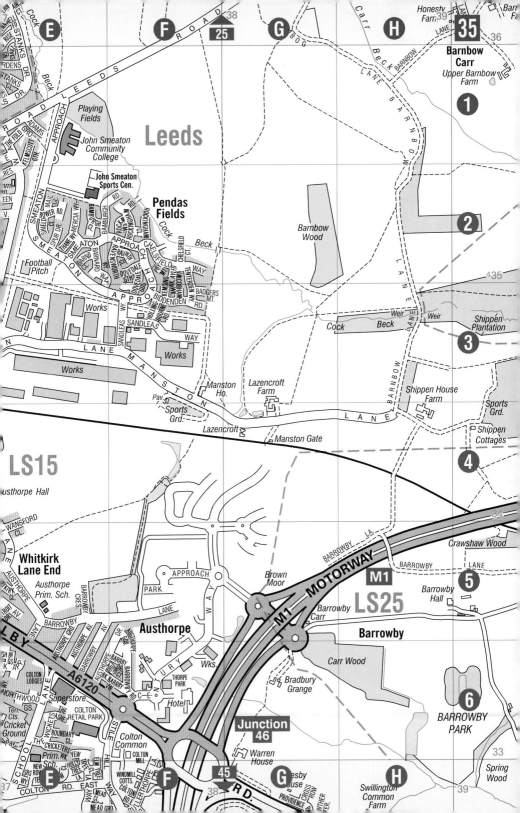

35
25
45
Leeds
LS15
LS25
Barnbow Carr
Upper Barnbow Farm
Honesty Farm
Playing Fields
John Smeaton Community College
John Smeaton Sports Cen.
Pendas Fields
Barnbow Wood
Football Pitch
Works
Cock Beck
Weir
Shippen Plantation
Manston Ho.
Lazencroft Farm
Shippen House Farm
Sports Grd.
Lazencroft
Manston Gate
Shippen Cottages
Austhorpe Hall
Whitkirk Lane End
Austhorpe Prim. Sch.
Crawshaw Wood
Brown Moor
M1 MOTORWAY
Barrowby Hall
Barrowby Carr
Barrowby
Austhorpe
Carr Wood
Bradbury Grange
Wks.
THORPE PARK
Hotel
Superstore
COLTON RETAIL PARK
Cricket Ground
Colton Common
COLTON MILL
Junction 46
Warren House
BARROWBY PARK
Spring Wood
Swillington Common Farm
A6120
LEEDS ROAD
MANSTON LANE
BARNBOW LANE
BARROWBY LANE
SMEATON APPROACH
COLTON RD. EAST
SCHOOL LANE
STILE HILL WAY

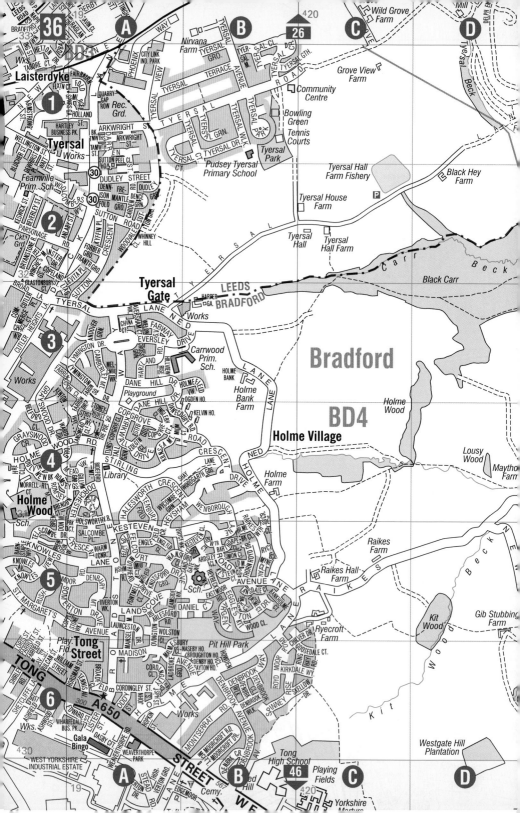
A
B
C
D
26
420
Wild Grove Farm
Nirvana Farm
Laisterdyke
BD3
Tyersal
Tyersal Works
Fearnville Prim. Sch.
CITY LINK IND. PARK
HARTLEY BUSINESS PK.
Rec. Grd.
Grove View Farm
Community Centre
Bowling Green
Tennis Courts
Tyersal Park
Pudsey Tyersal Primary School
Tyersal Hall Farm Fishery
Black Hey Farm
Tyersal House Farm
Tyersal Hall
Tyersal Hall Farm
Carr Beck
Black Carr
Tyersal Gate
LEEDS
BRADFORD
Works
Carrwood Prim. Sch.
Holme Bank Farm
Bradford
BD4
Holme Wood
Holme Village
Lousy Wood
Maytho Farm
Holme Farm
Playground
Library
Holme Wood
Sch.
Raikes Farm
Raikes Hall Farm
Ryecroft Farm
Kit Wood
Gib Stubbing Farm
Pit Hill Park
Tong Street
Play Fld.
TONG STREET
A650
Works
Wks.
Gala Bingo
WEST YORKSHIRE INDUSTRIAL ESTATE
WEAVERTHORPE PARK
WHARFEDALE BUS. PK.
Tong High School
Playing Fields
Westgate Hill Plantation
Kit Wood Beck
Cemy.
Yorkshire
46
1
2
3
4
5
6
30
430

37
PUDSEY
Pudsey
LS28
BD11
UPPERMOOR
CHAPELTOWN
B6154
Pudsey Park
Playing Field
Crawshaw School
Round Hill
Windmill Hill
Westroyd Hill
Littlemoor Bottom
Prim. Sch.
Community Centre
Turkey Hill
Woodlands
Sports Ground
Museum
Fulneck
Bankhouse
Nesbitt Hall
Willows Nook Farm
The Banks
Waterspride Kennels
Bank House Farm
Club House
Newstead House
Bankhouse Bottom
FULNECK GOLF COURSE
Sisters Wood
Burial Ground
Hope Farm
South Park House
South Park Farm
Reservoir
Hazeldene
North Wood
Pudsey Beck
Daffels Wood
Scholebrook Farm
Scholebrook
Beck
Park Wood
Acre Wood
Coney Wood
The Manor Ho.
Northfield Farm
Hill Green
Newlands Farm
Helicon Pond
Shackleton Wood
Home Farm
TONG HALL BUSINESS PARK
Tong
Cricket Grd.
Manor Farm
Corn Mill Farm
TONG PARK
Peter's Shrog
Garden Centre
Barron's Wood
Ringshaw Beck
Thick Thorn Bank
Cockersdale
Cockersdale Ho.
Farm
Dale Farm
Whiteley Wood
Doles Wood
TONG LANE
SCHOLEBROOK LANE
KEEPER LANE
MILL LANE
SPRINGFIELD LANE
KENT ROAD
VALLEY ROAD
LITTLEMOOR ROAD
FULNECK
BANKHOUSE LANE
27
38
47
1
2
3
4
5
6
E
F
G
H

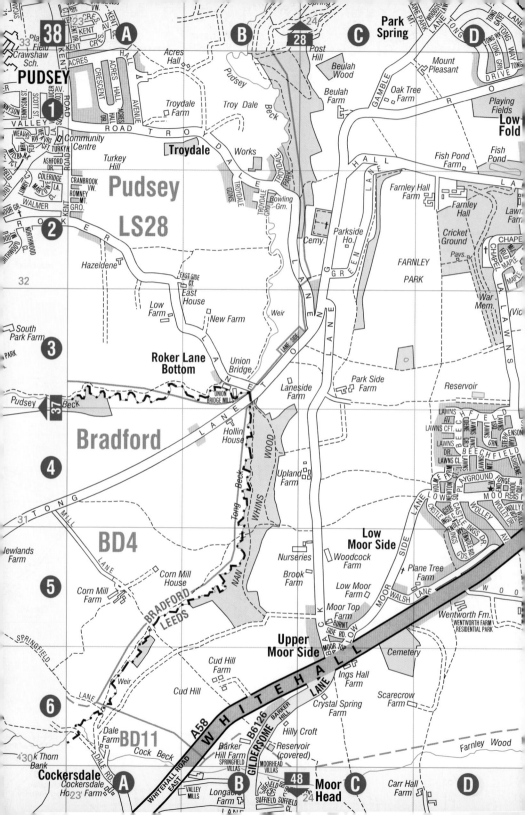

38
A
B
C
D
28
Park Spring
PUDSEY
Crawshaw Sch.
Acres Hall
Pudsey Beck
Troy Dale
Troydale Farm
Post Hill
Beulah Wood
Beulah Farm
Mount Pleasant
Oak Tree Farm
Playing Fields
Low Fold
Community Centre
Troydale
Works
Turkey Hill
Pudsey
LS28
Fish Pond Farm
Fish Pond
Farnley Hall Farm
Farnley Hall
Bowling Grn.
Cemy.
Parkside Ho.
Cricket Ground
FARNLEY PARK
War Mem.
Hazeldene
East Side Ct.
East House
Low Farm
New Farm
Weir
South Park Farm
Roker Lane Bottom
Union Bridge
Union Bridge Mills
Laneside Farm
Park Side Farm
Reservoir
Pudsey Beck
37
Bradford
Hollin House
Whins Wood
Tong Beck
Upland Farm
Tong Lane
Mill Lane
BD4
Newlands Farm
Nurseries
Woodcock Farm
Low Moor Side
Brook Farm
Plane Tree Farm
Corn Mill House
Corn Mill Farm
Bradford
Leeds
Low Moor Farm
Moor Top Farm
Wentworth Fm.
Wentworth Farm Residential Park
Upper Moor Side
Cemetery
Cud Hill Farm
Ings Hall Farm
Cud Hill
Scarecrow Farm
Crystal Spring Farm
Springfield
Weir
Whitehall
A58
Gildersome Lane
B6126
Hilly Croft
Reservoir (covered)
Barker Hill Farm
Dale Farm
BD11
Cock Beck
Farnley Wood
Cockersdale
Cockersdale Farm
Longacre Farm
Valley Mills
48
Moor Head
Carr Hall Farm
Whitehall Road East
Springfield Villas
Moorhead Villas
Low Moor Side Lane
Walsh Lane
Back Lane
Green Lane
Hall Lane
Gamble Lane
Lawns Lane
Chapel Lane
Roker Lane
Valley Road
Troydale Lane
Kent Road
Acres Hall Crescent
Acres Hall Avenue
1
2
3
4
5
6

RING ROAD FARNLEY
Reservoir
Silver Royd Hill
Stone Bri.
Ryecroft Prim. Sch.
Bawn
Gala Bingo
Warehouses
Wortley High Sch.
Play. Flds.
Cabbage Hill
Depot
Upper Wortley
WORTLEY
Prim. Sch.
Blue Hill
Town End
Recreation Grd.
Western Flatts Park
Cliff Park
Sports Grd.
New Blackpool
Farnley
Holly Farm
Playing Fields
Farnley Park Maths & Computing College
Lawns Pk. Prim. Sch.
Little Wood
Cobden Prim. Sch.
Lower Wortley Prim. Sch.
LS12
NEW FARNLEY
WHITEHALL IND. EST.
WHITEHALL PARK
WHITEHALL RD
A58
A6110
LOWER WORTLEY
RING ROAD
Ochre House Farm
Harper Farm
Castle Hill
Church Farm
Hypermarket
PAVILION BUS. PK.
CITY PARK INDUSTRIAL ESTATE
Leeds
Farnley Wood Farm
Beeston Royds
Hill Top Cemetery
Cottingley Spring
Spring End Farm
Reservoir
Works
Wood End Farm
Farnley Woodside Farm
Wood Farm
COTTINGLEY SPRINGS CARAVAN SITE
LS27
A62
GELDERD ROAD
Cemetery
Cemy.
Subway
M621
M621 MOTORWAY
Snittles Farm
Warehouses
Rooms Farm
Rooms
New Stables
E
F
G
H
1
2
3
4
5
6
29
40
49

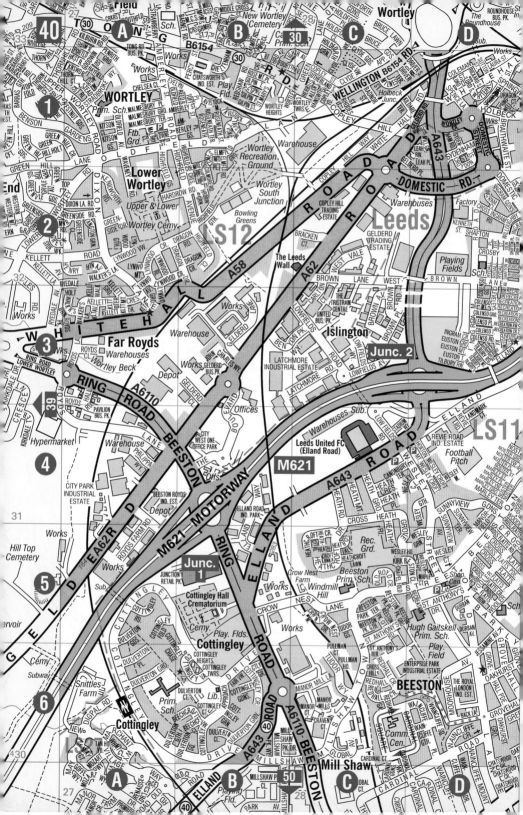
40
A
B
C
D
1
2
3
4
5
6
30
39
50
WORTLEY
Wortley
Lower Wortley
Upper & Lower Wortley Cemy.
Wortley Recreation Ground
Wortley South Junction
New Wortley Cemetery
The Roundhouse
ROUNDHOUSE BUS. PK.
Holbeck Junc.
HOLBECK
Leeds
LS12
LS11
Far Royds
Islington
Junc. 2
Junc. 1
Leeds United FC (Elland Road)
The Leeds Wall
Cottingley
Cottingley Hall Crematorium
BEESTON
Mill Shaw
Hill Top Cemetery
Hypermarket
WELLINGTON B6154 RD.
B6154
DOMESTIC RD.
GELDERD ROAD
WHITEHALL ROAD
RING ROAD BEESTON
RING ROAD LOWER WORTLEY
ELLAND ROAD
M621 MOTORWAY
M621
A58
A62
A643
A6110
LATCHMORE INDUSTRIAL ESTATE
GELDERD TRADING ESTATE
COPLEY HILL TRADING ESTATE
CITY PARK INDUSTRIAL ESTATE
CITY WEST ONE OFFICE PARK
ELLAND ROAD IND. PARK
REVIE ROAD IND. ESTATE
ENTERPRISE PARK INDUSTRIAL ESTATE
THE ROYAL LONDON IND. EST.
JUNCTION 1 RETAIL PK.
THE TRISTRAM CENTRE
Beeston Prim. Sch.
Hugh Gaitskell Prim. Sch.
Windmill Hill
Crow Nest Farm
Snittles Farm
Football Pitch
Playing Fields
Bowling Greens
Warehouse
Works
Depot
Offices

Holbeck
Whitehall Junction Warehouses
Canal Wharf
Camp Field
Crown Point
Brewery
Leeds City Office Park
Crown Point Retail Park
Sovereign Bus. Pk.
Fearn's Island
The Discovery Centre
Indoor Karting
Apex Business Centre
The Works
Pottery Field
Junc. 2a
M621 MOTORWAY
South Leeds Sports Cen.
Junc. 3
South Leeds Bus. Cen.
HUNSLET DISTRIBUTOR
A639
A61
A653
LS10
Hunslet
Play. Fld.
Crescent Towers Park
Hunslet Moor
Junc. 4
Beeston Hill
Holbeck Cemetery
Council Offs.
St. Francis of Assisi Catholic Prim. Sch.
Lib.
Shop. Cen.
TUNSTALL A61 RD.
Junc. 5
Tulip Retail Park
Balm Road Ind. Est.
Mecca Bingo
Hunslet Grn. Retail Cen.
Moor Rd.
M621
Junc. 6
Climax Works
Coll. of Building
Ashbrooke Park
Astra Business Park
Parkside Ind. Est.
Hunslet Carr
Cross Flatts Park
The Grange
Middleton Railway
Bowls & Athletic Cen.
South Leeds High Sch
Hunslet Hawks RLFC (John Charles Stadium)
Leeds College of Technology
Warehouses
Works
DEWSBURY ROAD
MIDDLETON GROVE
42
51
31
4
5
1
2
3
6
E
F
G
H
29
30
31
32
33
430

A
B
C
D
1
2
3
4
5
6
32
41
52
Cavalier Hill
Fearn's Island
The Discovery Centre
Indoor Karting
HUNSLET
EAST ST. A61
A61
Foundry
Warehouse
Wks.
Prim. Sch.
Comm. Cen.
Leeds Teaching & Learning Cen. (Copperfields)
Cross Green
AIRE A63 VALLEY WAY
PONTEFRACT
Ckt. Grd.
Yorkshire Produce Centre
HALTON MOOR ROAD
EAST END PARK
VICTORIA
Play-ground
Football World
CROSS GREEN IND. EST.
Knowsthorpe
Depot
Swing-bridge
Atkinson Hill
Leeds
RIVER AIRE
Knostrop Cut
Valley House
Knostrop Rifle Range
Sewage Works
Weir
Thwaite Mills Watermill Mus.
Thwaite Ho.
Thwaite Gate
THWAITE LANE
Aire & Calder
Hunslet
Play. Fld.
THE PENNY HILL CEN.
HUNSLET GRN. RETAIL CEN.
CHURCH
LOW ROAD A639
HUNSLET DISTRIBUTOR
GIBRALTAR ISLAND ROAD
HUNSLET TRADING ESTATE
CLAYTON BUSINESS CENTRE
MIDLAND ROAD
TULIP RETAIL PARK
Mecca Bingo
Works
Recreation Ground
Offices
THWAITE GA.
Thwaite Farm Trailer Park
WATERSIDE IND. PK.
Warehouses
Sorting Office
STOURTON BUS. PK.
MAYFLOWER HOUSE
QUEEN STREET
WAKEFIELD ROAD
A639
LS10
Junc. 6
M621 MOTORWAY
Woodhouse Hill
Cemetery
Rec. Grd.
Junction 7
M621
Stourton
Coll.
Freightliner Terminal
VALLEY FARM WAY
Skills Cen. Community Enterprise Resource Centre
BELLE ISLE ROAD
WINROSE GRO.
RING ROAD MIDDLETON
MIDDLETON ROAD
BELLE VUE CIRCUS

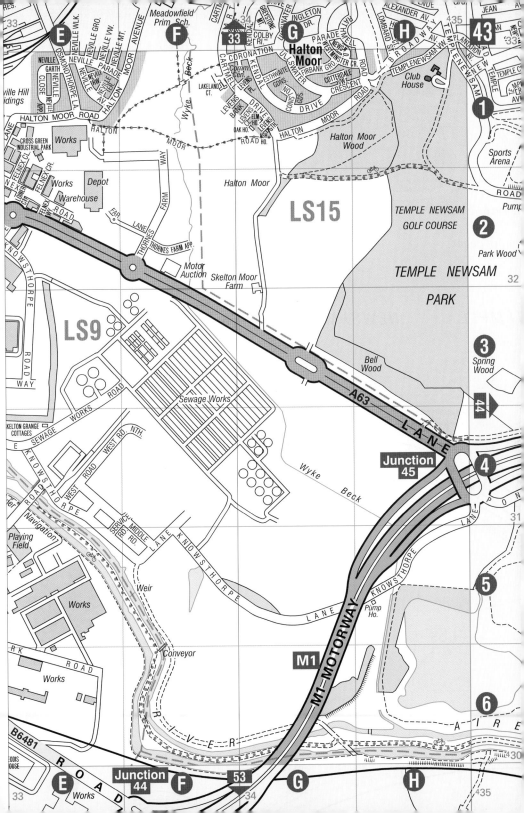
43
33
Meadowfield Prim. Sch.
Halton Moor
Halton Moor Road
Halton Moor Avenue
Neville Parade
Osmondthorpe La.
Coronation Parade
Ullswater Crescent
Kendal Drive
Cartmell Drive
Levens Bank
Lakeland Ct.
Comm. Cen.
Broadway
Templenewsam Vw.
Temple Newsam Road
Club House
Cross Green Industrial Park
Works
Depot
Warehouse
Felnex Road
Far Lane
Thornes Farm Way
Thornes Farm App.
Wyke Beck
Halton Moor Wood
Halton Moor
LS15
LS9
Temple Newsam Golf Course
Park Wood
Temple Newsam Park
Sports Arena
Motor Auction
Skelton Moor Farm
Bell Wood
Spring Wood
44
A63
Lane
Junction 45
Sewage Works
Sewage Works Road
Skelton Grange Cottages
Knowsthorpe Road
Knowsthorpe Way
West Road
West Rd. Nth.
Service Rd.
Middle Rd.
Knowsthorpe Lane
Pontefract Lane
Pump Ho.
M1
M1 Motorway
Navigation
Playing Field
Weir
Conveyor
River Aire
B6481
Road
Junction 44
53
33
34
435
430
31
32

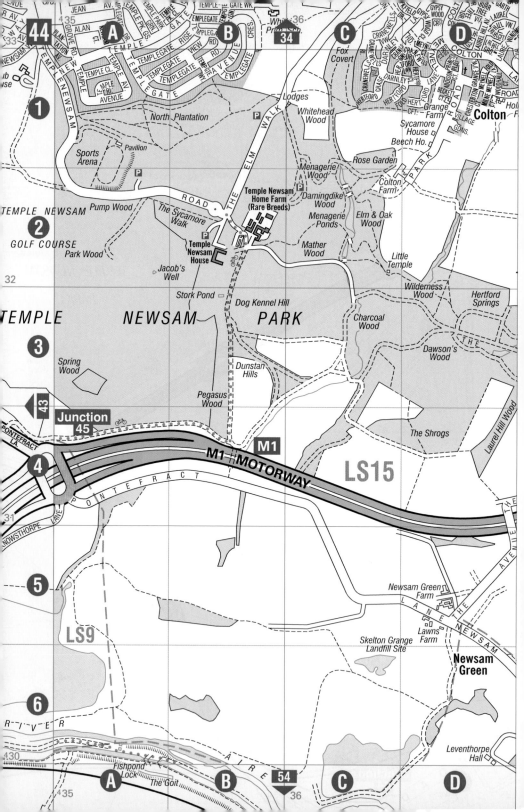

Temple Newsam Park
Temple Newsam Golf Course
Temple Newsam House
Temple Newsam Home Farm (Rare Breeds)
North Plantation
Sports Arena
Pavilion
Pump Wood
Park Wood
The Sycamore Walk
Jacob's Well
Stork Pond
Dog Kennel Hill
Spring Wood
Pegasus Wood
Dunstan Hills
Lodges
Whitehead Wood
Fox Covert
Menagerie Wood
Damingdike Wood
Menagerie Ponds
Rose Garden
Colton Farm
Elm & Oak Wood
Mather Wood
Little Temple
Wilderness Wood
Hertford Springs
Charcoal Wood
Dawson's Wood
The Shrogs
Laurel Hill Wood
Colton
Grange Farm
Sycamore House
Beech Ho.
Junction 45
M1 Motorway
Pontefract Lane
Knowsthorpe Lane
LS15
LS9
Newsam Green Farm
Lawns Farm
Skelton Grange Landfill Site
Newsam Green
Leventhorpe Hall
River Aire
Fishpond Lock
The Goit
The Avenue
Newsam Lane
The Elm Walk
Templegate
Temple Newsam Road
34
43
54

Leeds
LS25
LS26
Swillington Common
Hollinthorpe
SWILLINGTON
Garforth Bridge
Little Preston
Colton Common
Junction 46
M1
M1 MOTORWAY
SELBY ROAD
A63
A642
WAKEFIELD ROAD
LEEDS LANE
SWILLINGTON LANE
BULLERTHORPE LANE
COLTON RD. EAST
AVENUE WOOD
Avenue Ponds
Warren House
Ormesby House
Swillington Common Farm
Nurseries
Waterloo Manor
Brookfield Farm Ho.
Hollinthorpe Farm
Hollinthorpe Low Farm
Upperhall Farm
Syke Ho. Farm
Templethorpe Farm
Lower Hall Farm
Mount Pleasant Farm
Clay Quarry
Works
Mount Pleasant Picnic Site
New Covert
Whitecliffe
Smeaton House Farm
Parkinson's Wood
Woodside Farm
Gamblethorpe
Springwell Farm
Play. Flds.
Sch.
Comm. Cen.
Lib.
Hall Farm
PARKHOME ESTATE
LITTLE PRESTON HALL
Sports Ground
Football Ground
Lodge
Leventhorpe Cotts.
35
55
38
39
37
32
430

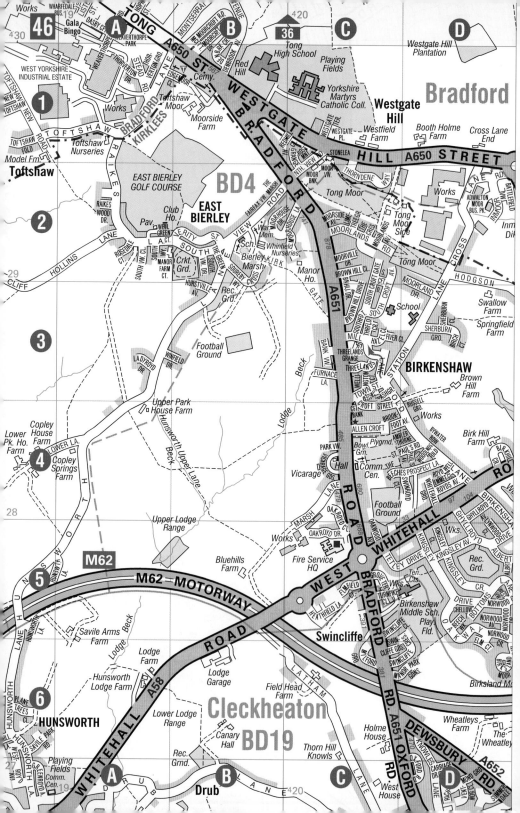
36
A650 TONG ST.
WESTGATE
BRADFORD RD.
HILL A650 STREET
Tong High School
Playing Fields
Yorkshire Martyrs Catholic Coll.
Westgate Hill
Westgate Hill Plantation
Bradford
Red Hill
Cemy.
WEST YORKSHIRE INDUSTRIAL ESTATE
Gala Bingo
Works
WEAVERTHORPE PARK
Toftshaw Moor
Moorside Farm
BRADFORD
KIRKLEES
TOFTSHAW RD.
Toftshaw Nurseries
Model Fm.
Toftshaw
TOFTSHAW FOLD
NEW ROAD
EAST BIERLEY GOLF COURSE
BD4
EAST BIERLEY
Club Ho.
Pav.
RAIKES LANE
RAIKES WOOD DR.
HOLLINS LANE
CLIFF
VERITY ST.
SOUTH VIEW ROAD
THE GREEN
Sch.
War Mem.
Whinfield Nurseries
Bierley Marsh
KIRK GATE
Manor Ho.
Crkt. Grd.
Rec. Grd.
HURSTVILLE AV.
SOUREBY CROSS WY.
LADYROYD DR.
WINFIELD DR.
Football Ground
Westfield Farm
Booth Holme Farm
Cross Lane End
STONELEA
THORNDENE WAY
Tong Moor
Tong Moor Side
Works
ADWALTON MOOR BUS. PK.
MOORLANDS RD.
MOORLAND DR.
HODGSON LANE
CROSS LANE
STATION LANE
A651
School
SHERBURN GRO.
Swallow Farm
Springfield Farm
BIRKENSHAW
Brown Hill Farm
THREELANDS GRANGE
FURNACE LA.
BANK VW.
TOWN ST.
CROFT STREET
ALLEN CROFT
BROOKFOOT AV.
RUSSELL GRO.
Works
BYWATER ROW
Birk Hill Farm
OLD LANE
Bowl. Grn.
Plygrnd.
Hall
Comm. Cen.
Vicarage
PARK VW.
VICARAGE GDS.
PROSPECT LA.
ROAD
Football Ground
MARSH LANE
OAKROYD DR.
Works
Fire Service HQ
WEST ROAD
WHITEHALL ROAD
KINGSLEY DRIVE
KINGSLEY AV.
GHYLL ROYD
BIRKENSHAW
Rec. Grd.
Wks.
TETLEY DRIVE
Ten. Cts.
Birkenshaw Middle Sch.
Play Fld.
Swincliffe
BRADFORD RD.
A651 OXFORD RD.
OAKWAY
DRIVE
BOTTOMS LANE
NORWOOD
Birksland Mo
M62
M62 MOTORWAY
Bluehills Farm
Upper Lodge Range
Upper Park House Farm
Hunsworth Beck
Upper Lane
Lodge Beck
Copley House Farm
Lower Pk. Ho. Farm
LOWER LA.
Copley Springs Farm
HUNSWORTH LANE
Savile Arms Farm
Lodge Farm
Hunsworth Lodge Farm
Lodge Garage
A58
WHITEHALL ROAD
LATHAM LANE
Field Head Farm
Cleckheaton
BD19
Lower Lodge Range
Canary Hall
Rec. Grnd.
Drub
DRUB LANE
Thorn Hill Knowls
Holme House
West House
DEWSBURY RD.
A652
Wheatleys Farm
The Wheatley
HUNSWORTH
PLANE TREES CL.
SAVILE PARK RD.
Playing Fields
Comm. Cen.
HUNSWORTH LA.
1
2
3
4
5
6
A
B
C
D
29
28
27
19
420
430

37
48
Garden Centre
Barron's Wood
Thick Thorn Bank
Dale Farm
Cockersdale House Farm
Cockersdale
Whiteley Wood
Doles Wood
Ringshaw Beck
Shawfield Farm
Lane End Farm
Tong Lane End
Golf Driving Range
THE MANOR GOLF COURSE
Club House
Lumb Wood
Lumb Hall Nurseries
Manor Farm
Westfield Farm
Tong Lane End Farm
BRADFORD & WAKEFIELD RD.
WESTGATE HILL STREET
BRADFORD ROAD
DRIGHLINGTON BY-PASS
A650
A58
B6135
BRADFORD
LEEDS
Nethertown
Lumb Bottom
Spring Gardens
Pitty Close Farm
KING STREET
WHITEHALL ROAD
EAST
Hill Top Farm
BD11
Kittle Point Wood
Upper Sunny Bank
Play. Fields
Lib.
DRIGHLINGTON
Drighlington Prim. Sch.
Battle Site 1643
Adwalton Moor
Adwalton
ADWALTON BUS. PK.
WAKEFIELD ROAD
MOORSIDE ROAD
STATION ROAD
B6125
Res.
Res. (covered)
Penfield
Moorside
Highlands
Reservoir (cov.)
Heightlands Farm
Birkenshaw Bottoms
Burnt Royd
Moorfield
Warehouse
Moor Fields
Batley
KIRKLEES
Foxhall Farm
Works
HOLDEN
Oakwell Beck
Oakwell Wood
M62
M62 MOTORWAY
Holly View Farm
Fieldhead Farm
Fieldhead Jun. & Inf. School
WF17
Springwell Farm
OAKWELL INDUSTRIAL PARK
Brecks Farm
Oakwell Hall
Oakwell
Oakwell Hall Country Park
Sewage Works
Oakwell House
St. Patrick's R.C. Prim. Sch.
FIELD HEAD LANE
GELDERD A62 RD.
Works

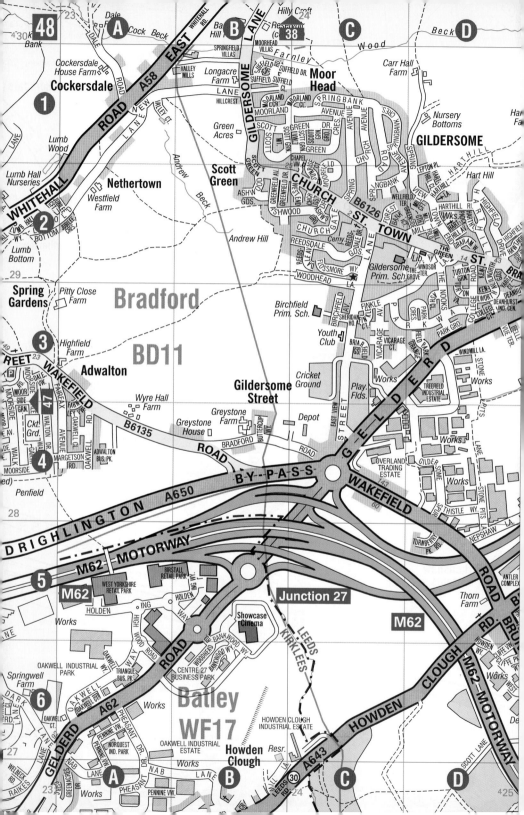48
A
B
C
D
38
47
1
2
3
4
5
6
Dale
Cock Beck
Hilly Croft
Reservoir
Beck
Wood
Farnley
Bank
Cockersdale House Farm
Cockersdale
WHITEHALL ROAD EAST A58
WHITEHALL RD.
DALE ROAD
NEW LANE
SPRINGFIELD VILLAS
VALLEY MILLS
MOORHEAD VILLAS
Longacre Farm
LANE
HILLCREST
GILDERSOME LANE
SUFFIELD DR.
SUFFIELD CL.
Moor Head
Carr Hall Farm
MOORLAND CR.
MOORLAND CL.
MOORLAND
SPRINGBANK
AVENUE
SPRINGBANK CRES.
Nursery Bottoms
GILDERSOME
VALLEY CT.
Green Acres
SCOTT
SCOTT GRN.
GREEN DR.
GREEN
CRES.
AVENUE
CHURCH AVENUE
SPRINGBANK AVENUE
SPRING VIEW
Lumb Wood
Lumb Hall Nurseries
Andrew Beck
Scott Green
CHAPEL VW.
SUNRISE CT.
MOORFIELD
LEPTON PL.
HART HILL
Hart Hill
Nethertown
Westfield Farm
ASHWOOD GDS.
GREENFIELD AV.
GREENFIELD DR.
WESTEND
CHURCH
B6126
ST. TOWN
SPRINGBANK
FOREST BANK
WELLFIELD TER.
MILL
HARTHILL RI.
HIGHFIELD DRIVE
HARTHILL
ASHWOOD
CHURCH GATE
SPRING
WHITEHALL
JUBILEE CT.
JUBILEE CRES.
LUMB HALL WY.
BOTTOM
Lumb Bottom
Andrew Hill
REEDSDALE
Cemy.
REEDSDALE DR.
LANE
THE GREEN
Lib.
TOWN END
GRAHAM W.
ST.
REEDSDALE AV.
FLOSSMORE WY.
GDS.
Gildersome Prim. Sch.
WINDSOR TER.
THE GROVE
THE NOOKS
TURTON GRN.
ROAD
KENILWORTH
DEANHURST IND. CEN.
WOODHEAD LA.
29
Spring Gardens
Pitty Close Farm
Bradford
Birchfield Prim. Sch.
BIRCHFIELD AV.
SHERIDAN HO.
FINKLE CT.
FINKLE AV.
PARKWAY
CRES.
PARK
ASH CL.
TURTON VA.
COLLEGE
COLLEGE CT.
PARK GRO.
Youth Club
BRIAR GS.
BRIAR FIELD
VICARAGE
VICARAGE CT.
FIELD PARK GRANGE
GELDERD ROAD
WINDMILL LA.
STONE PITS LANE
Works
BD11
Highfield Farm
STREET
WAKEFIELD
Adwalton
MOORSIDE
DALE VW.
MOORSIDE GRN.
Ckt. Grd.
WALTON DR.
FAIRFAX AVENUE
FARNLEY VW.
OAKWELL CL.
Cricket Ground
Play. Flds.
TREEFIELD INDUSTRIAL ESTATE
Gildersome Street
Wyre Hall Farm
Greystone Farm
Greystone House
BUTTERCUP WY.
Depot
EAST VIEW STREET
B6135
ROAD
BRADFORD
OAKWELL RD.
ADWALTON BUS. PK.
MARGETSON RD.
MOORSIDE
WALK
OVERLAND TRADING ESTATE
GILDERSOME
LANE
BY-PASS
A650
DRIGHLINGTON
WAKEFIELD
Penfield
28
143
60
THISTLE WY.
SPUR
NEPSHAW LA.
TURNBERRY PK. RD.
M62 MOTORWAY
BIRSTALL RETAIL PARK
WEST YORKSHIRE RETAIL PARK
M62
HOLDEN ING WY.
Junction 27
ANTLER COMPLEX
Thorn Farm
M62
HOLDEN ING
HIGH WOOD
ROAD
Showcase Cinema
LEEDS
KIRKLEES
BANKWOOD WY.
WOODHEAD RD.
CENTRE 27 BUSINESS PARK
OAKWELL WY.
TRIANGLE BUS. PK.
OAKWELL INDUSTRIAL PARK
Springwell Farm
OAKWELL
OAKWELL CT.
Batley
WF17
Works
A62
PHEASANT DR.
PENNINE VW.
NORQUEST IND. PARK
HOWDEN CLOUGH INDUSTRIAL ESTATE
OAKWELL INDUSTRIAL ESTATE
Howden Clough
Resr.
HOWDEN CLOUGH RD.
A643
LEEDS RD.
MILL LA.
30
M62 MOTORWAY
SCOTT LANE
HOWDEN WY.
CLIFFE VW.
GELDERD
DARK LANE
RD.
LANE
NAB LANE
PHEASANT DR.
PENNINE VW.
WELBECK RD.
RAIKES
GREENACRES DR.
27
23
24
425
Works

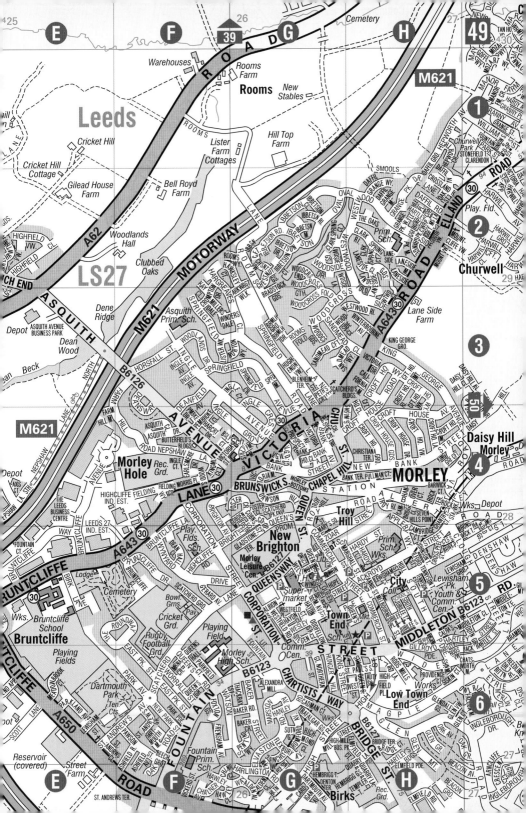

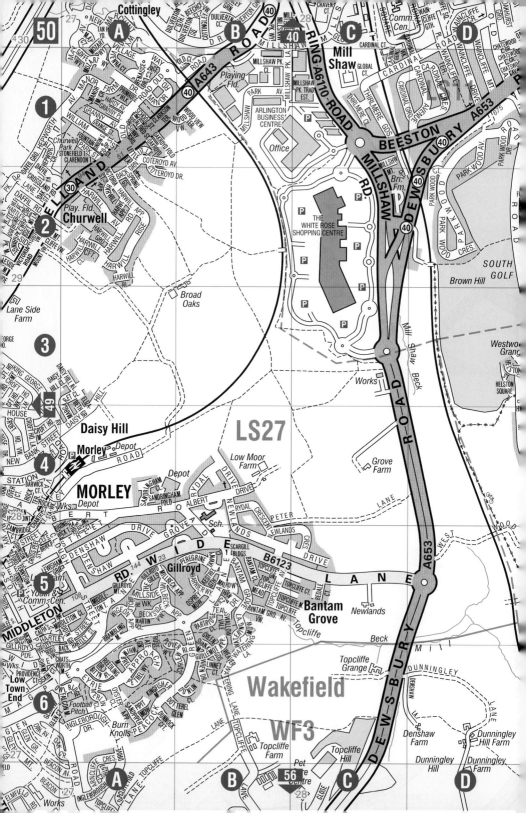

50
Cottingley
A
B
C
D
1
2
3
4
5
6
40
Mill Shaw
LS11
A643
ELLAND ROAD
RING A6110 ROAD
MILLSHAW
BEESTON
DEWSBURY ROAD
A653
Churwell
Play. Fld.
Playing Fld.
Churwell Park
ARLINGTON BUSINESS CENTRE
Office
MILLSHAW PK. TRAD. EST.
THE WHITE ROSE SHOPPING CENTRE
MILLSHAW RD.
Bri. Fm.
PARK WOOD AV.
PARK WOOD CRES.
SOUTH GOLF
Brown Hill
Broad Oaks
Lane Side Farm
Westwood Grange
HELSTON SQUARE
Mill Shaw Beck
Works
49
Daisy Hill
LS27
Morley
Depot
MORLEY
Low Moor Farm
Grove Farm
ALBERT ROAD
PETER LANE
NEWLANDS CRES.
Sch.
WIDE LANE
B6123
Gillroyd
SCARGILL BLDGS.
Bantam Grove
Newlands
Topcliffe
Beck
Topcliffe Grange
DUNNINGLEY LANE
Youth & Comm. Cen.
MIDDLETON
Low Town End
Football Pitch
Burn Knolls
Wakefield
WF3
Topcliffe Farm
Pet Care Centre
56
Topcliffe Hill
Denshaw Farm
Dunningley Hill Farm
Dunningley Hill
Dunningley Farm
Works

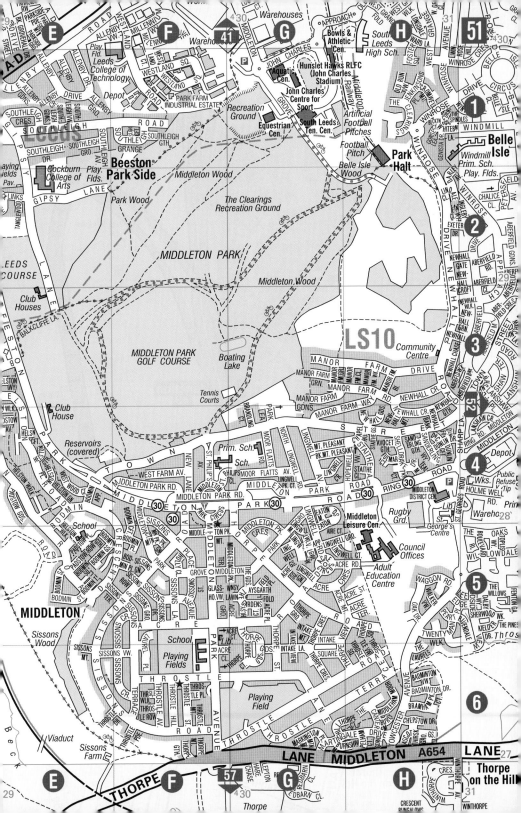

51
41
52
57
E
F
G
H
1
2
3
4
5
6
Leeds
LS10
Beeston Park Side
Belle Isle
Park Halt
MIDDLETON
Thorpe on the Hill
Leeds College of Technology
Cockburn College of Arts
Hunslet Hawks RLFC (John Charles Stadium)
John Charles Centre for Sport
Aquatic Cen.
Equestrian Cen.
South Leeds Ten. Cen.
Bowls & Athletic Cen.
South Leeds High Sch.
Artificial Football Pitches
Football Pitch
Belle Isle Wood
Windmill Prim. Sch. Play. Flds.
Recreation Ground
Middleton Railway
PARK FARM INDUSTRIAL ESTATE
Warehouses
Depot
Middleton Wood
Park Wood
The Clearings Recreation Ground
MIDDLETON PARK
MIDDLETON PARK GOLF COURSE
Boating Lake
Tennis Courts
Club Houses
Club House
Reservoirs (covered)
Community Centre
Prim. Sch.
Sch.
Middleton Leisure Cen.
Council Offices
Adult Education Centre
Rugby Grd.
MIDDLETON DISTRICT CEN.
Lib.
St. George's Centre
Wks.
Public Refuse Tip
School
Playing Fields
Playing Field
Sissons Wood
Sissons Farm
Viaduct
Beck
GIPSY LANE
SOUTHLEIGH ROAD
ALLENBY DRIVE
WESTLAND ROAD
JOHN CHARLES APPROACH
MIDDLETON GROVE
WINROSE DRIVE
WINDMILL LA.
NEWHALL ROAD
NEWHALL DRIVE
MANOR FARM DRIVE
MANOR FARM WAY
TOWN STREET
MIDDLETON PARK RD.
MIDDLETON PARK ROAD
RING ROAD MIDDLETON
SHARP LA.
ST. GEORGES ROAD
BODMIN ROAD
BODMIN CRESCENT
SISSONS ROAD
SISSONS PLACE
SISSONS AVENUE
MIDDLETON PARK CIRCUS
THORPE ROAD
ACRE ROAD
ACRE CRES.
THROSTLE ROAD
THROSTLE LANE
THROSTLE TERRACE
MIDDLETON PARK AVENUE
WAGGON RD.
TOWCESTER AVENUE
WESTWOOD AV.
BALKCLIFFE LA.
HELSTON ROAD
LANE MIDDLETON A654 LANE
THORPE
Thorpe
30
29
28
27
31

A
B
C
D
42
32
31
30
Skills Cen.
Community Enterprise Resource Centre
ENTERPRISE WY.
LOW GRANGE
WINROSE GRO.
WINROSE CRES.
BELLE ISLE CIRCUS
RING ROAD MIDDLETON
Urn Farm
M621
MOTORWAY
Junc. 8
Depot
LEEDS VALLEY PK.
SAVANNAH WAY
Bell Hill
1
WINDMILL ROAD
Belle Isle
Windmill Prim. Sch.
Play. Flds.
Comm. Cen.
ORION WLK.
HIGHLANDS DR.
MIDDLECROFT
LEA PARK DR.
WINROSE
CHALICE CL.
LS10
2
EXETER DR.
ABERFIELD GDNS.
SOUTH HILL WAY
MANDARIN WY.
Works
Haigh House Farm
PELICAN WKS.
NEWHALL GATE
ABERFIELD RD.
BROOM GTH.
BROOM PLACE
BROOM NOOK
HOPES FARM MT.
Lib.
Sch.
29
Haigh House
Fish Pond
NESFIELD CREST
NESFIELD GDNS.
NESFIELD CR.
BROOM VIEW
MIDDLETON WAY
RAYLANDS
GRANGE FIELDS
3
Community Centre
ABERFIELD
LANSHAW
DRIVE
NEWHALL CR.
Glebe Farm
Junction 43
RAYLANDS DRIVE
CRANMORE
Comm. Cen.
Prim. Sch.
Play. Fld.
CLAPGATE LA.
Works
Chimney
Factory
51
TOWN
SHARP LA.
DUNLIN DR.
MIDDLETON RING ROAD
Depot
DOLPHIN RD.
THROSTLE RD.
CRANMORE RISE
Sub.
4
MIDDLETON LA.
MIDDLETON AV.
Hope's Farm
Football Grd.
GLEBE CT.
30
P
MIDDLETON DISTRICT CEN.
Wks.
HOLME WELL RD.
Public Refuse Tip
Sharp Lane Prim. Sch.
Warehouse
ST. GEORGES ROAD
Lib.
28
St. George's Centre
CASTLE FIELDS
ANGEL ROW
Council Offices
THE OAKS
WIL-LOWDALE
SALAMANCA CRES.
MURRAY WY.
LEDBURY
MELTON AV.
WAKEFIELD
LEEDS
HOPEFIELD
5
M1
WAGGON
WOODSIDE
THE WILLOWS
FENTON GA.
NEW BLEN
KINSOP
WOODLAND
ROAD
THE PINES
SHERWOOD WK.
KIELDER
Throstle
Carr
Beck
CUNNINGHAM CT.
LANE
DANBY CT.
Rec. Grd.
SHERWOOD GRN.
COPLEY
LEADWELL
TWENTY WLK.
THE LAURELS
Kiddow Spring
Howley Cross
Robin Hood
AVENUE
BADMINTON VW.
BADMINTON DR.
6
CHEPSTOW DR.
FORMAN'S DR.
LANE
A61
BARLEY M.
OAST HO. CFT.
West
Wakefield
MIDDLETON
A654
Thorpe Hall
LOWER
MILNER
Robin Hood-Bri.
SHERWOOD IND. EST.
FORESTER CT.
27
A
Thorpe on the Hill
LANE
B
THORPE
58
C
D
Prim. Sch.
ROAD
31
32
Thorpe Ho. Fm.
WINTHORPE
Playing
ST. MARTINS FOLD

53
E
F
G
H
33
34
435
430
43
Junction 44
M1
M1-MOTORWAY
A639
PONTEFRACT RD.
B6481
Works
PONTEFRACT ROAD
LEEDS ROAD
A639
ROTHWELL COUNTRY PARK
Sub.
Piggery
Rose Cottage Farm
Haigh Cottage Farm
Rothwell Haigh
Haigh Farm
John O'Gaunts
LS26
MILL PIT LANE
JOHN O'GAUNTS TRADING ESTATE
Auction Mart
Warehouses
TEMPLE AV.
FIRST AV.
SECOND AV.
THIRD AV.
FOURTH
CRESCENT
CROSS AV.
KINGS CHASE
BULLOUGH LANE
STYE BANK
Comm. Cen.
Football Grou
29
ROSEWOOD CT.
RICHMOND CT.
ST. GEORGE'S AV.
HAIGH GDNS.
LAWFIELD AV.
HAIGHSIDE DRIVE
HAIGHSIDE WY.
WOOD CR.
HOME LEA
OAKWOOD DR.
SPIBEY LANE
HIGH RIDGE AV.
HIGH RIDGE PARK
WILLANS AVENUE
HAIGH ROAD
VICTORIA RD.
Victoria Jun. Sch.
CASTLE LODGE
LOW SHOPS LANE
Haigh Side Fm.
Leeds
Beck
COTSWOLD DRIVE
CORNWALL CRES.
MANOR
ALBANY ROAD
CASTLE ROAD
COTSWOLD RD.
PASTURE VIEW RD.
Recreation Ground
HAIGH WOOD ROAD
QUEENSWAY
CHURCHFIELD CR.
ORCHARD WAY
SANDYACRES
SANDYACRES DR.
WINDSOR DR.
Cemy.
NEW
FERNLEA
ROSEDALE
THORNE
SANDY BANK AV.
PARK LANE
Rothwell CE Prim. Sch.
THE PADDOCK
GILLETT DR.
ST. PETER'S AV.
ST. CHRIST'S AV.
Gillett Bri.
Springhead Park
Playgrd.
Pav.
Oulton
54
Haigh Beck
Rothwell Castle (Rems. of)
ROTHWELL
CHURCH ST.
INGRAM PDE.
WEST PARK
Superstore
COMMERCIAL ST.
COMMERCIAL STREET
OULTON
OULTON LANE
Coll. Lib.
BUTCHER
MARSH ST.
THE OVAL
WHITEHALL CFT.
ROYDS
SKYE VW.
ARRAN WAY
ISLAY CL.
28
Football Grd.
Cricket Grd.
Prim. Sch.
Hopefield Farm
STONE BRIG LANE
ST. CLEMENTS
BRIG LANE
MILL HILL
LAY GARTH
LAY GTH. FOLD
Prim. Sch.
SPRINGFIELD ST.
BENNETTS YD.
SWITHEN'S ST.
SWITHEN'S LANE
ELMROYD
OAKROYD
ASHROYD
BIRCHROYD
HAWTHORN GRO.
HAZEL CT.
WINDMILL LANE
WINDMILL FIELD
SWITHEN'S GRO.
SWITHEN'S CT.
TALBOT
ARMITAGE
CARLTON LANE
A654
THE GATEWAY
Rec. Grd.
Middle Shutts
Carlton Fields
SHUTTS
NORTHFIELD
Stone Bridge
STAINTON LANE
Carlton Bri.
Carlton Beck
Bridge End Farm
WESTFIELD CT.
WESTFIELD ROAD
Swithen's Plantation
Swithen's Farm
Beck
West Bridge
THE GRANGE
CHAPEL ST.
MAIN ST.
ALBION ST.
LITTLE LA.
CARR LA.
Nursery
PIT FIELD ROAD
WF3
Sch.
Carlton Hall
QUEEN ST.
Carlton
UNITY ST.
ASHTON CR.
SHAYFIELD LANE
QUEENS DR.
TOWN STREET
Spts. Grd.
Depot
Football Ground
59
27
1
2
3
4
5
6

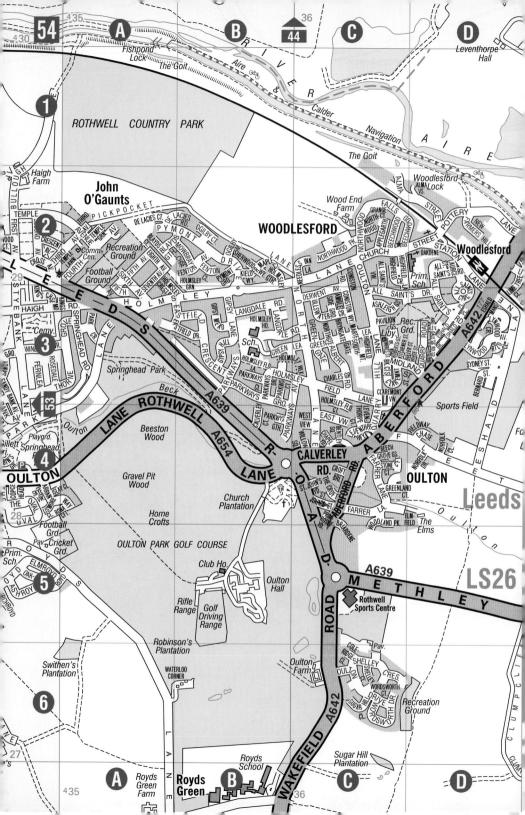
44
53
ROTHWELL COUNTRY PARK
Fishpond Lock
The Goit
RIVER Aire & Calder Navigation
AIRE
Leventhorpe Hall
Haigh Farm
John O'Gaunts
PICKPOCKET
WOODLESFORD
Wood End Farm
Woodlesford Lock
Woodlesford
Recreation Ground
Football Ground
Prim. Sch.
Rec. Grd.
Liby.
Sch.
Springhead Park
Oulton Beck
Beeston Wood
Gravel Pit Wood
Church Plantation
Home Crofts
OULTON PARK GOLF COURSE
Club Ho.
Oulton Hall
Rifle Range
Golf Driving Range
Robinson's Plantation
Swithen's Plantation
WATERLOO CORNER
Sports Field
OULTON
Leeds
LS26
The Elms
Rothwell Sports Centre
Oulton Farm
Recreation Ground
Sugar Hill Plantation
Royds School
Royds Green
Royds Green Farm
Football Grd.
Cricket Grd.
Prim. Sch.
Playgrd.
Springhead
Cemy.
LEEDS RD.
A639
ROTHWELL LANE A654
CALVERLEY RD.
ABERFORD RD. A642
WAKEFIELD ROAD A642
METHLEY LANE A639
CHURCH LANE
OULTON LANE
HOLMSLEY LANE
PYMONT DRIVE
STATION LANE
PARKWAYS
NORTH LANE
MIDLAND ST.
FARRER LANE
ROYDS LANE
ESHALD LANE
CLUMPCLIFFE
A
B
C
D
1
2
3
4
5
6
435
430
36
29
28
27

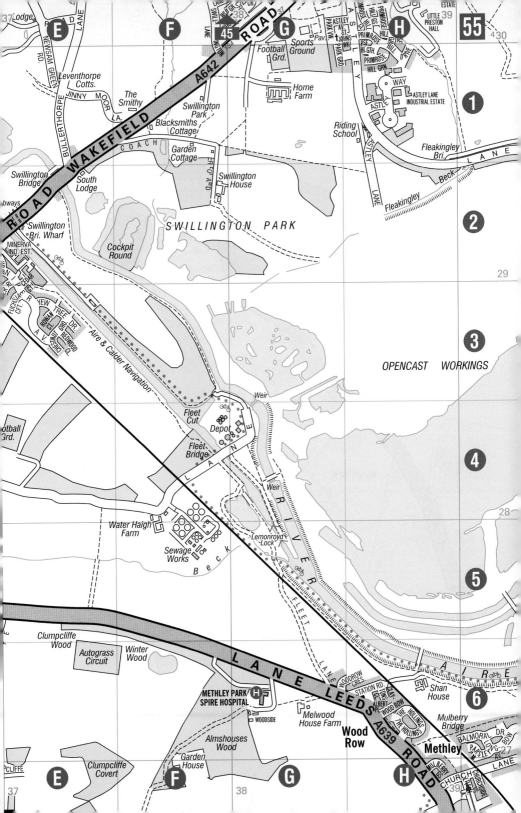
WAKEFIELD ROAD
A642
LEEDS ROAD
A639
Leventhorpe Cotts.
The Smithy
Swillington Park
Blacksmiths Cottage
Garden Cottage
Swillington House
South Lodge
Swillington Bridge
Swillington Bri. Wharf
SWILLINGTON PARK
Cockpit Round
Football Grd.
Sports Ground
Home Farm
Riding School
ASTLEY LANE INDUSTRIAL ESTATE
LITTLE PRESTON HALL
Fleakingley Bri.
Fleakingley Beck
MINERVA IND. EST.
Aire & Calder Navigation
OPENCAST WORKINGS
Weir
Fleet Cut
Depot
Fleet Bridge
RIVER AIRE
Water Haigh Farm
Sewage Works
Lemonroyd Lock
Clumpcliffe Wood
Autograss Circuit
Winter Wood
METHLEY PARK SPIRE HOSPITAL
WOODSIDE
Melwood House Farm
Wood Row
Shan House
Mulberry Bridge
Methley
Almshouses Wood
Garden House
Clumpcliffe Covert

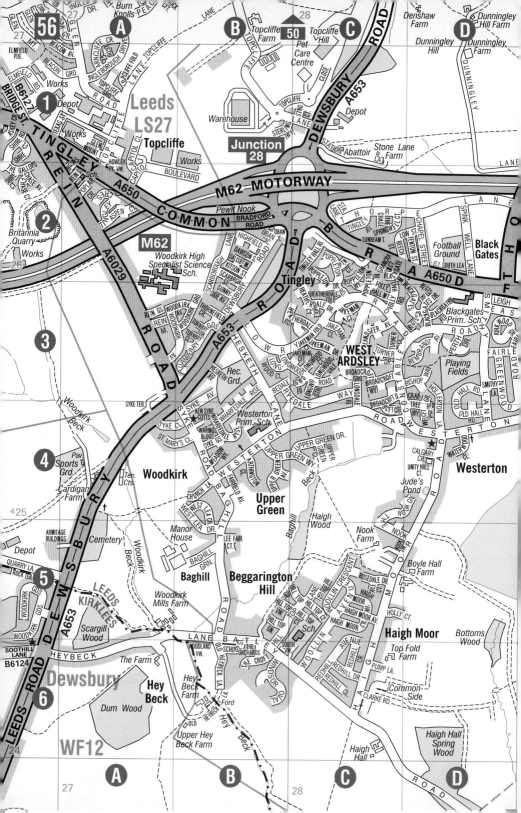

Leeds LS27
Topcliffe
Junction 28
M62 MOTORWAY
TINGLEY COMMON
A650
A6029
REIN ROAD
DEWSBURY ROAD
A653
BRADFORD ROAD
Woodkirk High Specialist Science Sch.
Tingley
WEST ARDSLEY
Westerton
Woodkirk
Upper Green
Baghill
Beggarington Hill
Haigh Moor
Hey Beck
Dewsbury
WF12
Dum Wood
Scargill Wood
Haigh Wood
Bottoms Wood
Haigh Hall Spring Wood
Haigh Hall
Common Side
Top Fold Farm
Boyle Hall Farm
Nook Farm
Jude's Pond
Playing Fields
Football Ground
Black Gates
Blackgates Prim. Sch.
Westerton Prim. Sch.
Rec. Grd.
Sports Grd.
Cardigan Farm
Cemetery
Manor House
Woodkirk Mills Farm
Upper Hey Beck Farm
The Farm
Britannia Quarry
Warehouse
Pet Care Centre
Topcliffe Farm
Topcliffe Hill
Denshaw Farm
Dunningley Hill Farm
Dunningley Hill
Dunningley Farm
Stone Lane Farm
Abattoir
Pewit Nook
LEEDS
KIRKLEES
LEEDS ROAD
HEYBECK LANE
BATLEY ROAD
WESTERTON ROAD
HAIGH MOOR ROAD

50

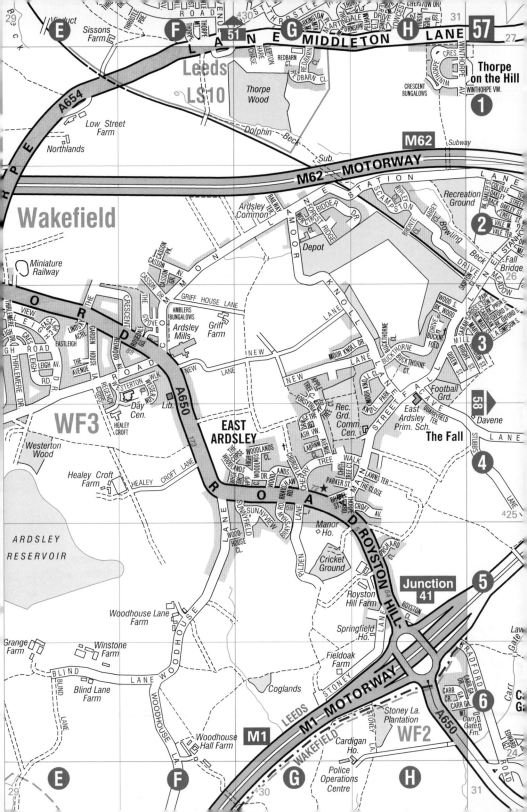

MIDDLETON LANE
Thorpe on the Hill
Leeds LS10
Thorpe Wood
Sissons Farm
Viaduct
Low Street Farm
Northlands
Dolphin Beck
M62 MOTORWAY
Subway
Sub.
STATION LANE
Recreation Ground
Ardsley Common
Wakefield
Miniature Railway
Depot
Bowling Beck
Fall Bridge
GRIFF HOUSE LANE
AMBLERS BUNGALOWS
Ardsley Mills
Griff Farm
NEW LANE
MOOR KNOLL LANE
BUCKTHORNE CT.
Football Grd.
Davene
East Ardsley Prim. Sch.
The Fall
Rec. Grd.
Comm. Cen.
Lib.
Day Cen.
WF3
A650
EAST ARDSLEY
Westerton Wood
Healey Croft Farm
HEALEY CROFT LANE
ARDSLEY RESERVOIR
Manor Ho.
Cricket Ground
ROYSTON HILL
Royston Hill Farm
Junction 41
Springfield Ho.
Fieldoak Farm
Woodhouse Lane Farm
Grange Farm
Winstone Farm
BLIND LANE
Blind Lane Farm
Coglands
M1 MOTORWAY
Stoney La. Plantation
WF2
Carr Gate Fm.
Cardigan Ho.
Woodhouse Hall Farm
Police Operations Centre
A654
A650
M1
M62
51
58
E F G H
1 2 3 4 5 6

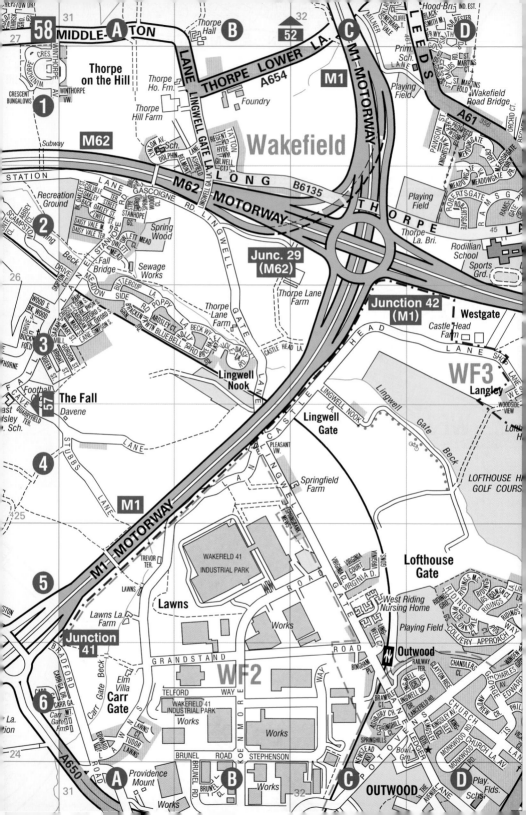
MIDDLETON
Thorpe Hall
52
THORPE LOWER LA.
A654
LANE
Thorpe on the Hill
Thorpe Ho. Fm.
Foundry
Thorpe Hill Farm
LINGWELL GATE LA.
M1
M1 MOTORWAY
Wakefield
M62
Subway
CRESCENT BUNGALOWS
WINTHORPE AV.
WINTHORPE VW.
STATION LANE
LONG THORPE LA.
B6135
M62 MOTORWAY
Recreation Ground
Spring Wood
Sewage Works
Fall Bridge
Junc. 29 (M62)
Thorpe Lane Farm
Junction 42 (M1)
Westgate
Castle Head Farm
CASTLE HEAD LA.
LANE SHOP LANE
WF3
Langley
Lingwell Nook
Lingwell Gate
Lingwell Gate Beck
The Fall
57
Davene
STUBBS LANE
Springfield Farm
LOFTHOUSE HALL GOLF COURSE
M1 MOTORWAY
WAKEFIELD 41 INDUSTRIAL PARK
Lofthouse Gate
Lawns
West Riding Nursing Home
Playing Field
Works
Junction 41
Outwood
Lawns La. Farm
GRANDSTAND ROAD
WF2
Elm Villa
Carr Gate
TELFORD WAY
KENMORE WAY
BRUNEL ROAD
STEPHENSON
Providence Mount
A650
OUTWOOD
Leeds
A61
Rodillian School
Sports Grd.
Thorpe La. Bri.
Playing Field
Wakefield Road Bridge
Prim. Sch.
Hood Bri. Ind. Est.
ROBERTSGATE
RAMSGATE
MEADOWGATE
COLLIERY APPROACH
CHURCH LA.
POTOVENS LANE
Bowl. Grn.
Play. Flds.
Schs.
A
B
C
D
1
2
3
4
5
6
31
32
27
26
425
24

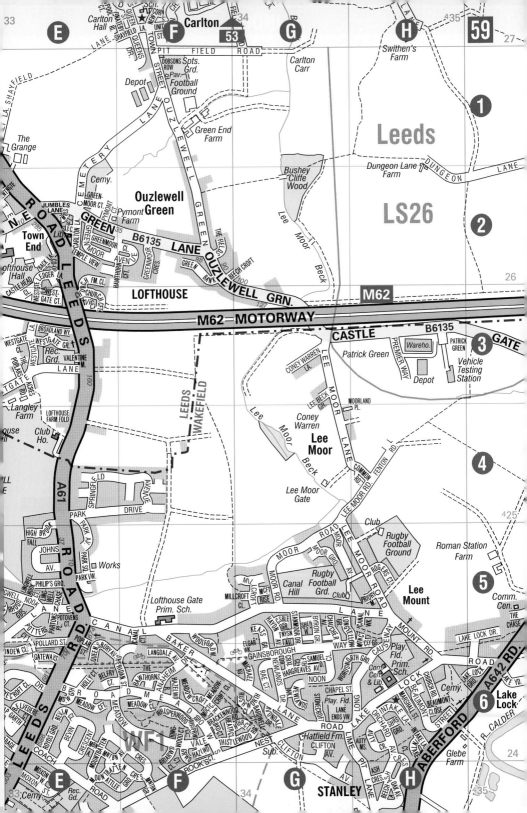

59
53
Carlton
Carlton Hall
E
F
G
H
33
34
435
27
26
425
24
Swithen's Farm
PIT FIELD ROAD
DOBSONS ROW
Spts. Grd.
Pav.
Football Ground
Depot
Carlton Carr
Green End Farm
SHAYFIELD LA.
The Grange
CEMETERY LANE
TOWN STREET
OUZLEWELL GREEN
Cemy.
Bushey Cliffe Wood
Dungeon Lane Farm
DUNGEON LANE
Leeds
LS26
Ouzlewell Green
Pymont Farm
JUMBLES LANE
GREEN LANE
B6135
Town End
Lib.
Lofthouse Hall
LOFTHOUSE
Lee Moor Beck
THE FIELDS
BEECH CROFT
GREEN BANK
OUZLEWELL GRN.
M62
M62 MOTORWAY
CASTLE GATE
Patrick Green
PREMIER WAY
Wareho.
Depot
PATRICK GREEN
Vehicle Testing Station
CONEY WARREN LA.
LEE MOOR LANE
LEE BECK GR.
MOORLAND PL.
Coney Warren
Lee Moor
LEEDS
WAKEFIELD
WESTGATE
BROADLAND WY.
Rec. Grd.
VALENTINE M.
LANE
Langley Farm
LOFTHOUSE FARM FOLD
Club Ho.
LEEDS ROAD
A61
SPRINGFIELD AVENUE
PARK DRIVE
PARK AV.
PARK SQ.
PARK VW.
Works
HIGH BROOK FALL
JOHNS AV.
PHILIP'S GRO.
LINGWELL NOOK LANE
COMMON RD.
FENTON RD.
LEE MOOR RD.
Lee Moor Gate
MOOR ROAD
MOOR GRO.
MOOR AV.
Club
Rugby Football Ground
ROGERS CT.
Roman Station Farm
Canal Hill
Rugby Football Grd.
MOOR RD.
MILLCROFT CL.
MCFT RISE
Lofthouse Gate Prim. Sch.
PRIORY M.
Lee Mount
Comm. Cen.
THE CHASE
LAKE LOCK DR.
CANAL LANE
BAKER LANE
POTTERS CFT.
POLLARD ST.
GATEWAYS
QUEENSBURY AV.
SHERIDAN ST.
LANGDALE AV.
THE HAWTHORNS
BELFRY CT.
HOLLY CT.
WOOLFORD W.
ELGAR WK.
KEATS GR.
GAINSBOROUGH WAY
NEWLANDS DR.
HARGREAVES AV.
SAMUEL
NOON CL.
WORDSWORTH GRO.
CAUSEWAY
MOUNT RD.
Play. Fld. Prim. Sch.
Com. Cen. & Lib.
LOCK ROAD
CHURCH RD.
BEAUMONT STREET
Cemy.
LAKE LOCK GRO.
A642 RD.
ABERFORD
Lake Lock
LAKE YD.
R. CALDER
Glebe Farm
BROADMEADOW
MEADOW CFT.
MEADOW CL.
WHISPERWOOD
MEADOWCROFT
RUSHWORTH CL.
BARDWELL
AVONDALE DR.
BRACKENWOOD RD.
THISTLEWOOD RD.
NEST LANE
CHAPEL ST.
Play. Fld.
LANE ENDS VW.
STONECROFT
LONG LANE
Hatfield Fm.
CLIFTON AV.
CLIFTON ROAD
LIME PIT LANE
AUTY MS.
AUTY CR.
ORCHARD
INTAKE LA.
MARSHALL ST.
ASH CRES.
BEECH CRES.
OAK AV.
STANLEY
WF1
Sub.
BRIARWD.
ROOKS CT.
CRESCENT
BEVIN
MOUNTBATTEN
ATTLEE GRO.
COACH ROAD
LEEDS RD.
MOXON ST.
Rec. Gd.
Cemy.
BELVEDERE CT.
ROYDS GRO.
INDEN CL.
POPLAR

INDEX

Including Streets, Places & Areas, Hospitals etc., Industrial Estates,
Selected Flats & Walkways, Stations and Selected Places of Interest.

HOW TO USE THIS INDEX

1. Each street name is followed by its Postcode District, then by its Locality abbreviation(s) and then by its map reference;
   e.g. **Abbey Rd.** LS5: Leeds . . . .5D **18** is in the LS5 Postcode District and the Leeds Locality and is to be found in square 5D on page **18**.
   The page number is shown in bold type.

2. A strict alphabetical order is followed in which Av., Rd., St., etc. (though abbreviated) are read in full and as part of the street name;
   e.g. **Ashroyd** appears after **Ash Rd.** but before **Ash Ter.**

3. Streets and a selection of flats and walkways that cannot be shown on the mapping, appear in the index with the thoroughfare to which they are connected
   shown in brackets; e.g. **Abbey Gth.** *LS19: Yead* . . . .*3D 8 (off Well Hill)*

4. Addresses that are in more than one part are referred to as not continuous.

5. Places and areas are shown in the index in BLUE TYPE and the map reference is to the actual map square in which the town centre or area is located and not
   to the place name shown on the map; e.g. ADEL MILL 3B 12

6. An example of a selected place of interest is **Abbey House Mus.** 6G 19

7. An example of a station is **Bramley Station (Rail)** . . . .4B 28, also included is **Park & Ride**.
   e.g. **King Lane (Park & Ride)** 6F 13

8. An example of a Hospital, Treatment Centre, Walk-in Centre or Hospice is CHAPEL ALLERTON HOSPITAL 6A 22

9. Map references for entries that appear on large scale pages **4 & 5** are shown first, with small scale map references shown in brackets;
   e.g. **Ahlux Ct.** LS2: Leeds 2H **5** (4H **31**)

GENERAL ABBREVIATIONS

All. : Alley	**E.** : East	**Mus.** : Museum
App. : Approach	**Est.** : Estate	**Nth.** : North
Arc. : Arcade	**Fld.** : Field	**Pde.** : Parade
Av. : Avenue	**Flds.** : Fields	**Pk.** : Park
Bk. : Back	**Gdn.** : Garden	**Pas.** : Passage
Blvd. : Boulevard	**Gdns.** : Gardens	**Pl.** : Place
Bri. : Bridge	**Gth.** : Garth	**Prom.** : Promenade
Bldg. : Building	**Ga.** : Gate	**Res.** : Residential
Bldgs. : Buildings	**Gt.** : Great	**Ri.** : Rise
Bungs. : Bungalows	**Grn.** : Green	**Rd.** : Road
Bus. : Business	**Gro.** : Grove	**Shop.** : Shopping
Cvn. : Caravan	**Hgts.** : Heights	**Sth.** : South
C'way. : Causeway	**Ho.** : House	**Sq.** : Square
Cen. : Centre	**Ind.** : Industrial	**St.** : Street
Chu. : Church	**Info.** : Information	**Ter.** : Terrace
Circ. : Circle	**Junc.** : Junction	**Trad.** : Trading
Cir. : Circus	**La.** : Lane	**Up.** : Upper
Cl. : Close	**Lit.** : Little	**Va.** : Vale
Comn. : Common	**Lwr.** : Lower	**Vw.** : View
Cnr. : Corner	**Mnr.** : Manor	**Vs.** : Villas
Cotts. : Cottages	**Mans.** : Mansions	**Vis.** : Visitors
Ct. : Court	**Mkt.** : Market	**Wlk.** : Walk
Cres. : Crescent	**Mdw.** : Meadow	**W.** : West
Cft. : Croft	**M.** : Mews	**Yd.** : Yard
Dr. : Drive	**Mt.** : Mount	

LOCALITY ABBREVIATIONS

Bail : **Baildon**	Esh : **Esholt**	Pud : **Pudsey**
Bard : **Bardsey**	Fars : **Farsley**	Raw : **Rawdon**
Bar E : **Barwick in Elmet**	Gar : **Garforth**	Rob H : **Robin Hood**
Bat : **Batley**	Gil : **Gildersome**	Rothw : **Rothwell**
Birk : **Birkenshaw**	Gom : **Gomersal**	S'cft : **Scarcroft**
Birs : **Birstall**	Guis : **Guiseley**	Scho : **Scholes**
B'frd : **Bradford**	Hawk : **Hawksworth**	Shad : **Shadwell**
B'hpe : **Bramhope**	H'fth : **Horsforth**	S'ley : **Stanley**
Burl W : **Burley in Wharfedale**	Hun : **Hunsworth**	Stan : **Stanningley**
Cal : **Calverley**	Kirk : **Kirkhamgate**	Swil : **Swillington**
Carl : **Carlton**	Leeds : **Leeds**	Swil C : **Swillington Common**
Carr G : **Carr Gate**	Loft : **Lofthouse**	T'ner : **Thorner**
Chur : **Churwell**	Men : **Menston**	Thpe H : **Thorpe on the Hill**
Cleck : **Cleckheaton**	Meth : **Methley**	Ting : **Tingley**
Dew : **Dewsbury**	Morl : **Morley**	W Ard : **West Ardsley**
Drig : **Drighlington**	N Far : **New Farnley**	Wike : **Wike**
E Ard : **East Ardsley**	Otley : **Otley**	Wood : **Woodlesford**
E Bier : **East Bierley**	Oul : **Oulton**	Wren : **Wrenthorpe**
Ecc : **Eccup**	Out : **Outwood**	Yead : **Yeadon**

A

	Abbey Gth. *LS19: Yead* *3D 8*	**Abbott Rd.** LS12: Leeds 6B **30**
	(off Well Hill)	**Abbott Vw.** LS12: Leeds 5B **30**
Abbey Av. LS5: Leeds .2F **29**	**Abbey Gorse** LS5: Leeds 6G **19**	**Aberdeen Dr.** LS12: Leeds 6G **29**
Abbey Cl. WF3: E Ard 2H **57**	**Abbey House Mus.** 6G **19**	**Aberdeen Gro.** LS12: Leeds 6G **29**
Abbey Ct. LS18: H'fth .5B **18**	**Abbey Light Railway** .1G **29**	**Aberdeen Rd.** LS12: Leeds 6G **29**
Abbeydale Gdns. LS5: Leeds 5E **19**	**Abbey Mt.** LS5: Leeds .2F **29**	**Aberdeen Wlk.** LS12: Leeds 6G **29**
Abbeydale Gth. LS5: Leeds 5E **19**	**Abbey Rd.** LS5: Leeds .5D **18**	**Aberfield Bank** LS10: Leeds 3A **52**
Abbeydale Gro. LS5: Leeds 5E **19**	**Abbey St.** LS3: Leeds .5D **30**	**Aberfield Cl.** LS10: Leeds 2A **52**
Abbeydale Mt. LS5: Leeds 5E **19**	**Abbey Ter.** LS5: Leeds 2F **29**	**Aberfield Crest** LS10: Leeds 3A **52**
Abbeydale Oval LS5: Leeds 5E **19**	**Abbey Vw.** LS5: Leeds 6G **19**	**Aberfield Dr.** LS10: Leeds 3A **52**
Abbeydale Va. LS5: Leeds 5E **19**	**Abbey Wlk.** LS5: Leeds 6F **19**	**Aberfield Gdns.** LS10: Leeds 2A **52**
Abbeydale Way LS5: Leeds 5E **19**	**Abbots M.** LS4: Leeds .3B **30**	**Aberfield Ga.** LS10: Leeds 2A **52**
	Abbott Ct. LS12: Leeds 5B **30**	**Aberfield Mt.** LS10: Leeds 3A **52**

Aberfield Ri.—Andrew St.

Aberfield Ri. LS10: Leeds 3A **52**
Aberfield Rd. LS10: Leeds 2A **52**
Aberfield Wlk. LS10: Leeds 3H **51**
Aberford Rd. LS26: Oul, Wood 4C **54**
WF3: S'ley 6H **59**
Abraham Hill LS26: Rothw 4H **53**
Acacia Pk. Cres. BD10: B'frd 1B **16**
Acacia Pk. Dr. BD10: B'frd 1B **16**
Acacia Pk. Ter. BD10: B'frd 1C **16**
Accommodation Rd. LS9: Leeds 4A **32**
Ackroyd St. LS27: Morl 5H **49**
Ackworth Av. LS19: Yead 3E **9**
Ackworth Cres. LS19: Yead 3E **9**
Ackworth Dr. LS19: Yead 3E **9**
Acorn Bus. Pk. LS14: Leeds 4G **33**
Acorn Dr. LS14: Leeds 3C **24**
Acre Cir. LS10: Leeds 5G **51**
Acre Cl. LS10: Leeds 6F **51**
Acre Ct. LS10: Leeds 5G **51**
Acre Cres. LS10: Leeds 5G **51**
Acre Gro. LS10: Leeds 5G **51**
Acre Mt. LS10: Leeds 5G **51**
Acre Pl. LS10: Leeds 5G **51**
Acre Rd. LS10: Leeds 5F **51**
Acres, The *LS17: Leeds 4D **12***
(off The Avenue)
Acres Hall Av. LS28: Pud 1A **38**
Acres Hall Cres. LS28: Pud 1A **38**
Acres Hall Dr. LS28: Pud 1A **38**
Acre Sq. LS10: Leeds 5G **51**
Acres Rd. WF3: Loft 3E **59**
Acre St. LS10: Leeds 5H **51**
Acre Ter. LS10: Leeds 5H **51**
Acrewood Cl. LS17: Leeds 6C **14**
Adams Gro. LS15: Leeds 1E **35**
Adams Gym ***2D 30***
(off Brudenell Av.)
Adam's Wlk. LS6: Leeds 3D **30**
Ada's Pl. LS28: Stan 3G **27**
Addingham Gdns. LS12: Leeds 6G **29**
Addison Av. BD3: B'frd 4A **26**
Addison Ct. LS15: Leeds 1D **44**
ADEL **6B 12**
ADEL EAST MOOR **6C 12**
Adel Gth. LS16: Leeds 4B **12**
Adel Grange Cl. LS16: Leeds 1A **20**
Adel Grange Cft. LS16: Leeds 1A **20**
Adel Grange M. LS16: Leeds 1A **20**
(not continuous)
Adel Grn. LS16: Leeds 5B **12**
Adel La. LS16: Leeds 5A **12**
Adel Mead LS16: Leeds 5B **12**
ADEL MILL **3B 12**
Adel Mill LS16: Leeds 3B **12**
Adel Pk. Cl. LS16: Leeds 6A **12**
Adel Pk. Ct. LS16: Leeds 6A **12**
Adel Pk. Cft. LS16: Leeds 6A **12**
Adel Pk. Dr. LS16: Leeds 6A **12**
Adel Pk. Gdns. LS16: Leeds 6A **12**
Adel Pasture LS16: Leeds 6A **12**
Adel Towers Cl. LS16: Leeds 6B **12**
Adel Towers Ct. LS16: Leeds 6B **12**
Adel Va. LS16: Leeds 5B **12**
Adel Wood Cl. LS16: Leeds 6B **12**
Adel Wood Dr. LS16: Leeds 6B **12**
Adel Wood Gdns. LS16: Leeds 6B **12**
Adel Wood Gro. LS16: Leeds 6B **12**
Adel Wood Pl. LS16: Leeds 6B **12**
Adel Wood Rd. LS16: Leeds 6B **12**
Admiral St. LS11: Leeds 3G **41**
Admirals Yd. LS10: Leeds 3B **42**
ADWALTON **3A 48**
Adwalton Bus. Pk. BD11: Drig 4A **48**
Adwalton Cl. BD11: Drig 4F **47**
Adwalton Grn. BD11: Drig 4F **47**
Adwalton Moor Bus. Pk. BD11: Birk 2D **46**
Adwick Pl. LS4: Leeds 3A **30**
Ahlux Ct. LS2: Leeds 2H **5** (4H **31**)
Ahlux Ho. LS2: Leeds 2H **5** (4H **31**)
Ainsley Ct. LS14: Leeds 6E **25**
Ainsley M. LS14: Leeds 6E **25**
Ainsley Vw. LS14: Leeds 6E **25**
Aintree Ct. LS10: Leeds 3A **42**
Airdale Ter. *LS13: Leeds 6H **17***
(off Airedale Cft.)
Aireborough Leisure Cen. **5G 7**
Aire Ct. LS10: Leeds 5G **51**
Airedale Cliff LS13: Leeds 6C **18**
Airedale Ct. LS14: Leeds 6H **23**
Airedale Cft. LS13: Leeds 6H **17**
Airedale Dr. LS18: H'fth 3H **17**
Airedale Gdns. LS13: Leeds 1H **27**
Airedale Gro. LS18: H'fth 3H **17**
LS26: Wood 3D **54**
Airedale Ho. LS13: Leeds 1B **28**
Airedale Mt. LS13: Leeds 6G **17**
Airedale Quay LS13: Leeds 1A **28**
Airedale Rd. LS26: Wood 3D **54**
Airedale Ter. LS26: Wood 3D **54**
*LS27: Morl 5H **49***
(off Gillroyd Pde.)
Airedale Vw. *LS13: Leeds 6H **17***
(off Town St.)
LS19: Raw 6F **9**
LS26: Wood 3D **54**
Airedale Wharf LS13: Leeds 6H **17**
Aire Gro. LS19: Yead 3E **9**
Aire Pl. LS3: Leeds 4C **30**
Aire St. LS1: Leeds 5C **4** (6F **31**)
Aire Valley Marina LS4: Leeds 4H **29**
Aire Valley Rd. LS9: Leeds 2B **42**
Aire Vw. LS19: Yead 3E **9**
Aire Vw. Gdns. LS5: Leeds 5F **19**
Aire Vw. Ter. LS13: Leeds 1A **28**
Airlie Av. LS8: Leeds 1B **32**
Airlie Pl. LS8: Leeds 1B **32**
Airport West LS19: Yead 1G **9**
Alan Cres. LS15: Leeds 6A **34**
Alaska Pl. LS7: Leeds 5A **22**
Albany Rd. LS26: Rothw 3F **53**
Albany St. LS12: Leeds 6G **29**
Albany Ter. LS12: Leeds 6G **29**
Alberta Av. LS7: Leeds 5A **22**
Albert Cres. BD11: Birk 5D **46**
Albert Dr. LS27: Morl 4B **50**
Albert Gro. LS6: Leeds 5B **20**
Albert Mt. *LS18: H'fth 3D **18***
(off Broadgate La.)
Albert Pl. BD3: B'frd 5A **26**
LS18: H'fth 2C **18**
LS26: Meth 6H **55**
Albert Rd. LS26: Oul 3C **54**
LS27: Morl 4H **49**
Albert Sq. LS19: Yead 2E **9**
Albert St. LS28: Pud 1F **37**
Albert Ter. *LS19: Yead 2E **9***
(off Rockfield Ter.)
Albert Way BD11: Birk 5D **46**
Albion Arc. LS1: Leeds 4E **5**
Albion Av. LS12: Leeds 6B **30**
Albion Pk. LS12: Leeds 5C **30**
Albion Pl. LS1: Leeds 4E **5** (5G **31**)
LS20: Guis 4G **7**
Albion Rd. LS28: Stan 3G **27**
Albion St. LS1: Leeds 4E **5** (5G **31**)
(not continuous)
LS2: Leeds 4E **5** (5G **31**)
LS27: Morl 5G **49**
(Corporation St.)
LS27: Morl 5G **49**
(Windsor Ct.)
WF3: Carl 6F **53**
Albion Way LS12: Leeds 5C **30**
Alcester Pl. LS8: Leeds 1B **32**
Alcester Rd. LS8: Leeds 1B **32**
Alcester Ter. LS8: Leeds 1B **32**
Alden Av. LS27: Morl 6G **49**
Alden Cl. LS27: Morl 6G **49**
Alder Dr. LS28: Pud 5C **26**
Alder Gth. LS28: Pud 5D **26**
Alder Hill Av. LS6: Leeds 4E **21**
Alder Hill Cotts. LS6: Leeds 4D **20**
Alder Hill Gro. LS7: Leeds 4E **21**
Alders, The LS7: Leeds 4H **21**
Aldersgate *LS12: Leeds 6A **30***
(off Wesley Rd.)
Aldersyde Rd. LS20: Guis 5F **7**
Aldersyde Way LS20: Guis 5F **7**
Alderton Bank LS17: Leeds 1D **20**
Alderton Cres. LS17: Leeds 1D **20**
Alderton Hgts. LS17: Leeds 1D **20**
Alderton Mt. LS17: Leeds 1D **20**
Alderton Pl. LS17: Leeds 1D **20**
Alderton Ri. LS17: Leeds 1E **21**
Alexander Av. LS15: Leeds 6H **33**
Alexander Ct. LS1: Leeds 3D **4** (5F **31**)
Alexander St. LS1: Leeds 3D **4** (5F **31**)
Alexandra Gro. LS6: Leeds 3C **30**
LS28: Pud 1F **37**
Alexandra Mill LS27: Morl 6G **49**
Alexandra Rd. LS6: Leeds 3C **30**
LS18: H'fth 2C **18**
LS28: Pud 1E **37**
Alexandra Ter. LS19: Yead 2E **9**
(not continuous)
Alfred St. LS27: Chur 1A **50**
Allenby Cres. LS11: Leeds 1E **51**
Allenby Dr. LS11: Leeds 1E **51**
Allenby Gdns. LS11: Leeds 1E **51**
Allenby Gro. LS11: Leeds 1E **51**
Allenby Pl. LS11: Leeds 1E **51**
Allenby Rd. LS11: Leeds 1E **51**
Allenby Vw. LS11: Leeds 6F **41**
Allen Cft. BD11: Birk 4C **46**
Allerton Av. LS17: Leeds 1H **21**
Allerton Ct. *LS17: Leeds 1H **21***
(off Allerton Gro.)
Allerton Cft. *LS7: Leeds 6A **22***
(off Harehills La.)
Allerton Grange Av. LS17: Leeds 2A **22**
Allerton Grange Cl. LS17: Leeds 3G **21**
Allerton Grange Cres. LS17: Leeds 3H **21**
Allerton Grange Cft. LS8: Leeds 3A **22**
Allerton Grange Dr. LS17: Leeds 3H **21**
Allerton Grange Gdns. LS17: Leeds 3H **21**
Allerton Grange Ri. LS17: Leeds 3G **21**
Allerton Grange Va. LS17: Leeds 3H **21**
Allerton Grange Wlk. LS17: Leeds 3H **21**
Allerton Grange Way LS8: Leeds 3A **22**
LS17: Leeds 3H **21**
Allerton Gro. LS17: Leeds 1H **21**
Allerton Hall LS7: Leeds 4G **21**
Allerton Hill LS7: Leeds 4G **21**
Allerton M. LS17: Leeds 2H **21**
Allerton Pk. LS7: Leeds 4H **21**
Allerton Pl. LS17: Leeds 1H **21**
Allerton St. LS4: Leeds 3B **30**
Allerton Ter. LS4: Leeds 4B **30**
Alliance St. LS12: Leeds 6G **29**
Allinson St. LS12: Leeds 1C **40**
All Saints Av. *LS9: Leeds 5B **32***
(off Aysgarth Mt.)
All Saint's Circ. LS26: Wood 3D **54**
All Saint's Dr. LS26: Wood 3C **54**
All Saints Rd. LS9: Leeds 5B **32**
LS26: Wood 2D **54**
All Saints Ter. *LS9: Leeds 5B **32***
(off Aysgarth Mt.)
All Saint's Vw. LS26: Wood 2C **54**
Alma Cl. LS28: Fars 2E **27**
Alma Cotts. LS6: Leeds 6B **20**
Alma Rd. LS6: Leeds 6B **20**
Alma St. LS9: Leeds 4B **32**
LS19: Yead 2E **9**
LS26: Wood 2C **54**
Alma Ter. LS26: Rothw 3F **53**
Alma Vs. LS26: Wood 2D **54**
Alnwick Vw. LS16: Leeds 4A **20**
Alpine Ter. LS26: Rothw 3G **53**
Alston La. LS14: Leeds 2A **34**
Alva Cl. LS20: Guis 3F **7**
Alva Ct. LS20: Guis 3F **7**
ALWOODLEY **5G 13**
Alwoodley Chase LS17: Leeds 4A **14**
Alwoodley Ct. LS17: Leeds 4D **12**
Alwoodley Ct. Gdns. LS17: Leeds 3E **13**
Alwoodley Gdns. LS17: Leeds 4E **13**
ALWOODLEY GATES **3A 14**
Alwoodley Gates LS17: Leeds 3A **14**
Alwoodley La. LS17: Leeds 3D **12**
ALWOODLEY PARK **3E 13**
Amberley Gdns. LS12: Leeds 1B **40**
Amberley Rd. LS12: Leeds 1A **40**
Amberley St. LS12: Leeds 1A **40**
Amberton App. LS8: Leeds 1E **33**
Amberton Cl. LS8: Leeds 6E **23**
Amberton Cres. LS8: Leeds 1E **33**
Amberton Gdns. LS8: Leeds 1E **33**
Amberton Gth. LS8: Leeds 1E **33**
Amberton Gro. LS8: Leeds 1E **33**
Amberton La. LS8: Leeds 1E **33**
Amberton Mt. LS8: Leeds 1E **33**
Amberton Pl. LS8: Leeds 1D **32**
Amberton Rd. LS8: Leeds 1D **32**
LS9: Leeds 1D **32**
Amberton St. LS8: Leeds 1E **33**
Amberton Ter. LS8: Leeds 1E **33**
Amblers Bldgs. *LS28: Pud 1G **37***
(off Amblers Ct.)
Amblers Bungs. WF3: E Ard 3F **57**
Amblers Ct. LS28: Pud 1G **37**
Amblerthorne BD11: Birk 4D **46**
Ambleside Gdns. LS28: Pud 6E **27**
Ambleside Gro. LS26: Wood 3C **54**
AMF Bowling
Leeds **2E 5 (4G 31)**
Amspool Ct. WF3: Carl 6E **53**
Anaheim Dr. WF1: Out 6F **59**
Ancaster Cres. LS16: Leeds 4H **19**
Ancaster Rd. LS16: Leeds 4H **19**
Ancaster Vw. LS16: Leeds 4H **19**
Anderson Av. LS8: Leeds 3A **32**
Anderson Mt. LS8: Leeds 3A **32**
Andover Grn. BD4: B'frd 3A **36**
Andrew Cres. WF1: Out 6D **58**
Andrew Ho. *LS28: Fars 2F **27***
(off Water La.)
Andrews Mnr. *LS19: Yead 2D **8***
(off Haworth La.)
Andrew Sq. LS28: Fars 2F **27**
Andrew St. LS28: Fars 3F **27**

A-Z Leeds 61

Angel Ct. LS3: Leeds 4D **30**
Angel Inn Yd. LS1: Leeds 4E **5**
Angel Row LS26: Rothw 4C **52**
Anlaby St. BD4: B'frd 2A **36**
Annie St. LS27: Morl 5H **49**
Anstey Ho. LS3: Leeds 3A **4**
Antler Complex LS27: Morl 5D **48**
Apex Bus. Cen. LS11: Leeds 2G **41**
Apex Vw. LS11: Leeds 2F **41**
Apex Way LS11: Leeds 2G **41**
APPERLEY BRIDGE .3A **16**
Apperley Gdns. BD10: B'frd 3A **16**
Apperley La. BD10: B'frd, Yead 3A **16**
   LS19: Raw 2B **16**
Apperley Rd. BD10: B'frd 3A **16**
   (not continuous)
Appleby Pl. LS15: Leeds 5G **33**
Appleby Wlk. LS15: Leeds 5G **33**
Appleby Way LS27: Morl 4H **49**
Applegarth LS26: Wood 2C **54**
Appleton Cl. LS9: Leeds 5B **32**
Appleton Ct. LS9: Leeds 5B **32**
Appleton Gro. LS9: Leeds 5D **32**
Appleton Sq. LS9: Leeds 5B **32**
Appleton Way LS9: Leeds 5B **32**
Apple Tree Cl. WF3: E Ard 3G **57**
Apple Tree Ct. WF3: E Ard 4G **57**
Approach, The LS15: Scho 4F **25**
Aragon Ct. LS7: Leeds 4E **21**
Archery Pl. LS2: Leeds 3F **31**
Archery Rd. LS2: Leeds 3F **31**
Archery St. LS2: Leeds 3F **31**
Archery Ter. LS2: Leeds 3F **31**
Arden Grange LS16: Leeds 1A **20**
Ardsley Cl. BD4: B'frd . . . .
   (not continuous)
Ardsley Cl. WF3: E Ard 3A **58**
Arena Pk. LS17: Leeds 2H **15**
Argent Way BD4: B'frd 5B **36**
Argie Av. LS4: Leeds 2H **29**
Argie Gdns. LS4: Leeds 3A **30**
Argie Rd. LS4: Leeds 3A **30**
Argie Ter. LS4: Leeds 3A **30**
Argyle Rd. LS9: Leeds 3H **5** (5H **31**)
Argyll Cl. LS18: H'fth 5B **10**
Arksey Pl. LS12: Leeds 5A **30**
Arksey Ter. LS12: Leeds 5A **30**
Arkwright St. BD4: B'frd 1A **36**
Arkwright Wlk. LS27: Morl 3G **49**
Arlesford Rd. BD4: B'frd 5A **36**
Arley Gro. LS12: Leeds 5A **30**
Arley Pl. LS12: Leeds 5A **30**
Arley St. LS12: Leeds 5A **30**
Arley Ter. LS12: Leeds 5A **30**
Arlington Bus. Cen. LS11: Leeds 1B **50**
Arlington Gro. LS8: Leeds 6D **22**
Arlington Rd. LS8: Leeds 1D **32**
Armitage Bldgs. WF12: Dew 5A **56**
Armitage Sq. LS28: Pud 1F **37**
Armitage St. LS26: Rothw 5G **53**
ARMLEY 5B **30**
Armley Ct. LS12: Leeds 5B **30**
Armley Grange Av. LS12: Leeds 4F **29**
Armley Grange Cres. LS12: Leeds 5F **29**
Armley Grange Dr. LS12: Leeds 5F **29**
Armley Grange Mt. LS12: Leeds 5F **29**
Armley Grange Oval LS12: Leeds 4F **29**
Armley Grange Ri. LS12: Leeds 5F **29**
Armley Grange Vw. LS12: Leeds 5G **29**
Armley Grange Wlk. LS12: Leeds 5G **29**
Armley Gro. Pl. LS12: Leeds 6B **30**
Armley Ho. LS14: Leeds 5G **23**
   (off Kingsdale Ct.)
Armley Leisure Cen. 6H **29**
Armley Lodge Rd. LS12: Leeds 4A **30**
Armley Mills Leeds Industrial Mus. 4A **30**
Armley Pk. Ct. LS12: Leeds 5A **30**
   (off Cecil Rd.)
Armley Pk. Rd. LS12: Leeds 4A **30**
Armley Ridge Cl. LS12: Leeds 5G **29**
Armley Ridge Rd. LS12: Leeds 4A **30**
   (not continuous)
Armley Ridge Ter. LS12: Leeds 4G **29**
Armley Rd. LS12: Leeds 5A **30**
   (not continuous)
Armouries Dr. LS10: Leeds 1H **41**
Armouries Way LS10: Leeds 6H **5** (6H **31**)
   LS28: Fars 3F **27**
Armstrong St. BD4: B'frd 1A **36**
   LS28: Fars 3F **27**
Arncliffe Cres. LS27: Morl 1A **56**
Arncliffe Gth. LS28: Stan 3F **27**
Arncliffe Grange LS17: Leeds 1H **21**
Arncliffe Rd. LS16: Leeds 3G **19**
Arncliffe St. LS28: Stan 3F **27**
Arndale Cen. LS6: Leeds 6B **20**
Arran Dr. LS18: H'fth 5B **10**
Arran Way LS26: Rothw 4H **53**

Arthington Av. LS10: Leeds 5H **41**
Arthington Cl. WF3: W Ard 4B **56**
Arthington Ct. LS10: Leeds 5H **41**
Arthington Gro. LS10: Leeds 5H **41**
Arthington Pl. LS10: Leeds 5H **41**
Arthington Rd. LS16: Leeds 1A **12**
Arthington St. LS10: Leeds 5H **41**
Arthington Ter. LS10: Leeds 5H **41**
Arthington Vw. LS10: Leeds 5H **41**
ARTHURSDALE 3F **25**
Arthursdale Cl. LS15: Scho 4F **25**
Arthursdale Dr. LS15: Scho 4F **25**
Arthursdale Grange LS15: Scho 4F **25**
Arthur St. LS28: Fars 3F **27**
   LS28: Stan 3G **27**
Arthur Ter. LS28: Fars 3F **27**
   (off Arthur St.)
Artist St. LS12: Leeds 6D **30**
Aruba LS12: Leeds 5A **4**
Arundel St. LS28: Pud 6G **27**
Arundel Ter. LS15: Leeds 3C **34**
   (off Tranquility Av.)
Ascot Gdns. LS10: Leeds 6H **51**
Ascot Ter. LS9: Leeds 6B **32**
Asda Ho. LS11: Leeds 6E **5** (1G **41**)
Ash Av. LS6: Leeds 6B **20**
Ashbrooke Pk. LS11: Leeds 5G **41**
Ashbury Chase WF1: Out 6C **58**
Ashby Av. LS13: Leeds 3D **28**
Ashby Cres. LS13: Leeds 4D **28**
Ashby Mt. LS13: Leeds 3D **28**
Ashby Sq. LS13: Leeds 3D **28**
Ashby Ter. LS13: Leeds 3D **28**
Ashby Vw. LS13: Leeds 3D **28**
Ash Cl. LS27: Gil 3D **48**
Ash Ct. LS14: Leeds .3G **33**
Ash Cres. LS6: Leeds .6B **20**
   WF3: S'ley 6H **59**
Ashdene LS12: N Far .4D **38**
Ashdene Cl. LS28: Pud 2G **37**
Ashdene Cres. LS28: Pud 2G **37**
Ashdown St. LS13: Leeds 4C **28**
Ashfield BD4: B'frd 6A **36**
   LS12: N Far 3G **39**
Ashfield Av. LS27: Morl 6F **49**
Ashfield Cl. LS12: N Far 3F **39**
   LS15: Leeds 1D **34**
Ashfield Cres. LS28: Stan 4F **27**
Ashfield Gro. LS28: Stan 4G **27**
Ashfield Pk. LS6: Leeds 6C **20**
Ashfield Rd. LS27: Morl 6F **49**
   LS28: Stan 4F **27**
Ashfield Ter. LS15: Leeds 1D **34**
   WF3: Thpe H 1B **58**
Ashfield Way LS12: N Far 3E **39**
Ashford Dr. LS28: Pud 1H **37**
Ash Gdns. LS6: Leeds 6B **20**
Ash Gro. BD11: Birk .3C **46**
   LS6: Leeds 2D **30**
   LS18: H'fth 1C **18**
   LS28: Pud 1G **37**
Ashgrove BD10: B'frd 4A **16**
Ashgrove M. LS3: Leeds 1H **27**
Ash Hill Dr. LS17: Shad 5H **15**
Ash Hill Gdns. LS17: Shad 5H **15**
Ash Hill Gth. LS17: Shad 5H **15**
Ash Hill La. LS17: Shad 5H **15**
Ash Ho. LS15: Leeds .1G **43**
Ashington Cl. BD2: B'frd 1A **26**
Ashlea Ct. LS13: Leeds 1C **28**
   (off Ashlea Ga.)
Ashlea Ga. LS13: Leeds 2C **28**
Ashlea Grn. LS13: Leeds 2C **28**
Ashleigh Gdns. LS26: Oul 3C **54**
Ashleigh Rd. LS16: Leeds 3G **19**
Ashley Av. LS9: Leeds 3C **32**
Ashley Ind. Est. LS7: Leeds 2G **31**
   LS12: Leeds 1H **39**
Ashley Rd. LS9: Leeds 3B **32**
Ashley Ter. LS9: Leeds 3C **32**
Ash M. BD10: B'frd .4A **16**
Ash Rd. LS6: Leeds 1A **30**
Ashroyd LS26: Rothw 5H **53**
Ash Ter. LS6: Leeds 6B **20**
Ashtofts Mt. LS20: Guis 4G **7**
Ashton Av. LS8: Leeds 3B **32**
Ashton Cres. WF3: Carl 6F **53**
Ashton Gro. LS8: Leeds 3B **32**
Ashton Mt. LS8: Leeds 3B **32**
Ashton Pl. LS8: Leeds 3B **32**
Ashton Rd. LS8: Leeds 2C **32**
Ashton Rd. Ind. Est. LS8: Leeds 2C **32**
Ashton Ter. LS8: Leeds 3B **32**
   WF3: Rob H 5D **52**
Ashton Vw. LS8: Leeds 3B **32**

Ash Tree App. LS14: Leeds 1D **34**
Ash Tree Bank LS14: Leeds 6D **24**
Ash Tree Cl. LS14: Leeds 6D **24**
Ash Tree Ct. LS14: Leeds 6D **24**
Ash Tree Gdns. LS14: Leeds 6D **24**
Ash Tree Gro. LS14: Leeds 6D **24**
Ash Tree Vw. LS14: Leeds 6D **24**
   (off Stanks Gdns.)
Ash Tree Wlk. LS14: Leeds 6D **24**
   (off Ash Tree Gdns.)
Ash Vw. LS6: Leeds 6B **20**
   WF3: E Ard 4G **57**
Ash Vs. LS15: Leeds .1D **34**
Ashville Av. LS6: Leeds 2B **30**
Ashville Gro. LS6: Leeds 2B **30**
Ashville Rd. LS4: Leeds 2B **30**
   LS6: Leeds 2B **30**
Ashville Ter. LS6: Leeds 2B **30**
   LS28: Fars 3F **27**
   (off New St.)
Ashville Vw. LS6: Leeds 3C **30**
Ashwood LS14: Leeds 2B **24**
Ashwood Dr. LS27: Gil 2B **48**
Ashwood Gdns. LS27: Gil 2B **48**
Ashwood Gro. LS27: Gil 2C **48**
Ashwood Pde. LS27: Gil 2B **48**
   (off Ashwood Gdns.)
Ashwood St. BD4: B'frd 6A **36**
Ashwood Ter. LS6: Leeds 1D **30**
Ashwood Vs. LS6: Leeds 1D **30**
Asket Av. LS14: Leeds 6G **23**
Asket Cl. LS14: Leeds 5G **23**
Asket Cres. LS14: Leeds 6G **23**
Asket Dr. LS14: Leeds 5G **23**
Asket Gdns. LS8: Leeds 5F **23**
Asket Gth. LS14: Leeds 5G **23**
Asket Grn. LS14: Leeds 5G **23**
Asket Hill LS8: Leeds .4F **23**
Asket Pl. LS14: Leeds 6G **23**
Asket Wlk. LS14: Leeds 6G **23**
Askey Cres. LS27: Morl 1A **56**
Askrigg Ct. LS29: Men 3D **6**
Aspect 14 LS7: Leeds 1F **5** (4G **31**)
Aspect Gdns. LS28: Pud 5E **27**
Aspect Ter. LS28: Pud 5E **27**
Aspen Cl. WF3: Ting .2A **56**
Aspen Mt. LS16: Leeds 1E **19**
Asquith Av. LS27: Morl 3E **49**
Asquith Av. Bus. Pk. LS27: Gil 3E **49**
Asquith Cl. LS27: Morl 4F **49**
Asquith Dr. LS27: Morl 4F **49**
Assembly St. LS2: Leeds 5F **5** (6G **31**)
Astley Av. LS26: Swil 6G **45**
Astley La. LS26: Swil 6H **45**
Astley La. Ind. Est. LS26: Swil 1H **55**
Astley Way LS26: Swil 1H **55**
Aston Av. LS13: Leeds 3D **28**
Aston Cres. LS13: Leeds 3E **29**
Aston Dr. LS13: Leeds 3E **29**
Aston Gro. LS13: Leeds 3E **29**
Aston Mt. LS13: Leeds 3E **29**
Aston Pl. LS13: Leeds 3D **28**
Aston Rd. LS13: Leeds 3D **28**
Aston St. LS13: Leeds 3D **28**
Aston Ter. LS13: Leeds 3E **29**
Aston Vw. LS13: Leeds 3D **28**
Astor Gro. LS13: Leeds 3A **28**
Astoria Ct. LS8: Leeds 6C **22**
Astor St. LS13: Leeds 3A **28**
Astra Bus. Pk. LS11: Leeds 5G **41**
Astura Ct. LS7: Leeds 6F **21**
Atha Cl. LS11: Leeds .6E **41**
Atha Cres. LS11: Leeds 6E **41**
Atha Ho. LS2: Leeds .1D **4**
Atha St. LS11: Leeds .6E **41**
Athens LS20: Guis 4F **7**
Athlone Gro. LS12: Leeds 6A **30**
Athlone St. LS12: Leeds 6A **30**
Athlone Ter. LS12: Leeds 6A **30**
ATKINSON HILL 3B **42**
Atkinson St. LS10: Leeds 2A **42**
Atlanta St. LS13: Leeds 3A **28**
Atlantic Apartments LS1: Leeds 5C **4**
Attlee Gro. WF1: Out 5E **35**
AUSTHORPE 5E **35**
Austhorpe Av. LS15: Leeds 6E **35**
Austhorpe Ct. LS15: Leeds 6E **35**
   (off Austhorpe Dr.)
Austhorpe Dr. LS15: Leeds 6E **35**
Austhorpe Gdns. LS15: Leeds 5F **35**
Austhorpe Gro. LS15: Leeds 6E **35**
Austhorpe La. LS15: Leeds 4D **34**
Austhorpe Rd. LS15: Leeds 3C **34**
Austhorpe Ter. LS15: Leeds 5D **34**
Authorpe Rd. LS6: Leeds 5D **20**
Autumn Av. LS6: Leeds 3C **30**
Autumn Cres. LS18: H'fth 4D **18**

Autumn Gro. LS6: Leeds 3C 30
Autumn Pl. LS6: Leeds 3C 30
Autumn St. LS6: Leeds 3C 30
Autumn Ter. LS6: Leeds 3C 30
Auty Cres. WF3: S'ley 6H 59
Auty M. WF3: S'ley 6H 59
Auty Sq. LS27: Morl 6H 49
Avenue, The BD10: B'frd 6A 8
   BD17: Esh 6A 8
   LS8: Leeds 3C 22
   LS9: Leeds 6A 32
   LS15: Leeds 2D 34
   LS15: Leeds, Swil 5D 44
   (not continuous)
   LS15: Scho 3F 25
   LS17: Leeds 4D 12
   LS18: H'fth 2H 17
   WF1: Out 6D 58
   WF3: Ting 3E 57
Avenue Ct. LS17: Leeds 4D 12
Avenue Cres. LS8: Leeds 1B 32
Avenue Gdns. LS17: Leeds 4E 13
Avenue Hill LS8: Leeds 1A 32
Avenue Lawns LS17: Leeds 4D 12
Avenue St. BD4: B'frd 6A 36
Avenue Ter. LS19: Yead 2F 9
Avenue Victoria LS18: Leeds 3C 22
Avenue Wlk. LS2: Leeds 2E 31
   LS6: Leeds 2E 31
Aviary Gro. LS12: Leeds 5A 30
Aviary Mt. LS12: Leeds 5A 30
Aviary Pl. LS12: Leeds 5A 30
Aviary Rd. LS12: Leeds 5A 30
Aviary Row LS12: Leeds 5A 30
Aviary St. LS12: Leeds 5A 30
Aviary Ter. LS12: Leeds 5A 30
Aviary Vw. LS12: Leeds 5A 30
Avocet Gth. LS10: Leeds 4H 51
Avon Cl. LS17: Shad 5H 15
Avon Ct. LS17: Shad 4G 15
Avondale Ct. LS17: Leeds 6H 13
Avondale Dr. WF3: S'ley 6G 59
Avondale St. LS13: Leeds 4C 28
Axis Ct. LS27: Gil 4E 49
Aylesford Mt. LS15: Leeds 2F 35
Ayresome Av. LS8: Leeds 1C 22
Ayresome Ter. LS8: Leeds 1B 22
Aysgarth Cl. LS9: Leeds 6B 32
Aysgarth Dr. LS9: Leeds 6B 32
Aysgarth Fold LS10: Leeds 5G 51
Aysgarth Pl. LS9: Leeds 6B 32
Aysgarth Wlk. LS9: Leeds 6B 32
Ayton Ho. BD4: B'frd 6B 36

B

Bachelor La. LS18: H'fth 2C 18
Bk. Airlie Av. LS8: Leeds 1B 32
   (off Airlie Av.)
Bk. Airlie Pl. LS8: Leeds 1B 32
   (off Airlie Pl.)
Bk. Albert Gro. LS6: Leeds 5B 20
Bk. Albert Ter. LS6: Leeds 3C 30
   (off Spring Gro. Ter.)
Bk. Alcester Pl. LS8: Leeds 1B 32
   (off Alcester Pl.)
Bk. Alcester Rd. LS8: Leeds 1B 32
   (off Alcester Rd.)
Bk. Alcester Ter. LS8: Leeds 1B 32
   (off Alcester Ter.)
Bk. Allerton Ter. LS7: Leeds 4H 21
Bk. Alma St. LS19: Yead 2E 9
   (off Alma St.)
Bk. Archery Pl. LS2: Leeds 3F 31
   (off Archery Rd.)
Bk. Archery Rd. LS2: Leeds 3F 31
   (off Archery Rd.)
Bk. Archery St. LS2: Leeds 3F 31
   (off Archery Rd.)
Bk. Archery Ter. LS2: Leeds 3F 31
   (off Archery Rd.)
Bk. Ash Gro. LS6: Leeds 2D 30
   (not continuous)
Bk. Ashley Av. LS9: Leeds 3C 32
   (off Ashley Rd.)
Bk. Ashley St. LS9: Leeds 3C 32
   (off Ashley Rd.)
Bk. Ashville Av. LS6: Leeds 2C 30
   (off Cardigan Rd.)
Bk. Ashville Gro. LS6: Leeds 2B 30
   (off Cardigan Rd.)
Bk. Ashville Rd. LS6: Leeds 2B 30
   (off Cardigan Rd.)
Bk. Ashville Ter. LS6: Leeds 2B 30
   (off Cardigan Rd.)
Bk. Ashwood Ter. LS6: Leeds 1D 30

Bk. Aston Pl. LS13: Leeds 3E 29
   (off Aston Rd.)
Bk. Aston Rd. LS13: Leeds 3D 28
Bk. Aston St. LS13: Leeds 3D 28
Bk. Aston Ter. LS13: Leeds 3E 29
   (off Aston Av.)
Bk. Aston Vw. LS13: Leeds 3E 29
   (off Aston Av.)
Bk. Athlone Av. LS12: Leeds 6A 30
Bk. Athlone Gro. LS12: Leeds 6A 30
   (off Athlone St.)
Bk. Athlone Ter. LS12: Leeds 6A 30
   (off Athlone St.)
Bk. Atlanta St. LS13: Leeds 3A 28
   (off Fairfield Av.)
Bk. Austhorpe Rd. LS15: Leeds 3C 34
   (off Austhorpe Rd.)
Bk. Autumn Rd. LS6: Leeds 3C 30
   (off Autumn Gro.)
Bk. Autumn Ter. LS6: Leeds 3C 30
   (off Alexandra Rd.)
Bk. Aviary Rd. LS12: Leeds 5A 30
   (off Aviary Gro.)
Bk. Bailey's Pl. LS16: Leeds 5B 20
Bk. Baldovan Ter. LS8: Leeds 1B 32
   (off Baldovan Ter.)
Bk. Bank Ter. LS28: Stan 3G 27
Bk. Banstead St. LS8: Leeds 2B 32
   (off Harehills Rd.)
Bk. Barden Pl. LS12: Leeds 6G 29
   (off Conference Rd.)
Bk. Barkly Gro. LS11: Leeds 5E 41
   (off Theodore St.)
Bk. Barkly Pde. LS11: Leeds 5E 41
   (off Barkly Dr.)
Bk. Barkly Ter. LS11: Leeds 5E 41
   (off Barkly Dr.)
Bk. Barrowby Vw. LS15: Leeds 6E 35
Bk. Bath Rd. LS13: Leeds 3C 28
   (off Cross Bath Rd.)
Bk. Beamsley Gro. LS6: Leeds 3C 30
   (off Harold Gro.)
Bk. Beamsley Mt. LS6: Leeds 3C 30
   (off Royal Pk. Rd.)
Bk. Beamsley Ter. LS6: Leeds 3C 30
   (off Royal Pk. Rd.)
Bk. Beechwood Gro. LS4: Leeds 2B 30
Bk. Beechwood Rd. LS4: Leeds 2B 30
   (off Beechwood Pl.)
Bk. Bellbrooke Gro. LS9: Leeds 3D 32
   (off Bellbrooke St.)
Bk. Bellbrooke Pl. LS9: Leeds 3D 32
   (off Bellbrooke St.)
Bk. Bellbrooke Ter. LS9: Leeds 3D 32
   (off Coldcotes Av.)
Bk. Belvedere Av. LS11: Leeds 5F 41
   (off Harlech Rd.)
Bk. Bentley Av. LS6: Leeds 5D 20
   (off Bentley Mt.)
Bk. Bentley Gro. LS6: Leeds 5D 20
   (off Bentley Mt.)
Bk. Berkeley Av. LS8: Leeds 2C 32
   (off Berkeley Rd.)
Bk. Berkeley Ter. LS8: Leeds 2C 32
   (off Berkeley Rd.)
Bk. Beverley Ter. LS11: Leeds 4F 41
Bk. Blenheim Av. LS2: Leeds 3F 31
Bk. Blenheim St. LS2: Leeds 3F 31
Bk. Boundary Ter. LS3: Leeds 4C 30
   (off Woodsley Rd.)
Bk. Branch Pl. LS12: Leeds 3G 39
   (off Branch Rd.)
Bk. Breary Av. LS18: H'fth 2D 18
Bk. Breary Ter. LS18: H'fth 2D 18
   (off Breary Av.)
Bk. Broad La. LS13: Leeds 1D 28
Bk. Broomfield Cres. LS6: Leeds 1B 30
Bk. Broomfield Pl. LS6: Leeds 2B 30
   (off Newport Rd.)
Bk. Broomfield Rd. LS6: Leeds 2B 30
   (off Newport Rd.)
Bk. Broughton Av. LS9: Leeds 3C 32
   (off Foundry App.)
Bk. Broughton Ter. LS9: Leeds 3C 32
   (off Foundry App.)
Bk. Brudenell Gro. LS6: Leeds 3D 30
   (off Royal Pk. Rd.)
Bk. Brudenell Mt. LS6: Leeds 2C 30
   (off Royal Pk. Rd.)
Bk. Brudenell Rd. LS6: Leeds 2C 30
   (off Thornville Rd.)
Bk. Brunswick St. LS2: Leeds 2F 5 (4G 31)
Bk. Burchett Gro. LS6: Leeds 1E 31
   (off Hartley Av.)
Bk. Burchett Pl. LS6: Leeds 1E 31
   (off Hartley Av.)

Bk. Burley Hill LS4: Leeds 3A 30
Bk. Burley Lodge Rd. LS6: Leeds 3C 30
   (off Chiswick St.)
Bk. Burley Lodge Ter. LS4: Leeds 4C 30
   (off Woodsley Rd.)
Bk. Burley St. LS3: Leeds 3A 4
Bk. Burlington Pl. LS11: Leeds 5F 41
   (off Tempest Rd.)
Bk. Burlington Rd. LS11: Leeds 5F 41
   (off Harlech Av.)
Bk. Burton Cres. LS6: Leeds 5B 20
Bk. Burton Ter. LS11: Leeds 4G 41
Bk. Camberley St. LS11: Leeds 4F 41
   (off Camberley St.)
Bk. Carberry Pl. LS6: Leeds 3C 30
   (off Carberry Rd.)
Bk. Carberry Rd. LS6: Leeds 3C 30
   (off Chiswick St.)
Bk. Carberry Ter. LS6: Leeds 3C 30
   (off Carberry Rd.)
Bk. Carter Mt. LS15: Leeds 5C 34
   (off Carter La.)
Bk. Carter Ter. LS15: Leeds 4C 34
   (off Carter La.)
Bk. Chapel La. LS6: Leeds 1B 30
   (off Broomfield Rd.)
Bk. Charlton Rd. LS9: Leeds 6C 32
Bk. Chatsworth Rd. LS8: Leeds 2C 32
   (off Harehills La.)
Bk. Chestnut Av. LS15: Leeds 3D 34
   (off Railway Rd.)
Bk. Chiswick Ter. LS6: Leeds 3C 30
   (off Carberry Rd.)
Bk. Christ Chu. Vw. LS12: Leeds 5H 29
   (off Stanningley Rd.)
Bk. Church La. LS5: Leeds 1G 29
   (off Hesketh Rd.)
   LS16: Leeds 4B 12
Bk. Claremont Av. LS3: Leeds 2A 4
Bk. Claremont Gro. LS3: Leeds 2A 4
Bk. Claremont St. LS26: Oul 3C 54
Bk. Claremont Ter. LS3: Leeds 2A 4
Bk. Clarence Rd. LS18: H'fth 4B 18
Bk. Clarence St. LS13: Leeds 4C 28
Bk. Clarkson Vw. LS6: Leeds 1E 31
   (off Quarry St.)
Bk. Cliff Mt. LS6: Leeds 1E 31
   (off Cliff Mt. Ter.)
Bk. Clifton Ter. LS9: Leeds 3D 32
   (off Clifton Av.)
Bk. Clipston Av. LS6: Leeds 5D 20
   (off Clipston Av.)
Bk. Clovelly Pl. LS11: Leeds 4F 41
   (off Rowland Rd.)
Bk. Colenso Mt. LS11: Leeds 3D 40
   (off Cleveleys Av.)
Bk. Colenso Rd. LS11: Leeds 3D 40
   (off Cleveleys Av.)
Bk. Colton Rd. LS12: Leeds 6A 30
Bk. Colwyn Vw. LS11: Leeds 5F 41
   (off Colwyn Av.)
Bk. Conway St. LS8: Leeds 2B 32
   (off Harehills Rd.)
Bk. Cowper Gro. LS8: Leeds 2C 32
   (off Ashley Rd.)
Bk. Cowper St. LS7: Leeds 2A 32
   (off Cross Cowper St.)
Bk. Craggwood Rd. LS18: H'fth 4C 18
Bk. Cranbrook Av. LS11: Leeds 4E 41
   (off Wickham St.)
Bk. Cranbrook Ter. LS11: Leeds 4E 41
   (off Hird St.)
Back Cres., The LS6: Leeds 2E 31
   (off Highbury St.)
Bk. Cromer Ter. LS2: Leeds 1B 4 (3E 31)
Bk. Cross Flatts Av. LS11: Leeds 5E 41
   (off Theodore St.)
Bk. Cross Flatts Cres. LS11: Leeds 5D 40
   (off Wooler St.)
Bk. Cross Flatts Gro. LS11: Leeds 5E 41
   (off Cross Flatts Gro.)
Bk. Cross Flatts Mt. LS11: Leeds 5E 41
   (off Wooler Gro.)
Bk. Cross Flatts Pl. LS11: Leeds 5D 40
   (off Wooler St.)
Bk. Cross Flatts Row LS11: Leeds 5D 40
   (off Wooler St.)
Bk. Cross Grn. La. LS9: Leeds 1B 42
   (off Cross Grn. La.)
Bk. Dalton Gro. LS11: Leeds 5E 41
   (off Cross Flatts Av.)
Bk. Dalton Rd. LS11: Leeds 5E 41
Bk. Dargai St. LS7: Leeds 2G 31
Bk. Dawlish Av. LS9: Leeds 5D 32
   (off Ivy Av.)
Bk. Dawlish Mt. LS9: Leeds 5D 32
   (off Ivy Av.)

Bk. Dawlish Rd. LS9: Leeds 5D 32
(off Dawlish Cres.)
Bk. De Lacy Mt. LS5: Leeds 6G 19
(off Morris La.)
Bk. Delph Mt. LS6: Leeds 1E 31
(off Delph La.)
Bk. Dent St. LS9: Leeds 6B 32
(off Kippax Mt.)
Bk. Devonshire La. LS8: Leeds 1C 22
Bk. Dewsbury Dr. LS11: Leeds 5G 41
(off Dewsbury Rd.)
Bk. Dorset Mt. LS8: Leeds 1C 32
(off Dorset St.)
Bk. Dorset Rd. LS8: Leeds 1C 32
(off Dorset Av.)
Bk. Dorset Ter. LS8: Leeds 2C 32
(off Harehills La.)
Bk. East Pk. Rd. LS9: Leeds 6C 32
(off Garton Rd.)
Bk. Ecclesburn Gro. LS9: Leeds 6D 32
(off Ivy St.)
Bk. Ecclesburn St. LS9: Leeds 6C 32
(off Park Pde.)
Bk. Edinburgh Rd. LS12: Leeds 5G 29
(off Moorfield St.)
Bk. Elford Pl. LS8: Leeds 2B 32
(off Roundhay Rd., not continuous)
Bk. Ellers Gro. LS8: Leeds 1B 32
(off Ellers Gro.)
Bk. Ellers Rd. LS8: Leeds 1B 32
(off Ellers Rd.)
Bk. Elsworth St. LS12: Leeds 6B 30
Bk. Eric St. LS13: Leeds 6C 18
Bk. Eshald Pl. LS26: Wood 3D 54
Bk. Esmond Ter. LS12: Leeds 6A 30
Bk. Estcourt Av. LS6: Leeds 6A 20
(off Canterbury Dr.)
Bk. Estcourt Ter. LS6: Leeds 1A 30
(off Canterbury Dr.)
Bk. Fairford Pl. LS11: Leeds 4G 41
Bk. Featherbank Ter. LS18: H'frth 4B 18
Bk. Garton Rd. LS9: Leeds 6C 32
(off East Pk. Rd.)
Bk. Garton Ter. LS9: Leeds 6C 32
(off East Pk. Pde.)
Bk. Gathorne St. LS7: Leeds 2A 32
(off Gathorne St.)
Bk. Gillett La. LS26: Rothw 4H 53
Bk. Glebe Ter. LS16: Leeds 5B 20
(off Weetwood La.)
Bk. Glenthorpe Ter. LS9: Leeds 5C 32
(off Walford Rd.)
Bk. Glossop St. LS6: Leeds 5D 20
(off Elm St.)
Bk. Gordon Ter. LS6: Leeds 5D 20
(off Gordon Vw.)
Bk. Graham Gro. LS4: Leeds 2B 30
Bk. Granby Gro. LS6: Leeds 1B 30
(off Granby Rd.)
Bk. Grange Av. LS7: Leeds 1H 31
(off Grange Av.)
Bk. Grange Cres. LS7: Leeds 1A 32
(off Hamilton Ter.)
Bk. Grange Ter. LS7: Leeds 1H 31
(off Nassau Pl.)
Bk. Grange Vw. LS7: Leeds 1A 32
(off Nassau Pl.)
Back Grn. LS27: Chur 2A 50
Bk. Greenhow Wlk. LS4: Leeds 3B 30
(off Greenhow Wlk.)
Bk. Greenmount Ter. LS11: Leeds 4F 41
(off Greenmount La.)
Bk. Grosvenor Ter. LS6: Leeds 1D 30
(off Cliff La.)
Bk. Grove Gdns. LS6: Leeds 5C 20
(off Grove Av.)
Bk. Grovehall Av. LS11: Leeds 6E 41
Bk. Grovehall Dr. LS11: Leeds 6E 41
Bk. Haigh Av. LS26: Rothw 2F 53
Bk. Haigh St. LS26: Rothw 2E 53
Bk. Haigh Vw. LS26: Rothw 2E 53
Bk. Halliday Gro. LS12: Leeds 5G 29
Bk. Halliday Pl. LS12: Leeds 5G 29
Bk. Hamilton Av. LS7: Leeds 1A 32
(off Nassau Pl.)
Bk. Hamilton Vw. LS7: Leeds 1A 32
(off Hamilton Ter.)
Bk. Harehills Av. LS7: Leeds 1A 32
(off Nassau Pl.)
Bk. Harehills La. LS8: Leeds 2B 32
(off Harehills Rd.)
Bk. Harehills Pk. Vw. LS9: Leeds 3D 32
(off Foundry App.)
Bk. Harehills Pl. LS8: Leeds 2B 32
(off Harehills Pl.)
Bk. Hares Av. LS8: Leeds 1B 32
(off Hares Av.)

Bk. Hares Mt. LS8: Leeds 1A 32
(off Hares Rd.)
Bk. Hares Ter. LS8: Leeds 1B 32
(off Hares Ter.)
Bk. Hares Vw. LS8: Leeds 1B 32
(off Hares Rd.)
Bk. Harold Gro. LS6: Leeds 3C 30
(off Cardigan Rd.)
Bk. Hartley Av. LS6: Leeds 1F 31
(off Burchett Ter.)
Bk. Hartley Gro. LS6: Leeds 1E 31
(off Glossop Vw.)
Bk. Hartley St. LS27: Morl 6A 50
Bk. Hawksworth Gro. LS5: Leeds 5D 18
Bk. Headingley Av. LS6: Leeds 6A 20
(off Canterbury Dr.)
Bk. Headingley Mt. LS6: Leeds 6A 20
(off Canterbury Dr.)
Bk. Heathfield Ter. LS6: Leeds 5B 20
(off Heathfield Ter.)
Bk. Heddon St. LS6: Leeds 5C 20
(off Brookfield Rd.)
Bk. Hessle Av. LS6: Leeds 2C 30
(off Walmsley Rd.)
Bk. Hessle Mt. LS6: Leeds 2C 30
(off Brundenell Rd.)
Bk. Hessle Ter. LS6: Leeds 2C 30
(off Walmsley Rd.)
Bk. Hessle Vw. LS6: Leeds 2C 30
(off Welton Rd.)
Bk. Highbury Ter. LS6: Leeds 5C 20
(off Highbury Mt.)
Bk. Highfield Rd. LS13: Leeds 3D 28
(off Aston Rd.)
Bk. High St. LS19: Yead 2D 8
Bk. Highthorne Gro. LS12: Leeds 5G 29
(off Highthorne St.)
Bk. Highthorne St. LS12: Leeds 5G 29
(off Armley Ridge Rd.)
Bk. Hillcrest Av. LS7: Leeds 1A 32
(off Grange Av.)
Bk. Hillcrest Vw. LS7: Leeds 1A 32
(off Hillcrest Pl.)
Bk. Hilltop Av. LS8: Leeds 1B 32
(off Hilltop Mt.)
Bk. Hill Top Mt. LS8: Leeds 1B 32
(off Hill Top Mt.)
Bk. Hilton Pl. LS8: Leeds 6B 22
(off Hilton Pl.)
Bk. Hilton Rd. LS8: Leeds 1B 32
(off Avenue Cres.)
Bk. Hollyshaw Ter. LS15: Leeds 5C 34
Bk. Holywell La. LS17: Shad 4F 15
Bk. Hovingham Gro. LS8: Leeds 1C 32
(off Sandhurst Mt.)
Bk. Hovingham Mt. LS8: Leeds 1C 32
(off Dorset Av.)
Bk. Hovingham Ter. LS8: Leeds 1C 32
(off Dorset Av.)
Bk. Hyde Ter. LS2: Leeds 1A 4 (4E 31)
Bk. Ibbetson Pl. LS1: Leeds 1C 4
Bk. Ingledew Cres. LS8: Leeds 1D 22
Bk. Ivy Av. LS9: Leeds 5C 32
(off Ivy Av.)
Bk. Ivy Gro. LS9: Leeds 6D 32
(off Victoria Av.)
Bk. Ivy Mt. LS9: Leeds 5C 32
(off Ivy Vw.)
Bk. Ivy St. LS9: Leeds 5C 32
(off Ivy Av.)
Bk. Karnac Rd. LS8: Leeds 1B 32
(off Nice St.)
Bk. Kelso Rd. LS2: Leeds 1A 4 (3D 30)
Bk. Kendal La. LS2: Leeds 2A 4
Bk. Kennerleigh Wlk. LS15: Leeds 4C 34
(off Kennerleigh Wlk.)
Bk. Kensington Ter. LS6: Leeds 2D 30
Bk. Kings Av. LS6: Leeds 3C 30
(off Alexandra Rd.)
Bk. Kitson St. LS9: Leeds 6B 32
(off Kippax Mt.)
Bk. Knowle Mt. LS4: Leeds 2B 30
(off Stanmore Hill)
Bk. Lake St. LS10: Leeds 5H 41
Bk. Lambton Gro. LS8: Leeds 1C 32
(off Lambton Gro.)
Bk. Landseer Av. LS13: Leeds 2E 29
(off Victoria Pk. Av.)
Bk. Landseer Gro. LS13: Leeds 2E 29
(off Victoria Pk. Av.)
Bk. Landseer Ter. LS13: Leeds 2E 29
(off Victoria Pk. Av.)
Back La. BD11: Drig 2H 47
LS11: Leeds 6D 40
LS12: N Far 5C 38
LS13: Leeds 4D 28
LS18: H'fth 3B 18

Back La. LS19: Yead 3C 8
LS20: Guis .4E 7
LS28: Fars 2F 27
WF3: Loft 2E 59
Bk. Langdale Gdns. LS6: Leeds 1A 30
(off Canterbury Dr.)
Bk. Langdale Ter. LS6: Leeds 1A 30
(off Canterbury Dr.)
Bk. Laurel Mt. LS7: Leeds 6H 21
Bk. Linden Gro. LS11: Leeds 4G 41
(off Linden Gro.)
Bk. Lodge La. LS11: Leeds 5F 41
(off Stratford Ter.)
Bk. Lombard St. LS19: Raw 5C 8
Bk. Longroyd Ter. LS11: Leeds 4G 41
(off Burton Av.)
Bk. Low La. LS18: H'fth 2D 18
(off Bk. Breary Av.)
Bk. Lucas St. LS6: Leeds 1E 31
(off Delph La.)
Bk. Lunan Pl. LS8: Leeds 1B 32
(off Lunan Pl.)
Bk. Lunan Ter. LS8: Leeds 1B 32
(off Lunan Ter.)
Bk. Mafeking Av. LS11: Leeds 6E 41
(off Dewsbury Rd.)
Bk. Mafeking Mt. LS11: Leeds 6E 41
Bk. Manor Dr. LS6: Leeds 1C 30
(off Manor Av.)
Bk. Manor Gro. LS7: Leeds 5H 21
(off St Martin's Dr.)
Bk. Markham Av. LS8: Leeds 1B 32
(off Markham Av.)
Bk. Marshall Av. LS15: Leeds 3D 34
(off Railway Rd.)
Bk. Marshall St. LS15: Leeds 3C 34
(off Austhorpe Rd.)
Bk. Marshall Ter. LS15: Leeds 3C 34
(off Railway Rd.)
Bk. Mary St. WF3: E Ard 3A 58
Bk. Masham St. LS12: Leeds 6B 30
(off Bk. Middle Cross St.)
Bk. Maud Av. LS11: Leeds 5F 41
(off Maud Pl.)
Bk. Mayville Av. LS6: Leeds 2C 30
(off Mayville Rd.)
Bk. Mayville Pl. LS6: Leeds 2C 30
(off Cardigan La.)
Bk. Mayville St. LS6: Leeds 2C 30
(off Mayville St.)
Bk. Mayville Ter. LS6: Leeds 2C 30
(off Mayville St.)
Bk. Meadow Vw. LS6: Leeds 2C 30
(off Brundenell Rd.)
Bk. Methley Dr. LS7: Leeds 5H 21
Bk. Mexborough Av. LS7: Leeds 1H 31
(off Savile Av.)
Bk. Mexborough Dr. LS7: Leeds 1H 31
(off Savile Av.)
Bk. Mexborough Gro. LS7: Leeds 1H 31
(off Savile Av.)
Bk. Mexborough St. LS7: Leeds 1H 31
(off Savile Av.)
Bk. Meynell Av. LS26: Rothw 4G 53
Bk. Middle Cross St.
LS12: Leeds 6B 30
Bk. Middleton Vw. LS11: Leeds 4E 41
Bk. Midland Rd. LS6: Leeds 2D 30
(off Hyde Pk. Ter.)
Bk. Milan Av. LS8: Leeds 2B 32
(off Milan Rd.)
Bk. Milan Rd. LS8: Leeds 2B 32
(off Harehills Rd.)
Bk. Milan St. LS8: Leeds 2C 32
(off Harehills La.)
Bk. Mitford Rd. LS12: Leeds 6B 30
Bk. Model Rd. LS12: Leeds 6B 30
Bk. Model Ter. LS12: Leeds 6B 30
Bk. Model Vw. LS12: Leeds 6B 30
Bk. Monk Bri. Dr. LS6: Leeds 5D 20
(off Bentley Mt.)
Bk. Monk Bri. St. LS6: Leeds 5D 20
(off Monk Bri. St.)
Bk. Montpelier Ter. LS6: Leeds 1E 31
(off Cliff Rd.)
Bk. Moorfield Ter. LS12: Leeds 5G 29
Bk. Moorland Ter. LS2: Leeds 3E 31
Bk. Morritt Dr. LS15: Leeds 5H 33
Bk. Mount Pleasant LS10: Leeds 4G 51
Bk. Mount Vw. LS6: Leeds 1D 30
(off Regent Pk. Ter.)
Bk. Nansen St. LS13: Leeds 3A 28
(off Fairfield Av.)
Bk. Newport Gdns. LS6: Leeds 2B 30
(off Newport Rd.)
Bk. Newport Mt. LS6: Leeds 2B 30
(off Newport Rd.)

Bk. Newport Pl. LS6: Leeds 2B 30
(off Newport Rd.)
Bk. Newton Gro. LS7: Leeds 1H 31
Bk. New York St. LS2: Leeds 5G 5 (6H 31)
Bk. Nice Vw. LS8: Leeds 1B 32
(off Nice Vw.)
Bk. Norman Mt. LS5: Leeds 1G 29
(off Morris La.)
Bk. Norman Pl. LS8: Leeds 1C 22
(off Norton Rd.)
Bk. Norman Ter. LS8: Leeds 1C 22
(off Norton Rd.)
Bk. Northbrook St. LS7: Leeds 4H 21
(off Northbrook St.)
Bk. North Pk. Av. LS8: Leeds 3B 22
Bk. Norwood Gro. LS6: Leeds 2C 30
(off Norwood Mt.)
Bk. Norwood Pl. LS6: Leeds 2C 30
(off Norwood Mt.)
Bk. Norwood Rd. LS6: Leeds 2C 30
(off Norwood Vw.)
Bk. Norwood Ter. LS6: Leeds 2C 30
Bk. Nowell Cres. LS9: Leeds 4D 32
(off Harehills La.)
Bk. Nowell Mt. LS9: Leeds 4D 32
(off Harehills La.)
Bk. Nowell Pl. LS9: Leeds 4D 32
(off Harehills La.)
Bk. Nowell Ter. LS9: Leeds 4D 32
(off Harehills La.)
Bk. Nunington St. LS12: Leeds 5B 30
(off Armley Pk. Rd.)
Bk. Nunington Vw. LS12: Leeds 4A 30
(off Nunnington Vw.)
Bk. Nunroyd Rd. LS17: Leeds 2H 21
(off Nunroyd Ter.)
Bk. Oakfield Ter. LS6: Leeds 5C 20
(off Brookfield Rd.)
Bk. Oakley St. WF3: Thpe H 2A 58
Bk. Oakley Ter. LS11: Leeds 5G 41
(off Garnet Rd.)
Bk. Oak Rd. LS7: Leeds 6H 21
(off St Mary's Rd.)
Bk. Oakwood Av. LS8: Leeds 5D 22
(off Oakwood Av.)
Bk. Oakwood Dr. LS8: Leeds 5D 22
(off Oakwood Boundary Rd.)
Bk. Osmondthorpe La. LS9: Leeds 5E 33
(off Cross Osmondthorpe La.)
Bk. Outwood La. LS18: H'fth 4C 16
Bk. Overdale Ter. LS15: Leeds 5A 34
(off Cross St.)
Bk. Oxford Pl. LS1: Leeds 3C 4
Bk. Oxford St. WF3: E Ard 3A 58
Bk. Park Cres. LS8: Leeds 1D 22
Bk. Parkfield Pl. LS11: Leeds 4E 41
(off Parkfield Row)
Bk. Parkfield Rd. LS11: Leeds 4E 41
(off Parkfield Row)
Bk. Park Vw. LS11: Leeds 4E 41
(off Dawson Rd.)
Bk. Park Vw. Av. LS4: Leeds 2B 30
Bk. Parkville Rd. LS13: Leeds 2C 28
Bk. Parnaby Av. LS10: Leeds 6B 42
(off Parnaby Rd.)
Bk. Parnaby St. LS10: Leeds 6B 42
Bk. Parnaby Ter. LS10: Leeds 6B 42
(off Parnaby Rd.)
Bk. Pasture Gro. LS7: Leeds 4H 21
(off Hillside Rd.)
Bk. Pasture Rd. LS8: Leeds 1B 32
(off Ellers Rd.)
Bk. Pawson St. WF3: E Ard 3A 58
Bk. Pollard La. LS13: Leeds 6C 18
Bk. Poplar Av. LS15: Leeds 3D 34
(off Railway Rd.)
Bk. Potternewton La. LS7: Leeds 5G 21
Bk. Potters St. LS7: Leeds 5H 21
(off St Martin's Dr.)
Bk. Prospect Ter. LS9: Leeds 6B 32
Bk. Providence Av. LS6: Leeds 1E 31
(off Delph La.)
Bk. Quarry Mt. Ter. LS6: Leeds 1E 31
(off Providence Rd.)
Bk. Raglan Rd. LS2: Leeds 2E 31
(off Raglan Rd.)
Bk. Ravenscar Av. LS8: Leeds 5C 22
(off Ravenscar Wlk.)
Bk. Raynville Mt. LS13: Leeds 2E 29
(off Victoria Pk. Av.)
Bk. Regent Pk. Ter. LS6: Leeds 1D 30
(off Regent Pk. Av.)
Bk. Regent Ter. LS6: Leeds 3D 30
Bk. Reginald Mt. LS7: Leeds 1H 31
(off Hall La.)
Bk. Reginald Pl. LS7: Leeds 1H 31
(off Reginald Row)

Bk. Reginald St. LS7: Leeds 1H 31
(off Reginald St.)
Bk. Richmond Mt. LS6: Leeds 1C 30
(off Manor Av.)
Bk. Ridge Mt. Ter. LS6: Leeds 1E 31
(off Cliff Rd.)
Bk. Ridge Vw. LS7: Leeds 6E 21
Bk. Roberts St. LS26: Wood 3C 54
Bk. Rochester Ter. LS6: Leeds 1B 30
(off Broomfield Rd.)
Bk. Rokeby Gdns. LS6: Leeds 6A 20
(off Ash Rd.)
Bk. Roman Gro. LS8: Leeds 1C 22
Bk. Roman Pl. LS8: Leeds 1D 22
Bk. Roman St. LS8: Leeds 1D 22
Bk. Rose Av. LS18: H'fth 4B 18
(off Rose St.)
Bk. Rosebank Cres. LS3: Leeds 3D 30
Bk. Rosemont Wlk. LS13: Leeds 3C 28
Bk. Rossall Rd. LS8: Leeds 1C 32
(off Nice St.)
Bk. Rossington Rd. LS8: Leeds 1A 32
(off Rossington Gro.)
Bk. Roundhay Cres. LS8: Leeds 6B 22
(off Cross Roundhay Av.)
Bk. Roundhay Gro. LS8: Leeds 6B 22
(off Cross Roundhay Av., not continuous)
Bk. Roundhay Pl. LS8: Leeds 6B 22
(off Harehills La.)
Bk. Roundhay Vw. LS8: Leeds 6B 22
(off Cross Roundhay Av.)
Back Row LS11: Leeds 1F 41
Bk. Rowland Ter. LS11: Leeds 4G 41
(off Rowland Pl.)
Bk. Ruthven Vw. LS8: Leeds 2C 32
(off Strathmore Ter.)
Bk. St Alban Cres. LS9: Leeds 4E 33
(off Harehills La.)
Bk. St Elmo Gro. LS9: Leeds 5C 32
(off Vinery Av.)
Bk. St Ives Mt. LS12: Leeds 5G 29
Bk. St Luke's Cres. LS11: Leeds 3E 41
(off St Luke's Cres.)
Bk. St Mary's Rd. LS7: Leeds 6H 21
Bk. Salisbury Gro. LS12: Leeds 5A 30
Bk. Salisbury Ter. LS12: Leeds 5A 30
(off Armley Lodge Rd.)
Bk. Salisbury Vw. LS12: Leeds 5A 30
(off Armley Lodge Rd.)
Bk. Sandhurst Gro. LS8: Leeds 2C 32
(off Harehills La.)
Bk. Sandhurst Pl. LS8: Leeds 2C 32
(off Harehills La.)
Bk. Sandhurst Rd. LS8: Leeds 2C 32
(off Harehills La.)
Bk. Savile Pl. LS7: Leeds 2H 31
(off Savile Av.)
Bk. Savile Rd. LS7: Leeds 2H 31
(off Savile Av.)
Bk. School St. LS27: Morl 5H 49
(off South St.)
Bk. School Vw. LS6: Leeds 2C 30
(off Welton Rd.)
Bk. Seaforth Av. LS9: Leeds 3D 32
(off Foundry App.)
Bk. Seaforth Pl. LS9: Leeds 2C 32
(off Strathmore Ter.)
Bk. Seaforth Ter. LS9: Leeds 2C 32
(off Strathmore Ter.)
Bk. Sefton Av. LS11: Leeds 4E 41
(off Wickham St.)
Bk. Sefton Ter. LS11: Leeds 4E 41
(off Wickham St.)
Bk. Shaftesbury Av. LS8: Leeds 2C 22
Bk. Shepherd's Pl. LS8: Leeds 1B 32
(off Shepherd's Pl.)
Bk. Sholebroke Av. LS7: Leeds 6H 21
Bk. Sholebroke Pl. LS7: Leeds 1H 31
(off Hall La.)
Bk. Sholebroke Vw. LS7: Leeds 1H 31
(off Hall La.)
Bk. Sidlaw Ter. LS8: Leeds 1B 32
(off Markham Av.)
Bk. South End Gro. LS13: Leeds 3E 29
(off South End Av.)
Bk. Spencer Mt. LS7: Leeds 1A 32
(off Gathorne St.)
Bk. Springfield Mt. LS12: Leeds 5G 29
Bk. Spring Gro. Wlk. LS6: Leeds 3C 30
(off Harold St.)
Bk. Stanley St. LS9: Leeds 3B 32
(off Ashley Rd.)
Bk. Stanmore Pl. LS4: Leeds 2A 30
(off St Michael's La.)
Bk. Stanmore St. LS4: Leeds 2A 30
(off St Michael's La.)
Bk. Stonegate Rd. LS6: Leeds 4D 20

Backstone Gill La. LS17: Wike 1F 15
Bk. Storey Pl. LS14: Leeds 4G 33
Bk. Stratford Av. LS11: Leeds 4E 41
(off Wickham St.)
Bk. Stratford St. LS11: Leeds 4F 41
(off Rowland Pl.)
Bk. Stratford Ter. LS11: Leeds 4F 41
(off Bude Rd.)
Bk. Strathmore Dr. LS9: Leeds 2C 32
(off Seaforth Dr.)
Back Sunnydene LS14: Leeds 4H 33
Bk. Sutton App. LS14: Leeds 4G 33
Bk. Tamworth St. BD4: B'frd 1A 36
Bk. Tempest Rd. LS11: Leeds 4E 41
(off Sefton Ter.)
Bk. Temple Vw. LS11: Leeds 4E 41
Bk. Thornhill St. LS28: Cal 5D 16
Bk. Thornville Row LS6: Leeds 2C 30
(off Thornville St.)
Bk. Tower Gro. LS12: Leeds 5G 29
Bk. Trafford Av. LS9: Leeds 3D 32
(off Foundry App.)
Bk. Trentham Pl. LS11: Leeds 5F 41
(off Trentham St.)
Bk. Vicars Rd. LS8: Leeds 1B 32
(off Shepherd's La.)
Bk. Victoria Av. LS9: Leeds 5C 32
(off Dawlish Cres.)
Bk. Victoria Gro. LS9: Leeds 5D 32
(off Dawlish Cres.)
Bk. Walmsley Rd. LS6: Leeds 2C 30
(off Mayville Rd.)
Bk. Welburn Av. LS16: Leeds 4H 19
Bk. Welton Av. LS6: Leeds 2C 30
(off Welton Rd.)
Bk. Welton Gro. LS6: Leeds 2C 30
(off Welton Rd.)
Bk. Welton Mt. LS6: Leeds 2C 30
(off Welton Rd.)
Bk. Welton Pl. LS6: Leeds 2C 30
(off Welton Rd.)
Bk. Wesley Rd. LS12: Leeds 6A 30
Bk. Westbury St. LS10: Leeds 6B 42
Bk. Westfield Rd. LS3: Leeds 4D 30
(off Westfield Cres.)
Bk. Westlock Av. LS9: Leeds 4C 32
(off Burton Way)
Bk. Westmorland Mt. LS13: Leeds 1D 28
Bk. Westover Rd. LS13: Leeds 2C 28
Bk. Wetherby Gro. LS4: Leeds 3A 30
(off Argie Av.)
Bk. Wetherby Rd. LS8: Leeds 5D 22
(off Wetherby Rd.)
Bk. Wickham St. LS11: Leeds 4E 41
(off Wickham St.)
Bk. William Av. LS15: Leeds 5G 33
(off Selby Rd.)
Bk. Wilton Gro. LS6: Leeds 5C 20
(off Monk Bri. Rd.)
Bk. Winfield Gro. LS2: Leeds 3F 31
(off Devon Rd.)
Bk. Winston Gdns. LS6: Leeds 6A 20
(off Ash Rd.)
Bk. Woodbine Ter. LS6: Leeds 5C 20
Bk. Woodland Pk. Rd. LS6: Leeds 6C 20
(off Coniston Av.)
Bk. Woodstock St. LS2: Leeds 3F 31
(off Bk. Blenheim Ter.)
Bk. Wood St. WF3: E Ard 3H 57
Bk. York Pl. LS1: Leeds 5B 4 (6E 31)
(not continuous)
Bk. York St. LS2: Leeds 5G 5 (6H 31)
Bacon St. LS20: Guis .5H 7
Baden Ter. LS13: Leeds 5C 28
(off Pudsey Rd.)
Badgers Mt. LS15: Leeds 3F 35
Badminton Dr. LS10: Leeds 6H 51
Badminton Vw. LS10: Leeds 6H 51
BAGBY FIELDS 2F 31
BAGHILL 5B 56
Baghill Grn. WF3: W Ard 5B 56
Baghill Rd. WF3: W Ard 4B 56
BAGLEY 1G 27
Bagley La. LS13: Fars, Leeds 1G 27
LS28: Fars 1F 27
Baildon Chase LS14: Leeds 4C 24
Baildon Cl. LS14: Leeds 5C 24
Baildon Dr. LS14: Leeds 5C 24
Baildon Grn. LS14: Leeds 5C 24
Baildon Path LS14: Leeds 5C 24
Baildon Pl. LS14: Leeds 5C 24
Baildon Rd. LS14: Leeds 4C 24
Baildon Wlk. LS14: Leeds 5C 24
Bailes Rd. LS7: Leeds 6E 21
Bailey's Cl. LS14: Leeds 5A 24
Bailey's Hill LS14: Leeds 6A 24
Bailey's La. LS14: Leeds 6A 24

Bailey's Lawn—Bedford Vw.

Bailey's Lawn LS14: Leeds 6A **24**
Bailey Towers LS14: Leeds 6A **24**
Bainbrigge Rd. LS6: Leeds 1B **30**
Baines St. LS26: Rothw 4G **53**
Baker Cres. LS27: Morl 6G **49**
Baker La. WF3: S'ley 5F **59**
Baker Rd. LS27: Morl 6G **49**
Bakers Cotts. *LS28: Pud 6G* ***27***
(off Park Vw.)
Baker St. LS27: Morl 6G **49**
Balbec Av. LS6: Leeds 6C **20**
Balbec St. LS6: Leeds 6C **20**
Baldovan Mt. LS8: Leeds 1B **32**
Baldovan Pl. LS8: Leeds 1B **32**
Baldovan Ter. LS8: Leeds 1B **32**
Balkcliffe La. LS10: Leeds 3E **51**
Balmoral Chase LS10: Leeds 4B **42**
Balmoral Dr. LS26: Meth 6H **55**
Balmoral Ho. LS17: Leeds 4H **13**
Balmoral Ter. LS6: Leeds 5C **20**
Balmoral Way LS19: Yead 3F **9**
Balm Pl. LS11: Leeds 2E **41**
Balm Rd. LS10: Leeds 5A **42**
Balm Rd. Ind. Est. LS10: Leeds 4H **41**
Balm Wlk. LS11: Leeds 2D **40**
Bamburgh Cl. LS15: Leeds 2E **35**
Bamburgh Rd. LS15: Leeds 2E **35**
Bamford Ho. *BD4: B'frd 6A* ***36***
(off Tong St.)
Bangor Gro. LS12: Leeds 3G **39**
Bangor Pl. LS12: Leeds 3G **39**
Bangor St. LS12: Leeds 3G **39**
Bangor Ter. LS12: Leeds 3G **39**
Bangor Vw. LS12: Leeds 3G **39**
BANK 5H **5** (6A **32**)
Bank, The BD10: B'frd 5A **16**
Bank Av. LS18: H'fth 3B **18**
LS27: Morl 4G **49**
Banker St. LS4: Leeds 4B **30**
Bankfield Gdns. LS4: Leeds 3A **30**
Bankfield Gro. LS4: Leeds 2A **30**
Bankfield Rd. LS4: Leeds 3A **30**
Bankfield Ter. LS4: Leeds 3A **30**
LS28: Stan 4G ***27***
(off Richardshaw Rd.)
Bank Gdns. LS18: H'fth 3B **18**
Bankholme Ct. BD4: B'frd 5B **36**
BANKHOUSE 2F **37**
Bank Ho. *LS27: Morl 5G* ***49***
(off Queen St.)
Bankhouse LS28: Pud 2F **37**
BANKHOUSE BOTTOM 3F **37**
Bank Ho. Cl. LS27: Morl 4G **49**
Bankhouse Ct. LS28: Pud 2F **37**
Bankhouse La. LS28: Pud 2F **37**
Banksfield Av. LS19: Yead 1D **8**
Banksfield Cl. LS19: Yead 1D **8**
Banksfield Cres. LS19: Yead 1D **8**
Banksfield Gro. LS19: Yead 1D **8**
Banksfield Mt. LS19: Yead 1D **8**
Banksfield Ri. LS19: Yead 1D **8**
Banksfield Ter. LS19: Yead 2D **8**
Bank Side St. LS8: Leeds 2B **32**
(not continuous)
Bank Sq. LS27: Morl 4G **49**
Bank St. LS1: Leeds 5E **5** (6G **31**)
(Boar La.)
LS1: Leeds 4E **5**
(Commercial St.)
LS27: Morl 4G **49**
Bank Ter. LS27: Morl 4H **49**
LS28: Stan 3G **27**
Bank Vw. BD11: Birk 3C **46**
LS7: Leeds 4F **21**
Bankwood Way WF17: Birs 5B **48**
Banstead St. E. LS8: Leeds 2B **32**
Banstead St. W. LS8: Leeds 2B **32**
Banstead Ter. E. LS8: Leeds 2B **32**
Banstead Ter. W. LS8: Leeds 2B **32**
Bantam Cl. LS27: Morl 5B **50**
BANTAM GROVE 5B **50**
Bantam Gro. La. LS27: Morl 5B **50**
Bantam Gro. Vw. LS27: Morl 5B **50**
Baptist Way LS28: Stan 3A **28**
Barberry Av. BD3: B'frd 5A **26**
Barclay St. LS7: Leeds 1G **5**
Barcroft Gro. LS19: Yead 3C **8**
Barden Cl. LS12: Leeds 6G **29**
Barden Grn. LS12: Leeds 6G **29**
Barden Gro. LS12: Leeds 6G **29**
Barden Mt. LS12: Leeds 6G **29**
Barden Pl. LS12: Leeds 6G **29**
Barden Ter. LS12: Leeds 6G **29**
Bardon Hall Gdns. LS16: Leeds 3A **20**
Bardon Hall M. LS16: Leeds 3A **20**
Bardwell Ct. WF3: S'ley 6G **59**
Barfield Av. LS19: Yead 3C **8**
Barfield Cres. LS17: Leeds 4B **14**
Barfield Dr. LS19: Yead 3C **8**
Barfield Gro. LS17: Leeds 4C **14**
Barfield Mt. LS17: Leeds 4C **14**
Barham Ter. BD10: B'frd 1A **26**
Baring Av. BD3: B'frd 4A **26**
Barker Hill LS12: Gil 6B **38**
Barker Pl. LS13: Leeds 4D **28**
Barkers Well Fold LS12: N Far 4D **38**
Barkers Well Gth. LS12: N Far 4E **39**
Barkers Well Ga. LS12: N Far 4E **39**
Barkers Well Lawn LS12: N Far 4E **39**
Barkly Av. LS11: Leeds 6E **41**
Barkly Dr. LS11: Leeds 6E **41**
Barkly Gro. LS11: Leeds 5E **41**
Barkly Pde. LS11: Leeds 6E **41**
Barkly Pl. LS11: Leeds 6E **41**
Barkly Rd. LS11: Leeds 5D **40**
Barkly St. LS11: Leeds 6E **41**
Barkly Ter. LS11: Leeds 6E **41**
Bar La. LS18: H'fth 3G **17**
Barlby Way LS8: Leeds 5E **23**
Barleycorn Yd. LS12: Leeds 6H **29**
Barley Fld. Ct. LS15: Leeds 5A **34**
Barley M. WF3: Rob H 6D **52**
Barnard Cl. LS15: Leeds 2E **35**
Barnard Way LS15: Leeds 2E **35**
BARNBOW CARR 6H **25**
Barnbow La. LS15: Leeds 1H **35**
Barnbrough St. LS4: Leeds 3A **30**
Barn Cl. LS29: Men 1B **6**
Barncroft Cl. LS14: Leeds 4H **23**
Barncroft Ct. LS14: Leeds 5G **23**
Barncroft Dr. LS14: Leeds 5G **23**
Barncroft Gdns. LS14: Leeds 5H **23**
Barncroft Grange LS14: Leeds 5G **23**
Barncroft Hgts. LS14: Leeds 4G **23**
Barncroft Mt. LS14: Leeds 5G **23**
Barncroft Ri. LS14: Leeds 5H **23**
Barncroft Rd. LS14: Leeds 5H **23**
Barncroft Towers LS14: Leeds 5G **23**
Barnet Gro. LS27: Morl 6G **49**
Barnet Rd. LS12: Leeds 6B **30**
Barnstaple Way BD4: B'frd 5A **36**
Barnswick Vw. LS16: Leeds 5E **11**
Baron Cl. LS11: Leeds 3E **41**
Baronscourt LS15: Leeds 5D **34**
Baronsmead LS15: Leeds 5C **34**
Baronsway LS15: Leeds 5C **34**
Barrack Rd. LS7: Leeds 2H **31**
Barrack St. LS7: Leeds 3H **31**
Barraclough Bldgs. BD10: B'frd 4A **16**
Barran Ct. LS8: Leeds 2B **32**
Barras Gth. Ind. Est.
LS12: Leeds 1H **39**
Barras Gth. Pl. LS12: Leeds 1H **39**
Barras Gth. Rd. LS12: Leeds 1H **39**
Barras Pl. LS12: Leeds 1H **39**
Barras St. LS12: Leeds 1H **39**
Barras Ter. LS12: Leeds 1H **39**
BARROWBY 5H **35**
Barrowby Av. LS15: Leeds 6E **35**
Barrowby Cl. LS29: Men 1D **6**
Barrowby Cres. LS15: Leeds 5E **35**
Barrowby Dr. LS15: Leeds 6F **35**
Barrowby La. LS15: Leeds 5E **35**
LS25: Gar, Leeds 5G **35**
Barrowby Rd. LS15: Leeds 6F **35**
Barthorpe Av. LS17: Leeds 3F **21**
Barthorpe Cl. BD4: B'frd 5B **36**
Barthorpe Cres. LS17: Leeds 3G **21**
Barton Ct. LS15: Leeds 6C **34**
Barton Gro. LS11: Leeds 3E **41**
Barton Hill LS11: Leeds 3E **41**
Barton Mt. LS11: Leeds 3E **41**
Barton Pl. LS11: Leeds 3E **41**
Barton Rd. LS11: Leeds 3E **41**
Barton Ter. LS11: Leeds 3E **41**
Barton Vw. LS11: Leeds 3E **41**
Barwick Ct. LS27: Morl 4H **49**
Barwick Rd. LS15: Leeds 2B **34**
Basilica LS1: Leeds 4E **5**
Batcliffe Dr. LS6: Leeds 5A **20**
Batcliffe Mt. LS6: Leeds 6A **20**
Bateson St. BD10: B'frd 4A **16**
Bath Cl. LS13: Leeds 3C **28**
Bath Gro. LS13: Leeds 3C **28**
Bath La. LS13: Leeds 4C **28**
Bath Rd. LS11: Leeds 1E **41**
LS13: Leeds 4C **28**
Batley Rd. WF3: W Ard 5B **56**
Batter La. LS19: Raw 5E **9**
Battlefield Vw. BD11: Birk 2D **46**
BAWN 2F **39**
Bawn App. LS12: Leeds 2E **39**
Bawn Av. LS12: Leeds 1E **39**
Bawn Chase LS12: Leeds 1E **39**
Bawn Dr. LS12: Leeds 1E **39**
Bawn Gdns. LS12: Leeds 1E **39**
Bawn La. LS12: Leeds 1E **39**
Bawn Path *LS12: Leeds 1F* ***39***
(off Bawn Av.)
Bawn Va. *LS12: Leeds 1E* ***39***
(off Bawn Gdns.)
Bawn Wlk. *LS12: Leeds 1F* ***39***
(off Bawn Gdns.)
Baxendale Dr. LS13: Leeds 5B **18**
Bay Horse La. LS14: S'cft 2H **15**
LS17: Leeds, S'cft 2H **15**
Bay Horse Yd. LS1: Leeds 4F **5**
LS28: Fars 2F **27**
Bayswater Cres. LS8: Leeds 2B **32**
Bayswater Gro. LS8: Leeds 2B **32**
Bayswater Mt. LS8: Leeds 2B **32**
Bayswater Pl. LS8: Leeds 2B **32**
Bayswater Rd. LS8: Leeds 2A **32**
Bayswater Row LS8: Leeds 2B **32**
Bayswater Ter. LS8: Leeds 2B **32**
Bayswater Vw. LS8: Leeds 3B **32**
Bayton La. LS18: H'fth 3F **9**
LS19: H'fth, Yead 3F **9**
Beacon Av. LS27: Morl 6H **49**
Beacon Gro. LS27: Morl 6H **49**
Beacon Vw. *LS27: Morl 1A* ***56***
(off Tingley Comn.)
Beamsley Cl. LS29: Men 2C **6**
Beamsley Ct. LS29: Men 3C **6**
Beamsley Cft. LS29: Men 3C **6**
Beamsley Gro. LS6: Leeds 3C **30**
Beamsley Mt. LS6: Leeds 3C **30**
Beamsley Pl. LS6: Leeds 3C **30**
Beamsley Ter. LS6: Leeds 3C **30**
Beamsley Wlk. LS29: Men 2C **6**
Bearing Av. LS11: Leeds 5G **41**
Bear Pit Gdns. *LS6: Leeds 2B* ***30***
(off Chapel La.)
Beaumont Av. LS8: Leeds 1C **22**
Beaumont Cl. WF3: S'ley 6H **59**
Beaumont Sq. LS28: Pud 1F **37**
Beaumont St. WF3: S'ley 6H **59**
Beck Bottom LS28: Cal 5A **16**
LS28: Fars 1G **27**
Beckbury Cl. LS28: Fars 3F **27**
Beckbury St. LS28: Fars 3F **27**
Becket La. WF3: Loft 1D **58**
Beckett Ct. LS15: Leeds 1D **44**
BECKETT PARK 5B **20**
Becketts, The *LS6: Leeds 5D* ***20***
(off Monk Bri. Rd.)
Beckett's Pk. Cres. LS6: Leeds 6A **20**
Beckett's Pk. Dr. LS6: Leeds 6A **20**
Beckett's Pk. Rd. LS6: Leeds 6B **20**
Beckett St. LS9: Leeds 4A **32**
Beckhill App. LS7: Leeds 5E **21**
Beckhill Av. LS7: Leeds 5E **21**
Beckhill Chase LS7: Leeds 5E **21**
Beckhill Cl. LS7: Leeds 5E **21**
Beckhill Dr. LS7: Leeds 4E **21**
Beckhill Fold LS7: Leeds 4E **21**
Beckhill Gdns. LS7: Leeds 5E **21**
Beckhill Gth. LS7: Leeds 5E **21**
Beckhill Ga. LS7: Leeds 5E **21**
Beckhill Grn. LS7: Leeds 5E **21**
Beckhill Gro. LS7: Leeds 5E **21**
Beckhill Lawn LS7: Leeds 5E **21**
Beckhill Pl. LS7: Leeds 4E **21**
Beckhill Row LS7: Leeds 4E **21**
Beckhill Va. LS7: Leeds 4E **21**
(not continuous)
Beckhill Vw. LS7: Leeds 5E **21**
Beckhill Wlk. LS7: Leeds 4E **21**
Beck Rd. LS8: Leeds 1B **32**
Beckside Gdns. LS16: Leeds 4B **20**
Beckside Vw. LS27: Morl 5A **50**
Beck Way WF3: E Ard 3B **58**
Beckwith Dr. BD10: B'frd 6A **16**
Bedale WF3: W Ard 3B **56**
Bedale Ct. LS27: Morl 5C **50**
Bedford Chambers LS1: Leeds 4D **4**
Bedford Cl. LS16: Leeds 6E **11**
Bedford Ct. LS8: Leeds 5E **23**
Bedford Dr. LS16: Leeds 6E **11**
Bedford Fld. LS6: Leeds 1E **31**
Bedford Gdns. LS16: Leeds 6E **11**
Bedford Gth. LS16: Leeds 6E **11**
Bedford Grn. LS16: Leeds 6E **11**
Bedford Gro. LS16: Leeds 1E **19**
Bedford Mt. LS16: Leeds 1E **19**
(not continuous)
Bedford Pl. LS16: Leeds 6E **11**
LS20: Guis 5G **7**
Bedford Row LS10: Leeds 3H **41**
Bedford St. LS1: Leeds 4D **4** (5F **31**)
Bedford Vw. LS16: Leeds 6E **11**

66 A-Z Leeds

Beech Av. LS12: Leeds 5A 30
  LS18: H'fth 4C 18
  WF3: S'ley 6H 59
Beech Cres. LS9: Leeds 2F 33
Beech Cft. WF3: Loft 2G 59
Beechcroft Cl. LS11: Leeds 6B 40
Beechcroft Mead LS17: Leeds 5C 14
Beechcroft Vw. LS11: Leeds 6B 40
Beech Dr. LS12: Leeds 2C 56
  LS18: H'fth 4B 18
Beeches, The BD11: Birk 4C 46
  LS20: Guis 3G 7
  LS28: Pud 5D 26
Beechfield LS12: N Far 4D 38
Beech Gro. LS6: Leeds 4E 9
  LS26: Rothw 3H 53
  LS27: Morl 6F 49
  LS29: Men 2C 6
Beech Gro. Gdns. LS26: Oul 4C 54
Beech Gro. Ter. LS2: Leeds 3E 31
Beech Ho. LS16: Leeds 3A 20
Beech La. LS9: Leeds 2F 33
Beech Lees LS28: Fars 1E 27
Beech Mt. LS9: Leeds 2F 33
Beechroyd LS28: Pud 1G 37
Beech St. WF3: Ting 3D 58
Beech Wlk. BD11: Birk 5D 46
  LS9: Leeds 2F 33
  LS16: Leeds 1B 20
BEECHWOOD
  LS14 . . . . .5H 23
  LS18 . . . . .6B 10
Beechwood LS26: Wood 2C 54
Beechwood Av. BD11: Drig 2F 47
  LS4: Leeds 2B 30
Beechwood Cen. *LS26: Wood* 2C 54
                    (off Beechwood)
Beechwood Cl. LS17: Shad 5G 15
  LS18: H'fth 6A 10
Beechwood Ct. *LS4: Leeds* 2B 30
              (off Beechwood Gro.)
  LS14: Leeds 5G 23
  LS16: Leeds 4H 11
Beechwood Cres. LS4: Leeds 2B 30
Beechwood Gro. BD11: Drig 2F 47
  LS4: Leeds 2B 30
Beechwood Mt. LS4: Leeds 2B 30
Beechwood Pl. LS4: Leeds 2B 30
Beechwood Rd. LS4: Leeds 2B 30
Beechwood Row LS4: Leeds 2B 30
  LS28: Stan 4E 27
Beechwood Ter. LS4: Leeds 2B 30
Beechwood Vw. LS4: Leeds 2B 30
Beechwood Wlk. LS4: Leeds 2B 30
Beecroft Cl. LS13: Leeds 2A 28
Beecroft Cres. LS13: Leeds 2A 28
Beecroft Gdns. LS13: Leeds 2A 28
Beecroft Mt. LS13: Leeds 2A 28
Beecroft St. LS5: Leeds 2G 29
BEESTON 6D 40
BEESTON HILL 3E 41
Beeston Pk. Cft. LS11: Leeds 5C 40
Beeston Pk. Gth. LS11: Leeds 5C 40
Beeston Pk. Gro. LS11: Leeds 5C 40
BEESTON PARK SIDE 1E 51
Beeston Pk. Ter. LS11: Leeds 5C 40
Beeston Rd. LS11: Leeds 5D 40
BEESTON ROYDS .5H 39
Beeston Royds Ind. Est. LS12: Leeds 4A 40
Beevers Ct. LS16: Leeds 1G 19
BEGGARINGTON HILL 5B 56
Belford Cl. BD4: B'frd 4A 36
Belford Ct. LS6: Leeds 2C 20
Belfry, The LS19: Yead 3E 9
Belfry Ct. WF1: Out .6E 59
Belfry Rd. LS9: Leeds 2C 42
Belgrave M. LS19: Raw 5C 8
Belgrave St. LS2: Leeds 3E 5 (5G 31)
Belgravia Gdns. LS8: Leeds 4E 23
Belinda St. LS10: Leeds 3A 42
Bellbrooke Av. LS9: Leeds 3D 32
Bellbrooke Gro. LS9: Leeds 3D 32
Bellbrooke Pl. LS9: Leeds 3D 32
Bellbrooke St. LS9: Leeds 3C 32
BELLE ISLE 1A 52
Belle Isle Cir. LS10: Leeds 1A 52
Belle Isle Cl. LS10: Leeds 1A 52
Belle Isle Pde. LS10: Leeds 6A 42
Belle Isle Rd. LS10: Leeds 5A 42
Belle Vue Av. LS8: Leeds 5F 23
  LS15: Scho 4F 25
Belle Vue Ct. *LS3: Leeds* 4D 30
                (off Consort Ter.)
Belle Vue Dr. LS28: Fars 2E 27
Belle Vue Est. LS15: Scho 5F 25

Belle Vue Rd. LS3: Leeds 3A 4 (4D 30)
  LS15: Scho 5F 25
Belle Vue Ter. LS20: Guis 5G 7
  LS27: Gil 3D 48
Bell Gro. LS13: Leeds 2C 28
Bell La. LS13: Leeds 2C 28
Bellmount Cl. LS13: Leeds 2D 28
Bellmount Gdns. LS13: Leeds 1C 28
Bellmount Grn. LS13: Leeds 2D 28
Bellmount Pl. LS13: Leeds 1C 28
Bellmount Vw. LS13: Leeds 2D 28
Bell Rd. LS13: Leeds 2C 28
Bell St. LS9: Leeds 3H 5 (5H 31)
Belmont Gro. LS2: Leeds 2B 4 (4E 31)
  LS19: Raw 4E 9
Belmont Ter. WF3: Thpe H 1B 58
Belvedere Av. LS11: Leeds 5F 41
  LS17: Leeds 5H 13
Belvedere Ct. *LS7: Leeds* 6A 22
            (off Harehills La.)
  LS17: Leeds 5A 14
  WF1: Out 6E 59
Belvedere Gdns. LS17: Leeds 5A 14
Belvedere Gro. LS17: Leeds 5H 13
Belvedere Mt. LS11: Leeds 5F 41
Belvedere Rd. LS17: Leeds 5H 13
Belvedere Ter. LS11: Leeds 5F 41
Belvedere Vw. LS17: Leeds 5A 14
Benbow Av. BD10: B'frd 6A 16
Bennet Ct. LS15: Leeds 5D 34
Bennett Rd. LS6: Leeds 6B 20
Bennetts Yd. LS26: Rothw 5G 53
Benson Gdns. LS12: Leeds 5H 39
Benson St. LS7: Leeds 1G 5 (3H 31)
Bentcliffe Av. LS17: Leeds 1H 21
Bentcliffe Cl. LS17: Leeds 2A 22
Bentcliffe Ct. LS17: Leeds 2A 22
Bentcliffe Dr. LS17: Leeds 1A 22
Bentcliffe Gdns. LS17: Leeds 2A 22
Bentcliffe Gro. LS17: Leeds 2A 22
Bentcliffe La. LS17: Leeds 2H 21
Bentcliffe Mt. LS17: Leeds 2A 22
Bentley Ct. LS7: Leeds 5D 20
Bentley Gdns. LS7: Leeds 5D 20
Bentley Gro. LS6: Leeds 5D 20
Bentley La. LS6: Leeds 5D 20
  LS7: Leeds 5D 20
Bentley Mt. LS6: Leeds 5D 20
Bentley Pde. LS6: Leeds 5D 20
Bentley Sq. LS26: Oul 4C 54
Benton Pk. Av. LS19: Raw 4E 9
Benton Pk. Cres. LS19: Raw 4E 9
Benton Pk. Dr. LS19: Raw 4E 9
Benton Pk. Rd. LS19: Raw 4E 9
Benyon Pk. Way LS12: Leeds 3B 40
Beringa LS12: Leeds 5A 4 (6E 31)
Berkeley Av. LS8: Leeds 2C 32
Berkeley Ct. LS2: Leeds 1A 4 (4D 30)
  LS8: Leeds 2C 32
             (off Chatsworth Rd.)
Berkeley Cres. LS8: Leeds 2C 32
Berkeley Gro. LS8: Leeds 2C 32
Berkeley Ho. *BD4: B'frd* 4A 36
             (off Stirling Cres.)
Berkeley Mt. LS8: Leeds 2C 32
Berkeley Rd. LS8: Leeds 2C 32
Berkeley St. LS8: Leeds 2C 32
Berkeley Ter. LS8: Leeds 2C 32
Berkeley Vw. LS8: Leeds 2C 32
Berking Av. LS9: Leeds 5B 32
Berking Row LS9: Leeds 5B 32
Bernard St. LS26: Wood 3D 54
Bertha St. LS28: Fars 3F 27
Bertrand St. LS11: Leeds 2E 41
Bessbrook St. LS10: Leeds 4H 41
Beulah Gro. LS6: Leeds 2F 31
Beulah Mt. LS6: Leeds 2F 31
Beulah St. LS6: Leeds 2F 31
Beulah Ter. *LS6: Leeds* 1F 31
              (off Beulah St.)
  LS15: Leeds 3C 34
             (off Austhorpe Rd.)
Beulah Vw. LS6: Leeds 2F 31
Beverley Av. LS11: Leeds 4F 41
Beverley Ct. LS17: Leeds 1H 21
  LS28: Fars 3F 27
Beverley Mt. LS11: Leeds 4F 41
Beverley St. BD4: B'frd 2A 36
Beverley Ter. LS11: Leeds 4F 41
Bevin Cl. WF1: Out 6E 59
Bevin Cres. WF1: Out 6E 59
Bewerley Cft. LS11: Leeds 3F 41
Bewick Gro. LS10: Leeds 2B 52
Bexley Av. LS8: Leeds 3B 32
Bexley Gro. LS8: Leeds 3B 32

Bexley Mt. LS8: Leeds 3B 32
Bexley Pl. LS8: Leeds 3B 32
Bexley Rd. LS8: Leeds 3B 32
Bexley Ter. LS8: Leeds 3B 32
Bexley Vw. LS8: Leeds 3B 32
Beza Ct. LS10: Leeds 5H 41
Beza Rd. LS10: Leeds 4H 41
Beza St. LS10: Leeds 4H 41
Biddenden Rd. LS15: Leeds 3F 35
Bidder Dr. WF3: E Ard 2G 57
Bideford Av. LS8: Leeds 6B 14
Bideford Mt. BD4: B'frd 4A 36
Billey La. LS12: Leeds 2E 39
             (not continuous)
Billingbauk Ct. LS13: Leeds 4D 28
Billingbauk Dr. LS13: Leeds 4D 28
Billing Ct. LS19: Raw .6F 9
Billing Dr. LS19: Raw .6G 9
Billington Cl. LS13: Leeds 5B 18
Billing Vw. LS19: Raw 6F 9
Billingwood Dr. LS19: Raw 6F 9
Bingham Pl. WF3: Loft 6C 58
Bingley Rd. LS20: Hawk 2A 6
  LS29: Men 2A 6
Bingley St. LS3: Leeds 4A 4 (5D 30)
Birch Av. LS15: Leeds 5A 34
Birch Ct. BD11: Birk .3D 46
Birch Cres. LS15: Leeds 5A 34
Birches, The LS20: Guis 3G 7
Birchfield Av. LS27: Gil 3C 48
Birchfields Av. LS14: Leeds 3C 24
Birchfields Cl. LS14: Leeds 4C 24
Birchfields Ct. LS14: Leeds 3C 24
Birchfields Cres. LS14: Leeds 3C 24
Birchfields Gth. LS14: Leeds 4C 24
Birchfields Ri. LS14: Leeds 4C 24
Birch Hill Ri. LS18: H'fth 3E 19
Birch Ho. LS17: Leeds 4H 21
Birch M. LS16: Leeds 1B 20
Birchroyd LS26: Rothw 5H 53
Birchtree Way LS16: Leeds 1E 19
Birchwood Av. LS17: Leeds 6C 14
Birchwood Hill LS17: Leeds 5C 14
Birchwood Mt. LS17: Leeds 5C 14
Birfed Cres. LS4: Leeds 2H 29
Birkdale Cl. LS17: Leeds 5F 13
Birkdale Dr. LS17: Leeds 5F 13
Birkdale Grn. LS17: Leeds 5F 13
Birkdale Gro. LS17: Leeds 5F 13
Birkdale Pl. LS17: Leeds 5E 13
Birkdale Ri. LS17: Leeds 5E 13
Birkdale Wlk. LS17: Leeds 5E 13
Birkdale Way LS17: Leeds 5F 13
BIRKENSHAW 4C 46
BIRKENSHAW BOTTOMS 5E 47
Birkenshaw La. BD11: Birk 4D 46
Birkhill Cres. BD11: Birk 4D 46
Birk La. LS27: Morl 5E 49
BIRKS 6G 49
Birksland Moor BD11: Birk 6D 46
Birkwith Cl. LS14: Leeds 3B 24
Birstall Cl. BD11: Drig 4G 47
Birstall Retail Pk. WF17: Birs 5A 48
Bishopsgate St. LS1: Leeds 5D 4 (6F 31)
Bishops Way LS14: Leeds 6G 23
Bishop Way WF3: Ting 3D 56
Bismarck Ct. LS11: Leeds 3F 41
Bismarck Dr. LS11: Leeds 3F 41
Bismarck St. LS11: Leeds 3F 41
Bittern Ri. LS27: Morl 6A 50
Black Bull St. LS10: Leeds 6G 5 (1H 41)
Blackburn Ct. LS26: Rothw 4H 53
Blackett St. LS28: Cal 4D 16
Blackgate M. WF3: Ting 2C 56
BLACK GATES 2D 56
Blackgates Cft. WF3: Ting 3D 56
Blackgates Cres. WF3: Ting 3D 56
Blackgates Dr. WF3: Ting 3D 56
Blackgates Fold WF3: Ting 3D 56
Blackgates Ri. WF3: Ting 3D 56
Blackman La. LS2: Leeds 1D 4 (3F 31)
  LS7: Leeds 3F 31
BLACK MOOR 5E 13
BLACKMOOR 2H 15
Blackmoor Ct. LS17: Leeds 4D 12
Blackmoor La. LS17: Bard, S'cft 1H 15
Black Moor Rd. LS17: Leeds 6D 12
Blackpool Gro. LS12: Leeds 3G 39
Blackpool Pl. LS12: Leeds 3G 39
Blackpool Ter. LS12: Leeds 3G 39
Blackpool Vw. LS12: Leeds 3G 39
Black Shepherd's La. *LS7: Leeds* 1A 32
             (off Shepherd's Gro.)
Blacksmith M. WF3: Rob H 6D 52
Blackthorn Ct. LS10: Leeds 1H 51

Blackwood Av. LS16: Leeds 6D 10
Blackwood Gdns. LS16: Leeds 6D 10
Blackwood Gro. LS16: Leeds 6D 10
Blackwood Mt. LS16: Leeds 6D 10
Blackwood Ri. LS16: Leeds 6D 10
Blairsville Gdns. LS13: Leeds 1B 28
Blairsville Gro. LS13: Leeds 1C 28
Blake Cres. LS20: Guis 5H 7
Blake Gro. LS7: Leeds 5H 21
Blakeney Gro. LS10: Leeds 6H 41
Blakeney Rd. LS10: Leeds 6H 41
Blandford Gdns. LS2: Leeds 3F 31
Blandford Gro. *LS2: Leeds* 3F 31
(off Bk. Blenheim Ter.)
Blayds Gth. LS26: Wood 2A 54
Blayd's M. LS1: Leeds 6E 5 (6G 31)
Blayds St. LS9: Leeds 6H 32
Blayd's Yd. LS1: Leeds 6E 5 (6G 31)
Bleach Mill La. LS29: Men 1A 6
Blencarn Cl. LS14: Leeds 1H 33
Blencarn Gth. LS14: Leeds 1H 33
Blencarn Lawn LS14: Leeds 1H 33
Blencarn Path LS14: Leeds 1H 33
Blencarn Rd. LS14: Leeds 1H 33
Blencarn Vw. LS14: Leeds 1H 33
Blencarn Wlk. LS14: Leeds 1H 33
Blenheim Av. LS2: Leeds 3F 31
Blenheim Ct. *LS2: Leeds* 3F 31
(off Blackman La.)
Blenheim Cres. *LS2: Leeds* 3F 31
(off Blenheim Av.)
Blenheim Gro. LS2: Leeds 3F 31
Blenheim Sq. LS2: Leeds 3F 31
Blenheim Ter. LS2: Leeds 1D 4
  LS27: Morl 3G 49
Blenheim Vw. LS2: Leeds 3F 31
Blenheim Wlk. LS2: Leeds 3F 31
Blenkinsop Dr. LS10: Leeds 5A 52
Blenkinsop Way LS10: Leeds 5A 52
Blind La. BD11: Drig 2H 47
  LS17: Shad 5G 15
  WF3: E Ard 6E 57
Blucher St. BD4: B'frd 2A 36
Bluebell Ct. LS14: Leeds 3A 24
Bluebell Rd. WF3: E Ard 3A 58
Blue Hill Cres. LS12: Leeds 1G 39
Blue Hill Grange LS12: Leeds 2G 39
Blue Hill Gro. LS12: Leeds 1G 39
Blue Hill La. LS12: Leeds 1G 39
Blundell St. LS1: Leeds 2C 4 (4F 31)
Boar La. LS1: Leeds 5E 5 (6G 31)
Bodley Ter. LS4: Leeds 4B 30
Bodmin App. LS10: Leeds 4E 51
Bodmin Cres. LS10: Leeds 4E 51
Bodmin Cft. LS10: Leeds 4F 51
Bodmin Gdns. LS10: Leeds 5E 51
Bodmin Gth. LS10: Leeds 5E 51
Bodmin Pl. LS10: Leeds 5F 51
(not continuous)
Bodmin Rd. LS10: Leeds 3D 50
Bodmin Sq. LS10: Leeds 5E 51
Bodmin St. LS10: Leeds 5E 51
Bodmin Ter. LS10: Leeds 5E 51
Body Balance 3A 28
Bodylines Gym 4A 32
(in Mabgate Mills Ind. & Commercial Cen.)
Body Mania Fitness 4H 53
(off Marsh St.)
Bodytech 4H 51
(within Middleton District Cen.)
Boggart Hill LS14: Leeds 5G 23
Boggart Hill Cres. LS14: Leeds 5G 23
Boggart Hill Dr. LS14: Leeds 5G 23
Boggart Hill Gdns. LS14: Leeds 5G 23
Boggart Hill Rd. LS14: Leeds 5G 23
Bog La. LS15: Leeds, Scho 6G 25
Boldmere Rd. LS15: Leeds 6G 33
Bolton Grange LS19: Yead 3E 9
Bolton Rd. LS19: Yead 3E 9
Bonaire LS12: Leeds 5A 4 (6D 30)
Bond Ct. LS1: Leeds 4D 4
Bond St. LS1: Leeds 4D 4 (5F 31)
Bonham Ct. *LS27: Morl* 5G 49
(off Queen St.)
Boocock St. *LS28: Stan* 4G 27
(off Varley St.)
Bookbinders, The *LS2: Leeds* 5G 5
(off Bk. York St.)
Boothroyd Dr. LS6: Leeds 6D 20
Booth's Yd. LS28: Pud 5G 27
Borrough Av. LS8: Leeds 3A 22
Borrough Vw. LS8: Leeds 3A 22
Borrowdale Cl. LS12: Leeds 3F 29
Borrowdale Cres. LS12: Leeds 3F 29
Borrowdale Cft. LS19: Yead 2D 8
Borrowdale Ter. LS14: Leeds 2H 33
Boston Av. LS5: Leeds 2F 29

Boston Towers *LS9: Leeds* 4A 32
(off Lindsey Gdns.)
Bottoms La. BD11: Birk 5D 46
Boulevard, The LS10: Leeds 1H 41
  LS12: Leeds 4B 40
  LS28: Fars 3F 27
Boulevard Ri. LS10: Leeds 5A 52
Boundary Cl. LS15: Leeds 6E 35
Boundary Farm Rd. LS17: Leeds 6E 13
Boundary Pl. LS7: Leeds 3A 32
Boundary St. LS7: Leeds 3A 32
Bourse, The LS1: Leeds 5E 5
Bowater Ct. BD4: B'frd 5B 36
Bowcliffe Rd. LS10: Leeds 3B 42
Bower Rd. LS15: Leeds 2E 35
Bowfell Cl. LS14: Leeds 1A 34
Bowland Cl. LS15: Leeds 6G 33
Bowling Grn. Ter. LS11: Leeds 2F 41
Bowling Grn. Vw. BD11: Drig 3G 47
Bowman La. LS10: Leeds 6G 5 (6H 31)
Bowness Av. BD10: B'frd 1A 26
Bowood Av. LS7: Leeds 4E 21
Bowood Cres. LS7: Leeds 4E 21
Bowood Gro. LS7: Leeds 4E 21
Bow St. LS9: Leeds .6A 32
Boyd Av. BD3: B'frd .4A 26
Bracken Ct. LS12: Leeds 2C 40
  LS17: Leeds 2G 21
Bracken Edge LS8: Leeds 6B 22
Bracken Grn. WF3: E Ard 3A 58
Bracken Hill LS17: Leeds 2G 21
Brackenhurst Dr. LS17: Leeds 1G 21
Brackenhurst Pl. LS17: Leeds 1G 21
Bracken Pk. LS14: S'cft 1H 15
Brackenwood Cl. LS8: Leeds 4A 22
Brackenwood Ct. WF1: Out 6F 59
Brackenwood Dr. LS8: Leeds 3A 22
Brackenwood Grn. LS8: Leeds 3A 22
Brackenwood Rd. WF3: Rob H 6C 52
Brackenwood Wlk. WF1: Out 6F 59
Bradburn Rd. WF3: Rob H 6C 52
Bradford & Wakefield Rd.
  BD4: B'frd 2E 47
Bradford La. BD3: B'frd 6A 26
Bradford Rd. BD3: B'frd 4B 26
  BD4: E Bier 1B 46
  BD11: Birk 5C 46
  BD11: Drig 4B 48
(Buttercup Way)
  BD11: Drig 2F 47
(Woodview)
  BD19: Gom 5C 46
  LS20: Guis 1D 6
  LS27: Gil 4B 48
  LS28: Pud, Stan .4B 26
  LS29: Men 1D 6
  WF2: Carr G, Wren 6A 58
(not continuous)
  WF3: E Ard, Ting .2B 56
BRADLEY HILL 3A 28
Bradley Hill Vw. *LS28: Stan* 3A 28
(off Swinnow La.)
Bradley La. LS28: Pud 6D 26
Bradley Ter. LS17: Leeds 5C 14
Bradstock Gdns. LS27: Morl 3G 49
Braithwaite Row LS10: Leeds 5A 42
Braithwaite St. LS11: Leeds 1D 40
Bramble Ct. WF1: Out 6C 58
Bramble M. LS17: Leeds 4E 15
Bramble Sq. WF3: E Ard 3B 58
Brambling M. LS27: Morl 5A 50
Bramham Pk. Ct. LS14: Leeds 6H 51
Bramleigh Dr. LS27: Morl 3G 49
Bramleigh Gro. LS27: Morl 3G 49
BRAMLEY 2D 28
Bramley Baths (Swimming Pool) 2B 28
Bramley Cen. LS13: Leeds 2D 28
Bramley Gdns. LS14: Leeds 2C 24
Bramley Station (Rail) 4B 28
Bramley's Yd. LS1: Leeds 4F 5
Bramston Av. LS13: Leeds 2A 28
Bramston Cl. LS13: Leeds 2A 28
Bramston Gdns. LS13: Leeds 2A 28
Bramston Recreation Cen. 1H 27
Brancepeth Pl. LS12: Leeds 6C 30
Branch End LS27: Gil 2D 48
Branch Cl. LS12: Leeds 3G 39
Branch Pl. LS12: Leeds 3G 39
Branch Rd. LS12: Leeds 3G 39
(Branch Pl.)
  LS12: Leeds 3G 39
(Stocks Hill)
Brander App. LS9: Leeds 4F 33
Brander Cl. LS9: Leeds 4F 33
Brander Dr. LS9: Leeds 4E 33
Brander Gro. LS9: Leeds 4E 33

Brander Rd. LS9: Leeds 3F 33
Brander St. LS9: Leeds 3F 33
Brandling Ct. LS10: Leeds 4G 51
BRANDON 4G 15
Brandon Cl. LS17: Leeds 2H 23
Brandon Ct. LS17: Leeds 4E 15
Brandon Cres. LS17: Leeds 2G 15
Brandon La. LS17: Leeds 2H 15
  LS17: Wike 1F 15
Brandon Rd. LS3: Leeds 3A 4 (5E 31)
Brandon St. LS12: Leeds 6D 30
Brandon Ter. LS17: Leeds 4D 14
Brandon Vw. LS17: Shad 4F 15
Brandon Way LS7: Leeds 6H 21
Brandon Way Cres. LS7: Leeds 6A 22
Branksome Pl. LS6: Leeds 3C 30
Branksome St. *LS6: Leeds* 3C 30
(off Queen's Rd.)
Branksome Ter. *LS6: Leeds* 3C 30
(off Queen's Rd.)
Bransby Cl. LS28: Fars 3G 27
Bransby Ct. LS28: Fars 3G 27
Bransby Ri. LS28: Fars 2G 27
Bransdale Av. LS20: Guis 5G 7
Bransdale Cl. LS20: Guis 5G 7
Bransdale Gdns. LS20: Guis 5G 7
Bransdale Gth. LS20: Guis 5G 7
Brantford St. LS7: Leeds 5H 21
Branwell Av. WF17: Birs 6G 47
Branwell Wlk. WF17: Birs 6H 47
Brathay Gdns. LS14: Leeds 2A 34
Braunstone Ct. LS29: Men 1B 6
Brayshaw Rd. WF3: E Ard 5G 57
Brayton App. LS14: Leeds 6C 24
Brayton Cl. LS14: Leeds 6C 24
Brayton Gth. LS14: Leeds 6D 24
Brayton Grange LS14: Leeds 1H 37
Brayton Grn. LS14: Leeds 6D 24
(not continuous)
Brayton Gro. LS14: Leeds 6C 24
Brayton Pl. LS14: Leeds 6C 24
Brayton Sq. LS14: Leeds 6D 24
Brayton Ter. LS14: Leeds 6C 24
Brayton Wlk. LS14: Leeds 6C 24
Breary Av. LS18: H'fth 2D 18
(not continuous)
Breary Ter. LS18: H'fth 2D 18
Breary Wlk. LS18: H'fth 2D 18
Brecks La. LS26: Swil 3H 45
Brecon App. LS9: Leeds 4F 33
Brecon Cl. LS9: Leeds 4F 33
Brecon Ri. LS9: Leeds 4F 33
Brendon Ct. BD4: B'frd 4A 36
Brendon Ho. *BD4: B'frd* 5A 36
(off Fontmell Cl.)
Brendon Wlk. BD4: B'frd 5A 36
(not continuous)
Brentwood Ct. LS16: Leeds 3G 19
Brentwood Gro. LS12: Leeds 6A 30
Brentwood St. LS12: Leeds 6A 30
Brentwood Ter. LS12: Leeds 6A 30
Brett Gdns. LS11: Leeds 3F 41
Brewery Pl. LS10: Leeds 6G 5
Brewery Wharf LS10: Leeds 6G 5 (6H 31)
(Bowman La.)
  LS10: Leeds 6F 5
(Waterloo St.)
Brian Cres. LS15: Leeds 3B 34
Brian Pl. LS15: Leeds 2B 34
BRIANSIDE 2A 34
Brian Vw. LS15: Leeds 2C 34
Briar Cl. LS28: Fars .3F 27
Briardene LS26: Oul .5C 54
Briarfield Gdns. LS27: Gil 3C 48
Briarlea Cl. LS19: Yead 4B 8
Briarmains Rd. WF17: Birs 6H 47
Briarsdale Ct. LS8: Leeds 2E 33
Briarsdale Cft. LS8: Leeds 2E 33
Briarsdale Gth. LS8: Leeds 2E 33
Briarsdale Hgts. LS9: Leeds 2E 33
Briarsdale M. LS8: Leeds 2D 32
Briarwood Cl. WF1: Out 6F 59
Brick Mill Rd. LS28: Pud 1H 37
Brick St. LS9: Leeds 5H 5 (6H 31)
Bridge, The LS10: Leeds 6F 5
Bridge Ct. LS11: Leeds 2E 41
  LS27: Morl 6H 49
Bridge End LS1: Leeds 5E 5 (6G 31)
  LS11: Leeds 6F 5
Bridge Fold LS5: Leeds 1F 29
Bridge Pl. LS18: H'fth 1C 18
Bridge Rd. LS5: Leeds 1F 29
  LS11: Leeds 2E 41
  LS13: Leeds 6G 17
Bridge St. LS2: Leeds 4G 5 (5H 31)
  LS27: Morl . . . . .6H 49 & 1A 56
Bridge Ter. LS27: Morl 6H 49

Bridge Vw. LS13: Leeds 6G 17
Bridgewater Ct. LS6: Leeds 5D 20
Bridgewater Pl. LS11: Leeds 6D 4 (1F 41)
Bridgewater Rd. LS9: Leeds 2B 42
Bridge Wood Cl. LS18: H'fth 2D 18
Bridge Wood Vw. LS18: H'fth 1D 18
Bridle Path LS15: Leeds 3A 34
Bridle Path Rd. LS17: Leeds 4F 15
Bridle Path Wlk. LS15: Leeds 3A 34
Briggate LS1: Leeds 5E 5 (6G 31)
Briggs Bldgs. LS27: Morl 5H 49
(off Melbourne St.)
Brighton Av. LS27: Morl 4F 49
Brighton Cliff LS13: Leeds 3C 28
Brighton Gro. LS13: Leeds 4D 28
Bright St. LS27: Morl 5F 49
LS28: Stan 3H 27
WF3: E Ard 3H 57
Brignall Cft. LS9: Leeds 4B 32
Brignall Gth. LS9: Leeds 4B 32
Brignall Way LS9: Leeds 4B 32
Brinsmead Ct. LS26: Rothw 2H 53
Bristol St. LS7: Leeds 1H 5 (4H 31)
Britannia Cl. LS28: Stan 3H 27
Britannia Ct. LS13: Leeds 5A 28
Britannia Ho. LS1: Leeds 4C 4
Britannia M. LS2: Pud 5A 28
Britannia St. LS1: Leeds 5C 4 (6F 31)
LS28: Stan 3H 27
Broadcasting Pl. LS2: Leeds 1D 4
Broadcroft Chase
WF3: Ting 4C 56
Broadcroft Dr. WF3: Ting 4C 56
Broadcroft Gro. WF3: Ting 3C 56
Broadcroft Way WF3: Ting 3C 56
Broadfield Cl. BD4: B'frd 6A 36
Broadfields LS18: H'fth 2D 18
Broadgate LS2: Leeds 3E 5 (5G 31)
Broadgate Av. LS18: H'fth 2D 18
Broadgate Ct. LS18: H'fth 3D 18
Broadgate Cres. LS18: H'fth 3C 18
Broadgate Dr. LS18: H'fth 2D 18
Broadgate La. LS18: H'fth 2C 18
Broadgate M. LS18: H'fth 3D 18
Broadgate Ri. LS18: H'fth 3D 18
Broadgate Wlk. LS18: H'fth 3C 18
Broadlands Av. LS28: Pud 6H 27
Broadlands Ct. LS28: Pud 6H 27
Broadlands Gdns. LS28: Pud 6A 28
Broadlands Pl. LS28: Pud 6H 27
Broadlands Vw. LS28: Pud 6A 28
Broadland Way WF3: Loft 3E 59
Broad La. BD4: B'frd 3A 36
LS5: Leeds 1C 28
LS13: Leeds 3A 28
LS28: Leeds 3A 28
Broad La. Cl. LS13: Leeds 1E 29
Broadlea Av. LS13: Leeds 1E 29
Broadlea Cl. LS13: Leeds 1E 29
Broadlea Cres. LS13: Leeds 1E 29
Broadlea Gdns. LS13: Leeds 1E 29
Broadlea Gro. LS13: Leeds 1E 29
Broadlea Hill LS13: Leeds 1E 29
Broadlea Mt. LS13: Leeds 2F 29
Broadlea Oval LS13: Leeds 1E 29
Broadlea Pl. LS13: Leeds 2E 29
Broadlea Rd. LS13: Leeds 1E 29
Broadlea St. LS13: Leeds 1E 29
Broadlea Ter. LS13: Leeds 1E 29
Broadlea Vw. LS13: Leeds 1D 28
Broadmeadows WF1: Out 6E 59
Broadstone Way BD4: B'frd 6A 36
Broad St. LS28: Fars 2E 27
Broad Wlk. LS2: Leeds 2E 31
Broadway LS5: Leeds 4E 19
LS15: Leeds 1H 43
LS18: H'fth 4H 17
LS20: Guis 5E 7
Broadway Av. LS6: Leeds 3C 30
Broadway Dr. LS18: H'fth 3B 18
Brodrick Ct. LS6: Leeds 6B 20
Brodwell Grange LS18: H'fth 3E 19
Brompton Gro. LS11: Leeds 5F 41
Brompton Mt. LS11: Leeds 5F 41
Brompton Row LS11: Leeds 5F 41
Brompton Ter. LS11: Leeds 5F 41
Brompton Vw. LS11: Leeds 5F 41
Bronte Cl. WF3: E Ard 2H 57
Bronte Ho. LS7: Leeds 2G 31
Brookfield Av. LS8: Leeds 1B 32
LS13: Leeds 5F 17
Brookfield Ct. LS13: Leeds 5F 17
Brookfield Gdns. LS13: Leeds 6F 17
Brookfield Pl. LS6: Leeds 5C 20
(not continuous)
Brookfield Rd. LS6: Leeds 5C 20
Brookfield St. LS10: Leeds 2H 41

Brookfield Ter. LS6: Leeds 5C 20
(off Brookfield Rd.)
LS10: Leeds 2H 41
Brookfoot Av. BD11: Birk 4C 46
Brookhill Av. LS17: Leeds 5A 14
Brookhill Cl. LS17: Leeds 5A 14
Brookhill Cres. LS17: Leeds 5A 14
Brookhill Dr. LS17: Leeds 5A 14
Brookhill Gro. LS17: Leeds 5A 14
Brookhouse Gdns. BD10: B'frd 3B 16
BROOKLANDS 1H 33
Brooklands Av. LS14: Leeds 1H 33
LS29: Men 1D 6
Brooklands Ct. LS14: Leeds 1H 33
Brooklands Cres. LS14: Leeds 1G 33
LS19: Yead 3D 8
Brooklands Dr. LS14: Leeds 1G 33
LS19: Yead 3D 8
Brooklands Gth. LS14: Leeds 1H 33
Brooklands Gro. LS29: Men 1D 6
Brooklands La. LS14: Leeds 1H 33
LS29: Men 1C 6
Brooklands Towers LS14: Leeds 6A 24
Brooklands Vw. LS14: Leeds 1H 33
(not continuous)
Brookleigh LS28: Cal 5D 16
Brooklyn Av. LS12: Leeds 6A 30
Brooklyn Pl. LS12: Leeds 6A 30
Brooklyn St. LS12: Leeds 6A 30
Brooklyn Ter. LS12: Leeds 6A 30
Brooksbank Dr. LS15: Leeds 5A 34
Brookside LS17: Leeds 4A 14
Broom Cl. LS10: Leeds 2B 52
Broom Cres. LS10: Leeds 3B 52
Broom Cross LS10: Leeds 2A 52
Broomfield LS16: Leeds 5H 11
Broomfield Cres. LS6: Leeds 1B 30
Broomfield Pl. LS6: Leeds 2B 30
Broomfield Rd. LS6: Leeds 1B 30
Broomfield Ter. LS6: Leeds 2B 30
Broomfield Vw. LS6: Leeds 2B 30
Broom Gdns. LS10: Leeds 2A 52
Broom Gth. LS10: Leeds 2B 52
Broom Gro. LS10: Leeds 3B 52
Broomhill Av. LS17: Leeds 1H 21
Broomhill Cres. LS17: Leeds 1H 21
Broomhill Dr. LS17: Leeds 2G 21
Broom Hill Rd. LS9: Leeds 4D 32
Broom Lawn LS10: Leeds 2A 52
Broom Mills Rd. LS28: Fars 2G 27
Broom Mt. LS10: Leeds 3B 52
Broom Nook LS10: Leeds 2B 52
Broom Pl. LS10: Leeds 2B 52
Broom Rd. LS10: Leeds 3A 52
Broom Ter. LS10: Leeds 2B 52
Broom Vw. LS10: Leeds 2B 52
Broom Wlk. LS10: Leeds 3B 52
Broughton Av. LS9: Leeds 3C 32
Broughton Ho. BD4: B'frd 6B 36
Broughton Ter. LS9: Leeds 3C 32
LS28: Stan 5G 27
Brown Av. LS11: Leeds 3C 40
Brownberrie Av. LS18: H'fth 6C 10
Brownberrie Cres. LS18: H'fth 6B 10
Brownberrie Dr. LS18: H'fth 6B 10
(not continuous)
Brownberrie Gdns. LS18: H'fth 6B 10
Brownberrie La. LS18: H'fth 6H 9
Brownberrie Wlk. LS18: H'fth 6C 10
Brown Hill Av. LS9: Leeds 3C 32
Brown Hill Cl. BD11: Birk 2C 46
Brown Hill Cres. LS9: Leeds 3C 32
Brown Hill Dr. BD11: Birk 3C 46
Brown Hill Ter. LS9: Leeds 3C 32
Brown La. E. LS11: Leeds 2D 40
Brown La. W. LS11: Leeds 2C 40
LS12: Leeds 2C 40
Brownlea Cl. LS19: Yead 4B 8
Brown Pl. LS11: Leeds 3C 40
Brown Rd. LS11: Leeds 3C 40
Bruce Gdns. LS12: Leeds 6C 30
Bruce Lawn LS12: Leeds 6C 30
Brudenell Av. LS6: Leeds 2D 30
Brudenell Gro. LS6: Leeds 2D 30
Brudenell Mt. LS6: Leeds 2C 30
Brudenell Rd. LS6: Leeds 2C 30
Brudenell Vw. LS6: Leeds 2D 30
Brunel Cl. WF2: Carr G 6B 58
Brunel Rd. WF2: Carr G 6B 58
Brunswick Ct. LS2: Leeds 2G 5 (4H 31)
Brunswick Pl. BD10: B'frd 4A 16
LS27: Morl 5H 49
Brunswick Rd. LS28: Pud 5G 27

Brunswick Row LS2: Leeds 2G 5 (4H 31)
Brunswick St. LS27: Morl 4G 49
Brunswick Ter. LS2: Leeds 2E 5 (4G 31)
(not continuous)
LS27: Morl 5A 50
BRUNTCLIFFE 5D 48
Bruntcliffe Av. LS27: Morl 5E 49
Bruntcliffe Cl. LS27: Morl 5F 49
Bruntcliffe Dr. LS27: Morl 5F 49
Bruntcliffe La. LS27: Morl 5E 49
Bruntcliffe Rd. LS27: Morl 5D 48
Bruntcliffe Way LS27: Morl 5E 49
Brussels St. LS9: Leeds 5H 5 (6H 31)
Bryanstone Rd. BD4: B'frd 2A 36
Bryan St. LS28: Fars 1F 27
Bryan St. Nth. LS28: Fars 1F 27
Bryngate LS26: Oul .3C 54
Bryony Ct. LS10: Leeds 4B 52
Buckden Ct. LS29: Men 2D 6
(off Jackson Wlk.)
Buckingham Av. LS6: Leeds 1C 30
Buckingham Dr. LS6: Leeds 1C 30
Buckingham Gro. LS6: Leeds 1C 30
Buckingham Ho. LS6: Leeds 1C 30
Buckingham Mt. LS6: Leeds 2C 30
Buckingham Rd. LS6: Leeds 1C 30
Buckle La. LS29: Men 2D 6
Buckley Av. LS11: Leeds 4F 41
Buck Stone Av. LS17: Leeds 5D 12
Buck Stone Cl. LS17: Leeds 5E 13
Buck Stone Cres. LS17: Leeds 5E 13
Buck Stone Dr. LS17: Leeds 5D 12
Buckstone Dr. LS19: Raw 6C 8
(not continuous)
Buck Stone Gdns. LS17: Leeds 5E 13
Buck Stone Grn. LS17: Leeds 5D 12
Buck Stone Gro. LS17: Leeds 5D 12
Buck Stone Mt. LS17: Leeds 5D 12
Buck Stone Oval LS17: Leeds 5D 12
Buck Stone Ri. LS17: Leeds 5D 12
Buck Stone Rd. LS17: Leeds 5D 12
Buck Stone Vw. LS17: Leeds 5D 12
Buck Stone Way LS17: Leeds 5D 12
Buckthorne Cl. WF3: E Ard 3H 57
Buckthorne Ct. WF3: E Ard 3H 57
Buckthorne Dr. WF3: E Ard 3H 57
Buckthorne Fold WF3: E Ard 3H 57
Buckton Cl. LS11: Leeds 3E 41
Buckton Mt. LS11: Leeds 3E 41
Buckton Vw. LS11: Leeds 3E 41
Bude Rd. LS11: Leeds 4F 41
Buller Cl. LS9: Leeds 4E 33
Buller Ct. LS9: Leeds 4E 33
Buller Gro. LS9: Leeds 4D 32
Buller St. LS26: Wood 3D 54
Bullerthorpe La. LS15: Leeds 1F 45
LS26: Swil 1E 55
Bullough La. LS26: Rothw 2H 53
Bungalows, The LS15: Leeds 2D 34
(off Church La.)
Burchett Gro. LS6: Leeds 1E 31
Burchett Pl. LS6: Leeds 1E 31
Burchett Ter. LS6: Leeds 1F 31
Burdett Ter. LS4: Leeds 3A 30
Burghley M. LS10: Leeds 6H 51
Burland Ter. LS26: Swil 5G 45
BURLEY 3B 30
Burley Grange Rd. LS4: Leeds 3A 30
Burley Hill Cres. LS4: Leeds 2H 29
Burley Hill Dr. LS4: Leeds 2H 29
Burley Hill Trad. Est.
LS4: Leeds 2A 30
Burley La. LS18: H'fth 3B 18
LS29: Men 1B 6
Burley Lodge Pl. LS6: Leeds 4C 30
(off Burley Lodge Rd.)
Burley Lodge Rd. LS6: Leeds 3C 30
Burley Lodge St. LS6: Leeds 4C 30
Burley Lodge Ter. LS6: Leeds 4C 30
Burley Pl. LS4: Leeds 4B 30
Burley Rd. LS3: Leeds 3C 30
LS4: Leeds 2A 30
Burley St. LS3: Leeds 3A 4 (5D 30)
Burley Wood Ct. LS4: Leeds 2H 29
Burley Wood Cres. LS4: Leeds 2H 29
Burley Wood La. LS4: Leeds 2A 30
Burley Wood Mt. LS4: Leeds 2H 29
Burley Wood Vw. LS4: Leeds 2A 30
Burlington Av. BD3: B'frd 4A 26
Burlington Pl. LS11: Leeds 5F 41
Burlington Rd. LS11: Leeds 5F 41
BURMANTOFTS 4B 32
Burmantofts St. LS9: Leeds 5A 32
Burnsall Ct. LS12: Leeds 5H 29
Burnsall Cft. LS12: Leeds 5H 29
Burnsall Gdns. LS12: Leeds 5H 29

Burnsall Grange—Castle Vw.

Burnsall Grange *LS12: Leeds* . . . . *5H* ***29*** *(off Theaker La.)*
Burnshaw M. LS10: Leeds 6G **51**
Burnstall Cres. LS29: Men 3D **6**
Burnt Side Rd. LS12: N Far 5C **38**
Burr Tree Dr. LS15: Leeds 6D **34**
Burr Tree Gth. LS15: Leeds 6D **34**
Burr Tree Va. LS15: Leeds 6D **34**
Burton Av. LS11: Leeds 4G **41**
Burton Cres. LS6: Leeds 5B **20**
Burton Ho. LS17: Leeds 5B **14**
Burton M. LS17: Leeds 4H **13**
Burton Rd. LS11: Leeds 4G **41**
Burton Row LS11: Leeds 3G **41**
Burton St. LS11: Leeds 3G **41**
LS28: Fars 2F **27**
Burton Ter. LS11: Leeds 4G **41**
Burton Way LS9: Leeds 4C **32**
Busely Ct. LS27: Morl 4F **49**
BUSLINGTHORPE **1G 31**
Buslingthorpe Grn. LS7: Leeds 2G **31**
Buslingthorpe La. LS7: Leeds 1G **31**
Buslingthorpe Va. LS7: Leeds 1G **31**
Bussey Ct. LS6: Leeds 2E **31**
Butcher Hill LS5: Leeds 3E **19**
LS16: Leeds 3E **19**
LS18: H'fth 3E **19**
Butcher La. LS26: Rothw 4G **53**
Butchers Row LS2: Leeds 4F **5**
Butcher St. LS11: Leeds 1F **41**
Butler Way LS28: Stan 3G **27**
Butterbowl Dr. LS12: Leeds 2E **39**
Butterbowl Gdns. LS12: Leeds 2F **39**
Butterbowl Gth. LS12: Leeds 2E **39**
Butterbowl Gro. LS12: Leeds 2E **39**
Butterbowl Lawn LS12: Leeds 2E **39**
Butterbowl Mt. LS12: Leeds 2F **39**
Butterbowl Rd. LS12: Leeds 2F **39**
Buttercup La. WF3: E Ard 2A **58**
Buttercup Way BD11: Drig 4B **48**
Butterfield's Bldgs. LS27: Morl 4F **49**
Butterfield St. LS9: Leeds 6B **32**
Butterley St. LS10: Leeds 2G **41**
Butt La. LS12: Leeds .1D **38**
LS13: Leeds 6E **29**
Button Hill LS7: Leeds 1H **31**
Butt Row LS12: Leeds 1E **39**
Butts Ct. LS1: Leeds 4E **5** (5G **31**)
Butts La. LS20: Guis .4G **7**
Butts Mt. LS12: Leeds 6B **30**
Butts Ter. LS20: Guis 4G **7**
Byeway LS20: Guis 4E **7**
Byron Gro. WF3: S'ley 5G **59**
Byron St. LS2: Leeds 2G **5** (4H **31**)
Bywater Row BD11: Birk 4D **46**

C

CABBAGE HILL **1G 39**
Cabbage Hill LS12: Leeds 1H **39**
Cad Beeston LS11: Leeds 4E **41**
Cad Beeston M. LS11: Leeds 4E **41**
Cadman Ct. LS27: Morl 6G **49**
Cain Cl. LS9: Leeds . . . . .6B **32** (not continuous)
Cairn Av. LS20: Guis .3E **7**
Cairn Gth. LS20: Guis 3E **7**
Caister Cl. WF17: Birs 6A **48**
Calgary Cres. WF3: W Ard 4D **56**
Calgary Pl. LS7: Leeds 5H **21**
California M. LS27: Morl 3H **49**
California St. LS27: Morl 5H **49**
Call La. LS1: Leeds 6F **5** (6G **31**)
Calls, The LS2: Leeds 5F **5** (6G **31**)
CALVERLEY **4C 16**
Calverley Av. BD3: B'frd 5A **26**
LS13: Leeds 2B **28**
CALVERLEY BRIDGE **5G 17**
Calverley Ct. LS13: Leeds 2B **28**
LS26: Oul 4B **54**
Calverley Cutting LS28: Cal 3B **16**
Calverley Dr. LS13: Leeds 2B **28**
Calverley Gdns. LS13: Leeds 1A **28**
Calverley Gth. LS13: Leeds 2B **28**
Calverley Gro. LS13: Leeds 2B **28**
Calverley La. LS13: Leeds 1H **27**
LS18: H'fth 4G **17**
LS28: Cal, Fars . . . . .5E **17** (not continuous)
Calverley Moor Av. LS28: Pud 4C **26**
Calverley Rd. LS26: Oul 4C **54**
Calverley St. LS1: Leeds 2C **4** (4F **31**)
Calverley Ter. LS13: Leeds 2B **28**
Camberley Cl. LS28: Pud 1G **37**
Camberley Mt. BD4: B'frd 3A **36**
Camberley St. LS11: Leeds 4G **41**
Camberley Way LS28: Pud 1G **37**
Cambrian St. LS11: Leeds 3E **41**
Cambrian Ter. LS11: Leeds 3E **41**
Cambridge Cl. LS27: Morl 4H **49**
Cambridge Ct. LS27: Morl 5H **49**
Cambridge Dr. LS13: Leeds 2B **28**
Cambridge Gdns. LS13: Leeds 2B **28**
Cambridge Rd. LS6: Leeds 2F **31**
Cambridge St. LS20: Guis 4G **7**
Campbell St. LS28: Stan 3F **27**
CAMP FIELD **1F 41**
CAMP TOWN **5F 13**
Canada Cres. LS19: Raw 5E **9**
Canada Dr. LS19: Raw 4E **9**
Canada Rd. LS19: Raw 4E **9**
Canada Ter. LS19: Raw 5E **9**
Canalbank Vw. LS13: Leeds 6H **17**
Canal Ct. WF3: Loft .5F **59**
Canal Gdns. **2D 22**
Canal La. WF3: Loft, S'ley 5E **59**
Canal Pl. LS12: Leeds 6D **30**
Canal Rd. LS12: Leeds 5A **30**
LS13: Leeds 5G **17**
Canal St. LS12: Leeds 6C **30**
Canal Wlk. WF3: S'ley 5H **59**
Canal Wharf LS5: Leeds 2F **29**
LS11: Leeds 6C **4** (6F **31**)
Candle Ho. LS1: Leeds 6C **4**
Cannon Wlk. LS2: Leeds 3E **31**
Canonbury Ter. LS11: Leeds 4C **40**
Canter, The LS10: Leeds 6H **51**
Canterbury Dr. LS6: Leeds 1A **30**
Canterbury Rd. LS6: Leeds 1A **30**
Cape Ind. Est. LS28: Fars 2G **27**
Capel Ct. LS28: Cal .5D **16**
Capel St. LS28: Cal .5D **16**
Capitol Blvd. LS27: Morl 2A **56**
Capitol Cl. LS27: Morl 1A **56**
Capitol Pde. LS6: Leeds 4D **20**
Caraway Ct. LS6: Leeds 2D **20**
Caraway Dr. LS6: Leeds 2D **20**
Caraway M. LS6: Leeds 2D **20**
Carberry Pl. LS6: Leeds 3C **30**
Carberry Rd. LS6: Leeds 3C **30**
Carberry Ter. *LS6: Leeds* . . . .*3C* ***30*** *(off Carberry Rd.)*
Carden Av. LS15: Leeds 6G **33**
Carden Gro. LS15: Leeds 6G **33**
Carden Rd. BD4: B'frd 2A **36**
Cardigan Av. LS27: Morl 6G **49**
Cardigan Ct. LS6: Leeds 1C **30**
Cardigan Flds. Rd. LS4: Leeds 4A **30**
Cardigan La. LS4: Leeds . . . . .3B **30** (not continuous)
LS6: Leeds 2C **30**
Cardigan Rd. LS6: Leeds 1B **30**
Cardigan Ter. WF3: E Ard 3A **58**
Cardigan Trad. Est. LS4: Leeds 4B **30**
Cardinal Av. LS11: Leeds 1D **50**
Cardinal Ct. LS11: Leeds 6C **40**
Cardinal Cres. LS11: Leeds 1D **50**
Cardinal Gdns. LS11: Leeds 1C **50**
Cardinal Gro. LS11: Leeds 1C **50**
Cardinal Rd. LS11: Leeds 1C **50**
Cardinal Sq. LS11: Leeds 6D **40**
Cardinal Wlk. LS11: Leeds 6C **40**
Carisbrooke Rd. LS16: Leeds 4H **19**
Carlisle Av. LS19: Yead 3E **9**
Carlisle Dr. LS28: Pud 1F **37**
Carlisle Gro. LS28: Pud 1F **37**
Carlisle Rd. LS10: Leeds 1H **41**
LS28: Pud 1F **37**
Carlisle St. LS28: Stan 4E **27**
CARLTON **6F 53**
Carlton Av. LS28: Pud 6G **27**
Carlton Carr LS7: Leeds 1E **5** (3G **31**)
Carlton Cl. *LS7: Leeds* . . . .*3G* ***31*** *(off Carlton Ri.)*
Carlton Ct. LS12: Leeds 3C **40**
Carlton Cft. *LS7: Leeds* . . . .*3G* ***31*** *(off Carlton Gdns.)*
Carlton Dr. LS20: Guis 3H **7**
Carlton Gdns. LS7: Leeds 3G **31**
Carlton Gth. LS7: Leeds 3G **31**
LS17: Leeds 4C **14**
Carlton Ga. LS7: Leeds 1E **5** (3G **31**)
Carlton Grange LS19: Yead 2E **9**
Carlton Gro. LS7: Leeds 3G **31**
Carlton Hill LS2: Leeds 1E **5** (3G **31**)
LS7: Leeds 3G **31**
Carlton La. LS20: Guis 3H **7**
LS26: Rothw 5F **53**
WF3: Loft 2E **59**
Carlton M. LS20: Guis 4H **7**
Carlton Moor M. LS10: Leeds 4B **52**
Carlton Mt. LS19: Yead 1E **9**
Carlton Pde. LS7: Leeds 1F **5** (3G **31**)
Carlton Pl. LS7: Leeds 3G **31**
Carlton Ri. LS7: Leeds 3G **31**
LS28: Pud 6G **27**
Carlton Row LS12: Leeds 6G **29**
Carlton Ter. LS19: Yead 2E **9**
LS28: Pud 5G **27**
Carlton Towers LS7: Leeds 3G **31**
Carlton Trad. Est. LS12: Leeds 5B **30**
Carlton Vw. LS7: Leeds 3G **31**
Carlton Wlk. LS7: Leeds 3G **31**
Carnegie Regional Indoor Tennis Cen. **5H 19**
Carr Bottom Rd. BD10: B'frd 4A **16**
Carr Bri. Av. LS16: Leeds 6D **10**
Carr Bri. Cl. LS16: Leeds 6D **10**
Carr Bri. Dr. LS16: Leeds 6D **10**
Carr Bri. Vw. LS16: Leeds 6D **10**
Carr Cl. LS19: Raw .6F **9**
CARR CROFTS **6H 29**
Carr Crofts LS12: Leeds 6H **29**
Carr Crofts Dr. LS12: Leeds 6H **29**
CARR GATE **6A 58**
Carr Ga. Cres. WF2: Carr G 6H **57**
Carr Ga. Dr. WF2: Carr G 6A **58**
Carr Ga. Mt. WF2: Carr G 6H **57**
Carr Hill Av. LS28: Cal 5C **16**
Carr Hill Dr. LS28: Cal 5C **16**
Carr Hill Gro. LS28: Cal 5C **16**
Carr Hill Nook LS28: Cal 5C **16**
Carr Hill Ri. LS28: Cal 5C **16**
Carr Hill Rd. LS28: Cal 5C **16**
Carrholm Cres. LS7: Leeds 4F **21**
Carrholm Dr. LS7: Leeds 4F **21**
Carrholm Gro. LS7: Leeds 4F **21**
Carrholm Mt. LS7: Leeds 4F **21**
Carrholm Rd. LS7: Leeds 4F **21**
Carrholm Vw. LS7: Leeds 4F **21**
Carriage Dr. BD19: Gom 6D **46**
Carriage Dr., The LS8: Leeds 2E **23**
Carriageworks Theatre, The . . . .**3D 4 (5F 31)**
Carrington Ter. LS20: Guis 5F **7**
Carr La. LS19: Raw 6F **9**
WF3: Carl 6G **53**
Carr Mnr. Av. LS17: Leeds 3F **21**
Carr Mnr. Cres. LS17: Leeds 2F **21**
Carr Mnr. Cft. LS17: Leeds 4F **21**
Carr Mnr. Dr. LS17: Leeds 3F **21**
Carr Mnr. Gdns. LS17: Leeds 3F **21**
Carr Mnr. Gth. LS17: Leeds 2F **21**
Carr Mnr. Gro. LS17: Leeds 3F **21**
Carr Mnr. Mt. LS17: Leeds 3F **21**
Carr Mnr. Pde. LS17: Leeds 3F **21**
Carr Mnr. Pl. LS17: Leeds 3F **21**
Carr Mnr. Rd. LS17: Leeds 4F **21**
Carr Mnr. Vw. LS17: Leeds 2F **21**
Carr Mnr. Wlk. LS17: Leeds 4F **21**
Carr Mills LS7: Leeds 1F **31**
Carr Moor Side LS11: Leeds 4G **41**
Carr Moor St. LS10: Leeds 5H **41**
Carr Rd. LS28: Cal 4B **16**
Carr Wood Cl. LS28: Cal 5C **16**
Carr Wood Gdns. LS28: Cal 5C **16**
Carr Wood Way LS28: Cal 4C **16**
Carter Av. LS15: Leeds 5C **34**
Carter La. LS15: Leeds 4C **34**
Carter Mt. LS15: Leeds 5C **34**
Carter Ter. LS15: Leeds 4C **34**
Cartier Ho. LS10: Leeds 1H **41**
Cartmell Ct. LS15: Leeds 6F **33**
Cartmell Dr. LS15: Leeds 6F **33**
Caspar Apartments
LS2: Leeds 2F **5**
Casson Av. WF3: E Ard 2F **57**
Casson Dr. WF3: E Ard 2F **57**
Casson Gro. WF3: E Ard 2F **57**
Castlefields LS26: Rothw 4D **52**
Castle Ga. LS26: Oul 3H **59**
Castle Grange LS19: Yead 3F **9**
Castle Gro. Av. LS6: Leeds 4B **20**
Castle Gro. Dr. LS6: Leeds 5B **20**
Castle Head Cl. WF3: Loft 3E **59**
Castle Head La. WF3: Loft 4B **58**
WF3: Thpe H 3B **58**
Castle Ings Cl. LS12: N Far 4D **38**
Castle Ings Dr. LS12: N Far 4D **38**
Castle Ings Gdns. LS12: N Far 4D **38**
Castle Lodge Av. LS26: Rothw 2D **52**
Castle Lodge Ct. LS26: Rothw 3E **53**
Castle Lodge Gdns. LS26: Rothw 3D **52**
Castle Lodge Gth. LS26: Rothw 2E **53**
Castle Lodge M. LS26: Rothw 3E **53**
Castle Lodge Sq. LS26: Rothw 2E **53**
Castle Lodge Way LS26: Rothw 3D **52**
Castle Rd. LS26: Rothw 4F **53**
Castle St. LS1: Leeds 4B **4** (5E **31**)
Castleton Cl. LS12: Leeds 6D **30**
Castleton Rd. LS12: Leeds 5C **30**
Castle Vw. LS17: Leeds 2F **21**

70 A-Z Leeds

Castle Wood Cl. LS18: H'fth 3D 18
Catalina LS12: Leeds 6A 4 (6E 31)
Cathcart St. LS6: Leeds 2E 31
Catherine Gro. LS11: Leeds 4F 41
Cautley Rd. LS9: Leeds 1B 42
Cavalier App. LS9: Leeds 1B 42
Cavalier Cl. LS9: Leeds 1B 42
Cavalier Ct. LS9: Leeds 1B 42
Cavalier Dr. BD10: B'frd 3A 16
Cavalier Gdns. LS9: Leeds 1B 42
Cavalier Ga. LS9: Leeds 1B 42
Cavalier Grn. LS9: Leeds 1B 42
CAVALIER HILL 6A 32
Cavalier M. LS9: Leeds 1B 42
Cavalier Vw. LS9: Leeds 1B 42
Cave La. WF3: E Ard 3H 57
Cavendish App. BD11: Drig 3G 47
Cavendish Ct. *BD11: Drig* *3G 47*
(off Cavendish App.)
Cavendish Dr. LS20: Guis 5F 7
Cavendish Gro. LS20: Guis 5F 7
Cavendish M. BD11: Drig 3G 47
LS17: Leeds 5H 13
Cavendish Pl. LS28: Stan 4F 27
Cavendish Ri. LS28: Pud 6A 28
Cavendish Rd. LS2: Leeds 1C 4 (3F 31)
LS20: Guis 5F 7
Cavendish Sq. LS28: Stan 4G 27
Cavendish St. LS3: Leeds 3A 4 (5D 30)
LS19: Yead 2E 9
LS28: Pud 6A 28
Caythorpe Rd. LS16: Leeds 4H 19
Cecil Gro. LS12: Leeds 5A 30
Cecil Mt. LS12: Leeds 5A 30
Cecil Rd. LS12: Leeds 5A 30
Cecil St. LS12: Leeds 5A 30
Cedar Av. LS12: Leeds 6H 29
Cedar Cl. LS12: Leeds 6A 30
Cedar Ct. *LS17: Leeds* *1H 21*
(off Harrogate Rd.)
LS26: Wood 2E 55
Cedar Dr. LS14: Leeds 3G 33
Cedar Mt. LS12: Leeds 6H 29
Cedar Pl. LS12: Leeds 6H 29
Cedar Rd. LS12: Leeds 6H 29
Cedar St. LS12: Leeds 6H 29
Cedar Ter. LS12: Leeds 6H 29
Cemetery La. WF3: Carl 2E 59
Cemetery Rd. LS11: Leeds 3E 41
LS19: Yead 2E 9
LS28: Pud 5E 27
Centaur Ho. LS1: Leeds 3B 4 (4E 31)
Central Pk. LS11: Leeds 1F 41
Central Rd. LS1: Leeds 5F 5 (6G 31)
Central St. LS1: Leeds 4C 4 (5F 31)
Centre 27 Bus. Pk. WF17: Birs 6B 48
Century Way LS15: Leeds 6F 35
Chaddle Wood Cl. LS18: H'fth 2C 18
Chadwick St. LS10: Leeds 1H 41
Chadwick St. Sth. LS10: Leeds 1H 41
Chalfont Rd. LS16: Leeds 3H 19
Chalice Cl. LS10: Leeds 2A 52
Challenge Way BD4: B'frd 3A 36
Chalner Av. LS27: Morl 6F 49
Chalner Cl. LS27: Morl 6F 49
Chancellor Ct. LS2: Leeds 5F 5 (6G 31)
Chancellor St. LS6: Leeds 2F 31
Chancel Sq. LS6: Leeds 2D 20
Chandlers, The LS2: Leeds 6G 5
Chandlers Cl. WF1: Out 6D 58
Chandlers Wharf
LS13: Leeds 5G 17
Chandos Av. LS8: Leeds 3A 22
Chandos Fold LS8: Leeds 4A 22
Chandos Gdns. LS8: Leeds 3A 22
Chandos Gth. LS8: Leeds 3A 22
Chandos Grn. LS8: Leeds 3A 22
Chandos M. LS8: Leeds 3A 22
Chandos Pl. LS8: Leeds 3B 22
Chandos Ter. LS8: Leeds 3B 22
Chandos Wlk. LS8: Leeds 3A 22
Change All. LS1: Leeds 4E 5
Chantrell Ct. LS2: Leeds 5G 5 (6H 31)
Chantry Ct. LS27: Morl 4H 49
Chantry Cft. LS15: Leeds 6D 34
Chantry Gth. LS15: Leeds 6D 34
Chapel, The *LS26: Oul* *4C 54*
(off Calverley Rd.)
CHAPEL ALLERTON 5F 21
CHAPEL ALLERTON HOSPITAL 6A 22
Chapel Allerton Lawn Tennis & Squash Club
. . . . .4G 21
Chapel Ct. LS15: Leeds 5A 34
Chapel Fold LS6: Leeds 2B 30
LS11: Leeds 5C 40
LS12: *Leeds* *6A 30*
(off Wesley Rd.)

Chapel Fold LS15: Leeds 5A 34
LS28: Pud *1G 37*
(off Littlemoor Rd.)
Chapel Grn. LS28: Pud 1F 37
Chapel Hill LS10: Leeds 4H 51
LS19: Yead 2D 8
LS27: Morl 4G 49
Chapel La. LS6: Leeds 1B 30
(not continuous)
LS12: Leeds .6A 30
LS12: N Far 2D 38
LS19: Yead 2D 8
Chapel Lofts *LS27: Morl* *5H 49*
(off Commercial St.)
Chapel Pl. LS6: Leeds 6B 20
Chapel Rd. LS7: Leeds 6H 21
Chapel Sq. *LS6: Leeds* *6B 20*
(off Chapel St.)
Chapel St. LS6: Leeds 6B 20
LS13: Leeds 6G 17
LS15: Leeds 5A 34
LS19: Raw 5D 8
LS28: Cal 4D 16
LS28: Stan 4G 27
WF3: Carl 6F 53
WF3: E Ard 4G 57
WF3: S'ley 6G 59
WF3: Ting 2D 56
Chapel Ter. *LS6: Leeds* *6B 20*
(off Chapel St.)
CHAPELTOWN 1H 31
Chapeltown LS28: Pud 1F 37
Chapeltown Bus. Cen. *LS7: Leeds* *1H 31*
(off Chapeltown Rd.)
Chapeltown Rd. LS7: Leeds 2H 31
Chapel Vw. LS27: Gil 1C 48
Chapel Yd. *LS15: Leeds* *1D 44*
(off Meynell Rd.)
LS26: Oul 4C 54
Charles Av. BD3: B'frd 6A 26
LS9: Leeds 1B 42
WF1: Out 6D 58
Charles Gdns. LS11: Leeds 2E 41
Charles Gro. LS26: Oul 3C 54
Charles Morris Hall LS2: Leeds 1A 4 (4E 31)
Charles St. LS18: H'fth 3B 18
LS27: Morl 5H 49
LS28: Fars 2F 27
Charlotte Cl. WF17: Birs 6H 47
Charlotte Gro. LS15: Leeds 5B 34
Charlton Gro. LS9: Leeds 6C 32
Charlton Pl. LS9: Leeds 6C 32
Charlton Rd. LS9: Leeds 6C 32
Charlton St. LS9: Leeds 6C 32
Charnley Dr. LS7: Leeds 5A 22
Chartist's Ct. *LS27: Morl* *6G 49*
(off Gt. Northern St.)
Chartists Way LS27: Morl 6G 49
Chartwell Ct. *LS17: Leeds* *4D 14*
(off Shadwell La.)
Charville Gdns. LS17: Shad 6H 15
Chase, The LS19: Raw 5C 8
WF3: S'ley 5H 59
WF3: Ting 2C 56
Chase Av. LS27: Morl 2A 56
Chase Ct. LS27: Morl 2A 56
Chatswood Av. LS11: Leeds 1D 50
Chatswood Cres. LS11: Leeds 1D 50
Chatswood Dr. LS11: Leeds 6D 40
Chatsworth Av. LS28: Pud 5C 26
Chatsworth Cl. LS8: Leeds 2C 32
Chatsworth Cres. LS28: Pud 5C 26
Chatsworth Dr. LS28: Pud 5C 26
Chatsworth Fall LS28: Pud 5C 26
Chatsworth Ind. Est.
LS12: Leeds 1B 40
Chatsworth M. LS27: Morl 6A 50
Chatsworth Ri. LS28: Pud 1G 26
Chatsworth Rd. LS8: Leeds 2C 32
LS28: Pud 5C 26
Chaucer Av. LS28: Pud 1H 37
WF3: S'ley 5G 59
Chaucer Gdns. LS28: Pud 1H 37
Chaucer Gro. LS28: Pud 1H 37
Cheapside *LS27: Morl* *4G 49*
(off Chapel Hill)
Chellow Ter. BD11: Birk 5D 46
Chelsea Cl. LS12: Leeds 1A 40
Chelsfield Ct. LS15: Leeds 2F 35
Chelsfield Way LS15: Leeds 2F 35
Cheltenham St. LS12: Leeds 1B 40
Chelwood Av. LS8: Leeds 6B 14
Chelwood Cres. LS8: Leeds 1B 22
Chelwood Dr. LS8: Leeds 6B 14
Chelwood Gro. LS8: Leeds 6B 14
Chelwood Mt. LS8: Leeds 6B 14
Chelwood Pl. LS8: Leeds 6A 14

Chenies Cl. LS14: Leeds 4G 33
Chepstow Dr. LS10: Leeds 6H 51
Cherry Ct. LS6: Leeds 5D 20
LS9: Leeds *4A 32*
(off Cherry Row)
Cherry Gro. LS6: Leeds 6D 20
Cherry Lea Ct. LS19: Raw 4D 8
Cherry Pl. LS9: Leeds 4A 32
Cherry Ri. LS14: Leeds 3C 24
Cherry Row LS9: Leeds 2H 5 (4A 32)
Cherry Tree Av. BD10: B'frd 4A 16
Cherry Tree Ct. WF3: E Ard 4G 57
Cherry Tree Cres. LS28: Fars 2F 27
Cherry Tree Dr. LS28: Fars 2F 27
Cherry Tree Wlk. LS2: Leeds 5F 5
WF3: E Ard 4G 57
Cherrywood Cl. LS14: Leeds 2B 24
Cherrywood Gdns. LS14: Leeds 2B 24
Chervana Ct. BD4: B'frd 3A 36
Chesney Av. LS10: Leeds 3H 41
Chesney Pk. Ind. Est. *LS10: Leeds* *3H 41*
(off Hillidge Rd.)
Chester St. LS12: Leeds 5A 30
Chesterton Ct. LS15: Leeds 1D 44
Chestnut Av. LS6: Leeds 2C 30
LS15: Leeds 3D 34
Chestnut Dr. LS16: Leeds 4H 11
Chestnut Gdns. LS12: Leeds 1A 40
LS27: Chur 2G 49
Chestnut Gro. LS6: Leeds 2C 30
LS26: Wood 3E 55
LS28: Cal 5D 16
Chestnut La. LS14: Leeds 3G 33
Chestnut Pl. LS6: Leeds 2C 30
Chestnut Ri. LS12: Leeds 1H 39
Chestnut St. LS6: Leeds 2C 30
Chestnut Vw. LS27: Chur 2G 49
Chestnut Way LS16: Leeds 4H 11
Chevin Av. LS29: Men 1D 6
Chevin End LS29: Guis, Men 2D 6
Chevin End Rd. LS20: Guis 2F 7
Chevington Ct. LS19: Raw 6C 8
Chevin Ho. *LS29: Men* *2D 6*
(off High Royds Dr.)
Chichester St. LS12: Leeds 5A 30
Chiltern Ct. LS13: Leeds 6G 17
Chilver Dr. BD4: B'frd 5C 36
Chippendale Ct. LS29: Men 1D 6
Chirton Gro. LS8: Leeds 6C 22
Chiswick St. LS6: Leeds 4C 30
Chiswick Ter. *LS6: Leeds* *3C 30*
(off Carberry Rd.)
Chorley La. LS2: Leeds 2B 4 (4E 31)
LS3: Leeds 3B 4 (5E 31)
Christ Chu. Av. LS12: Leeds 5H 29
Christ Chu. Mt. LS12: Leeds 5H 29
Christ Chu. Pde. LS12: Leeds 5H 29
Christ Chu. Pl. LS12: Leeds 5H 29
Christ Chu. Rd. LS12: Leeds 5H 29
Christ Chu. Ter. LS12: Leeds 5H 29
Christ Chu. Vw. LS12: Leeds 5H 29
Christiana Ter. LS27: Morl 4H 49
Christopher Rd. LS6: Leeds 2F 31
Church Av. LS6: Leeds 4D 20
LS18: H'fth 2B 18
LS26: Swil 5G 45
LS27: Gil 1C 48
Church Cl. LS14: Leeds 1B 34
(not continuous)
LS26: Swil 5G 45
Church Ct. LS19: Yead 3D 8
LS27: Morl 4G 49
Church Cres. LS17: Leeds 6G 13
LS18: H'fth 2B 18
LS19: Yead 3C 8
LS26: Swil 6H 45
Church Cft. LS29: Men 1B 6
WF3: Loft 3E 59
Church Farm Cl. WF3: Loft 3E 59
Church Farm Gth. LS17: Shad 5H 15
Churchfield Cft. LS26: Rothw 4H 53
Churchfield Gro. LS26: Rothw 3G 53
Churchfield La. LS26: Rothw 3G 53
Churchfield Rd. LS26: Rothw 4G 53
Church Gdns. LS17: Leeds 6H 13
LS27: Gil 2C 48
Church Ga. LS18: H'fth 2B 18
Churchgate LS27: Gil 2C 48
Church Gro. LS6: Leeds 4C 20
LS18: H'fth 2B 18
Church Hill LS16: Leeds 3H 27
Church Hill Grn. LS28: Stan 3H 27
Church Hill Mt. LS28: Stan 3H 27
Churchill Gdns. *LS2: Leeds* *3F 31*
(off Bk. Blenheim Ter.)
Churchill Ho. *BD4: B'frd* *3A 36*
(off Tyersal La.)

Church La.—Colton St.

Church La. LS2: Leeds 5G 5 (6H 31)
LS6: Leeds 4D 20
LS7: Leeds 5H 21
LS15: Leeds 3C 34
LS16: Leeds 5A 12
LS18: H'fth 2B 18
LS26: Meth 6H 55
LS26: Swil 6F 45
LS28: Pud 6G 27
WF1: Out 6D 58
WF3: E Ard 4G 57
WF3: W Ard 4B 56
Church La. Av. WF1: Out 6D 58
Church M. LS5: Leeds 5E 19
Church Mt. LS18: H'fth 2B 18
Church Rd. *LS9: Leeds 6A 32*
(off Cross Catherine St.)
LS12: Leeds 6A 30
LS18: H'fth 3B 18
WF3: S'ley 6H 59
Church Row LS2: Leeds 5G 5 (6H 31)
Churchside Vs. LS26: Meth 6H 55
Church St. LS5: Leeds 1G 29
LS10: Leeds 3H 41
LS19: Yead 3C 8
LS20: Guis 4G 7
LS26: Rothw 4G 53
LS26: Wood 2C 54
LS27: Gil 2C 48
LS27: Morl 4G 49
Church Vw. LS5: Leeds 1H 29
LS16: Leeds 4A 12
LS29: Men 1B 6
Church Wlk. LS2: Leeds 5G 5 (6H 31)
Church Way LS27: Morl 4G 49
Church Wood Av. LS16: Leeds 5A 20
Church Wood Mt. LS16: Leeds 4A 20
Church Wood Rd. LS16: Leeds 5A 20
CHURWELL 1A 50
CITY 5H 49
City Ga. LS3: Leeds 5D 30
City Link Ind. Pk. BD4: B'frd 1A 36
City Mills *LS27: Morl 5H 49*
(off Peel St.)
City Pk. Ind. Est. LS12: Leeds 4A 40
City Sq. LS1: Leeds 5D 4 (6F 31)
City Varieties Music Hall 4E 5 (5G 31)
City Vw. LS11: Leeds 5D 40
City Wlk. LS11: Leeds 1F 41
City West One Office Pk. LS12: Leeds 4B 40
Clapgate La. LS10: Leeds 4B 52
Clapham Dene Rd. LS15: Leeds 4B 34
Clara Dr. LS28: Cal 4B 16
Clara St. LS28: Fars 3F 27
Claremont LS28: Pud 6H 27
Claremont Av. LS3: Leeds 2A 4 (4E 31)
Claremont Ct. LS6: Leeds 5C 20
Claremont Cres. LS6: Leeds 6D 20
Claremont Dr. LS6: Leeds 5C 20
Claremont Gdns. LS28: Fars 3F 27
Claremont Gro. LS3: Leeds 2A 4 (4E 31)
LS28: Pud 6G 27
Claremont Pl. LS12: Leeds 6G 29
Claremont Rd. LS6: Leeds 5C 20
Claremont St. LS12: Leeds 6G 29
LS26: Oul 3C 54
Claremont Ter. LS12: Leeds 6G 29
Claremont Vw. LS3: Leeds 2A 4 (4E 31)
LS26: Oul 3C 54
Claremont Vs. *LS2: Leeds 2B 4*
(off Clarendon Rd.)
Claremount LS6: Leeds 5C 20
Clarence Dock LS10: Leeds 6H 5 (1H 41)
Clarence Dr. LS18: H'fth 4B 18
Clarence Gdns. LS18: H'fth 4B 18
Clarence Gro. LS18: H'fth 4B 18
Clarence Ho. LS10: Leeds 1H 41
Clarence M. LS18: H'fth 4B 18
Clarence Rd. LS10: Leeds 1A 42
LS18: H'fth 4B 18
Clarence St. LS13: Leeds 4C 28
Clarence Ter. LS28: Pud 5G 27
Clarendon Pl. LS2: Leeds 3E 31
Clarendon Rd. LS2: Leeds 1A 4 (3E 31)
Clarendon Ter. LS27: Chur 1A 50
LS28: Pud 1G 37
Clarendon Way LS2: Leeds 2B 4 (4E 31)
Clarion Camp LS29: Men 1F 7
Clark Av. LS9: Leeds 6B 32
Clark Cres. LS9: Leeds 6B 32
Clarke Rd. WF3: W Ard 6C 56
Clarke St. LS28: Cal 5D 16
Clark Gro. LS9: Leeds 1B 42
Clark La. LS9: Leeds 6B 32
(not continuous)
Clark Mt. LS9: Leeds 6B 32
Clark Rd. LS9: Leeds 6B 32
Clark Row LS9: Leeds 1B 42
Clarkson Ter. LS27: Chur 1A 50
Clarkson Vw. LS6: Leeds 1E 31
Clark Spring Cl. LS27: Morl 2G 49
Clark Spring Ct. LS27: Morl 2H 49
Clark Spring Ri. LS27: Morl 2H 49
Clark Ter. LS9: Leeds 6B 32
Clark Vw. LS9: Leeds 1B 42
Clay Pit La. LS2: Leeds 2E 5 (4G 31)
LS7: Leeds 1F 5 (4G 31)
Clayton Bus. Cen. LS10: Leeds 4A 42
Clayton Cl. LS10: Leeds 5B 42
Clayton Ct. LS10: Leeds 5B 42
LS16: Leeds 3F 19
Clayton Dr. LS10: Leeds 5B 42
Clayton Grange LS16: Leeds 3F 19
Clayton Gro. LS19: Yead 2D 8
Clayton Ri. WF1: Out 6D 58
Clayton Rd. LS10: Leeds 5B 42
Claytons Cl. LS26: Meth 6H 55
Clayton St. LS26: Rothw 4H 53
Clayton Way LS10: Leeds 5B 42
Clayton Wood Bank LS16: Leeds 2F 19
Clayton Wood Cl. LS16: Leeds 2F 19
Clayton Wood Ct. LS16: Leeds 2F 19
Clayton Wood Ri. LS16: Leeds 2F 19
Clayton Wood Rd. LS16: Leeds 2E 19
Clearings, The LS10: Leeds 1H 51
Cleasby Rd. LS29: Men 2C 6
Cleeve Hill LS19: Raw 5D 8
Clement Ter. LS26: Rothw 5G 53
Cleveleys Av. LS11: Leeds 3D 40
Cleveleys Ct. *LS11: Leeds 3D 40*
(off Cleveleys Av.)
Cleveleys Mt. LS11: Leeds 3D 40
Cleveleys Rd. LS11: Leeds 3D 40
Cleveleys St. *LS11: Leeds 3D 40*
(off Cleveleys Rd.)
Cleveleys Ter. LS11: Leeds 3D 40
Cliff Ct. LS6: Leeds 1E 31
Cliffdale Rd. LS7: Leeds 1F 31
Cliffdale Rd. Light Ind. Est.
LS7: Leeds 1F 31
Cliffe Ct. *LS19: Yead 2E 9*
(off Harper La.)
Cliffe Dr. LS19: Raw 6C 8
Cliffe La. LS19: Raw 1E 17
Cliffe Pk. Chase LS12: Leeds 1G 39
Cliffe Pk. Cl. LS12: Leeds 1G 39
Cliffe Pk. Cres. LS12: Leeds 1G 39
Cliffe Pk. Dr. LS12: Leeds 1G 39
Cliffe Pk. Mt. LS12: Leeds 1G 39
Cliffe Pk. Ri. LS12: Leeds 1G 39
Cliffe Pk. Way LS27: Morl 6D 48
Cliffe Ter. WF3: Rob H 6C 52
Cliffe Vw. LS27: Morl 6D 48
Cliffe Wood Dr. LS19: Raw 1C 16
Cliff Hollins La. BD4: E Bier 3A 46
Cliff La. LS6: Leeds 1D 30
Cliff Mt. LS6: Leeds 1E 31
Cliff Mt. Ter. LS6: Leeds 1E 31
Clifford Dr. LS29: Men 2D 6
Clifford Pl. LS27: Chur 2H 49
Cliff Rd. LS6: Leeds 1E 31
Cliff Rd. Gdns. LS6: Leeds 1E 31
Cliff Side Gdns. LS6: Leeds 1E 31
Cliff Ter. LS6: Leeds 1E 31
Clifton Av. LS9: Leeds 4C 32
WF3: S'ley 6G 59
Clifton Ct. *LS28: Pud 5G 27*
(off Clifton Rd.)
Clifton Dr. LS28: Pud 5G 27
Clifton Gro. LS9: Leeds 4C 32
Clifton Hill LS28: Pud 5G 27
Clifton M. LS28: Pud 5G 27
Clifton Mt. LS9: Leeds 4C 32
Clifton Pl. LS28: Pud 5H 27
Clifton Rd. LS28: Pud 5G 27
Clifton Ter. LS9: Leeds 4C 32
Climax Works LS11: Leeds 5G 41
Clipston Av. LS6: Leeds 5D 20
Clipstone Mt. LS6: Leeds 5D 20
Clipstone Ter. LS6: Leeds 5D 20
Clipston St. LS6: Leeds 5D 20
Clive Mt. Ho. *LS5: Leeds 2F 29*
(off Broad La.)
Cloberry St. LS2: Leeds 1A 4 (3E 31)
Clock Bldgs. LS8: Leeds 1C 32
Close, The LS9: Leeds 6A 32
LS17: Leeds 4E 13
LS20: Guis 5E 7
WF3: E Ard 4H 57
Cloth Hall St. LS1: Leeds 5F 5 (6G 31)
Clough St. LS27: Morl 5H 49
Clovelly Av. LS11: Leeds 4F 41
Clovelly Gro. LS11: Leeds 4F 41
Clovelly Pl. LS11: Leeds 4F 41
Clovelly Row LS11: Leeds 4F 41
Clovelly Ter. LS11: Leeds 4F 41
Clover Ct. LS28: Cal 5C 16
Clover Cres. LS28: Cal 4C 16
Club La. LS13: Leeds 6G 17
Club Row LS7: Leeds 4G 21
LS19: Yead 2E 9
Clumpcliffe LS26: Meth 6D 54
Clyde App. LS12: Leeds 1C 40
Clyde Chase *LS12: Leeds 1C 40*
(off Clyde App.)
Clyde Ct. *LS12: Leeds 1C 40*
(off Copley St.)
Clyde Gdns. LS12: Leeds 1C 40
Clyde Grange *LS12: Leeds 1C 40*
(off Clyde Vw.)
Clyde Vw. LS12: Leeds 1C 40
Clyde Wlk. LS12: Leeds 1C 40
Coach Rd. LS12: N Far 4E 39
LS20: Guis 6F 7
LS26: Swil 1F 55
WF1: Out 6E 59
Coal Hill Dr. LS13: Leeds 1H 27
Coal Hill Fold LS13: Leeds 1H 27
Coal Hill Gdns. LS13: Leeds 1H 27
Coal Hill Ga. *LS13: Leeds 1H 27*
(off Coal Hill Dr.)
Coal Hill Grn. LS13: Leeds 1H 27
Coal Hill La. LS13: Leeds 1G 27
LS28: Fars 1G 27
Coal Rd. LS14: Leeds 1A 24
LS17: Wike 1F 15
Cobden Av. LS12: Leeds 3F 39
Cobden Gro. LS12: Leeds 3F 39
Cobden M. LS27: Morl 4G 49
Cobden Pl. LS12: Leeds 3F 39
Cobden Rd. LS12: Leeds 3F 39
Cobden St. LS12: Leeds 3F 39
LS27: Morl 4G 49
Cobden Ter. LS12: Leeds 3F 39
Cobham Wlk. LS15: Leeds 3F 35
Cockburn Cl. LS11: Leeds 4G 41
Cockburn Way LS11: Leeds 4G 41
Cockcroft Ho. *LS6: Leeds 2B 30*
(off Chapel La.)
COCKERSDALE 1A 48
Cockshott Cl. LS12: Leeds 4F 29
Cockshott Dr. LS12: Leeds 4F 29
Cockshott Hill LS28: Fars 2F 27
Cockshott La. LS12: Leeds 4F 29
(not continuous)
Colby Ri. LS15: Leeds 6G 33
Coldcotes Av. LS9: Leeds 3D 32
Coldcotes Cir. LS9: Leeds 3E 33
Coldcotes Cl. LS9: Leeds 3E 33
Coldcotes Cres. LS9: Leeds 3F 33
Coldcotes Dr. LS9: Leeds 3E 33
Coldcotes Gth. LS9: Leeds 3F 33
Coldcotes Gro. LS9: Leeds 3F 33
Coldcotes Vw. LS9: Leeds 3F 33
Coldcotes Wlk. LS9: Leeds 3F 33
Coldwell Rd. LS15: Leeds 4B 34
Coldwell Sq. LS15: Leeds 4B 34
Coleman St. LS12: Leeds 1D 40
Colenso Gdns. LS11: Leeds 3D 40
Colenso Gro. LS11: Leeds 3D 40
Colenso Mt. LS11: Leeds 3D 40
Colenso Pl. LS11: Leeds 3D 40
Colenso Rd. LS11: Leeds 3D 40
Colenso Ter. LS11: Leeds 3D 40
Coleridge Cl. LS26: Oul 6C 54
Coleridge La. LS28: Pud 2H 37
College Ct. LS27: Gil 3D 48
College Lawns LS12: Leeds 5F 29
College Rd. LS27: Gil 3D 48
College Vw. LS12: Leeds 6F 29
Colley Gdns. WF3: S'ley 5H 59
Colliers La. LS17: Shad 5G 15
Colliery App. WF3: Loft 5D 58
Collindale Cl. BD10: B'frd 5A 16
Collin Rd. LS14: Leeds 4H 33
Colmore Gro. LS12: Leeds 2B 40
Colmore Rd. LS12: Leeds 2B 40
Colmore St. LS12: Leeds 1B 40
COLTON 1D 44
Colton Ct. LS15: Leeds 6D 34
Colton Cft. LS15: Leeds 6D 34
Colton Gth. LS15: Leeds 6D 34
Colton La. LS15: Leeds 6D 34
Colton Lodges LS15: Leeds 6E 35
Colton Mill LS15: Leeds 6F 35
Colton Retail Pk. LS15: Leeds 6E 35
Colton Rd. LS12: Leeds 6A 30
LS15: Leeds 6C 34
Colton Rd. E. LS15: Leeds 1E 45
(not continuous)
Colton St. LS12: Leeds 6A 30

72 A-Z Leeds

Colville Ter. LS11: Leeds 3F 41
  WF3: Thpe H 2A 58
Colwyn Av. LS11: Leeds 5F 41
Colwyn Mt. LS11: Leeds 5F 41
Colwyn Pl. LS11: Leeds 5F 41
Colwyn Rd. LS11: Leeds 5F 41
Colwyn Ter. LS11: Leeds 5F 41
Colwyn Vw. LS11: Leeds 5F 41
Commerce Ct. BD4: B'frd 3A 36
Commercial Rd. LS5: Leeds 1G 29
Commercial St. LS1: Leeds 4E 5 (5G 31)
  LS26: Rothw 4G 53
  LS27: Morl 5G 49
Commercial Vs. LS28: Pud 1F 37
Commercial Way LS28: Pud 5H 27
Common La. WF3: E Ard 3F 57
Common Rd. WF3: S'ley 4H 59
Compton Av. LS9: Leeds 3C 32
Compton Cres. LS9: Leeds 3C 32
Compton Pl. LS9: Leeds 3C 32
Compton Rd. LS9: Leeds 3C 32
Compton Row LS9: Leeds 3C 32
Compton Ter. LS9: Leeds 3C 32
Compton Vw. LS9: Leeds 3C 32
Concept LS7: Leeds .4G 21
Concept Pl. LS3: Leeds 4D 30
Concordia St. LS1: Leeds 6E 5 (6G 31)
Concord St. LS2: Leeds 2G 5 (4H 31)
Concourse Ho. LS11: Leeds 1D 50
         (off Dewsbury Rd.)
Coney Warren La. WF3: S'ley 3G 59
Conference Pl. LS12: Leeds 6G 29
Conference Rd. LS12: Leeds 6G 29
Conference Ter. LS12: Leeds 6G 29
Congress Mt. LS12: Leeds 6G 29
Congress St. LS12: Leeds 6G 29
Coniston Av. LS6: Leeds 6C 20
Coniston Ct. WF3: Loft 5D 58
Coniston Gdns. LS15: Leeds 1G 43
Coniston Rd. LS26: Wood 2C 54
Coniston Way LS26: Wood 3C 54
Consort St. LS3: Leeds 2A 4 (4D 30)
Consort Ter. LS3: Leeds 4D 30
Consort Vw. LS3: Leeds 4D 30
Consort Wlk. LS3: Leeds 4D 30
         (not continuous)
Constable Gro. WF3: S'ley 5G 59
Constable Rd. WF3: Ting 3C 56
Constance Gdns. LS7: Leeds 3F 31
Constance Way LS7: Leeds 3F 31
Conway Av. LS8: Leeds 2B 32
Conway Dr. LS8: Leeds 2B 32
Conway Gro. LS8: Leeds 2B 32
Conway Mt. LS8: Leeds 2B 32
Conway Pl. LS8: Leeds 2B 32
Conway Rd. LS8: Leeds 2B 32
Conway St. LS8: Leeds 2B 32
  LS28: Stan 4F 27
Conway Ter. LS8: Leeds 2B 32
Conway Vw. LS8: Leeds 2B 32
COOKRIDGE 4D 10
Cookridge Av. LS16: Leeds 3E 11
Cookridge Dr. LS16: Leeds 3D 10
Cookridge Gro. LS16: Leeds 3E 11
Cookridge La. LS16: Leeds 1D 10
Cookridge St. LS1: Leeds 3D 4 (5F 31)
  LS2: Leeds 2D 4 (5F 31)
         (not continuous)
Co-operation St. LS12: Leeds 3G 39
Co-operative St. LS27: Chur 1A 50
  LS27: Morl 4G 49
  WF3: Loft 2E 59
Cooper Hill LS28: Pud 2H 37
Copeland St. BD4: B'frd 2A 36
Copgrove Cl. BD4: B'frd 4A 36
Copgrove Ct. BD4: B'frd 4A 36
Copgrove Rd. BD4: B'frd 4A 36
  LS8: Leeds 1C 32
Copley Hill LS12: Leeds 1C 40
Copley Hill Trad. Est. LS12: Leeds 2C 40
Copley Hill Way LS12: Leeds 2C 40
Copley La. WF3: Rob H 5D 52
Copley St. LS12: Leeds 1C 40
Copley Yd. LS12: Leeds 1C 40
Copperfield Av. LS9: Leeds 1B 42
Copperfield Cres. LS9: Leeds 1B 42
Copperfield Dr. LS9: Leeds 1B 42
Copperfield Gro. LS9: Leeds 1B 42
Copperfield Mt. LS9: Leeds 1C 42
Copperfield Pl. LS9: Leeds 1B 42
Copperfield Row LS9: Leeds 1B 42
Copperfield Ter. LS9: Leeds 1B 42
Copperfield Vw. LS9: Leeds 1B 42
Copperfield Wlk. LS9: Leeds 1B 42
Coppice, The LS19: Yead 4B 8
Coppice Grange LS19: Yead 1D 8
Coppice Head LS26: Rothw 4H 53

Coppice Way LS8: Leeds 5C 22
Coppice Wood Av. LS19: Yead 1C 8
  LS20: Guis, Yead .1C 8
Coppice Wood Cl. LS20: Guis 4H 7
Coppice Wood Cres. LS19: Yead 1C 8
Coppice Wood Gro. LS20: Guis 1C 8
Coppice Wood Ri. LS19: Yead 1D 8
Copplestone Wlk. BD4: B'frd 5A 36
Coppy La. LS13: Leeds 1C 28
Copt Royd Gro. LS19: Yead 2C 8
Cordingley Cl. BD4: B'frd 6A 36
Cordingley St. BD4: B'frd 6A 36
Core Shop. Cen., The LS1: Leeds 4E 5 (5G 31)
Corner Ho. Shops LS17: Leeds 1H 21
Corn Mill LS29: Men .1D 6
Corn Mill Ct. LS13: Leeds 5D 28
Cornmill Vw. LS18: H'fth 3E 19
Cornstone Fold LS12: Leeds 6C 28
Cornus Gdns. LS10: Leeds 1H 51
Cornwall Cl. LS26: Rothw 3F 53
Cornwall Cres. LS26: Rothw 3F 53
Coronation Av. BD17: Esh 6A 8
Coronation Pde. LS15: Leeds 1G 43
Coronation St. WF3: Carl 6F 53
Corporation St. LS27: Morl 4F 49
Cote, The LS28: Fars .3E 27
Cotefields Av. LS28: Fars 2E 27
Cote La. LS28: Fars 3E 27
Coteroyd Av. LS27: Chur 1A 50
Coteroyd Dr. LS27: Chur 2A 50
Cotswold Dr. LS26: Rothw 3F 53
Cotswold Rd. LS26: Rothw 3G 53
Cottage Rd. BD10: B'frd 4A 16
  LS6: Leeds 5B 20
Cottage Road Cinema 5B 20
Cotterdale Vw. LS15: Leeds 1G 43
COTTINGLEY 6B 40
Cottingley App. LS11: Leeds 6B 40
Cottingley Chase LS11: Leeds 6A 40
Cottingley Ct. LS11: Leeds 6B 40
Cottingley Cres. LS11: Leeds 6B 40
Cottingley Dr. LS11: Leeds 5A 40
Cottingley Fold LS11: Leeds 5A 40
Cottingley Gdns. LS11: Leeds 6B 40
Cottingley Grn. LS11: Leeds 6B 40
Cottingley Gro. LS11: Leeds 6B 40
Cottingley Hall Crematorium LS11: Leeds 6B 40
Cottingley Hgts. LS11: Leeds 6B 40
Cottingley Rd. LS11: Leeds 5A 40
Cottingley Springs Cvn. Site LS27: Gil 6G 39
Cottingley Station (Rail) 6A 40
Cottingley Towers LS11: Leeds 6B 40
Cottingley Va. LS11: Leeds 6B 40
Cotton St. LS9: Leeds 5H 5 (6A 32)
Coultas Cl. LS29: Men 1D 6
County Arc. LS1: Leeds 4F 5 (5G 31)
Coupland Pl. LS11: Leeds 3F 41
Coupland Rd. LS11: Leeds 3F 41
Coupland St. LS11: Leeds 4F 41
Court, The LS17: Leeds 4D 12
Courtenay Cl. BD3: B'frd 6A 26
Courtenays LS14: Leeds 1B 34
Courtyard, The LS10: Leeds 3H 41
  LS12: Leeds 4F 29
Courtyards, The LS14: Leeds 4B 24
Coverdale Cl. LS12: Leeds 3F 29
Coverley Gth. LS19: Yead 6H 7
Coverley Ri. LS19: Yead 6H 7
Cow Cl. Gro. LS12: Leeds 3G 39
Cow Cl. Rd. LS12: Leeds 3F 39
Cowper Av. LS9: Leeds 6H 17
Cowper Cres. LS9: Leeds 3C 32
Cowper Gro. LS8: Leeds 2C 32
Cowper Mt. LS9: Leeds 3C 32
Cowper Rd. LS9: Leeds 3C 32
Cowper St. LS7: Leeds 1H 31
Cowper Ter. LS9: Leeds 3C 32
Crab La. LS12: Leeds .5A 30
Crabtree Way WF3: W Ard 3D 56
Cragg Av. LS18: H'fth .3B 18
Cragg Hill LS18: H'fth 3C 18
Cragg Rd. LS18: H'fth 3C 18
Cragg Ter. LS18: H'fth 3B 18
         (not continuous)
  LS19: Raw 1D 16
Craggwell Ter. LS18: H'fth 4C 18
         (off Wood La.)
Craggwood Cl. LS18: H'fth 4C 18
Craggwood Rd. LS18: H'fth 4C 18
Craggwood Ter. LS18: H'fth 4C 18
         (off Craggwood Rd.)
Crag Hill Av. LS16: Leeds 2E 11
Crag Hill Vw. LS16: Leeds 3E 11
Crag La. LS17: Leeds .4C 12
Cragside Cl. LS5: Leeds 4E 19

Cragside Cres. LS5: Leeds 4E 19
Cragside Gdns. LS5: Leeds 4E 19
Cragside Gro. LS5: Leeds 5D 18
Cragside Mt. LS5: Leeds 4E 19
Cragside Pl. LS5: Leeds 4E 19
Cragside Wlk. LS5: Leeds 5D 18
Craigmore Ct. BD4: B'frd 5B 36
Cranbrook Av. LS11: Leeds 4E 41
Cranbrook Vw. LS28: Pud 2A 38
Cranewells Dr. LS15: Leeds 1D 44
Cranewells Grn. LS15: Leeds 1C 44
Cranewells Ri. LS15: Leeds 1C 44
Cranewells Va. LS15: Leeds 1C 44
Cranewells Vw. LS15: Leeds 6C 34
Cranmer Bank LS17: Leeds 6E 13
Cranmer Cl. LS17: Leeds 6E 13
Cranmer Gdns. LS17: Leeds 6E 13
Cranmer Ri. LS17: Leeds 5E 13
Cranmer Rd. LS17: Leeds 6E 13
         (not continuous)
Cranmore Cres. LS10: Leeds 4B 52
Cranmore Dr. LS10: Leeds 4B 52
Cranmore Gdns. LS10: Leeds 4A 52
Cranmore Gth. LS10: Leeds 4A 52
Cranmore Grn. LS10: Leeds 4A 52
Cranmore Gro. LS10: Leeds 4A 52
Cranmore La. LS10: Leeds 4B 52
Cranmore Ri. LS10: Leeds 4B 52
Cranmore Rd. LS10: Leeds 4A 52
Craven Ct. LS11: Leeds 6C 40
Craven Pk. LS29: Men 1B 6
Craven Rd. LS6: Leeds 2F 31
Crawshaw Av. LS28: Pud 6H 27
Crawshaw Cl. LS28: Pud 6G 27
Crawshaw Gdns. LS28: Pud 6H 27
Crawshaw Hill LS28: Pud 6G 27
Crawshaw Pk. LS28: Pud 6G 27
Crawshaw Ri. LS28: Pud 1G 37
Crawshaw Rd. LS28: Pud 6G 27
Crescent, The BD11: Birk 2C 46
  LS6: Leeds 2E 31
       (off Woodhouse La.)
  LS13: Leeds 2C 28
  LS15: Leeds 5B 34
  LS16: Leeds 5G 11
  LS17: Leeds 3D 12
  LS18: H'fth 2H 17
  LS20: Guis 5E 7
  LS28: Pud 5H 27
  LS29: Men 1D 6
  WF3: Ting 3E 57
Crescent Av. LS26: Rothw 2H 53
Crescent Bungs. WF3: Thpe H 1H 57
Crescent Ct. LS17: Leeds 3D 12
Crescent Gdns. LS17: Leeds 5H 13
Crescent Grange LS11: Leeds 3G 41
Crescent Towers LS11: Leeds 3G 41
Crescent Vw. LS17: Leeds 3D 12
Crest, The LS26: Swil .6G 45
Cricketers, The LS5: Leeds 1H 29
Cricketers Fold LS17: Shad 5G 15
Cricketers Ter. LS12: Leeds 6A 30
Cricketers Vw. LS17: Shad 5G 15
Cricketers Wlk. LS15: Leeds 6E 35
Cricklegate LS15: Leeds 5B 34
CRIMBLES 6H 27
Crimbles Ct. LS28: Pud 6H 27
Crimbles Pl. LS28: Pud 6H 27
Crimbles Rd. LS28: Pud 6H 27
Crimbles Ter. LS28: Pud 6H 27
Cripple Syke LS18: H'fth 1C 18
Croft, The BD11: Drig .4G 47
  LS15: Leeds 4B 34
  LS26: Oul 4C 54
  WF3: W Ard 6B 56
Croft Av. LS28: Fars 2F 27
  WF3: E Ard 4H 57
Croft Bank BD11: Birk 4C 46
Croft Bri. LS26: Oul 4C 54
Croft Cl. LS29: Men 1B 6
Croft Cotts. LS12: N Far 4E 39
Croft Ct. LS18: H'fth .2C 18
  LS29: Men 1C 6
Croftdale Gro. LS15: Leeds 3D 34
Croft Dr. LS29: Men 1C 6
Crofters Lea LS19: Yead 3B 8
Croft Head LS20: Guis 4G 7
Croft Ho. Av. LS27: Morl 4H 49
Croft Ho. Cl. LS27: Morl 3H 49
Croft Ho. Ct. LS28: Pud 5G 27
Croft Ho. Dr. LS27: Morl 4H 49
Croft Ho. Gdns. LS27: Morl 4H 49
Croft Ho. Gro. LS27: Morl 4H 49
Croft Ho. La. LS27: Morl 4H 49
Croft Ho. M. LS27: Morl 4H 49
Croft Ho. Mt. LS27: Morl 3H 49

Croft Ho. Ri.—Dean Head

Croft Ho. Ri. LS27: Morl 3H **49**
Croft Ho. Rd. LS27: Morl 4H **49**
Croft Ho. Vw. LS27: Morl 4H **49**
Croft Ho. Wlk. LS27: Morl 3H **49**
Croft Ho. Way LS27: Morl 3H **49**
Crofton Ri. LS17: Shad 5H **15**
Crofton Ter. LS17: Shad 5H **15**
Croft Pk. LS29: Men 1B **6**
Croft Ri. LS29: Men 1C **6**
Croft's Ct. LS1: Leeds 4D **4** (5F **31**)
Croftside Cl. LS14: Leeds 2B **34**
Croft St. BD11: Birk 4C **46**
(not continuous)
LS28: Fars 2F **27**
Croft Ter. LS12: N Far 4E **39**
Croft Way LS29: Men 1C **6**
Cromack Vw. LS28: Pud 6E **27**
Cromer Pl. LS2: Leeds 3E **31**
(not continuous)
Cromer Rd. LS2: Leeds 1A **4** (3E **31**)
Cromer St. LS2: Leeds 1A **4** (3E **31**)
Cromer Ter. LS2: Leeds 1A **4** (4E **31**)
Crompton Dr. LS27: Morl 3F **49**
Cromwell Ct. BD11: Drig 4F **47**
Cromwell Hgts. *LS9: Leeds 4A **32***
(off Thealby Lawn)
Cromwell M. LS9: Leeds 4A **32**
Cromwell Mt. LS9: Leeds 4A **32**
LS10: Leeds 1H **51**
Cromwell St. LS9: Leeds 3H **5** (5A **32**)
Crooklands *LS20: Guis 4G **7***
(off Kelcliffe La.)
Cropper Ga. LS1: Leeds 4A **4** (5E **31**)
Crosby Av. LS11: Leeds 3D **40**
Crosby Pl. LS11: Leeds 2E **41**
Crosby Rd. LS11: Leeds 3D **40**
Crosby St. LS11: Leeds 2D **40**
Crosby Ter. LS11: Leeds 2E **41**
Crosby Vw. LS11: Leeds 2E **41**
Cross Albert Pl. LS12: Leeds 1B **40**
Cross Arc. LS1: Leeds 4F **5**
Cross Aston Gro. LS13: Leeds 3E **29**
Cross Av. LS26: Rothw 2H **53**
Cross Aysgarth Mt. LS9: Leeds 5B **32**
Cross Banstead St. LS8: Leeds 2B **32**
Cross Bath Rd. LS13: Leeds 3C **28**
Cross Belgrave St. LS2: Leeds 3F **5** (5G **31**)
Cross Bellbrooke Av. *LS9: Leeds 3D **32***
(off Bellbrooke Av.)
Cross Bell St. LS9: Leeds 3H **5**
Cross Bentley La. LS6: Leeds 5D **20**
Cross Burley Lodge Rd. *LS6: Leeds 3C **30***
(off Broadway Av.)
Cross Cardigan Ter. LS4: Leeds 4A **30**
Cross Catherine St. LS9: Leeds 6A **32**
Cross Chancellor St. LS6: Leeds 2F **31**
Cross Chapel St. LS6: Leeds 6B **20**
Cross Chestnut Gro. *LS6: Leeds 2C **30***
(off Chestnut Gro.)
Cross Cliff Rd. LS6: Leeds 1D **30**
Cross Conway Mt. LS8: Leeds 2B **32**
Cross Cowper St. LS7: Leeds 2H **31**
Cross Dawlish Gro. LS9: Leeds 5D **32**
Cross Easy Rd. LS9: Leeds 1B **42**
Cross Elford St. *LS8: Leeds 2B **32***
(off Elford Gro.)
Crossfield St. LS2: Leeds 2E **31**
Cross Flatts Av. LS11: Leeds 5E **41**
Cross Flatts Cres. LS11: Leeds 5D **40**
Cross Flatts Dr. LS11: Leeds 4D **40**
Cross Flatts Gro. LS11: Leeds 5D **40**
Cross Flatts Mt. LS11: Leeds 5E **41**
Cross Flatts Pde. LS11: Leeds 5D **40**
Cross Flatts Pl. LS11: Leeds 5D **40**
Cross Flatts Rd. LS11: Leeds 5D **40**
Cross Flatts Row LS11: Leeds 5D **40**
Cross Flatts St. LS11: Leeds 5D **40**
Cross Flatts Ter. LS11: Leeds 5D **40**
Cross Francis St. LS7: Leeds 2H **31**
CROSS GATES **3C 34**
Cross Gates Av. LS15: Leeds 2C **34**
Cross Gates La. LS15: Leeds 2B **34**
Cross Gates Rd. LS15: Leeds 3A **34**
(not continuous)
Crossgates Shop. Cen. LS15: Leeds 3C **34**
Cross Gates Station (Rail) **4C 34**
Cross Glen Rd. LS16: Leeds 4A **20**
Cross Granby Ter. LS6: Leeds 6B **20**
Cross Grange Av. LS7: Leeds 2A **32**
Cross Grasmere St. LS12: Leeds 6B **30**
CROSS GREEN **2C 42**
Cross Grn. BD4: B'frd 3A **36**
Cross Grn. App. LS9: Leeds 2C **42**
Cross Grn. Av. LS9: Leeds 1B **42**
Cross Grn. Cl. LS9: Leeds 2C **42**
Cross Grn. Ct. LS9: Leeds 2D **42**
Cross Grn. Cres. LS9: Leeds 1B **42**
Cross Grn. Dr. LS9: Leeds 2C **42**
Cross Grn. Gth. LS9: Leeds 2C **42**
Cross Grn. Gro. LS9: Leeds 1B **42**
Cross Grn. Ind. Est. LS9: Leeds 2D **42**
Cross Grn. Ind. Pk. LS9: Leeds 1E **43**
Cross Grn. La. LS9: Leeds 1A **42**
LS15: Leeds 5A **34**
Cross Grn. Ri. LS9: Leeds 2C **42**
Cross Grn. Rd. LS9: Leeds 1B **42**
Cross Grn. Row LS6: Leeds 4C **20**
Cross Grn. Va. LS9: Leeds 3C **42**
Cross Grn. Way LS9: Leeds 2C **42**
Cross Greenwood Mt.
LS6: Leeds 4C **20**
Cross Hartley Av. *LS6: Leeds 1E **31***
(off Lucas Pl.)
Cross Heath Gro. LS11: Leeds 4C **40**
Cross Henley Rd. LS13: Leeds 3C **28**
Cross Hill LS11: Leeds 6C **40**
Cross Hilton Gro. LS8: Leeds 6B **22**
Cross Ingledew Cres. LS8: Leeds 1D **22**
Cross Ingram Rd. LS11: Leeds 2D **40**
Cross Kelso Rd. LS2: Leeds 1A **4** (4D **30**)
Crossland Ct. LS11: Leeds 1E **41**
Crossland Rd. LS27: Chur 2H **49**
Crossland Ter. LS11: Leeds 4G **41**
Cross La. BD11: Birk 2D **46**
LS12: Leeds 6H **29**
(Privilege St.)
LS12: Leeds 2E **39**
(Stonebridge La.)
LS20: Guis 1H **7**
Cross Lea Farm Rd. LS5: Leeds 4F **19**
Cross Lidgett Pl. LS8: Leeds 3B **22**
Cross Louis St. LS7: Leeds 2H **31**
Cross Maude St. LS2: Leeds 5G **5**
Cross Mitford Rd. LS12: Leeds 6B **30**
Cross Osmondthorpe La.
LS9: Leeds 5E **33**
Cross Pk. St. LS15: Leeds 5A **34**
Cross Peel St. LS27: Morl 5H **49**
Cross Quarry St. LS6: Leeds 1E **31**
Cross Regent Pk. Av. *LS6: Leeds 1D **30***
(off Regent Pk. Av.)
Cross Reginald Mt. LS7: Leeds 1H **31**
Cross Rd. LS18: H'fth 3A **18**
Cross Roseville Rd. *LS8: Leeds 2A **32***
(off Bayswater Rd.)
Cross Roundhay Av. LS8: Leeds 6B **22**
Cross Row LS15: Swil C 1G **45**
Cross St Michaels La. LS6: Leeds 1B **30**
Cross Speedwell St. LS6: Leeds 2F **31**
Cross Stamford St. LS7: Leeds 1H **5** (4H **31**)
Cross St. LS15: Leeds 5A **34**
LS26: Rothw 4G **53**
WF3: E Ard 3A **58**
Cross Ter. LS26: Rothw 4G **53**
Cross Valley Dr. LS15: Leeds 4B **34**
Cross Westfield Rd. *LS3: Leeds 4D **30***
(off Westfield Rd.)
Cross Wingham St. LS7: Leeds 3H **31**
Cross Woodstock St. *LS2: Leeds 3F **31***
(off Blenheim Wlk.)
Cross Woodview St. *LS11: Leeds 5F **41***
(off Woodview St.)
Cross York St. LS2: Leeds 5G **5** (6H **31**)
Crown Court
Leeds **3C 4 (5F 31)**
Crown Ct. LS2: Leeds 5F **5** (6G **31**)
Crow Nest Dr. LS11: Leeds 5C **40**
Crow Nest La. LS11: Leeds 5B **40**
Crow Nest M. LS11: Leeds 5C **40**
CROWN POINT **6G 5 (6H 31)**
Crown Point Retail Pk.
LS10: Leeds 1G **41**
Crown Point Rd.
LS2: Leeds 6G **5** (1G **41**)
LS9: Leeds 6H **5** (1G **41**)
LS10: Leeds 6G **5** (1G **41**)
Crown St. LS2: Leeds 5F **5** (6G **31**)
Crown St. Bldg. LS2: Leeds 5F **5**
Crowther Av. LS28: Cal 5B **16**
Crowther Pl. LS6: Leeds 2F **31**
Crowther St. BD10: B'frd 4A **16**
Crowthers Yd. LS28: Pud 1G **37**
Crowtrees Ct. LS19: Raw 5E **9**
Crow Trees Pk. LS19: Raw 5D **8**
Croxall Dr. WF3: S'ley 6G **59**
Croydon St. LS11: Leeds 1D **40**
Crozier Ho. LS10: Leeds 1H **41**
Cudbear St. LS10: Leeds 1H **41**
Cumberland Ct. LS6: Leeds 2B **30**
Cumberland Rd. LS6: Leeds 1D **30**
Cunningham Ct. WF3: Rob H 5C **52**
Curlew Ri. LS27: Morl 6B **50**
Cutler Hgts. La. BD4: B'frd 3A **36**
Cutler Pl. BD4: B'frd 3A **36**
Cypress Point LS7: Leeds 1G **5**
Czar St. LS11: Leeds 1E **41**

D

Daby Ct. WF3: Rob H 5C **52**
Daffil Av. LS27: Chur 2H **49**
Daffil Grange M. LS27: Morl 2H **49**
Daffil Grange Way LS27: Morl 2H **49**
Daffil Gro. LS27: Chur 2H **49**
Daffil Rd. LS27: Chur 2H **49**
Daisyfield Grange *LS13: Leeds 4D **28***
(off Rossefield App.)
Daisyfield Rd. LS13: Leeds 3D **28**
DAISY HILL **4A 50**
Daisy Hill LS27: Morl 4A **50**
Daisy Hill Av. LS27: Morl 3A **50**
Daisy Hill Cl. LS27: Morl 3H **49**
Daisy La. WF3: E Ard 3B **58**
Daisy Row LS13: Leeds 4D **28**
Daisy Va. M. WF3: Thpe H 2A **58**
Daisy Va. Ter. WF3: Thpe H 2A **58**
Dalby Way LS10: Leeds 5A **52**
Dale Cl. LS20: Guis 5D **6**
Dale Pk. Av. LS16: Leeds 5D **10**
Dale Pk. Cl. LS16: Leeds 5D **10**
Dale Pk. Gdns. LS16: Leeds 5D **10**
Dale Pk. Ri. LS16: Leeds 5D **10**
Dale Pk. Vw. LS16: Leeds 5D **10**
Dale Pk. Wlk. LS16: Leeds 5D **10**
Dale Rd. BD11: Drig 6A **38**
Dales Dr. LS20: Guis 5D **6**
Daleside Av. LS28: Pud 5C **26**
Daleside Cl. LS28: Pud 4B **26**
Daleside Gro. LS28: Pud 5C **26**
Daleside Rd. LS28: Pud 4B **26**
Dales Way LS20: Guis 5D **6**
Dale Vw. BD11: Drig 3H **47**
Dale Vs. LS18: H'fth 4D **18**
Dalton Av. LS11: Leeds 5E **41**
Dalton Gro. LS11: Leeds 5E **41**
Dalton Rd. LS11: Leeds 5E **41**
Dam La. LS19: Yead 2E **9**
Damon Av. BD10: B'frd 1A **26**
Danby Wlk. LS9: Leeds 6B **32**
Danecourt Rd. BD4: B'frd 4A **36**
Dane Hill Dr. BD4: B'frd 3A **36**
Daniel Ct. BD4: B'frd 5B **36**
Darcy Ct. LS15: Leeds 5C **34**
Darfield Av. LS8: Leeds 2C **32**
Darfield Cres. LS8: Leeds 2C **32**
Darfield Gro. LS8: Leeds 2B **32**
Darfield Pl. LS8: Leeds 2C **32**
Darfield Rd. LS8: Leeds 2C **32**
Darfield St. LS8: Leeds 2C **32**
Darfield Vs. *LS8: Leeds 3C **32***
(off Darfield Cres.)
Dark La. WF17: Birs 6H **47**
Darkwood Cl. LS17: Leeds 5C **14**
Darkwood Way LS17: Leeds 5C **14**
Darley Av. LS10: Leeds 2H **51**
Darnley La. LS15: Leeds 1C **44**
Darnley Rd. LS16: Leeds 4H **19**
Darren St. BD4: B'frd 1A **36**
Dartmouth Av. LS27: Morl 6G **49**
Dartmouth M. LS27: Morl 6F **49**
Dartmouth Way LS11: Leeds 5G **41**
David Lloyd Leisure
Leeds **1F 21**
David St. LS11: Leeds 1F **41**
Davies Av. LS8: Leeds 3B **22**
Dawlish Av. LS9: Leeds 5D **32**
Dawlish Cres. LS9: Leeds 5D **32**
Dawlish Gro. LS9: Leeds 6D **32**
Dawlish Mt. LS9: Leeds 5D **32**
Dawlish Pl. LS9: Leeds 5D **32**
Dawlish Rd. LS9: Leeds 5D **32**
Dawlish Row LS9: Leeds 5D **32**
Dawlish St. LS9: Leeds 5D **32**
Dawlish Ter. LS9: Leeds 5D **32**
Dawlish Wlk. LS9: Leeds 5D **32**
Dawson Hill LS27: Morl 4G **49**
Dawson La. BD4: B'frd 5G **37**
LS26: Rothw 3G **53**
Dawson Rd. LS11: Leeds 4E **41**
Dawsons Cnr. LS28: Stan 3E **27**
Dawsons Ct. LS14: Leeds 1B **34**
Dawsons Mdw. LS28: Stan 3E **27**
Dawsons Ter. LS28: Stan 3E **27**
Dawson St. LS28: Stan 4F **27**
WF3: Ting 2B **56**
Dean Av. LS8: Leeds 5C **22**
Dean Ct. LS8: Leeds 5C **22**
Deanfield Av. LS27: Morl 4F **49**
Dean Hall Cl. LS27: Morl 5F **49**
Dean Head LS18: H'fth 1A **10**

74 A-Z Leeds

Deanhurst Gdns.—E. Moor Cl.

Deanhurst Gdns. LS27: Gil 3D **48**
Deanhurst Ind. Cen. LS27: Gil 3D **48**
Dean La. LS18: H'fth, Yead 1A **10**
LS20: Hawk 5B **6**
Dean M. LS18: H'fth 1B **10**
Dean Pk. Av. BD11: Drig 2G **47**
Dean Pk. Dr. BD11: Drig 2G **47**
Dean Pastures BD11: Drig 3G **47**
Deansway LS27: Morl 3F **49**
Deanswood Cl. LS17: Leeds 6E **13**
Deanswood Dr. LS17: Leeds 6D **12**
Deanswood Gdns. LS17: Leeds 6D **12**
Deanswood Gth. LS17: Leeds 6E **13**
Deanswood Grn. LS17: Leeds 6D **12**
Deanswood Hill LS17: Leeds 6D **12**
Deanswood Pl. LS17: Leeds 6E **13**
Deanswood Ri. LS17: Leeds 6E **13**
Deanswood Vw. LS17: Leeds 6E **13**
Dean Vw. WF17: Birs 6H **47**
Deighton Vw. LS6: Leeds 2C **20**
De Lacies Ct. LS26: Wood 2A **54**
De Lacies Rd. LS26: Wood 2A **54**
De Lacy Mt. LS5: Leeds 1G **29**
Delius Av. BD10: B'frd 6A **16**
Delph Ct. LS6: Leeds 1E **31**
DELPH END 6E **27**
Delph End LS28: Pud 6D **26**
Delph Hill *LS28: Pud 5G 27*
(off Clifton Hill)
Delph La. LS6: Leeds 1E **31**
Delph Mt. LS6: Leeds 1E **31**
Delph Vw. LS6: Leeds 1E **31**
Denbigh App. LS9: Leeds 3F **33**
Denbigh Cft. LS9: Leeds 3F **33**
Denbigh Hgts. LS9: Leeds 3F **33**
Denbrook Av. BD4: B'frd 6B **36**
Denbrook Cl. BD4: B'frd 6B **36**
Denbrook Cres. BD4: B'frd 1B **46**
Denbrook Wlk. BD4: B'frd 6B **36**
Denbrook Way BD4: B'frd 6B **36**
Denbury Mt. BD4: B'frd 5A **36**
Denby Ho. BD4: B'frd 6B **36**
Dence Grn. BD4: B'frd 2A **36**
Dence Pl. LS15: Leeds 5G **33**
Dene Ho. Ct. LS2: Leeds 3F **31**
Deneway LS28: Stan 3E **27**
Denison Hall LS3: Leeds 2A **4** (4E **31**)
Denison Rd. LS3: Leeds 3A **4** (5E **31**)
Denison St. LS19: Yead 2D **8**
Dennil Cres. LS15: Leeds 1D **34**
Dennil Rd. LS15: Leeds 2D **34**
Dennison Fold BD4: B'frd 2A **36**
Dennistead Cres. LS6: Leeds 6B **20**
Denshaw Dr. LS27: Morl 5A **50**
Denshaw Gro. LS27: Morl 5A **50**
Denshaw La. WF3: Ting 6D **50**
Denton Av. LS8: Leeds 3B **22**
Denton Gro. LS8: Leeds 3B **22**
Denton Ho. *LS14: Leeds 5G 23*
(off Kingsdale Ct.)
Denton Row LS12: Leeds 1G **39**
Denton Ter. LS27: Morl 6G **49**
Dent St. LS9: Leeds 6B **32**
Derby Pl. BD3: B'frd 6A **26**
LS19: Raw 5D 8
(off North St.)
Derby Rd. BD3: B'frd 6A **26**
LS19: Raw 5D **8**
Derbyshire St. LS10: Leeds 4B **42**
Derby Ter. BD10: B'frd 3A **16**
Derry Hill LS29: Men 2B **6**
Derry Hill Gdns. LS29: Men 1B **6**
Derry La. LS29: Men 1B **6**
Derwent Av. LS26: Wood 3C **54**
Derwent Dr. LS16: Leeds 5B **12**
Derwent Pl. LS11: Leeds 1E **41**
Derwentwater Gro. LS6: Leeds 6B **20**
Derwentwater Ter. LS6: Leeds 6B **20**
Detroit Av. LS15: Leeds 5D **34**
Detroit Dr. LS15: Leeds 5E **35**
Devon Cl. LS2: Leeds 3F **31**
Devon Rd. LS2: Leeds 3F **31**
Devonshire Av. LS8: Leeds 2C **22**
Devonshire Cl. LS8: Leeds 1C **22**
(not continuous)
Devonshire Cres. LS8: Leeds 2C **22**
Devonshire Gdns. LS2: Leeds 2F **31**
Devonshire La. LS8: Leeds 1C **22**
Devonshire Pl. LS19: Yead 2D **8**
Devro Ct. LS9: Leeds 3D **42**
Dewhirst Pl. BD4: B'frd 2A **36**
Dewsbury Rd. BD19: Gom 6D **46**
LS11: Leeds 1G **41**
(Meadow La.)
LS11: Leeds 2D **50**
(Park Wood Cl.)
LS27: Leeds, Morl 1C **56**
Dewsbury Rd. WF3: Ting 3B **56**
(not continuous)
WF12: Dew, E Ard 5A **56**
Diadem Dr. LS14: Leeds 4G **33**
Dial St. LS9: Leeds 1B **42**
Dibb La. LS19: Yead 6H **7**
Dib Cl. LS8: Leeds 6F **23**
Dib La. LS8: Leeds 6F **23**
Dickinson St. LS18: H'fth 1C **18**
Dick La. BD3: B'frd 6A **26**
BD4: B'frd 3A **36**
Dick's Gth. Rd. LS29: Men 1B **6**
Digby Rd. LS29: Men 1C **6**
Digpal Rd. LS27: Chur 6A **40**
Dinsdale Bldgs. LS19: Yead 3C **8**
Discovery Cen., The
Leeds 1A 42
Disraeli Gdns. LS11: Leeds 3F **41**
Disraeli Ter. LS11: Leeds 3F **41**
Dixon Ct. LS12: N Far 4H **39**
Dixon La. LS12: Leeds 2A **40**
Dixon La. Rd. LS12: Leeds 2A **40**
Dobson Av. LS11: Leeds 4G **41**
Dobson Gro. LS11: Leeds 4G **41**
Dobson Locks BD10: B'frd 2A **16**
Dobson Pl. LS11: Leeds 4G **41**
Dobsons Row WF3: Carl 1F **59**
Dobson Ter. LS11: Leeds 4G **41**
Dobson Vw. LS11: Leeds 4G **41**
Dock St. LS10: Leeds 6F **5** (6G **31**)
Dodgson Av. LS7: Leeds 2A **32**
Dolly La. LS9: Leeds 4A **32**
Dolphin Ct. LS9: Leeds 6A **32**
LS13: Leeds 4B **28**
Dolphin La. WF3: Thpe H 2A **58**
(not continuous)
Dolphin Rd. LS10: Leeds 4A **52**
Dolphin St. LS9: Leeds 6A **32**
Domestic Court
Leeds 3D 4 (5F 31)
Domestic Rd. LS12: Leeds 2D **40**
Domestic St. LS11: Leeds 1D **40**
Dominion Av. LS7: Leeds 5H **21**
Dominion Cl. LS7: Leeds 5H **21**
Donald St. LS28: Fars 3F **27**
Donisthorpe St. LS10: Leeds 2A **42**
Dorchester Ct. BD4: B'frd 4A **36**
Dorchester Cres. BD4: B'frd 4A **36**
Dorchester Dr. LS19: Yead 3F **9**
Dorset Av. LS8: Leeds 1C **32**
Dorset Gro. LS28: Stan 5G **27**
Dorset Mt. LS8: Leeds 2C **32**
Dorset Rd. LS8: Leeds 1C **32**
Dorset St. LS8: Leeds 1C **32**
Dorset Ter. LS8: Leeds 2C **32**
Dortmund Sq. LS2: Leeds 3E **5**
Dotterel Glen LS27: Morl 6A **50**
Dovedale Gdns. LS15: Leeds 3F **35**
Dovedale Gth. LS15: Leeds 2F **35**
Dragon Ct. LS12: Leeds 1D **40**
Dragon Cres. LS12: Leeds 2B **40**
Dragon Dr. LS12: Leeds 2A **40**
Dragon Rd. LS12: Leeds 2B **40**
Dragons Health Club
Yeadon 2D 8
Drake La. BD11: Drig 4G **47**
Draycott Wlk. BD4: B'frd 5A **36**
Drayton Mnr. Yd. *LS11: Leeds 3G 41*
(off Moor Cres.)
Driftholme Rd. BD11: Drig 2H **47**
DRIGHLINGTON 3G **47**
Drighlington By-Pass BD11: Drig 2E **47**
LS27: Gil 4F **47**
Drive, The BD10: B'frd 5A **16**
LS8: Leeds 3B **22**
LS9: Leeds 6A **32**
LS15: Leeds 3D **34**
LS16: Leeds 6G **11**
LS17: Leeds 3D **12**
LS26: Swil 6G **45**
Driver Pl. LS12: Leeds 1C **40**
Driver St. LS12: Leeds 1D **40**
Driver Ter. LS12: Leeds 1C **40**
DRUB 6A **46**
Drub La. BD19: Cleck 6A **46**
Drummond Av. LS16: Leeds 5A **20**
Drummond Ct. LS16: Leeds 5A **20**
Drummond Rd. LS16: Leeds 4A **20**
Drury Av. LS18: H'fth 3B **18**
Drury Cl. LS18: H'fth 3B **18**
Drury La. LS18: H'fth 3B **18**
(not continuous)
Duckett Gro. LS28: Pud 5B **26**
Dudley Gro. BD4: B'frd 2A **36**
Dudley St. BD4: B'frd 2A **36**
Dufton App. LS14: Leeds 2A **34**
Duke St. LS9: Leeds 5H **5** (6H **31**)
Dulverton Cl. LS11: Leeds 6B **40**
Dulverton Ct. LS11: Leeds 6B **40**
Dulverton Gdns. LS11: Leeds 5A **40**
Dulverton Gth. LS11: Leeds 6A **40**
Dulverton Grn. LS11: Leeds 6B **40**
Dulverton Gro. BD4: B'frd 4A **36**
LS11: Leeds 6A **40**
Dulverton Pl. LS11: Leeds 6A **40**
Dulverton Sq. LS11: Leeds 6B **40**
Duncan St. LS1: Leeds 5F **5** (6G **31**)
Duncombe St. LS1: Leeds 3A **4** (5E **31**)
Dungeon La. LS26: Oul 1H **59**
Dunhill Cres. LS9: Leeds 5G **33**
Dunhill Ri. LS9: Leeds 5G **33**
Dunkirk Hill LS12: Leeds 4B **30**
Dunlin Cl. LS27: Morl 6B **50**
Dunlin Ct. LS10: Leeds 4H **51**
Dunlin Cft. LS10: Leeds 4H **51**
Dunlin Dr. LS10: Leeds 4H **51**
Dunlin Fold LS10: Leeds 4H **51**
Dunlop Av. LS12: N Far 3G **39**
Dunningley La. WF3: Ting 6D **50**
Dunnock Cft. LS27: Morl 6A **50**
Dunstarn Ct. LS16: Leeds 6B **12**
Dunstarn Dr. LS16: Leeds 6B **12**
Dunstarn Gdns. LS16: Leeds 6C **12**
Dunstarn La. LS16: Leeds 1B **20**
Durban Av. LS11: Leeds 5D **40**
Durban Cres. LS11: Leeds 5D **40**
Durham Ct. LS28: Fars 2F **27**
Dutton Grn. LS14: Leeds 3A **24**
Dutton Way LS14: Leeds 4A **24**
Duxbury Ri. LS7: Leeds 3F **31**
Dyehouse La. LS28: Pud 3G **37**
(not continuous)
Dyers Ct. LS6: Leeds 1D **30**
Dyer St. LS2: Leeds 4G **5** (5H **31**)
Dyson Ho. LS4: Leeds 2H **29**

E

Earlsmere Dr. LS27: Morl 4F **49**
Earlswood Av. LS8: Leeds 1B **22**
Earlswood Chase LS28: Pud 1G **37**
Earlswood Mead LS28: Pud 1F **37**
Easdale Cl. LS14: Leeds 6H **23**
Easdale Cres. LS14: Leeds 6A **24**
Easdale Mt. LS14: Leeds 1H **33**
Easdale Rd. LS14: Leeds 1H **33**
EAST ARDSLEY 4G **57**
EAST BIERLEY 2B **46**
East C'way. LS16: Leeds 4B **12**
E. Causeway Cl. LS16: Leeds 4B **12**
E. Causeway Cres. LS16: Leeds 5B **12**
E. Causeway Va. LS16: Leeds 5C **12**
East Ct. *LS28: Fars 2F 27*
(off Water La.)
Eastdean Bank LS14: Leeds 5A **24**
Eastdean Dr. LS14: Leeds 5A **24**
Eastdean Gdns. LS14: Leeds 5B **24**
Eastdean Ga. LS14: Leeds 6B **24**
Eastdean Grange LS14: Leeds 6B **24**
Eastdean Gro. LS14: Leeds 5B **24**
Eastdean Ri. LS14: Leeds 5B **24**
Eastdean Rd. LS14: Leeds 5A **24**
Easterly Av. LS8: Leeds 1C **32**
Easterly Cl. LS8: Leeds 2D **32**
Easterly Cres. LS8: Leeds 1C **32**
Easterly Cross LS8: Leeds 1D **32**
Easterly Gth. LS8: Leeds 1D **32**
Easterly Gro. LS8: Leeds 1C **32**
Easterly Mt. LS8: Leeds 1D **32**
Easterly Rd. LS8: Leeds 1C **32**
Easterly Sq. LS8: Leeds 1D **32**
Easterly Vw. LS8: Leeds 1D **32**
Eastfield Cres. LS26: Wood 3B **54**
Eastfield Dr. LS26: Wood 3B **54**
Eastfield Gdns. BD4: B'frd 4A **36**
East Fld. St. LS9: Leeds 6A **32**
Eastgate LS2: Leeds 4F **5** (5G **31**)
E. Grange Cl. LS10: Leeds 6A **42**
E. Grange Dr. LS10: Leeds 6A **42**
E. Grange Gth. LS10: Leeds 6A **42**
E. Grange Ri. LS10: Leeds 6A **42**
E. Grange Rd. LS10: Leeds 6A **42**
E. Grange Sq. LS10: Leeds 6A **42**
E. Grange Vw. LS10: Leeds 6A **42**
E. King St. LS9: Leeds 6H **5** (6A **32**)
Eastland Wlk. LS13: Leeds 4E **29**
East Leeds Leisure Cen. 6G **33**
Eastleigh WF3: Ting 3E **57**
Eastleigh Ct. WF3: Ting 3E **57**
Eastleigh Dr. WF3: Ting 3D **56**
EAST MOOR 5B **12**
E. Moor Av. LS8: Leeds 2B **22**
E. Moor Cl. LS8: Leeds 2B **22**

A-Z Leeds 75

E. Moor Cres. LS8: Leeds 1B 22	Edinburgh Gro. LS12: Leeds 5G 29	Elmfield LS26: Oul .4D 54
E. Moor Dr. LS8: Leeds 2C 22	Edinburgh Pl. LS12: Leeds 5G 29	Elmfield Ct. BD11: Birk 5C 46
Eastmoor Ho. BD4: B'frd 5B 36	Edinburgh Rd. LS12: Leeds 5G 29	LS13: Leeds .4D 28
E. Moor La. LS16: Leeds 5B 12	Edinburgh Ter. LS12: Leeds 5G 29	LS27: Morl .6H 49
E. Moor Rd. LS8: Leeds 1B 22	Edison Gdns. LS20: Guis 3F 7	Elmfield Gro. LS12: Leeds 1B 40
East Pde. LS1: Leeds 4D 4 (5F 31)	(off Netherfield Rd.)	Elmfield Pde. LS27: Morl 6H 49
LS29: Men .1C 6	Edison Way LS20: Guis 3F 7	Elmfield Pl. LS12: Leeds 1B 40
East Pk. Dr. LS9: Leeds 6B 32	Edlington Cl. BD4: B'frd 4A 36	Elmfield Rd. LS12: Leeds 1B 40
East Pk. Gro. LS9: Leeds 6C 32	Edmonton Pl. LS7: Leeds 5H 21	LS27: Morl .6H 49
East Pk. Mt. LS9: Leeds 6C 32	Edroyd Pl. LS28: Fars 2F 27	Elmfield Way LS13: Leeds 4D 28
East Pk. Pde. LS9: Leeds 6C 32	Edroyd St. LS28: Fars 2F 27	Elm Ho. LS7: Leeds 4A 22
East Pk. Pl. LS9: Leeds 6C 32	Education Rd. LS7: Leeds 2G 31	(off Allerton Pk.)
East Pk. Rd. LS9: Leeds 6B 32	Edward Cl. LS28: Pud 6F 27	LS15: Leeds .1G 43
East Pk. St. LS9: Leeds 6C 32	Edward Ct. WF2: Carr G 6A 58	Elmhurst Cl. LS17: Leeds 5C 14
LS27: Morl .6F 49	Edward Dr. WF1: Out 6D 58	Elmhurst Gdns. LS17: Leeds 5C 14
East Pk. Ter. LS9: Leeds 6C 32	Edward St. BD4: B'frd 6A 36	Elmroyd LS26: Rothw 5H 53
East Pk. Vw. LS9: Leeds 6C 32	LS2: Leeds 3F 5 (5G 31)	Elms, The LS7: Leeds 5H 21
E. Side Ct. LS28: Pud 2B 38	Edwin Rd. LS20: Guis 4F 7	LS13: Leeds .4E 29
East St. LS2: Leeds 5H 5 (6H 31)	Edwin Rd. LS6: Leeds 3C 30	LS20: Guis .4G 7
LS9: Leeds 6H 5 (6H 31)	Egerton Ter. LS19: Raw 6F 9	Elm St. LS6: Leeds 1F 31
East Vw. LS15: Leeds 3C 34	(off Town St.)	Elmton Cl. LS10: Leeds 2H 51
LS19: Yead .3E 9	Eggleston Dr. BD4: B'frd 5B 36	Elm Tree Cl. LS15: Leeds 1E 45
LS26: Oul .4C 54	Eggleston St. LS13: Leeds 6H 17	LS28: Pud .1G 37
LS27: Gil .4C 48	Eighth Av. LS12: Leeds 1B 40	Elmtree La. LS10: Leeds 3H 41
LS28: Pud .2G 37	LS26: Rothw .2A 54	Elm Wlk., The LS15: Leeds 2B 44
(Greaves Yd.)	Eightlands Av. LS13: Leeds 3D 28	Elmwood La. LS2: Leeds 1F 5 (4G 31)
LS28: Pud 5H 27	Eightlands La. LS13: Leeds 3D 28	Elsham Ter. LS4: Leeds 3A 30
(off Lane End)	Ekota Pl. LS8: Leeds 1B 32	Elsham Ter. LS4: Leeds 3A 30
East Vw. Cotts. LS28: Pud 5H 27	Elba La. LS12: Leeds 5A 4 (6D 30)	Elsworth Av. BD3: B'frd 4A 26
(off Priestley Gdns.)	Elder Cft. LS13: Leeds 4C 28	Elsworth Ho. LS5: Leeds 2F 29
East Vw. Rd. LS19: Yead 3E 9	Elder Mt. LS13: Leeds 4C 28	Elsworth St. LS12: Leeds 6B 30
Eastwood Cres. LS14: Leeds 1D 34	Elder Pl. LS13: Leeds 4C 28	Eltham Av. LS6: Leeds 2F 31
Eastwood Dr. LS14: Leeds 6D 24	Elder Ri. LS26: Wood 3E 55	Eltham Cl. LS6: Leeds 2F 31
Eastwood Gdns. LS14: Leeds 1C 34	Elder Rd. LS13: Leeds 4C 28	Eltham Ct. LS6: Leeds 2F 31
Eastwood Gth. LS14: Leeds 1D 34	Elder St. BD10: B'frd 4A 16	Eltham Dr. LS6: Leeds 2F 31
Eastwood La. LS14: Leeds 1D 34	LS13: Leeds 4C 28	Eltham Gdns. LS6: Leeds 2F 31
Eastwood Nook LS14: Leeds 1D 34	Elderwood Gdns. BD10: B'frd 6A 16	Eltham Ri. LS6: Leeds 2F 31
Easy Rd. LS9: Leeds 1B 42	Eldon Ct. LS2: Leeds 3F 31	Elvaston Rd. LS27: Morl 6G 49
Eaton Hill LS16: Leeds 6E 11	Eldon Mt. LS20: Guis 4G 7	Elwell St. WF3: Thpe H 2A 58
Eaton M. LS10: Leeds 4G 51	Eldon Ter. LS2: Leeds 3F 31	Ely St. LS12: Leeds 5A 30
Eaton Sq. LS10: Leeds 5G 51	(off Eldon Ct.)	Embankment, The LS1: Leeds 6E 5 (6G 31)
Ebberston Gro. LS6: Leeds 2D 30	Eleanor Dr. LS28: Cal 4B 16	LS4: Leeds 3B 30
Ebberston Pl. LS6: Leeds 2D 30	Elford Gro. LS8: Leeds 2B 32	Emmanuel Trad. Est. LS12: Leeds 1E 41
Ebberston Ter. LS6: Leeds 2D 30	Elford Pl. E. LS8: Leeds 2B 32	Emmet Cl. BD11: Birk 4D 46
Ebenezer Ho. LS27: Morl 5G 49	Elford Pl. W. LS8: Leeds 2B 32	Emmott Dr. LS19: Raw 6F 9
(off Fountain St.)	Elford Rd. LS8: Leeds 2B 32	Emmott Vw. LS19: Raw 6F 9
Ebenezer St. LS28: Fars 2F 27	Elgar Wlk. WF3: S'ley 6G 59	Emsley Pl. LS10: Leeds 2A 42
WF3: Rob H 6D 52	Eliot Gro. LS20: Guis 5H 7	Emsley's Vis. Cen. 4C 8
Ebor Mt. LS6: Leeds 3D 30	Elizabeth Ct. LS28: Pud 6F 27	Emville Av. LS17: Leeds 4E 15
Ebor Pl. LS6: Leeds 3D 30	Elizabeth Gro. LS27: Morl 3A 50	Endecliff M. LS6: Leeds 1E 31
Ebor St. LS6: Leeds 3D 30	Elizabeth Pl. LS14: Leeds 6A 24	Enfield LS19: Yead 3D 8
Ebor Ter. LS10: Leeds 5A 42	Elizabeth St. LS6: Leeds 2C 30	Enfield Av. LS7: Leeds 3A 32
(off Woodhouse Hill Rd.)	Elland Ho. LS14: Leeds 5S 23	Enfield Pl. LS7: Leeds 3H 31
Ecclesburn Av. LS9: Leeds 6C 32	(off Kingsdale Ct.)	Enfield Ter. LS7: Leeds 3A 32
Ecclesburn Rd. LS9: Leeds 6C 32	Elland Road 4C 40	Engine Fields Nature Reserve 3C 8
Ecclesburn St. LS9: Leeds 6C 32	Elland Rd. LS11: Leeds 5B 40	Englefield Cl. BD4: B'frd 5A 36
Ecclesburn Ter. LS9: Leeds 6C 32	(Crow Nest La.)	Englefield Cres. BD4: B'frd 5A 36
ECCLESHILL COMMUNITY HOSPITAL 6A 16	LS11: Leeds 2H 49	Ennerdale Rd. LS12: N Far 5D 38
ECCLESHILL NHS TREATMENT CENTRE 6A 16	(Daffil Rd.)	Ennerdale Way LS12: N Far 4D 38
Eccleshill Swimming Pool 5A 16	LS11: Leeds 3D 40	Enterprise Pk. Ind. Est. LS11: Leeds 6D 40
Eccup La. LS16: Ecc, Leeds 3B 12	(Tilbury Rd.)	Enterprise Way LS10: Leeds 6B 42
Eccup Moor Rd. LS16: Ecc 1C 12	LS27: Chur 2H 49	Envoy St. LS11: Leeds 3G 41
Echo Central LS9: Leeds 1A 42	Elland Rd. Ind. Pk. LS11: Leeds 4B 40	Epworth Pl. LS10: Leeds 3A 42
Echo Central Two LS9: Leeds 1A 42	Elland Ter. LS11: Leeds 2F 41	Eric St. LS13: Leeds 6C 18
(off Cross Grn. La.)	Elland Way LS11: Leeds 5B 40	Escroft Ct. LS29: Men 2D 6
Edale Way LS16: Leeds 6F 11	Ellerby La. LS9: Leeds 1A 42	(off Clifford Dr.)
Eddison Cl. LS16: Leeds 4B 12	Ellerby Rd. LS9: Leeds 6A 32	Eshald La. LS26: Wood 4D 54
Eddison Cl. LS28: Fars 3F 27	Eller Cl. LS8: Leeds 5E 23	Eshald Mans. LS26: Wood 3D 54
Eddison Wlk. LS16: Leeds 4B 12	Ellers Gro. LS8: Leeds 1B 32	Eshald Pl. LS26: Wood 3D 54
Eden Cres. LS4: Leeds 1H 29	Ellerslie Hall LS2: Leeds 3E 31	Esholt Av. LS20: Guis 6F 7
Eden Dr. LS4: Leeds 2H 29	(off Lyddon Ter.)	Esholt Hall Est. BD17: Esh 5A 8
Eden Gdns. LS4: Leeds 2H 29	Ellers Rd. LS8: Leeds 1B 32	Eskdale Cl. LS20: Guis 5G 7
Eden Gro. LS4: Leeds 2H 29	Ellicott Ct. LS29: Men 1C 6	Eskdale Cft. LS20: Guis 5G 7
Eden Mt. LS4: Leeds 2H 29	Ellies Ct. LS17: Leeds 5C 14	Esmond St. LS12: Leeds 6A 30
Eden Rd. LS4: Leeds 1H 29	Elliot Ct. LS13: Leeds 1A 28	Esmond Ter. LS12: Leeds 6A 30
Eden Wlk. LS4: Leeds 2H 29	Ellis Fold LS12: Leeds 6H 29	Esporta Health & Fitness Club
Eden Way LS4: Leeds 2H 29	Ellis Ter. LS6: Leeds 5B 20	Bradford 5B 26
Ederoyd Av. LS28: Stan 4D 26	(off Glebe Ter.)	Cookridge 3F 11
Ederoyd Cres. LS28: Stan 4C 26	Ellwood Cl. LS7: Leeds 4D 20	Leeds 3D 4
Ederoyd Dr. LS28: Stan 4D 26	Elm Ct. BD11: Birk 5D 46	Estcourt Av. LS6: Leeds 6A 20
Ederoyd Gro. LS28: Stan 4D 26	Elm Cft. LS14: Leeds 3C 24	Estcourt Ter. LS6: Leeds 6A 20
Ederoyd Mt. LS28: Stan 4D 26	Elmete Av. LS8: Leeds 4E 23	Esthwaite Gdns. LS15: Leeds 1G 43
Ederoyd Ri. LS28: Stan 4D 26	LS15: Scho 5F 25	Eton Ct. LS7: Leeds 4A 22
Edgbaston Cl. LS17: Leeds 3E 13	Elmete Cl. LS8: Leeds 5F 23	Euston Gro. LS11: Leeds 3D 40
Edgbaston Wlk. LS17: Leeds 3E 13	Elmete Cft. LS15: Scho 5F 25	Euston Mt. LS11: Leeds 3D 40
Edgemoor Cl. BD4: B'frd 1A 46	Elmete Dr. LS8: Leeds 4F 23	Euston Ter. LS11: Leeds 3D 40
Edgerton Rd. LS16: Leeds 3H 19	Elmete Grange LS29: Men 1C 6	Evanston Av. LS4: Leeds 4A 30
Edgware Av. LS8: Leeds 3B 32	Elmete Hill LS8: Leeds 5F 23	Evelyn Av. BD3: B'frd 5A 26
Edgware Gro. LS8: Leeds 3B 32	Elmete La. LS8: Leeds 4F 23	Evelyn Pl. LS12: Leeds 1A 40
Edgware Mt. LS8: Leeds 3B 32	LS17: Shad 6G 15	Everleigh St. LS9: Leeds 5C 32
Edgware Pl. LS8: Leeds 3B 32	Elmete Mt. LS8: Leeds 5F 23	Eversley Dr. BD4: B'frd 3A 36
Edgware Row LS8: Leeds 3B 32	Elmete Wlk. LS8: Leeds 5E 23	Exeter Dr. LS10: Leeds 2H 51
Edgware St. LS8: Leeds 3B 32	Elmete Way LS8: Leeds 5F 23	Eyres Av. LS12: Leeds 5A 30
Edgware Ter. LS8: Leeds 3B 32	LS14: Leeds 1C 34	Eyres Gro. LS12: Leeds 5A 30
Edgware Vw. LS8: Leeds 3B 32	Elmet Towers LS14: Leeds 1C 34	(off Eyres Ter.)
Edinburgh Av. LS12: Leeds 5G 29		Eyres Mill Side LS12: Leeds 5H 29
		Eyres St. LS12: Leeds 5A 30
		(off Eyres Ter.)

Eyres Ter.—Fir Tree La.

Eyres Ter. LS12: Leeds 5A **30**
Eyrie App. LS27: Morl 6A **50**

F

FAGLEY 3A **26**
Fagley La. BD2: B'frd 2A **26**
Fagley Rd. BD2: B'frd 3A **26**
Fairbairn Fold BD4: B'frd 1A **36**
Fairburn Ho. *LS18: H'fth 4B **18***
(off Regent Cres.)
Fairfax Av. BD11: Drig 3A **48**
LS29: Men 1C **6**
Fairfax Cl. LS14: Leeds 2B **34**
Fairfax Ct. LS11: Leeds 4E **41**
Fairfax Gdns. LS29: Men 1C **6**
Fairfax Gro. LS19: Yead 6H **7**
Fairfax Rd. LS11: Leeds 4E **41**
LS29: Men 1B **6**
Fairfax Vw. BD4: E Bier 2B **46**
LS18: H'fth 5B **10**
Fairfield LS18: H'fth 2C **18**
Fairfield Av. LS13: Leeds 3A **28**
LS28: Pud 5G **27**
WF3: W Ard 4B **56**
Fairfield Cl. LS13: Leeds 3B **28**
LS26: Rothw 5D **52**
Fairfield Ct. LS17: Leeds 4A **14**
Fairfield Cres. LS13: Leeds 3A **28**
Fairfield Dr. LS26: Rothw 5D **52**
Fairfield Gdns. LS26: Rothw 5D **52**
Fairfield Gro. LS13: Leeds 3B **28**
LS26: Rothw 5D **52**
Fairfield Hill LS13: Leeds 3B **28**
Fairfield La. LS26: Rothw 5D **52**
Fairfield Mt. LS13: Leeds 3B **28**
Fairfield Rd. LS13: Leeds 3A **28**
Fairfield Sq. LS13: Leeds 3B **28**
Fairfield St. BD4: B'frd 6A **36**
LS13: Leeds 3A **28**
Fairfield Ter. LS13: Leeds 3B **28**
Fairford Av. LS11: Leeds 4G **41**
Fairford Mt. LS6: Leeds 2C **20**
Fairford Ter. LS11: Leeds 4G **41**
Fairleigh Cres. WF3: Ting 3D **56**
Fairleigh Rd. WF3: Ting 3D **56**
Fair Vw. LS11: Leeds 6B **40**
Fairway BD10: B'frd 2C **16**
LS20: Guis 4D **6**
Fairway, The LS17: Leeds 3F **13**
LS28: Stan 4D **26**
Fairway Cl. LS20: Guis 5E **7**
Fairwood Gro. BD10: B'frd 2A **26**
Falcon M. LS27: Morl 6A **50**
Falkland Ct. LS17: Leeds 2G **21**
Falkland Cres. LS17: Leeds 2G **21**
Falkland Gdns. LS17: Leeds 2H **21**
Falkland Gro. LS17: Leeds 2G **21**
Falkland Mt. LS17: Leeds 2G **21**
Falkland Ri. LS17: Leeds 2G **21**
Falkland Rd. BD10: B'frd 1A **26**
LS17: Leeds 2G **21**
FALL, THE 3H **57**
Fall La. WF3: E Ard 3H **57**
Fall Pk. Ct. LS13: Leeds 6D **18**
Fallswood Gro. LS13: Leeds 1D **28**
Fallwood Marina LS13: Leeds 6B **18**
Falmers Cotts. *LS6: Leeds 1D **30***
(off Cliff La.)
Falsgrave Av. BD2: B'frd 3A **26**
Faraday *LS20: Guis 3F **7***
(off Netherfield Rd.)
Far Cft. Ter. LS12: Leeds 1B **40**
Farfield Av. LS28: Fars 2E **27**
Farfield Dr. LS28: Fars 3E **27**
Farfield Gro. LS28: Fars 2E **27**
Farfield Ri. LS28: Fars 2E **27**
FAR FOLD 5H **29**
FAR HEADINGLEY 5D **20**
Far La. LS9: Leeds 2E **43**
Farm Ct. LS15: Leeds 3B **34**
Farm Hill Cres. LS7: Leeds 6E **21**
Farm Hill M. LS27: Morl 4E **49**
Farm Hill Nth. LS7: Leeds 5E **21**
Farm Hill Ri. LS7: Leeds 6E **21**
Farm Hill Rd. LS27: Morl 3F **49**
Farm Hill Sth. LS7: Leeds 6E **21**
Farm Hill Way LS7: Leeds 6E **21**
Farm Mt. LS15: Leeds 3C **34**
Far Moss LS17: Leeds 4E **13**
Farm Rd. LS15: Leeds 3B **34**
Farndale App. LS14: Leeds 6C **24**
Farndale Cl. LS14: Leeds 6C **24**
Farndale Gdns. LS14: Leeds 5C **24**
Farndale Gth. LS14: Leeds 5C **24**
Farndale Pl. LS14: Leeds 5C **24**
Farndale Sq. LS14: Leeds 6C **24**
Farndale Ter. LS14: Leeds 6C **24**
Farndale Vw. *LS14: Leeds 5C **24***
(off Stanks Dr.)
Farnham Cl. LS14: Leeds 2B **24**
LS16: Leeds 4A **20**
Farnham Cft. LS14: Leeds 2B **24**
FARNLEY 2E **39**
Farnley Cl. LS29: Men 1D **6**
Farnley Cres. LS12: Leeds 1E **39**
Farnley Ho. *LS14: Leeds 5G **23***
(off Kingsdale Ct.)
Farnley Rd. LS29: Men 1C **6**
Farnley Vw. BD11: Drig 4A **48**
Faroe LS12: Leeds 6A **4** (6E **31**)
Farrar Ct. LS13: Leeds 2C **28**
Farrar Cft. LS16: Leeds 5G **11**
Farrar Gro. LS16: Leeds 5G **11**
Farrar La. LS16: Leeds 5F **11**
(not continuous)
Far Reef Cl. LS18: H'fth 1C **18**
Farrer La. LS26: Oul 4C **54**
Farriers Ct. BD11: Drig 3G **47**
Farrier Way WF3: Rob H 6D **52**
Farringdon Cl. BD4: B'frd 3A **36**
Farringdon Dr. BD4: B'frd 4A **36**
Farringdon Sq. BD4: B'frd 3A **36**
Farrow Bank LS12: Leeds 6E **29**
Farrow Grn. LS12: Leeds 6F **29**
Farrow Hill LS12: Leeds 6F **29**
Farrow Rd. LS12: Leeds 6E **29**
Farrow Va. LS12: Leeds 6E **29**
FAR ROYDS 3A **40**
FARSLEY 2F **27**
FARSLEY BECK BOTTOM 2G **27**
Farsley Beck M. LS13: Leeds 2G **27**
Farsley Celtic FC 3G **27**
Fartown LS28: Pud 1F **37**
Fartown Cl. LS28: Pud 2G **37**
Farway BD4: B'frd 3A **36**
Far Well Fold LS19: Raw 6F **9**
Far Well Rd. LS19: Raw 6F **9**
Faversham Wlk. BD4: B'frd 3A **36**
Fawcett Av. LS12: Leeds 2H **39**
Fawcett Bank LS12: Leeds 2G **39**
Fawcett Cl. LS12: Leeds 2G **39**
Fawcett Dr. LS12: Leeds 2G **39**
Fawcett Gdns. LS12: Leeds 2G **39**
Fawcett La. LS12: Leeds 2G **39**
Fawcett Pl. LS12: Leeds 2G **39**
Fawcett Rd. LS12: Leeds 2G **39**
Fawcett Va. LS12: Leeds 2G **39**
Fawcett Vw. *LS12: Leeds 2G **39***
(off Fawcett Va.)
Fawcett Way LS12: Leeds 2G **39**
Fawdon Dr. LS14: Leeds 6D **24**
Fawdon Pl. LS14: Leeds 6D **24**
Fearnley Cl. LS12: Leeds 6B **30**
Fearnley Pl. LS12: Leeds 6B **30**
FEARN'S ISLAND 1A **42**
FEARNVILLE 1F **33**
Fearnville Av. LS8: Leeds 1F **33**
Fearnville Cl. LS8: Leeds 6F **23**
Fearnville Dr. LS8: Leeds 1F **33**
Fearnville Gro. LS8: Leeds 6F **23**
Fearnville Mt. LS8: Leeds 6F **23**
Fearnville Pl. LS8: Leeds 6G **23**
Fearnville Rd. LS8: Leeds 1F **33**
Fearnville Sports Cen. 2F **33**
Fearnville Ter. LS8: Leeds 6G **23**
Fearnville Vw. LS8: Leeds 1F **33**
Feast Fld. LS18: H'fth 2B **18**
Featherbank Av. LS18: H'fth 4B **18**
Featherbank Ct. *LS18: H'fth 4B **18***
(off Featherbank Av.)
Featherbank Gro. LS18: H'fth 3B **18**
Featherbank La. LS18: H'fth 3B **18**
Featherbank Mt. LS18: H'fth 3B **18**
Featherbank Ter. LS18: H'fth 4B **18**
Featherbank Wlk. LS18: H'fth 4B **18**
Felcourt Dr. BD4: B'frd 5A **36**
Felcourt Fold BD4: B'frd 5A **36**
Felnex Cl. LS9: Leeds 2E **43**
Felnex Cres. LS9: Leeds 2E **43**
Felnex Rd. LS9: Leeds 2D **42**
Felnex Sq. LS9: Leeds 2D **42**
Felnex Way LS9: Leeds 2E **43**
Fencote Cres. BD2: B'frd 2A **26**
Fenton Av. LS26: Wood 2B **54**
Fenton Cl. LS26: Wood 2B **54**
Fenton Ga. LS10: Leeds 5A **52**
Fenton Pl. LS10: Leeds 5A **52**
Fenton Rd. WF3: S'ley 4H **59**
Fentonsgate WF3: Loft 2E **59**
Fenton St. LS1: Leeds 1D **4** (4F **31**)
WF3: Ting 2D **56**
Fernbank Av. LS13: Leeds 2H **27**
Fernbank Cl. LS13: Leeds 2H **27**
Fernbank Dr. LS13: Leeds 2H **27**
Fernbank Gdns. LS13: Leeds 2H **27**
Fernbank Pl. LS13: Leeds 2H **27**
Fernbank Rd. LS13: Leeds 2H **27**
Fern Bank Ter. *LS19: Yead 2C **8***
(off Park Av.)
Fernbank Wlk. LS13: Leeds 2H **27**
Ferncliffe Rd. LS13: Leeds 3C **28**
Ferncliffe Ter. LS13: Leeds 3B **28**
Fern Cft. LS14: S'cft 2H **15**
Ferndene Av. WF17: Birs 6H **47**
Ferndene Wlk. WF17: Birs 6H **47**
Fern Gro. *LS5: Leeds 1G **29***
(off Tordoff Pl.)
Fernlea LS26: Rothw 3H **53**
Fern Lea Vw. LS28: Stan 3G **27**
Fern Ter. LS28: Stan 3G **27**
Fern Way LS14: S'cft 2H **15**
Fernwood LS8: Leeds 2C **22**
Fernwood Ct. LS8: Leeds 2C **22**
Ferriby Cl. BD2: B'frd 2A **26**
Ferriby Towers *LS9: Leeds 4A **32***
(off Granville Rd.)
Fewston Av. LS9: Leeds 1B **42**
Fewston Ct. LS9: Leeds 1B **42**
Field End LS15: Leeds 6A **34**
Field End Cl. LS15: Leeds 6A **34**
Field End Ct. LS15: Leeds 6A **34**
Field End Cres. LS15: Leeds 6A **34**
Field End Gdns. LS15: Leeds 6A **34**
Field End Gth. LS15: Leeds 6A **34**
Field End Grn. LS15: Leeds 6A **34**
Field End Gro. LS15: Leeds 5B **34**
Field End Mt. LS15: Leeds 6A **34**
Field End Rd. LS15: Leeds 6A **34**
Fieldgate Rd. BD10: B'frd 4A **16**
Fieldhead WF17: Birs 6G **47**
Fieldhead Cres. WF17: Birs 6G **47**
Fieldhead Dr. LS20: Guis 5E **7**
Fieldhead Gro. LS20: Guis 5E **7**
Field Head La. BD11: Drig 5G **47**
WF17: Birs 6G **47**
Fieldhead Rd. LS20: Guis 5E **7**
Fieldhouse Cl. LS17: Leeds 1G **21**
Fieldhouse Dr. LS17: Leeds 1G **21**
Fieldhouse Gro. LS28: Fars 3E **27**
Fieldhouse Lawn LS17: Leeds 1G **21**
Fieldhouse Wlk. LS17: Leeds 1G **21**
(not continuous)
Fielding Ct. LS27: Morl 4F **49**
Fielding Ga. LS12: Leeds 5B **30**
Fielding Ga. M. LS12: Leeds 5B **30**
Fielding Way LS27: Morl 4F **49**
Fieldmoor Lodge LS28: Pud 1G **37**
Field Pk. Grange LS27: Gil 3D **48**
Fields, The WF3: Loft 2F **59**
Fieldside Cl. BD4: B'frd 5B **36**
Field Ter. LS15: Leeds 5A **34**
(Cross St.)
LS15: Leeds 4B **34**
(Hermon Rd.)
Fieldway Av. LS13: Leeds 1A **28**
Fieldway Chase LS26: Oul 4D **54**
Fieldway Cl. LS13: Leeds 1A **28**
Fieldway Ri. LS13: Leeds 1A **28**
Fifth Av. LS26: Rothw 2A **54**
Fillingfir Dr. LS16: Leeds 3F **19**
Fillingfir Rd. LS16: Leeds 3F **19**
Fillingfir Wlk. LS16: Leeds 3F **19**
Finch Dr. LS15: Leeds 1F **45**
Finchley Way LS27: Morl 6G **49**
Findon Ter. BD10: B'frd 1A **26**
Fink Hill LS18: H'fth 3A **18**
Finkle Ct. LS27: Gil 3C **48**
Finkle La. LS27: Gil 3C **48**
Finsbury Rd. LS1: Leeds 1C **4** (4F **31**)
Firbank Gro. LS15: Leeds 1G **43**
First Av. LS12: Leeds 6B **30**
LS19: Raw 4E **9**
LS26: Rothw 2H **53**
LS28: Stan 4G **27**
First Av. Ind. Est. LS28: Stan 4G **27**
Firth Av. LS11: Leeds 5E **41**
Firth Cl. WF3: S'ley 6G **59**
Firth Gro. LS11: Leeds 5E **41**
Firth Mt. LS11: Leeds 5E **41**
Firth Rd. LS11: Leeds 5E **41**
Firth St. LS9: Leeds 1H **5** (4A **32**)
Firth Ter. LS9: Leeds 1H **5** (4A **32**)
Firth Vw. LS11: Leeds 5E **41**
Fir Tree App. LS17: Leeds 5F **13**
Fir Tree Cl. LS17: Leeds 5G **13**
Fir Tree Gdns. LS17: Leeds 5F **13**
Fir Tree Grn. LS17: Leeds 5G **13**
Fir Tree Gro. LS17: Leeds 6G **13**
Fir Tree La. LS17: Leeds 6H **13**

A-Z Leeds 77

Fir Tree Ri.—Gate Way Dr.

Fir Tree Ri. LS17: Leeds 6G **13**
Fir Tree Va. LS17: Leeds 6G **13**
Fish St. LS1: Leeds 4F **5** (5G **31**)
Fitness First Health Club
Leeds 4A **30**
Fitzroy Dr. LS8: Leeds 5C **22**
Flats, The LS19: Yead 3E **9**
Flawith Dr. BD2: B'frd 3A **26**
Flax Mill Rd. LS10: Leeds 4A **42**
Flax Pl. LS9: Leeds 6H **5** (6A **32**)
Flaxton Cl. LS11: Leeds 4F **41**
Flaxton Ct. BD4: B'frd 1A **36**
Flaxton Gdns. LS11: Leeds 4F **41**
Flaxton Grn. BD2: B'frd 3A **26**
Flaxton St. LS11: Leeds 4F **41**
Flaxton Vw. LS11: Leeds 4F **41**
Fleet La. LS26: Meth 5G **55**
LS26: Oul 4D **54**
Fleet Thro' Rd. LS18: H'fth 5B **18**
Flexbury Av. LS27: Morl 6G **49**
Flinton Gro. BD2: B'frd 2A **26**
Floral Av. LS7: Leeds 5G **21**
Florence Av. LS9: Leeds 3C **32**
Florence Gro. LS9: Leeds 3C **32**
Florence Mt. LS9: Leeds 3C **32**
Florence Pl. LS9: Leeds 3C **32**
Florence St. LS9: Leeds 3C **32**
Florence Ter. *LS27: Morl 5H **49***
(off Gillroyd Pde.)
Flossmore Way LS27: Gil 2C **48**
Flower Chase LS20: Guis 4H **7**
Flower Cl. LS19: Yead 2C **8**
Flower Ct. LS18: H'fth 4B **18**
Flower Gth. BD10: B'frd 5A **16**
*LS18: H'fth 3B **18***
(off Stanhope Dr.)
Flower Mt. *LS19: Yead 2E **9***
(off Alexandra Ter.)
Focus Way LS19: Raw 4D **8**
Fold, The LS15: Leeds 1E **35**
Folly Hall Mt. WF3: Ting 3C **56**
Folly Hall Rd. WF3: Ting 3C **56**
Folly La. LS11: Leeds 3F **41**
Fontmell Cl. BD4: B'frd 5A **36**
Football LS19: Yead 2E **9**
Football Cen. 4A **30**
Football World 2D **42**
Forber Gro. BD4: B'frd 2A **36**
Forber Pl. LS15: Leeds 6G **33**
Forbes Ho. *BD4: B'frd 4A **36***
(off Stirling Cres.)
Forest Bank LS27: Gil 2C **48**
Forest Ridge WF3: E Ard 2G **57**
Forge La. LS12: Leeds 5B **30**
LS17: Wike 1F **15**
Forge Row LS12: N Far 4D **38**
Forman's Dr. WF3: Rob H 6C **52**
Forrester Ct. WF3: Rob H 6D **52**
Forster Loft LS12: Leeds 3H **39**
Forster M. LS12: Leeds 3G **39**
Forster Pl. LS12: Leeds 3G **39**
Forster St. LS10: Leeds 2A **42**
Forsythia Av. WF3: E Ard 3G **57**
Forth Ct. LS11: Leeds 1E **41**
Forum Leisure Cen., The 4H **5** (5H **31**)
Foster Cl. LS27: Morl 4G **49**
Foster Cres. LS27: Morl 4G **49**
Foster Sq. LS10: Leeds 1H **51**
Foster St. LS27: Morl 4G **49**
Foster Ter. LS13: Leeds 2D **28**
Foston Cl. BD2: B'frd 3A **26**
Foston La. BD2: B'frd 3A **26**
Foundry App. LS9: Leeds 3D **32**
Foundry Av. LS8: Leeds 2D **32**
LS9: Leeds 2D **32**
Foundry Dr. LS9: Leeds 2D **32**
Foundry Ind. Est. LS28: Stan 4G **27**
Foundry La. LS9: Leeds 2F **33**
LS14: Leeds 2F **33**
LS28: Stan 3G **27**
Foundry Mill Cres. LS14: Leeds 2H **33**
Foundry Mill Dr. LS14: Leeds 2G **33**
(not continuous)
Foundry Mill Gdns. LS14: Leeds 6G **23**
Foundry Mill Mt. LS14: Leeds 2H **33**
Foundry Mill St. LS14: Leeds 2G **33**
Foundry Mill Ter. LS14: Leeds 2H **33**
Foundry Mill Vw. LS14: Leeds 2H **33**
Foundry Mill Wlk. LS14: Leeds 2H **33**
Foundry Pl. LS9: Leeds 2D **32**
Foundry Rd. LS28: Stan 4G **27**
Foundry Sq. *LS11: Leeds 1F **41***
(off Foundry St.)
Foundry St. LS9: Leeds 5H **5** (6A **32**)
LS11: Leeds 1F **41**
Foundry Wlk. LS8: Leeds 2C **32**
Fountain Ct. LS27: Morl 5E **49**
Fountain Hall *LS27: Morl 6F **49***
(off Fountain St.)
Fountain St. LS1: Leeds 3B **4** (5E **31**)
LS27: Chur 1A **50**
LS27: Morl 6F **49**
Fourteenth Av. LS12: Leeds 1B **40**
Fourth Av. LS26: Rothw 2A **54**
Fowler's Pl. LS28: Stan 3G **27**
Foxcroft Cl. LS6: Leeds 6H **19**
Foxcroft Gth. LS6: Leeds 6H **19**
Foxcroft Grn. LS6: Leeds 6H **19**
Foxcroft Mt. LS6: Leeds 6H **19**
Foxcroft Rd. LS6: Leeds 6H **19**
Foxcroft Wlk. LS6: Leeds 6H **19**
Foxcroft Way LS6: Leeds 6H **19**
Foxglove Av. LS8: Leeds 5E **23**
Foxglove Rd. WF17: Birs 6G **47**
Foxhill Av. LS16: Leeds 2A **20**
Foxhill Ct. LS16: Leeds 2A **20**
Foxhill Cres. LS16: Leeds 2B **20**
Foxhill Dr. LS16: Leeds 2A **20**
Foxhill Grn. LS16: Leeds 2B **20**
Foxhill Gro. LS16: Leeds 2B **20**
Foxhills, The LS16: Leeds 5D **10**
Foxholes Cres. LS28: Cal 5D **16**
Foxholes La. LS28: Cal 5D **16**
Foxton Gdns. LS27: Morl 6F **49**
Fox Way LS10: Leeds 2A **42**
Foxwood LS8: Leeds 3E **23**
Foxwood Av. LS8: Leeds 6G **23**
Foxwood Cl. LS8: Leeds 6G **23**
Foxwood Farm Way LS8: Leeds 6G **23**
Foxwood Gro. LS8: Leeds 6G **23**
Foxwood Ri. LS8: Leeds 6G **23**
Foxwood Wlk. LS8: Leeds 6G **23**
Fraisthorpe Mead BD2: B'frd 3A **26**
Frances St. LS28: Fars 3F **27**
Francis Ct. *LS7: Leeds 2H **31***
(off Francis St.)
Francis Gro. LS11: Leeds 4F **41**
Francis St. LS7: Leeds 2H **31**
Frankland Gro. LS7: Leeds 2A **32**
Frankland Pl. LS7: Leeds 2A **32**
(not continuous)
Frank Parkinson Ct. *LS20: Guis 4G **7***
(off W. Villa Rd.)
Frank Parkinson Homes *LS20: Guis 4G **7***
(off Oxford St.)
Fraser Av. LS18: H'fth 3H **17**
Fraser Rd. LS28: Cal 5B **16**
Fraser St. LS9: Leeds 4B **32**
Frederick Av. LS9: Leeds 1C **42**
Frederick St. LS28: Fars 2E **27**
Freemantle Pl. LS15: Leeds 6G **33**
Freemont St. LS13: Leeds 3A **28**
Freestone M. LS12: Leeds 6C **28**
Fremantle Gro. BD4: B'frd 2A **36**
Frensham Av. LS27: Morl 6F **49**
Frodingham Vs. BD2: B'frd 3A **26**
Frontline Cl. LS8: Leeds 5C **22**
Front Row LS11: Leeds 1F **41**
(not continuous)
Front St. LS11: Leeds 1F **41**
Fuchsia Cft. LS26: Wood 3E **55**
Fulford Wlk. BD2: B'frd 3A **26**
Fulham Pl. LS11: Leeds 4F **41**
Fulham Sq. *LS11: Leeds 4F **41***
(off Fulham St.)
Fulham St. LS11: Leeds 4F **41**
Fullers Ho. *LS9: Leeds 6H **5***
(off East St.)
Fulmar Ct. LS10: Leeds 4H **51**
FULNECK 2G **37**
Fulneck LS28: Pud 3F **37**
Fulneck Cl. LS11: Leeds 2E **51**
Fulneck Ct. LS28: Pud 2H **37**
Fulneck M. LS28: Pud 2H **37**
Fulneck Moravian Settlement & Moravian Mus.
2G **37**
Fulton Pl. LS16: Leeds 4A **20**
Furnace La. BD11: Birk 3C **46**
Future Bodies Gym & Fitness Cen. *5H **49***
(off Commercial St.)

G

Gable End Ter. LS28: Pud 6H **27**
Gables, The LS17: Leeds 5C **14**
LS18: H'fth 6C **10**
Gabriel Ct. *LS10: Leeds 3H **41***
(off Hunslet Grn. Way)
Gain La. BD3: B'frd 4A **26**
Gainsborough Flds. *LS12: N Far 4E **39***
(off Coach Rd.)
Gainsborough Pl. *LS12: N Far 4E **39***
(off Well Holme Mead)
Gainsborough Way WF3: S'ley 6G **59**
Gainsbro' Av. LS16: Leeds 4H **11**
Gainsbro' Dr. LS16: Leeds 4H **11**
Gaitskell Ct. LS11: Leeds 2E **41**
Gaitskell Grange LS11: Leeds 2E **41**
Gaitskell Wlk. LS11: Leeds 2E **41**
Gala Bingo
Bradford 6A **36**
Leeds 1F **39**
Gala Casino
Leeds 4A **4** (5D **30**)
Gallagher Leisure Pk. BD3: B'frd 5B **26**
Gallery & Studio Theatre 1C **4** (4F **31**)
Gallops, The LS27: Morl 2A **56**
Galloway Ct. LS28: Pud 5C **26**
Galloway La. LS28: Pud 4C **26**
Galloway Rd. BD10: B'frd 4A **16**
GAMBLE HILL 5D **28**
Gamble Hill LS13: Leeds 5D **28**
Gamble Hill Chase LS13: Leeds 5D **28**
Gamble Hill Cl. LS13: Leeds 5D **28**
Gamble Hill Cft. *LS13: Leeds 5D **28***
(off Gamble Hill Vw.)
Gamble Hill Cross *LS13: Leeds 5D **28***
(off Gamble Hill Lawn)
Gamble Hill Dr. LS13: Leeds 5D **28**
Gamble Hill Fold *LS13: Leeds 5D **28***
(off Gamble Hill Lawn)
Gamble Hill Grange *LS13: Leeds 5D **28***
(off Gamble Hill Dr.)
Gamble Hill Grn. LS13: Leeds 5D **28**
Gamble Hill Lawn LS13: Leeds 5D **28**
Gamble Hill Path *LS13: Leeds 5D **28***
(off Gamble Hill Grn.)
Gamble Hill Pl. LS13: Leeds 5D **28**
Gamble Hill Ri. LS13: Leeds 5D **28**
Gamble Hill Va. LS13: Leeds 5D **28**
Gamble Hill Vw. LS13: Leeds 5D **28**
Gamble Hill Wlk. *LS13: Leeds 5D **28***
(off Gamble Hill Ri.)
Gamble La. LS12: Leeds 1C **38**
Gambles Hill LS28: Fars 2F **27**
Gang, The *LS12: Leeds 6A **30***
(off Town St.)
Gangster's Gym & Smokey's Place 3B **30**
Ganners Cl. LS13: Leeds 1C **28**
Ganners Gth. LS13: Leeds 1D **28**
Ganners Grn. LS13: Leeds 1C **28**
Ganners Gro. LS13: Leeds 1D **28**
Ganners Hill LS13: Leeds 1D **28**
Ganners La. LS13: Leeds 1C **28**
Ganners Mt. LS13: Leeds 1C **28**
Ganners Ri. LS13: Leeds 1D **28**
Ganners Rd. LS13: Leeds 1C **28**
Ganners Wlk. LS13: Leeds 1C **28**
Ganners Way LS13: Leeds 1C **28**
Ganton Cl. LS6: Leeds 1F **31**
Gardeners Ct. LS10: Leeds 3H **41**
Garden Ho. La. WF3: Ting 3E **57**
Gardenhurst LS6: Leeds 1C **30**
Gardens, The LS10: Leeds 5G **51**
LS28: Fars 2E **27**
Garden Vw. Ct. LS8: Leeds 2D **22**
GARFORTH BRIDGE 2H **45**
Gargrave App. LS9: Leeds 5B **32**
Gargrave Ct. LS9: Leeds 4B **32**
Gargrave Pl. LS9: Leeds 4B **32**
Garibaldi St. BD3: B'frd 6A **26**
(not continuous)
Garland Dr. LS15: Leeds 6D **34**
Garmont M. LS7: Leeds 5H **21**
Garmont Rd. LS7: Leeds 5H **21**
Garnet Av. LS11: Leeds 4G **41**
Garnet Cres. LS11: Leeds 4G **41**
Garnet Gro. LS11: Leeds 4G **41**
Garnet Pde. LS11: Leeds 4G **41**
Garnet Pl. LS11: Leeds 4G **41**
Garnet Rd. LS11: Leeds 5G **41**
Garnet Ter. LS11: Leeds 4G **41**
Garnet Vw. LS11: Leeds 4G **41**
Garth, The LS9: Leeds 6A **32**
Garth Av. LS17: Leeds 2F **21**
Garth Dr. LS17: Leeds 2F **21**
Garth Gro. LS29: Men 1C **6**
Garth Rd. LS17: Leeds 2F **21**
Garth Wlk. LS17: Leeds 2F **21**
Garton Av. LS9: Leeds 6C **32**
Garton Gro. LS9: Leeds 6C **32**
Garton Rd. LS9: Leeds 6C **32**
Garton Ter. LS9: Leeds 6C **32**
Garton Vw. LS9: Leeds 6C **32**
Gascoigne Rd. WF3: Thpe H 2A **58**
Gate Ho. Ct. LS26: Wood 2E **55**
Gateland Dr. LS17: Shad 5G **15**
Gateland La. LS17: Shad 6G **15**
Gateway, The LS26: Rothw 5G **53**
Gate Way Dr. LS19: Yead 2C **8**

78 A-Z Leeds

Gateways WF1: Out 6E **59**
Gathorne Cl. LS8: Leeds 2A **32**
Gathorne St. LS8: Leeds 2A **32**
(not continuous)
Gathorne Ter. LS8: Leeds 2A **32**
(not continuous)
Gaunts Pl. LS25: Fars 2G **27**
Gavin Cl. BD3: B'frd 6A **26**
Gelderd Bus. Pk. LS12: Leeds 3B **40**
Gelderd Cl. LS12: Leeds 3B **40**
Gelderd La. LS12: Leeds 3B **40**
Gelderd Pl. LS12: Leeds 1C **40**
Gelderd Rd. LS12: Gil, Leeds 6G **39**
LS12: Leeds 1D **40**
LS27: Gil 4C **48**
WF17: Birs 6H **47**
Gelderd Trad. Est. LS12: Leeds 2C **40**
Gelder Rd. LS12: Leeds 6H **29**
Gemini Bus. Pk. LS7: Leeds 2H **31**
Genista Dr. LS10: Leeds 1H **51**
George Mann Rd. LS10: Leeds 4C **42**
George Mann Way LS10: Leeds 4B **42**
George St. LS2: Leeds 4F **5** (5G **31**)
LS19: Raw 5D **8**
WF1: Out 6D **58**
Georgian Sq. LS13: Leeds 6G **17**
Gerard Av. LS27: Morl 5F **49**
Ghyll Beck Dr. LS19: Raw 6G **9**
Ghyll Mt. LS19: Yead 3B **8**
Ghyll Rd. LS6: Leeds 5G **19**
Ghyll Royd LS20: Guis 6G **7**
(not continuous)
Ghyllroyd LS19: Yead 4C **8**
Ghyllroyd Av. BD11: Birk 4D **46**
Ghyllroyd Dr. BD11: Birk 4D **46**
Gibraltar Island Rd. LS10: Leeds 3B **42**
Gibraltar Rd. LS28: Pud 6D **26**
Gibson Dr. LS15: Leeds 6C **34**
Gilbert Chase LS5: Leeds 2G **29**
Gilbert Cl. LS5: Leeds 2H **29**
Gilbert Mt. LS5: Leeds 2H **29**
Gilbert St. LS28: Fars 3F **27**
GILDERSOME 2C **48**
Gildersome La. LS12: Gil, N Far 1B **48**
LS27: Gil 1B **48**
Gildersome Spur LS27: Gil 4D **48**
GILDERSOME STREET 4B **48**
Gillett Dr. LS26: Rothw 4H **53**
Gillett La. LS26: Rothw 4H **53**
Gillingham Grn. BD4: B'frd 4A **36**
Gill La. LS19: Yead 5A **8**
GILLROYD 5A **50**
Gillroyd Mt. LS27: Morl 5A **50**
Gillroyd Pde. LS27: Morl 6H **49**
Gillroyd Pl. LS27: Morl 5H **49**
Gillroyd Ter. LS27: Morl 5A **50**
Gills, The LS27: Morl 5A **50**
Gillstead Ho. LS14: Leeds 5H **23**
(off Kingsdale Ct.)
Gilpin Pl. LS12: Leeds 1B **40**
Gilpin St. LS12: Leeds 1B **40**
Gilpin Ter. LS12: Leeds 1B **40**
Gilpin Vw. LS12: Leeds 1B **40**
Gilwell Ct. WF3: Thpe H 1B **58**
Gipsy Hill LS26: Wood 3B **54**
Gipsy La. LS11: Leeds 1E **51**
LS26: Wood .3B **54**
Gipsy Mead LS26: Wood 3B **54**
Gipsy St. BD3: B'frd 5A **26**
GIPTON 2D **32**
Gipton App. LS9: Leeds 4E **33**
Gipton Av. LS7: Leeds 2A **32**
Gipton Ga. E. LS9: Leeds 2E **33**
Gipton Ga. W. LS9: Leeds 2D **32**
Gipton Lodge LS8: Leeds 1C **32**
(off Copgrove Rd.)
Gipton Sq. LS9: Leeds 4F **33**
Gipton St. LS8: Leeds 2A **32**
GIPTON WOOD 6D **22**
Gipton Wood Av. LS8: Leeds 6D **22**
Gipton Wood Cres. LS8: Leeds 6D **22**
Gipton Wood Gro. LS8: Leeds 6D **22**
Gipton Wood Pl. LS8: Leeds 6D **22**
Gipton Wood Rd. LS8: Leeds 6D **22**
Glade, The LS28: Stan 3C **26**
Glade Wlk. LS10: Leeds 5B **52**
Gladstone Ct. LS28: Stan 3H **27**
(off Gladstone Ter.)
Gladstone Cres. LS19: Raw 4D **8**
Gladstone Ho. BD4: B'frd 3A **36**
(off Tyersal La.)
Gladstone Rd. LS19: Raw 5D **8**
Gladstone St. LS28: Fars 2F **27**
Gladstone Ter. LS27: Morl 5G **49**
LS28: Stan .3H **27**
Gladstone Vs. LS17: Shad 6G **15**
Glanville Ter. LS26: Rothw 4G **53**

Glasshouse St. LS10: Leeds 2H **41**
Glasshouse Vw. LS10: Leeds 5F **51**
Glastonbury Ct. BD4: B'frd 3A **36**
Glebe Av. LS5: Leeds 1H **29**
Glebe Ct. LS26: Rothw 4C **52**
Glebe Mt. LS28: Pud 1G **37**
Glebe Pl. LS5: Leeds 1H **29**
Glebe St. LS28: Pud 1G **37**
Glebe Ter. LS16: Leeds 4B **20**
GLEDHOW 4B **22**
Gledhow Av. LS8: Leeds 3B **22**
Gledhow Ct. LS7: Leeds 4A **22**
Gledhow Grange Vw. LS8: Leeds 4B **22**
Gledhow Grange Wlk. LS8: Leeds 4B **22**
Gledhow La. LS7: Leeds 4H **21**
LS8: Leeds .4A **22**
Gledhow La. End LS7: Leeds 4H **21**
Gledhow Mt. LS8: Leeds 3A **32**
Gledhow Pk. Av. LS7: Leeds 5A **22**
Gledhow Pk. Cres. LS7: Leeds 5A **22**
Gledhow Pk. Dr. LS7: Leeds 5H **21**
Gledhow Pk. Gro. LS7: Leeds 5A **22**
Gledhow Pk. Rd. LS7: Leeds 5A **22**
Gledhow Pk. Vw. LS7: Leeds 5A **22**
Gledhow Pl. LS8: Leeds 3A **32**
Gledhow Ri. LS8: Leeds 5D **22**
Gledhow Rd. LS8: Leeds 3A **32**
Gledhow Ter. LS8: Leeds 3A **32**
Gledhow Towers LS8: Leeds 4A **22**
Gledhow Valley Rd. LS7: Leeds 3H **21**
LS8: Leeds .4A **22**
Gledhow Wood Av. LS8: Leeds 4B **22**
Gledhow Wood Cl. LS8: Leeds 4B **22**
Gledhow Wood Ct. LS8: Leeds 6C **22**
Gledhow Wood Gro. LS8: Leeds 4B **22**
Gledhow Wood Rd. LS8: Leeds 4B **22**
Glencoe Vw. LS9: Leeds 1B **42**
Glen Ct. LS27: Morl 6H **49**
Glendale Gdns. LS27: Morl 6H **49**
Glen Dene LS29: Men 1D **6**
Glendower Pk. LS16: Leeds 1B **20**
Gleneagles Rd. LS17: Leeds 5F **13**
Glenfield Cvn. Pk. LS17: Bard 1H **15**
Glen Gro. LS27: Morl 6H **49**
Glenholme Rd. LS28: Fars 3E **27**
Glenhurst BD4: B'frd 6A **36**
Glenlea Cl. LS28: Stan 2A **28**
Glenlea Gdns. LS28: Stan 2A **28**
Glenmere Mt. LS19: Yead 2F **9**
Glen Mt. LS27: Morl 6H **49**
LS29: Men 2D **6**
Glenmount Ter. LS27: Morl 1A **56**
Glen Rd. LS16: Leeds 4A **20**
LS27: Morl .6H **49**
Glenroyd Cl. LS28: Pud 6E **27**
Glensdale Gro. LS9: Leeds 6B **32**
Glensdale Mt. LS9: Leeds 6B **32**
Glensdale Rd. LS9: Leeds 6B **32**
Glensdale St. LS9: Leeds 6B **32**
Glensdale Ter. LS9: Leeds 6B **32**
Glenthorpe Av. LS9: Leeds 5C **32**
Glenthorpe Cres. LS9: Leeds 5C **32**
Glenthorpe Ter. LS9: Leeds 5C **32**
Glen Vw. LS27: Morl 6H **49**
Global Av. LS11: Leeds 6C **40**
Global Ct. LS11: Leeds 1C **50**
Globe Rd. LS11: Leeds 6A **4** (6E **31**)
Glossop Gro. LS6: Leeds 1F **31**
(off Glossop Vw.)
Glossop Mt. LS6: Leeds 1F **31**
Glossop St. LS6: Leeds 1F **31**
Glossop Vw. LS6: Leeds 1F **31**
Gloucester Ct. LS12: Leeds 6C **30**
Gloucester Ter. LS12: Leeds 5C **30**
Glover Way LS11: Leeds 5G **41**
Goffee Way LS27: Chur 1A **50**
Golden Bank LS18: H'fth 2C **18**
Golden Ter. LS12: Leeds 3G **39**
Goldsmith Dr. WF3: Rob H 6D **52**
Gomersall Ho. BD11: Drig 3F **47**
Goodman St. LS10: Leeds 2A **42**
Goodrick La. LS17: Leeds 3F **13**
Goodwin Rd. LS12: Leeds 1A **40**
Goodwood LS10: Leeds 6H **51**
Goody Cross La. LS26: Swil 5H **45**
Goody Cross Va. LS26: Swil 5H **45**
Goosedale Ct. BD4: B'frd 6C **36**
Goose La. LS20: Hawk 4A **6**
Gordon Dr. LS6: Leeds 5C **20**
Gordon Pl. LS6: Leeds 5D **20**
Gordon St. WF3: E Ard 3A **58**
Gordon Ter. LS6: Leeds 5D **20**
Gorse Lea LS10: Leeds 1H **51**
Gotts Pk. Av. LS12: Leeds 4F **29**
Gotts Pk. Cres. LS12: Leeds 4F **29**

Gotts Pk. Vw. LS12: Leeds 3F **29**
Gotts Rd. LS12: Leeds 5A **4** (6D **30**)
Gower St. LS2: Leeds 3G **5** (5H **31**)
Grace St. LS1: Leeds 4B **4** (5E **31**)
Grafton St. LS7: Leeds 2F **5** (4G **31**)
Grafton Vs. LS15: Leeds 1D **34**
Graham Av. LS4: Leeds 2B **30**
Graham Gro. LS4: Leeds 2B **30**
Graham Ho. LS5: Leeds 2F **29**
(off Broad La.)
Graham Mt. LS4: Leeds 2B **30**
Graham St. LS4: Leeds 2B **30**
Graham Ter. LS4: Leeds 2B **30**
Graham Vw. LS4: Leeds 2B **30**
Graham Wlk. LS27: Gil 2D **48**
Graingers Way LS12: Leeds 6A **4** (6D **30**)
Granary Wharf LS1: Leeds 6D **4** (6F **31**)
Granby Av. LS6: Leeds 6B **20**
Granby Cl. LS6: Leeds 1B **30**
Granby Gro. LS6: Leeds 1B **30**
Granby Mt. LS6: Leeds 6B **20**
Granby Pl. LS6: Leeds 6B **20**
Granby Rd. LS6: Leeds 1B **30**
Granby St. LS6: Leeds 6B **20**
Granby Ter. LS6: Leeds 6B **20**
Granby Vw. LS6: Leeds 6B **20**
Grand Arc. LS1: Leeds 3F **5**
Grandstand Rd. WF2: Carr G 6A **58**
WF3: Loft 6A **58**
Grand Theatre & Opera House 3F **5** (5G **31**)
Grange, The LS6: Leeds 6C **20**
LS11: Leeds 5E **41**
LS12: Leeds 4F **29**
LS13: Leeds 4C **28**
WF3: Carl 6F **53**
Grange Av. BD3: B'frd 5B **26**
BD4: E Bier .1C **46**
LS7: Leeds .1A **32**
LS19: Yead 3E **9**
LS29: Men 1B **6**
Grange Bldgs. LS27: Morl 1A **56**
(off Hodgson St.)
Grange Cl. LS10: Leeds 3H **41**
LS18: H'fth .3H **17**
Grange Ct. LS6: Leeds 6D **20**
LS15: Scho .5F **25**
LS17: Leeds 4G **13**
LS26: Wood .2C **54**
Grange Cres. LS7: Leeds 1A **32**
LS19: Yead 3E **9**
Grange Cft. LS17: Leeds 4G **13**
Grange Dr. LS18: H'fth 3H **17**
Grange Farm Cl. LS29: Men 1B **6**
Grangefield Ind. Est. LS28: Stan 4G **27**
Grangefield Rd. LS28: Stan 3G **27**
(not continuous)
Grange Flds. Mt. LS10: Leeds 2B **52**
Grange Flds. Rd. LS10: Leeds 3B **52**
Grange Flds. Way LS10: Leeds 3B **52**
Grange Gro. BD3: B'frd 5B **26**
Grange Holt LS17: Leeds 4G **13**
Grange Mt. LS19: Yead 3E **9**
Grange Pk. Av. LS8: Leeds 6F **23**
Grange Pk. Cl. LS8: Leeds 6G **23**
Grange Pk. Ct. LS27: Morl 2H **49**
(off Grange Pk. Dr.)
Grange Pk. Cres. LS8: Leeds 6F **23**
Grange Pk. Dr. LS27: Morl 2H **49**
Grange Pk. Gro. LS8: Leeds 6F **23**
Grange Pk. M. LS8: Leeds 6F **23**
LS27: Morl .2H **49**
Grange Pk. Pl. LS8: Leeds 6F **23**
Grange Pk. Ri. LS8: Leeds 6F **23**
Grange Pk. Rd. LS8: Leeds 6F **23**
Grange Pk. Ter. LS8: Leeds 6G **23**
Grange Pk. Wlk. LS8: Leeds 6F **23**
Grange Pk. Way LS27: Morl 2H **49**
Grange Rd. LS10: Leeds 3H **41**
LS19: Yead 3E **9**
Grange Rd., The LS16: Leeds 2H **19**
Grange St. LS27: Chur 1A **50**
Grange Ter. LS7: Leeds 1H **31**
LS19: Yead 3E **9**
(off Grange Rd.)
LS27: Morl .2H **49**
LS28: Pud 5G **27**
Grange Vw. BD3: B'frd 5B **26**
LS7: Leeds .1A **32**
LS15: Leeds 1D **44**
LS28: Pud 5G **27**
Grange Vw. Gdns. LS17: Leeds 2H **23**
Grangewood Ct. LS16: Leeds 2H **19**
WF1: Out 6F **59**
Grangewood Gdns. LS16: Leeds 2H **19**
Granhamthorpe LS13: Leeds 3C **28**
Granny Av. LS27: Chur 1A **50**

Granny La.—Half Mile

Granny La. LS12: Leeds 2G **39**
Granny Pl. LS27: Chur 1A **50**
Grant Av. LS7: Leeds 3A **32**
Grantham Towers *LS9: Leeds* *4A 32*
(off Lindsey Gdns.)
Granton Rd. LS7: Leeds 6H **21**
Granville Rd. LS9: Leeds 4A **32**
Granville St. LS28: Pud 5E **27**
LS28: Stan 3H **27**
Granville Ter. LS19: Yead 2E **9**
LS20: Guis 3H **7**
Grape St. LS10: Leeds 2H **41**
Grasmere Cl. LS12: Leeds 1B **40**
Grasmere Ct. LS12: Leeds 6B **30**
Grasmere Rd. LS12: Leeds 1B **40**
GRAVELEYTHORPE **5A** 34
Graveleythorpe Ri. LS15: Leeds 4B **34**
Graveleythorpe Rd. LS15: Leeds 4B **34**
Gray Ct. LS15: Leeds 5D **34**
Grayrigg Cl. LS15: Leeds 6G **33**
Grayshon St. BD11: Drig 4H **47**
Grayson Crest LS4: Leeds 2H **29**
Grayson Hgts. LS4: Leeds 2H **29**
Grayswood Cres. BD4: B'frd 4A **36**
Grayswood Dr. BD4: B'frd 3A **36**
Gt. George St. LS1: Leeds 3C **4** (5F **31**)
LS2: Leeds 3C **4** (5F **31**)
Gt. Northern St. LS27: Morl 6G **49**
Gt. Wilson St. LS11: Leeds 1F **41**
Greaves Yd. LS28: Pud 2G **37**
Greek St. LS1: Leeds 4D **4** (5F **31**)
GREEN, THE
LS14 ....**1A** 34
LS28 ....**1F** 27
Green, The BD4: E Bier 2B **46**
LS14: Leeds 6A **24**
(not continuous)
LS17: Leeds 1A **22**
LS18: H'fth 3B **18**
LS19: Yead *2D 8*
(off Town St.)
LS20: Guis 5G **7**
LS27: Gil 2D **48**
LS28: Fars 1F **27**
Greenacre Pk. LS19: Raw 4D **8**
Greenacre Pk. Av. LS19: Raw 4D **8**
Greenacre Pk. M. LS19: Raw 4E **9**
Greenacre Pk. Ri. LS19: Raw 4D **8**
Greenacres Dr. WF17: Birs 6A **48**
Green Bank WF3: Loft 2F **59**
Greenbanks Av. LS18: H'fth 1C **18**
Greenbanks Cl. LS18: H'fth 1C **18**
Greenbanks Dr. LS18: H'fth 1B **18**
GREENBOTTOM **5G** 7
Green Chase LS6: Leeds 4C **20**
Green Cl. LS6: Leeds 4D **20**
Green Ct. LS15: Scho 4F **25**
LS17: Leeds 1H **21**
Green Cres. LS6: Leeds 4C **20**
Greencroft M. *LS20: Guis* *4G 7*
(off The Green)
Green Dragon Yd. LS1: Leeds 4D **4**
Greenfield Av. LS20: Guis 6D **6**
LS27: Gil 2B **48**
Greenfield Ct. LS16: Leeds 5H **11**
Greenfield Dr. LS27: Gil 2B **48**
Greenfield La. LS20: Guis 6C **6**
Greenfield Rd. LS9: Leeds 6A **32**
Greengate LS26: Oul 3C **54**
GREENGATES **4A** 16
Greenhead Rd. LS16: Leeds 3H **19**
Green Hill Chase LS12: Leeds 1H **39**
Green Hill Cl. LS12: Leeds 4F **29**
Green Hill Cres. LS12: Leeds 1A **40**
Green Hill Cft. LS12: Leeds 1H **39**
Green Hill Dr. LS13: Leeds 4E **29**
Green Hill Gdns. LS12: Leeds 1H **39**
Green Hill Holt LS12: Leeds 1H **39**
Green Hill La. LS12: Leeds 2G **39**
Green Hill Mt. LS13: Leeds 4E **29**
Green Hill Pl. LS13: Leeds 4E **29**
Green Hill Rd. LS12: Leeds 4F **29**
LS13: Leeds 4E **29**
Greenhills LS19: Raw 6E **9**
Green Hill Way LS13: Leeds 4E **29**
Greenholme Ct. BD4: B'frd 5B **36**
Greenhouse *LS11: Leeds* *3F 41*
(off Beeston Rd.)
Greenhouse, The LS11: Leeds 3F **41**
Greenhow Cl. LS4: Leeds 3B **30**
Greenhow Gdns. LS4: Leeds 3B **30**
Greenhow Rd. LS4: Leeds 3B **30**
Greenhow Wlk. LS4: Leeds 3B **30**
Greenland Ct. LS26: Oul 4C **54**
Green La. BD2: B'frd 2A **26**
LS11: Leeds 6D **40**
LS12: Leeds 1C **40**
Green La. LS12: N Far 2C **38**
LS14: Leeds 3A **24**
LS15: Leeds 4B **34**
LS16: Leeds 5D **10**
LS18: H'fth 4B **18**
LS19: Yead 4D **8**
LS28: Pud 1F **37**
WF3: Loft 2E **59**
Green Lea LS26: Oul 3B **54**
Greenlea Av. LS19: Yead 3B **8**
Greenlea Cl. LS19: Yead 4B **8**
Greenlea Fold LS19: Yead 4B **8**
Greenlea Mt. LS19: Yead 3B **8**
Greenlea Rd. LS19: Yead 3B **8**
Greenmoor Av. LS12: Leeds 6D **28**
WF3: Loft 2E **59**
Greenmoor Cl. WF3: Loft 2E **59**
Greenmoor Ct. WF3: Carl, Loft 2E **59**
Greenmoor Cres. WF3: Loft 2F **59**
Greenmount Ct. *LS11: Leeds* *4F 41*
(off Fulham St.)
Greenmount La. LS11: Leeds 4F **41**
Greenmount Pl. LS11: Leeds 4F **41**
Greenmount St. LS11: Leeds 4F **41**
Greenmount Ter. LS11: Leeds 4F **41**
Greenock Pl. LS12: Leeds 5G **29**
Greenock Rd. LS12: Leeds 5G **29**
Greenock St. LS12: Leeds 5G **29**
Greenock Ter. LS12: Leeds 5G **29**
Green Pk. LS17: Leeds 1A **22**
Green Pasture Cl. LS9: Leeds 5E **33**
Green Rd. LS6: Leeds 3C **20**
Green Row LS6: Leeds 4C **20**
Greenroyd Av. BD19: Hun 6A **46**
Greenshank M. LS27: Morl 5B **50**
Greenshaw Ter. LS20: Guis 4F **7**
Greenside *LS19: Yead* *4C 8*
(off Warm La.)
LS28: Pud 1F **37**
Greenside Av. LS12: Leeds 2H **39**
Greenside Cl. LS12: Leeds 2A **40**
Greenside Ct. LS27: Gil 2D **48**
Greenside Dr. LS12: Leeds 2A **40**
Greenside Gro. LS28: Pud 1F **37**
Greenside Rd. LS12: Leeds 2A **40**
Greenside Ter. LS12: Leeds 2H **39**
Greenside Wlk. LS12: Leeds 2H **39**
Green Ter. LS11: Leeds 4G **41**
LS20: Guis 5G **7**
Greenthorpe Ct. LS13: Leeds 6E **29**
Greenthorpe Hill LS13: Leeds 6E **29**
Greenthorpe Mt. LS13: Leeds 5E **29**
Greenthorpe Rd. LS13: Leeds 5E **29**
Greenthorpe St. LS13: Leeds 6E **29**
Greenthorpe Wlk. LS13: Leeds 5E **29**
Green Top LS12: Leeds 2H **39**
Greentop LS28: Pud 1F **37**
Green Top Gdns. LS12: Leeds 2H **39**
Green Vw. LS6: Leeds 4C **20**
Greenview Cl. LS9: Leeds 3E **33**
Greenview Ct. LS8: Leeds 3C **22**
Greenville Av. LS12: Leeds 2H **39**
Greenville Gdns. LS12: Leeds 2H **39**
Greenway LS15: Leeds 4C **34**
LS20: Guis 6E **7**
Greenway Cl. LS15: Leeds 4C **34**
Greenwell Ct. LS9: Leeds 5E **33**
Greenwood Ct. LS6: Leeds 3C **20**
Greenwood Mt. LS6: Leeds 4C **20**
Greenwood Pk. LS6: Leeds 4C **20**
Greenwood Rd. WF3: Ting 3D **56**
Greenwood Row LS28: Pud 6H **27**
Grenfell Dr. BD3: B'frd 5A **26**
Grenfell Ter. BD3: B'frd 5A **26**
Gresley Ho. *LS18: H'fth* *6C 10*
(off Sussex Av.)
Greyshiels Av. LS6: Leeds 1A **30**
Greyshiels Cl. LS6: Leeds 1A **30**
Greystone Mt. LS15: Leeds 6G **33**
Greystones Ct. LS8: Leeds 4E **23**
LS17: Leeds 5G **13**
Griff Ho. La. WF3: E Ard 3F **57**
Grimthorpe Av. LS6: Leeds 6A **20**
Grimthorpe Pl. LS6: Leeds 6B **20**
Grimthorpe St. LS6: Leeds 6A **20**
Grimthorpe Ter. LS6: Leeds 6B **20**
Grosmont Pl. LS13: Leeds 2C **28**
Grosmont Rd. LS13: Leeds 3C **28**
Grosmont Ter. LS13: Leeds 2C **28**
Grosvenor Ct. LS16: Leeds 5D **10**
Grosvenor Hill LS7: Leeds 3G **31**
Grosvenor M. LS19: Raw 5C **8**
Grosvenor Mt. LS6: Leeds 1D **30**
Grosvenor Pk. LS7: Leeds 4G **21**
Grosvenor Pk. Gdns.
LS6: Leeds 1D **30**
Grosvenor Rd. LS6: Leeds 1D **30**
Grosvenor Ter. LS6: Leeds 1D **30**
Grove, The BD10: B'frd 4A **16**
LS8: Leeds 5F **23**
LS17: Leeds 4D **12**
LS18: H'fth 3B **18**
LS19: Yead 3D **8**
LS26: Swil 5H **45**
LS27: Gil 2D **48**
LS28: Pud 6F **27**
WF3: E Ard 3F **57**
Grove Av. LS6: Leeds 5C **20**
LS28: Pud 6F **27**
Grove Ct. LS6: Leeds 5C **20**
LS28: Pud 6F **27**
Grove Farm Cl. LS16: Leeds 5F **11**
Grove Farm Cres. LS16: Leeds 6E **11**
Grove Farm Cft. LS16: Leeds 5E **11**
Grove Farm Dr. LS16: Leeds 5E **11**
Grove Gdns. LS6: Leeds 5C **20**
Grovehall Av. LS11: Leeds 6D **40**
Grovehall Dr. LS11: Leeds 6D **40**
Grovehall Pde. LS11: Leeds 6D **40**
Grovehall Rd. LS11: Leeds 6D **40**
Grove Ho. *LS7: Leeds* *1A 32*
(off Woodland Gro.)
Grove Ho. Ct. *LS8: Leeds* *5F 23*
(off Nth. Grove Cl.)
Grove La. LS6: Leeds 5B **20**
Grove Ri. LS17: Leeds 4D **12**
Grove Rd. LS6: Leeds 6C **20**
LS10: Leeds 4A **42**
LS15: Leeds 6A **34**
LS18: H'fth 3B **18**
LS28: Pud 6F **27**
LS29: Men 1C **6**
Grove St. LS1: Leeds 4A **4**
LS28: Stan 3G **27**
Grove Ter. BD11: Birk 5C **46**
LS28: Pud 6F **27**
Grovewood LS6: Leeds 5B **20**
Grunberg Pl. LS6: Leeds 6B **20**
Grunberg St. LS6: Leeds 6B **20**
Guardian M. *LS12: Leeds* *2A 40*
(off Lynwood Gth.)
Guillemot App. LS27: Morl 6B **50**
GUISELEY **4G** 7
Guiseley Dr. LS29: Men 3D **6**
Guiseley Retail Pk. LS20: Guis 5G **7**
Guiseley Station (Rail) 4F **7**
Guiseley Theatre **5G** 7
Gurbax Ct. BD3: B'frd 6A **26**
Gwynne Av. BD3: B'frd 4A **26**
Gym and Tonic **1B** 22
Gym Health & Fitness Club, The **3C** 32
Gypsy Wood Cl. LS15: Leeds 6D **34**
Gypsy Wood Crest LS15: Leeds 6D **34**

H

Haddon Av. LS4: Leeds 3A **30**
Haddon Pl. LS4: Leeds 3A **30**
Haddon Rd. LS4: Leeds 3B **30**
Hadleigh Ct. LS17: Leeds 1H **21**
Hadley's Ct. *LS27: Gil* *3D 48*
(off Gelderd Rd.)
Haigh Av. LS26: Rothw 2E **53**
Haigh Gdns. LS26: Rothw 2E **53**
Haigh Hall BD10: B'frd 4A **16**
Haigh Hall Rd. BD10: B'frd 4A **16**
HAIGH MOOR **5C** 56
Haigh Moor Av. WF3: W Ard 5C **56**
Haigh Moor Cres. WF3: W Ard 5C **56**
Haigh Moor Rd. WF3: W Ard 6C **56**
Haigh Moor Vw. WF3: W Ard 5C **56**
Haigh Pk. Rd. LS10: Leeds 5D **42**
Haigh Rd. LS26: Rothw 3G **53**
Haighside LS26: Rothw 3E **53**
Haighside Cl. LS26: Rothw 3E **53**
Haighside Dr. LS26: Rothw 3E **53**
Haighside Way LS26: Rothw 3E **53**
Haigh Ter. LS26: Rothw 2E **53**
Haigh Vw. LS26: Rothw 2E **53**
Haigh Wood Cres. LS16: Leeds 6D **10**
Haigh Wood Grn. LS16: Leeds 1D **18**
Haigh Wood Rd. LS16: Leeds 6C **10**
Haines Pk. LS7: Leeds 3A **32**
Hainsworth Ct. *LS28: Fars* *2F 27*
(off Ebenezer St.)
Hainsworth Sq. LS28: Fars 2F **27**
Hainsworth St. LS12: Leeds 1C **40**
LS26: Rothw 5G **53**
Halcyon Hill LS7: Leeds 3G **21**
Hales Rd. LS12: Leeds 2H **39**
Halesworth Cres. BD4: B'frd 4A **36**
Haley's Yd. LS13: Leeds 2C **28**
HALF MILE **2H** 27

80 A-Z Leeds

Half Mile—Hawthorn Dr.

Half Mile LS13: Leeds 3H **27**
Half Mile Cl. LS28: Stan 3H **27**
Half Mile Ct. LS28: Stan 3H **27**
Half Mile Gdns. LS13: Leeds 3H **27**
Half Mile Grn. LS28: Stan 3H **27**
Half Mile La. LS13: Leeds 2H **27**
LS28: Fars 2H **27**
Hall, The LS7: Leeds 4G **21**
Hallamfield LS20: Guis 5G **7**
Hallam St. LS20: Guis 5F **7**
Hall Ct. LS7: Leeds 1H **31**
Hall Gro. LS6: Leeds 3D **30**
Halliday Av. LS12: Leeds 5G **29**
Halliday Dr. LS12: Leeds 5G **29**
Halliday Gro. LS12: Leeds 5G **29**
Halliday Mt. LS12: Leeds 5G **29**
Halliday Pl. LS12: Leeds 5G **29**
Halliday Rd. LS12: Leeds 5G **29**
Halliday St. LS28: Pud 5G **27**
Hall La. LS7: Leeds 6H **21**
LS12: Leeds 6A **30**
LS12: N Far 1C **38**
LS16: Leeds 3E **11**
LS18: H'fth 3H **17**
Hall Pk. Av. LS18: H'fth 2A **18**
Hall Pk. Cl. LS18: H'fth 2A **18**
Hall Pk. Gth. LS18: H'fth 2A **18**
Hall Pk. Mt. LS18: H'fth 2A **18**
Hall Pk. Ri. LS18: H'fth 2A **18**
Hall Pl. LS9: Leeds 6B **32**
Hall Rd. LS12: Leeds 6A **30**
LS26: Swil 6H **45**
Hall Sq. LS28: Cal 4D **16**
Hallwood Grn. BD10: B'frd 6A **16**
HALTON 5H **33**
Halton Dr. LS15: Leeds 5A **34**
Halton Hill LS15: Leeds 5H **33**
HALTON MOOR 6G **33**
Halton Moor Av. LS9: Leeds 1F **43**
Halton Moor Rd. LS9: Leeds 1C **42**
(not continuous)
LS15: Leeds 1G **43**
Hamilton Av. LS7: Leeds 1A **32**
Hamilton Gdns. LS7: Leeds 2H **31**
Hamilton Pl. LS7: Leeds 2A **32**
Hamilton Ter. LS7: Leeds 1A **32**
Hamilton Vw. LS7: Leeds 1A **32**
Hammerton Gro. LS28: Pud 6H **27**
Hammerton St. LS28: Pud 6G **27**
Hammond Cres. BD11: Drig 2F **47**
Hampton Cres. *LS9: Leeds 6B* ***32***
(off Long La. Cl.)
Hampton Pl. LS9: Leeds 6B **32**
Hampton Ter. LS9: Leeds 6B **32**
Hanley Rd. LS27: Morl 6G **49**
Hanover Av. LS3: Leeds 2A **4** (5E **31**)
Hanover Ct. LS27: Morl 4H **49**
Hanover Ho. *LS19: Yead 2E* ***9***
(off Harper La.)
Hanover La. LS3: Leeds 3B **4** (5E **31**)
Hanover Mt. LS3: Leeds 2A **4** (4E **31**)
Hanover Sq. LS3: Leeds 2A **4** (4E **31**)
Hanover Wlk. LS3: Leeds 3B **4** (5E **31**)
Hanover Way LS3: Leeds 3A **4** (5E **31**)
Hansby Av. LS14: Leeds 6B **24**
Hansby Bank LS14: Leeds 6B **24**
Hansby Cl. LS14: Leeds 1B **34**
Hansby Dr. LS14: Leeds 6B **24**
Hansby Gdns. LS14: Leeds 1B **34**
Hansby Ga. LS14: Leeds 6B **24**
Hansby Grange LS14: Leeds 6B **24**
Hansby Pl. LS14: Leeds 6B **24**
Harborough Grn.
BD10: B'frd 3A **16**
Harcourt Dr. LS27: Morl 4F **49**
Harcourt Pl. LS1: Leeds 4A **4** (5D **30**)
Harden Gro. BD10: B'frd 2A **26**
Hardrow Grn. LS12: Leeds 2B **40**
Hardrow Gro. LS12: Leeds 2B **40**
Hardrow Rd. LS12: Leeds 2A **40**
Hardrow Ter. LS12: Leeds 2B **40**
Hardwick Cft. LS7: Leeds 5H **21**
Hardy Av. LS27: Chur 1A **50**
Hardy Ct. LS27: Morl 5H **49**
Hardy Gro. LS11: Leeds 4E **41**
Hardy St. LS11: Leeds 4E **41**
LS27: Morl 5H **49**
Hardy Ter. LS11: Leeds 4F **41**
Hardy Vw. LS11: Leeds 4E **41**
Hare Farm Av. LS12: Leeds 6D **28**
Hare Farm Cl. LS12: Leeds 5D **28**
Harefield E. LS15: Leeds 6G **33**
Harefield W. LS15: Leeds 6G **33**
HAREHILLS 3D **32**
Harehills Av. LS7: Leeds 1A **32**
LS8: Leeds 1A **32**
HAREHILLS CORNER 1B **32**
Harehills La. LS7: Leeds 6A **22**
LS8: Leeds 1B **32**
LS9: Leeds 1C **32**
Harehills Pk. Av. LS9: Leeds 3D **32**
Harehills Pk. Cotts. LS9: Leeds 3E **33**
Harehills Pk. Rd. LS9: Leeds 3D **32**
Harehills Pk. Ter. LS9: Leeds 3D **32**
Harehills Pk. Vw. LS9: Leeds 3D **32**
Harehills Pl. LS8: Leeds 2B **32**
Harehills Rd. LS8: Leeds 1B **32**
Hare La. LS28: Pud 2G **37**
Hare Pk. Mt. LS12: Leeds 6C **28**
Hares Av. LS8: Leeds 1B **32**
Hares Mt. LS8: Leeds 1A **32**
Hares Rd. LS8: Leeds 1A **32**
Hares Ter. LS8: Leeds 1B **32**
Hares Vw. LS8: Leeds 1B **32**
Harewood Ct. LS14: Leeds 1A **34**
LS17: Leeds 2H **21**
Harewood St. LS2: Leeds 4F **5** (5G **31**)
Harewood Way LS13: Leeds 5B **28**
Hargrave Cres. LS29: Men 1B **6**
Hargreaves Av. WF3: S'ley 6G **59**
Hargreaves Cl. LS27: Morl 2F **49**
Hargreaves St. LS26: Rothw 4H **53**
Harker Ter. LS28: Stan 4F **27**
Harland Sq. *LS2: Leeds 2E* ***31***
(off Moorfield St.)
Harlech Av. LS11: Leeds 5F **41**
Harlech Cres. LS11: Leeds 5F **41**
Harlech Gro. LS11: Leeds 5F **41**
Harlech Mt. LS11: Leeds 5F **41**
Harlech Pk. Ct. LS11: Leeds 5F **41**
Harlech Rd. LS11: Leeds 5F **41**
Harlech St. LS11: Leeds 5F **41**
Harlech Ter. LS11: Leeds 5F **41**
Harley Cl. LS13: Leeds 5A **28**
Harley Ct. LS13: Leeds 5A **28**
Harley Dr. LS13: Leeds 5A **28**
Harley Gdns. LS13: Leeds 5A **28**
Harley Grn. LS13: Leeds 5A **28**
Harley Ri. LS13: Leeds 5A **28**
Harley Rd. LS13: Leeds 5A **28**
Harley Ter. LS13: Leeds 5A **28**
Harley Vw. LS13: Leeds 5A **28**
Harley Wlk. LS13: Leeds 5A **28**
Harlington Ct. LS27: Morl 6G **49**
Harlington Rd. LS27: Morl 6G **49**
Harlow Ct. LS8: Leeds 4E **23**
Harold Av. LS6: Leeds 3C **30**
Harold Gdns. LS27: Morl 5A **50**
Harold Gro. LS6: Leeds 3C **30**
Harold Mt. LS6: Leeds 3C **30**
Harold Pl. LS6: Leeds 3C **30**
Harold Rd. LS6: Leeds 3C **30**
Harold Sq. LS6: Leeds 3C **30**
Harold St. LS6: Leeds 3C **30**
Harold Ter. LS6: Leeds 3C **30**
Harold Vw. LS6: Leeds 3C **30**
Harold Wlk. LS6: Leeds 3C **30**
Harper Ga. BD4: B'frd 3B **36**
Harper La. LS19: Yead 3D **8**
Harper Rock *LS19: Yead 3D* ***8***
(off Harper La.)
Harper St. LS2: Leeds 5G **5** (6H **31**)
Harper Ter. *LS19: Yead 3D* ***8***
(off Harper La.)
Harrier Way LS27: Morl 5B **50**
Harriet St. LS7: Leeds 2H **31**
Harrison and Potter Trust Homes, The
LS2: Leeds 2F **5**
Harrison Cres. LS9: Leeds 4F **33**
Harrison Potter Trust Almshouses
LS2: Leeds 2E ***31***
(off Raglan Rd.)
Harrison's Av. LS28: Stan 3H **27**
Harrison St. LS1: Leeds 3F **5** (5G **31**)
Harrogate Pde. LS17: Leeds 1H **21**
Harrogate Rd. BD10: B'frd 6A **16**
LS7: Leeds 3G **21**
LS17: Leeds 2G **21**
LS17: Leeds, Wike 6H **13**
LS19: B'hpe, Yead 1G **9**
LS19: Raw 5D **8**
(not continuous)
Harrogate Vw. LS17: Leeds 4E **15**
Harrowby Cres. LS16: Leeds 4H **19**
Harrowby Rd. LS16: Leeds 4H **19**
Harthill LS27: Gil 2D **48**
Harthill Av. LS27: Gil 2D **48**
Harthill Cl. LS27: Gil 2D **48**
Harthill La. LS27: Gil 2D **48**
Harthill Paddock LS27: Gil 2D **48**
Harthill Pde. *LS27: Gil 2D* ***48***
(off Town St.)
Harthill Ri. LS27: Gil 2D **48**
Hartland Rd. BD4: B'frd 3A **36**
Hartley Av. LS6: Leeds 1E **31**
Hartley Bus. Pk. BD4: B'frd 1A **36**
Hartley Cres. LS6: Leeds 1E **31**
Hartley Gdns. LS6: Leeds 1F **31**
Hartley Gro. LS6: Leeds 1E **31**
Hartley Hill LS2: Leeds 2F **5** (4G **31**)
Hartley Pl. LS27: Morl 6H **49**
Hartley's Bldgs. LS27: Morl 6H **49**
Hartley St. LS27: Chur 2H **49**
LS27: Morl 5H **49**
Hartley's Yd. LS12: Leeds 6H **29**
Hartwell Rd. LS6: Leeds 3C **30**
Harwill App. LS27: Chur 2A **50**
Harwill Av. LS27: Chur 2A **50**
Harwill Cft. LS27: Chur 2A **50**
Harwill Gro. LS27: Chur 2A **50**
Harwill Ri. LS27: Chur 2A **50**
Harwill Rd. LS27: Chur 2A **50**
Haslemere Cl. BD4: B'frd 4A **36**
Haslewood Cl. LS9: Leeds 5A **32**
Haslewood Ct. LS9: Leeds 5B **32**
Haslewood Dene LS9: Leeds 5B **32**
Haslewood Dr. LS9: Leeds 5A **32**
Haslewood Gdns. LS9: Leeds 5B **32**
Haslewood Grn. LS9: Leeds 5B **32**
Haslewood M. LS9: Leeds 5B **32**
Haslewood Pl. LS9: Leeds 5B **32**
Haslewood Sq. LS9: Leeds 5B **32**
Haslewood Vw. LS9: Leeds 5B **32**
Hastings Ct. LS17: Shad 5G **15**
Hathaway Dr. LS14: Leeds 2B **24**
Hathaway La. LS14: Leeds 3B **24**
Hathaway M. LS14: Leeds 2B **24**
Hathaway Wlk. LS14: Leeds 3B **24**
Hauxwell Dr. LS19: Yead 3D **8**
Haven, The LS15: Leeds 5D **34**
Haven Chase LS16: Leeds 6E **11**
Haven Cl. LS16: Leeds 5F **11**
Haven Ct. LS16: Leeds 6F **11**
Haven Cft. LS16: Leeds 6F **11**
Haven Gdns. LS16: Leeds 6E **11**
Haven Gth. LS16: Leeds 6E **11**
Haven Grn. LS16: Leeds 6E **11**
Haven Mt. LS16: Leeds 6E **11**
Haven Ri. LS16: Leeds 6E **11**
Haven Vw. LS16: Leeds 6E **11**
Havercroft LS12: Leeds 2E **39**
Havercroft Gdns. LS12: Leeds 2E **39**
Haw Av. LS19: Yead 1E **9**
Hawkhill Av. LS15: Leeds 3B **34**
LS20: Guis 5F **7**
Hawkhill Dr. LS15: Leeds 2B **34**
Hawkhill Gdns. LS15: Leeds 2B **34**
Hawkhills LS7: Leeds 4A **22**
Hawkhurst Rd. LS12: Leeds 1A **40**
Hawkins Dr. LS7: Leeds 3G **31**
Hawkshead Cres. LS14: Leeds 2H **33**
Hawksley Ct. LS27: Morl 2F **49**
Hawk's Nest Gdns. E. LS17: Leeds 5H **13**
Hawk's Nest Gdns. Sth. LS17: Leeds 5H **13**
Hawk's Nest Gdns. W. LS17: Leeds 5H **13**
Hawk's Nest Ri. LS17: Leeds 5H **13**
Hawkstone Av. LS20: Guis 6E **7**
Hawkstone Vw. LS20: Guis 6E **7**
Hawkswood Av. LS5: Leeds 4E **19**
Hawkswood Cres. LS5: Leeds 4E **19**
Hawkswood Gro. LS5: Leeds 4E **19**
Hawkswood Mt. LS5: Leeds 4E **19**
Hawkswood Pl. LS5: Leeds 5E **19**
Hawkswood St. LS5: Leeds 5F **19**
Hawkswood Ter. LS5: Leeds 5F **19**
Hawkswood Vw. LS5: Leeds 4E **19**
HAWKSWORTH
LS5 5E **19**
LS20 5B **6**
Hawksworth Av. LS20: Guis 6F **7**
Hawksworth Cl. LS29: Men 2C **6**
Hawksworth Commercial Pk. LS13: Leeds 4C **28**
Hawksworth Dr. LS20: Guis 6F **7**
LS29: Men 1B **6**
Hawksworth Gro. LS5: Leeds 5D **18**
Hawksworth La. LS20: Guis 5B **6**
Hawksworth Rd. LS18: H'fth 4D **18**
Haw La. LS19: Yead 2D **8**
Hawley Cl. LS27: Morl 6F **49**
Hawley Ter. BD10: B'frd 1A **26**
Hawley Way LS27: Morl 6F **49**
Haworth Ct. *LS19: Yead 2D* ***8***
(off Chapel La.)
Haworth La. LS19: Yead 2D **8**
Haworth Rd. WF17: Birs 6H **47**
Hawthorn Av. LS19: Yead 2D **8**
Hawthorn Cres. LS7: Leeds 4H **21**
LS19: Yead 2D **8**
Hawthorn Cft. WF3: Loft 2E **59**
Hawthorn Dr. LS13: Leeds 5F **17**
LS19: Yead 1E **9**

A-Z Leeds 81

Hawthorne Av.—High St.

Hawthorne Av. BD3: B'frd 5A 26
Hawthorne Cl. LS27: Gil 2D 48
Hawthorne Dr. LS27: Gil 2E 49
Hawthorne Gdns. LS16: Leeds 4H 11
Hawthorne Mills *LS12: Leeds 3G 39*
(off Cobden Rd.)
Hawthorne Ri. LS14: Leeds 3C 24
Hawthorne Vw. LS27: Gil 2E 49
Hawthorn Gro. LS13: Leeds 6F 17
LS26: Rothw 5H 53
Hawthorn La. LS7: Leeds 4H 21
Hawthorn M. LS14: Leeds 3B 24
Hawthorn Mt. LS7: Leeds 4H 21
Hawthorn Pk. LS14: Leeds 3A 24
Hawthorn Rd. LS7: Leeds 4H 21
LS19: Yead 2D 8
Hawthorns, The WF1: Out 6F 59
Hawthorn Sq. WF3: E Ard 3A 58
Hawthorn St. BD3: B'frd 5A 26
Hawthorn Ter. LS25: Gar 2H 45
Hawthorn Va. LS7: Leeds 4H 21
Hawthorn Vw. LS7: Leeds 4H 21
Haw Vw. LS19: Yead 1E 9
Haydn Av. WF3: S'ley 5G 59
Haydn Cl. LS27: Morl 5G 49
Haydn Ct. LS27: Morl 5G 49
Haydn's Ter. LS28: Stan 3G 27
Hayfield Ter. LS12: Leeds 1A 40
Hayleigh Av. LS13: Leeds 2C 28
Hayleigh Mt. LS13: Leeds 2C 28
Hayleigh St. LS13: Leeds 2C 28
Hayleigh Ter. LS13: Leeds 3C 28
Hazel Av. LS14: Leeds 3C 24
Hazel Cl. BD11: Birk 3C 46
Hazel Ct. LS26: Rothw 5H 53
Hazelcroft BD2: B'frd 1A 26
Hazelhurst Ct. LS28: Pud 6H 27
Hazel La. WF3: E Ard 3B 58
Hazelwood Ct. WF1: Out 6F 59
Hazelwood Rd. WF1: Out 6F 59
HEADINGLEY 6B 20
Headingley 1B 30
Headingley Av. LS6: Leeds 6A 20
Headingley Ct. LS6: Leeds 1D 30
Headingley Cres. LS6: Leeds 1B 30
HEADINGLEY HILL 1C 30
Headingley La. LS6: Leeds 1C 30
Headingley Mt. LS6: Leeds 6A 20
Headingley Office Pk. LS6: Leeds 1D 30
Headingley Ri. *LS6: Leeds 2D 30*
(off Welton Rd.)
Headingley Station (Rail) 1H 29
Headingley Ter. LS6: Leeds 1D 30
Headingley Vw. LS6: Leeds 1B 30
Headrow, The LS1: Leeds 3D 4 (5F 31)
Healey Cft. WF3: W Ard 4F 57
Healey Cft. La. WF3: E Ard 4F 57
Heathcliffe Cl. WF17: Birs 6H 47
Heathcliffe Ct. *LS27: Morl 5D 48*
(off Bruntcliffe Rd.)
Heath Cres. LS11: Leeds 4C 40
Heathcroft Bank LS11: Leeds 5C 40
Heathcroft Cres. LS11: Leeds 5C 40
Heathcroft Dr. LS11: Leeds 5C 40
Heathcroft Lawn LS11: Leeds 5C 40
Heathcroft Ri. LS11: Leeds 5C 40
Heathcroft Va. LS11: Leeds 5C 40
Heather Cl. WF1: Out 6F 59
Heather Ct. WF1: Out 6G 59
Heathercroft LS7: Leeds 5A 22
Heatherdale Ct. WF3: Ting 3C 56
Heatherdale Dr. WF3: Ting 3C 56
Heatherdale Fold WF3: Ting 3C 56
Heatherdale Rd. WF3: Ting 3B 56
Heather Gdns. LS13: Leeds 5E 29
Heather Gro. LS13: Leeds 4E 29
Heathfield LS16: Leeds 5G 11
Heathfield Cl. WF3: W Ard 4D 56
Heathfield La. BD11: Birk 5C 46
Heathfield Ter. LS6: Leeds 5B 20
Heathfield Wlk. LS16: Leeds 4G 11
Heath Gro. LS11: Leeds 4C 40
LS28: Pud 1E 37
Heath Mt. LS11: Leeds 4C 40
Heath Pl. LS11: Leeds 4C 40
Heath Ri. LS11: Leeds 5C 40
Heath Rd. LS11: Leeds 4C 40
Heaton Av. LS12: Leeds 2A 40
Heaton Ct. *LS14: Leeds 5H 23*
(off Kingsdale Ct.)
Heaton's Ct. LS1: Leeds 6E 5 (6G 31)
Hebden App. LS14: Leeds 5B 24
Hebden Chase LS14: Leeds 5B 24
Hebden Cl. LS14: Leeds 5B 24
Hebden Grn. LS14: Leeds 5B 24
Hebden Path LS14: Leeds 5B 24
Hebden Pl. LS14: Leeds 5B 24
Hebden Wlk. LS14: Leeds 5B 24
Heddon Pl. LS6: Leeds 5C 20
Heddon St. LS6: Leeds 5C 20
Hedley Chase LS12: Leeds 6C 30
Hedley Gdns. LS12: Leeds 6C 30
Hedley Grn. LS12: Leeds 6C 30
Heights Bank LS12: Leeds 6F 29
Heights Cl. LS12: Leeds 6E 29
Heights Dr. LS12: Leeds 5E 29
Heights East, The LS12: Leeds 6F 29
Heights Gth. LS12: Leeds 6E 29
Heights Grn. LS12: Leeds 6F 29
Heights La. LS12: Leeds 6F 29
Heights Pde. LS12: Leeds 6E 29
Heights Wlk. LS12: Leeds 6F 29
Heights Way LS12: Leeds 6E 29
Heights West, The LS12: Leeds 6E 29
Helmsley Ct. LS10: Leeds 5G 51
Helmsley Dr. LS16: Leeds 4H 19
Helmsley Rd. LS16: Leeds 4H 19
Helston Cft. LS10: Leeds 4E 51
Helston Gth. LS10: Leeds 4E 51
Helston Grn. LS10: Leeds 4E 51
Helston Pl. LS10: Leeds 4E 51
Helston Rd. LS10: Leeds 3E 51
Helston Sq. LS10: Leeds 3D 50
Helston St. LS10: Leeds 3D 50
Helston Wlk. LS10: Leeds 4E 51
(not continuous)
Helston Way LS10: Leeds 3E 51
Hembrigg Gdns. LS27: Morl 6G 49
Hembrigg Ter. LS27: Morl 6G 49
Hemingway Cl. LS10: Leeds 3A 42
Hemingway Gth. LS10: Leeds 4A 42
Hemingway Grn. LS10: Leeds 4A 42
Henbury St. LS7: Leeds 1H 5 (4H 31)
Henconner Av. LS7: Leeds 5G 21
Henconner Cres. LS7: Leeds 5G 21
Henconner Dr. LS7: Leeds 5G 21
Henconner Gdns. LS7: Leeds 5G 21
Henconner Gth. LS7: Leeds 5G 21
Henconner Gro. LS7: Leeds 5G 21
Henconner La. LS7: Leeds 5G 21
LS13: Leeds 4E 29
Henconner Rd. LS7: Leeds 5G 21
Henley Av. LS13: Leeds 3C 28
LS19: Raw 6F 9
Henley Cl. LS19: Raw 6F 9
Henley Cres. LS13: Leeds 3C 28
LS19: Raw 6F 9
Henley Dr. LS19: Raw 6E 9
Henley Gro. LS13: Leeds 3C 28
Henley Hill LS19: Raw 6E 9
Henley Mt. LS19: Raw 6F 9
Henley Pl. LS13: Leeds 3C 28
Henley Rd. LS13: Leeds 3C 28
Henley St. LS13: Leeds 3C 28
Henley Ter. LS13: Leeds 3C 28
Henley Vw. LS13: Leeds 3C 28
LS19: Raw 6E 9
Henley Vs. *LS19: Raw 6E 9*
(off Well La.)
Henry Av. LS12: Leeds 2A 40
Henry Gro. LS28: Pud 6F 27
Henry Moore Institute 3D 4
Henry Pl. LS27: Morl 5G 49
Henry Price Bldgs. LS2: Leeds 3E 31
Henry Ter. LS19: Yead 6H 7
HENSHAW 3C 8
Henshaw Av. LS19: Yead 3D 8
Henshaw Cres. LS19: Yead 3D 8
Henshaw La. LS19: Yead 4C 8
Henshaw M. LS19: Yead 4D 8
Henshaw Oval LS19: Yead 3D 8
Hepton Ct. LS9: Leeds 5D 32
Hepworth Av. LS27: Chur 1H 49
Hepworth Cres. LS27: Chur 1H 49
Herbalist St. LS12: Leeds 1C 40
Herbert Pl. BD3: B'frd 5A 26
Hereford St. LS12: Leeds 5A 30
Hermon Rd. LS15: Leeds 4B 34
Hermon St. LS15: Leeds 4B 34
Heron Cl. LS17: Leeds 5B 14
Heron Ct. LS27: Morl 5B 50
Heron Gro. LS17: Leeds 5B 14
Herries Ct. *LS29: Men 1D 6*
(off Leathley Rd.)
Hertford Chase LS15: Leeds 1C 44
Hertford Cl. LS15: Leeds 1D 44
Hertford Cft. LS15: Leeds 1D 44
Hertford Fold LS15: Leeds 1C 44
Hertford Lawn LS15: Leeds 1C 44
Hesketh Av. LS5: Leeds 6G 19
WF3: Ting 3B 56
Hesketh La. WF3: Ting, W Ard 3B 56
Hesketh Mt. LS5: Leeds 6G 19
Hesketh Pl. LS5: Leeds 6G 19
Hesketh Rd. LS5: Leeds 6G 19
Hesketh Ter. LS5: Leeds 1G 29
Hessle Av. LS6: Leeds 2C 30
Hessle Mt. LS6: Leeds 2C 30
Hessle Pl. LS6: Leeds 2C 30
Hessle Rd. LS6: Leeds 2C 30
Hessle St. LS6: Leeds 2C 30
Hessle Ter. LS6: Leeds 2C 30
Hessle Vw. LS6: Leeds 2C 30
Hessle Wlk. LS6: Leeds 2C 30
Hetton Ct. LS10: Leeds 4H 41
Hetton Dr. BD3: B'frd 1A 36
Hetton Rd. LS8: Leeds 6D 22
HEY BECK 6A 56
Heybeck La. WF12: Dew 6A 56
Heybeck Wlk. BD4: B'frd 5B 36
Heydon Cl. LS6: Leeds 2D 20
Heysham Dr. BD4: B'frd 4A 36
High Ash Av. LS17: Leeds 4A 14
High Ash Cres. LS17: Leeds 4A 14
High Ash Dr. LS17: Leeds 4A 14
High Ash Mt. LS17: Leeds 4A 14
High Bank App. LS15: Leeds 6D 34
High Bank Cl. LS15: Leeds 6D 34
High Bank Gdns. LS15: Leeds 6E 35
High Bank Ga. LS15: Leeds 6D 34
High Bank Pl. LS15: Leeds 6D 34
High Bank St. *LS28: Fars 2F 27*
(off Low Bank St.)
High Bank Vw. LS15: Leeds 6D 34
High Bank Way LS15: Leeds 6D 34
High Brook Fall WF3: Loft 5E 59
Highbury Cl. LS6: Leeds 5C 20
Highbury La. LS6: Leeds 5C 20
Highbury Mt. LS6: Leeds 5C 20
Highbury Pl. LS6: Leeds 5C 20
LS13: Leeds 5A 28
Highbury Rd. LS6: Leeds 5C 20
Highbury St. LS6: Leeds 5C 20
Highbury Ter. LS6: Leeds 5C 20
High Cliffe *LS4: Leeds 2A 30*
(off St Michael's La.)
Highcliffe Ind. Est. LS27: Morl 4E 49
Highcliffe Rd. LS27: Morl 5F 49
High Cl. LS19: Raw 6D 8
LS20: Guis 5D 6
High Ct. LS2: Leeds 5G 5 (6H 31)
High Ct. La. LS2: Leeds 5G 5 (6H 31)
Highcroft Cl. LS28: Pud 5E 27
Higher Grange Rd. LS28: Pud 5G 27
Highfield WF3: Ting 2B 56
Highfield Av. LS12: Leeds 1A 40
Highfield Cl. LS12: Leeds 2B 40
LS27: Gil 2E 49
Highfield Ct. *LS12: Leeds 2A 40*
(off Highfield Av.)
Highfield Cres. LS12: Leeds 1B 40
LS26: Wood 2C 54
LS28: Pud 5F 27
Highfield Dr. LS19: Raw 6E 9
LS27: Gil 2D 48
WF17: Birs 6G 47
Highfield Gdns. LS12: Leeds 1A 40
LS27: Gil 2D 48
Highfield Gth. LS12: Leeds 2B 40
Highfield Grn. LS28: Pud 5F 27
Highfield La. LS26: Wood 2C 54
Highfield Mt. LS26: Oul 3C 54
Highfield Pl. LS27: Morl 6H 49
Highfield Rd. LS13: Leeds 3D 28
LS28: Pud 5E 27
Highfield St. LS13: Leeds 3D 28
LS28: Pud 5E 27
Highfield Ter. LS19: Raw 6E 9
LS28: Pud 5E 27
Highfield Vw. LS27: Gil 2E 49
Highfold LS19: Yead 4C 8
High Gate St. LS10: Leeds 3A 42
Highlands Cl. LS10: Leeds 1B 52
Highlands Dr. LS10: Leeds 1B 52
Highlands Gro. LS10: Leeds 1B 52
Highlands Wlk. LS10: Leeds 1B 52
Highlea Cl. LS19: Yead 4B 8
High Mill Bus. Pk. LS27: Morl 6G 49
High Moor Av. LS17: Leeds 1A 22
High Moor Cl. LS17: Leeds 6A 14
High Moor Ct. LS17: Leeds 1A 22
High Moor Cres. LS17: Leeds 6A 14
High Moor Dr. LS17: Leeds 6A 14
High Moor Gro. LS17: Leeds 6A 14
High Ridge Av. LS26: Rothw 2F 53
High Ridge Ct. LS26: Rothw 3G 53
High Ridge Pk. LS26: Rothw 2F 53
High Royds Dr. LS29: Men 2C 6
High St. LS19: Yead 2D 8
LS27: Morl 6G 49
LS28: Fars 2F 27

82 A-Z Leeds

Highthorne Ct. LS17: Leeds 5B **14**
Highthorne Dr. LS17: Leeds 5B **14**
Highthorne Gro. LS12: Leeds 5G **29**
LS17: Leeds 5C **14**
Highthorne Mt. LS17: Leeds 5B **14**
Highthorne St. LS12: Leeds 5G **29**
Highthorne Vw. LS12: Leeds 5G **29**
Highway LS20: Guis 4D **6**
Highways LS14: Leeds 4G **33**
Highwood Av. LS17: Leeds 6G **13**
Highwood Ct. LS6: Leeds 6C **20**
Highwood Cres. LS17: Leeds 6G **13**
Highwood Gro. LS17: Leeds 1G **21**
High Woodlands WF3: E Ard 4G **57**
High Wood Rd. WF17: Birs 5A **48**
Hillary Pl. LS2: Leeds 1C **4** (3F **31**)
Hill Ct. Av. LS13: Leeds 1C **28**
Hillcourt Cft. LS13: Leeds 1C **28**
Hill Ct. Dr. LS13: Leeds 1C **28**
Hill Ct. Fold LS13: Leeds 1C **28**
Hill Ct. Gro. LS13: Leeds 1C **28**
Hill Ct. Vw. LS13: Leeds 1B **28**
Hill Cres. LS19: Raw 4E **9**
Hill Crest LS26: Swil 6G **45**
Hillcrest LS27: Gil .1B **48**
Hillcrest Av. LS7: Leeds 2A **32**
Hill Crest Cl. LS26: Swil 6F **45**
Hillcrest Ct. LS16: Leeds 5E **11**
Hillcrest Mt. LS16: Leeds 5E **11**
Hillcrest Pl. LS7: Leeds 1A **32**
Hillcrest Ri. LS16: Leeds 5D **10**
Hillcrest Vw. LS7: Leeds 1A **32**
HILL END 5E **29**
Hill End Cl. LS12: Leeds 5F **29**
Hill End Cres. LS12: Leeds 5F **29**
Hill End Rd. LS12: Leeds 5F **29**
HILLFOOT 5D **26**
Hillfoot Av. LS28: Pud 5D **26**
Hillfoot Cotts. LS28: Pud 5C **26**
Hillfoot Cres. LS28: Pud 5D **26**
Hillfoot Dr. LS28: Pud 5D **26**
Hillfoot Ri. LS28: Pud 5D **26**
HILL GREEN 5G **37**
Hill Grn. Ct. BD4: B'frd 5G **37**
Hillidge Rd. LS10: Leeds 3H **41**
Hillidge Sq. LS10: Leeds 3H **41**
Hillingdon Way LS17: Leeds 3E **13**
Hillings La. LS20: Hawk, Men 4A **6**
LS29: Men 1A **6**
Hill Ri. Av. LS13: Leeds 1C **28**
Hill Ri. Gro. LS13: Leeds 1C **28**
Hillside Av. LS20: Guis 2F **7**
Hillside Bldgs. LS11: Leeds 4E **41**
(off Beeston Rd.)
Hillside Ct. LS7: Leeds 4A **22**
LS29: Men 1B **6**
Hillside Gro. LS28: Pud 6H **27**
Hill Side Mt. LS28: Stan 3G **27**
Hillside Mt. LS28: Pud 6A **28**
Hillside Ri. LS20: Guis 2F **7**
Hillside Rd. LS7: Leeds 4H **21**
Hillside Vw. LS28: Pud 6A **28**
Hill St. LS9: Leeds 4A **32**
LS11: Leeds 4F **41**
Hillthorpe LS28: Pud 2G **37**
Hillthorpe Ct. LS10: Leeds 6G **51**
Hillthorpe Ri. LS28: Pud 2G **37**
Hillthorpe Rd. LS28: Pud 2G **37**
Hillthorpe Sq. LS28: Pud 2G **37**
Hillthorpe St. LS28: Pud 2G **37**
Hillthorpe Ter. LS28: Pud 2G **37**
HILL TOP
LS6 . . . . .3C **20**
LS12 . . . . .5F **29**
Hill Top Av. LS8: Leeds 1B **32**
WF3: W Ard 5C **56**
Hill Top Ct. WF3: W Ard 5C **56**
Hill Top Gdns. WF3: W Ard 5C **56**
Hill Top Grn. WF3: W Ard 5C **56**
Hill Top Gro. WF3: W Ard 5C **56**
Hill Top La. WF3: W Ard 6B **56**
Hill Top Mt. LS8: Leeds 1B **32**
Hill Top Pl. LS6: Leeds 3D **30**
LS8: Leeds 1B **32**
Hill Top Rd. LS6: Leeds 3D **30**
LS12: Leeds 5F **29**
Hill Top St. LS6: Leeds 3D **30**
Hill Top Vw. WF3: W Ard 5B **56**
Hill Vw. Av. LS7: Leeds 4H **21**
Hill Vw. Mt. LS7: Leeds 4H **21**
Hill Vw. Pl. LS7: Leeds 4H **21**
Hillview Ri. BD4: B'frd 3A **36**
Hill Vw. Ter. LS7: Leeds 4H **21**
Hillway LS20: Guis 6E **7**
Hilton Gro. LS8: Leeds 6B **22**
Hilton Pl. LS8: Leeds 1B **32**

Hilton Rd. LS8: Leeds 1B **32**
Hilton St. LS8: Leeds 1B **32**
Hilton Ter. LS8: Leeds 1B **32**
Hindle Pl. LS27: Chur 2H **49**
Hinsley Ct. LS6: Leeds 6C **20**
Hird St. LS11: Leeds 4E **41**
Hirst's Yd. LS1: Leeds 5F **5**
HMP Leeds LS12: Leeds 6B **30**
Hobberley La. LS17: Leeds, Shad 5H **15**
Hodgson Av. BD3: B'frd 5A **26**
LS17: Leeds 6C **14**
Hodgson Cres. LS17: Leeds 6C **14**
Hodgson La. BD11: Birk 2D **46**
BD11: Drig .3F **47**
Hodgson Pl. LS27: Chur 2H **49**
Hodgson St. LS27: Morl 2A **56**
HOLBECK 2E **41**
Holbeck La. LS11: Leeds 1D **40**
Holbeck Moor Rd. LS11: Leeds 2E **41**
Holbeck Towers LS11: Leeds 2E **41**
Holborn App. LS6: Leeds 2E **31**
Holborn Central LS6: Leeds *2E 31*
(off Rampart Rd.)
Holborn Ct. LS6: Leeds 2F **31**
Holborn Gdns. LS6: Leeds 2E **31**
Holborn Grn. LS6: Leeds 2E **31**
Holborn Gro. LS6: Leeds 2E **31**
Holborn Ter. LS6: Leeds 2F **31**
Holborn Towers LS6: Leeds 2F **31**
Holborn Vw. LS6: Leeds 2E **31**
Holborn Wlk. LS6: Leeds 2E **31**
Holden Ing Way WF17: Birs 5A **48**
Holdforth Cl. LS12: Leeds 6C **30**
Holdforth Gdns. LS12: Leeds 6C **30**
Holdforth Grn. LS12: Leeds 6C **30**
Holdforth Pl. LS12: Leeds 6C **30**
Holdsworth Pl. LS12: Leeds 6H **29**
Holland St. BD4: B'frd 1A **36**
Hollerton La. WF3: W Ard 3D **56**
Hollies, The WF3: W Ard 6A **30**
Hollin Ct. LS16: Leeds 4B **20**
Hollin Cres. LS16: Leeds 4B **20**
Hollin Dr. LS16: Leeds 4C **20**
Hollin Gdns. LS16: Leeds 4A **20**
Hollingbourne Rd. LS15: Leeds 3F **35**
Hollings, The LS26: Meth 6H **55**
Hollin Hill Av. LS8: Leeds 6E **23**
Hollin Hill Cotts. LS8: Leeds 6E **23**
Hollin Hill Dr. LS8: Leeds 6E **23**
Hollin La. LS16: Leeds 4B **20**
Hollin M. LS16: Leeds 4B **20**
HOLLIN PARK 6F **23**
Hollin Pk. Av. LS8: Leeds 6F **23**
Hollin Pk. Ct. LS28: Cal 5C **16**
Hollin Pk. Cres. LS8: Leeds 6F **23**
Hollin Pk. Dr. LS28: Cal 5C **16**
Hollin Pk. Mt. LS8: Leeds 5F **23**
Hollin Pk. Pde. LS8: Leeds 6E **23**
Hollin Pk. Pl. LS8: Leeds 6E **23**
Hollin Pk. Rd. LS8: Leeds 6E **23**
LS28: Cal .5C **16**
Hollin Pk. Ter. LS8: Leeds 6E **23**
Hollin Pk. Vw. LS8: Leeds 6E **23**
Hollin Rd. LS16: Leeds 4B **20**
Hollins Hill LS20: Guis 6E **7**
HOLLINTHORPE .3G **45**
Hollin Vw. LS16: Leeds 4B **20**
Hollis Pl. LS3: Leeds 4D **30**
Holly Av. LS16: Leeds 6D **10**
Holly Bank LS6: Leeds 5B **20**
LS20: Guis 4F **7**
Holly Cl. LS10: Leeds 5F **51**
Holly Ct. LS20: Guis 5F **7**
WF1: Out 6E **59**
WF3: W Ard 5C **56**
Holly Cres. WF3: E Ard 3B **58**
Hollycroft Ct. LS16: Leeds 6G **11**
Holly Dr. LS16: Leeds 6D **10**
Holly Pk. LS18: H'fth 2H **17**
Holly Pk. Mills LS28: Cal 5C **16**
Hollyshaw Cres. LS15: Leeds 5C **34**
Hollyshaw Gro. LS15: Leeds 4C **34**
Hollyshaw La. LS15: Leeds 5C **34**
Hollyshaw St. LS15: Leeds 5C **34**
Hollyshaw Ter. LS15: Leeds 5C **34**
Hollyshaw Wlk. LS15: Leeds 4C **34**
Holly Tree La. LS15: Leeds 1E **45**
Hollywell Gro. LS12: Leeds 5H **29**
Hollywell La. LS12: Leeds 6H **29**
Hollywood Bowl
Leeds 4B **30**
Holme Bank BD4: B'frd 3B **36**
Holme Bank Cl. BD4: B'frd 5B **36**
Holme Farm Ct. LS12: N Far 4D **38**
Holmefield Vw. BD4: B'frd 3B **36**

Holme La. BD4: B'frd 4B **36**
Holmelea Cft. LS6: Leeds 4C **20**
(off Church Gro.)
Holmes St. LS11: Leeds 1G **41**
HOLME VILLAGE 4B **36**
Holme Well Rd. LS10: Leeds 4A **52**
HOLME WOOD 4A **36**
Holme Wood Rd. BD4: B'frd 4A **36**
Holmfield Dr. LS8: Leeds 2C **22**
Holmsley Crest LS26: Wood 2A **54**
Holmsley Fld. Ct. LS26: Oul 3C **54**
Holmsley Fld. La. LS26: Oul 3B **54**
Holmsley Gth. LS26: Wood 2B **54**
Holmsley Grn. LS26: Wood 2B **54**
Holmsley Ho. LS26: Wood 3B **54**
Holmsley La. LS26: Wood 2B **54**
Holmsley Wlk. LS26: Oul 3B **54**
Holmwood LS6: Leeds 1C **22**
Holmwood Av. LS6: Leeds 3C **20**
Holmwood Cl. LS6: Leeds 3D **20**
Holmwood Cres. LS6: Leeds 3D **20**
Holmwood Dr. LS6: Leeds 3C **20**
Holmwood Gro. LS6: Leeds 3D **20**
Holmwood Mt. LS6: Leeds 3D **20**
Holmwood Vw. LS6: Leeds 3C **20**
Holroyd St. LS7: Leeds 3H **31**
Holsworthy Rd. BD4: B'frd 5A **36**
Holt Av. LS16: Leeds 4A **12**
Holt Cl. LS16: Leeds 4A **12**
Holt Cres. LS16: Leeds 4F **11**
Holtdale App. LS16: Leeds 4E **11**
Holtdale Av. LS16: Leeds 4F **11**
Holtdale Cl. LS16: Leeds 4F **11**
Holtdale Cft. LS16: Leeds 4F **11**
Holtdale Dr. LS16: Leeds 4F **11**
Holtdale Fold LS16: Leeds 4F **11**
Holtdale Gdns. LS16: Leeds 4F **11**
Holtdale Gth. LS16: Leeds 4F **11**
Holtdale Grn. LS16: Leeds 4F **11**
Holtdale Gro. LS16: Leeds 4F **11**
Holtdale Lawn LS16: Leeds 4F **11**
Holtdale Pl. LS16: Leeds 4F **11**
Holtdale Rd. LS16: Leeds 4F **11**
Holtdale Vw. LS16: Leeds 4F **11**
Holtdale Way LS16: Leeds 4F **11**
Holt Dr. LS16: Leeds 4G **11**
Holt Farm Cl. LS16: Leeds 4G **11**
Holt Farm Ri. LS16: Leeds 4G **11**
Holt Gdns. LS16: Leeds 4A **12**
Holt Gth. LS16: Leeds 4G **11**
Holt Ga. LS16: Leeds 4G **11**
Holt Grn. LS16: Leeds 4G **11**
Holt La. LS16: Leeds 4G **11**
Holt La. Ct. LS16: Leeds 5H **11**
HOLT PARK 4F **11**
Holt Pk. App. LS16: Leeds 4G **11**
Holt Pk. Av. LS16: Leeds 4G **11**
Holt Pk. Cl. LS16: Leeds 4F **11**
Holt Pk. Cres. LS16: Leeds 4F **11**
Holt Pk. Dr. LS16: Leeds 4G **11**
Holt Pk. Gdns. LS16: Leeds 4G **11**
Holt Pk. Ga. LS16: Leeds 4G **11**
Holt Pk. Grange LS16: Leeds 4G **11**
Holt Pk. Grn. LS16: Leeds 4G **11**
Holt Pk. Gro. LS16: Leeds 4F **11**
Holt Pk. La. LS16: Leeds 4G **11**
Holt Pk. Leisure Cen. 4F **11**
Holt Pk. Ri. LS16: Leeds 4G **11**
Holt Pk. Rd. LS16: Leeds 4F **11**
Holt Pk. Va. LS16: Leeds 4F **11**
Holt Pk. Vw. LS16: Leeds 4F **11**
Holt Pk. Way LS16: Leeds 4G **11**
Holt Ri. LS16: Leeds 4G **11**
Holt Rd. LS16: Leeds 4G **11**
Holt Va. LS16: Leeds 4G **11**
Holt Wlk. LS16: Leeds 4G **11**
Holt Way LS16: Leeds 4G **11**
Holybrook Av. BD10: B'frd 5A **16**
Holywell La. LS17: Shad 4F **15**
Holywell Vw. LS17: Shad 4F **15**
Home Farm Dr. LS29: Men 2B **6**
Home Farm M. LS29: Men 2C **6**
Home Lea LS26: Rothw 2F **53**
Home Lea Dr. LS26: Rothw 2F **53**
Hopefield Chase LS26: Rothw 5D **52**
Hopefield Cl. LS26: Rothw 5D **52**
Hopefield Ct. LS26: Rothw 5D **52**
WF3: E Ard 4G **57**
Hopefield Cres. LS26: Rothw 5D **52**
Hopefield Dr. LS26: Rothw 5D **52**
Hopefield Gdns. LS26: Rothw 5D **52**
Hopefield Grn. LS26: Rothw 5D **52**
Hopefield Gro. LS26: Rothw 5D **52**
Hopefield M. LS26: Rothw 5D **52**
Hopefield Pl. LS26: Rothw 5D **52**
Hopefield Vw. LS26: Rothw 5D **52**
Hopefield Wlk. LS26: Rothw 5D **52**

Hopefield Way LS26: Rothw 5D **52**
Hope Pastures 1A **20**
Hope Rd. LS9: Leeds 3H **5** (5H **31**)
Hopes Farm Mt. LS10: Leeds 2B **52**
Hopes Farm Rd. LS10: Leeds 2B **52**
Hopes Farm Vw. LS10: Leeds 2B **52**
Hope St. LS27: Morl 5G **49**
Hopewell Pl. LS6: Leeds 3C **30**
Hopewell Ter. LS18: H'fth 4B **18**
Hopewell Vw. LS10: Leeds 4H **51**
Hopkin St. BD4: B'frd 6A **36**
Hopton Ct. LS12: Leeds 6H **29**
(off Hopton M.)
Hopton M. LS12: Leeds 6H **29**
Hopwood Bank LS18: H'fth 1C **18**
Hopwood Cl. LS18: H'fth 1C **18**
Hopwood Rd. LS18: H'fth 1C **18**
Horf Orde Vw. LS13: Leeds 5B **18**
Hornbeam Ct. LS20: Guis 4F **7**
Hornbeam Way LS14: Leeds 3C **24**
Horsfall St. LS27: Morl 3F **49**
HORSFORTH 3B **18**
Horsforth New Rd. LS13: Leeds 5G **17**
Horsforth Station (Rail) 6C **10**
Horsforth Village Mus. 3B **18**
(off The Green)
Horsham Rd. BD4: B'frd 5A **36**
Horsman St. BD4: B'frd 6A **36**
Horton Cl. LS13: Leeds 1H **27**
Horton Gth. LS13: Leeds 1H **27**
Horton Ri. LS13: Leeds 1H **27**
Hospital La. LS16: Leeds 6F **11**
Hough Cl. LS13: Leeds 5B **28**
HOUGH END 5C **28**
Hough End Av. LS13: Leeds 4D **28**
Hough End Cl. LS13: Leeds 4D **28**
Hough End Ct. LS13: Leeds 4D **28**
Hough End Cres. LS13: Leeds 4C **28**
Hough End Gdns. LS13: Leeds 4D **28**
Hough End Gth. LS13: Leeds 4C **28**
Hough End La. LS13: Leeds 4C **28**
Hough Gro. LS13: Leeds 3C **28**
Hough La. LS13: Leeds 3C **28**
Houghley Av. LS12: Leeds 3F **29**
Houghley Cl. LS13: Leeds 3E **29**
Houghley Cres. LS12: Leeds 3F **29**
Houghley La. LS13: Leeds 3E **29**
Houghley Rd. LS12: Leeds 3F **29**
Houghley Sq. LS12: Leeds 3F **29**
HOUGH SIDE 6B **28**
Hough Side Cl. LS28: Pud 6B **28**
Hough Side La. LS28: Pud 6A **28**
Hough Side Rd. LS28: Pud 6H **27**
Hough Ter. LS13: Leeds 3C **28**
Hough Top LS13: Leeds 6A **28**
Hough Tree Rd. LS13: Leeds 5C **28**
Hough Tree Ter. LS13: Leeds 5C **28**
Hovingham Av. LS8: Leeds 1C **32**
Hovingham Gro. LS8: Leeds 1C **32**
Hovingham Mt. LS8: Leeds 1C **32**
Hovingham Ter. LS8: Leeds 1C **32**
Howard Av. LS15: Leeds 6H **33**
Howard Ct. LS15: Leeds 6H **33**
Howden Cl. BD4: B'frd 6B **36**
HOWDEN CLOUGH 6B **48**
Howden Clough Ind. Est. WF17: Birs ..6B **48**
Howden Clough Rd. LS27: Morl 6C **48**
Howden Gdns. LS6: Leeds 3C **30**
Howden Pl. LS6: Leeds 3C **30**
Howden Way LS27: Morl 5D **48**
Howley Pk. Vw. LS27: Morl 1A **56**
Howson Cl. LS20: Guis 4H **7**
Hoxton Mt. LS11: Leeds 4D **40**
Hudson Gro. LS9: Leeds 4C **32**
Hudson Pl. LS9: Leeds 4C **32**
Hudson Rd. LS9: Leeds 3C **32**
Hudson's Ter. LS19: Yead 2E **9**
Hudson St. LS9: Leeds 4C **32**
LS28: Fars 4F **27**
Hudswell Rd. LS10: Leeds 3H **41**
Huggan Row LS28: Pud 6H **27**
(off Hammerton Gro.)
Hughenden Vw. LS27: Morl 3G **49**
Hull St. LS27: Morl 5H **49**
Hunger Hill LS27: Morl 6G **49**
Hunger Hills Av. LS18: H'fth 2A **18**
Hunger Hills Dr. LS18: H'fth 2A **18**
HUNSLET 3H **41**
Hunslet Bus. Pk. LS10: Leeds 2A **42**
HUNSLET CARR 6H **41**
Hunslet Distributor LS10: Leeds 3H **41**
Hunslet Grn. Retail Cen.
LS10: Leeds 4H **41**
Hunslet Grn. Way LS10: Leeds 3H **41**
Hunslet Hall Rd. LS11: Leeds 3F **41**
Hunslet Hawks RLFC 1G **51**
Hunslet Ho. LS10: Leeds 6F **5**

Hunslet La. LS10: Leeds 1G **41**
(Crown Point Rd.)
LS10: Leeds 6F **5** (1G **41**)
(Salem Pl.)
Hunslet Rd. LS10: Leeds 1H **41**
(Sheaf St.)
LS10: Leeds 6F **5** (6G **31**)
(Waterloo St.)
Hunslet Trad. Est. LS10: Leeds 3B **42**
HUNSWORTH 6A **46**
Hunsworth La. LS10: E Bier 5A **46**
BD19: Cleck, Hun 6A **46**
(not continuous)
Hunters Ct. LS15: Leeds 6A **34**
Hunters Way LS15: Leeds 6A **34**
Huntington Cres. LS16: Leeds 4A **20**
Huntsman Ho. LS10: Leeds 1G **41**
Hurstville Av. BD4: E Bier 3B **46**
Husler Gro. LS7: Leeds 2H **31**
Husler Pl. LS7: Leeds 2H **31**
Hustler's Row LS6: Leeds 3B **20**
Hutchinson Pl. LS5: Leeds 2G **29**
Hutton Ter. LS28: Pud 6G **27**
HYDE PARK 2C **30**
Hyde Pk. Cl. LS6: Leeds 3D **30**
Hyde Pk. Cnr. LS6: Leeds 2D **30**
Hyde Pk. Pl. LS6: Leeds 2D **30**
Hyde Pk. Rd. LS6: Leeds 3D **30**
Hyde Pk. Ter. LS6: Leeds 2D **30**
Hyde Pk. Vs. LS6: Leeds 2D **30**
(off Bk. Kensington Ter.)
Hyde Pl. LS2: Leeds 2A **4** (4E **31**)
Hyde St. LS2: Leeds 2A **4** (4E **31**)
Hyde Ter. LS2: Leeds 1A **4** (4E **31**)
Hyde Way WF3: Thpe H 1B **58**

I

Ibbetson Cl. LS27: Chur 2G **49**
Ibbetson Ct. LS27: Chur 2G **49**
Ibbetson Cft. LS27: Chur 2G **49**
Ibbetson Dr. LS27: Chur 2G **49**
Ibbetson M. LS27: Chur 2G **49**
Ibbetson Oval LS27: Chur 2G **49**
Ibbetson Ri. LS27: Chur 2G **49**
Ibbetson Rd. LS27: Chur 2G **49**
Ida's, The LS10: Leeds 5C **42**
Ida St. LS10: Leeds 5C **42**
Ilford St. LS27: Morl 5H **49**
Illingworth Cl. LS19: Yead 4E **9**
Imperial Ter. LS12: Leeds 5H **29**
Indigoblu LS10: Leeds 1G **41**
(off Crown Point Rd.)
Indoor Bowls & Athletic Cen. 6G **41**
Industrial St. LS9: Leeds 4B **32**
Infirmary St. LS1: Leeds 4D **4** (5F **31**)
Inghams Av. LS28: Pud 6D **26**
Inghams Ter. LS28: Pud 5D **26**
Inghams Vw. LS28: Pud 5D **26**
Ingle Av. LS27: Morl 3F **49**
Ingleborough Cl. BD4: B'frd 4A **36**
Ingleborough Dr. LS27: Morl 6A **50**
(not continuous)
Ingleby Way LS10: Leeds 2A **52**
Ingle Ct. LS27: Morl 4F **49**
(Earlsmere Dr.)
LS27: Morl 3F **49**
(Springfield Av.)
Ingle Cres. LS27: Morl 3G **49**
Ingledew Ct. LS17: Leeds 5H **13**
Ingledew Cres. LS8: Leeds 1D **22**
Ingledew Dr. LS8: Leeds 2D **22**
Ingle Gro. LS27: Morl 4F **49**
Ingle La. LS29: Men 2D **6**
Ingle Row LS7: Leeds 5H **21**
Ingleton Cl. LS11: Leeds 4F **41**
Ingleton Dr. LS15: Leeds 6G **33**
Ingleton Gro. LS11: Leeds 4F **41**
Ingleton Pl. LS11: Leeds 4F **41**
Ingleton St. LS11: Leeds 4F **41**
Inglewood App. LS14: Leeds 2B **34**
Inglewood Dr. LS14: Leeds 2B **34**
Inglewood Pl. LS14: Leeds 2B **34**
Inglewood Ter. LS6: Leeds 1E **31**
(off Delph La.)
Ingram Cl. LS11: Leeds 2D **40**
Ingram Ct. LS11: Leeds 2D **40**
Ingram Cres. LS11: Leeds 3D **40**
Ingram Gdns. LS11: Leeds 2D **40**
Ingram Pde. LS26: Rothw 4G **53**
Ingram Rd. LS11: Leeds 3D **40**
Ingram Row LS11: Leeds 1F **41**
Ingram Vw. LS11: Leeds 2D **40**
Ings Av. LS20: Guis 3F **7**
Ings Ct. LS20: Guis 3E **7**

Ings Cres. LS9: Leeds 6D **32**
LS20: Guis 4E **7**
Ings La. LS20: Guis 4E **7**
Ings Rd. LS9: Leeds 6D **32**
Ing St. BD3: B'frd 1A **36**
Inkerman St. BD2: B'frd 1A **26**
Inmoor Rd. BD11: Birk 2D **46**
Inner Ring Rd. LS1: Leeds 2B **4** (4E **31**)
LS2: Leeds 1D **4** (4E **31**)
INTAKE 1A **28**
Intake Cl. WF3: S'ley 6H **59**
Intake La. LS10: Leeds 6G **51**
LS13: Leeds 2H **27**
LS14: T'ner 1D **24**
LS19: Raw 6F **9**
LS28: Stan 2H **27**
WF3: S'ley 6H **59**
(not continuous)
Intake Mt. LS10: Leeds 5G **51**
Intake Rd. LS28: Pud 5H **27**
Intake Sq. LS10: Leeds 5G **51**
Intake Vw. LS10: Leeds 5G **51**
LS13: Leeds 2A **28**
Intercity Way LS13: Leeds 4H **27**
Intermezzo Dr. LS10: Leeds 6D **42**
Invertrees Av. LS19: Raw 5E **9**
Iqbal Ct. BD3: B'frd 1A **36**
Ireland Cres. LS16: Leeds 6F **11**
IRELAND WOOD 1F **19**
Iron Stone Dr. LS12: N Far 3G **39**
Iron Stone Gdns. LS12: N Far 4G **39**
Ironwood App. LS14: Leeds 2A **34**
Ironwood Cres. LS14: Leeds 2A **34**
Ironwood Vw. LS14: Leeds 1A **34**
Irwin App. LS15: Leeds 6H **33**
Irwin St. LS28: Fars 3F **27**
(not continuous)
Islay Cl. LS26: Rothw 4H **53**
ISLINGTON 3B **40**
Ivegate LS19: Yead 2D **8**
Iveson App. LS16: Leeds 1F **19**
Iveson Cl. LS16: Leeds 1F **19**
Iveson Ct. LS16: Leeds 1F **19**
Iveson Cres. LS16: Leeds 1F **19**
Iveson Dr. LS16: Leeds 1F **19**
Iveson Gdns. LS16: Leeds 1F **19**
Iveson Gth. LS16: Leeds 1G **19**
Iveson Grn. LS16: Leeds 1F **19**
Iveson Gro. LS16: Leeds 1F **19**
Iveson Lawn LS16: Leeds 1G **19**
Iveson Ri. LS16: Leeds 1G **19**
Iveson Rd. LS16: Leeds 1F **19**
Iveson Wood Ri. LS16: Leeds 1G **19**
Ivies, The LS28: Pud 6G **27**
(off Lidget Hill)
Ivory St. LS10: Leeds 2G **41**
Ivy Av. LS9: Leeds 5C **32**
Ivy Bank LS19: Yead 2C **8**
Ivy Chase LS28: Pud 5B **28**
Ivy Ct. LS7: Leeds 5H **21**
Ivy Cres. LS9: Leeds 5C **32**
Ivy Gdns. LS13: Leeds 1D **28**
Ivy Gth. LS7: Leeds 5H **21**
Ivy Gro. LS9: Leeds 6D **32**
Ivy Mt. LS9: Leeds 5C **32**
Ivy Pl. LS13: Leeds 1D **28**
Ivy Rd. LS9: Leeds 6C **32**
Ivy St. LS9: Leeds 5C **32**
Ivy Vw. LS9: Leeds 5C **32**
Ivy View Studios 5C **32**
(off Ivy Vw.)

J

Jackie Smart Ct. LS7: Leeds 2A **32**
Jack La. LS10: Leeds 2G **41**
(Parkfield St.)
LS10: Leeds 3A **42**
(Whitfield Sq.)
LS11: Leeds 2F **41**
(Nineveh Rd.)
LS11: Leeds 1F **41**
(Parkfield St.)
Jackman Dr. LS18: H'fth 3D **18**
Jackson Av. LS8: Leeds 4B **22**
Jackson Rd. LS7: Leeds 2G **31**
Jackson Wlk. LS29: Men 2D **6**
Jacobs Ct. LS5: Leeds 2H **29**
Jacob St. LS2: Leeds 2F **5** (4G **31**)
Jail Yd. LS26: Rothw 4H **53**
Jail Yd. Pde. LS26: Rothw 4H **53**
(off Jail Yd.)
Jakeman Cl. WF3: Ting 3C **56**
Jakeman Ct. WF3: Ting 3C **56**
Jakeman Cft. WF3: Ting 3C **56**
Jakeman Dr. WF3: Ting 3C **56**

Jakeman Fold WF3: Ting 3C 56
James Av. LS8: Leeds 3B 22
James Baillie Pk. LS6: Leeds 6D 20
James Ct. LS27: Morl 4A 50
James St. BD11: Birk 3C 46
   LS19: Raw 5D 8
Jamie Ct. BD10: B'frd 5A 16
Jaques Cl. LS6: Leeds 1H 29
Jarvis Sq. WF3: Rob H 6C 52
Jarvis Wlk. WF3: Rob H 6C 52
Jean Av. LS15: Leeds 6A 34
Jenkinson Cl. LS11: Leeds 2E 41
Jenkinson Lawn LS11: Leeds 2E 41
Jenkinsons Pl. LS10: Leeds 1H 51
Jesmond Sq. LS28: Fars 2G 27
Jessamine Av. LS11: Leeds 6D 40
Jessop Row LS12: Leeds 6G 29
Jinny Moor La. LS26: Swil 1E 55
Joe Dean Recreation Cen. 6F 29
Joffre Mt. LS19: Yead 3E 9
   (off Springwell Cl.)
John Charles App. LS11: Leeds 1G 51
John Charles Cen. for Sport 1G 51
John Charles Stadium 1G 51
John Charles Way LS12: Leeds 3B 40
JOHN O'GAUNTS 2H 53
John O'Gaunts Trad. Est. LS26: Rothw .2G 53
John O'Gaunts Wlk. LS26: Rothw 3H 53
Johns Av. WF3: Loft 5E 59
Johnson Ter. LS27: Morl 5H 49
Johnston St. LS6: Leeds 2F 31
John St. BD4: B'frd 6A 36
   LS6: Leeds 2C 30
   LS19: Raw 5D 8
Jordan Rd. LS28: Stan 3A 28
Joseph Stones Ho. LS2: Leeds 4H 5
   (off St Cecilia St.)
Joseph St. BD4: B'frd 6A 36
   LS10: Leeds 3A 42
Joseph's Well LS3: Leeds 3B 4
Jubilee Cl. LS27: Morl 5H 49
   (off Marshall St.)
Jubilee Cres. BD11: Drig 2A 48
Jubilee Cft. BD11: Drig 2H 47
Jubilee Pl. LS27: Morl 5H 49
Jubilee St. LS27: Morl 5H 49
Jubilee Ter. LS27: Morl 5H 49
Jude Cl. LS13: Leeds 2E 29
Jumbles Ct. WF3: Loft 2E 59
Jumbles La. WF3: Loft 2E 59
Junction 1 Retail Pk. LS11: Leeds 5A 40
Junction St. LS10: Leeds 1G 41
Juniper Av. LS26: Wood 2D 54
Juniper Pl. LS9: Leeds 4D 32
Junxion, The LS5: Leeds 1H 29
   (off Station App.)
Juvenile Court
   Leeds 3D 4 (5F 31)

K

K2 LS9: Leeds 3E 5 (5E 33)
Karnac Rd. LS8: Leeds 1B 32
Kay Cl. LS27: Morl 2F 49
Kearsley Ter. LS10: Leeds 5A 42
Keats Gro. WF3: S'ley 5G 59
Kedleston Rd. LS8: Leeds 6B 14
Keeble Ho. BD2: B'frd 3A 26
   (off St Clare's Av.)
Keelham Dr. LS19: Raw 5E 9
Keel Moorings LS13: Leeds 6H 17
Keeper La. BD4: B'frd 4F 37
Keeton St. LS9: Leeds 5B 32
Keighley Pl. LS28: Stan 3G 27
KELCLIFFE 3F 7
Kelcliffe Av. LS20: Guis 4G 7
Kelcliffe Gro. LS20: Guis 4G 7
Kelcliffe La. LS20: Guis 3F 7
Keldholme Cl. LS13: Leeds 6G 17
Keldholme Rd. LS13: Leeds 6G 17
Kellett Av. LS12: Leeds 3A 40
Kellett Cres. LS12: Leeds 3A 40
Kellett Dr. LS12: Leeds 3A 40
Kellett Gro. LS12: Leeds 3A 40
Kellett La. LS12: Leeds 2H 39
Kellett Mt. LS12: Leeds 3A 40
Kellett Pl. LS12: Leeds 3A 40
Kellett Rd. LS12: Leeds 2H 39
Kellett Ter. LS12: Leeds 3A 40
Kellett Wlk. LS12: Leeds 3A 40
Kelmscott Av. LS15: Leeds 2D 34
Kelmscott Cres. LS15: Leeds 2D 34
Kelmscott Gdns. LS15: Leeds 2D 34
Kelmscott Gth. LS15: Leeds 1E 35
Kelmscott Grn. LS15: Leeds 2D 34

Kelmscott Gro. LS15: Leeds 2D 34
Kelmscott La. LS15: Leeds 2D 34
Kelsall Av. LS6: Leeds 3C 30
Kelsall Gro. LS6: Leeds 4C 30
Kelsall Pl. LS6: Leeds 3C 30
Kelsall Rd. LS6: Leeds 3C 30
Kelsall Ter. LS6: Leeds 3C 30
Kelso Ct. LS3: Leeds 4D 30
Kelso Gdns. LS2: Leeds 1A 4 (4D 30)
Kelso Hgts. LS3: Leeds 3D 30
Kelso Ho. BD4: B'frd 4A 36
   (off Stirling Cres.)
Kelso Pl. LS2: Leeds 3D 30
Kelso Rd. LS2: Leeds 1A 4 (3D 30)
Kelso St. LS2: Leeds 1A 4 (4D 30)
Kelvin Ho. BD4: B'frd 4B 36
Kemsing Wlk. LS15: Leeds 3F 35
Kendal Bank LS3: Leeds 2A 4 (4D 30)
Kendal Carr LS3: Leeds 2A 4 (4D 30)
Kendal Cl. LS3: Leeds 2A 4 (4D 30)
Kendal Dr. LS15: Leeds 6G 33
Kendal Gro. LS3: Leeds 2A 4 (4E 31)
Kendal La. LS3: Leeds 2A 4 (4D 30)
Kendal Ri. LS3: Leeds 3A 4
Kendal Rd. LS3: Leeds 2A 4 (4E 31)
Kendal Wlk. LS3: Leeds 3A 4
Kendell St. LS10: Leeds 6F 5 (6G 31)
Kenilworth Av. LS27: Gil 3D 48
Kenilworth Gdns. LS27: Gil 2D 48
Kenilworth Rd. LS12: Leeds 2A 40
Kenmore Rd. WF2: Carr G 6B 58
Kennerleigh Av. LS15: Leeds 4C 34
Kennerleigh Cres. LS15: Leeds 4D 34
Kennerleigh Dr. LS15: Leeds 4C 34
Kennerleigh Gth. LS15: Leeds 4D 34
Kennerleigh Glen LS15: Leeds 4C 34
Kennerleigh Gro. LS15: Leeds 4D 34
Kennerleigh Ri. LS15: Leeds 4D 34
Kennerleigh Wlk. BD4: B'frd 5B 36
   (off Wenborough La.)
   LS15: Leeds 4C 34
Kenneth St. LS11: Leeds 2D 40
Kensington Ct. LS6: Leeds 2D 30
   LS10: Leeds 1B 52
Kensington Gdns. LS10: Leeds 2B 52
Kensington Ter. LS6: Leeds 2D 30
Kensington Way LS10: Leeds 2B 52
Ken Syke Cotts. WF3: W Ard 4B 56
KENT 6G 27
Kent Av. LS28: Pud 6A 28
Kent Cl. LS28: Pud 6A 28
Kent Cres. LS28: Pud 6H 27
Kent Dr. LS28: Pud 6A 28
Kentmere App. LS14: Leeds 6G 23
Kentmere Av. LS14: Leeds 4H 23
Kentmere Cl. LS14: Leeds 6A 24
Kentmere Cres. LS14: Leeds 5H 23
Kentmere Gdns. LS14: Leeds 5H 23
Kentmere Ga. LS14: Leeds 5H 23
Kentmere Grn. LS14: Leeds 5H 23
Kentmere Ri. LS14: Leeds 6A 24
Kenton Way BD4: B'frd 3A 36
Kent Rd. LS28: Pud 6H 27
Kenwood M. LS18: H'fth 3D 18
Kenworthy Cl. LS16: Leeds 4G 11
Kenworthy Gdns. LS16: Leeds 4G 11
Kenworthy Gth. LS16: Leeds 4G 11
Kenworthy Ga. LS16: Leeds 4G 11
Kenworthy Ri. LS16: Leeds 4G 11
Kenworthy Va. LS16: Leeds 4G 11
Kepler Gro. LS8: Leeds 3A 32
Kepler Mt. LS8: Leeds 3A 32
Kepler Ter. LS8: Leeds 3A 32
Keplestone M. LS17: Leeds 3A 14
Kepstorn Cl. LS5: Leeds 6G 19
Kepstorn Ri. LS5: Leeds 6G 19
Kepstorn Rd. LS16: Leeds 4H 19
Kerry Ct. LS18: H'fth 2B 18
   (off Kerry Gth.)
Kerry Gth. LS18: H'fth 2B 18
Kerry Hill LS18: H'fth 3B 18
   (not continuous)
Kerry St. LS18: H'fth 2B 18
Kerry Vw. LS18: H'fth 2C 18
Kershaw St. BD3: B'frd 6A 26
Kesteven Cl. BD4: B'frd 5B 36
Kesteven Ct. BD4: B'frd 5A 36
Kesteven Rd. BD4: B'frd 5B 36
Kestrel Cl. LS17: Leeds 5B 14
Kestrel Gth. LS27: Morl 5B 50
Kestrel Gro. LS17: Leeds 5B 14
Keswick St. BD4: B'frd 2A 36
Keys Ct. LS11: Leeds 1F 41
   (off Saw Mill St.)
Kidacre St. LS10: Leeds 1G 41
   LS11: Leeds 1G 41
Kielder Dr. LS10: Leeds 5A 52

Kielder Way LS26: Wood 2B 54
Kilburn Rd. LS12: Leeds 6A 30
Kildare Ter. LS12: Leeds 1C 40
KILLINGBECK 4G 33
Killingbeck Bri. LS14: Leeds 4F 33
Killingbeck Dr. LS14: Leeds 4G 33
Killingbeck Retail Pk. LS14: Leeds .. .3G 33
Kilner Ho. BD2: B'frd 3A 26
   (off St Clare's Av.)
Kilnsea Mt. BD4: B'frd 4A 36
Kimberley Pl. LS9: Leeds 3D 32
Kimberley Rd. LS9: Leeds 3D 32
Kimberley Vw. LS9: Leeds 4D 32
King Alfred's Dr. LS6: Leeds 2E 21
King Alfred's Grn. LS6: Leeds 2E 21
King Alfred's Wlk. LS6: Leeds 2E 21
King Alfred's Way LS6: Leeds 2E 21
King Charles St. LS1: Leeds 4E 5 (5G 31)
King Charles Wlk. LS1: Leeds 4E 5
   (within The Core Shop. Cen.)
King Cl. LS17: Leeds 5E 13
King Dr. LS17: Leeds 5D 12
King Edward Av. LS18: H'fth 3B 18
King Edward Cres. LS18: H'fth 2C 18
King Edward St. LS1: Leeds 4F 5 (5G 31)
King Edwins Ct. LS8: Leeds 6C 22
Kingfield LS20: Guis 3H 7
Kingfisher Cl. LS17: Leeds 5B 14
Kingfisher M. LS27: Morl 5B 50
Kingfisher Way LS17: Leeds 5B 14
King George Av. LS7: Leeds 4H 21
   LS18: H'fth 2C 18
   LS27: Morl 3H 49
King George Cft. LS27: Morl 4H 49
King George Gdns. LS7: Leeds 4H 21
King George Gro. LS27: Morl 3H 49
King George Rd. LS18: H'fth 2C 18
King La. LS16: Leeds 1B 12
   LS17: Leeds 4D 12
King Lane (Park & Ride) 6F 13
Kings App. LS13: Leeds 3E 29
Kings Av. LS6: Leeds 4C 30
Kings Chase LS26: Rothw 3H 53
Kings Cft. LS17: Leeds 2G 21
King's Cft. Gdns. LS17: Leeds 2H 21
Kingsdale Av. BD11: Drig 3G 47
   LS29: Men 2C 6
Kingsdale Ct. LS14: Leeds 5G 23
   (not continuous)
Kingsdale Dr. LS29: Men 2D 6
Kingsdale Gdns. BD11: Drig 3G 47
Kingsfield LS26: Rothw 4D 52
Kingsley Av. BD11: Birk 5D 46
   LS16: Leeds 4H 11
   WF1: Out 6D 58
Kingsley Cl. BD11: Birk 5D 46
   WF1: Out 6D 58
Kingsley Cres. BD11: Birk 5D 46
Kingsley Dr. BD11: Birk 5D 46
   LS16: Leeds 4H 11
Kingsley Gth. WF1: Out 6D 58
Kingsley Rd. LS16: Leeds 4H 11
Kings Mead LS26: Rothw 3A 54
Kingsmead LS14: Leeds 3A 24
Kingsmead Dr. LS14: Leeds 2H 23
Kingsmill Cl. LS27: Morl 4F 49
King's Mt. LS17: Leeds 3G 21
Kings Pl. LS6: Leeds 1B 30
King's Rd. LS6: Leeds 3C 30
Kingston Gdns. LS15: Leeds 3B 34
Kingston Ter. LS2: Leeds 3F 31
King St. BD11: Drig 3G 47
   LS1: Leeds 5C 4 (6F 31)
   LS19: Raw 5C 8
   LS19: Yead 2E 9
   LS27: Morl 6G 49
   LS28: Stan 4F 27
Kingsway BD11: Drig 3G 47
   LS15: Leeds 5C 34
Kingsway Ct. LS17: Leeds 2H 21
Kingswear Cl. LS15: Leeds 4D 34
Kingswear Cres. LS15: Leeds 4D 34
Kingswear Gth. LS15: Leeds 4D 34
Kingswear Glen LS15: Leeds 4D 34
Kingswear Gro. LS15: Leeds 4D 34
Kingswear Pde. LS15: Leeds 4D 34
Kingswear Ri. LS15: Leeds 4D 34
Kingswear Vw. LS15: Leeds 4D 34
Kingswood Av. LS8: Leeds 6C 14
Kingswood Cres. LS8: Leeds 6B 14
Kingswood Dr. LS8: Leeds 6B 14
Kingswood Gdns. LS8: Leeds 6B 14
Kingswood Gro. LS8: Leeds 6C 14
Kingswood Rd. LS12: Leeds 1A 40
Kipling Ct. BD10: B'frd 4A 16
Kippax Mt. LS9: Leeds 6B 32

Kippax Pl. LS9: Leeds 6B 32
Kirk Beston Cl. LS11: Leeds 5C 40
Kirkdale Av. LS12: Leeds 3H 39
Kirkdale Cres. LS12: Leeds 4H 39
Kirkdale Dr. LS12: Leeds 3H 39
Kirkdale Gdns. LS12: Leeds 3H 39
Kirkdale Gro. LS12: N Far 3G 39
Kirkdale Mt. LS12: Leeds 4H 39
Kirkdale Ter. LS12: Leeds 4H 39
Kirkdale Vw. LS12: Leeds 4H 39
Kirkdale Way BD4: B'frd 6B 36
Kirkfield Dr. LS15: Leeds 6D 34
Kirkfield Gdns. LS15: Leeds 6D 34
Kirkfields Ind. Cen. LS19: Yead 2C 8
Kirkfield Vw. LS15: Leeds 6D 34
Kirk Ga. BD11: Birk 2B 46
Kirkgate LS1: Leeds 4F 5 (5G 31)
(not continuous)
LS2: Leeds 5G 5 (6G 31)
Kirkgate Mkt. LS1: Leeds 4F 5 (5G 31)
Kirkham St. LS13: Leeds 6H 17
Kirklands Cl. LS19: Yead 1C 8
LS29: Men .1C 6
Kirkland Vs. LS28: Pud 1G 37
Kirk La. LS19: Yead 6H 7
Kirklees Cl. LS28: Fars 1F 27
Kirklees Cft. LS28: Fars 1F 27
Kirklees Dr. LS28: Fars 1F 27
Kirklees Gth. LS28: Fars 1F 27
Kirklees Ri. LS28: Fars 1F 27
KIRKSTALL 1G 29
Kirkstall Abbey (remains) 6F 19
Kirkstall Av. LS5: Leeds 2F 29
Kirkstall Brewery LS5: Leeds 1F 29
(off Broad La.)
Kirkstall Hill LS4: Leeds 1H 29
LS5: Leeds 1H 29
Kirkstall Ind. Pk. LS4: Leeds 4B 30
Kirkstall La. LS5: Leeds 1G 29
LS6: Leeds 1G 29
Kirkstall Leisure Cen. 1G 29
Kirkstall Mt. LS5: Leeds 2F 29
Kirkstall Rd. LS3: Leeds 5D 30
LS4: Leeds 2H 29
Kirkstall Valley Nature Reserve 3H 29
Kirkstall Valley Retail Pk.
LS5: Leeds 2G 29
Kirkwall Av. LS9: Leeds 6D 32
Kirkwall Dr. BD4: B'frd 4A 36
Kirkwood Av. LS16: Leeds 5D 10
Kirkwood Cl. LS16: Leeds 4D 10
Kirkwood Cres. LS16: Leeds 4E 11
Kirkwood Dr. LS16: Leeds 4D 10
Kirkwood Gdns. LS16: Leeds 4E 11
Kirkwood Gro. LS16: Leeds 5D 10
WF3: Ting .3D 56
Kirkwood La. LS16: Leeds 4D 10
Kirkwood Ri. LS16: Leeds 4E 11
Kirkwood Vw. LS16: Leeds 4E 11
Kirkwood Way LS16: Leeds 4E 11
Kitchener Av. LS9: Leeds 4D 32
Kitchener Gro. LS9: Leeds 3D 32
Kitchener Mt. LS9: Leeds 4D 32
Kitchener Pl. LS9: Leeds 4D 32
Kitchener St. LS9: Leeds 4D 32
LS26: Wood 3C 54
Kitson Cl. LS12: Leeds 1A 40
Kitson Gdns. LS12: Leeds 1A 40
Kitson Rd. LS10: Leeds 2H 41
Kitson St. LS9: Leeds 6B 32
WF3: Ting .2B 56
Kit Wood Cl. BD4: B'frd 5B 36
Knavesmire LS26: Rothw 4D 52
(not continuous)
Knights Cl. LS15: Leeds 5C 34
Knightscroft Av. LS26: Rothw 3G 53
Knightscroft Dr. LS26: Rothw 3G 53
Knightshill LS15: Leeds 5D 34
Knightsway LS15: Leeds 4C 34
WF3: Loft .1D 58
Knightsway Ct. BD3: B'frd 4B 26
Knoll, The LS28: Cal 3C 26
Knoll Pk. WF3: E Ard 4H 57
Knoll Wood Pk. LS18: H'fth 3D 18
Knostrop La. LS9: Leeds 3D 42
Knott La. LS19: Raw 3F 17
Knowle Av. LS4: Leeds 2B 30
Knowle Gro. LS4: Leeds 2B 30
Knowle Mt. LS4: Leeds 2B 30
Knowle Pl. LS4: Leeds 2B 30
Knowle Rd. LS4: Leeds 2B 30
Knowles Av. BD4: B'frd 5A 36
Knowles La. BD4: B'frd 5A 36
BD19: Gom 6D 46
Knowles Vw. BD4: B'frd 5A 36
Knowle Ter. LS4: Leeds 3A 30
KNOWSTHORPE .2A 42

Knowsthorpe Cres. LS9: Leeds 2B 42
Knowsthorpe Ga. LS9: Leeds 3D 42
Knowsthorpe La. LS9: Leeds 2B 42
Knowsthorpe Rd. LS9: Leeds 2E 43
Knowsthorpe Way LS9: Leeds 3D 42
Knox St. LS13: Leeds 6F 17
Knutsford Gro. BD4: B'frd 5A 36
Kyffin Av. LS15: Leeds 6G 33
Kyffin Pl. BD4: B'frd 2A 36

L

LA Bowl
Leeds 1F 41
Laburnum Cl. WF3: E Ard 4G 57
Laburnum Pl. BD10: B'frd 3A 16
Laburnum St. LS28: Fars 4F 27
LS28: Pud .5E 27
Ladbroke Gro. BD4: B'frd 6A 36
Ladybeck Cl. LS2: Leeds 3G 5 (5H 31)
Lady La. LS2: Leeds 3F 5 (5G 31)
Lady Pk. Ct. LS17: Leeds 5B 14
Lady Pit Ct. LS11: Leeds 3F 41
(off Lady Pit La.)
Lady Pit La. LS11: Leeds 3F 41
(not continuous)
Ladyroyd Dr. BD4: E Bier 3A 46
LADY WOOD 4E 23
Ladywood Grange
LS8: Leeds 5F 23
Ladywood Mead LS8: Leeds 5F 23
Ladywood Rd. LS8: Leeds 5D 22
LA Fitness
Leeds 5E 5
LAISTERDYKE 1A 36
Laith Cl. LS16: Leeds 6F 11
Laith Gdns. LS16: Leeds 6G 11
Laith Gth. LS16: Leeds 6F 11
Laith Rd. LS16: Leeds 6F 11
Laith Grn. LS16: Leeds 6F 11
Laith Wlk. LS16: Leeds 6F 11
Lakeland Ct. LS15: Leeds 1F 43
Lakeland Cres. LS17: Leeds 3E 13
Lakeland Dr. LS17: Leeds 3F 13
LAKE LOCK 6H 59
Lake Lock Dr. WF3: S'ley 5H 59
Lake Lock Gro. WF3: S'ley 5H 59
Lake Lock Rd. WF3: S'ley 6H 59
Lakeside Chase LS19: Raw 5E 9
Lakeside Cl. LS10: Leeds 5H 41
Lakeside Gdns. LS19: Raw 5E 9
Lakeside Ind. Est.
LS12: Leeds 6E 29
Lakeside Rd. LS12: Leeds 1E 39
Lakeside Ter. LS19: Raw 5E 9
Lakeside Vw. LS19: Raw 5E 9
Lakeside Wlk. LS19: Raw 5E 9
(off Lakeside Ter.)
Lake St. LS10: Leeds 5H 41
(off Norwich Av.)
Lake Ter. LS10: Leeds 5H 41
Lakeview Ct. LS8: Leeds 3E 23
Lake Yd. WF3: S'ley 6H 59
Lambert Av. LS8: Leeds 5B 22
Lambert Dr. LS8: Leeds 5B 22
Lambert's Arc. LS1: Leeds 5F 5
Lamberts Yd. LS26: Rothw 4G 53
Lambert Ter. LS18: H'fth 3A 18
(Parkside)
LS18: H'fth 2E 19
(Springfield Cl.)
Lambourne Av. BD10: B'frd 6A 16
Lambrigg Cres. LS14: Leeds 1A 34
Lambton Gro. LS8: Leeds 1B 32
Lambton Pl. LS8: Leeds 1B 32
Lambton St. LS8: Leeds 1B 32
Lambton Ter. LS8: Leeds 1B 32
Lambton Vw. LS8: Leeds 1B 32
Lanark Dr. LS18: H'fth 5B 10
Lancaster Pl. LS26: Rothw 5H 53
(off Royds La.)
Lancaster Way LS19: Yead 1G 9
Lancastre Av. LS5: Leeds 2F 29
(not continuous)
Lancastre Gro. LS5: Leeds 2F 29
Lancefield Ho. WF1: Out 6D 58
Lancet Ri. WF3: Rob H 6C 52
Landmark Ct. LS11: Leeds 4D 40
Landscove Av. BD4: B'frd 5A 36
Landseer Av. LS13: Leeds 2E 29
WF3: Ting .3C 56
Landseer Cl. LS13: Leeds 2D 28
Landseer Cres. LS13: Leeds 2E 29
Landseer Dr. LS13: Leeds 2D 28
Landseer Gdns. LS13: Leeds 2D 28
Landseer Grn. LS13: Leeds 2D 28

Landseer Gro. LS13: Leeds 2E 29
Landseer Mt. LS13: Leeds 2E 29
Landseer Ri. LS13: Leeds 2D 28
Landseer Rd. LS13: Leeds 2D 28
Landseer Ter. LS13: Leeds 2E 29
Landseer Vw. LS13: Leeds 2E 29
Landseer Wlk. LS13: Leeds 2D 28
(off Landseer Way)
Landseer Way LS13: Leeds 2D 28
Landsholme Ct. BD4: B'frd 5B 36
Lands La. LS1: Leeds 4E 5 (5G 31)
LS20: Guis .4G 7
Land St. LS28: Fars 2F 27
Lane, The LS9: Leeds 6A 32
LS17: Leeds 4D 12
Lane End LS28: Pud 5H 27
(not continuous)
Lane End Ct. LS17: Leeds 4D 12
Lane End Cft. LS17: Leeds 4D 12
Lane End Fold LS28: Pud 5H 27
Lane End Mt. LS28: Pud 5H 27
Lane End Pl. LS11: Leeds 2F 41
LANE ENDS 6H 9
Lane Ends Vw. WF3: S'ley 6G 59
Lane Fox Ct. LS19: Raw 3D 8
(off Harper La.)
Lanes, The LS28: Pud 5H 27
Lane Side LS12: Pud 3B 38
Laneside LS27: Chur 2H 49
Laneside Cl. LS27: Morl 2H 49
Laneside Fold LS27: Morl 2H 49
Laneside Gdns. LS27: Morl 2H 49
Laneside Mt. LS27: Chur 2H 49
Laneside Ter. LS27: Chur 2H 49
Langbar App. LS14: Leeds 5D 24
Langbar Cl. LS14: Leeds 5D 24
Langbar Gdns. LS14: Leeds 6D 24
Langbar Grn. LS14: Leeds 5D 24
Langbar Gro. LS14: Leeds 6D 24
Langbar Pl. LS14: Leeds 5D 24
Langbar Rd. LS14: Leeds 6D 24
Langbar Sq. LS14: Leeds 6D 24
Langbar Vw. LS14: Leeds 5D 24
Langdale Av. LS6: Leeds 6A 20
WF1: Out .6F 59
Langdale Gdns. LS6: Leeds 1A 30
Langdale Rd. BD10: B'frd 1A 26
LS26: Wood 3B 54
Langdale Ter. LS6: Leeds 1A 30
LANGLEY 3D 58
Langley Av. LS13: Leeds 1A 28
Langley Cl. LS13: Leeds 1A 28
Langley Cres. LS13: Leeds 1B 28
Langley Gth. LS13: Leeds 1A 28
Langley Mt. LS13: Leeds 1B 28
Langley Pl. LS13: Leeds 1A 28
Langley Rd. LS13: Leeds 1A 28
Langley Ter. LS13: Leeds 1A 28
Langthorne Ct. LS27: Morl 1A 56
Langton Grn. LS12: Leeds 2A 40
Langtons Wharf LS2: Leeds 6G 5
Lansdale Ct. BD4: B'frd 5B 36
Lansdowne St. LS12: Leeds 1A 40
Lanshaw Cl. LS10: Leeds 3A 52
Lanshaw Cres. LS10: Leeds 4A 52
Lanshaw Pl. LS10: Leeds 3A 52
Lanshaw Rd. LS10: Leeds 3A 52
Lanshaw Ter. LS10: Leeds 4A 52
Lanshaw Vw. LS10: Leeds 3A 52
Lanshaw Wlk. LS10: Leeds 3A 52
Larches, The LS13: Leeds 1C 34
Larchfield Home LS10: Leeds 3A 42
Larchfield Rd. LS10: Leeds 2A 42
Larchwood LS19: Raw 1E 17
LARKFIELD 5E 9
Larkfield Av. LS19: Raw 5E 9
Larkfield Cres. LS19: Raw 5E 9
Larkfield Dr. LS19: Raw 5E 9
Larkfield Mt. LS19: Raw 5E 9
Larkfield Rd. LS19: Raw 5E 9
LS28: Pud .5G 27
Larkhill Cl. LS8: Leeds 3A 22
Larkhill Grn. LS8: Leeds 2A 22
Larkhill Rd. LS8: Leeds 2A 22
Larkhill Vw. LS8: Leeds 3A 22
Larkhill Wlk. LS8: Leeds 2A 22
Larkhill Way LS8: Leeds 2A 22
Larwood Av. BD10: B'frd 1A 26
La Salle LS10: Leeds 1H 41
Lascelles Mt. LS8: Leeds 2B 32
(off Lascelles Rd. E.)
Lascelles Pl. LS8: Leeds 2B 32
Lascelles Rd. E. LS8: Leeds 2B 32
Lascelles Rd. W. LS8: Leeds 2B 32
Lascelles St. LS8: Leeds 2B 32
Lascelles Ter. LS8: Leeds 2B 32

Lascelles Vw. LS8: Leeds 2B 32
Lastingham Rd. LS13: Leeds 6H 17
Latchmere Av. LS16: Leeds 3F 19
Latchmere Cl. LS16: Leeds 3G 19
Latchmere Crest LS16: Leeds 3F 19
Latchmere Cross LS16: Leeds 3F 19
Latchmere Dr. LS16: Leeds 3F 19
Latchmere Gdns. LS16: Leeds 2G 19
Latchmere Grn. LS16: Leeds 3F 19
Latchmere Rd. LS16: Leeds 3F 19
Latchmere Vw. LS16: Leeds 3F 19
        (not continuous)
Latchmere Wlk. LS16: Leeds 2G 19
Latchmore Ind. Est. LS12: Leeds 3B 40
Latchmore Rd. LS12: Leeds 3C 40
Latham La. BD19: Gom 6C 46
Latimer Cl. LS20: Guis 3F 7
Latimer Way LS20: Guis 3F 7
Launceston Dr. BD4: B'frd 5A 36
Laura St. LS12: Leeds 1D 40
Laureates, The LS20: Guis 5G 7
        (off Shakespeare La.)
Laurel Bank LS15: Leeds 1D 34
Laurel Bank Ct. LS6: Leeds 1A 30
Laurel Fold LS12: Leeds 6A 30
Laurel Gro. LS12: Leeds 6A 30
Laurel Hill Av. LS15: Leeds 6D 34
Laurel Hill Cft. LS15: Leeds 6D 34
Laurel Hill Gdns. LS15: Leeds 6D 34
Laurel Hill Gro. LS15: Leeds 6D 34
Laurel Hill Vw. LS15: Leeds 6D 34
Laurel Hill Way LS15: Leeds 1D 44
Laurel Mt. LS7: Leeds 6H 21
   LS28: Stan 5G 27
Laurel Pl. LS10: Leeds 5F 51
   LS12: Leeds 6A 30
Laurels, The LS8: Leeds 5B 22
   LS10: Leeds 6H 51
Laurel St. LS12: Leeds 6A 30
Laurel Ter. LS12: Leeds 6A 30
   LS15: Leeds 1D 34
        (off Stanks La. Sth.)
   LS28: Stan 5G 27
Laurence Ct. LS26: Wood 2D 54
Lavender Wlk. LS9: Leeds 6B 32
Lawfield Av. LS26: Rothw 3E 53
LAWNS 5A 58
Lawns WF2: Carr G .5A 58
Lawns Av. LS12: N Far 4D 38
Lawns Cl. LS12: N Far 4D 38
Lawns Ct. WF2: Carr G 6A 58
Lawns Cres. LS12: N Far 4D 38
Lawns Dene LS12: N Far 4D 38
Lawns Dr. LS12: N Far 4D 38
Lawns Grn. LS12: N Far 4D 38
Lawns Hall Cl. LS16: Leeds 6H 11
Lawns La. LS10: Leeds 4A 42
   LS12: N Far 3D 38
   WF2: Carr G 6A 58
Lawns Mt. LS12: N Far 4D 38
Lawns Sq. LS12: N Far 4D 38
Lawns Ter. LS12: N Far 4D 38
   WF3: E Ard 4H 57
LAWNSWOOD 1G 19
Lawnswood Bus. Pk. LS16: Leeds 2G 19
Lawns Wood Crematorium
   LS16: Leeds 6H 11
Lawnswood Gdns. LS16: Leeds 1H 19
Lawrence Av. LS8: Leeds 1E 33
Lawrence Ct. LS28: Pud 1F 37
Lawrence Cres. LS8: Leeds 1E 33
Lawrence Gdns. LS8: Leeds 6E 23
Lawrence Rd. LS8: Leeds 1E 33
Lawrence Wlk. LS8: Leeds 1E 33
Lawson Ct. LS8: Fars 2G 27
Lawson St. LS12: Leeds 6H 29
Lawson Wood Ct. LS6: Leeds 2D 20
Lawson Wood Dr. LS6: Leeds 2D 20
Laycock Pl. LS7: Leeds 2H 31
Lay Garth LS26: Rothw 5G 53
Lay Gth. Cl. LS26: Rothw 4G 53
Lay Gth. Ct. LS26: Rothw 5G 53
Lay Gth. Fold LS26: Rothw 5G 53
Lay Gth. Gdns. LS26: Rothw 5G 53
Lay Gth. Grn. LS26: Rothw 5G 53
Lay Gth. Mead LS26: Rothw 5G 53
Lay Gth. Pl. LS26: Rothw 5G 53
Lay Gth. Sq. LS26: Rothw 4G 53
Layton Av. LS19: Raw 6F 9
Layton Cl. LS19: Raw 1G 17
Layton Cres. LS19: Raw 6F 9
Layton Dr. LS19: Raw 6G 9
Layton La. LS19: Raw 6F 9
Layton Mt. LS19: Raw 6F 9
Layton Pk. Av. LS19: Raw 1G 17
Layton Pk. Cl. LS19: Raw 6F 9

Layton Pk. Cft. LS19: Raw 1G 17
Layton Pk. Dr. LS19: Raw 6F 9
Layton Ri. LS18: H'fth 6H 9
Layton Rd. LS18: H'fth 6G 9
   LS19: Raw 6G 9
Leadwell La. LS26: Rothw 6D 52
   WF3: Rob H 6D 52
Lea Farm Cres. LS5: Leeds 5F 19
Lea Farm Dr. LS5: Leeds 4F 19
Lea Farm Gro. LS5: Leeds 5F 19
Lea Farm Mt. LS5: Leeds 4F 19
Lea Farm Pl. LS5: Leeds 5F 19
Lea Farm Rd. LS5: Leeds 4E 19
Lea Farm Row LS5: Leeds 5F 19
Lea Farm Wlk. LS5: Leeds 4F 19
Leafield Cl. LS17: Leeds 1F 21
Leafield Dr. LS17: Leeds 1F 21
   LS28: Pud 2H 37
Leafield Grange LS17: Leeds 1F 21
Leafield Pl. LS19: Yead 6H 7
Leafield Towers LS17: Leeds 1F 21
Leafield Vs. LS19: Yead 6H 7
        (off Leafield Pl.)
Leah Pl. LS12: Leeds 1D 40
Leah Row LS12: Leeds 1D 40
Lea Mill Pk. Cl. LS19: Yead 2C 8
Lea Mill Pk. Dr. LS19: Yead 2C 8
Leamside Wlk. BD4: B'frd 5A 36
Lea Pk. Cl. LS10: Leeds 2B 52
Lea Pk. Cft. LS10: Leeds 2B 52
Lea Pk. Dr. LS10: Leeds 2B 52
Lea Pk. Gdns. LS10: Leeds 2B 52
Lea Pk. Gth. LS10: Leeds 2B 52
Lea Pk. Gro. LS10: Leeds 2B 52
Lea Pk. Va. LS10: Leeds 2C 52
Leasowe Av. LS10: Leeds 5A 42
Leasowe Cl. LS10: Leeds 5A 42
        (off Springfield Pl.)
Leasowe Gdns. LS10: Leeds 5B 42
Leasowe Gth. LS10: Leeds 5A 42
Leasowe Rd. LS10: Leeds 5A 42
Lea Ter. LS17: Leeds 2G 21
Leathley Av. LS29: Men 2D 6
Leathley Cres. LS29: Men 2D 6
Leathley La. LS29: Men 1D 6
Leathley Rd. LS10: Leeds 2G 41
   LS29: Men 1D 6
Leavens, The BD10: B'frd 3A 16
Lea Vw. LS18: H'fth .2B 18
Ledbury Av. LS10: Leeds 5B 52
Ledbury Cl. LS10: Leeds 5B 52
Ledbury Cft. LS10: Leeds 5B 52
Ledbury Dr. LS10: Leeds 5B 52
Ledbury Grn. LS10: Leeds 5B 52
Ledbury Gro. LS10: Leeds 5B 52
Ledgard Way LS12: Leeds 5A 30
Ledger La. WF1: Out 6D 58
   WF3: Loft 2E 59
Lee Beck Gro. WF3: S'ley 3G 59
LEEDS .4E 5 (5G 31)
Leeds 27 Ind. Est. LS27: Morl 4E 49
Leeds and Bradford Rd.
   LS5: Leeds 6C 18
   LS13: Leeds 2A 28
   LS28: Stan 3H 27
Leeds Aquatic Cen. 1G 51
LEEDS BRADFORD INTERNATIONAL AIRPORT
   . . . . .2G 9
Leeds Bus. Cen., The LS27: Morl 4E 49
Leeds Carnegie RUFC
   Headingley Carnegie Stadium 1B 30
Leeds City Art Gallery 3D 4 (5F 31)
Leeds City Mus. 2D 4 (4H 31)
Leeds City Office Pk. LS11: Leeds 1G 41
Leeds Corn Exchange LS2: Leeds 5F 5
LEEDS DENTAL INSTITUTE 2B 4 (4E 31)
LEEDS GENERAL INFIRMARY 2C 4 (4F 31)
Leeds La. LS26: Swil 2G 45
Leeds Metropolitan University
   Civic Quarter Campus 1D 4 (4F 31)
   Headingley Beckett Pk. Campus 5H 19
   Leslie Silver Building 1D 4 (4F 31)
Leeds Metropolitan University Sports Cen. . . .5H 19
LEEDS NUFFIELD HEALTH HOSPITAL
   . . . . .3B 4 (5E 31)
Leeds Old Rd. BD3: B'frd 5A 26
Leeds Rhinos RLFC 1B 30
Leeds Rd. BD3: B'frd 6A 26
   LS15: Bar E, Scho 6H 25
   LS15: Leeds, Scho 1E 35
   LS16: B'hpe 1H 11
   LS19: Raw 5D 8
   LS20: Guis 5G 7
   LS26: Meth 6G 55
   LS26: Oul, Rothw 2H 53
   WF1: Out 6E 59

Leeds Rd. WF3: Loft 2E 59
   WF12: Dew 6A 56
   WF17: Birs 6B 48
Leeds Sailing & Activity Cen. 2E 9
Leeds Shop. Plaza LS1: Leeds 5E 5 (6G 31)
LEEDS SPIRE HOSPITAL 4C 22
Leeds Station (Rail) 6D 4 (6F 31)
Leeds United FC 4C 40
Leeds University Business School 3D 30
Leeds Valley Pk. LS10: Leeds 1D 52
Leeds Wall, The 2B 40
Lee Edge LS10: Leeds 5H 51
Lee Fair Ct. WF3: W Ard 5B 56
Lee La. E. LS18: H'fth 1B 18
Lee La. W. LS18: H'fth 1H 17
LEE MOOR 4G 59
Lee Moor La. WF3: S'ley 3G 59
Lee Moor Rd. WF3: S'ley 4G 59
LEE MOUNT 5H 59
Lees La. LS28: Fars .1F 27
Leicester Cl. LS7: Leeds 3F 31
Leicester Gro. LS7: Leeds 3F 31
Leicester Pl. LS2: Leeds 3F 31
   LS7: Leeds 3F 31
Leigh Av. WF3: Ting .3E 57
Leigh Rd. WF3: Ting 3E 57
Leighton Pl. LS1: Leeds 3C 4
Leighton St. LS1: Leeds 3B 4 (5F 31)
Leigh Vw. WF3: Ting 3D 56
Leith Ho. BD4: B'frd .4A 36
        (off Stirling Cres.)
Lenham Cl. LS27: Morl 6G 49
Lenhurst Av. LS12: Leeds 2F 29
Lennox Gdns. LS15: Leeds 6C 34
Lennox Rd. LS4: Leeds 4B 30
Lenton Dr. LS11: Leeds 5G 41
Leodis Ct. LS11: Leeds 1F 41
Leodis Ho. LS10: Leeds 6E 43
Leodis Residences LS6: Leeds 2F 31
Leodis Way LS10: Leeds 1D 52
Leopold Gdns. LS7: Leeds 2A 32
Leopold Gro. LS7: Leeds 2H 31
Leopold St. LS7: Leeds 2H 31
Lepton Hare Chase
   LS10: Leeds 1G 57
Lepton Pl. LS27: Gil 2D 48
Leslie Av. LS19: Yead 1E 9
Leslie Ter. LS6: Leeds 2E 31
Levens Bank LS15: Leeds 1F 43
Levens Cl. LS15: Leeds 1G 43
Levens Gth. LS15: Leeds 1G 43
Levens Pl. LS15: Leeds 1G 43
Leventhorpe Ct. LS26: Oul 4C 54
Leventhorpe Way LS26: Oul 4C 54
Levita Gro. BD4: B'frd 3A 36
Levita Pl. BD4: B'frd 2A 36
   LS15: Leeds 5G 33
Lewisham Ct. LS27: Morl 5H 49
Lewisham Gro. LS27: Morl 5H 49
Lewisham St. LS27: Morl 6E 49
LEYLANDS, THE 2F 5 (4G 31)
Leylands Rd. LS2: Leeds 2H 5 (4H 31)
Ley La. LS12: Leeds .5B 30
Leysholme Cres. LS12: Leeds 1G 39
Leysholme Dr. LS12: Leeds 1H 39
Leysholme Ter. LS12: Leeds 1H 39
Leysholme Vw. LS12: Leeds 1H 39
Leywell Ter. LS12: Leeds 5G 29
Liberty Pk. LS1: Leeds 4A 4
Lickless Av. LS18: H'fth 2D 18
Lickless Dr. LS18: H'fth 2D 18
Lickless Gdns. LS18: H'fth 2D 18
Lickless Ter. LS18: H'fth 2D 18
Lidget Hill LS28: Pud 6G 27
Lidgett Cl. LS8: Leeds 4B 22
Lidgett Ct. LS8: Leeds 3B 22
Lidgett Cres. LS8: Leeds 3B 22
Lidgett Gro. LS8: Leeds 4B 22
Lidgett Hill LS8: Leeds 4B 22
Lidgett La. LS8: Leeds 4B 22
   LS17: Leeds 2H 21
Lidgett Mt. LS8: Leeds 2B 22
LIDGETT PARK 3C 22
Lidgett Pk. Av. LS8: Leeds 2B 22
Lidgett Pk. Ct. LS8: Leeds 2B 22
Lidgett Pk. Gdns. LS8: Leeds 3B 22
Lidgett Pk. Gro. LS8: Leeds 3B 22
Lidgett Pk. M. LS8: Leeds 2C 22
Lidgett Pk. Rd. LS8: Leeds 3B 22
        (not continuous)
Lidgett Pk. Vw. LS8: Leeds 2B 22
Lidgett Pl. LS8: Leeds 3B 22
Lidgett Towers LS8: Leeds 2A 22
Lidgett Wlk. LS8: Leeds 4B 22
        (not continuous)
Lifton Pl. LS2: Leeds 3E 31
Light, The LS2: Leeds 3D 4 (5F 31)

Lighthouse Fold. WF3: Loft 3E **59**
(off The Poplars)
Lilac Ct. LS14: Leeds 3G **33**
Lilacs, The LS20: Guis 4G **7**
Lime Gro. LS7: Leeds 5H **21**
LS19: Yead 5C **8**
Lime Tree Av. LS17: Leeds 6G **59**
Lime Tree Cl. LS26: Wood 3D **54**
Limetree Gro. BD11: Birk 2C **46**
Limewood App. LS14: Leeds 4A **24**
Limewood Ct. LS14: Leeds 4A **24**
Limewood Rd. LS14: Leeds 5A **24**
Limewood Way LS14: Leeds 5A **24**
Lincoln Ct. LS28: Fars 3F **27**
(off South Dr.)
Lincoln Grn. Ct. LS9: Leeds 4A **32**
Lincoln Grn. Rd. LS9: Leeds 4A **32**
Lincoln Rd. LS9: Leeds 4A **32**
Lincoln Towers LS9: Leeds 4A **32**
(off Lincoln Rd.)
Lincombe Bank LS8: Leeds 3A **22**
Lincombe Dr. LS8: Leeds 3A **22**
Lincombe Mt. LS8: Leeds 3A **22**
Lincombe Ri. LS8: Leeds 3A **22**
Lincroft Cres. LS13: Leeds 1D **28**
Lindale Cl. LS10: Leeds 2H **51**
Linden Av. BD3: B'frd 5A **26**
LS11: Leeds 4F **41**
Linden Ct. LS16: Leeds 4B **20**
LS26: Rothw 5D **52**
Linden Gdns. LS11: Leeds 4G **41**
Linden Gro. LS11: Leeds 4G **41**
Linden Mt. LS11: Leeds 4F **41**
Linden Pl. LS11: Leeds 4G **41**
Linden Rd. LS11: Leeds 4F **41**
Linden St. LS11: Leeds 4F **41**
Linden Ter. LS11: Leeds 4G **41**
Lindsay Acre WF3: Ting 3E **57**
Lindsey Ct. LS9: Leeds 4A **32**
Lindsey Gdns. LS9: Leeds 4A **32**
Lindsey Mt. LS9: Leeds 4A **32**
(off Lindsey Rd.)
Lindsey Rd. LS9: Leeds 4A **32**
Linfield LS6: Leeds .1B **6**
Ling Ct. LS29: Men .6C **20**
Lingfield App. LS17: Leeds 6F **13**
Lingfield Bank LS17: Leeds 6F **13**
Lingfield Cl. LS17: Leeds 6G **13**
Lingfield Cres. LS17: Leeds 6F **13**
Lingfield Dr. LS17: Leeds 6G **13**
Lingfield Gdns. LS17: Leeds 6F **13**
Lingfield Ga. LS17: Leeds 6F **13**
Lingfield Grn. LS17: Leeds 6F **13**
Lingfield Gro. LS17: Leeds 6G **13**
Lingfield Hill LS17: Leeds 5F **13**
Lingfield Mt. LS17: Leeds 6G **13**
Lingfield Rd. LS17: Leeds 6F **13**
Lingfield Vw. LS17: Leeds 6F **13**
Lingfield Wlk. LS17: Leeds 6F **13**
Ling La. LS14: S'cft .2H **15**
LS17: Leeds 2H **15**
Lingmell Cres. BD4: B'frd 5B **36**
(off Simon Cl.)
Lingwell App. LS10: Leeds 5G **51**
Lingwell Av. LS10: Leeds 4G **51**
Lingwell Chase WF3: Loft 5E **59**
Lingwell Ct. LS10: Leeds 5G **51**
WF3: Loft 5C **58**
Lingwell Cres. LS10: Leeds 4G **51**
Lingwell Gdns. LS10: Leeds 5G **51**
LINGWELL GATE 4C **58**
Lingwell Ga. Cres. WF1: Out 6D **58**
Lingwell Ga. Dr. WF1: Out 6C **58**
Lingwell Ga. La. WF1: Out 6B **58**
WF3: Loft, Thpe H 1B **58**
Lingwell Grn. LS10: Leeds 5G **51**
Lingwell Gro. LS10: Leeds 5G **51**
Lingwell M. LS10: Leeds 5G **51**
LINGWELL NOOK 3B **58**
Lingwell Nook Ct. WF3: Loft 5E **59**
Lingwell Nook Crest WF3: Loft 5E **59**
(off Lingwell Nook La.)
Lingwell Nook La. WF3: Loft 3C **58**
(Castle Head La.)
WF3: Loft 5D **58**
(Ridings La.)
Lingwell Pk. Ct. LS10: Leeds 4G **51**
Lingwell Rd. LS10: Leeds 4G **51**
Lingwell Vw. LS10: Leeds 5G **51**
Lingwell Wlk. LS10: Leeds 5G **51**
Link, The LS26: Swil 6F **45**
Links, The LS11: Leeds 2E **51**
Linnet Ct. LS27: Morl 6B **50**
Linton Av. LS17: Leeds 5B **14**
Linton Cl. LS17: Leeds 5A **14**

Linton Cres. LS17: Leeds 5B **14**
Linton Cft. LS16: Leeds 3F **19**
Linton Dr. LS17: Leeds 5A **14**
Linton Gro. LS17: Leeds 5A **14**
Linton Ri. LS17: Leeds 5A **14**
Linton Rd. LS17: Leeds 5A **14**
Linton Vw. LS17: Leeds 4A **14**
Lisbon Sq. LS1: Leeds 4A **4**
Lisbon St. LS1: Leeds 4B **4** (5E **31**)
Lismore Cl. LS26: Rothw 4H **53**
Lister Hill LS18: H'fth 1C **18**
Lister St. BD4: B'frd .6A **36**
Lister Wlk. LS27: Morl 3F **49**
Lit. Church La. LS26: Meth 6H **55**
Lit. Cross St. LS1: Leeds 4E **5**
Lit. Fountain St. LS27: Morl 5G **49**
Lit. King St. LS1: Leeds 5C **4** (6F **31**)
Little La. LS27: Chur 1A **50**
LS27: Morl 5G **49**
WF3: Carl 6G **53**
Lit. Lane Ct. LS27: Chur 1A **50**
LITTLE LONDON
LS7 . . . . .1F **5** (3G **31**)
LS19 . . . . .5C **8**
LITTLEMOOR BOTTOM 2G **37**
Littlemoor Ct. LS28: Pud 1G **37**
Littlemoor Cres. LS28: Pud 2G **37**
Littlemoor Cres. Sth. LS28: Pud 2G **37**
Littlemoor Gdns. LS28: Pud 2G **37**
Lit. Moor La. LS14: T'ner 1F **25**
Lit. Moor Pl. LS12: Leeds 6H **29**
Littlemoor Rd. LS28: Pud 1G **37**
Littlemoor Vw. LS28: Pud 1H **37**
Lit. Neville St. LS1: Leeds 6D **4** (6F **31**)
Little Park BD10: B'frd 2A **16**
LITTLE PRESTON 6H **45**
Lit. Preston Hall LS26: Swil 6H **45**
Lit. Queen St. LS1: Leeds 5B **4** (6E **31**)
Littleway LS17: Leeds 2G **21**
LITTLE WOODHOUSE 1A **4** (4E **31**)
Lit. Woodhouse St. LS2: Leeds 2B **4** (4E **31**)
Litton Ct. LS29: Men 2D **6**
Litton Way LS14: Leeds 3B **24**
Livinia Gro. LS7: Leeds 3G **31**
Lockside Rd. LS10: Leeds 4C **42**
Lockwood Cl. LS11: Leeds 6G **41**
Lockwood Ct. LS11: Leeds 6G **41**
Lockwood Pk. LS11: Leeds 6G **41**
Lockwood Way LS11: Leeds 6G **41**
Lodge Hill Cl. LS12: N Far 4E **39**
Lodge Hill Wlk. LS12: N Far 4E **39**
Lodge La. LS11: Leeds 4F **41**
Lodge Rd. LS28: Pud 5F **27**
Lodge Row LS15: Leeds 3C **34**
(off Tranquility Av.)
Lodge St. LS2: Leeds 1C **4** (3F **31**)
(not continuous)
Lodge Ter. LS11: Leeds 5F **41**
LOFTHOUSE 2E **59**
Lofthouse Farm Fold WF3: Loft 4E **59**
LOFTHOUSE GATE 5D **58**
Lofthouse Pl. LS2: Leeds 3F **31**
Loiner Ct. LS9: Leeds 2E **43**
Lombard St. LS15: Leeds 6H **33**
LS19: Raw 5C **8**
Lomond Av. LS18: H'fth 5B **10**
Londesboro Gro. LS9: Leeds 6C **32**
Londesboro Ter. LS9: Leeds 6C **32**
London La. LS19: Raw 5C **8**
London Sq. LS19: Raw 5C **8**
London St. LS19: Raw 5C **8**
Longbow Av. LS26: Meth 6H **55**
Long Causeway LS9: Leeds 2B **42**
LS16: Leeds 1B **20**
WF3: S'ley 6H **59**
Long Cl. La. LS9: Leeds 6B **32**
Longfellow Gro. WF3: S'ley 5G **59**
Longfield Av. LS28: Pud 6H **27**
Longfield Ct. LS28: Pud 6H **27**
Longfield Dr. LS13: Leeds 6H **17**
LS15: Leeds 5A **34**
Longfield Gth. LS13: Leeds 6H **17**
Longfield Gro. LS28: Pud 6H **27**
Longfield Mt. LS28: Pud 6H **27**
Longfield Rd. LS28: Pud 6G **27**
Longfield Ter. LS28: Pud 6G **27**
Longfield Vw. LS28: Fars 2F **27**
(off Croft St.)
Longley's Yd. LS10: Leeds 5A **42**
Long Preston Chase BD10: B'frd 4A **16**
Long Row LS18: H'fth 2C **18**
(not continuous)
Longroyd Av. LS11: Leeds 4G **41**
Longroyd Cres. LS11: Leeds 4G **41**
Longroyd Cres. Nth. LS11: Leeds 4G **41**
Longroyd Gro. LS11: Leeds 4G **41**
Longroyd Pl. LS11: Leeds 4G **41**

Longroyd St. LS11: Leeds 4G **41**
Longroyd St. Nth. LS11: Leeds 4G **41**
Longroyd Ter. LS11: Leeds 4G **41**
Longroyd Vw. LS11: Leeds 4G **41**
Long Thorpe La. WF3: Loft, Thpe H 2B **58**
Longwood Cl. LS17: Leeds 4D **14**
WF3: Ting 3B **56**
Longwood Ct. WF3: Ting 3C **56**
Longwood Cres. LS17: Leeds 4D **14**
Longwood Fold WF3: Ting 3C **56**
Longwood Gth. WF3: Ting 3C **56**
Longwood Rd. WF3: Ting 3C **56**
Longwood Va. WF3: Ting 3B **56**
Longwood Way LS17: Leeds 4D **14**
Lonsdale Ri. WF3: W Ard 3C **56**
Lonsdale Sq. LS10: Leeds 6H **41**
Loom Ho. LS9: Leeds 6H **5**
Lord St. LS12: Leeds 1D **40**
Lord Ter. LS12: Leeds 1D **40**
Loris St. BD4: B'frd .6A **36**
Lorry Bank LS7: Leeds 1G **31**
Louis Ct. LS7: Leeds 2H **31**
Louis Gro. LS7: Leeds 2A **32**
Louis Ho. LS27: Morl 4H **49**
(off Pullman Ct.)
Louis Le Prince Ct. LS8: Leeds 2B **32**
(off Bayswater Rd.)
Louis St. LS7: Leeds 2H **31**
Lounge Picture House, The 6B **20**
Love La. LS26: Rothw 4G **53**
Lovell Ho. LS7: Leeds 1G **5**
Lovell Pk. Cl. LS7: Leeds 1G **5** (4H **31**)
Lovell Pk. Ct. LS7: Leeds 1F **5** (4H **31**)
Lovell Pk. Ga. LS7: Leeds 1F **5** (4G **31**)
Lovell Pk. Grange LS7: Leeds 1G **5**
Lovell Pk. Hgts. LS7: Leeds 1G **5**
Lovell Pk. Hill LS7: Leeds 1F **5** (4G **31**)
Lovell Pk. M. LS7: Leeds 1G **5** (4H **31**)
Lovell Pk. Rd. LS2: Leeds 2F **5** (4G **31**)
LS7: Leeds 2F **5** (4G **31**)
Lovell Pk. Towers LS7: Leeds 1F **5**
Lovell Pk. Vw. LS7: Leeds 1G **5** (4H **31**)
Low Bank St. LS28: Fars 2F **27**
Low Cl. St. LS2: Leeds 2E **31**
Lowell Gro. LS13: Leeds 5A **28**
Lowell Pl. LS13: Leeds 5A **28**
Lower Bankhouse LS28: Pud 3F **37**
Lwr. Basinghall St. LS1: Leeds 4D **4** (5F **31**)
Lwr. Brunswick St. LS2: Leeds 2G **5** (4H **31**)
LOWER FAGLEY .2A **26**
Lower La. BD4: E Bier 4A **46**
Lwr. Rushton Rd. BD3: B'frd 6A **26**
Lwr. Tofts Rd. LS28: Pud 6G **27**
Lwr. Town St. LS13: Leeds 2D **28**
LOWER WORTLEY 2A **40**
Lwr. Wortley Rd. LS12: Leeds 3G **39**
LOW FARM 5F **11**
Lowfields Av. LS12: Leeds 3C **40**
Lowfields Rd. LS12: Leeds 3C **40**
(not continuous)
Low Flds. Way LS12: Leeds 3C **40**
LOW FOLD
LS12 . . . . .1E **39**
LS18 . . . . .3A **18**
Low Fold LS9: Leeds 1A **42**
LS18: H'fth 4A **18**
LS19: Raw 5D **8**
Low Grange Cres. LS10: Leeds 6A **42**
Low Grange Vw. LS10: Leeds 1A **52**
LOW GREEN 6E **9**
Low Green LS19: Raw 6E **9**
Low Hall Cl. LS29: Men 1C **6**
Low Hall Pl. LS11: Leeds 1E **41**
Low Hall Rd. LS18: H'fth 3G **17**
LS29: Men 1D **6**
LS18: H'fth 1C **18**
Low Mills Rd. LS12: Leeds 3H **39**
LOW MOOR SIDE 5C **38**
Low Moor Side LS12: N Far 4D **38**
Low Moorside Cl. LS12: N Far 4E **39**
Low Moorside La. LS12: N Far 5C **38**
Low Moor Ter. LS11: Leeds 5F **41**
Lowood La. WF17: Birs 6G **47**
Lowry Rd. WF3: Ting 3B **56**
Low Shops La. LS26: Rothw 3E **53**
Low St. WF3: Ting 2D **56**
Lowther Cres. LS26: Swil 5G **45**
Lowther Dr. LS26: Swil 5F **45**
Lowther St. LS8: Leeds 1B **32**
Lowther Ter. LS15: Swil C 1G **45**
Lowtown LS28: Pud .5H **27**
LOW TOWN END .6H **49**
Low Whitehouse Row LS10: Leeds 2H **41**
Lucas Ct. LS6: Leeds 2G **31**
Lucas Pl. LS6: Leeds 1E **31**

Lucas St. LS6: Leeds 1E 31
Lucy Av. LS15: Leeds 5G 33
Ludgate Hill LS2: Leeds 4F 5 (5G 31)
Ludolf Dr. LS17: Shad 5G 15
Lulworth Av. LS15: Leeds 4D 34
Lulworth Cl. LS15: Leeds 4D 34
Lulworth Cres. LS15: Leeds 4D 34
Lulworth Dr. LS15: Leeds 5D 34
Lulworth Gth. LS15: Leeds 5D 34
Lulworth Vw. LS15: Leeds 4D 34
Lulworth Wlk. LS15: Leeds 4D 34
Lumb Bottom BD11: Drig 2H 47
Lumb Hall Way BD11: Drig 2H 47
Lumby Cl. LS28: Pud 2H 37
Lumby La. LS28: Pud 2H 37
Lumley Av. LS4: Leeds 2B 30
Lumley Gro. LS4: Leeds 2B 30
Lumley Mt. LS4: Leeds 2B 30
Lumley Pl. LS4: Leeds 2B 30
Lumley Rd. LS4: Leeds 2B 30
Lumley St. LS4: Leeds 2B 30
Lumley Ter. LS4: Leeds 2B 30
Lumley Vw. LS4: Leeds 2B 30
Lumley Wlk. LS4: Leeds 2B 30
Lunan Pl. LS8: Leeds 1B 32
Lunan Ter. LS8: Leeds 1B 32
Lupton Av. LS9: Leeds 5C 32
Lupton Flats LS6: Leeds 6B 20
Lupton's Bldgs. LS12: Leeds 6H 29
Lupton St. LS10: Leeds 4A 42
Luther St. LS13: Leeds 6G 17
Luttrell Cl. LS16: Leeds 1G 19
Luttrell Cres. LS16: Leeds 1G 19
Luttrell Gdns. LS16: Leeds 1G 19
Luttrell Pl. LS16: Leeds 1G 19
Luttrell Rd. LS16: Leeds 1G 19
Luxor Av. LS8: Leeds 1B 32
Luxor Rd. LS8: Leeds 1B 32
Luxor St. LS8: Leeds 1B 32
Luxor Vw. LS8: Leeds 1B 32
Lyddon Hall LS2: Leeds 1B 4 (3E 31)
Lyddon Ter. LS2: Leeds 1A 4 (3E 31)
Lydgate LS9: Leeds 4B 32
Lydgate Pl. LS28: Cal 4C 16
Lydgate St. LS28: Cal 4C 16
Lydia St. LS2: Leeds .4G 5
Lyme Chase LS14: Leeds 3H 33
Lymington Dr. BD4: B'frd 3A 36
Lyndhurst Cl. LS15: Scho 4F 25
Lyndhurst Cres. LS15: Scho 4F 25
Lyndhurst Rd. LS15: Scho 5F 25
Lyndhurst Vw. LS15: Scho 5F 25
Lynnfield Gdns. LS15: Scho 5F 25
Lynnwood Gdns. LS28: Pud 6E 27
Lynton Av. WF3: Thpe H 1A 58
Lynwood Av. LS12: Leeds 2A 40
LS26: Wood .3D 54
Lynwood Cl. BD11: Birk 5D 46
Lynwood Cres. LS12: Leeds 2A 40
LS26: Wood .3D 54
Lynwood Gth. LS12: Leeds 2A 40
Lynwood Gro. LS12: Leeds 3A 40
Lynwood M. BD4: B'frd 5B 36
Lynwood Mt. LS12: Leeds 2A 40
Lynwood Ri. LS12: Leeds 2A 40
Lynwood Vw. LS12: Leeds 2A 40
Lytham Gro. LS12: Leeds 3G 39
Lytham Pl. LS12: Leeds 3G 39
Lytton St. LS10: Leeds 4H 41

M

M1 Ind. Est. LS10: Leeds 4H 5
MABGATE 2G 5 (4H 31)
Mabgate LS9: Leeds 3H 5 (5H 31)
Mabgate Grn. LS9: Leeds 3H 5 (5H 31)
Mabgate Mills Ind. & Commercial Cen.
LS9: Leeds 2H 5 (4A 32)
Macaulay St. LS9: Leeds 3H 5 (4A 32)
McClintock Ho. LS10: Leeds 1H 41
(off The Boulevard)
McClure Ho. LS10: Leeds 1H 41
(off The Boulevard)
Mackenzie Ho. LS10: Leeds 6H 5
McLaren Flds. LS13: Leeds 3D 28
Madeline Joy Apartments LS6: Leeds . . .1B 30
(off Broomfield Cres.)
Madison Av. BD4: B'frd 6A 36
Mafeking Av. LS11: Leeds 6E 41
Mafeking Gro. LS11: Leeds 6E 41
Mafeking Mt. LS11: Leeds 6E 41
Magdalene Cl. LS16: Leeds 6G 11
Magdalin Dr. LS28: Stan 3A 26
Magellan Ho. LS10: Leeds 6H 5 (1H 41)
Magistrates' Court
Leeds 3C 4 (5F 31)

Magpie La. LS27: Morl 6H 49
Mail Cl. LS15: Leeds 2E 35
Main St. LS15: Scho 5F 25
LS17: Shad 4F 15
LS20: Hawk 5A 6
LS29: Men 1B 6
WF3: Carl 6F 53
WF3: E Ard .4H 57
Maitland Pl. LS11: Leeds 3E 41
Malden Rd. LS6: Leeds 2D 20
Malham Cl. LS14: Leeds 1A 34
Malham Ho. LS29: Men 2C 6
MALHAM HOUSE DAY HOSPITAL 2A 4 (4E 31)
Mallard Cl. LS10: Leeds 2B 52
Mallard Way LS27: Morl 5B 50
Malmesbury Cl. BD4: B'frd 6A 36
LS12: Leeds .1A 40
Malmesbury Gro. LS12: Leeds 1A 40
Malmesbury Pl. LS12: Leeds 1A 40
Malmesbury Ter. LS12: Leeds 1A 40
Maltby Ct. LS15: Leeds 6D 34
Malting Cl. WF3: Rob H 6D 52
Malting Ri. WF3: Rob H 6D 52
Maltings, The LS6: Leeds 3C 30
(off Spring Gro. Wlk.)
WF3: Rob H .6D 52
Maltings Ct. LS11: Leeds 3G 41
(off Maltings Rd.)
Maltings Rd. LS11: Leeds 4G 41
Malvern Gro. LS11: Leeds 3E 41
Malvern Ri. LS11: Leeds 3E 41
Malvern Rd. LS11: Leeds 3E 41
Malvern St. LS11: Leeds 3E 41
Malvern Vw. LS11: Leeds 3E 41
Mandarin Way LS10: Leeds 2B 52
Mandela Ct. LS7: Leeds 6H 21
Mandela Ho. LS7: Leeds 2H 31
Manderston Chase LS12: Leeds 3F 29
Manitoba Pl. LS7: Leeds 5A 22
Manor, The LS8: Leeds 5E 23
(off Ladywood Rd.)
Manor Av. LS6: Leeds 1C 30
Manor Cl. BD11: Drig 2G 47
LS19: Yead 2D 8
LS26: Rothw 3G 53
Manor Ct. LS11: Leeds 6C 40
LS17: Shad 5H 15
Manor Cres. LS26: Rothw 3F 53
Manor Cft. LS15: Leeds 6C 34
Manor Dr. LS6: Leeds 2C 30
(not continuous)
Mnr. Farm Cl. LS10: Leeds 3H 51
Mnr. Farm Ct. BD4: E Bier 2A 46
LS20: Guis 4G 7
Mnr. Farm Cres. LS27: Chur 1A 50
Mnr. Farm Dr. LS10: Leeds 3G 51
LS27: Chur 1A 50
Mnr. Farm Gdns. LS10: Leeds 3G 51
Mnr. Farm Gth. LS10: Leeds 3G 51
Mnr. Farm Gro. LS10: Leeds 3G 51
Mnr. Farm Ho. LS10: Leeds 3H 51
Mnr. Farm Rd. LS10: Leeds 3G 51
Mnr. Farm Wlk. LS10: Leeds 3H 51
Mnr. Farm Way LS10: Leeds 4G 51
Manorfield LS11: Leeds 4D 40
Manor Fold LS18: H'fth 3A 18
Manor Gth. LS15: Leeds 6C 34
Manor Gro. LS7: Leeds 5H 21
Manor Ho. Cft. LS16: Leeds 6B 12
Manor Ho. La. LS17: Leeds 2B 14
Manor Ho. St. LS28: Pud 6G 27
Manor La. LS26: Oul 4C 54
(off Aberford Rd.)
Mnr. Mill La. LS11: Leeds 6C 40
Manor Mills LS11: Leeds 6C 40
(Manor Ct.)
LS11: Leeds .1F 41
(Manor Rd.)
Manor Pk. Gdns. BD19: Gom 6D 46
Manor Rd. LS11: Leeds 1F 41
LS12: Leeds .2A 40
LS18: H'fth 3A 18
LS26: Rothw 3F 53
LS27: Chur 1A 50
Manor Sq. LS19: Yead 2D 8
Manor St. LS7: Leeds 3H 31
Manor St. Ind. Est. LS7: Leeds 3A 32
(not continuous)
Manor Ter. LS6: Leeds 1C 30
LS19: Yead 2D 8
Manor Vw. LS6: Leeds 1C 30
LS28: Pud 6G 27
Mansel M. BD4: B'frd 6A 36
Mansfield Pl. LS6: Leeds 5B 20
Mansion Ga. LS7: Leeds 5A 22
Mansion Ga. Dr. LS7: Leeds 5A 22
Mansion Ga. M. LS7: Leeds 5A 22

Mansion Ga. Sq. LS7: Leeds 5A 22
Mansion La. LS8: Leeds 2D 22
MANSTON 2D 34
Manston App. LS15: Leeds 2C 34
Manston Av. LS15: Leeds 2C 34
Manston Cres. LS15: Leeds 2D 34
Manston Dr. LS15: Leeds 2C 34
Manston Gdns. LS15: Leeds 2D 34
Manston Gro. LS15: Leeds 3C 34
Manston La. LS15: Leeds 3D 34
Manston Ri. LS15: Leeds 2C 34
Manston Ter. LS15: Leeds 2D 34
Manston Way LS15: Leeds 2C 34
Maple Av. BD3: B'frd 5A 26
Maple Ct. LS11: Leeds 5D 40
LS14: Leeds .3H 33
LS26: Wood .2B 54
Maple Cft. LS12: N Far 2D 38
LS17: Leeds .6A 14
Maple Dr. LS12: N Far 2D 38
Maple Fold LS12: N Far 2D 38
Maple Gro. LS12: N Far 2D 38
Maple Ri. LS26: Rothw 5G 53
Maple Ter. LS19: Yead 6H 7
Maple Way LS14: Leeds 3C 24
Marchant Way LS27: Chur 6A 40
Mardale Cres. LS14: Leeds 2A 34
Margaret Cl. LS27: Morl 4A 50
Margate LS26: Oul .3C 54
Margetson Rd. BD11: Drig 4A 48
Marian Gro. LS11: Leeds 4F 41
Marian Rd. LS6: Leeds 2F 31
Marian Ter. LS6: Leeds 2F 31
Marina Cres. LS27: Morl 6F 49
Market Bldgs. LS2: Leeds 4G 5 (5H 31)
Market Hall LS27: Morl 5G 49
(off Hope St.)
Market Pl. LS28: Pud 6G 27
Market Sq. LS27: Morl 5H 49
(off Hope St.)
Market St. Arc. LS1: Leeds 5F 5 (6G 31)
Markham Av. LS8: Leeds 1B 32
LS19: Raw 4E 9
Markham Cres. LS19: Raw 4E 9
Markham Cft. LS19: Raw 4E 9
Markington M. LS10: Leeds 6G 51
Markington Pl. LS10: Leeds 6G 51
Mark La. LS2: Leeds 3E 5 (5G 31)
Marlborough Cotts. LS29: Men 1D 6
(off Marlborough Ct.)
Marlborough Ct. LS29: Men 1D 6
Marlborough Gdns. LS2: Leeds 3F 31
(off Bk. Blenheim Ter.)
Marlborough Grange LS1: Leeds 3A 4
Marlborough Gro. LS2: Leeds 3F 31
(off Bk. Blenheim Ter.)
Marlborough St. LS1: Leeds 4A 4 (5E 31)
Marlborough Towers
LS1: Leeds 3A 4 (5E 31)
Marlborough Vs. LS29: Men 1D 6
Marley Gro. LS11: Leeds 4D 40
Marley Pl. LS11: Leeds 4D 40
Marley St. LS11: Leeds 4D 40
Marley Ter. LS11: Leeds 4D 40
Marley Vw. LS11: Leeds 4D 40
Marlowe Cl. LS28: Fars 2H 37
Marlowe Ct. LS20: Guis 4F 7
(off Holly Bank)
Marsden Av. LS11: Leeds 5E 41
Marsden Cl. LS28: Fars 2F 27
(off Water La.)
Marsden Gro. LS11: Leeds 5E 41
Marsden Memorial Homes LS28: Fars 3F 27
(off Newlands)
Marsden Mt. LS11: Leeds 5E 41
Marsden Pl. LS11: Leeds 5E 41
Marsden Vw. LS11: Leeds 5E 41
Marsett Way LS14: Leeds 3B 24
Marsh LS28: Pud 6E 27
Marsh, The BD4: E Bier 2B 46
Marshall Av. LS15: Leeds 3D 34
Marshall Cl. LS27: Morl 5G 49
(off Marshall St.)
Marshall Ct. LS11: Leeds 1E 41
LS19: Yead 2D 8
Marshall Mills LS11: Leeds 1E 41
Marshall St. LS11: Leeds 1F 41
LS15: Leeds .3C 34
LS19: Yead 2D 8
LS27: Morl 5G 49
WF3: S'ley 6H 59
Marshall Ter. LS15: Leeds 3C 34
Marsh Ct. LS28: Pud 6E 27
Marsh La. BD11: Birk 4C 46
LS9: Leeds 5H 5 (6H 31)
(not continuous)
Marsh Ri. LS28: Pud 6E 27

Marsh St.—Mill Grn.

Marsh St. LS6: Leeds .2E 31
LS26: Rothw .5G 53
Marsh Ter. LS28: Pud .6E 27
Marsh Va. LS6: Leeds .2E 31
Marsland Pl. BD3: B'frd .6A 26
Marston Av. LS27: Morl .6G 49
Marston Mt. LS9: Leeds .4A 32
(off Lincoln Rd.)
Martin Cl. LS27: Morl .5A 50
Martin Ct. LS15: Leeds .5D 34
Martindale Cl. BD2: B'frd .2A 26
Martindale Dr. LS13: Leeds .4E 29
Martingale Dr. LS10: Leeds .6G 51
Martin Ter. LS4: Leeds .3A 30
Marton Ct. BD3: B'frd .6A 26
Marwood Rd. LS13: Leeds .6E 29
Maryfield Av. LS15: Leeds .3A 34
Maryfield Cl. LS15: Leeds .3A 34
Maryfield Ct. LS15: Leeds .3B 34
Maryfield Cres. LS15: Leeds .3B 34
Maryfield Gdns. LS15: Leeds .3A 34
Maryfield Grn. LS15: Leeds .3A 34
Maryfield M. LS15: Leeds .3A 34
Maryfield Va. LS15: Leeds .3A 34
Mary St. LS28: Fars .1G 27
WF3: E Ard .3A 58
Mary Sunley Ho. LS8: Leeds .2B 32
(off Banstead St. W.)
Masefield St. LS20: Guis .5H 7
Masham Ct. LS6: Leeds .5B 20
Masham Gro. LS12: Leeds .6B 30
Masham St. LS12: Leeds .6B 30
Matrix Ct. LS11: Leeds .5F 41
Matty La. LS26: Rothw .5D 52
Maud Av. LS11: Leeds .5F 41
Maude St. LS2: Leeds .5G 5 (6H 31)
Maud Pl. LS11: Leeds .5F 41
Mavis Av. LS16: Leeds .3E 11
Mavis Gro. LS16: Leeds .4E 11
Mavis La. LS16: Leeds .3E 11
Mawcroft Cl. LS19: Yead .4C 8
Mawcroft Grange Dr. LS19: Yead .4C 8
Mawcroft M. LS19: Yead .4D 8
May Av. LS27: Chur .1A 50
Maybrook Ind. Pk. LS12: Leeds .5C 30
May Ct. LS27: Chur .6A 40
Mayfield Ct. LS18: H'fth .2C 18
Mayfield Rd. LS15: Leeds .5B 34
Mayflower Ho. LS10: Leeds .5C 42
Mayo Cl. LS8: Leeds .5F 23
May Ter. LS9: Leeds .1B 42
Maythorne Cl. BD4: B'frd .5B 36
Mayville Av. LS6: Leeds .2C 30
Mayville Pl. LS6: Leeds .2C 30
Mayville Rd. LS6: Leeds .2C 30
Mayville St. LS6: Leeds .2C 30
Mayville Ter. LS6: Leeds .2C 30
Mead Cl. LS15: Leeds .1E 45
Mead Gro. LS15: Leeds .1E 45
Meadowbrook Ct. LS27: Morl .6E 49
Meadow Cl. WF1: Out .6F 59
Meadow Cft. BD11: Drig .3F 47
LS11: Leeds .2F 41
LS29: Men .2C 6
WF1: Out .6E 59
Meadowcroft Cl. WF1: Out .6F 59
Meadowcroft Ct. WF1: Out .6F 59
Meadowcroft M. LS9: Leeds .6A 32
Meadowcroft Rd. WF1: Out .6F 59
Meadow Gth. WF1: Out .6E 59
Meadowgate Cft. WF3: Loft .1D 58
Meadowgate Dr. WF3: Loft .1D 58
Meadowgate Va. WF3: Loft .2D 58
Meadowhurst Gdns. LS28: Pud .6F 27
Meadow La. LS11: Leeds .6E 5 (1G 41)
Meadow Pk. Cres. LS28: Stan .3D 26
Meadow Pk. Dr. LS28: Stan .3D 26
Meadow Rd. BD10: B'frd .3A 16
LS11: Leeds .1F 41
Meadows, The LS16: Leeds .6A 12
Meadow Side Rd. WF3: E Ard .2A 58
Meadow Va. WF1: Out .6E 59
Meadow Valley LS17: Leeds .4F 13
Meadow Vw. LS6: Leeds .2C 30
LS28: Pud .6E 27
Meadow Wlk. LS7: Leeds .5A 22
Meadow Way LS17: Leeds .4E 13
WF3: W Ard .4B 56
Mead Rd. LS15: Leeds .1E 45
Mead Vw. BD4: B'frd .4A 36
Mead Way LS15: Leeds .1E 45
MEANWOOD .4D 20
Meanwood Cl. LS7: Leeds .1F 31
MEANWOOD GROVE .2C 20
Meanwood Gro. LS6: Leeds .2C 20
Meanwood Rd. LS6: Leeds .5D 20
LS7: Leeds .5D 20
Meanwood Towers LS6: Leeds .3E 21
Meanwood Valley Cl. LS7: Leeds .5D 20
Meanwood Valley Dr. LS7: Leeds .5D 20
Meanwood Valley Grn. LS7: Leeds .5D 20
Meanwood Valley Gro. LS7: Leeds .5D 20
Meanwood Valley Mt. LS7: Leeds .5D 20
Meanwood Valley Urban Farm .6F 21
Meanwood Valley Wlk. LS7: Leeds .5D 20
Mecca Bingo
Leeds, Balm Rd. .4H 41
Leeds, Cross Gates Rd. .3C 34
Leeds, New York St. .5G 5
Medeway LS28: Stan .3E 27
Melbourne Gro. BD3: B'frd .5A 26
LS13: Leeds .3C 28
Melbourne Mills LS27: Morl .5H 49
(off Melbourne St.)
Melbourne Mill Yd. LS27: Morl .5H 49
(off Middleton Rd.)
Melbourne St. LS2: Leeds .2G 5 (4H 31)
LS13: Leeds .3C 28
LS27: Morl .5H 49
LS28: Fars .3F 27
Melcombe Wlk. BD4: B'frd .3A 36
Melrose Gro. LS18: H'fth .3E 19
Melrose Pl. LS18: H'fth .3D 18
LS28: Pud .1F 37
Melrose Ter. LS18: H'fth .3D 18
Melrose Vs. LS18: H'fth .3D 18
(off Broadgate La.)
Melrose Wlk. LS18: H'fth .3D 18
Melton Av. LS10: Leeds .5B 52
Melton Cl. LS10: Leeds .5B 52
Melton Gth. LS10: Leeds .5B 52
Melton Ter. BD10: B'frd .1A 26
Melville Cl. LS6: Leeds .2F 31
Melville Gdns. LS6: Leeds .1F 31
Melville Pl. LS6: Leeds .1F 31
Melville Rd. LS6: Leeds .2F 31
Memorial Cotts. LS12: N Far .4D 38
(off Lawn La.)
Memorial Dr. LS6: Leeds .4D 20
MENSTON .1B 6
Menston Dr. LS29: Men .2C 6
Menston Hall LS29: Men .1D 6
Menston Ho. LS29: Men .2C 6
(off High Royds Dr.)
Menston Station (Rail) .1C 6
Merchants Ho. LS2: Leeds .2G 5
(off North St.)
Merchants Quay LS9: Leeds .6H 5 (6H 31)
Mercia Way LS15: Leeds .2E 35
Merlin Cl. LS27: Morl .6A 50
Merlyn-Rees Av. LS27: Morl .5G 49
Merrion Cen. LS2: Leeds .2E 5 (4G 31)
Merrion Cen. Superstore LS2: Leeds .4G 31
(off Wade La.)
Merrion Pl. LS1: Leeds .3F 5 (5G 31)
(not continuous)
LS2: Leeds .5G 31
Merrion St. LS1: Leeds .3F 5 (5G 31)
LS2: Leeds .3E 5 (5G 31)
(not continuous)
Merrion Way LS2: Leeds .2E 5 (4G 31)
Merriville LS18: H'fth .4D 18
Merton Av. LS28: Fars .3F 27
Merton Dr. LS28: Fars .3E 27
Merton Gdns. LS28: Fars .3E 27
METHLEY .6H 55
Methley Dr. LS7: Leeds .5G 21
Methley Gro. LS7: Leeds .5G 21
Methley La. LS7: Leeds .5H 21
LS26: Oul .5C 54
Methley Mt. LS7: Leeds .5H 21
METHLEY PARK SPIRE HOSPITAL .6G 55
Methley Pl. LS7: Leeds .5G 21
Methley Ter. LS7: Leeds .5H 21
Methley Vw. LS7: Leeds .5H 21
Mexborough Av. LS7: Leeds .1H 31
Mexborough Dr. LS7: Leeds .1H 31
Mexborough Gro. LS7: Leeds .1H 31
Mexborough Pl. LS7: Leeds .2H 31
Mexborough Rd. LS7: Leeds .2H 31
Mexborough St. LS7: Leeds .1H 31
Meynell App. LS11: Leeds .2E 41
Meynell Av. LS26: Rothw .4G 53
Meynell Ct. LS15: Leeds .6D 34
Meynell Fold LS15: Leeds .1D 44
Meynell Hgts. LS11: Leeds .2E 41
Meynell La. LS15: Leeds .1D 44
Meynell Mt. LS26: Rothw .4H 53
Meynell Rd. LS15: Leeds .6D 34
Meynell Sq. LS11: Leeds .2E 41
Meynell Wlk. LS11: Leeds .2E 41
Michael Av. WF3: S'ley .6G 59
Micklefield Ct. LS19: Raw .5D 8
Micklefield La. LS19: Raw .5C 8
Micklefield Rd. LS19: Raw .5D 8
Mickley St. LS12: Leeds .6B 30
Middlecroft Cl. LS10: Leeds .1B 52
Middlecroft Rd. LS10: Leeds .1B 52
Middle Cross St. LS12: Leeds .6B 30
(not continuous)
Middle Fold LS9: Leeds .3H 5 (5H 31)
Middleham Ct. BD4: B'frd .4A 36
Middleham Moor LS10: Leeds .6H 51
Middlemoor LS14: Leeds .3B 24
Middle Rd. LS9: Leeds .5F 43
Middlethorne Cl. LS17: Leeds .4D 14
Middlethorne Ct. LS17: Leeds .4C 14
Middlethorne M. LS17: Leeds .4D 14
Middlethorne Ri. LS17: Leeds .4C 14
MIDDLETON .4F 51
Middleton Av. LS9: Leeds .4B 32
LS26: Rothw .4C 52
Middleton Cl. LS27: Morl .5A 50
Middleton Cres. LS11: Leeds .5F 41
Middleton District Cen. LS10: Leeds .4H 51
Middleton Gro. LS11: Leeds .6F 41
LS27: Morl .5A 50
Middleton La. LS26: Rothw .4C 52
(not continuous)
WF3: Thpe H .6H 51
Middleton Leisure Cen. .4H 51
Middleton Pk. Av. LS10: Leeds .5F 51
Middleton Pk. Cir. LS10: Leeds .4F 51
Middleton Pk. Ct. LS10: Leeds .5F 51
Middleton Pk. Cres. LS10: Leeds .5G 51
Middleton Pk. Equestrian Cen. .1G 51
Middleton Pk. Grn. LS10: Leeds .5F 51
Middleton Pk. Gro. LS10: Leeds .4F 51
Middleton Pk. Mt. LS10: Leeds .5F 51
Middleton Pk. Rd. LS10: Leeds .4F 51
Middleton Pk. Ter. LS10: Leeds .5G 51
Middleton Railway
Moor Road Station .4H 41
Park Halt Station .1H 51
Middleton Rd. LS10: Leeds .2A 52
LS27: Morl .5H 49
Middleton Ter. LS27: Morl .5A 50
Middleton Way LS10: Leeds .3B 52
Middle Wlk. LS8: Leeds .2E 23
Midgley Gdns. LS6: Leeds .2E 31
Midgley Pl. LS6: Leeds .2F 31
Midgley Ter. LS6: Leeds .2F 31
Midland Cl. LS10: Leeds .4B 42
Midland Gth. LS10: Leeds .4A 42
Midland Ho. LS26: Wood .3D 54
(off Midland St.)
Midland Pas. LS6: Leeds .2D 30
Midland Pl. LS11: Leeds .1E 41
Midland Rd. LS6: Leeds .2D 30
LS10: Leeds .4A 42
Midland St. LS26: Oul .3C 54
Mid Point BD3: B'frd .5B 26
Mid Point Bus. Pk. BD3: B'frd .5B 26
Milan Rd. LS8: Leeds .2B 32
Milan St. LS8: Leeds .2C 32
MILES HILL .5F 21
Miles Hill Av. LS7: Leeds .5F 21
Miles Hill Cres. LS7: Leeds .5F 21
Miles Hill Gro. LS7: Leeds .5F 21
Miles Hill Mt. LS7: Leeds .4E 21
Miles Hill Pl. LS7: Leeds .4F 21
Miles Hill Rd. LS7: Leeds .4F 21
Miles Hill Sq. LS7: Leeds .5F 21
Miles Hill St. LS7: Leeds .5F 21
Miles Hill Ter. LS7: Leeds .5F 21
Miles Hill Vw. LS7: Leeds .5F 21
Milestone Ct. LS28: Stan .3H 27
Milford Gro. BD19: Gom .6C 46
Milford Pl. LS4: Leeds .4B 30
Millbank LS19: Yead .1D 8
Millbank Ct. LS28: Pud .1H 37
Millbank Fold LS28: Pud .1H 37
Millbank Vw. LS28: Pud .1H 37
Millbeck App. LS27: Morl .5A 50
Mill Cft. LS27: Gil .2D 48
Millcroft WF3: Loft .5G 59
Millcroft Cl. WF3: Loft .5F 59
Millcroft Ri. WF3: Loft .5G 59
Mill Dale Ct. BD11: Drig .3H 47
(off Moorside Va.)
Millennium Ct. LS28: Pud .5H 27
(off Lowtown)
Millennium Dr. LS11: Leeds .6F 41
Millennium Sq. LS2: Leeds .2D 4 (4F 31)
Millennium Way LS11: Leeds .6F 41
Millers Dale LS27: Morl .3F 49
Mill Fold LS27: Gil .2D 48
Mill Garth LS27: Gil .2D 48
Millgarth St. LS2: Leeds .4G 5 (5H 31)
MILL GREEN .6B 24
Mill Grn. LS12: Leeds .1D 40

90 A-Z Leeds

Mill Grn. Cl.—Morritt Dr.

Mill Grn. Cl. LS14: Leeds 6C **24**
Mill Grn. Gdns. LS14: Leeds 6C **24**
Mill Grn. Gth. LS14: Leeds 6C **24**
Mill Grn. Pl. LS14: Leeds 6C **24**
Mill Grn. Rd. LS14: Leeds 6C **24**
Mill Grn. Vw. LS14: Leeds 6C **24**
Mill Hill LS1: Leeds 5E **5** (6G **31**)
LS26: Rothw 4G **53**
LS28: Pud 2G **37**
Mill Hill Grn. LS26: Rothw 4G **53**
Mill Hill Sq. LS26: Rothw 4G **53**
Mill La. BD4: B'frd 4H **37**
BD11: Birk 3C **46**
BD19: Cleck, Hun 6A **46**
LS13: Leeds 2A **28**
LS20: Hawk 5A **6**
LS27: Gil 2D **48**
WF3: E Ard 3H **57**
WF17: Birs 6B **48**
Mill Pit La. LS26: Rothw 2F **53**
Mill Pond Cl. LS6: Leeds 5C **20**
Millpond Gdns. *LS12: Leeds 5H* ***29***
(off Eyres Mill Side)
Mill Pond Gro. LS6: Leeds 5C **20**
Mill Pond La. LS6: Leeds 4C **20**
Mill Pond Sq. LS6: Leeds 4C **20**
MILL SHAW 6C **40**
Millshaw LS11: Leeds 6B **40**
Millshaw Mt. LS11: Leeds 1C **50**
Millshaw Pk. Av. LS11: Leeds 1B **50**
Millshaw Pk. Cl. LS11: Leeds 1B **50**
Millshaw Pk. Dr. LS11: Leeds 6B **40**
Millshaw Pk. La. LS11: Leeds 1B **50**
Millshaw Pk. Trad. Est. LS11: Leeds 1C **50**
Millshaw Pk. Way LS11: Leeds 6B **40**
Millshaw Rd. LS11: Leeds 2C **50**
Millside Wlk. LS27: Morl 5A **50**
Mill St. LS9: Leeds 5H **5** (6A **32**)
LS27: Morl 6G **49**
Millwright St. LS2: Leeds 2H **5** (4H **31**)
Milne Ct. LS15: Leeds 1D **44**
Milner Fold LS28: Pud 2F **37**
Milner Gdns. LS9: Leeds 1B **42**
Milner La. WF3: Rob H 6C **52**
Milner's Rd. LS19: Yead 6H **7**
Milnes St. LS12: Leeds 1C **40**
Milton Ct. WF3: S'ley 5H **59**
Milton Dr. LS15: Scho 4F **25**
Milton Ter. LS5: Leeds 1G **29**
LS19: Yead 6H **7**
Minerva Ind. Est. LS26: Wood 2E **55**
Minor and Scurr's Yd. LS1: Leeds 4E **5**
Minster Dr. BD4: B'frd 2A **36**
Mirycarr La. LS14: Leeds, T'ner 1E **25**
Miry La. LS19: Yead 2D **8**
Mistress La. LS12: Leeds 5A **30**
Mitford Pl. LS12: Leeds 6B **30**
Mitford Rd. LS12: Leeds 6B **30**
Mitford Ter. LS12: Leeds 6B **30**
Mitford Vw. LS12: Leeds 6B **30**
Modder Av. LS12: Leeds 6H **29**
Modder Pl. LS12: Leeds 6H **29**
Model Av. LS12: Leeds 6B **30**
Model Rd. LS12: Leeds 6B **30**
Model Ter. LS12: Leeds 6B **30**
Monk Bri. Av. LS6: Leeds 5D **20**
Monk Bri. Dr. LS6: Leeds 5D **20**
Monk Bri. Gro. LS6: Leeds 5C **20**
Monk Bri. Mt. LS6: Leeds 5D **20**
Monk Bri. Pl. LS6: Leeds 5C **20**
Monk Bri. Rd. LS6: Leeds 5C **20**
Monk Bri. St. LS6: Leeds 5D **20**
Monk Bri. Ter. LS6: Leeds 5C **20**
Monkswood LS5: Leeds 5F **19**
Monkswood Av. LS14: Leeds 3H **23**
Monkswood Bank LS14: Leeds 3H **23**
Monkswood Cl. LS14: Leeds 3H **23**
Monkswood Dr. LS14: Leeds 3H **23**
Monkswood Ga. LS14: Leeds 3A **24**
Monkswood Grn. LS14: Leeds 3H **23**
Monkswood Hill LS14: Leeds 3H **23**
Monkswood Ho. LS5: Leeds 1F **29**
Monkswood Ri. LS14: Leeds 3H **23**
Monkswood Wlk. LS14: Leeds 3A **24**
Monkwood Rd. WF1: Out 6D **58**
Monson Av. LS28: Cal 5D **16**
Montagu Av. LS8: Leeds 6D **22**
Montagu Ct. LS8: Leeds 5D **22**
Montagu Cres. LS8: Leeds 6E **23**
Montagu Dr. LS8: Leeds 5D **22**
Montague LS12: Leeds 5A **4**
Montague Ct. LS12: Leeds 6G **29**
Montagu Gdns. LS8: Leeds 6D **22**
Montagu Gro. LS8: Leeds 6E **23**
Montagu Pl. LS8: Leeds 6D **22**
Montagu Ri. LS8: Leeds 6E **23**
Montagu Vw. LS8: Leeds 6D **22**
Montcalm Cres. LS10: Leeds 5A **42**
Montfort Cl. LS18: H'fth 6B **10**
Montgomery Av. LS16: Leeds 4A **20**
Montpelier Ter. LS6: Leeds 1E **31**
Montreal Av. LS7: Leeds 5H **21**
Montreal Ter. LS13: Leeds 5A **28**
Montserrat Rd. BD4: B'frd 6B **36**
MOOR ALLERTON 6G **13**
Moor Allerton Av. LS17: Leeds 1A **22**
Moor Allerton Cen. LS17: Leeds 1F **21**
Moor Allerton Cres. LS17: Leeds 1A **22**
Moor Allerton Dr. LS17: Leeds 1A **22**
Moor Allerton Gdns. LS17: Leeds 1H **21**
Moor Allerton Hall LS8: Leeds 2B **22**
Moor Allerton Way LS17: Leeds 1A **22**
Moor Av. LS15: Leeds 6H **33**
WF3: S'ley 5G **59**
Moor Bank BD4: B'frd 2C **46**
Moorbank Ct. LS6: Leeds 6C **20**
Moor Cl. LS10: Leeds 5H **41**
Moor Cres. LS11: Leeds 3G **41**
Moor Cres. Chase LS11: Leeds 3G **41**
Moor Cft. LS16: Leeds 5B **12**
Moorcroft Av. BD3: B'frd 4A **26**
Moorcroft Dr. BD4: B'frd 6B **36**
Moorcroft Rd. BD4: B'frd 6B **36**
Moorcroft Ter. BD4: B'frd 6B **36**
Moor Dr. LS6: Leeds 5C **20**
LS28: Pud 2H **37**
Moorehouse Gro. LS9: Leeds 4A **32**
MOOR END 6G **29**
Moor Farm Gdns. LS7: Leeds 4G **21**
Moorfield LS27: Gil 2C **48**
Moorfield Av. BD3: B'frd 4A **26**
LS12: Leeds 5G **29**
LS29: Men 1B **6**
Moorfield Bus. Pk. LS19: Yead 3F **9**
Moorfield Cl. LS19: Yead 3F **9**
Moorfield Ct. LS19: Yead 3F **9**
Moorfield Cres. LS12: Leeds 5G **29**
LS19: Yead 3E **9**
LS28: Pud 1F **37**
Moorfield Cft. LS19: Yead 3F **9**
Moorfield Dr. LS19: Yead 3F **9**
Moorfield Gdns. LS28: Pud 1E **37**
Moorfield Gro. LS12: Leeds 5G **29**
LS28: Pud 1E **37**
Moorfield Ind. Est. LS19: Yead 2F **9**
Moorfield Rd. LS12: Leeds 5G **29**
LS19: Yead 3F **9**
Moorfields LS13: Leeds 2C **28**
LS17: Leeds 1H **21**
Moorfield St. LS2: Leeds 2E **31**
LS12: Leeds 5G **29**
Moorfield Ter. LS19: Yead 2E **9**
Moor Flatts Av. LS10: Leeds 4G **51**
Moor Flatts Rd. LS10: Leeds 4G **51**
Moorgarth Av. BD3: B'frd 4A **26**
Moor Grange LS19: Yead 3F **9**
Moor Grange Ct. LS16: Leeds 3F **19**
Moor Grange Dr. LS16: Leeds 3G **19**
Moor Grange Ri. LS16: Leeds 3G **19**
Moor Grange Vw. LS16: Leeds 3G **19**
Moor Gro. LS28: Pud 2H **37**
WF3: S'ley 5G **59**
Moor Haven LS17: Leeds 6E **13**
Moorhaven Ct. LS17: Leeds 6E **13**
MOOR HEAD 1C **48**
Moorhead Vs. LS27: Gil 6B **38**
Moorhouse Av. LS11: Leeds 6D **40**
Moor Ho. Ct. LS17: Leeds 5D **14**
Moorhouse Dr. BD11: Birk 2B **46**
Moorhouse La. BD11: Birk 2C **46**
Moorings, The BD10: B'frd 3A **16**
LS10: Leeds 4D **42**
LS17: Leeds 4A **14**
Moor Knoll Cl. WF3: E Ard 3H **57**
Moor Knoll Dr. WF3: E Ard 3G **57**
Moor Knoll La. WF3: E Ard 2G **57**
Moorland Av. LS6: Leeds 3D **30**
LS20: Guis 4G **7**
LS27: Gil 1B **48**
Moorland Cl. LS17: Leeds 2H **21**
LS27: Gil 1C **48**
Moorland Cres. LS17: Leeds 2G **21**
LS20: Guis 3G **7**
LS27: Gil 1B **48**
LS28: Pud 5C **26**
LS29: Men 3E **7**
Moorland Dr. BD11: Birk 2D **46**
LS17: Leeds 2G **21**
LS20: Guis 3G **7**
LS28: Pud 4C **26**
Moorland Gdns. LS17: Leeds 2H **21**
Moorland Gth. LS17: Leeds 2G **21**
Moorland Gro. LS17: Leeds 1G **21**
LS28: Pud 4C **26**
Moorland Ings LS17: Leeds 2G **21**
Moorland Leys LS17: Leeds 2G **21**
Moorland Pl. WF3: S'ley 3H **59**
Moorland Ri. LS17: Leeds 2G **21**
Moorland Rd. BD11: Drig 3G **47**
LS6: Leeds 3D **30**
LS28: Pud 4C **26**
Moorlands, The LS17: Leeds 5A **14**
Moorlands Av. BD11: Birk 2C **46**
LS19: Yead 3F **9**
Moorlands Dr. LS19: Yead 3F **9**
Moorlands Rd. BD11: Birk 2C **46**
Moorland Vw. LS13: Leeds 1B **28**
LS17: Leeds 1G **21**
Moorland Wlk. LS17: Leeds 1G **21**
Moor La. BD11: Birk 5E **47**
BD19: Gom 6E **47**
LS20: Guis 2G **7**
LS29: Men 1A **6**
Moor Pk. Av. LS6: Leeds 5B **20**
Moor Pk. Dr. BD3: B'frd 5A **26**
LS6: Leeds 5B **20**
Moor Pk. Mt. LS6: Leeds 5B **20**
Moor Pk. Vs. LS6: Leeds 5C **20**
Moor Rd. LS6: Leeds 5B **20**
LS10: Leeds 3H **41**
LS11: Leeds 3G **41**
(not continuous)
LS16: B'hpe 1D **10**
WF3: S'ley 5G **59**
Moor Road Station
Middleton Railway 4H **41**
MOORSIDE
LS13 1C **28**
WF17 4H **47**
Moorside App. BD11: Drig 4H **47**
Moorside Av. BD11: Birk 2C **46**
BD11: Drig 4H **47**
Moorside Cl. BD11: Drig 4H **47**
Moorside Cres. BD11: Drig 4G **47**
Moorside Dr. BD11: Drig 4H **47**
LS13: Leeds 1C **28**
Moorside Gdns. BD11: Drig 4H **47**
Moorside Grn. BD11: Drig 3H **47**
Moorside Maltings
LS11: Leeds 3G **41**
Moorside Mt. BD11: Drig 4G **47**
Moorside Pde. BD11: Drig 4H **47**
Moorside Rd. BD11: Drig 4G **47**
Moorside St. LS13: Leeds 1C **28**
Moorside Ter. BD11: Drig 4H **47**
LS13: Leeds 1C **28**
Moorside Va. BD11: Drig 3H **47**
Moorside Vw. BD11: Drig 4H **47**
Moorside Wlk. BD11: Drig 3H **47**
MOOR TOP 6H **29**
Moor Top BD11: Drig 3F **47**
(not continuous)
LS12: N Far 5C **38**
LS20: Guis 1F **7**
LS21: Men 1F **7**
MOORTOWN 6H **13**
Moortown Cnr. LS17: Leeds 1H **21**
Moor Vw. BD4: B'frd 2C **46**
LS6: Leeds 2D ***30***
(off Hyde Pk. Rd.)
LS11: Leeds 2E **41**
LS12: Leeds 6H **29**
LS19: Yead 2F **9**
Moorview Cft. LS29: Men 1B **6**
Moorville Cl. LS11: Leeds 3F **41**
Moorville Ct. LS11: Leeds 3F **41**
Moorville Dr. BD11: Birk 2C **46**
Moorville Gro. LS11: Leeds 3E **41**
Moorville Rd. LS11: Leeds 3F **41**
Moorway LS20: Guis 4D **6**
Moravia Bank *LS28: Pud 2G* ***37***
(off Fartown)
Moresdale La. LS14: Leeds 2H **33**
MORLEY 5G **49**
Morley Av. BD3: B'frd 4A **26**
Morley Bottoms LS27: Morl 4G **49**
MORLEY HOLE 4F **49**
Morley Leisure Cen. 5G **49**
Morley Mkt. *LS27: Morl 5G* ***49***
(off Hope St.)
Morley Station (Rail) 4A **50**
Morpeth Pl. LS9: Leeds 6A **32**
Morrell Ct. BD4: B'frd 4A **36**
Morris Av. LS5: Leeds 6G **19**
Morris Gro. LS5: Leeds 1G **29**
Morris La. LS5: Leeds 6G **19**
Morris Mt. LS5: Leeds 1G **29**
Morris Pl. LS27: Morl 4F **49**
Morris Vw. LS5: Leeds 1G **29**
Morritt Av. LS15: Leeds 4B **34**
Morritt Dr. LS15: Leeds 5H **33**

A-Z Leeds 91

Morritt Gro. LS15: Leeds	.5H 33
Mortec Pk. LS15: Leeds	.4E 25
Mortimer Av. BD3: B'frd	.4A 26
Morton Ter. LS20: Guis	.4F 7
Morwick Gro. LS15: Scho	.5F 25
Morwick Ter. LS14: Leeds	.3E 25
Moseley Pl. LS6: Leeds	.2F 31
Moseley Wood App. LS16: Leeds	.5D 10
Moseley Wood Av. LS16: Leeds	.3D 10
Moseley Wood Bank LS16: Leeds	.4D 10
Moseley Wood Cl. LS16: Leeds	.5D 10
Moseley Wood Cres. LS16: Leeds	.4D 10
Moseley Wood Cft. LS16: Leeds	.5C 10
Moseley Wood Dr. LS16: Leeds	.4D 10
Moseley Wood Gdns. LS16: Leeds	.4D 10
Moseley Wood Grn. LS16: Leeds	.4D 10
Moseley Wood Gro. LS16: Leeds	.4D 10
Moseley Wood La. LS16: Leeds	.4E 11
Moseley Wood Ri. LS16: Leeds	.4D 10
Moseley Wood Vw. LS16: Leeds	.3E 11
Moseley Wood Wlk. LS16: Leeds	.4D 10
Moseley Wood Way LS16: Leeds	.3D 10
Moss Bri. Rd. LS13: Leeds	.6H 17
Moss Gdns. LS17: Leeds	.4E 13
Moss Lea LS27: Chur	.2H 49
Moss Ri. LS17: Leeds	.4E 13
Moss Valley LS17: Leeds	.4E 13
Motley La. LS20: Guis	.3G 7
Motley Row LS20: Guis	.3G 7
(off Motley La.)	
Mount, The LS15: Leeds	.4B 34
LS17: Leeds	.3F 13
LS19: Raw	.6F 9
LS26: Rothw	.2H 53
LS27: Chur	.2H 49
(off Elland Rd.)	
Mountbatten Av. WF1: Out	.6E 59
Mountbatten Cres. WF1: Out	.6E 59
Mountbatten Gro. WF1: Out	.6F 59
Mt. Cliffe Vw. LS27: Chur	.2H 49
Mount Dr. LS17: Leeds	.3F 13
Mountfields LS2: Leeds	.1A 4
Mount Gdns. LS17: Leeds	.3F 13
Mt. Pleasant LS10: Leeds	.4G 51
LS13: Leeds	.1B 28
LS18: H'fth	.3D 18
(off Broadgate La.)	
LS20: Guis	.3G 7
LS28: Stan	.4F 27
(off Westbourne Pl.)	
Mt. Pleasant Av. LS8: Leeds	.6B 22
Mt. Pleasant Ct. LS28: Pud	.5G 27
Mt. Pleasant Gdns. LS8: Leeds	.6B 22
(off Sycamore Av.)	
Mt. Pleasant Hgts. LS28: Pud	.5G 27
(off Mt. Pleasant Rd.)	
Mt. Pleasant Rd. LS28: Pud	.5G 27
Mt. Pleasant St. LS28: Pud	.5H 27
Mt. Preston LS2: Leeds	.1A 4
Mt. Preston St. LS2: Leeds	.1A 4 (4E 31)
Mount Ri. LS17: Leeds	.3F 13
Mount Rd. WF3: S'ley	.5H 59
Mount Royal LS18: H'fth	.3B 18
Mt. Tabor St. LS28: Pud	.6E 27
Mt. Vernon Rd. LS19: Raw	.5E 9
Mount Vw. LS27: Chur	.2H 49
Mowbray Chase LS26: Wood	.2B 54
Mowbray Ct. LS14: Leeds	.2A 34
Mowbray Cres. LS14: Leeds	.2A 34
Moxon St. WF1: Out	.6E 59
Moxon Way WF1: Out	.6E 59
Moynihan Cl. LS8: Leeds	.1D 32
Mozart Way LS27: Chur	.1A 50
Muir Ct. LS6: Leeds	.1B 30
(off Sagar Pl.)	
Muirhead Ct. BD4: B'frd	.5A 36
Muirhead Dr. BD4: B'frd	.5A 36
Muirhead Fold BD4: B'frd	.5A 36
Mulberry Av. LS16: Leeds	.5B 12
Mulberry Gdns. LS26: Meth	.6H 55
Mulberry Gth. LS16: Leeds	.6C 12
Mulberry Ri. LS16: Leeds	.5B 12
Mulberry St. LS28: Pud	.6G 27
Mulberry Vw. LS16: Leeds	.6B 12
Mullins Ct. LS9: Leeds	.6B 32
Murray Av. LS10: Leeds	.5A 52
Murray Ct. LS18: H'fth	.3E 19
Murray Dr. LS10: Leeds	.5A 52
Murray Way LS10: Leeds	.5A 52
Murton Cl. LS14: Leeds	.1A 34
Museum St. LS9: Leeds	.4B 32
Musgrave Bank LS13: Leeds	.3E 29
Musgrave Ct. LS28: Pud	.5H 27
Musgrave Mt. LS13: Leeds	.3E 29
Musgrave Ri. LS13: Leeds	.3E 29
Musgrave Vw. LS13: Leeds	.3E 29

Musgrave Ho. LS5: Leeds	.1F 29
(off Broad La.)	
Mushroom St. LS9: Leeds	.1H 5 (4H 31)
Myers Dr. LS13: Leeds	.5B 18

N

Nab La. WF17: Birs	.6A 48
(not continuous)	
Naburn App. LS14: Leeds	.2B 24
Naburn Chase LS14: Leeds	.4C 24
Naburn Cl. LS14: Leeds	.4C 24
Naburn Ct. LS14: Leeds	.3B 24
Naburn Dr. LS14: Leeds	.4B 24
Naburn Fold LS14: Leeds	.4C 24
Naburn Gdns. LS14: Leeds	.4B 24
Naburn Grn. LS14: Leeds	.4B 24
Naburn Pl. LS14: Leeds	.3B 24
Naburn Rd. LS14: Leeds	.4B 24
Naburn Vw. LS14: Leeds	.4C 24
Naburn Wlk. LS14: Leeds	.4B 24
Nancroft Cres. LS12: Leeds	.6A 30
Nancroft Mt. LS12: Leeds	.6A 30
Nancroft Ter. LS12: Leeds	.6A 30
Nansen Av. LS13: Leeds	.3B 28
Nansen Gro. LS13: Leeds	.3B 28
Nansen Mt. LS13: Leeds	.3B 28
Nansen Pl. LS13: Leeds	.3B 28
Nansen St. LS13: Leeds	.3A 28
Nansen Ter. LS13: Leeds	.3B 28
Nansen Vw. LS13: Leeds	.3B 28
Napier St. BD3: B'frd	.6A 26
Narrowboat Wharf	
LS13: Leeds	.6H 17
Naseby Gdns. LS9: Leeds	.5A 32
Naseby Gth. LS9: Leeds	.4A 32
Naseby Grange LS9: Leeds	.5A 32
(off Naseby Gdns.)	
Naseby Ho. BD4: B'frd	.6B 36
Naseby Pl. LS9: Leeds	.5A 32
Naseby Ter. LS9: Leeds	.5A 32
Naseby Vw. LS9: Leeds	.5A 32
Naseby Wlk. LS9: Leeds	.5A 32
Nassau Pl. LS7: Leeds	.2A 32
Nateby Ri. WF3: Carl	.4F 53
National Pk. LS10: Leeds	.3A 42
National Rd. LS10: Leeds	.2A 42
Navigation Ct. LS13: Leeds	.5G 17
Navigation Dr. BD10: B'frd	.3A 16
Navigation Wlk. LS10: Leeds	.6F 5 (6G 31)
Naylor Gth. LS6: Leeds	.6D 20
Naylor Pl. LS11: Leeds	.3F 41
Neath Gdns. LS9: Leeds	.2F 33
Ned La. BD4: B'frd	.3A 36
Needless Inn La. LS26: Wood	.2C 54
Nelson Pl. LS27: Morl	.4G 49
(off Croft Ho. Rd.)	
Nepshaw La. LS27: Gil	.5D 48
LS27: Morl	.4F 49
Nepshaw La. Nth. LS27: Morl	.4E 49
Nepshaw La. Sth. LS27: Gil	.4E 49
Neptune St. LS9: Leeds	.6H 5 (6H 31)
Nesfield Cl. LS10: Leeds	.3B 52
Nesfield Cres. LS10: Leeds	.3B 52
Nesfield Gdns. LS10: Leeds	.3A 52
Nesfield Gth. LS10: Leeds	.3A 52
Nesfield Grn. LS10: Leeds	.3A 52
Nesfield Rd. LS10: Leeds	.3A 52
Nesfield Vw. LS10: Leeds	.3A 52
Nesfield Wlk. LS10: Leeds	.3A 52
Nethercliffe Cres. LS20: Guis	.3F 7
Nethercliffe Rd. LS20: Guis	.3F 7
Netherfield Cl. LS19: Yead	.2D 8
Netherfield Ct. LS20: Guis	.4F 7
(off Netherfield Rd.)	
Netherfield Dr. LS20: Guis	.3F 7
Netherfield Ri. LS20: Guis	.4F 7
Netherfield Rd. LS20: Guis	.4F 7
Netherfield Ter. LS19: Yead	.2D 8
LS20: Guis	.4F 7
(off Netherfield Rd.)	
Nether St. LS28: Fars	.2F 27
NETHERTOWN	.2A 48
NETHER YEADON	.5D 8
Nettleton Cl. BD4: B'frd	.5G 37
Nettleton Ct. LS15: Leeds	.5D 34
Neville App. LS9: Leeds	.1E 43
Neville Av. LS9: Leeds	.1E 43
Neville Cl. LS9: Leeds	.1E 43
Neville Cres. LS9: Leeds	.5F 33
Neville Gdns. LS9: Leeds	.1E 43
Neville Gro. LS9: Leeds	.6E 33
LS26: Swil	.5G 45
Neville Mt. LS9: Leeds	.1E 43
Neville Pde. LS9: Leeds	.1E 43
Neville Pl. LS9: Leeds	.6F 33

Neville Rd. LS9: Leeds	.5F 33
LS15: Leeds	.5F 33
Neville Row LS9: Leeds	.1E 43
Neville Sq. LS9: Leeds	.6F 33
Neville St. LS1: Leeds	.6D 4 (1F 41)
LS11: Leeds	.6D 4 (6F 31)
Neville Ter. LS9: Leeds	.1E 43
Neville Vw. LS9: Leeds	.6E 33
Neville Wlk. LS9: Leeds	.6E 33
New Adel Av. LS16: Leeds	.6G 11
New Adel Gdns. LS16: Leeds	.6G 11
New Adel La. LS16: Leeds	.1G 19
Newark Va. WF3: Rob H	.6C 52
New Bank Ri. BD4: B'frd	.4A 36
New Bank St. LS27: Morl	.4H 49
NEW BLACKPOOL	.3G 39
New Briggate LS1: Leeds	.3F 5 (5G 31)
LS2: Leeds	.3F 5 (5G 31)
NEW BRIGHTON	.5G 49
Newby Cl. LS29: Men	.2D 6
Newby Ct. LS29: Men	.2D 6
Newby Gth. LS17: Leeds	.4D 14
Newcastle Cl. BD11: Drig	.4F 47
New Centaur Ho. LS11: Leeds	.6D 4 (6F 31)
New Cote Cotts. LS28: Fars	.2G 27
New Craven Ga. LS11: Leeds	.2G 41
New Cres. LS18: H'fth	.3B 18
New Cft. LS18: H'fth	.3B 18
Newell Sq. LS28: Pud	.1F 37
(off Smalewell Rd.)	
New Farmers Hill LS26: Wood	.2D 54
NEW FARNLEY	.4D 38
Newfield Dr. LS29: Men	.1C 6
New Forest Way LS10: Leeds	.5A 52
Newhall Bank LS10: Leeds	.4H 51
Newhall Chase LS10: Leeds	.3H 51
Newhall Cl. LS10: Leeds	.3H 51
Newhall Cres. LS10: Leeds	.3H 51
Newhall Cft. LS10: Leeds	.2A 52
Newhall Gdns. LS10: Leeds	.4H 51
Newhall Gth. LS10: Leeds	.4H 51
Newhall Ga. LS10: Leeds	.2H 51
Newhall Grn. LS10: Leeds	.3A 52
Newhall Mt. LS10: Leeds	.4H 51
Newhall Rd. LS10: Leeds	.3H 51
Newhall Wlk. LS10: Leeds	.3A 52
New Inn St. LS12: Leeds	.6G 29
Newlaithes Gdns. LS18: H'fth	.4B 18
Newlaithes Gth. LS18: H'fth	.5A 18
Newlaithes Rd. LS18: H'fth	.5A 18
Newlands LS28: Fars	.3F 27
Newlands Av. BD3: B'frd	.4A 26
LS19: Yead	.1C 8
Newlands Cres. LS27: Morl	.5B 50
Newlands Dr. LS27: Morl	.5B 50
WF3: S'ley	.6G 59
Newlands Pl. LS19: Yead	.2C 8
Newlands Wlk. WF3: S'ley	.6G 59
New La. BD3: B'frd	.1A 36
BD4: B'frd	.1A 36
(Armstrong St.)	
BD4: B'frd	.5D 36
(Raikes La.)	
BD11: Drig	.1A 48
LS10: Leeds	.4F 51
LS11: Leeds	.1F 41
LS27: Gil	.1A 48
WF3: E Ard	.3F 57
NEWLAY	.5B 18
Newlay Bridle Path LS18: H'fth	.4B 18
Newlay Cl. BD10: B'frd	.4A 16
Newlay Gro. LS18: H'fth	.5B 18
Newlay La. LS13: Leeds	.1C 28
LS18: H'fth	.4B 18
Newlay La. Pl. LS13: Leeds	.1C 28
Newlay Mt. LS18: H'fth	.5B 18
Newlay Wood Av. LS18: H'fth	.4C 18
Newlay Wood Cl. LS18: H'fth	.4C 18
Newlay Wood Cres. LS18: H'fth	.4C 18
Newlay Wood Dr. LS18: H'fth	.4B 18
Newlay Wood Fold LS18: H'fth	.4B 18
Newlay Wood Gdns. LS18: H'fth	.4C 18
Newlay Wood Ri. LS18: H'fth	.4C 18
Newlay Wood Rd. LS18: H'fth	.4B 18
New Leeds LS13: Leeds	.6B 18
New Line BD10: B'frd	.4A 16
Newmarket App. LS9: Leeds	.2D 42
Newmarket Grn. LS9: Leeds	.1D 42
Newmarket La. LS9: Leeds	.2D 42
New Mkt. St. LS1: Leeds	.5F 5 (6G 31)
New Moon Apartments LS6: Leeds	.6C 20
New Occupation La. LS28: Pud	.1E 37
New Pk. Av. LS28: Fars	.2G 27
New Pk. Cl. LS28: Fars	.2G 27
New Pk. Cft. LS28: Fars	.2G 27
New Pk. Gro. LS28: Fars	.2F 27
New Pk. Pl. LS28: Fars	.2G 27

New Pk. St. LS27: Morl 6F 49
New Pk. Va. LS28: Fars 2G 27
New Pk. Vw. LS28: Fars 3G 27
New Pk. Wlk. LS28: Fars 3F 27
New Pk. Way LS28: Fars 2G 27
New Pepper Rd. LS10: Leeds 4B 42
Newport Av. LS13: Leeds 3A 28
Newport Cres. LS6: Leeds 2B 30
Newport Gdns. LS6: Leeds 2B 30
Newport Mt. LS6: Leeds 2B 30
Newport Rd. LS6: Leeds 2B 30
Newport Vw. LS6: Leeds 1B 30
New Princess St. LS11: Leeds 2F 41
New Pudsey Sq. LS28: Stan 4E 27
New Pudsey Station (Rail) 4E 27
New Rd. LS19: Yead 6H 7
    WF3: Carl 6F 53
New Rd. Side LS18: H'fth 3A 18
    LS19: Raw 4D 8
New Row LS15: Leeds 1E 45
    LS28: Cal 2B 26
Newsam Ct. LS15: Leeds 6A 34
Newsam Dr. LS15: Leeds 6G 33
NEWSAM GREEN 5D 44
Newsam Grn. Rd. LS26: Wood 5D 44
NEW SCARBOROUGH
    LS13 ....4D 28
    LS19 ....6H 7
New Scarbro' Rd. LS13: Leeds 3D 28
New Station St. LS1: Leeds 5D 4 (6F 31)
Newstead Av. WF1: Out 6C 58
New St. LS18: H'fth 3B 18
    LS28: Fars 4F 27
    LS28: Pud 1F 37
New St. Cl. LS28: Pud 1G 37
New St. Gdns. LS28: Pud 1G 37
New St. Gro. LS28: Pud 1G 37
New Temple Ga. LS15: Leeds 1A 44
New Toftshaw BD4: B'frd 1A 46
Newton Cl. LS26: Rothw 5D 52
Newton Ct. LS8: Leeds 5E 23
    LS26: Rothw 5D 52
Newton Gth. LS7: Leeds 6A 22
Newton Gro. LS7: Leeds 1A 32
Newton Hill Rd. LS7: Leeds 6H 21
Newton Lodge Cl. LS7: Leeds 6G 21
Newton Lodge Dr. LS7: Leeds 6G 21
Newton Pde. LS7: Leeds 6H 21
Newton Pk. Ct. LS7: Leeds 6A 22
Newton Pk. Dr. LS7: Leeds 6A 22
Newton Pk. Vw. LS7: Leeds 1A 32
Newton Rd. LS7: Leeds 1H 31
Newton Sq. LS12: N Far 4D 38
Newton Ter. LS7: Leeds 5G 21
Newton Vw. LS7: Leeds 6H 21
Newton Vs. LS7: Leeds 5G 21
Newton Wlk. LS7: Leeds 1A 32
NEW TOWN 3A 32
New Village M. LS27: Chur 1A 50
    (off New Village Way)
New Village Way LS27: Chur 6A 40
New Wlk. LS8: Leeds 2D 22
New Way LS20: Guis 4D 6
New Windsor Dr. LS26: Rothw 3H 53
NEW WORTLEY 6C 30
New York Cotts. LS19: Raw 1F 17
New York La. LS19: Raw 1F 17
New York Rd. LS2: Leeds 3G 5 (5H 31)
    (not continuous)
    LS9: Leeds 3G 5 (5H 31)
New York St. LS2: Leeds 5F 5 (6H 31)
NHS WALK-IN CENTRE
    Leeds General Infirmary 2C 4
    (within Leeds General Infirmary)
    The Headrow 3D 4
    (within The Light)
Nice Av. LS8: Leeds 1B 32
Nice St. LS8: Leeds 1C 32
Nice Vw. LS8: Leeds 1B 32
Nicholson Ct. LS8: Leeds 5C 22
Nickleby Rd. LS9: Leeds 5C 32
Nijinsky Way LS10: Leeds 6D 42
Nile St. LS2: Leeds 2G 5 (4H 31)
Nineveh Gdns. LS11: Leeds 2E 41
Nineveh Pde. LS11: Leeds 2E 41
Nineveh Rd. LS11: Leeds 2E 41
Nippet La. LS9: Leeds 5A 32
Nixon Av. LS9: Leeds 6D 32
Nook, The LS17: Leeds 4H 13
    WF3: W Ard 5C 56
Nook Gdns. LS15: Scho 3F 25
Nook Grn. WF3: W Ard 4D 56
Nook Rd. LS15: Scho 3F 25
Nooks, The LS27: Gil 2D 48
Nook Vw. WF3: W Ard 5C 56
Noon Cl. WF3: S'ley 6G 59
Nora Pl. LS13: Leeds 2A 28

Nora Rd. LS13: Leeds 2A 28
Nora Ter. LS13: Leeds 2A 28
Norbury Rd. BD10: B'frd 6A 16
Norfolk Cl. LS7: Leeds 4H 21
    LS26: Oul 4D 54
Norfolk Dr. LS26: Oul 4D 54
Norfolk Gdns. LS7: Leeds 4H 21
Norfolk Grn. LS7: Leeds 4H 21
Norfolk Mt. LS7: Leeds 4H 21
Norfolk Pl. LS7: Leeds 4H 21
Norfolk Ter. LS7: Leeds 4H 21
Norfolk Vw. LS7: Leeds 4H 21
Norfolk Wlk. LS7: Leeds 4H 21
Norman Gro. LS5: Leeds 1G 29
Norman Mt. LS5: Leeds 1G 29
Norman Pl. LS8: Leeds 1C 22
Norman Row LS5: Leeds 1G 29
Norman St. LS5: Leeds 1G 29
Norman Ter. LS8: Leeds 1C 22
Normanton Gro. LS11: Leeds 3E 41
Normanton Pl. LS11: Leeds 3E 41
Normanton Towers LS16: Leeds 5G 19
Norman Vw. LS5: Leeds 1G 29
Normington Ho. LS13: Leeds 6G 17
Norquest Ind. Pk. WF17: Birs 6A 48
Nortech Cl. LS7: Leeds 3H 31
Nth. Broadgate La. LS18: H'fth 2C 18
Northbrook Cft. LS7: Leeds 4H 21
    (off Hill Vw. Mt.)
Northbrook Pl. LS7: Leeds 4H 21
Northbrook St. LS7: Leeds 4H 21
Northcote Cres. LS11: Leeds 3F 41
Northcote Dr. LS11: Leeds 3F 41
Northcote Grn. LS11: Leeds 3F 41
Northcote St. LS28: Fars 3F 27
North Ct. LS2: Leeds 3F 5 (5G 31)
Northern Ballet Theatre 4G 19
    (off Spen La.)
Northern St. LS1: Leeds 5B 4 (6E 31)
Northern St. Apartments LS1: Leeds 5C 4
Nth. Farm Rd. LS8: Leeds 2D 32
    LS9: Leeds 2D 32
Northfield Av. LS26: Rothw 5E 53
Northfield Pl. LS26: Rothw 5D 52
Northgate LS26: Oul 3C 54
Nth. Grange M. LS6: Leeds 1D 30
Nth. Grange Mt. LS6: Leeds 6C 20
Nth. Grange Rd. LS6: Leeds 1C 30
North Gro. Cl. LS8: Leeds 5F 23
North Gro. Dr. LS8: Leeds 5F 23
North Gro. Ri. LS8: Leeds 5F 23
Nth. Hill Cl. LS8: Leeds 5E 23
Nth. Hill Ct. LS6: Leeds 6D 20
Nth. Hill Rd. LS6: Leeds 1D 30
North La. LS6: Leeds 6B 20
    LS8: Leeds 4E 23
    LS26: Oul, Wood 3C 54
North La. Gdns. LS8: Leeds 5E 23
Nth. Lingwell Rd. LS10: Leeds 4G 51
Northolme Av. LS16: Leeds 4H 19
Northolme Cres. LS16: Leeds 4H 19
North Pde. LS16: Leeds 3G 19
    LS27: Morl 6H 49
    (off Gillroyd Pde.)
North Pk. Av. LS8: Leeds 3B 22
North Pk. Gro. LS8: Leeds 3C 22
North Pk. Pde. LS8: Leeds 2B 22
North Pk. Rd. LS8: Leeds 3C 22
    (not continuous)
North Parkway LS14: Leeds 6G 23
North Rd. LS15: Leeds 3C 34
    LS18: H'fth 6B 10
Northrops Yd. LS28: Pud 6G 27
Northside Bus. Pk. LS7: Leeds 3H 31
Northside Retail Pk. LS7: Leeds 4D 20
North St. LS2: Leeds 2G 5 (4H 31)
    LS7: Leeds 2G 5 (3H 31)
    LS19: Raw 5D 8
    LS28: Stan 5G 27
North Ter. LS15: Leeds 3C 34
    (off Tranquility Av.)
    LS19: Yead 2D 8
North Vw. LS8: Leeds 5F 23
    LS26: Rothw 4H 53
    (off Royds La.)
    LS29: Men 1C 6
North Vw. Ct. LS28: Stan 3G 27
    (off North Vw. St.)
North Vw. Rd. BD4: B'frd 2C 46
North Vw. St. LS28: Stan 3G 27
North Vw. Ter. LS28: Stan 3G 27
North Way LS8: Leeds 5F 23
Northwest Bus. Pk. LS6: Leeds 2F 31
Nth. West Rd. LS6: Leeds 2F 31
Northwood Cl. LS26: Wood 2C 54
    LS28: Pud 2H 37

Northwood Falls LS26: Wood 2C 54
Northwood Gdns. LS15: Leeds 6E 35
Northwood Grn. LS28: Pud 2H 37
    (off Roker La.)
Northwood Mt. LS28: Pud 2H 37
Northwood Pk. LS26: Wood 2C 54
Northwood Vw. LS28: Pud 2H 37
Norton Rd. LS8: Leeds 1C 22
Norton Way LS27: Morl 3G 49
Norville Ter. LS6: Leeds 1C 30
    (off Headingley La.)
Norwich Av. LS10: Leeds 5H 41
Norwood Av. BD11: Birk 5D 46
    LS29: Men 2C 6
Norwood Cl. LS29: Men 2C 6
    LS29: Men 3C 6
Norwood Cres. BD11: Birk 5D 46
    LS28: Stan 3H 27
Norwood Cft. LS28: Stan 3H 27
Norwood Dr. BD11: Birk 5D 46
Norwood Gro. BD11: Birk 5D 46
    LS6: Leeds 2C 30
Norwood Mt. LS6: Leeds 2C 30
Norwood Pl. LS6: Leeds 2C 30
Norwood Rd. LS6: Leeds 2C 30
Norwood Ter. LS6: Leeds 2C 30
Norwood Vw. LS6: Leeds 2C 30
Noster Gro. LS11: Leeds 4D 40
Noster Hill LS11: Leeds 4D 40
Noster Pl. LS11: Leeds 4D 40
Noster Rd. LS11: Leeds 4D 40
Noster St. LS11: Leeds 4D 40
Noster Ter. LS11: Leeds 4D 40
Noster Vw. LS11: Leeds 4D 40
Nottingham Cl. WF3: Rob H 6C 52
Nottingham St. BD3: B'frd 6A 26
Nova La. WF17: Birs 6F 47
Nowell App. LS9: Leeds 4D 32
Nowell Av. LS9: Leeds 4D 32
Nowell Cl. LS9: Leeds 4D 32
Nowell Ct. LS9: Leeds 4D 32
Nowell Cres. LS9: Leeds 4D 32
Nowell End Row LS9: Leeds 4D 32
Nowell Gdns. LS9: Leeds 4D 32
Nowell Gro. LS9: Leeds 4D 32
Nowell La. LS9: Leeds 4D 32
Nowell Mt. LS9: Leeds 4D 32
Nowell Pde. LS9: Leeds 4D 32
Nowell Pl. LS9: Leeds 4D 32
Nowell St. LS9: Leeds 4D 32
Nowell Ter. LS9: Leeds 4D 32
Nowell Vw. LS9: Leeds 4D 32
Nowell Wlk. LS9: Leeds 4D 32
Nuffield Health Fitness & Wellbeing Cen.
    Guiseley 4E 7
Nunnington Av. LS12: Leeds 5A 30
Nunnington St. LS12: Leeds 5A 30
Nunnington Ter. LS12: Leeds 5A 30
Nunnington Vw. LS12: Leeds 4A 30
Nunroyd Av. LS17: Leeds 2H 21
    LS20: Guis 5H 7
Nunroyd Gro. LS17: Leeds 2H 21
Nunroyd Lawn LS17: Leeds 2H 21
Nunroyd Rd. LS17: Leeds 2H 21
Nunroyd St. LS17: Leeds 2H 21
Nunroyd Ter. LS17: Leeds 2H 21
Nunthorpe Rd. LS13: Leeds 6H 17
Nursery Cl. LS17: Leeds 5G 13
Nursery Gro. LS17: Leeds 5E 13
Nursery La. LS17: Leeds 5E 13
Nursery Mt. LS10: Leeds 6A 42
Nursery Mt. Rd. LS10: Leeds 5A 42
Nursery Rd. LS20: Guis 2F 7
Nussey Av. WF17: Birs 6G 47
Nutter La. WF17: Birs 6F 47
Nutting Gro. Ter. LS12: Leeds 2E 39

O

Oak Av. LS27: Morl 6H 49
    WF3: S'ley 6H 59
Oak Cres. LS15: Leeds 6H 33
Oakdale Cl. BD10: B'frd 2A 26
    WF3: Loft 5D 58
Oakdale Dr. BD10: B'frd 2A 26
Oakdale Gth. LS14: Leeds 2B 24
Oakdale Mdw. LS14: Leeds 2B 24
Oakdene LS26: Wood 2D 54
Oakdene Cl. LS28: Pud 2H 37
Oakdene Ct. LS17: Leeds 5C 14
Oakdene Dr. LS17: Leeds 5C 14
Oakdene Gdns. LS17: Leeds 5C 14
Oakdene Va. LS17: Leeds 5C 14
Oakdene Way LS17: Leeds 5C 14
Oak Dr. LS10: Leeds 5H 51
    LS16: Leeds 1H 19

Oakfield LS6: Leeds 1C 30
Oakfield Av. LS26: Rothw 3G 53
Oakfield Ter. LS18: H'fth 3E 19
         (off Woodville St.)
Oakford Ter. LS18: H'fth 2E 19
Oak Gro. LS27: Morl 6H 49
Oakham Gth. LS9: Leeds 6E 33
Oakham M. LS9: Leeds 6D 32
Oakhampton Ct. LS8: Leeds 3E 23
Oakham Way LS9: Leeds 6D 32
Oak Ho. LS5: Leeds 1F 29
  LS7: Leeds 4H 21
        (off Allerton Pk.)
  LS15: Leeds 1G 43
Oakhurst LS6: Leeds 1C 30
Oakhurst Av. LS11: Leeds 6E 41
Oakhurst Gro. LS11: Leeds 6D 40
Oakhurst Mt. LS11: Leeds 6D 40
Oakhurst Rd. LS11: Leeds 6D 40
Oakhurst St. LS11: Leeds 6E 41
Oaklands WF3: Rob H 6C 52
Oaklands Av. LS13: Leeds 6G 17
  LS16: Leeds 6B 12
Oaklands Cl. LS8: Leeds 1E 33
  LS16: Leeds 6B 12
Oaklands Ct. LS8: Leeds 2E 33
Oaklands Cres. LS8: Leeds 2E 33
Oaklands Dr. LS8: Leeds 2E 33
  LS16: Leeds 1B 20
Oaklands Fold LS8: Leeds 1E 33
  LS16: Leeds 6B 12
Oaklands Gro. LS8: Leeds 2E 33
  LS13: Leeds 6G 17
  LS16: Leeds 6B 12
Oaklands Pl. LS8: Leeds 2E 33
Oaklands Rd. LS13: Leeds 6G 17
Oaklands St. LS8: Leeds 2E 33
Oaklea Gdns. LS16: Leeds 1B 20
Oaklea Hall Cl. LS16: Leeds 1B 20
Oaklea Rd. LS15: Scho 5F 25
Oakley Gro. LS11: Leeds 4G 41
Oakley St. WF3: Thpe H 2A 58
Oakley Ter. LS11: Leeds 5G 41
Oakley Vw. LS11: Leeds 5G 41
Oakridge Av. LS29: Men 1D 6
Oak Rd. LS7: Leeds 6H 21
  LS12: Leeds 6C 30
  LS15: Leeds 5H 33
  LS27: Morl 6F 49
Oakroyd LS26: Rothw 5H 53
Oakroyd Cl. BD11: Birk 4C 46
Oakroyd Dr. BD11: Birk 5C 46
Oakroyd Fold LS27: Chur 1A 50
Oakroyd Mt. LS28: Stan 5G 27
Oakroyd Ter. LS27: Chur 1A 50
  LS28: Stan 5G 27
Oaks, The LS10: Leeds 5A 52
  LS20: Guis 3G 7
  LS27: Chur 2H 49
Oak St. LS27: Chur 2H 49
  LS28: Pud 5E 27
Oak Ter. LS15: Leeds 2D 34
        (off Church La.)
Oak Tree Bus. Pk. LS14: Leeds 4A 24
Oak Tree Cl. LS9: Leeds 2E 33
Oak Tree Ct. LS9: Leeds 2E 33
        (off Oak Tree Pl.)
Oak Tree Cres. LS9: Leeds 2E 33
Oak Tree Dr. LS8: Leeds 2E 33
Oak Tree Gro. LS9: Leeds 2E 33
Oak Tree La. LS14: Leeds 3G 33
Oak Tree Mt. LS9: Leeds 2E 33
Oak Tree Pl. LS9: Leeds 2E 33
Oak Tree Wlk. LS9: Leeds 2E 33
Oakway BD11: Birk 5D 46
OAKWELL 6F 47
Oakwell Av. LS8: Leeds 5C 22
  LS12: Leeds 6B 30
Oakwell Cl. BD11: Drig 4A 48
Oakwell Ct. LS13: Leeds 2B 28
  LS28: Fars 2F 27
        (off Water La.)
  WF17: Birs 6A 48
        (not continuous)
Oakwell Cres. LS8: Leeds 5C 22
Oakwell Dr. LS8: Leeds 5C 22
Oakwell Gdns. LS8: Leeds 5C 22
Oakwell Gro. LS13: Leeds 2C 28
Oakwell Hall 6F 47
Oakwell Hall Country Pk. 6E 47
Oakwell Ind. Est. WF17: Birs 6A 48
Oakwell Ind. Pk. WF17: Birs 6A 48
Oakwell Mt. LS8: Leeds 5C 22
Oakwell Oval LS8: Leeds 5C 22
Oakwell Rd. BD11: Drig 4A 48
Oakwell Ter. LS28: Fars 2F 27
Oakwell Way WF17: Birs 6A 48

OAKWOOD 5E 23
Oakwood Av. BD11: Birk 5C 46
  LS8: Leeds 5D 22
Oakwood Boundary Rd.
  LS8: Leeds 5D 22
Oakwood Ct. LS8: Leeds 5E 23
Oakwood Dr. LS8: Leeds 5D 22
  LS26: Rothw 2F 53
Oakwood Fitness Cen. 6E 23
Oakwood Gdns. LS8: Leeds 5D 22
  LS28: Pud 1G 37
Oakwood Gth. LS8: Leeds 5E 23
Oakwood Grange LS8: Leeds 5E 23
Oakwood Grange La. LS8: Leeds 5E 23
Oakwood Grn. LS8: Leeds 5E 23
Oakwood Ho. LS13: Leeds 5F 17
        (off Rodley La.)
Oakwood La. LS8: Leeds 5D 22
  LS9: Leeds 2F 33
Oakwood Mt. LS8: Leeds 5D 22
Oakwood Nook LS8: Leeds 5D 22
Oakwood Pk. LS8: Leeds 6E 23
Oakwood Pl. LS8: Leeds 5D 22
Oakwood Ri. LS8: Leeds 5E 23
Oakwood Ter. LS28: Pud 1G 37
Oakwood Vw. LS8: Leeds 5E 23
Oakwood Wlk. LS8: Leeds 5E 23
Oasby Cft. BD4: B'frd 6A 36
Oast Ho. Cft. WF3: Rob H 6D 52
Oastler Rd. LS28: Cal 5D 16
Oatland Cl. LS7: Leeds 3G 31
Oatland Ct. LS7: Leeds 1F 5 (3G 31)
        (not continuous)
Oatland Dr. LS7: Leeds 3G 31
Oatland Gdns. LS7: Leeds 3G 31
Oatland Grn. LS7: Leeds 3G 31
Oatland Hgts. LS7: Leeds 1G 5
Oatland La. LS7: Leeds 3G 31
Oatland Pl. LS7: Leeds 2G 31
Oatland Rd. LS7: Leeds 3G 31
Oatland Towers LS7: Leeds 1F 5 (3G 31)
Oban Cl. WF3: Ting 2B 56
Oban Pl. LS12: Leeds 5G 29
Oban St. LS12: Leeds 5H 29
Oban Ter. LS12: Leeds 5H 29
  WF3: Ting 2B 56
Occupation La. LS28: Pud 1E 37
Odda La. LS20: Hawk 4A 6
Oddfellow St. LS27: Morl 5G 49
Oddy Pl. LS6: Leeds 5B 20
Oddy's Fold LS6: Leeds 3C 20
Oddy St. BD4: B'frd 6A 36
Odeon Cinema
  Bradford .5B 26
Ogden Ho. BD4: B'frd 3B 36
Ogilby Ct. LS26: Wood 2B 54
Ogilby M. LS26: Wood 2B 54
O'Grady Sq. LS9: Leeds 6B 32
Old Barn Cl. LS17: Leeds 4E 13
Old Brandon La. LS17: Shad 5G 15
Old Cl. LS11: Leeds 1B 50
Old Farm App. LS16: Leeds 3F 19
Old Farm Cl. LS16: Leeds 3G 19
Old Farm Cross LS16: Leeds 3G 19
Old Farm Dr. LS16: Leeds 3F 19
Old Farm Gth. LS16: Leeds 3G 19
Old Farm Pde. LS16: Leeds 3G 19
Old Farm Wlk. LS16: Leeds 3F 19
Oldfield Av. LS12: Leeds 1A 40
Oldfield Ct. LS7: Leeds 5A 22
Oldfield La. LS12: Leeds 1A 40
Oldfield St. LS12: Leeds 1A 40
Old Fold LS28: Fars 2F 27
Old Hall Rd. WF3: Ting 3D 56
Old Haworth La. LS19: Yead 2D 8
Old Heybeck La. WF3: W Ard 6B 56
Old Hollings Hill BD17: Esh 6E 7
  LS20: Guis 6E 7
Old La. BD11: Birk 3C 46
  BD11: Drig 2H 47
  LS11: Leeds 5D 40
  LS20: Hawk 5A 6
Old Marsh LS28: Pud 6E 27
Old Mill Bus. Pk. LS10: Leeds 3B 42
Old Mill La. LS10: Leeds 3A 42
Old Oak Cl. LS16: Leeds 4G 19
Old Oak Dr. LS16: Leeds 4G 19
Old Oak Gth. LS16: Leeds 4F 19
Old Oak Lawn LS16: Leeds 4G 19
Old Orchard, The LS13: Leeds 1B 28
  LS29: Men 1D 6
        (off Station Rd.)
Old Park Rd. LS8: Leeds 3C 22
        (not continuous)
Old Rd. LS27: Chur 1A 50
  LS28: Fars, Stan 4E 27

Oldroyd Cres. LS11: Leeds 5C 40
Old Run Rd. LS10: Leeds 5H 41
Old Run Vw. LS10: Leeds 1H 51
Old School Lofts LS12: Leeds 6G 29
Old School M. LS27: Chur 1A 50
Old Smithy Ct. LS28: Cal 5D 16
        (off Blackett St.)
Old Whack Ho. La. LS19: Yead 3B 8
Olive Lodge LS18: H'fth 2C 18
        (off Broadgate La.)
Oliver Ct. BD11: Drig 4F 47
Oliver Hill LS18: H'fth 4C 18
Olrika Ct. LS7: Leeds 1H 31
Ontario Pl. LS7: Leeds 5H 21
Opal One LS3: Leeds 5D 30
Opal Three LS2: Leeds 2F 5
Open University
  Leeds 5E 5
Orange Tree Gro. WF3: E Ard 4G 57
Orchard Av. WF3: S'ley 6H 59
Orchard Cl. WF3: E Ard 5H 57
Orchard Ct. LS16: Leeds 4B 20
        (off St Chads Rd.)
  LS20: Guis 4G 7
        (off Orchard La.)
Orchard Cft. LS15: Leeds 3B 34
Orchard Dr. LS28: Pud 5D 26
Orchard Gro. BD10: B'frd 5A 16
  LS29: Men 1D 6
Orchard La. LS20: Guis 4G 7
Orchard M. LS13: Leeds 6G 17
Orchard Mt. LS15: Leeds 3C 34
Orchard Rd. LS15: Leeds 3B 34
Orchards, The LS15: Leeds 3B 34
  WF3: W Ard 6B 56
Orchard Sq. LS15: Leeds 3B 34
Orchard Way LS20: Guis 4G 7
  LS26: Rothw 3G 53
Orchid Ct. WF3: Loft 1D 58
Oriental St. LS12: Leeds 6A 30
Orion Cres. LS10: Leeds 2A 52
Orion Dr. LS10: Leeds 2A 52
Orion Gdns. LS10: Leeds 2B 52
Orion Vw. LS10: Leeds 2B 52
Orion Wlk. LS10: Leeds 1B 52
Ormonde Pl. LS7: Leeds 2G 31
Orrell Gro. LS10: Leeds 5A 52
Orville Gdns. LS6: Leeds 1C 30
Osbourne Ct. LS13: Leeds 4D 28
OSMONDTHORPE 5E 33
Osmondthorpe Cotts. LS9: Leeds 6E 33
Osmondthorpe La. LS9: Leeds 5E 33
Osmondthorpe Ter. LS9: Leeds 5D 32
Osprey Cl. LS17: Leeds 5B 14
Osprey Gro. LS17: Leeds 5B 14
Osprey Mdw. LS27: Morl 5B 50
Osterley Cres. BD10: B'frd 6A 16
Osterley Gro. BD10: B'frd 6A 16
Oswald Cl. LS20: Guis 4F 7
Oswaldthorpe Av. BD3: B'frd 4A 26
Otley La. LS19: Yead 2D 8
Otley Old Rd. LS16: Leeds 4E 11
  LS18: H'fth, Yead 1B 10
Otley Rd. LS6: Leeds 4A 20
  LS16: Leeds 1H 11
  LS20: Guis 4E 7
Ottawa Pl. LS7: Leeds 5H 21
Otterburn Gdns. LS16: Leeds 6H 11
OULTON 4C 54
Oulton Dr. LS26: Oul 6C 54
Oulton La. LS26: Oul 2C 54
  LS26: Rothw 4H 53
Out Gang LS13: Leeds 2D 28
Out Gang La. LS13: Leeds 2E 29
OUTWOOD 6D 58
Outwood Av. LS18: H'fth 4D 18
Outwood Chase LS18: H'fth 3D 18
Outwood La. LS18: H'fth 4C 18
Outwood Station (Rail) 6C 58
Outwood Wlk. LS18: H'fth 4C 18
OUZLEWELL GREEN 2F 59
Ouzlewell Grn. WF3: Loft 1F 59
OVAL, THE 3H 33
Oval, The LS10: Leeds 3H 41
  LS14: Leeds 3H 33
  LS20: Guis 5E 7
  LS26: Rothw 4H 53
  LS28: Fars 3G 27
Overdale Av. LS17: Leeds 4C 14
Overdale Ter. LS15: Leeds 5A 34
Overland Cres. BD10: B'frd 3A 16
Overland Trad. Est. LS27: Gil 4C 48
Over La. LS19: Raw 6E 9
Ovington Dr. BD4: B'frd 6A 36
Owlcotes Dr. LS28: Pud 5E 27
Owlcotes Gdns. LS28: Pud 5E 27
Owlcotes Gth. LS28: Pud 5D 26

Owlcotes La. LS28: Pud 5E 27
  LS28: Stan 4E 27
               (not continuous)
Owlcotes Rd. LS28: Pud 5D 26
Owlcotes Shop. Cen. LS28: Stan 4F 27
Owlcotes Ter. LS28: Pud 5E 27
Owler La. WF17: Birs 6G 47
Owlett Mead WF3: Thpe H 2A 58
Owlett Mead Cl. WF3: Thpe H 2A 58
Owl Ridge LS27: Morl 6A 50
Oxenford Ct. LS16: Leeds 6G 11
Oxford Av. LS20: Guis 3F 7
Oxford Pl. LS1: Leeds 3C 4 (5F 31)
  LS28: Stan 4G 27
Oxford Rd. BD19: Gom 6D 46
  LS7: Leeds 2G 31
  LS20: Guis 4F 7
Oxford Row LS1: Leeds 3C 4 (5F 31)
               (not continuous)
Oxford St. LS20: Guis 4G 7
  WF3: E Ard 3A 58
Oxford Vs. LS20: Guis 4G 7
Oxley St. LS9: Leeds 6B 32
Oxton Mt. LS9: Leeds 5B 32
Oxton Way LS9: Leeds 5B 32
Oyster Cl. LS27: Morl 6A 50

P

Pack Horse Yd. LS1: Leeds 4E 5
Paddock, The BD4: B'frd 6A 36
               (off Tennis Av.)
  LS6: Leeds 4D 20
  LS26: Rothw 4G 53
Paddock Cl. BD11: Drig 4G 47
Paddock Dr. BD11: Drig 4G 47
Padstow Av. LS10: Leeds 4E 51
Padstow Pl. LS10: Leeds 5E 51
Padstow Row LS10: Leeds 5E 51
Paignton Ct. LS13: Leeds 4D 28
Paisley Gro. LS12: Leeds 5G 29
Paisley Pl. LS12: Leeds 5G 29
Paisley Rd. LS12: Leeds 5G 29
Paisley St. LS12: Leeds 5G 29
Paisley Ter. LS12: Leeds 5G 29
Paisley Vw. LS12: Leeds 5G 29
Palmerston Ho. BD4: B'frd 3A 36
               (off Tyersal La.)
Parade, The BD4: B'frd 4A 36
  LS6: Leeds 6B 20
               (off North La.)
  LS9: Leeds 6A 32
  LS19: Yead 3B 8
               (off Westfield Dr.)
Paradise Gro. LS18: H'fth 3E 19
               (off Low La.)
Paradise Pl. LS18: H'fth 3E 19
Parc Mont LS8: Leeds 3E 23
Park & Ride
  King Lane 6F 13
Park App. LS15: Leeds 5F 35
Park Av. BD11: Drig 3G 47
  LS8: Leeds 3E 23
  LS12: Leeds 5H 29
  LS15: Leeds 3D 34
  LS19: Raw 5E 9
  LS19: Yead 2C 8
  LS26: Swil 6G 45
  LS27: Morl 6F 49
  LS28: Pud 6G 27
  WF3: Loft 5E 59
Park Cir. LS10: Leeds 4F 51
Park Cl. BD11: Drig 3G 47
  LS13: Leeds 2C 28
Park Copse LS18: H'fth 2A 18
Park Cotts. LS8: Leeds 2D 22
Park Cres. LS8: Leeds 1C 22
  LS12: Leeds 5H 29
  LS20: Guis 6E 7
  LS26: Rothw 3A 54
  LS27: Gil 3D 48
Parkcroft LS28: Fars 3F 27
Park Cross St. LS1: Leeds 4C 4 (5F 31)
Park Dale LS29: Men 1C 6
Park Dr. LS12: N Far 4G 39
  LS18: H'fth 3H 17
  WF3: Loft 4E 59
Park Edge Cl. LS8: Leeds 4E 23
Parker St. WF3: E Ard 4G 57
Park Farm Ind. Est. LS11: Leeds 1F 51
Park Fld. LS29: Men .1C 6
Parkfield Av. LS11: Leeds 4E 41
Parkfield Cl. LS28: Pud 6F 27
Parkfield Ct. LS14: Leeds 2G 33
  LS27: Morl 6F 49

Parkfield Gro. LS11: Leeds 4E 41
Parkfield Mt. LS11: Leeds 4E 41
  LS28: Pud 6G 27
Parkfield Pl. LS11: Leeds 4E 41
Parkfield Rd. LS11: Leeds 4E 41
Parkfield Row LS11: Leeds 4E 41
Parkfield St. LS11: Leeds 2G 41
Parkfield Ter. LS28: Pud 6G 27
  LS28: Stan 4G 27
               (not continuous)
Parkfield Vw. LS11: Leeds 4E 41
Parkfield Way LS14: Leeds 2G 33
Park Ga. Cl. LS18: H'fth 3B 18
Park Ga. Cres. LS20: Guis 5F 7
Park Gro. LS6: Leeds 5B 20
  LS10: Leeds 5G 51
  LS18: H'fth 3H 17
  LS19: Yead 2C 8
  LS26: Swil 1G 55
  LS27: Gil 3D 48
Park Halt Station
  Middleton Railway 1H 51
Park Holme LS7: Leeds 1A 32
Parkhome Est. LS26: Swil 6H 45
Parkin La. BD10: B'frd 3B 16
Parkinson Way LS20: Guis 3F 7
Parkland Av. LS27: Morl 6E 49
Parkland Cres. LS6: Leeds 2E 21
Parkland Dr. LS6: Leeds 2E 21
Parkland Gdns. LS6: Leeds 3E 21
PARKLANDS 1A 34
Parkland Ter. LS6: Leeds 3E 21
Parkland Vw. LS19: Yead 3D 8
               (not continuous)
Park La. LS1: Leeds 3B 4 (5E 31)
  LS3: Leeds 3A 4 (5D 30)
  LS8: Leeds 1D 22
  LS20: Guis 6E 7
  LS26: Rothw 4H 53
Park La. Central LS6: Leeds 6B 20
               (off Bennett Rd.)
Park La. Ct. LS17: Shad 4E 15
Park La. M. LS17: Shad 5D 14
Park Lea LS10: Leeds 4G 51
Park Mt. LS5: Leeds 1G 29
  LS12: Leeds 5G 29
Park Pde. LS9: Leeds 1C 42
  LS27: Morl 6F 49
Park Pl. LS1: Leeds 4C 4 (5F 31)
  LS8: Leeds 6F 23
Park Ri. LS13: Leeds 1C 28
Park Rd. BD10: B'frd 6A 16
  LS12: Leeds 5G 29
  LS13: Leeds 2C 28
  LS15: Leeds 1D 44
  LS19: Raw 5D 8
  LS19: Yead 2C 8
  LS20: Guis 6E 7
  LS29: Men 1C 6
Park Row LS1: Leeds 4D 4 (5F 31)
  LS28: Stan 4G 27
Park Row Apartments
  LS1: Leeds 4D 4
Parkside LS18: H'fth 3A 18
Parkside Av. LS6: Leeds 4D 20
Parkside Cl. LS4: Leeds 2H 29
  LS6: Leeds 3D 20
Parkside Ct. LS14: Leeds 1A 34
Parkside Cres. LS6: Leeds 3D 20
  LS14: Leeds 1A 34
Parkside Dr. LS14: Leeds 1A 34
Parkside Gdns. LS6: Leeds 4D 20
Parkside Grn. LS6: Leeds 4D 20
Parkside Gro. LS11: Leeds 6E 41
Parkside Hgts. LS4: Leeds 2H 29
Parkside Ind. Est. LS11: Leeds 6G 41
Parkside La. LS11: Leeds 5G 41
Parkside Lawns LS6: Leeds 4D 20
Parkside Mt. LS11: Leeds 6E 41
Parkside Pde. LS11: Leeds 6E 41
Parkside Pl. LS6: Leeds 3D 20
  LS16: Leeds 2B 20
  LS28: Fars 3F 27
Parkside Row LS11: Leeds 6E 41
Parkside Vw. LS6: Leeds 3D 20
  LS14: Leeds 1A 34
Parkside Wlk. LS28: Fars 3G 27
PARK SPRING 6D 28
Park Spring Gdns. LS13: Leeds 4B 28
Park Spring Ri. LS13: Leeds 5B 28
Park Sq. LS19: Raw 5E 9
               (off Batter La.)
  LS28: Pud 6G 27
  WF3: Loft 5E 59
Park Sq. E. LS1: Leeds 4C 4 (5F 31)
Park Sq. Nth. LS1: Leeds 4C 4 (5F 31)

Park Sq. Sth. LS1: Leeds 4C 4 (5F 31)
Park Sq. W. LS1: Leeds 4C 4 (5F 31)
Parkstone Av. LS16: Leeds 2G 19
Parkstone Grn. LS16: Leeds 2G 19
Parkstone Gro. LS16: Leeds 2G 19
Parkstone Mt. LS16: Leeds 2G 19
Parkstone Pl. LS16: Leeds 2G 19
Park St. LS1: Leeds 3C 4 (5F 31)
  LS12: Leeds 5G 29
  LS15: Leeds 5B 34
  LS19: Yead 2C 8
  LS27: Chur 1A 50
Park Ter. LS6: Leeds 5B 20
Park Top LS28: Stan 4G 27
Park Vw. BD11: Birk 4C 46
  LS11: Leeds 4E 41
  LS13: Leeds 2C 28
               (not continuous)
  LS16: Leeds 5A 12
  LS19: Yead 6H 7
               (off South Vw.)
  LS26: Swil 6G 45
  LS28: Pud 6G 27
  WF3: Loft 5E 59
Park Vw. Av. LS4: Leeds 2B 30
  LS19: Raw 5E 9
Parkview Ct. LS8: Leeds 1D 22
Park Vw. Cres. LS8: Leeds 2D 22
Park Vw. Gro. LS4: Leeds 3B 30
Park Vw. Rd. LS4: Leeds 3B 30
Park Vw. Ter. LS15: Leeds 5A 34
               (off Primrose La.)
  LS19: Raw 5D 8
Park Villa Ct. LS8: Leeds 2C 22
PARK VILLAS 1C 22
Park Vs. LS8: Leeds 2C 22
Parkville Pl. LS13: Leeds 1C 28
Parkville Rd. LS13: Leeds 2C 28
Park Way LS29: Men 1C 6
Parkway LS27: Gil .3C 48
Parkway Cl. LS14: Leeds 1G 33
Parkway Ct. LS14: Leeds 2G 33
Parkway Grange LS14: Leeds 2G 33
Parkways LS26: Oul 3B 54
Parkways Av. LS26: Oul 4B 54
Parkways Cl. LS26: Oul 3B 54
Parkways Dr. LS26: Oul 3B 54
Parkways Gth. LS26: Oul 4B 54
Parkways Gro. LS26: Oul 3B 54
Parkway Towers LS14: Leeds 1G 33
Parkway Va. LS14: Leeds 1B 34
               (Harewood Ct.)
  LS14: Leeds 2G 33
               (South Parkway)
Park W. LS26: Rothw 4G 53
Park Wood Av. LS11: Leeds 2D 50
Park Wood Cl. LS11: Leeds 2D 50
Parkwood Av. LS8: Leeds 4C 22
Park Wood Cl. LS11: Leeds 2D 50
Park Wood Cres. LS11: Leeds 2D 50
Park Wood Dr. LS11: Leeds 1D 50
Parkwood Gdns. LS8: Leeds 4C 22
  LS28: Cal 5C 16
Parkwood M. LS8: Leeds 4C 22
Parkwood Rd. LS11: Leeds 2D 50
  LS28: Cal 5D 16
Parkwood Vw. LS8: Leeds 4C 22
Parkwood Way LS8: Leeds 4C 22
Parliament Pl. LS12: Leeds 5B 30
Parliament Rd. LS12: Leeds 6B 30
Parnaby Av. LS10: Leeds 6B 42
Parnaby Rd. LS10: Leeds 6B 42
Parnaby St. LS10: Leeds 6B 42
Parnaby Ter. LS10: Leeds 6B 42
Parrott St. BD4: B'frd 6A 36
Parsley M. LS26: Meth 6H 55
Parsonage Rd. BD4: B'frd 2A 36
Partons Pl. WF3: Loft 5E 59
Partridge Cl. LS27: Morl 5B 50
Pasture Av. LS7: Leeds 4H 21
Pasture Cres. LS7: Leeds 4H 21
Pasture Gro. LS7: Leeds 4H 21
Pasture La. LS7: Leeds 4H 21
Pasture Mt. LS12: Leeds 5H 29
Pasture Pde. LS7: Leeds 4H 21
Pasture Pl. LS7: Leeds 4H 21
Pasture Rd. LS8: Leeds 1A 32
Pasture St. LS7: Leeds 4H 21
Pasture Ter. LS7: Leeds 4H 21
Pasture Vw. LS12: Leeds 5H 29
Pasture Vw. Rd. LS26: Rothw 4G 53
Patrick Grn. LS26: Oul 3H 59
Pavilion Bus. Pk. LS12: Leeds 4A 40
Pavilion Cl. LS28: Stan 3G 27
Pavilion Gdns. LS26: Wood 3C 54
  LS28: Fars 3G 27

Pavilion Ho. LS14: Leeds 1B **34**
    (off York Rd.)
Pavilion M. LS6: Leeds 2B **30**
Pavilion Way LS28: Pud 6F **27**
Pawson St. LS27: Morl 6F **49**
  WF3: E Ard .3A **58**
  WF3: Loft 1D **58**
Paxton Ct. LS12: Leeds 3F **29**
Peacock Ct. LS19: Yead 3F **9**
Peacock Grn. LS27: Morl 6A **50**
Pearson Av. LS6: Leeds 2C **30**
Pearson Gro. LS6: Leeds 2C **30**
Pearsons Cl. LS14: Leeds 1A **34**
Pearsons Ct. LS14: Leeds 1A **34**
Pearsons Dr. LS14: Leeds 1A **34**
Pearsons Fold LS14: Leeds 1A **34**
Pearson St. LS10: Leeds 2H **41**
  LS28: Cal 4D **16**
Pearsons Vw. LS14: Leeds 1A **34**
Pearsons Way LS14: Leeds 1A **34**
Pearson Ter. LS6: Leeds 2C **30**
Pearl Pl. LS10: Leeds 5H **51**
Peasehill Cl. LS19: Raw 5E **9**
Peasehill Pk. LS19: Raw 5E **9**
Peckover Dr. LS28: Pud 4B **26**
Peel Cl. BD4: B'frd 1A **36**
Peel Mills Bus. Cen. LS27: Morl 5H **49**
Peel Sq. LS5: Leeds 1G **29**
Peel St. LS27: Morl 5H **49**
Peel Vs. LS27: Morl 5H **49**
Pelham Ct. LS10: Leeds 6H **51**
  LS17: Leeds 6D **14**
Pelham Pl. LS7: Leeds 4G **21**
Pelican Works LS26: Rothw 2D **52**
Pembroke Cl. LS27: Morl 4F **49**
Pembroke Dr. LS27: Morl 4F **49**
  LS28: Pud .5G **27**
Pembroke Grange LS9: Leeds 3F **33**
Pembroke Rd. LS28: Pud 5G **27**
Pembroke Towers LS9: Leeds 2F **33**
Pembury Mt. LS15: Leeds 2F **35**
Penarth Rd. LS15: Leeds 3B **34**
Pendas Dr. LS15: Leeds 3D **34**
PENDAS FIELDS 2F **35**
Pendas Gro. LS15: Leeds 2D **34**
Pendas Wlk. LS15: Leeds 3D **34**
Pendas Way LS15: Leeds 3D **34**
Pendil Cl. LS15: Leeds 5C **34**
Pendragon Ter. LS20: Guis 4F **7**
Penfield Rd. BD11: Drig 3H **47**
Penlands Cres. LS15: Leeds 6D **34**
Penlands Lawn LS15: Leeds 6D **34**
Penlands Wlk. LS15: Leeds 6D **34**
Pennine Ind. Est. LS12: Leeds 6H **29**
Pennine Vw. WF17: Birs 6A **48**
Pennington Ct. LS6: Leeds 2E **31**
Pennington Gro. LS6: Leeds 1E **31**
Pennington Pl. LS6: Leeds 2E **31**
Pennington St. LS6: Leeds 2E **31**
Pennington Ter. LS6: Leeds 1E **31**
Pennwell Dean LS14: Leeds 6D **24**
Pennwell Fld. LS14: Leeds 6E **25**
Pennwell Gth. LS14: Leeds 6D **24**
Pennwell Ga. LS14: Leeds 6D **24**
Pennwell Grn. LS14: Leeds 6D **24**
Pennwell Lawn LS14: Leeds 6D **24**
Pennyfield Cl. LS6: Leeds 2D **20**
Penny Hill Cen., The LS10: Leeds 3A **42**
Penny La. LS10: Leeds 3H **41**
Pennythorne Ct. LS19: Yead 4C **8**
Pennythorne Dr. LS19: Yead 4C **8**
Penraevon 1 Light Ind. Est. LS7: Leeds 2G **31**
Penraevon Av. LS7: Leeds 2G **31**
Penraevon Ind. Est. LS7: Leeds 2G **31**
  (off Jackson Rd.)
Penrith Gro. LS12: Leeds 1A **40**
Pentland Gro. LS27: Morl 6G **49**
Pepper Gdns. LS13: Leeds 1E **29**
Pepper Hills LS17: Leeds 5H **13**
Pepper La. LS10: Leeds 4B **42**
  LS13: Leeds 1D **28**
Pepper Rd. LS10: Leeds 5H **42**
Percival St. LS2: Leeds 2D **4** (4F **31**)
Percy St. LS12: Leeds 1A **40**
Peregrine Av. LS27: Morl 5B **50**
Perseverance Mill LS6: Leeds 2F **31**
  (off Cross Chancellor St.)
Perseverance St. LS28: Pud 6E **27**
Perseverance Ter. LS26: Rothw 5G **53**
Perth Dr. WF3: Ting 3D **56**
Perth Mt. LS18: H'fth 5B **10**
Peter La. LS27: Morl 4B **50**
Peter Laylock Ind. Est. LS7: Leeds 2G **31**
Petersfield Av. LS10: Leeds 2A **52**
Petrel Way LS27: Morl 6A **50**
Petrie Cres. LS13: Leeds 6F **17**
Petrie Gro. BD3: B'frd 6A **26**
Petrie Rd. BD3: B'frd 6A **26**

Petrie St. LS13: Leeds 6F **17**
Peverell Cl. BD4: B'frd 4A **36**
Pheasant Dr. WF3: Birs 6A **48**
Philip Gth. WF1: Out 6D **58**
Philippa Way LS12: Leeds 4A **40**
Philip's Gro. WF3: Loft 5E **59**
Phillips Cl. LS18: H'fth 2C **18**
  (off Broadgate La.)
Phil May Ct. LS12: Leeds 1C **40**
  (off Holdforth Grn.)
Phoenix Cl. LS14: Leeds 2A **34**
Phoenix Way BD4: B'frd 1A **36**
Pickard Bank LS6: Leeds 6D **20**
Pickard Ct. LS15: Leeds 5C **34**
Pickering Mt. LS12: Leeds 5B **30**
Pickering St. LS12: Leeds 5B **30**
Pickpocket La. LS26: Rothw, Wood 2A **54**
Pickup Bus. Pk. LS28: Stan 3H **27**
Piece Wood Rd. LS16: Leeds 6D **10**
Pigeon Cote Cl. LS14: Leeds 5A **24**
Pigeon Cote Rd. LS14: Leeds 5A **24**
Pilden La. WF3: E Ard 5G **57**
Pilgrim Way LS28: Stan 3A **28**
Pilot St. LS9: Leeds 1H **5** (4A **32**)
Pinder Av. LS12: Leeds 3F **39**
Pinder Gro. LS12: Leeds 3F **39**
Pinder St. LS12: Leeds 3F **39**
Pinder Vw. LS12: Leeds 3F **39**
Pine Ct. LS2: Leeds 5G **5** (6H **31**)
Pines, The LS10: Leeds 5A **52**
Pinfold Ct. LS15: Leeds 5B **34**
Pinfold Gro. LS15: Leeds 5A **34**
Pinfold Hill LS15: Leeds 5B **34**
Pinfold La. LS12: Leeds 6H **29**
  LS15: Leeds 5A **34**
  LS16: Leeds 3E **11**
Pinfold Mt. LS15: Leeds 6B **34**
Pinfold Rd. LS15: Leeds 6B **34**
Pinfold Sq. LS15: Leeds 5A **34**
Pipe & Nook La. LS12: Leeds 6F **29**
Pipit Mdw. LS27: Morl 6A **50**
Pitchstone Ct. LS12: Leeds 6D **28**
Pitfall St. LS1: Leeds 6F **5** (6G **31**)
Pit Fld. Rd. WF3: Carl 1F **59**
Pitt Row LS1: Leeds 6E **5** (6G **31**)
Place, The LS17: Leeds 5H **13**
Place's Rd. LS9: Leeds 6A **32**
Plaid Row LS9: Leeds 5A **32**
Plane Tree Av. LS17: Leeds 5B **14**
Plane Tree Cl. LS17: Leeds 5B **14**
Plane Tree Cft. LS17: Leeds 5B **14**
Plane Tree Gdns. LS17: Leeds 5B **14**
Plane Tree Gro. LS19: Yead 3F **9**
Plane Tree Ri. LS17: Leeds 5B **14**
Plane Trees Cl. BD19: Hun 6A **46**
Plane Tree Vw. LS17: Leeds 5B **14**
Plantation Av. LS15: Leeds 6H **33**
  LS17: Leeds 4C **14**
Plantation Gdns. LS17: Leeds 4C **14**
Platform One LS5: Leeds 1H **29**
  (off Station App.)
Playfair Rd. LS10: Leeds 5H **41**
Playground LS12: N Far 4D **38**
Playhouse Sq. LS2: Leeds 5H **31**
  (off Eastgate)
Plaza, The LS2: Leeds 1E **5**
Pleasance, The LS26: Swil 6G **45**
Pleasant Ct. LS6: Leeds 2E **31**
  (off Woodhouse St.)
Pleasant Mt. LS11: Leeds 2E **41**
Pleasant Pl. LS11: Leeds 2E **41**
Pleasant St. LS11: Leeds 2E **41**
Pleasant Ter. LS11: Leeds 2E **41**
Pleasant Vw. WF3: Loft 4B **58**
Pleasant Vw. Ter. WF3: Rob H 5D **52**
  (off Copley La.)
Plevna St. LS10: Leeds 5C **42**
Plover Way LS27: Morl 6A **50**
Plowmans Wlk. LS19: Yead 3B **8**
Poets Pl. LS18: H'fth 1C **18**
Pogson's Cotts. LS14: Leeds 6B **24**
  (off York Rd.)
Point, The LS12: Leeds 1D **40**
  (off Whitehall Pl.)
Pole Position Indoor Karting
  Leeds 2H **41**
Pollard La. LS13: Leeds 5B **18**
Pollard St. WF3: Loft 5E **59**
Ponderosa Cl. LS8: Leeds 2B **32**
Pontefract Av. LS9: Leeds 6B **32**
Pontefract La. LS9: Leeds, Swil 3B **32**
  (not continuous)
  LS15: Leeds 4A **44**
Pontefract La. Cl. LS9: Leeds 6B **32**
Pontefract Rd. LS10: Leeds 5C **42**
  LS26: Rothw 1F **53**

Pontefract St. LS9: Leeds 6B **32**
Poole Cres. LS15: Leeds 3B **34**
Poole Mt. LS15: Leeds 4B **34**
Poole Rd. LS15: Leeds 3B **34**
Poole Sq. LS15: Leeds 4B **34**
Poplar Av. LS15: Leeds 3D **34**
Poplar Cl. LS13: Leeds 5F **29**
Poplar Ct. LS13: Leeds 5E **29**
Poplar Cres. WF3: Ting 2A **56**
Poplar Cft. LS13: Leeds 5E **29**
Poplar Dr. LS18: H'fth 3H **17**
Poplar Gdns. LS13: Leeds 5E **29**
Poplar Gth. LS13: Leeds 5E **29**
Poplar Ga. LS13: Leeds 5E **29**
Poplar Grn. LS13: Leeds 5E **29**
Poplar Gro. LS13: Leeds 5E **29**
Poplar Pl. LS28: Pud 6D **26**
Poplar Ri. LS13: Leeds 4E **29**
Poplars, The LS6: Leeds 1C **30**
  LS20: Guis .3G **7**
  WF3: Loft 3E **59**
Poplar Sq. LS28: Fars 3F **27**
Poplar St. WF3: Loft 5E **59**
Poplar Vw. LS12: N Far 4G **39**
  LS13: Leeds 5E **29**
Poplar Way LS13: Leeds 5E **29**
Poplarwood Gdns. BD10: B'frd 6A **16**
Poppleton Ct. WF3: Ting 2C **56**
Poppleton Cft. WF3: Ting 3C **56**
  (off Lowry Rd.)
Poppleton Dr. WF3: Ting 2C **56**
Poppleton Ri. WF3: Ting 3C **56**
Poppleton Rd. WF3: Ting 2C **56**
Poppleton Way WF3: Ting 2C **56**
Poppy La. WF3: E Ard 3A **58**
Portage Av. LS15: Leeds 6H **33**
Portage Cres. LS15: Leeds 6G **33**
Portland Cres. LS1: Leeds 2D **4** (4F **31**)
Portland Ga. LS1: Leeds 2D **4** (4F **31**)
  (not continuous)
  LS2: Leeds 2D **4** (4F **31**)
Portland Ho. LS12: Leeds 1A **40**
Portland St. LS1: Leeds 3C **4** (5F **31**)
  LS28: Pud .5A **28**
Portland Way LS1: Leeds 2D **4** (4F **31**)
Portman St. LS28: Cal 5D **16**
Post Hil Gdns. LS28: Pud 6A **28**
Post Hill Ct. LS28: Pud 6D **28**
Post Hill Vw. LS28: Pud 6A **28**
Potovens Ct. WF3: Loft 5E **59**
Potovens La. WF1: Out 6D **58**
  WF3: Loft 6C **58**
POTTERNEWTON 1H **31**
Potternewton Av. LS7: Leeds 5F **21**
Potternewton Ct. LS7: Leeds 5G **21**
Potternewton Cres. LS7: Leeds 6F **21**
Potternewton Gdns. LS7: Leeds 5G **21**
Potternewton Gro. LS7: Leeds 5F **21**
Potternewton Hgts. LS7: Leeds 5G **21**
Potternewton La. LS7: Leeds 5E **21**
Potternewton Mt. LS7: Leeds 5F **21**
Potternewton Vw. LS7: Leeds 5F **21**
Potters Cft. WF3: Loft 5E **59**
POTTERY FIELD .1H **41**
Pottery La. LS26: Wood 2D **54**
Pottery Rd. LS10: Leeds 3H **41**
Poulton Pl. LS11: Leeds 4G **41**
Premier Way LS26: Oul 3H **59**
Preston La. LS26: Swil 5E **41**
Preston Vw. LS26: Swil 6H **45**
Pretoria Rd. BD3: B'frd 6A **26**
PRIESTHORPE 1E **27**
Priesthorpe Av. LS28: Stan 3D **26**
Priesthorpe Ct. LS28: Fars 1F **27**
Priesthorpe La. LS28: Fars 2D **26**
Priesthorpe Rd. LS28: Cal, Fars 1C **26**
  (not continuous)
Priestley Cl. LS28: Pud 5H **27**
Priestley Ct. LS18: H'fth 3E **19**
  LS28: Pud .5H **27**
Priestley Dr. LS28: Pud 4H **27**
Priestley Gdns. LS28: Pud 5H **27**
Priestley Vw. LS28: Pud 5H **27**
Priestley Wlk. LS28: Pud 5H **27**
Primitive St. WF3: Carl 6F **53**
Primley Gdns. LS17: Leeds 5G **13**
Primley Pk. Av. LS17: Leeds 5G **13**
Primley Pk. Cl. LS17: Leeds 5G **13**
Primley Pk. Ct. LS17: Leeds 4G **13**
Primley Pk. Cres. LS17: Leeds 5G **13**
Primley Pk. Dr. LS17: Leeds 5G **13**
Primley Pk. Gth. LS17: Leeds 5H **13**
Primley Pk. Gro. LS17: Leeds 5G **13**
Primley Pk. La. LS17: Leeds 5G **13**
Primley Pk. Grn. LS17: Leeds 4H **13**
Primley Pk. Mt. LS17: Leeds 5H **13**
Primley Pk. Ri. LS17: Leeds 5H **13**

Primley Pk. Rd.—Raylands Way

Primley Pk. Rd. LS17: Leeds 5G **13**
Primley Pk. Vw. LS17: Leeds 4G **13**
Primley Pk. Wlk. LS17: Leeds 4H **13**
Primley Pk. Way LS17: Leeds 4G **13**
Primo Pl. LS8: Leeds 2F **33**
Primrose Av. LS15: Leeds 5A **34**
LS26: Swil 6H **45**
Primrose Cl. LS15: Leeds 5A **34**
Primrose Ct. LS17: Leeds 4H **13**
LS20: Guis 4G 7
(off Orchard Way)
Primrose Cres. LS15: Leeds 4A **34**
Primrose Dr. LS15: Leeds 5A **34**
Primrose Gdns. LS15: Leeds 4A **34**
Primrose Gth. LS15: Leeds 5H **33**
Primrose Gro. LS15: Leeds 4A **34**
Primrose Hill LS28: Stan 4G **27**
Primrose Hill Cl. LS26: Swil 6H **45**
Primrose Hill Dr. LS26: Swil 6H **45**
Primrose Hill Gdns. LS26: Swil 6H **45**
Primrose Hill Gth. LS26: Swil 1H **55**
Primrose Hill Grn. LS26: Swil 1H **55**
Primrose Hill Gro. LS26: Swil 6H **45**
Primrose La. LS11: Leeds 4G **41**
LS15: Leeds 5H **33**
(not continuous)
Primrose Rd. LS15: Leeds 5A **34**
Primrose Wlk. LS27: Chur 1A **50**
Primrose Yd. LS26: Oul 4C **54**
Prince Edward Gro. LS12: Leeds 3G **39**
Prince Edward Rd. LS12: Leeds 3G **39**
Princes Av. LS8: Leeds 4D **22**
Prince's Ct. LS17: Leeds 2G **21**
Prince's Gro. LS6: Leeds 6B **20**
Prince's Gym **3D 30**
Princess Ct. LS15: Leeds 1D **44**
LS17: Leeds 6H **13**
Princess Flds. LS15: Leeds 1D **44**
Princes Sq. LS1: Leeds 6C **4** (6F **31**)
Princess St. LS19: Raw 5C **8**
Priory M. WF3: S'ley 5H **59**
Privilege St. LS12: Leeds 6H **29**
Prospect Av. LS13: Leeds 2C **28**
LS28: Pud 5F **27**
Prospect Bldgs. *WF3: E Ard 4G 57*
(off Bradford Rd.)
Prospect Ct. *LS27: Morl 4G 49*
(off Prospect Pl.)
Prospect Cres. LS10: Leeds 4H **41**
Prospect Gdns. LS15: Leeds 5B **34**
Prospect Gro. LS28: Pud 5F **27**
Prospect La. BD11: Birk 4D **46**
Prospect M. *LS27: Morl 4G 49*
(off Prospect Pl.)
Prospect Pl. LS13: Leeds 2C **28**
LS18: H'fth 3B **18**
LS26: Rothw 5H **53**
LS27: Morl 4G **49**
WF3: Loft 1D **58**
Prospect Sq. LS28: Fars 3F **27**
Prospect St. LS19: Raw 6E **9**
LS28: Fars 2F **27**
LS28: Pud 5E **27**
Prospect Ter. *LS9: Leeds 6B 32*
(off Lavender Wlk.)
LS13: Leeds 6G **17**
(Airedale Mt.)
LS13: Leeds 2C **28**
(Prospect Vw.)
LS18: H'fth 2C **18**
LS26: Rothw 5H **53**
LS28: Fars 2F **27**
Prospect Vw. LS13: Leeds 2C **28**
Prosper St. LS10: Leeds 3A **42**
Providence Av. LS6: Leeds 1E **31**
Providence Ct. LS27: Morl 6H **49**
Providence Mt. *LS27: Morl 4G 49*
(off Bank St.)
Providence Pl. LS2: Leeds 1E **5** (4G **31**)
LS15: Swil C 1G **45**
LS27: Morl 5E **49**
LS28: Stan 4G **27**
Providence Rd. LS6: Leeds 1E **31**
Providence St. LS28: Fars 3F **27**
(not continuous)
Providence Ter. LS2: Leeds 2E **31**
Providence Works *LS27: Morl 5D 48*
(off Howden Clough Rd.)
PUDSEY 5H **27**
Pudsey Bus. Cen. LS28: Pud 6H **27**
Pudsey Leisure Cen. **6G 27**
Pudsey Rd. LS12: Leeds 5D **28**
LS13: Leeds, Pud 6B **28**
Pullman Ct. LS11: Leeds 6C **40**
LS27: Morl 4H **49**
Pullman Ho. LS11: Leeds 6C **40**
Pump La. WF3: W Ard 6C **56**
Purbeck Ct. BD4: B'frd 5A **36**
Pymont Ct. WF3: Loft 2E **59**
Pymont Dr. LS26: Wood 2A **54**
Pymont Gro. LS26: Wood 2B **54**
Pym St. LS10: Leeds 2H **41**

Q

Quaker Ho. LS2: Leeds 3E **31**
Quakers La. LS19: Raw 4D **8**
Quarrie Dene Ct. LS7: Leeds 5G **21**
Quarry, The LS17: Leeds 3E **13**
Quarry Bank Ct. LS5: Leeds 5F **19**
Quarry Cotts. LS18: H'fth 2B **18**
Quarry Dene LS16: Leeds 3A **20**
Quarry Dene Pk. LS16: Leeds 2A **20**
Quarryfield Ter. WF3: E Ard 4H **57**
Quarry Gap Row BD4: B'frd 1A **36**
Quarry Gdns. LS17: Leeds 3E **13**
QUARRY HILL 4H **5** (5H **31**)
Quarry Hill LS26: Oul 4C **54**
LS28: Fars 2F 27
(off Wesley St.)
Quarry Ho. LS2: Leeds 4H **5** (5A **32**)
Quarry La. LS27: Morl 6H **49**
WF12: Dew 5A **56**
Quarry Mt. LS6: Leeds 1E **31**
LS19: Yead 2E 9
(off King St.)
Quarry Mt. Pl. LS6: Leeds 1E **31**
Quarry Mt. St. LS6: Leeds 1E **31**
Quarry Mt. Ter. LS6: Leeds 1E **31**
Quarry Pl. LS6: Leeds 2E **31**
Quarry Rd. LS26: Wood 3D **54**
Quarry St. LS6: Leeds 2E **31**
Quarry Ter. LS18: H'fth 2B **18**
Quay One LS9: Leeds 6H **5**
Quayside, The BD10: B'frd 3A **16**
Quayside Ho. LS11: Leeds 6D **4**
Quebec St. LS1: Leeds 4D **4** (6F **31**)
Queen's Arc. LS1: Leeds 4E **5**
Queensbury Av. WF1: Out 6E **59**
Queen's Cl. LS7: Leeds 3G **21**
Queens Ct. LS1: Leeds 5F **5**
LS17: Leeds 2G **21**
LS28: Pud 5G **27**
Queenscourt LS27: Morl 5G **49**
Queens Dr. LS28: Pud 5F **27**
WF3: Carl 6F **53**
Queen's Gro. LS27: Morl 6F **49**
Queens Hall LS27: Morl 6F **49**
Queenshill App. LS17: Leeds 1G **21**
Queenshill Av. LS17: Leeds 1G **21**
Queenshill Cl. LS17: Leeds 1G **21**
Queenshill Ct. LS17: Leeds 1G **21**
Queenshill Cres. LS17: Leeds 6G **13**
Queenshill Dr. LS17: Leeds 1F **21**
Queenshill Gdns. LS17: Leeds 1F **21**
Queenshill Gth. LS17: Leeds 1G **21**
Queenshill Lawn *LS17: Leeds 1G 21*
(off Queenshill App.)
Queenshill Rd. LS17: Leeds 1G **21**
Queenshill Vw. LS17: Leeds 1G **21**
Queenshill Wlk. LS17: Leeds 1G **21**
Queenshill Way LS17: Leeds 1G **21**
Queen's Pl. LS27: Morl 5H **49**
Queen's Prom. LS27: Morl 4G **49**
Queen Sq. LS2: Leeds 2E **5** (4G **31**)
Queen Sq. Ct. LS2: Leeds 2D **4** (4F **31**)
Queen's Rd. LS6: Leeds 3C **30**
LS27: Morl 6F **49**
Queens Ter. LS20: Guis 4F **7**
Queensthorpe Av.
LS13: Leeds 5D **28**
Queensthorpe Cl. LS13: Leeds 5E **29**
Queensthorpe Ri. LS13: Leeds 5D **28**
Queen St. BD10: B'frd 4A **16**
LS1: Leeds 5B **4** (6E **31**)
LS10: Leeds 5C **42**
LS19: Raw 5D **8**
LS27: Morl 4G **49**
(not continuous)
WF3: Carl 6F **53**
WF3: E Ard 3H **57**
Queensview LS14: Leeds 6A **24**
Queen's Wlk. LS6: Leeds 5G **19**
Queensway LS15: Leeds 5C **34**
LS19: Yead 4G **7**
LS20: Guis, Yead 4G **7**
LS26: Rothw 3G **53**
LS27: Morl 5G **49**
Queenswood Cl. LS6: Leeds 5G **19**
Queenswood Ct. LS6: Leeds 1A **30**
Queenswood Dr. LS6: Leeds 4G **19**
Queenswood Gdns. LS6: Leeds 1A **30**
Queenswood Grn. LS6: Leeds 4G **19**
Queenswood Hgts. LS6: Leeds 6A **20**
Queenswood Mt. LS6: Leeds 6H **19**
Queenswood Ri. LS6: Leeds 6H **19**
Queenswood Rd. LS6: Leeds 6H **19**
Queen Victoria St. LS1: Leeds 4F **5**

R

Raby Av. LS7: Leeds 2H **31**
Raby St. LS7: Leeds 2H **31**
Raby Ter. LS7: Leeds 2H **31**
Rachel Ct. LS9: Leeds 3D **32**
Radcliffe Gdns. LS28: Pud 1G **37**
Radcliffe Gro. LS28: Pud 1G **37**
Radcliffe La. LS28: Pud 6G **27**
Radcliffe Ter. LS28: Pud 1G **37**
Radnor St. LS12: Leeds 1C **40**
Rae Ct. WF3: S'ley 6G **59**
Raglan Rd. LS2: Leeds 2E **31**
LS6: Leeds 2E **31**
Raglan St. BD3: B'frd 6A **26**
Raglan Ter. BD3: B'frd 6A **26**
Raikes Av. BD4: B'frd 4B **36**
Raikes La. BD4: B'frd 5C **36**
BD4: E Bier 1A **46**
WF17: Birs 6H **47**
Raikes Wood Dr. BD4: E Bier 2A **46**
Railsfield Cliff *LS13: Leeds 3C 28*
(off Brighton Cliff)
Railsfield Mt. LS13: Leeds 4C **28**
Railsfield Ri. LS13: Leeds 4C **28**
Railsfield Way LS13: Leeds 3D **28**
Railway Rd. LS15: Leeds 3C **34**
(not continuous)
Railway St. LS9: Leeds 5H **5** (6A **32**)
Railway Ter. WF1: Out 6D **58**
WF3: E Ard 2G **57**
Raincliffe Gro. LS9: Leeds 5C **32**
Raincliffe Mt. LS9: Leeds 6C **32**
Raincliffe Rd. LS9: Leeds 5C **32**
Raincliffe St. LS9: Leeds 5C **32**
Raincliffe Ter. LS9: Leeds 6C **32**
Rakehill Rd. LS15: Bar E, Scho 4F **25**
Rampart Rd. LS6: Leeds 2E **31**
Ramsgate WF3: Loft 2D **58**
Ramsgate Cres. WF3: Loft 2D **58**
Ramsgill Ho. LS29: Men 3D **6**
Ramshead App. LS14: Leeds 5A **24**
Ramshead Cl. LS14: Leeds 4A **24**
Ramshead Cres. LS14: Leeds 4H **23**
Ramshead Dr. LS14: Leeds 4H **23**
Ramshead Gdns. LS14: Leeds 4H **23**
Ramshead Gro. LS14: Leeds 5A **24**
Ramshead Hgts. LS14: Leeds 6A **24**
(Bailey's La.)
LS14: Leeds 5A **24**
(Eastdean Rd.)
Ramshead Hill LS14: Leeds 5A **24**
Ramshead Pl. LS14: Leeds 5A **24**
Ramshead Vw. LS14: Leeds 5A **24**
Randolph St. BD3: B'frd 5A **26**
LS13: Leeds 3A **28**
Ranelagh Av. BD10: B'frd 6A **16**
Rathmell Rd. LS15: Leeds 6G **33**
Raven Rd. LS6: Leeds 1C **30**
Ravenscar Av. LS8: Leeds 5C **22**
Ravenscar Mt. LS8: Leeds 5C **22**
Ravenscar Ter. LS8: Leeds 5C **22**
Ravenscar Vw. LS8: Leeds 5C **22**
Ravenscar Wlk. LS8: Leeds 5C **22**
RAVENSCLIFFE 1A 26
Ravenscliffe Av. BD10: B'frd 6A **16**
Ravenscliffe Rd. LS28: Cal 5B **16**
Ravens Mt. LS28: Pud 6H **27**
Ravensworth Cl. LS15: Leeds 2F **35**
Ravensworth Way LS15: Leeds 2F **35**
RAWDON 6F **9**
Rawdon Crematorium LS19: Raw 2G **17**
Rawdon Dr. LS19: Raw 6D **8**
Rawdon Hall Dr. LS19: Raw 6D **8**
Rawdon Pk. LS19: Raw 4D **8**
Rawdon Rd. LS18: H'fth, Yead 1G **17**
Rawfolds Av. WF17: Birs 6H **47**
Rawling Way LS6: Leeds 6E **21**
Rawson Av. BD3: B'frd 5A **26**
Rawson Pl. LS11: Leeds 4G **41**
Rawson Ter. LS11: Leeds 4G **41**
Raygill Cl. LS17: Leeds 4D **14**
Raylands Cl. LS10: Leeds 3B **52**
Raylands Ct. LS10: Leeds 3B **52**
Raylands Fold LS10: Leeds 3B **52**
Raylands Gth. LS10: Leeds 3B **52**
Raylands La. LS10: Leeds 3B **52**
Raylands Pl. LS10: Leeds 3B **52**
Raylands Rd. LS10: Leeds 3B **52**
Raylands Way LS10: Leeds 4A **52**

A-Z Leeds 97

Raynel App. LS16: Leeds 6G 11
Raynel Cl. LS16: Leeds 5F 11
Raynel Dr. LS16: Leeds 6G 11
Raynel Gdns. LS16: Leeds 5G 11
Raynel Gth. LS16: Leeds 6G 11
Raynel Grn. LS16: Leeds 6G 11
Raynel Mt. LS16: Leeds 5G 11
Raynel Way LS16: Leeds 5F 11
Rayner Gdns. LS28: Fars 2G 27
Raynor Ter. LS28: Pud 5H 27
Raynville App. LS13: Leeds 3E 29
Raynville Av. LS13: Leeds 2E 29
Raynville Cl. LS13: Leeds 2E 29
Raynville Ct. LS12: Leeds 3F 29
   LS13: Leeds .3E 29
Raynville Cres. LS12: Leeds 3F 29
Raynville Dene LS12: Leeds 2F 29
Raynville Dr. LS13: Leeds 2E 29
Raynville Gdns. LS12: Leeds 3F 29
Raynville Gth. LS12: Leeds 3F 29
Raynville Grange LS13: Leeds 3E 29
   (off Raynville Rd.)
Raynville Grn. LS13: Leeds 2E 29
Raynville Gro. LS13: Leeds 3E 29
Raynville Mt. LS13: Leeds 2E 29
Raynville Pl. LS13: Leeds 3E 29
Raynville Ri. LS13: Leeds 3E 29
Raynville Rd. LS12: Leeds 2E 29
   LS13: Leeds .2D 28
Raynville St. LS13: Leeds 2E 29
Raynville Ter. LS13: Leeds 2E 29
Raynville Wlk. LS13: Leeds 3E 29
Raynville Way LS12: Leeds 3F 29
Raywood Cl. LS19: Yead 1C 8
Recreation Av. LS11: Leeds 3E 41
Recreation Cres. LS11: Leeds 3D 40
Recreation Gro. LS11: Leeds 3D 40
Recreation Mt. LS11: Leeds 3D 40
Recreation Pl. LS11: Leeds 3D 40
Recreation Rd. LS11: Leeds 5D 40
Recreation Row LS11: Leeds 3D 40
Recreation St. LS11: Leeds 3D 40
Recreation Ter. LS11: Leeds 3D 40
Recreation Vw. LS11: Leeds 3D 40
Rectory St. LS9: Leeds 4A 32
Redbarn Cl. LS10: Leeds 1G 57
Redbarn Ct. LS10: Leeds 1G 57
Redbeck Cotts. LS18: H'fth 3G 17
Redcar Rd. BD10: B'frd 5A 16
Redcote La. LS4: Leeds 4H 29
   LS12: Leeds .5H 29
Redcourt LS12: Leeds 4A 30
   (off Athone Gro.)
Redesdale Gdns. LS16: Leeds 6G 11
Red Hall App. LS14: Leeds 2A 24
Red Hall Av. LS17: Leeds 2H 23
Red Hall Chase LS14: Leeds 2A 24
Redhall Cl. LS11: Leeds 6C 40
Red Hall Ct. LS14: Leeds 2A 24
Redhall Cres. LS11: Leeds 6C 40
Red Hall Cft. LS14: Leeds 2A 24
Red Hall Dr. LS14: Leeds 2A 24
Red Hall Gdns. LS17: Leeds 2H 23
Redhall Ga. LS11: Leeds 6C 40
Red Hall Grn. LS14: Leeds 2A 24
Red Hall La. LS14: Leeds 2A 24
   LS17: Leeds .2H 23
Red Hall Va. LS14: Leeds 3A 24
Red Hall Vw. LS14: Leeds 2A 24
Red Hall Wlk. LS14: Leeds 2A 24
Red Hall Way LS14: Leeds 2A 24
Redhill Av. WF3: W Ard 6C 56
Redhill Cl. BD4: B'frd 1C 46
   WF3: W Ard .6C 56
Redhill Cres. WF3: W Ard 6C 56
Redhill Dr. WF3: W Ard 6C 56
Red Ho. Gdns. LS29: Men 2C 6
Redhouse La. LS7: Leeds 4A 22
Red La. LS28: Fars 2E 27
Red Lodge Cl. LS8: Leeds 1F 33
Redmire Ct. LS14: Leeds 1A 34
Redmire Dr. LS14: Leeds 1A 34
Redmire St. BD3: B'frd 6A 26
Redmire Vw. LS14: Leeds 1A 34
Redshaw Rd. LS12: Leeds 1B 40
Red Va. BD19: Gom 6D 46
Redvers Cl. LS16: Leeds 2G 19
Redwald Dr. LS20: Guis 4F 7
Redwood Av. WF3: Ting 3E 57
Redwood Cl. LS19: Yead 6H 7
   LS26: Wood .3E 55
Redwood Gro. LS19: Yead 6H 7
Redwood Way LS19: Yead 6H 7
Reedling Dr. LS27: Morl 6A 50
Reed Rd. LS12: Leeds 1B 40
Reedsdale Av. LS27: Gil 2C 48

Reedsdale Dr. LS27: Gil 2C 48
Reedsdale Gdns. LS27: Gil 2C 48
Regal Pde. LS15: Leeds 3B 34
Regency Ct. LS6: Leeds 1C 30
Regency Gdns. WF3: W Ard 3E 57
Regency Pk. Gro. LS28: Pud 2G 37
Regency Pk. Rd. LS28: Pud 2G 37
Regent Av. LS18: H'fth 4C 18
Regent Cl. LS18: H'fth 4C 18
Regent Ct. LS1: Leeds 5F 5
   LS18: H'fth 4C 18
Regent Cres. LS18: H'fth 4B 18
Regent Pk. Av. LS6: Leeds 1D 30
Regent Pk. Ter. LS6: Leeds 1D 30
Regent Pl. WF3: Thpe H 1B 58
Regent Rd. LS18: H'fth 4B 18
Regent St. BD10: B'frd 4A 16
   LS2: Leeds 3H 5 (5H 31)
   LS7: Leeds 3H 5 (4H 21)
Regent Ter. LS6: Leeds 3D 30
   LS7: Leeds 4H 21
Regina Dr. LS7: Leeds 5H 21
Regina Ho. LS13: Leeds 5D 28
Reginald Mt. LS7: Leeds 1H 31
Reginald Row LS7: Leeds 1H 31
Reginald St. LS7: Leeds 1H 31
Reginald Ter. LS7: Leeds 1H 31
Reginald Vw. LS7: Leeds 1H 31
Reighton Cft. BD10: B'frd 5A 16
Rein, The LS14: Leeds 5H 23
Rein Gdns. WF3: Ting 3A 56
Rein M. WF3: Ting 3A 56
Rein Rd. LS18: H'fth 4B 18
   LS27: Morl 1A 56
   WF3: Ting 1A 56
Rein St. LS27: Morl 2A 56
Reinwood Av. LS8: Leeds 6F 23
Rembrandt Av. WF3: Ting 3D 56
Renaissance Ct. LS27: Chur 1A 50
Renaissance Dr. LS27: Chur 1A 50
Renton Av. LS20: Guis 4F 7
Renton Dr. LS20: Guis 5F 7
Renton Lea LS20: Guis 5F 7
Reservoir Ct. LS28: Cal 5C 16
Restmore Av. LS20: Guis 3F 7
Revie Rd. LS11: Leeds 4D 40
Revie Rd. Ind. Est.
   LS11: Leeds .4D 40
Reyden M. LS12: Leeds 1A 40
Rhodes Ct. LS27: Morl 6H 49
   (off High St.)
Rhodes Gdns. WF3: Loft 5E 59
Rhodes Ter. LS12: Leeds 1C 40
Rialto Ct. LS13: Leeds 6G 17
Riccall Nook BD10: B'frd 5A 16
Richardshaw Dr. LS28: Stan 4G 27
Richardshaw La. LS28: Pud, Stan 4G 27
Richardshaw Rd. LS28: Stan 4G 27
Richardson Cres. LS9: Leeds 6D 32
Richardson Rd. LS9: Leeds 6D 32
Richmond Av. LS6: Leeds 1C 30
Richmond Cl. LS13: Leeds 3A 28
   LS26: Rothw .3H 53
   LS27: Morl 6G 49
Richmond Ct. LS9: Leeds 6B 32
   LS13: Leeds .6G 17
   LS26: Rothw .3H 53
Richmond Cft. LS9: Leeds 6B 32
Richmond Gdns. LS28: Pud 6A 28
Richmond Grn. St. LS9: Leeds 6A 32
   (off Cross Catherine St.)
RICHMOND HILL 6B 32
Richmond Hill App. LS9: Leeds 6A 32
Richmond Hill Cl. LS9: Leeds 6A 32
Richmond Hill Sports & Recreation Cen. 5B 32
Richmond Ho. LS8: Leeds 1D 22
   (off Street La.)
Richmond Mt. LS6: Leeds 1C 30
Richmond Rd. LS6: Leeds 1C 30
   LS28: Fars 3E 27
Richmond St. LS9: Leeds 6H 5 (6A 32)
Richmond Ter. LS20: Guis 4F 7
   LS28: Pud 6A 28
Rickard St. LS12: Leeds 1D 40
Rider Rd. LS6: Leeds 1F 31
Rider St. LS9: Leeds 5A 32
Ridge Cl. LS20: Guis 5E 7
Ridge Gro. LS7: Leeds 6E 21
Ridge Mt. LS6: Leeds 1E 31
Ridge Rd. LS7: Leeds 1F 31
Ridge Ter. LS6: Leeds 6C 20
Ridge Vw. LS13: Leeds 5C 28
Ridgeway LS8: Leeds 5B 22
   LS20: Guis 5D 6
Ridge Way Cl. LS8: Leeds 5B 22

Ridgeway Ter. LS6: Leeds 1E 31
   (off Delph La.)
Ridings Cl. WF3: Loft 5D 58
Ridings Ct. WF3: Loft 5D 58
Ridings Gdns. WF3: Loft 5D 58
Ridings La. WF3: Loft 5D 58
Ridings M. WF3: Loft 5D 58
Ridings Way WF3: Loft 5D 58
Rigton App. LS9: Leeds 5A 32
Rigton Cl. LS9: Leeds 5B 32
Rigton Dr. LS9: Leeds 5A 32
Rigton Grn. LS9: Leeds 5A 32
Rigton Lawn LS9: Leeds 5A 32
Rigton M. LS9: Leeds 5A 32
Rillbank La. LS3: Leeds 4D 30
Rillbank St. LS3: Leeds 4D 30
   (off Woodsley Rd.)
Rillington Mead BD10: B'frd 5A 16
Rimswell Holt BD10: B'frd 5A 16
Ring Hay Rd. BD4: B'frd 6C 36
Ring Rd. Adel LS16: Leeds 1B 20
Ring Rd. Beeston LS11: Leeds 5B 40
   LS12: Leeds .3A 40
Ring Rd. Beeston Pk. LS10: Leeds 1D 50
   LS11: Leeds .1E 51
Ring Rd. Bramley LS13: Leeds 5D 28
Ring Rd. Cross Gates LS15: Leeds 2C 34
Ring Rd. Farnley LS12: Leeds 5D 28
Ring Rd. Farsley LS13: Leeds, Pud 3D 26
   LS28: Fars 3D 26
Ring Rd. Halton LS15: Leeds 4C 34
Ring Rd. Horsforth LS16: Leeds 3E 19
   LS18: H'fth, Leeds 3E 19
Ring Rd. Lwr. Wortley
   LS12: Leeds .1F 39
Ring Rd. Meanwood LS6: Leeds 1C 20
   LS16: Leeds .1C 20
   LS17: Leeds .1C 20
Ring Rd. Middleton LS10: Leeds 4H 51
Ring Rd. Moortown LS6: Leeds 1E 21
   LS17: Leeds .1E 21
Ring Rd. Seacroft LS14: Leeds 3H 23
Ring Rd. Shadwell LS17: Leeds 6E 15
Ring Rd. Weetwood LS16: Leeds 2H 19
Ring Rd. West Pk. LS16: Leeds 2F 19
Ringwood Av. LS14: Leeds 3H 23
Ringwood Ct. WF1: Out 6F 59
Ringwood Cres. LS14: Leeds 2A 24
Ringwood Dr. LS14: Leeds 3A 24
Ringwood Gdns. LS14: Leeds 3A 24
Ringwood Mt. LS14: Leeds 3A 24
Ripley Cl. WF3: E Ard 2H 57
Ripley La. LS20: Guis 2G 7
Ripon Ho. LS28: Fars 2F 27
Rise, The LS5: Leeds 6G 19
Rivendale LS10: Leeds 5A 52
Riverside Cl. LS1: Leeds 6F 5 (6G 31)
Riverside W. LS1: Leeds 6A 4 (6E 31)
River Vw. LS18: H'fth 2B 18
Riviera Gdns. LS7: Leeds 5G 21
Roans Brae BD10: B'frd 5A 16
Robb Av. LS11: Leeds 6E 41
Robb St. LS11: Leeds 6E 41
Robert Ho. LS27: Morl 4H 49
   (off Pullman Ct.)
Roberts Av. LS9: Leeds 3D 32
Roberts Ct. LS9: Leeds 3D 32
Robertsgate WF3: Loft 2D 58
Robertsgate Sq. WF3: Loft 2D 58
   (off Robertsgate)
Roberts Pl. LS9: Leeds 4D 32
Roberts St. LS26: Wood 3C 54
Roberts Wharf LS9: Leeds 6H 5 (1A 42)
Robin Chase LS28: Pud 6H 27
ROBIN HOOD 6D 52
Robin La. LS28: Pud 6G 27
Robin's Gro. LS26: Rothw 4H 53
Robinwood Ct. LS8: Leeds 2C 22
Rocheford Cl. LS10: Leeds 4B 42
Rocheford Ct. LS10: Leeds 4B 42
Rocheford Gdns. LS10: Leeds 4B 42
Rocheford Gro. LS10: Leeds 4B 42
Rocheford Wlk. LS10: Leeds 4B 42
Rochester Gdns. LS13: Leeds 1H 27
Rochester Rd. WF17: Birs 6G 47
Rochester Ter. LS6: Leeds 1B 30
Rochester Wynd LS17: Leeds 5C 14
Rock Ct. LS27: Morl 4H 49
Rockery Cft. LS18: H'fth 1C 18
Rockery Rd. LS18: H'fth 1C 18
Rockfield LS19: Yead 2E 9
   (off Rockfield Ter.)
Rockfield Ter. LS19: Yead 2E 9
Rockingham Cl. LS15: Leeds 2F 35
Rockingham Rd. LS15: Leeds 2F 35
Rockingham Way LS15: Leeds 2F 35
Rock La. LS13: Leeds 1B 28

Rockley Hall Yd. LS1: Leeds	4F 5
Rock Ter. LS15: Leeds	5H 33
LS27: Morl	4H 49
WF12: Dew	5A 56
Rockville Ter. *LS19: Yead*	*3E 9*
(off Rufford Ridge)	
Rockwood Cres. LS28: Cal	3C 26
Rockwood Gro. LS28: Cal	2D 26
Rockwood Hill Ct. LS28: Cal	3C 26
Rockwood Rd. LS28: Cal	3C 26
Roderick St. LS12: Leeds	6H 29
RODLEY	6G 17
Rodley Hall *LS13: Leeds*	*6H 17*
(off Club La.)	
Rodley La. LS13: Leeds	1A 28
(Airedale Quay)	
LS13: Leeds	5E 17
(Calverley La.)	
LS28: Cal	5E 17
Rods Mills La. LS27: Morl	6H 49
Rods Vw. LS27: Morl	6H 49
Rogers Ct. WF3: S'ley	5H 59
Rogers Pl. LS28: Pud	5H 27
Rokeby Gdns. BD10: B'frd	5A 16
LS6: Leeds	6A 20
Roker La. LS28: Pud	2H 37
ROKER LANE BOTTOM	3A 38
Roman Av. LS8: Leeds	1C 22
Romanby Shaw BD10: B'frd	5A 16
Roman Ct. LS8: Leeds	1D 22
Roman Cres. LS8: Leeds	1D 22
Roman Dr. LS8: Leeds	1D 22
Roman Gdns. LS8: Leeds	1C 22
Roman Gro. LS8: Leeds	1C 22
Roman Mt. LS8: Leeds	1D 22
Roman Pl. LS8: Leeds	1D 22
Roman Ter. LS8: Leeds	1C 22
Roman Vw. LS8: Leeds	1D 22
Rombalds Av. LS12: Leeds	5A 30
Rombalds Ct. LS29: Men	1B 6
Rombalds Cres. LS12: Leeds	4A 30
Rombalds Cft. *LS19: Yead*	*2D 8*
Rombalds Gro. LS12: Leeds	5A 30
Rombalds Pl. LS12: Leeds	4A 30
Rombalds St. LS12: Leeds	4A 30
Rombalds Ter. LS12: Leeds	5A 30
Rombalds Vw. LS12: Leeds	4A 30
Romford Av. LS27: Morl	6G 49
Romney Mt. LS28: Pud	2A 38
Romsey Gdns. BD4: B'frd	4A 36
Romsey M. BD4: B'frd	4A 36
Rona Cft. LS26: Rothw	4A 54
Rook's Nest Rd.	
WF1: Out	6F 59
WF3: S'ley	6F 59
Rookwith Pde. BD10: B'frd	5A 16
Rookwood Av. LS9: Leeds	5E 33
Rookwood Cres. LS9: Leeds	5E 33
Rookwood Cft. LS9: Leeds	6E 33
Rookwood Gdns. LS9: Leeds	5E 33
Rookwood Hill LS9: Leeds	5E 33
Rookwood Mt. LS9: Leeds	5E 33
Rookwood Pde. LS9: Leeds	5F 33
Rookwood Pl. LS9: Leeds	5E 33
Rookwood Rd. LS9: Leeds	5E 33
Rookwood Sq. LS9: Leeds	5F 33
Rookwood St. LS9: Leeds	6E 33
Rookwood Ter. LS9: Leeds	6E 33
Rookwood Va. LS9: Leeds	5E 33
Rookwood Vw. LS9: Leeds	5E 33
Rookwood Wlk. LS9: Leeds	5E 33
ROOMS	1F 49
Rooms Fold LS27: Morl	3G 49
Rooms La. LS27: Gil, Morl	1F 49
Rooms Way LS27: Morl	2F 49
Roper Av. LS8: Leeds	3B 22
Roper Gro. LS8: Leeds	3B 22
Roscoe St. LS7: Leeds	3H 31
Roscoe Ter. LS12: Leeds	6H 29
Roseate Grn. LS27: Morl	6A 50
Rose Av. LS18: H'fth	4B 18
Rosebank Cres. LS3: Leeds	3D 30
Rosebank Gdns. LS3: Leeds	4D 30
Rosebank Ho. *LS3: Leeds*	*3D 30*
(off Rosebank Rd.)	
Rosebank Rd. LS3: Leeds	4D 30
Rosebank Row LS3: Leeds	4D 30
Rosebery St. LS28: Pud	5E 27
Rosebery Ter. LS28: Stan	3H 27
Rosebud Wlk. LS8: Leeds	3A 32
Rosecliffe Mt. LS13: Leeds	2B 28
Rosecliffe Ter. LS13: Leeds	2B 28
Rosedale LS26: Rothw	3H 53
Rosedale Bank LS10: Leeds	6H 41
Rosedale Ct. BD4: E Bier	2A 46
WF3: W Ard	5C 56
Rosedale Dr. WF3: W Ard	5C 56

Rosedale Gdns. LS10: Leeds	6H 41
(not continuous)	
WF3: Ting	3F 57
Rosedale Grn. LS10: Leeds	6H 41
Rosedale Wlk. LS10: Leeds	6H 41
Rose Gro. LS26: Rothw	3F 53
Rosemary Av. *LS12: Leeds*	*6B 30*
(off Armley Gro. Pl.)	
Rosemont Av. LS13: Leeds	3C 28
LS28: Pud	5H 27
Rosemont Dr. LS28: Pud	5H 27
Rosemont Gro. LS13: Leeds	3B 28
Rosemont Pl. LS13: Leeds	3C 28
Rosemont Rd. LS13: Leeds	3C 28
Rosemont St. LS13: Leeds	3C 28
LS28: Pud	5H 27
Rosemont Ter. LS13: Leeds	3C 28
LS28: Pud	5H 27
Rosemont Vw. LS13: Leeds	3B 28
Rosemont Vs. LS28: Pud	5H 27
Rosemont Wlk. LS13: Leeds	3C 28
Rose Mt. BD4: B'frd	1C 46
Rosemount *LS7: Leeds*	*5G 21*
(off School La.)	
Rose Mt. Pl. LS12: Leeds	1B 40
Roseneath Pl. LS12: Leeds	1B 40
Roseneath St. LS12: Leeds	1B 40
Roseneath Ter. LS12: Leeds	1B 40
Rose St. LS18: H'fth	3B 18
Rose Ter. LS18: H'fth	3A 18
Roseville Bus. Pk. LS8: Leeds	3A 32
Roseville Rd. LS8: Leeds	1H 5 (3A 32)
Roseville St. LS8: Leeds	3A 32
Roseville Ter. *LS15: Leeds*	*2D 34*
(off Church La.)	
Roseville Way LS8: Leeds	3A 32
Rosewood Ct. *LS17: Leeds*	*6E 13*
(off Cranmer Cl.)	
LS26: Rothw	2H 53
Rosgill Dr. LS14: Leeds	6H 23
Rosgill Grn. LS14: Leeds	6A 24
Rosgill Wlk. LS14: Leeds	6H 23
Rossall Rd. LS8: Leeds	1B 32
Rossefield App. LS13: Leeds	4D 28
Rossefield Av. LS13: Leeds	3D 28
Rossefield Chase LS13: Leeds	3D 28
Rossefield Cl. LS13: Leeds	3D 28
Rossefield Dr. LS13: Leeds	3D 28
Rossefield Gdns. LS13: Leeds	3D 28
Rossefield Gth. LS13: Leeds	3D 28
Rossefield Grn. *LS13: Leeds*	*3D 28*
(off Rossefield Dr.)	
Rossefield Gro. LS13: Leeds	3D 28
Rossefield Lawn LS13: Leeds	3D 28
Rossefield Pde. *LS13: Leeds*	*3D 28*
(off Rossefield Wlk.)	
Rossefield Pl. LS13: Leeds	3D 28
Rossefield Ter. LS13: Leeds	3D 28
Rossefield Vw. LS13: Leeds	3D 28
Rossefield Wlk. LS13: Leeds	3D 28
Rossefield Way LS13: Leeds	3D 28
Rossett Bus. Pk. LS13: Leeds	1B 28
Ross Gro. LS13: Leeds	1A 28
Rossington Gro. LS8: Leeds	1A 32
Rossington Pl. LS8: Leeds	1A 32
Rossington Rd. LS8: Leeds	6C 22
Rossington St. LS2: Leeds	3D 4 (5F 31)
Ross Ter. LS13: Leeds	1A 28
Rothbury Gdns. LS16: Leeds	6H 11
ROTHWELL	4G 53
ROTHWELL HAIGH	3F 53
Rothwell Country Pk.	1A 54
Rothwell La. LS26: Rothw	3A 54
Rothwell Sports Cen.	5C 54
ROUNDHAY	2C 22
Roundhay Av. LS8: Leeds	6B 22
Roundhay Ct. LS8: Leeds	2C 22
Roundhay Cres. LS8: Leeds	6B 22
Roundhay Gdns. LS8: Leeds	6B 22
Roundhay Gro. LS8: Leeds	6B 22
Roundhay Mt. LS8: Leeds	6B 22
Roundhay Pk.	2D 22
Roundhay Pk. La. LS17: Leeds	4D 14
Roundhay Pl. LS8: Leeds	6B 22
Roundhay Rd. LS7: Leeds	3H 31
LS8: Leeds	1C 32
Roundhay Vw. LS8: Leeds	6B 22
Roundhead Fold BD10: B'frd	3A 16
Roundhouse Bus. Pk.	
LS12: Leeds	6A 4 (6D 30)
Roundway, The LS27: Morl	5E 49
Roundwood Av. BD10: B'frd	6A 16
Roundwood Glen BD10: B'frd	4A 16
Roundwood Vw. BD10: B'frd	5A 16
Row, The *LS19: Raw*	*5C 8*
(off Apperley La.)	
Rowan Av. BD3: B'frd	6A 26

Rowan Ct. LS19: Raw	4D 8
LS26: Wood	3E 55
Rowans, The LS13: Leeds	2H 27
Rowanwood Gdns. BD10: B'frd	6A 16
Rowland Pl. LS11: Leeds	4F 41
Rowland Rd. LS11: Leeds	4F 41
Rowland Ter. LS11: Leeds	4F 41
Rowlestone Ri. BD10: B'frd	5A 16
Rowton Thorpe BD10: B'frd	5A 16
Roxby Cl. LS9: Leeds	4A 32
Roxholme Av. LS7: Leeds	6A 22
Roxholme Gro. LS7: Leeds	6A 22
Roxholme Pl. LS7: Leeds	6A 22
Roxholme Rd. LS7: Leeds	6A 22
Roxholme Ter. LS7: Leeds	6A 22
Royal Armouries Mus., The	6H 5 (1H 41)
Royal Cl. LS10: Leeds	5H 41
Royal Ct. LS10: Leeds	5H 41
Royal Dr. LS10: Leeds	5H 41
Royal Gdns. LS10: Leeds	5H 41
Royal Gro. LS10: Leeds	5H 41
Royal London Ind. Est., The	
LS11: Leeds	6D 40
Royal Pk. Av. LS6: Leeds	3D 30
Royal Pk. Gro. LS6: Leeds	2D 30
Royal Pk. Mt. LS6: Leeds	2D 30
Royal Pk. Rd. LS6: Leeds	3C 30
Royal Pk. Ter. LS6: Leeds	3D 30
Royal Pk. Vw. LS6: Leeds	2D 30
Royal Pl. LS10: Leeds	5H 41
Royd Moor Rd. BD4: B'frd	6B 36
Royds Av. BD11: Birk	4D 46
Royds Cl. LS26: Rothw	3A 40
Royds Ct. *LS26: Rothw*	*4H 53*
(off Royds La.)	
Royds Farm Rd. LS12: Leeds	5A 40
ROYDS GREEN	6B 54
Royds Gro. WF1: Out	6E 59
Royds Hall Rd. LS12: Leeds	3A 40
Royds La. LS12: Leeds	3A 40
LS26: Oul, Rothw	5H 53
Royds Pk. LS12: Leeds	3A 40
Roydstone Rd. BD3: B'frd	5A 26
Royd Vw. LS28: Pud	1E 37
Royd Well BD11: Birk	4D 46
Royston Cl. WF3: E Ard	5H 57
Royston Hill WF3: E Ard	5H 57
Ruby St. LS9: Leeds	1H 5 (4A 32)
Rufford Av. LS19: Yead	3D 8
Rufford Bank LS19: Yead	3E 9
Rufford Cl. LS19: Yead	3E 9
Rufford Cres. LS19: Yead	3E 9
Rufford Dr. LS19: Yead	3E 9
Rufford Gdns. LS19: Yead	3D 8
RUFFORD PARK	3D 8
Rufford Ridge LS19: Yead	3E 9
Rufford Ri. LS19: Yead	3D 8
Rugby Training Cen.	2G 29
Runswick Av. LS11: Leeds	2D 40
Runswick Pl. LS11: Leeds	2D 40
Runswick St. LS11: Leeds	2D 40
Runswick Ter. LS11: Leeds	2E 41
Rushmoor Rd. BD4: B'frd	5A 36
Rusholme Dr. LS28: Fars	2E 27
Rushton Av. BD3: B'frd	5A 26
Rushton Rd. BD3: B'frd	6A 26
Rushton St. LS28: Cal	5D 16
Rushton Ter. BD3: B'frd	6A 26
Rushworth Cl. WF3: S'ley	6G 59
Ruskin Cres. LS20: Guis	5H 7
Ruskin St. LS28: Stan	4E 27
Russell Gro. BD11: Birk	4D 46
LS8: Leeds	1B 32
Russell St. LS1: Leeds	4D 4 (5F 31)
Ruswarp Cres. BD10: B'frd	5A 16
Ruthven Vw. LS8: Leeds	2C 32
Rutland Cl. LS26: Wood	3D 54
Rutland Ct. *LS28: Pud*	*5G 27*
(off Richardshaw La.)	
Rutland Mt. LS3: Leeds	3A 4 (5D 30)
Rutland St. LS3: Leeds	3A 4 (5E 31)
Rutland Ter. LS3: Leeds	3A 4 (5D 30)
Ryan Pl. LS8: Leeds	1C 32
Rycroft Av. LS13: Leeds	4A 28
Rycroft Cl. LS13: Leeds	4B 28
Rycroft Ct. LS13: Leeds	4B 28
Rycroft Dr. LS13: Leeds	4B 28
Rycroft Gdns. LS13: Leeds	4A 28
Rycroft Grn. LS13: Leeds	4B 28
Rycroft Pl. LS13: Leeds	4B 28
Rycroft Towers LS13: Leeds	4A 28
Rydal Cres. LS27: Morl	4B 50
Rydal Dr. LS27: Morl	4B 50
Rydall Pl. LS11: Leeds	2D 40
Rydall St. LS11: Leeds	2D 40
Rydall Ter. LS11: Leeds	2D 40
Ryder Gdns. LS8: Leeds	4C 22

Ryecroft Cl. BD4: B'frd 5B 36
  WF1: Out 6E 59
Ryedale Av. LS12: Leeds 3H 39
Ryedale Ct. LS14: Leeds 6H 23
Ryedale Holt LS12: Leeds 2A 40
Ryedale Way WF3: W Ard 3B 56
Rye Pl. LS14: Leeds 4H 33
Ryton Dale BD10: B'frd 5A 16

S

Sackville App. LS7: Leeds 2G 31
Sackville St. LS7: Leeds 1G 31
Sadler Cl. LS16: Leeds 5A 12
Sadler Copse LS16: Leeds 5A 12
Sadler Way LS16: Leeds 5A 12
Sagar Pl. LS6: Leeds 1B 30
St Alban App. LS9: Leeds 4E 33
St Alban Cl. LS9: Leeds 4E 33
St Alban Ct. LS9: Leeds 4E 33
St Alban Cres. LS9: Leeds 4E 33
St Alban Gro. LS9: Leeds 4E 33
St Alban Mt. LS9: Leeds 4E 33
St Alban Rd. LS9: Leeds 4E 33
St Alban's Pl. LS2: Leeds 2F 5 (4G 31)
St Alban Vw. LS9: Leeds 4E 33
St Andrews Av. LS27: Morl 6E 49
St Andrews Cl. LS13: Leeds 6G 17
  LS19: Yead 1E 9
  LS27: Morl 6E 49
St Andrew's Ct. LS3: Leeds 5D 30
               (off St Andrew's St.)
  LS19: Yead 1D 8
                  (off Haw La.)
St Andrew's Cft. LS17: Leeds 5F 13
St Andrew's Dr. LS17: Leeds 5G 13
St Andrew's Gro. LS27: Morl 6F 49
St Andrews Pl. LS3: Leeds 5D 30
St Andrew's Rd. LS19: Yead 2E 9
St Andrew's St. LS3: Leeds 5D 30
St Andrews Ter. LS27: Morl 6E 49
St Andrew's Wlk. LS17: Leeds 5G 13
St Annes Ct. LS5: Leeds 1A 30
St Anne's Dr. LS4: Leeds 1A 30
St Annes Pl. LS5: Leeds 1H 29
St Anne's Rd. LS6: Leeds 6A 20
St Anne's Roman Catholic Cathedral
  . . . . .3D 4 (5F 31)
St Anne's St. LS2: Leeds 3D 4 (5F 31)
St Ann's Av. LS4: Leeds 3B 30
St Ann's Cl. LS4: Leeds 2A 30
St Ann's Gdns. LS4: Leeds 2A 30
St Ann's Grn. LS4: Leeds 1A 30
St Ann's La. LS4: Leeds 1A 30
St Ann's Mt. LS4: Leeds 2B 30
St Ann's Ri. LS4: Leeds 2H 29
St Ann's Sq. LS4: Leeds 2A 30
St Ann's Way LS4: Leeds 2A 30
St Anthony's Dr. LS11: Leeds 5D 40
St Anthony's Rd. LS11: Leeds 5C 40
St Anthony's Ter. LS11: Leeds 6C 40
St Augustines Ct. LS8: Leeds 2B 32
               (off Harehills Pl.)
St Barnabas Rd. LS11: Leeds 1F 41
St Bartholomews Cl. LS12: Leeds 6A 30
St Benedicts Chase LS13: Leeds 6D 18
St Benedicts Dr. LS13: Leeds 6E 19
St Benedicts Gdns. LS13: Leeds 6E 19
St Catherine's Bus. Complex
  LS13: Leeds 1D 28
               (off Broad La.)
St Catherines Cres. LS13: Leeds 1D 28
St Catherine's Dr. LS13: Leeds 1D 28
St Catherines Grn. LS13: Leeds 1D 28
St Catherine's Hill LS13: Leeds 1D 28
St Catherines Wlk. LS8: Leeds 5C 22
St Cecilia St. LS2: Leeds 4H 5 (5H 31)
St Chad's Av. LS6: Leeds 5A 20
St Chad's Dr. LS6: Leeds 5A 20
St Chad's Gro. LS6: Leeds 5A 20
St Chad's Ri. LS6: Leeds 5A 20
St Chads Pde. LS16: Leeds 5B 20
St Chads Rd. LS16: Leeds 5B 20
St Chad's Vw. LS6: Leeds 6A 20
St Christopher's Av. LS26: Rothw 4H 53
St Clare's Av. BD2: B'frd 3A 26
St Clements Av. LS26: Rothw 4G 53
St Clements Cl. LS26: Rothw 5F 53
St Clements Ri. LS26: Rothw 4F 53
St Cyprian's Gdns. LS9: Leeds 3D 32
St Davids Cl. WF3: Rob H 1D 58
St David's Ct. LS11: Leeds 1F 41
               (off David St.)
St Davids Gth. WF3: Rob H 1D 58
St Davids Rd. WF3: Rob H 1D 58
St Edmunds Ct. LS8: Leeds 1C 22

St Elmo Gro. LS9: Leeds 5C 32
St Francis Pl. LS11: Leeds 1F 41
St Gabriel Ct. LS14: Leeds 6D 24
St Gabriels Ct. LS18: H'fth 5B 10
ST GEMMA'S HOSPICE 2H 21
St George's Av. LS26: Rothw 2E 53
St George's Cres. LS26: Rothw 2E 53
St Georges Rd. LS1: Leeds 2C 4 (4F 31)
  LS10: Leeds 4H 51
St Helenas Cvn. Pk.
  LS18: H'fth 1C 10
St Helens Av. LS16: Leeds 6B 12
St Helens Cl. LS16: Leeds 6B 12
              (not continuous)
St Helens Cft. LS16: Leeds 6A 12
St Helens Gdns. LS16: Leeds 6A 12
St Helens Gro. LS16: Leeds 6A 12
St Helens La. LS16: Leeds 6H 11
St Helens Way LS16: Leeds 6B 12
St Hilda's Av. LS9: Leeds 1B 42
St Hilda's Cres. LS9: Leeds 1B 42
St Hilda's Gro. LS9: Leeds 1B 42
St Hilda's Mt. LS9: Leeds 1B 42
St Hilda's Pl. LS9: Leeds 1B 42
St Hilda's Rd. LS9: Leeds 1B 42
St Hilda's Ter. BD3: B'frd 5A 26
St Hughes Lodge LS12: Leeds 5A 30
           (off Armley Lodge Rd.)
St Ives Gro. LS12: Leeds 5G 29
St Ives Mt. LS12: Leeds 5G 29
St James App. LS14: Leeds 1A 34
St James Av. LS18: H'fth 2C 18
St James Cl. LS12: Leeds 5F 29
St James Cres. LS28: Pud 6D 26
St James's Ct. LS9: Leeds 3A 32
St James M. LS12: Leeds 5F 29
  LS15: Leeds 2D 34
St James's Ct. LS9: Leeds 3A 32
ST JAMES'S UNIVERSITY HOSPITAL 3B 32
St James Ter. LS18: H'fth 2D 18
St James Wlk. LS18: H'fth 2D 18
St John's Av. LS6: Leeds 3D 30
  LS28: Fars 3F 27
St John's Cen. LS2: Leeds 3E 5 (5G 31)
St John's Church 3E 5 (5G 31)
St John's Cl. LS6: Leeds 3D 30
  LS7: Leeds 1H 31
  LS19: Yead 3C 8
St John's Dr. LS19: Yead 3C 8
St John's Gro. LS6: Leeds 3D 30
St John's Pk. LS29: Men 1B 6
St John's Pl. BD11: Birk 3C 46
  LS5: Leeds 1H 29
             (off Vicarage Ter.)
St John's Rd. LS3: Leeds 2A 4 (4D 30)
  LS19: Yead 3C 8
St John's St. LS26: Oul 4C 54
St John's Ter. LS3: Leeds 3D 30
St Johns Wlk. LS26: Swil 6H 45
St John's Way LS19: Yead 3C 8
St John's Yd. LS26: Oul 4C 54
St Joseph's Ct. LS19: Raw 1D 16
St Lawrence Cl. LS28: Pud 6F 27
St Lawrence St. LS7: Leeds 5H 21
St Lawrence Ter. LS28: Pud 6G 27
St Luke's Cres. LS11: Leeds 3E 41
St Luke's Grn. LS11: Leeds 3E 41
St Luke's Rd. LS11: Leeds 3E 41
St Luke's St. LS11: Leeds 3E 41
St Luke's Vw. LS11: Leeds 3E 41
St Margaret's Av. BD4: B'frd 5A 36
  LS8: Leeds 5C 22
  LS18: H'fth 2B 18
St Margaret's Cl. LS18: H'fth 1B 18
St Margaret's Dr. LS18: Leeds 5C 22
  LS18: H'fth 1B 18
St Margaret's Gro. LS8: Leeds 5C 22
St Margaret's Rd. LS18: H'fth 1B 18
St Margaret's Vw. LS8: Leeds 5C 22
St Mark's Av. LS2: Leeds 3E 31
St Mark's Ct. LS6: Leeds 2F 31
St Mark's Flats LS2: Leeds 2E 31
             (off Providence Ter.)
St Mark's Ho. LS2: Leeds 2F 31
             (off St Mark's Av.)
St Mark's Rd. LS2: Leeds 3F 31
  LS6: Leeds 2E 31
             (not continuous)
St Mark's St. LS2: Leeds 3E 31
St Martin's Av. LS7: Leeds 6G 21
St Martins Ct. WF3: Rob H 1D 58
St Martin's Cres. LS7: Leeds 6H 21
St Martin's Dr. LS7: Leeds 5H 21
St Martins Fold WF3: Rob H 1D 58
St Martin's Gdns. LS7: Leeds 6G 21
St Martin's Gro. LS7: Leeds 6H 21

St Martin's Rd. LS7: Leeds 6H 21
St Martin's Ter. LS7: Leeds 6H 21
St Martin's Vw. LS7: Leeds 6H 21
St Mary's Av. LS26: Swil 6G 45
St Mary's Cl. LS7: Leeds 6H 21
  LS12: Leeds .1B 40
  WF3: W Ard 4A 56
St Mary's Ct. LS7: Leeds 6H 21
ST MARY'S HOSPITAL 5F 29
St Mary's La. LS9: Leeds 5A 32
St Mary's Pk. App. LS12: Leeds 5F 29
St Mary's Pk. Ct. LS12: Leeds 5F 29
St Mary's Pk. Cres.
  LS12: Leeds 5F 29
St Mary's Pk. Grn. LS12: Leeds 5F 29
St Mary's Rd. LS7: Leeds 6H 21
St Mary's Sq. LS27: Morl 5G 49
St Mary's St. LS9: Leeds 3H 5 (5H 31)
St Matthew's St. LS11: Leeds 2E 41
St Matthews Wlk. LS7: Leeds 3G 21
St Matthew Way LS14: Leeds 6E 25
St Matthias Ct. LS4: Leeds 3B 30
St Matthias Gro. LS4: Leeds 3B 30
St Matthias St. LS4: Leeds 3B 30
             (not continuous)
St Matthias Ter. LS4: Leeds 3B 30
St Michael Ct. LS13: Leeds 2C 28
St Michael's Ct. LS6: Leeds 6B 20
St Michael's Cres. LS6: Leeds 1B 30
St Michael's Gro. LS6: Leeds 1B 30
St Michael's La. LS4: Leeds 2A 30
  LS6: Leeds 1B 30
St Michael's Rd. LS6: Leeds 1B 30
St Michael's Ter. LS6: Leeds 1B 30
St Michael's Vs. LS6: Leeds 1B 30
           (off St Michael's Cres.)
St Oswald's Gth. LS20: Guis 4H 7
St Oswald's Ter. LS20: Guis 4G 7
St Paul's Av. BD11: Birk 4D 46
St Paul's Pl. LS1: Leeds 4C 4 (5F 31)
St Paul's Rd. BD11: Birk 4D 46
St Paul's St. LS1: Leeds 4B 4 (5E 31)
  LS27: Morl 6H 49
St Peter's Av. LS26: Rothw 4H 53
St Peter's Bldgs. LS9: Leeds 4H 5 (6H 31)
St Peter's Ct. LS11: Leeds 3G 41
  LS13: Leeds .2D 28
St Peter's Cres. LS27: Morl 3G 49
St Peter's Gdns. LS13: Leeds 2C 28
St Peter's Mt. LS13: Leeds 3D 28
St Peter's Pl. LS9: Leeds 4H 5 (5H 31)
St Peter's Sq. LS9: Leeds 4H 5 (5H 31)
St Peter's St. LS2: Leeds 4G 5 (5H 31)
St Peters Vw. LS27: Morl 3G 49
             (off Rooms La.)
St Peter's Way LS29: Men 1B 6
St Philip's Av. LS10: Leeds 4F 51
St Philip's Cl. LS10: Leeds 4F 51
St Stephen's Ct. LS9: Leeds 5B 32
St Stephen's Rd. LS9: Leeds 5B 32
  LS28: Cal 4C 16
St Thomas Row LS2: Leeds 2G 5 (4H 31)
St Vincent Ct. LS28: Pud 1G 37
             (off Littlemoor Rd.)
St Vincent Rd. LS28: Pud 1G 37
St Wilfrid's Av. LS8: Leeds 1C 32
             (not continuous)
St Wilfrid's Cir. LS8: Leeds 2D 32
St Wilfrid's Cres. LS8: Leeds 1D 32
St Wilfrid's Dr. LS8: Leeds 1C 32
St Wilfrid's Gth. LS8: Leeds 2D 32
St Wilfrid's Gro. LS8: Leeds 1C 32
St Wilfrid's St. LS28: Cal 4D 16
Salamanca Cres. LS10: Leeds 5A 52
Salcombe Pl. BD4: B'frd 5A 36
Salem Pl. LS10: Leeds 6F 5 (1G 41)
Salisbury Av. LS12: Leeds 5A 30
Salisbury Cl. LS18: H'fth 2D 18
Salisbury Gro. LS12: Leeds 5A 30
Salisbury M. LS18: H'fth 2D 18
  WF3: Ting 2B 56
Salisbury Pl. LS28: Cal 5C 16
Salisbury Rd. LS12: Leeds 5A 30
Salisbury St. LS19: Raw 5D 8
  LS28: Cal 5C 16
Salisbury Ter. LS12: Leeds 5A 30
Salisbury Vw. LS12: Leeds 5A 30
  LS18: H'fth 2D 18
Salmon Cres. LS18: H'fth 2C 18
Salters Gdn. LS28: Pud 6G 27
             (off Crawshaw Rd.)
Samara W. Mt. LS2: Leeds 2A 4
Samuel Dr. WF3: S'ley 6G 59
Sandacre Cl. BD10: B'frd 2A 26
Sandbed Cl. LS15: Leeds 2D 34
Sandbed La. LS15: Leeds 2D 34
Sandbed Lawns LS15: Leeds 2D 34

Sanderling Gth. LS10: Leeds 4H 51
Sanderling Way LS10: Leeds 4H 51
Sandfield Av. LS6: Leeds 5C 20
Sandfield Gth. LS6: Leeds 5C 20
Sandfield Vw. LS6: Leeds 5C 20
 (off Sandfield Av.)
SANDFORD 1E 29
Sandford Pl. LS5: Leeds 1G 29
Sandford Rd. LS5: Leeds 2H 29
Sandgate Wlk. BD4: B'frd 5B 36
Sandhill Ct. LS17: Leeds 6H 13
Sandhill Cres. LS17: Leeds 5A 14
Sandhill Dr. LS17: Leeds 5H 13
Sandhill Gro. LS17: Leeds 4A 14
Sandhill La. LS17: Leeds 6H 13
Sandhill Lawns LS17: Leeds 6H 13
Sandhill Mt. LS17: Leeds 4A 14
Sandhill Oval LS17: Leeds 4A 14
Sandhill Vs. LS14: T'ner 1E 25
Sandhurst Av. LS8: Leeds 2C 32
Sandhurst Gro. LS8: Leeds 2C 32
Sandhurst Mt. LS8: Leeds 1C 32
Sandhurst Pl. LS8: Leeds 2C 32
Sandhurst Rd. LS8: Leeds 2C 32
Sandhurst St. LS28: Cal 4C 16
Sandhurst Ter. LS8: Leeds 2C 32
Sandiford Cl. LS15: Leeds 2D 34
Sandiford Ter. LS15: Leeds 2D 34
Sandleas Way LS15: Leeds 3F 35
Sandlewood Cl. LS11: Leeds 2E 41
Sandlewood Ct. LS6: Leeds 2D 20
Sandlewood Cres. LS6: Leeds 2D 20
Sandlewood Grn. LS11: Leeds 2F 41
Sandmead Cl. BD4: B'frd 4A 36
 LS27: Morl 3G 49
Sandmead Cft. LS27: Morl 3G 49
Sandmead Way LS27: Morl 3G 49
Sandmoor Av. LS17: Leeds 3H 13
Sandmoor Chase LS17: Leeds 4H 13
Sandmoor Cl. LS17: Leeds 4H 13
Sandmoor Dr. LS17: Leeds 3H 13
Sandmoor Grn. LS17: Leeds 3G 13
Sandmoor La. LS17: Leeds 3H 13
Sandmoor M. LS17: Leeds 4H 13
Sandon Gro. LS10: Leeds 5A 42
Sandon Mt. LS10: Leeds 5A 42
Sandon Pl. LS10: Leeds 5A 42
Sandpiper App. LS27: Morl 6A 50
Sandringham App. LS17: Leeds 6A 14
Sandringham Av. LS28: Pud 1G 37
Sandringham Cl. LS27: Morl 4A 50
Sandringham Ct. LS17: Leeds 5H 13
Sandringham Cres. LS17: Leeds 6H 13
Sandringham Dr. LS17: Leeds 6H 13
Sandringham Fold LS27: Morl 4A 50
Sandringham Gdns. LS17: Leeds 6H 13
Sandringham Grn. LS17: Leeds 5A 14
Sandringham Ho. LS17: Leeds 4H 13
Sandringham Mt. LS17: Leeds 6A 14
Sandringham Way LS17: Leeds 6H 13
Sandstone Dr. LS12: Leeds 6C 28
Sandway LS15: Leeds 3B 34
Sandway Gdns. LS15: Leeds 3B 34
Sandway Gro. LS15: Leeds 3B 34
Sandyacres LS26: Rothw 3H 53
Sandyacres Cres. LS26: Rothw 3H 53
Sandyacres Dr. LS26: Rothw 3H 53
Sandy Bank Av. LS26: Rothw 3H 53
Sandy Gro. LS26: Rothw 3H 53
Sandy Way LS19: Yead .2D 8
Sandywood Ct. LS18: H'fth 4H 7
Santorini LS12: Leeds 5A 4 (6E 31)
Sarah St. WF3: E Ard 3H 57
Sardinia St. LS10: Leeds 1D 52
Savannah Way LS10: Leeds 1D 52
Savile Av. LS7: Leeds 2H 31
Savile Dr. LS7: Leeds 1H 31
Savile Mt. LS7: Leeds 2H 31
Savile Pk. Rd. BD19: Hun 6A 46
Savile Pl. LS7: Leeds 2H 31
Savile Rd. LS7: Leeds 2H 31
Saville Cl. WF3: Loft 2E 59
Saville Grn. LS9: Leeds 5B 32
Saville's Sq. LS27: Morl 5G 49
 (off Queen St.)
Savins Mill Way LS5: Leeds 1G 29
Savoy Ct. LS28: Stan 4F 27
Saw Mill St. LS11: Leeds 1F 41
Saw Mill Yd. LS11: Leeds 1F 41
Saxon Ct. LS17: Leeds .6F 13
Saxon Ga. LS17: Leeds .1F 21
Saxon Grn. LS17: Leeds 1E 21
Saxon Gro. LS17: Leeds 6E 13
Saxon Mt. LS17: Leeds .6F 13
Saxon Rd. LS17: Leeds .1E 21
Saxstead Ri. LS12: Leeds 1A 40

Saxton Gdns. LS9: Leeds 6A 32
 (off The Close)
 LS9: Leeds 6A 32
 (off The Drive)
Saxton Ho. LS19: Yead 3D 8
Saxton La. LS9: Leeds 5H 5 (6A 32)
Sayers Cl. LS5: Leeds 1H 29
Sayner La. LS10: Leeds .1H 41
Sayner Rd. LS10: Leeds 1H 41
Scala Ct. LS10: Leeds 2H 41
Scampston Dr. WF3: E Ard 2H 57
Scarborough Junc. LS13: Leeds 4C 28
Scarborough La. WF3: Ting 3B 56
Scarborough St. WF3: Ting 2B 56
Scarcroft Vw. LS17: Leeds 3H 15
Scargill Bldgs. LS27: Morl 5B 50
Scargill Cl. LS9: Leeds .4B 32
Scargill Grange LS9: Leeds 5B 32
Scarth Av. LS9: Leeds 3C 32
Scatcherd Gro. LS27: Morl 5F 49
Scatcherd La. LS27: Morl 6F 49
Scatcherd Pk. Av. LS27: Morl 4G 49
Scatcherd's Bldgs. LS27: Morl 3G 49
Schofield Ct. LS27: Morl 5G 49
 (off Queenscourt)
Scholars Way LS15: Leeds 1E 45
Scholebroke La. LS28: Pud 4E 37
SCHOLEBROOK 4E 37
Scholebrook Ct. BD4: B'frd 6A 36
 (off Broadfield Cl.)
Scholebrook La. BD4: B'frd 4E 37
SCHOLES 4F 25
Scholes La. LS15: Leeds 3E 25
Scholes Lodge La. LS15: Scho 6G 25
School Cl. LS12: N Far 4D 38
School Cft. LS26: Rothw 3G 53
School La. LS6: Leeds 5C 20
 LS7: Leeds 5G 21
 LS15: Leeds 1E 45
 (Colton Rd. E.)
 LS15: Leeds 5A 34
 (Pinfold Gro.)
 LS17: Wike 1D 14
School M. LS12: Leeds .6A 30
School St. LS27: Chur 1A 50
 LS27: Morl 5H 49
 LS28: Fars 2F 27
 LS28: Pud 1F 37
 (not continuous)
 WF3: W Ard 6B 56
School Vw. LS6: Leeds .2C 30
Scotch Pk. Trad. Est. LS12: Leeds 5B 30
SCOTLAND 4B 10
Scotland Cl. LS18: H'fth .6B 10
Scotland La. LS18: H'fth 1A 10
Scotland Mill La. LS6: Leeds 1D 20
 LS17: Leeds 1D 20
Scotland Way LS18: H'fth 5A 10
Scotland Wood Rd. LS17: Leeds 1D 20
Scott Cl. LS26: Swil 6G 45
SCOTT GREEN 2B 48
Scott Grn. LS27: Gil 1B 48
Scott Grn. Cres. LS27: Gil 1B 48
Scott Grn. Dr. LS27: Gil .1B 48
Scott Grn. Gro. LS27: Gil 1C 48
Scott Grn. Mt. LS27: Gil 1B 48
Scott Grn. Vw. LS27: Gil 1C 48
SCOTT HALL 6G 21
Scott Hall Av. LS7: Leeds 6G 21
Scott Hall Cres. LS7: Leeds 5F 21
Scott Hall Dr. LS7: Leeds 1G 31
Scott Hall Grn. LS7: Leeds 6G 21
Scott Hall Gro. LS7: Leeds 6G 21
Scott Hall Pl. LS7: Leeds 6G 21
Scott Hall Rd. LS7: Leeds 4F 21
 LS17: Leeds 4F 21
Scott Hall Row LS7: Leeds 1H 31
Scott Hall Sports Cen. 5G 21
Scott Hall Sq. LS7: Leeds 6G 21
Scott Hall St. LS7: Leeds 1G 31
Scott Hall Ter. LS7: Leeds 6G 21
Scott Hall Wlk. LS7: Leeds 1G 31
Scott Hall Way LS7: Leeds 5G 21
Scott La. LS27: Morl 6D 48
Scotts Almshouse's
 LS10: Leeds 6A 42
Scotts Bldgs. LS6: Leeds 5B 20
 (off Mansfield Pl.)
Scott St. LS28: Pud 1H 37
Scott Wood La. LS7: Leeds 6F 21
SEACROFT 6A 24
Seacroft Av. LS14: Leeds 6B 24
Seacroft Cres. LS14: Leeds 6B 24
Seacroft Family Activity Cen. 2A 34
Seacroft Ga. LS14: Leeds 6B 24
 (not continuous)
SEACROFT HOSPITAL 4A 34

Seacroft Ind. Est. LS14: Leeds 4A 24
 (Limewood App.)
 LS14: Leeds 3B 24
 (Sherburn Rd. Nth., not continuous)
Seaforth Av. LS9: Leeds 2C 32
Seaforth Gro. LS9: Leeds 2C 32
Seaforth Mt. LS9: Leeds 2C 32
Seaforth Pl. LS9: Leeds 2C 32
Seaforth Rd. LS9: Leeds 2C 32
Seaforth Ter. LS9: Leeds 2C 32
Second Av. LS12: Leeds 6C 30
 LS19: Raw 4E 9
 LS26: Rothw 2H 53
Sedbergh Cl. LS15: Leeds 6G 33
Sefton Av. LS11: Leeds .4E 41
Sefton Ct. LS6: Leeds 5B 20
Sefton St. LS11: Leeds .4F 41
Sefton Ter. LS11: Leeds 4E 41
Selby Av. LS9: Leeds 5G 33
Selby Rd. LS9: Leeds 5G 33
 LS15: Leeds, Swil C 6A 34
 LS25: Gar 1G 45
Select Ct. LS28: Fars 1F 27
Seminary St. LS2: Leeds 1B 4 (4E 31)
Servia Dr. LS7: Leeds 2G 31
Servia Gdns. LS7: Leeds 2G 31
Servia Hill LS6: Leeds 2F 31
 LS7: Leeds 2F 31
Servia Rd. LS7: Leeds 2F 31
Service Rd. LS9: Leeds .5E 43
Seven Hills Point LS27: Morl 4H 49
Seventh Av. LS26: Rothw 2A 54
Severn Rd. LS10: Leeds .4B 42
Severn Way LS10: Leeds 3B 42
Sewage Works Rd. LS9: Leeds 4E 43
SHADWELL 5H 15
Shadwell La. LS17: Leeds 1H 21
Shadwell Pk. Av. LS17: Leeds 4E 15
Shadwell Pk. Cl. LS17: Shad 4E 15
Shadwell Pk. Ct. LS17: Shad 5E 15
Shadwell Pk. Dr. LS17: Shad 5E 15
Shadwell Pk. Gdns. LS17: Shad 4E 15
Shadwell Pk. Gro. LS17: Shad 5E 15
Shadwell Wlk. LS17: Leeds 6A 14
Shaftesbury Av. LS8: Leeds 2C 22
Shaftesbury Pde. LS9: Leeds 4E 33
Shaftesbury Rd. LS8: Leeds 1C 22
Shafton La. LS11: Leeds 2D 40
Shafton Pl. LS11: Leeds 2D 40
Shafton St. LS11: Leeds 2D 40
Shafton Vw. LS11: Leeds 2D 40
Shakespeare App. LS9: Leeds 4B 32
Shakespeare Av. LS9: Leeds 4B 32
Shakespeare Cl. LS9: Leeds 4B 32
 LS20: Guis 5H 7
Shakespeare Ct. LS9: Leeds 4B 32
 (off Shakespeare App.)
Shakespeare Gdns. LS9: Leeds 4B 32
Shakespeare Grange LS9: Leeds 4B 32
Shakespeare Lawn LS9: Leeds 4B 32
Shakespeare Rd. LS20: Guis 5G 7
Shakespeare St. LS9: Leeds 3B 32
Shakespeare Towers LS9: Leeds 4B 32
Shakespeare Va. LS9: Leeds 4B 32
Shakespeare Wlk. LS9: Leeds 4B 32
Shancara Ct. WF3: Ting .2C 56
Shannon Rd. LS9: Leeds 5A 32
Shannon St. LS9: Leeds .5A 32
Sharp Ho. Pl. LS10: Leeds 5B 52
Sharp Ho. Rd. LS10: Leeds 5A 52
Sharp La. LS10: Leeds 4A 52
 (Dolphin Rd.)
 LS10: Leeds 4H 51
 (Dunlin Dr.)
 WF3: Rob H 4A 52
Sharp M. LS6: Leeds 6D 20
Sharp Row LS28: Pud 1G 37
Shaw Cl. LS20: Guis 5H 7
SHAW LANE 1C 8
Shaw La. LS6: Leeds 6B 20
 LS20: Guis 4H 7
Shaw La. Gdns. LS20: Guis 4H 7
Shaw Leys LS19: Yead 1C 8
Shaw Royd LS19: Yead .1C 8
Shaw Royd Ct. LS19: Yead 1C 8
 (off Shaw Royd)
Shaw Vs. LS20: Guis 4H 7
 (off Queensway)
Shay Ct. LS6: Leeds 2F 31
Shayfield La. WF3: Carl, Loft 1E 59
Shay La. BD4: B'frd 4B 36
Shay St. LS6: Leeds 2F 31
Sheaf St. LS10: Leeds 1H 41
Shearers Ho. LS9: Leeds 6H 5
 (off East St.)
Shear's Yd. LS2: Leeds 5G 5 (6H 31)
SHEEPSCAR 2H 31

Sheepscar Ct.—Southleigh Rd.

Sheepscar Ct. LS7: Leeds 3H **31**
Sheepscar Gro. LS7: Leeds 1G **5** (4H **31**)
Sheepscar Row LS7: Leeds 3H **31**
Sheepscar St. Nth. LS7: Leeds 2G **31**
Sheepscar St. Sth. LS7: Leeds 1H **5** (3H **31**)
Sheepscar Way LS7: Leeds 2H **31**
Shelldrake Dr. LS10: Leeds 4H **51**
Shelley Cl. LS26: Oul 6C **54**
Shelley Cres. LS26: Oul 6C **54**
Shelley Wlk. WF3: S'ley 5G **59**
Shell La. LS28: Cal 5D **16**
Shepcote Cl. LS16: Leeds 6F **11**
Shepcote Cres. LS16: Leeds 6F **11**
Shepherd's Gro. LS7: Leeds 1A **32**
Shepherd's La. LS7: Leeds 1A **32**
LS8: Leeds 1A **32**
Shepherd's Pl. LS8: Leeds 1B **32**
Sherbourne Dr. LS6: Leeds 2C **20**
Sherbrooke Av. LS15: Leeds 6H **33**
Sherburn App. LS14: Leeds 5C **24**
Sherburn Cl. BD11: Birk 3D **46**
LS14: Leeds 5C 24
(off Sherburn App.)
Sherburn Ct. *LS14: Leeds 5C 24*
(off Sherburn App.)
Sherburn Gro. BD11: Birk 3D **46**
Sherburn Pl. LS14: Leeds 5C **24**
Sherburn Rd. LS14: Leeds 5C **24**
Sherburn Rd. Nth. LS14: Leeds 3B **24**
Sherburn Row *LS14: Leeds 5C 24*
(off Sherburn App.)
Sherburn Sq. *LS14: Leeds 5C 24*
(off Sherburn Pl.)
Sherburn Wlk. *LS14: Leeds 5C 24*
(off York Rd.)
Sheridan Cl. LS28: Pud 1H **37**
Sheridan Ct. LS28: Pud 1H **37**
Sheridan Ho. LS27: Gil 3C **48**
Sheridan St. WF1: Out 6E **59**
Sheridan Way LS28: Pud 1H **37**
Sherwood Gdns. WF3: Loft 1D **58**
Sherwood Grn. WF3: Rob H 6C **52**
Sherwood Ind. Est. WF3: Rob H 6D **52**
Sherwood Wlk. LS10: Leeds 5A **52**
Sherwood Way LS26: Wood 2B **54**
Shetcliffe La. BD4: B'frd 6A **36**
Shield Cl. LS15: Leeds 2E **35**
Shipton M. LS27: Morl 6H **49**
Ship Yd. LS1: Leeds 4E **5**
Shire Cl. LS27: Morl 1A **56**
Shire Ct. LS27: Morl 2A **56**
Shiredene LS6: Leeds 6C **20**
Shire Oak Rd. LS6: Leeds 6C **20**
Shire Oak St. LS6: Leeds 6B **20**
Shire Rd. LS27: Morl 1A **56**
Shires Gro. WF3: S'ley 6H **59**
Shires Rd. LS20: Guis 5G **7**
Shirley Dr. LS13: Leeds 1C **28**
Shirley Rd. BD4: B'frd 6A **36**
Sholebroke Av. LS7: Leeds 1H **31**
Sholebroke Ct. LS7: Leeds 1H **31**
Sholebroke Mt. LS7: Leeds 1G **31**
Sholebroke Pl. LS7: Leeds 1H **31**
Sholebroke St. LS7: Leeds 1G **31**
Sholebroke Ter. LS7: Leeds 6H **21**
Sholebroke Vw. LS7: Leeds 1H **31**
Shop La. WF3: Loft 3D **58**
Shoreham Rd. LS12: Leeds 6A **30**
Short La. LS7: Leeds 4G **21**
Shortway LS28: Stan 4C **26**
Showcase Cinema
Birstall 5B **48**
Shutts, The LS26: Rothw 4E **53**
Siddall St. LS11: Leeds 1F **41**
Sidings, The LS20: Guis 4F **7**
Sidney St. LS1: Leeds 4F **5** (5G **31**)
Siegen Cl. LS27: Morl 5G **49**
Siegen Mnr. *LS27: Morl 5G 49*
(off Wesley St.)
Silk Mill App. LS16: Leeds 1E **19**
Silk Mill Av. LS16: Leeds 6D **10**
Silk Mill Bank LS16: Leeds 1D **18**
Silk Mill Cl. LS16: Leeds 6D **10**
Silk Mill Dr. LS16: Leeds 1D **18**
Silk Mill Gdns. LS16: Leeds 1D **18**
Silk Mill Grn. LS16: Leeds 1E **19**
Silk Mill M. LS16: Leeds 1F **19**
Silk Mill Rd. LS16: Leeds 1D **18**
Silk Mill Way LS16: Leeds 1E **19**
Silkstone Ct. LS15: Leeds 4C **34**
Silkstone Way LS15: Leeds 4C **34**
Silver Ct. LS13: Leeds 4H **27**
Silver Cross Way LS20: Guis 4F **7**
Silverdale Av. LS17: Leeds 4D **14**
LS20: Guis 5G **7**
Silverdale Cl. LS20: Guis 6G **7**
Silverdale Cres. LS20: Guis 5G **7**
Silverdale Dr. LS20: Guis 6G **7**
Silverdale Grange LS20: Guis 6G **7**
Silverdale Gro. LS20: Guis 6F **7**
Silverdale Mt. LS20: Guis 6G **7**
Silverdale Rd. LS20: Guis 6F **7**
Silverhill Dr. BD3: B'frd 4A **26**
Silver Ho. LS2: Leeds 1E **5**
Silver La. LS19: Yead 2D **8**
Silver Royd Av. LS12: Leeds 1F **39**
Silver Royd Cl. LS12: Leeds 1F **39**
Silver Royd Dr. LS12: Leeds 1F **39**
Silver Royd Gth. LS12: Leeds 1F **39**
Silver Royd Gro. LS12: Leeds 1F **39**
SILVER ROYD HILL 1F **39**
Silver Royd Hill LS12: Leeds 1F **39**
Silver Royd Pl. LS12: Leeds 1F **39**
Silver Royd Rd. LS12: Leeds 1F **39**
Silver Royd St. LS12: Leeds 1F **39**
Silver Royd Ter. LS12: Leeds 1F **39**
Silver Royd Way LS12: Leeds 1F **39**
Silver St. LS11: Leeds 1E **41**
Simmons Ct. LS9: Leeds 1B **42**
Simmons Way LS8: Leeds 1D **32**
Simon Cl. BD4: B'frd 5B **36**
Simon Marks Ct. *LS12: Leeds 2A 40*
(off Lynwood Gth.)
Simpson Gro. LS12: Leeds 6B **30**
Simpsons Fold E. LS10: Leeds 6F **5** (6G **31**)
Simpsons Fold W. LS10: Leeds 6F **5**
Simpson St. WF3: E Ard 3A **58**
Sir George Martin Dr.
LS16: Leeds 5B **12**
Sir Karl Cohen Sq. LS12: Leeds 6H **29**
Siskin Ct. LS27: Morl 6H **49**
Sissons Av. LS10: Leeds 5F **51**
Sissons Cres. LS10: Leeds 5F **51**
Sissons Dr. LS10: Leeds 5F **51**
Sissons Grn. LS10: Leeds 5F **51**
Sissons Gro. LS10: Leeds 5F **51**
Sissons La. LS10: Leeds 5F **51**
Sissons Mt. LS10: Leeds 6E **51**
Sissons Pl. LS10: Leeds 4F **51**
Sissons Rd. LS10: Leeds 5E **51**
Sissons Row LS10: Leeds 5F **51**
Sissons St. LS10: Leeds 5F **51**
Sissons Ter. LS10: Leeds 5E **51**
Sissons Vw. LS10: Leeds 6E **51**
Sixth Av. LS26: Rothw 2A **54**
Sizers Ct. LS19: Yead 4C **8**
Skellow Dr. BD4: B'frd 6C **36**
Skelton Av. LS9: Leeds 5D **32**
Skelton Cres. LS9: Leeds 5D **32**
Skelton Grange Cotts. LS9: Leeds 4E **43**
Skelton Grange Rd. LS10: Leeds 5D **42**
Skelton Mt. LS9: Leeds 5D **32**
Skelton Pl. *LS9: Leeds 5D 32*
(off Ivy Av.)
Skelton Rd. LS9: Leeds 5D **32**
Skeltons La. LS14: T'ner, Leeds 2B **24**
Skelton St. LS9: Leeds 5D **32**
Skelton Ter. LS9: Leeds 5D **32**
Skelwith App. LS14: Leeds 3A **34**
Skelwith Wlk. LS14: Leeds 3A **34**
Skinner La. LS7: Leeds 1G **5** (4H **31**)
Skinner St. LS1: Leeds 4A **4**
Skipton Cl. WF3: E Ard 2H **57**
Skye Vw. LS26: Rothw 4H **53**
Skyline LS2: Leeds 4H **5** (5H **31**)
Sky Plaza LS2: Leeds 1E **5**
Slade Ho. *BD2: B'frd 3A 26*
(off St Clares Av.)
SLAID HILL 4D **14**
Slaid Hill Ct. LS17: Leeds 4D **14**
Slaters Rd. LS28: Stan 4G **27**
Sledmere Cft. LS14: Leeds 5C **24**
Sledmere Gth. LS14: Leeds 5C **24**
Sledmere Grn. *LS14: Leeds 5C 24*
(off Sledmere Pl.)
Sledmere La. LS14: Leeds 5C **24**
(not continuous)
Sledmere Pl. LS14: Leeds 5C **24**
Sledmere Sq. *LS14: Leeds 5C 24*
(off Sledmere Pl.)
Slingsby Cl. BD10: B'frd 3A **16**
Smalewell Cl. LS28: Pud 1F **37**
Smalewell Dr. LS28: Pud 1E **37**
Smalewell Gdns. LS28: Pud 1E **37**
Smalewell Grn. LS28: Pud 1F **37**
Smalewell Rd. LS28: Pud 1E **37**
(Smalewell Dr.)
LS28: Pud 1D **36**
(Tyersal La.)
Smeaton App. LS15: Leeds 2E **35**
Smeaton Ct. LS18: H'fth 3E **19**
Smeaton Gro. LS26: Swil 5G **45**
Smiths Cotts. *LS16: Leeds 5B 20*
(off Weetwood La.)
Smithson St. LS26: Rothw 5H **53**
Smithy La. LS16: Leeds 3E **11**
WF3: Ting 3D **56**
Smithy Mills La. LS16: Leeds 1B **20**
Smools La. LS27: Morl, Chur 2H **49**
Snaith Wood Dr. LS19: Raw 2E **17**
Snaith Wood M. LS19: Raw 2E **17**
Snake La. LS9: Leeds 1C **42**
Snowden App. LS13: Leeds 2E **29**
Snowden Cl. LS13: Leeds 3D **28**
Snowden Cres. LS13: Leeds 3D **28**
Snowden Fold LS13: Leeds 3D **28**
Snowden Gdns. LS13: Leeds 3E **29**
Snowden Grn. *LS13: Leeds 3D 28*
(off Snowden Cl.)
Snowden Gro. LS13: Leeds 3D **28**
Snowden Lawn LS13: Leeds 3D **28**
Snowden Royd LS13: Leeds 2D **28**
Snowden Va. LS13: Leeds 3D **28**
Snowden Wlk. LS13: Leeds 3D **28**
Snowden Way LS13: Leeds 2D **28**
Sofia Cl. LS9: Leeds 3D **32**
Sofia Ct. *LS13: Leeds 1D 28*
(off Wellington Gth.)
Somerdale Cl. LS13: Leeds 4D **28**
Somerdale Gdns. LS13: Leeds 4D **28**
Somerdale Gro. LS13: Leeds 4D **28**
Somerdale Wlk. LS13: Leeds 4D **28**
Somerset Rd. LS28: Pud 5G **27**
Somers Pl. LS1: Leeds 4C **4**
Somers St. LS1: Leeds 4B **4** (5F **31**)
Somerton Dr. BD4: B'frd 5A **36**
Somerville Av. LS14: Leeds 3H **33**
Somerville Dr. LS14: Leeds 3H **33**
Somerville Grn. LS14: Leeds 3H **33**
Somerville Gro. LS14: Leeds 2H **33**
Somerville Mt. LS14: Leeds 3H **33**
Somerville Vw. LS14: Leeds 3H **33**
Sommerville M. LS28: Stan 4E **27**
Soothill La. WF17: Bat, Dew 6A **56**
Soureby Cross Way BD4: E Bier 2B **46**
Sth. Accommodation Rd.
LS9: Leeds 2A **42**
LS10: Leeds 2H **41**
South Cl. LS20: Guis 5D **6**
Southcote St. *LS28: Fars 3F 27*
(off Northcote St.)
South Cft. Av. BD11: Birk 3C **46**
South Cft. Dr. BD11: Birk 2C **46**
South Cft. Ga. BD11: Birk 3C **46**
South Dr. LS20: Guis 5D **6**
LS28: Fars 2F **27**
South End Av. LS13: Leeds 4E **29**
South End Ct. LS13: Leeds 3E **29**
South End Gro. LS13: Leeds 4E **29**
South End Mt. LS13: Leeds 4E **29**
South End Ter. LS13: Leeds 4E **29**
Sth. Farm Cres. LS9: Leeds 3E **33**
Sth. Farm Rd. LS9: Leeds 3E **33**
Southfield Av. LS17: Leeds 1A **22**
Southfield Dr. LS17: Leeds 1A **22**
Southfield Mt. *LS10: Leeds 6A 42*
(off Woodville Mt.)
LS12: Leeds 6A **30**
Southfield St. LS12: Leeds 6A **30**
Southfield Ter. BD11: Birk 3C **46**
LS12: Leeds 6A 30
(off Southfield Mt.)
Southgate LS20: Guis 6D **6**
LS26: Oul 3C **54**
South Hill LS10: Leeds 2B **52**
South Hill Cl. LS10: Leeds 2B **52**
South Hill Cft. LS10: Leeds 2B **52**
South Hill Gdns. LS10: Leeds 2B **52**
South Hill Gro. LS10: Leeds 2B **52**
South Hill Ri. LS10: Leeds 2B **52**
South Hill Way LS10: Leeds 2B **52**
Southlands LS18: H'fth 2B **18**
Southlands Av. LS17: Leeds 3G **21**
LS19: Raw 1F **17**
Southlands Cl. LS17: Leeds 2G **21**
Southlands Cres. LS17: Leeds 3G **21**
Southlands Dr. LS17: Leeds 3G **21**
South Lea WF3: Ting 2D **56**
South Lee LS18: H'fth 2B **18**
Sth. Leeds Bus. Cen. LS11: Leeds 2G **41**
South Leeds Sports Cen. 2F **41**
South Leeds Tennis Cen. 1G **51**
Southleigh Av. LS11: Leeds 1E **51**
Southleigh Cres. LS11: Leeds 1E **51**
Southleigh Cft. LS11: Leeds 1F **51**
Southleigh Dr. LS11: Leeds 1E **51**
Southleigh Gdns. LS11: Leeds 1E **51**
Southleigh Gth. LS11: Leeds 1F **51**
Southleigh Grange LS11: Leeds 1F **51**
Southleigh Gro. LS11: Leeds 1E **51**
Southleigh Rd. LS11: Leeds 1E **51**

102 A-Z Leeds

Southleigh Vw. LS11: Leeds ...1E 51
Sth. Nelson St. LS27: Morl ...4G 49
Southolme Cl. LS5: Leeds ...5F 19
South Pde. LS1: Leeds ...4D 4 (5F 31)
LS6: Leeds ...6B 20
LS27: Morl ...5H 49
LS28: Pud ...1F 37
South Pde. Cl. LS28: Pud ...1G 37
South Pk. Ter. LS28: Pud ...3H 37
South Parkway LS14: Leeds ...2G 33
(not continuous)
Sth. Parkway App. LS14: Leeds ...2G 33
South Pl. LS27: Morl ...5H 49
(off South St.)
Sth. Queen St. LS27: Morl ...6H 49
South Row LS18: H'fth ...2C 18
Southroyd Gdns. LS28: Pud ...2H 37
Southroyd Pde. LS28: Pud ...2G 37
(off Fartown)
Southroyd Pk. LS28: Pud ...2G 37
(not continuous)
Southroyd Ri. LS28: Pud ...2G 37
Southroyd Vs. LS28: Pud ...2G 37
South St. LS19: Raw ...5D 8
LS27: Morl ...5H 49
South Vw. BD10: B'frd ...4A 16
LS15: Leeds ...3C 34
(off Church La.)
LS18: H'fth ...4C 18
LS19: Yead ...6H 7
LS20: Guis ...4G 7
LS26: Rothw ...3G 53
LS27: Chur ...2H 49
LS28: Pud ...6H 27
LS28: Stan ...4E 27
LS29: Men ...2C 6
WF3: W Ard ...6B 56
Southview Bus. Pk. LS20: Guis ...6G 7
South Vw. Cl. BD4: E Bier ...2A 46
LS19: Yead ...6H 7
South Vw. Cotts. LS17: Shad ...6H 15
South Vw. Cres. LS19: Yead ...6H 7
South Vw. Dr. BD4: E Bier ...2B 46
South Vw. Rd. BD4: E Bier ...2B 46
LS19: Yead ...2D 8
South Vw. Ter. LS19: Yead ...3E 9
Southwaite Cl. LS14: Leeds ...1H 33
Southwaite Gth. LS14: Leeds ...1H 33
Southwaite La. LS14: Leeds ...1H 33
Southwaite Lawn LS14: Leeds ...1H 33
Southwaite Pl. LS14: Leeds ...1H 33
South Way BD4: E Bier ...2A 46
Southway LS18: H'fth ...6A 10
LS20: Guis ...5C 6
Southwood Cl. LS14: Leeds ...1C 34
Southwood Cres. LS14: Leeds ...1C 34
Southwood Ga. LS14: Leeds ...1C 34
Southwood Rd. LS14: Leeds ...1C 34
Sovereign Bus. Pk. LS10: Leeds ...1H 41
Sovereign Ct. LS17: Leeds ...3A 14
Sovereign Quay LS1: Leeds ...6E 5
Sovereign St. LS1: Leeds ...6D 4 (6G 31)
Sowden's Yd. LS16: Leeds ...5B 20
Sowood St. LS4: Leeds ...3A 30
Spa Ind. Est. LS7: Leeds ...1G 31
Spalding Towers LS9: Leeds ...4A 32
(off Lindsey Gdns.)
Speedwell Mt. LS6: Leeds ...2F 31
Speedwell St. LS6: Leeds ...2F 31
Spen App. LS16: Leeds ...4F 19
Spen Bank LS16: Leeds ...4F 19
Spence La. LS12: Leeds ...1D 40
Spenceley St. LS2: Leeds ...2E 31
(not continuous)
Spencer Mt. LS8: Leeds ...2A 32
Spencer Pl. LS7: Leeds ...2A 32
Spen Cres. LS16: Leeds ...4F 19
Spen Dr. LS16: Leeds ...3G 19
Spen Gdns. LS16: Leeds ...3H 19
Spen Grn. LS16: Leeds ...4F 19
Spen Hill LS16: Leeds ...4G 19
Spen La. LS5: Leeds ...6G 19
LS6: Leeds ...5G 19
LS16: Leeds ...2G 19
(not continuous)
Spen Lawn LS16: Leeds ...4F 19
Spen M. LS16: Leeds ...4G 19
Spennithorne Av. LS16: Leeds ...1G 19
Spennithorne Dr. LS16: Leeds ...2G 19
Spen Rd. LS16: Leeds ...3G 19
Spenser Ri. LS20: Guis ...5H 7
Spenser Rd. LS20: Guis ...5H 7
Spens Ho. LS2: Leeds ...1D 4
Spen Wlk. LS16: Leeds ...4F 19
Spen Way LS16: Leeds ...5G 19
Spibey Cres. LS26: Rothw ...2F 53
Spibey La. LS26: Rothw ...2F 53

Spindles, The LS10: Leeds ...1H 51
Spinks Gdns. LS14: Leeds ...1B 34
Spink Well La. WF3: Ting ...2D 56
Spinners Chase LS28: Pud ...6G 27
Spinners Ga. BD4: B'frd ...1A 36
Spinney, The LS9: Leeds ...6A 32
LS17: Leeds ...1A 22
LS19: Raw ...1C 16
Spinneyfield Ct. LS9: Leeds ...6A 32
Spinney Ri. BD4: B'frd ...6B 36
Spring Av. LS27: Gil ...2C 48
Spring Bank LS5: Leeds ...1G 29
Springbank LS19: Raw ...6C 8
Springbank Av. LS27: Gil ...2C 48
LS28: Fars ...2G 27
Springbank Cl. LS28: Fars ...2F 27
Spring Bank Cres. LS6: Leeds ...1C 30
Springbank Cres. LS27: Gil ...1C 48
Springbank Dr. LS28: Fars ...2G 27
Springbank Gro. LS28: Fars ...2G 27
Springbank M. WF3: Loft ...4B 58
Springbank Rd. LS27: Gil ...1C 48
LS28: Fars ...2F 27
Spring Bank Ter. LS20: Guis ...4G 7
Spring Cl. Av. LS9: Leeds ...1B 42
Spring Cl. Gdns. LS9: Leeds ...1B 42
Spring Cl. St. LS9: Leeds ...1A 42
Spring Cl. Wlk. LS9: Leeds ...1B 42
Springfield Av. LS27: Morl ...3F 49
WF3: Loft ...4E 59
Springfield Cl. LS18: H'fth ...2E 19
Springfield Commercial Cen.
LS28: Fars ...1G 27
Springfield Ct. LS17: Leeds ...5C 14
LS19: Yead ...1C 8
LS20: Guis ...4G 7
(off West St.)
Springfield Cres. LS27: Morl ...3G 49
Springfield Gdns. LS18: H'fth ...2D 18
LS28: Pud ...1H 37
Springfield Grn. LS10: Leeds ...5A 42
Springfield La. BD4: B'frd ...5G 37
LS27: Morl ...3G 49
Springfield M. LS20: Guis ...4G 7
LS27: Morl ...3G 49
Springfield Mt. LS2: Leeds ...1A 4 (4E 31)
LS12: Leeds ...5G 29
LS18: H'fth ...2D 18
Springfield Pl. LS10: Leeds ...5A 42
(Leasowe Rd.)
LS10: Leeds ...5C 42
(Pontefract Rd.)
LS20: Guis ...4G 7
Springfield Ri. LS18: H'fth ...2D 18
LS26: Rothw ...5H 53
Springfield Rd. LS20: Guis ...5G 7
LS27: Morl ...3F 49
Springfield St. LS26: Rothw ...5H 53
Springfield Ter. LS17: Leeds ...5C 14
(off Springfield Ct.)
LS20: Guis ...5G 7
LS28: Stan ...4F 27
Springfield Vs. LS27: Gil ...1B 48
Springfield Wlk. LS18: H'fth ...2D 18
SPRING GARDENS ...3H 47
Spring Gdns. BD11: Drig ...3H 47
LS27: Chur ...2A 50
Spring Gro. Av. LS6: Leeds ...3C 30
Spring Gro. Vw. LS6: Leeds ...3C 30
Spring Gro. Wlk. LS6: Leeds ...3C 30
Springhead Rd. LS26: Rothw ...3A 54
Spring Hill LS7: Leeds ...1G 31
LS16: Leeds ...5C 12
Springhill Cl. WF1: Out ...6C 58
Spring Hill Cotts. LS6: Leeds ...5C 20
(off Monk Bri. Rd.)
Springhills WF1: Out ...6C 58
Spring Hill Ter. LS6: Leeds ...5C 20
(off Monk Bri. Rd.)
Spring Rd. LS6: Leeds ...1C 30
Springrove Ter. LS6: Leeds ...3C 30
Springs Rd. LS19: Yead ...3A 8
Spring Valley LS28: Stan ...4G 27
Spring Valley Av. LS13: Leeds ...4C 28
Spring Valley Cl. LS13: Leeds ...4C 28
Spring Valley Ct. LS13: Leeds ...4C 28
Spring Valley Cres. LS13: Leeds ...4C 28
Spring Valley Cft. LS13: Leeds ...4C 28
Spring Valley Dr. LS13: Leeds ...4C 28
Spring Valley Vw. LS13: Leeds ...4C 28
Spring Valley Wlk. LS13: Leeds ...4C 28
Spring Vw. LS27: Gil ...1D 48
Springwell Av. LS26: Swil ...6G 45
Springwell Cl. LS19: Yead ...3E 9
Springwell Ct. LS12: Leeds ...1D 40
WF3: Ting ...2C 56

Springwell Rd. LS12: Leeds ...1D 40
LS26: Swil ...6G 45
Springwell St. LS12: Leeds ...1D 40
Springwell Ter. LS19: Yead ...3E 9
Springwell Vw. LS12: Leeds ...1E 41
Springwood Cl. WF3: Thpe H ...2A 58
Springwood Ct. LS8: Leeds ...5D 22
(off Bk. Wetherby Rd.)
Springwood Gdns. LS8: Leeds ...5D 22
Springwood Gro. LS8: Leeds ...5E 23
Springwood M. LS8: Leeds ...5E 23
Springwood Rd. LS8: Leeds ...5D 22
LS19: Raw ...6C 8
Spur Dr. LS15: Leeds ...2E 35
Square, The LS18: H'fth ...3B 18
Squirrel Way LS17: Leeds ...5B 14
Stable Ct. LS28: Cal ...5D 16
(off Bk. Thornhill St.)
Stadium Way LS11: Leeds ...4C 40
Stafford St. LS10: Leeds ...3A 42
Stainbeck Av. LS7: Leeds ...5D 20
Stainbeck Cnr. LS7: Leeds ...4G 21
(off Harrogate Rd.)
Stainbeck Gdns. LS7: Leeds ...4F 21
Stainbeck La. LS7: Leeds ...4E 21
Stainbeck Rd. LS7: Leeds ...5D 20
Stainbeck Wlk. LS7: Leeds ...5F 21
Stainburn Av. LS17: Leeds ...2A 22
Stainburn Cres. LS17: Leeds ...2H 21
Stainburn Dr. LS17: Leeds ...2H 21
Stainburn Gdns. LS17: Leeds ...2A 22
Stainburn Mt. LS17: Leeds ...3A 22
Stainburn Pde. LS17: Leeds ...2H 21
Stainburn Rd. LS17: Leeds ...3H 21
Stainburn Ter. LS17: Leeds ...3H 21
Stainburn Vw. LS17: Leeds ...2A 22
Stainmore Cl. LS14: Leeds ...2A 34
Stainmore Pl. LS14: Leeds ...2A 34
Stainton La. WF3: Carl ...5F 53
Stairfoot Cl. LS16: Leeds ...4B 12
Stair Foot La. LS16: Leeds ...4B 12
LS17: Leeds ...4B 12
Stairfoot Vw. LS16: Leeds ...4B 12
Stairfoot Wlk. LS16: Leeds ...4B 12
Staithe Av. LS10: Leeds ...4H 51
Staithe Cl. LS10: Leeds ...4H 51
Staithe Gdns. LS10: Leeds ...4H 51
Stanbeck Ct. LS7: Leeds ...3G 21
Standale Av. LS28: Pud ...5F 27
Standale Cres. LS28: Pud ...5F 27
Standale Ri. LS28: Pud ...5F 27
Standard Vs. LS12: Leeds ...3H 39
Stanhall Av. LS28: Stan ...4F 27
Stanhall M. LS28: Stan ...4F 27
Stanhope Av. LS18: H'fth ...1C 18
Stanhope Cl. LS18: H'fth ...1C 18
Stanhope Cl. LS18: H'fth ...6B 10
Stanhope Dr. LS18: H'fth ...3B 18
Stanhope Gdns. WF3: Thpe H ...2A 58
Stanhope Gro. WF3: Thpe H ...2A 58
Stanhope Rd. WF3: Thpe H ...2A 58
STANKS ...6D 24
Stanks App. LS14: Leeds ...1D 34
Stanks Av. LS14: Leeds ...1D 34
Stanks Cl. LS14: Leeds ...1E 35
Stanks Cross LS14: Leeds ...1E 35
Stanks Dr. LS14: Leeds ...5C 24
Stanks Gdns. LS14: Leeds ...6D 24
Stanks Gth. LS14: Leeds ...1E 35
Stanks Grn. LS14: Leeds ...1E 35
Stanks Gro. LS14: Leeds ...1D 34
Stanks La. Nth. LS14: Leeds ...5C 24
Stanks La. Sth. LS14: Leeds ...1D 34
Stanks Pde. LS14: Leeds ...1D 34
Stanks Ri. LS14: Leeds ...1E 35
Stanks Rd. LS14: Leeds ...1D 34
Stanks Way LS14: Leeds ...1D 34
STANLEY ...6H 59
Stanley Av. LS9: Leeds ...3B 32
Stanley Dr. LS8: Leeds ...1D 22
Stanley Gro. LS20: Guis ...5G 7
Stanley Ho. LS10: Leeds ...1H 41
Stanley Pl. LS9: Leeds ...3C 32
Stanley Rd. LS7: Leeds ...2H 31
LS9: Leeds ...3B 32
Stanley St. BD10: B'frd ...4A 16
Stanley Ter. LS9: Leeds ...3C 32
(not continuous)
LS12: Leeds ...6A 30
Stanley Vw. LS12: Leeds ...6A 30
Stanmore Dr. WF3: S'ley ...5G 59
Stanmore Av. LS4: Leeds ...2A 30
Stanmore Cres. LS4: Leeds ...2A 30
Stanmore Gro. LS4: Leeds ...2A 30
Stanmore Hill LS4: Leeds ...2B 30
Stanmore Mt. LS4: Leeds ...2A 30
Stanmore Pl. LS4: Leeds ...2A 30

Stanmore Rd. LS4: Leeds 2A 30
Stanmore St. LS4: Leeds 2A 30
Stanmore Ter. LS4: Leeds 2A 30
Stanmore Vw. LS4: Leeds 2A 30
STANNINGLEY 3H 27
Stanningley By-Pass
  LS13: Leeds 4E 27
  LS28: Stan .4E 27
Stanningley Ct. LS28: Stan 3H 27
      (off Leeds & Bradford Rd.)
Stanningley Fld. Cl. LS13: Leeds 4A 28
Stanningley Ind. Est. LS28: Stan 4F 27
Stanningley Loft LS28: Stan 4E 50
      (off Town St.)
Stanningley Rd. LS12: Leeds 4E 29
  LS13: Leeds 3A 28
  LS28: Stan .3H 27
Stansfield Fold LS18: H'fth 1C 18
      (off Rockery Rd.)
Star Health & Fitness Club 5C 32
      (off Glenthorpe Cres.)
Station Apartments LS15: Leeds 3C 34
      (off Station Rd.)
Station Av. LS13: Leeds 3B 28
Station Ct. LS15: Leeds 4C 34
Station Cres. LS12: Leeds 6H 29
Station Gdns. LS15: Scho 4F 25
Station La. BD11: Birk 3C 46
  LS26: Wood 2D 54
  WF3: E Ard 2H 57
  WF3: Ting .1C 56
      (not continuous)
Station Mt. LS13: Leeds 3B 28
Station Pde. LS5: Leeds 1H 29
Station Pl. LS13: Leeds 3C 28
Station Rd. BD11: Drig 4G 47
  LS12: Leeds 6H 29
  LS15: Leeds 3C 34
  LS15: Scho 4F 25
  LS18: H'fth 1C 18
  LS20: Guis .4F 7
  LS26: Meth 6H 55
  LS27: Morl 4G 49
  LS29: Men .1D 6
Station Sq. LS28: Stan 4E 27
Station St. LS28: Pud 1F 37
Station Ter. LS13: Leeds 3C 28
Station Vw. LS15: Leeds 4C 34
Station Wlk. LS27: Morl 4H 49
Station Way LS12: Leeds 6H 29
Stead Rd. BD4: B'frd 1A 46
Steads Yd. LS18: H'fth 1C 18
Steel Grn. LS12: N Far 4G 39
Steel Ter. LS26: Rothw 4H 53
      (off Bk. Gillett La.)
Stephenson Dr. LS12: N Far 4D 38
Stephenson Ho. LS27: Morl 4H 49
      (off Pullman Ct.)
Stephenson Way LS12: N Far 4D 38
  WF2: Carr G 6B 58
Sterling Ct. WF3: Ting 1C 56
Sterling Way WF3: Ting 1B 56
Stewart Cl. LS15: Leeds 6C 34
Stile Hill Way LS15: Leeds 6F 35
Stirling Cres. BD4: B'frd 4A 36
  LS18: H'fth 5A 10
Stockheld La. LS15: Leeds, Scho 2F 25
Stockhill Fold BD10: B'frd 3A 16
      (not continuous)
Stockhill Rd. BD10: B'frd 4A 16
Stocks App. LS14: Leeds 1B 34
Stocks Hill LS11: Leeds 2E 41
  LS12: Leeds 5A 30
  LS29: Men .1B 6
Stocks Hill Gth. LS29: Men 1B 6
      (off Stocks Hill)
Stocks Ri. LS14: Leeds 1B 34
Stocks Rd. LS14: Leeds 1C 34
Stocks St. LS7: Leeds 2G 31
Stonebridge App. LS12: Leeds 1E 39
Stonebridge Av. LS12: Leeds 1F 39
Stone Bri. Ct. LS12: Leeds 1E 39
      (off Farnley Cres.)
Stonebridge Gro. LS12: Leeds 1E 39
Stonebridge La. LS12: Leeds 2E 39
Stone Bri. Lea LS12: Leeds 1E 39
      (off Farnley Cres.)
Stone Brig Grn. LS26: Rothw 5F 53
Stone Brig La. LS26: Rothw 5F 53
Stonechat Ri. LS27: Morl 5A 50
Stonecliffe Bank LS12: Leeds 1E 39
Stonecliffe Cl. LS12: Leeds 1E 39
Stonecliffe Cres. LS12: Leeds 1E 39
Stonecliffe Dr. LS12: Leeds 1E 39
Stonecliffe Gdns. LS12: Leeds 1E 39
Stonecliffe Gth. LS12: Leeds 1E 39
Stonecliffe Grn. LS12: Leeds 1E 39

Stonecliffe Gro. LS12: Leeds 1E 39
Stonecliffe Lawn LS12: Leeds 1E 39
Stonecliffe Mt. LS12: Leeds 1E 39
Stonecliffe Pl. LS12: Leeds 1E 39
      (off Stonebridge La.)
Stonecliffe Ter. LS12: Leeds 1E 39
Stonecliffe Vw. LS12: Leeds 1E 39
Stonecliffe Wlk. LS12: N Far 2E 39
Stonecliffe Way LS12: Leeds 1E 39
Stonecroft WF3: S'ley 6G 59
Stone Cft. Ct. LS26: Oul 4C 54
Stonedene LS6: Leeds 3D 20
Stonefield Ter. LS27: Chur 1A 50
Stonegate LS7: Leeds 2G 31
      (not continuous)
Stonegate App. LS7: Leeds 5D 20
Stonegate Chase LS7: Leeds 4D 20
Stonegate Cl. LS17: Leeds 6H 13
Stonegate Cres. LS7: Leeds 4E 21
Stonegate Dr. LS7: Leeds 4E 21
Stonegate Edge LS7: Leeds 4E 21
Stonegate Farm Cl. LS7: Leeds 4D 20
Stonegate Gdns. LS7: Leeds 4D 20
Stonegate Grn. LS7: Leeds 5D 20
Stonegate Gro. LS7: Leeds 4E 21
Stonegate La. LS7: Leeds 5D 20
Stonegate M. LS7: Leeds 5D 20
Stonegate Pl. LS7: Leeds 5D 20
Stonegate Rd. LS6: Leeds 4D 20
  LS17: Leeds 4D 20
Stonegate Vw. LS7: Leeds 4D 20
Stonegate Wlk. LS7: Leeds 5E 21
Stonehurst LS14: Leeds 1D 34
Stonelea BD4: B'frd 1C 46
Stonelea Ct. LS6: Leeds 6B 20
  LS7: Leeds 4E 21
Stoneleigh Av. LS17: Leeds 5B 14
Stoneleigh Cl. LS17: Leeds 5B 14
Stoneleigh Ct. LS17: Leeds 5B 14
Stoneleigh Gth. LS17: Leeds 6B 14
Stoneleigh La. LS17: Leeds 6B 14
Stoneleigh Way LS17: Leeds 6B 14
Stone Mill App. LS6: Leeds 4C 20
Stone Mill Ct. LS6: Leeds 4C 20
Stone Mill Way LS6: Leeds 4C 20
Stone Pits La. LS27: Gil 3D 48
Stone Vs. LS6: Leeds 5B 20
Stonecroft LS18: H'fth 3B 18
  LS19: Raw 5E 9
      (off Batter La.)
Stoneyhurst Sq. BD4: B'frd 4A 36
Stoneyhurst Way BD4: B'frd 4A 36
Stoney La. LS18: H'fth 3B 18
  WF2: Kirk .6H 57
  WF3: E Ard 6G 57
Stoney Ri. LS18: H'fth 3B 18
Stoney Rock Ct. LS9: Leeds 4B 32
Stoney Rock La. LS9: Leeds 4B 32
Stoneythorpe LS18: H'fth 3B 18
Stony Royd LS28: Fars 2E 27
Storey Pl. LS14: Leeds 4G 33
Stott Rd. LS6: Leeds 2C 30
Stott St. LS12: Leeds 6B 30
STOURTON 6D 42
Stourton Bus. Pk.
  LS10: Leeds 5C 42
Stowe Gro. LS9: Leeds 5E 33
Stradbroke Way LS12: Leeds 1A 40
Strafford Way BD10: B'frd 3A 16
Stratford Av. LS11: Leeds 4E 41
Stratford Ct. LS7: Leeds 5G 21
Stratford St. LS11: Leeds 5F 41
Stratford Ter. LS11: Leeds 4F 41
Strathmore Av. LS9: Leeds 3C 32
Strathmore Dr. LS9: Leeds 2C 32
Strathmore Rd. LS9: Leeds 3D 32
Strathmore Ter. LS9: Leeds 3C 32
Strathmore Vw. LS9: Leeds 3C 32
Stratton Vw. BD4: B'frd 3A 36
Strawberry La. LS12: Leeds 6A 30
      (not continuous)
Strawberry Rd. LS12: Leeds 6A 30
Streamside LS6: Leeds 5C 20
Street La. LS8: Leeds 1C 22
  LS17: Leeds 1G 21
  LS27: Gil 4C 48
Stretton Av. LS6: Leeds 2C 20
Strickland Av. LS17: Shad 5H 15
Strickland Cl. LS17: Shad 5H 15
Strickland Cres. LS17: Shad 5H 15
Strone, The BD10: B'frd 2B 16
Stubbs La. WF3: E Ard 4A 58
Stubley Farm M. LS27: Morl 4G 49
Studfold Vw. LS14: Leeds 3A 34
Studio Rd. LS3: Leeds 4C 30
Studley Ter. LS28: Pud 5G 27

Styebank La. LS26: Rothw 3H 53
Suffield Cl. LS27: Gil 1B 48
Suffield Cres. LS27: Gil 1B 48
Suffield Dr. LS27: Gil 1B 48
Suffield Rd. LS27: Gil 1B 48
Suffolk Ct. LS19: Yead 2D 8
Sugar Hill Cl. LS26: Oul 6C 54
Sugar Well App. LS7: Leeds 6E 21
Sugar Well Ct. LS7: Leeds 1F 31
Sugar Well Mt. LS7: Leeds 6E 21
Sugar Well Rd. LS7: Leeds 6E 21
Sulby Gro. BD10: B'frd 4A 16
Summerbank Cl. BD11: Drig 2H 47
Summerbridge Dr. BD10: B'frd 6A 16
Summerdale BD19: Gom 6D 46
Summerfield Av. LS13: Leeds 2A 28
Summerfield Dr. LS13: Leeds 2A 28
Summerfield Grn. LS13: Leeds 2A 28
Summerfield Pl. LS13: Leeds 2A 28
  LS28: Stan 5G 27
      (off Richardshaw La.)
Summerfield Rd. LS13: Leeds 2A 28
Summerfield Wlk. LS13: Leeds 2A 28
Summerhill Gdns. LS8: Leeds 1D 22
Summerhill Pl. LS8: Leeds 1D 22
Summerseat LS19: Raw 6F 9
Summersgill Sq. LS18: H'fth 3B 18
Summerville Rd. LS28: Stan 4E 27
Sunbeam Av. LS11: Leeds 4F 41
Sunbeam Gro. LS11: Leeds 4F 41
Sunbeam Pl. LS11: Leeds 4F 41
Sunbeam Ter. LS11: Leeds 4F 41
  WF3: Ting .2C 56
Sun Fld. LS28: Stan 4F 27
Sunfield Cl. LS28: Stan 3F 27
Sunfield Dr. LS28: Stan 3F 27
Sunfield Gdns. LS28: Stan 3F 27
Sunfield Pl. LS28: Stan 4F 27
Sunningdale Av. LS17: Leeds 5E 13
Sunningdale Cl. LS17: Leeds 5E 13
Sunningdale Dr. LS17: Leeds 5E 13
Sunningdale Grn. LS17: Leeds 5E 13
Sunningdale Wlk. LS17: Leeds 5E 13
Sunningdale Way LS17: Leeds 5E 13
Sunny Bank LS8: Leeds 6B 22
  LS27: Chur 1A 50
      (off Sunny Gro.)
Sunnybank Av. BD3: B'frd 4B 26
  LS18: H'fth 4B 18
Sunnybank Ct. LS19: Yead 2F 9
Sunnybank Cres. LS19: Yead 2F 9
Sunny Bank Gro. LS8: Leeds 6B 22
Sunny Bank Ho. LS28: Fars 2F 27
Sunnybank La. BD3: B'frd 4B 26
Sunny Bank Mills LS28: Fars 2F 27
Sunnybank Rd. LS18: H'fth 4B 18
Sunnybank St. LS18: H'fth 4B 18
Sunnybank Ter. LS18: H'fth 4B 18
Sunny Bank Vw. LS8: Leeds 6B 22
Sunnydene LS14: Leeds 4H 33
Sunnyfield WF3: E Ard 4G 57
Sunny Gro. LS27: Chur 1A 50
Sunnyridge Av. LS28: Pud 5D 26
Sunnyside WF3: Ting 3B 56
      (off Dewsbury Rd.)
Sunnyside Av. WF3: Ting 3B 56
Sunnyside Rd. LS13: Leeds 4B 28
Sunnyview WF3: E Ard 4G 57
Sunnyview Av. LS11: Leeds 4D 40
Sunnyview Ct. LS11: Leeds 4D 40
Sunnyview Ho. LS11: Leeds 4D 40
      (off Manorfield)
Sunnyview Ter. LS11: Leeds 4D 40
Sunrise Ct. LS27: Gil 2C 48
Sunset Av. LS6: Leeds 4C 20
Sunset Dr. LS6: Leeds 4C 20
Sunset Hill Top LS6: Leeds 3C 20
Sunset Mt. LS6: Leeds 4C 20
Sunset Ri. LS6: Leeds 3C 20
Sunset Rd. LS6: Leeds 3C 20
Sunset Ter. LS6: Leeds 3C 20
Sunset Vw. LS6: Leeds 3C 20
Sunshine Mills LS12: Leeds 6G 29
Sun St. LS19: Yead 2E 9
  LS28: Stan 4G 27
Surrey Gro. LS28: Pud 5G 27
Surrey Rd. LS28: Pud 5G 27
Sussex App. LS10: Leeds 4B 42
Sussex Av. LS10: Leeds 4B 42
  LS18: H'fth 6C 10
Sussex Gdns. LS10: Leeds 4B 42
Sussex Grn. LS10: Leeds 4B 42
Sussex Pl. LS10: Leeds 4B 42
Sussex St. LS9: Leeds 6A 32
      (not continuous)
Sutherland Av. LS8: Leeds 2C 22

Sutherland Cres. LS8: Leeds 1C 22
Sutherland Mt. LS9: Leeds 3C 32
Sutherland Rd. LS9: Leeds 3C 32
Sutherland St. LS12: Leeds 1C 40
Sutherland Ter. LS9: Leeds 3C 32
Sutton App. LS14: Leeds 4G 33
Sutton Cres. BD4: B'frd 3A 36
   LS14: Leeds 4G 33
Sutton Gro. BD4: B'frd 1A 36
   LS27: Morl 6G 49
Sutton Ho. BD4: B'frd 1A 36
Sutton Rd. BD4: B'frd 2A 36
Sutton St. LS12: Leeds 1D 40
Swaine Hill Cres. LS19: Yead 2C 8
Swaine Hill St. LS19: Yead 2C 8
Swaine Hill Ter. LS19: Yead 2C 8
Swallow Av. LS12: Leeds 1G 39
Swallow Cl. LS12: Leeds 5F 29
   LS17: Leeds 5B 14
Swallow Cres. LS12: Leeds 1F 39
Swallow Dr. LS17: Leeds 5B 14
SWALLOW HILL 6F 29
Swallow Mt. LS12: Leeds 1G 39
Swallow Va. LS27: Morl 5B 50
Swallow Vw. LS12: Leeds 5F 29
Swan Apartments
   LS1: Leeds 4E 5
Swan Ct. LS20: Guis 3F 7
Swan St. LS1: Leeds 4E 5
SWARCLIFFE 1C 34
Swarcliffe App. LS14: Leeds 1C 34
Swarcliffe Av. LS14: Leeds 1C 34
Swarcliffe Bank LS14: Leeds 6C 24
Swarcliffe Dr. LS14: Leeds 6C 24
Swarcliffe Dr. E. LS14: Leeds 1D 34
Swarcliffe Grn. LS14: Leeds 1D 34
Swarcliffe Pde. LS14: Leeds 6C 24
Swarcliffe Rd. LS14: Leeds 6C 24
Swardale Grn. LS14: Leeds 1C 34
Swardale Rd. LS14: Leeds 1C 34
Sweet St. LS11: Leeds 1F 41
Sweet St. W. LS11: Leeds 1E 41
   (not continuous)
SWILLINGTON 6G 45
SWILLINGTON COMMON 1G 45
Swillington La. LS15: Swil C 4G 45
   LS26: Swil 6F 45
Swincar Av. LS19: Yead 2C 8
SWINCLIFFE 5C 46
Swincliffe Cl. BD19: Gom 5C 46
Swincliffe Cres. BD19: Gom 6C 46
Swincliffe Gdns. BD19: Gom 6C 46
Swinegate LS1: Leeds 6E 5 (6G 31)
SWINNOW 3A 28
Swinnow Av. LS13: Leeds 4A 28
Swinnow Cl. LS13: Leeds 4A 28
Swinnow Cres. LS28: Stan 3A 28
Swinnow Dr. LS13: Leeds 4A 28
Swinnow Gdns. LS13: Leeds 4A 28
Swinnow Gth. LS13: Leeds 4A 28
Swinnow Grn. LS28: Pud 4H 27
Swinnow Gro. LS13: Leeds 4A 28
Swinnow La. LS13: Leeds 3A 28
   LS28: Stan 3A 28
SWINNOW MOOR 5B 28
Swinnow Rd. LS13: Leeds 5H 27
   LS28: Leeds, Pud 5H 27
Swinnow Shop. Cen.
   LS13: Leeds 5A 28
Swinnow Vw. LS13: Leeds 4A 28
Swinnow Wlk. LS13: Leeds 4A 28
Swinroyd Cl. BD11: Birk 4D 46
Swithen's Ct. LS26: Rothw 5H 53
Swithen's Dr. LS26: Rothw 5G 53
Swithen's Gro. LS26: Rothw 5G 53
Swithen's La. LS26: Rothw 5G 53
Swithen's St. LS26: Rothw 5H 53
Sycamore Av. LS8: Leeds 6B 22
   LS15: Leeds 5A 34
Sycamore Chase LS28: Pud 6H 27
Sycamore Cl. LS6: Leeds 1E 31
   LS7: Leeds 4D 20
   LS15: Leeds 5G 33
Sycamore Ct. LS8: Leeds 5E 23
Sycamore Cft. LS11: Leeds 4F 41
Sycamore Fold LS11: Leeds 4F 41
Sycamore Row LS13: Leeds 1A 28
Sycamores, The LS20: Guis 3G 7
Sycamore Wlk. LS28: Fars 3F 27
Sydenham Rd. LS11: Leeds 1D 40
Sydenham St. LS11: Leeds 1D 40
Sydney St. LS26: Wood 3D 54
   LS28: Fars 3F 27
Syke Av. WF3: W Ard 4B 56
Syke Cl. WF3: W Ard 4A 56
Syke Gdns. WF3: W Ard 4B 56
Syke La. LS7: S'cft 1H 15

Syke Rd. WF3: W Ard 4B 56
Syke Ter. WF3: W Ard 4A 56
Sylvan Vw. LS18: H'fth 2C 18

T

Tagore Ct. BD3: B'frd 1A 36
Talbot Av. LS4: Leeds 2A 30
   LS8: Leeds 1A 22
   LS17: Leeds 1A 22
Talbot Ct. LS8: Leeds 2B 22
Talbot Cres. LS8: Leeds 1B 22
Talbot Fold LS8: Leeds 2B 22
Talbot Gdns. LS8: Leeds 1B 22
Talbot Gro. LS8: Leeds 1B 22
Talbot Mt. LS4: Leeds 2A 30
Talbot Ri. LS17: Leeds 1B 22
Talbot Rd. LS8: Leeds 1B 22
Talbot Ter. LS4: Leeds 2A 30
   LS26: Rothw 5G 53
Talbot Vw. LS4: Leeds 2A 30
Tall Trees LS17: Leeds 6G 13
Tamworth St. BD4: B'frd 1A 36
Tandy Trad. Est., The
   LS12: Leeds 4B 30
Tanglewood LS11: Leeds 2E 51
Tanhouse Hill LS18: H'fth 3E 19
   (not continuous)
Tan Ho. Yd. LS27: Chur 6A 40
Tannery, The LS3: Leeds 5D 30
   (off Cavendish St.)
Tannery Sq. LS6: Leeds 4C 20
Tannery Yd. LS28: Pud 6H 27
Tarn La. LS17: Leeds, S'cft 3E 15
Tarnside Dr. LS14: Leeds 2H 33
Tarn Vw. Rd. LS19: Yead 2F 9
Tarran Way WF3: Rob H 5C 52
Tatham Way LS8: Leeds 5E 23
Tatton La. WF3: Thpe H 1B 58
Tavergate LS20: Hawk 5A 6
Tavistock Cl. LS12: Leeds 1B 40
Tavistock M. LS12: Leeds 1B 40
Tavistock Pk. LS12: Leeds 1B 40
Tavistock Way LS12: Leeds 1B 40
Tawny Beck LS13: Leeds 5C 28
Tawny Cl. BD4: B'frd 6A 36
   LS27: Morl 5B 50
Taylor La. LS15: Bar E 5H 25
Taylors Cl. LS14: Leeds 1B 34
Tealby Cl. LS16: Leeds 1E 19
Teal Dr. LS27: Morl 5B 50
Teale Cl. LS7: Leeds 6A 22
Teale Dr. LS7: Leeds 6A 22
Teal M. LS10: Leeds 4H 51
Teasel Bank LS28: Pud 6D 26
Teasel Row LS12: Leeds 5A 30
   (off Eyres Mill Side)
Teasel Vw. LS28: Pud 6D 26
   (off Bradley La.)
Techno Cen. LS18: H'fth 1C 18
Telephone Pl. LS7: Leeds 1H 5 (4H 31)
Telford Cl. LS10: Leeds 5A 42
Telford Gdns. LS10: Leeds 5A 42
Telford Pl. LS10: Leeds 5A 42
Telford Ter. LS10: Leeds 5A 42
Telford Wlk. LS10: Leeds 5A 42
Telford Way WF2: Carr G 6A 58
Telscombe Dr. BD4: B'frd 5A 36
Temperance Ct. LS18: H'fth 3B 18
Temperance St. LS28: Stan 4G 27
Tempest Pl. LS11: Leeds 4E 41
Tempest Rd. LS11: Leeds 4E 41
Templar La. LS2: Leeds 3G 5 (5H 31)
   LS15: Leeds 1D 34
Templar Pl. LS2: Leeds 3G 5 (5H 31)
Templar St. LS2: Leeds 3F 5 (5G 31)
Temple Av. LS15: Leeds 1A 44
   LS26: Rothw 2H 53
Temple Cl. LS15: Leeds 6H 33
   LS26: Rothw 2H 53
Temple Cres. LS11: Leeds 4E 41
Temple Ga. LS15: Leeds 6B 34
Temple Ga. Dr. LS15: Leeds 6A 34
Templegate Av. LS15: Leeds 1A 44
Templegate Cl. LS15: Leeds 1B 44
Templegate Cres. LS15: Leeds 1B 44
Temple Ga. Grn. LS15: Leeds 1A 44
Templegate Ri. LS15: Leeds 1A 44
Templegate Rd. LS15: Leeds 1A 44
Templegate Vw. LS15: Leeds 1A 44
Templegate Wlk. LS15: Leeds 6B 34
Templegate Way LS15: Leeds 1B 44

Temple Grn. LS26: Rothw 2A 54
Temple Gro. LS15: Leeds 6A 34
Temple La. LS15: Leeds 6B 34
Temple Lawn LS26: Rothw 2A 54
Temple Lea LS15: Leeds 6B 34
Temple M. LS15: Leeds 6A 34
   (off Selby Rd.)
Temple Newsam Home Farm (Rare Breeds)
   ....2B 44
Temple Newsam House 2B 44
Temple Newsam Pk. 1H 43
Templenewsam Rd. LS15: Leeds 6H 33
Templenewsam Vw. LS15: Leeds 1H 43
Temple Pk. Cl. LS15: Leeds 6A 34
Temple Pk. Gdns. LS15: Leeds 6A 34
Temple Pk. Grn. LS15: Leeds 6A 34
Temple Ri. LS15: Leeds 1A 44
Temple Row LS15: Leeds 1E 45
   (off Colton Rd. E.)
Temple Row Cl. LS15: Leeds 1E 45
Templer Ter. LS27: Morl 6H 49
Templestowe Cres. LS15: Leeds 4C 34
Templestowe Dr. LS15: Leeds 5C 34
Templestowe Gdns.
   LS15: Leeds 5B 34
Templestowe Hill LS15: Leeds 4B 34
Temple Vw. WF3: Loft 2E 59
Temple Vw. Gro. LS9: Leeds 6C 32
   (not continuous)
Temple Vw. Pl. LS9: Leeds 6B 32
Temple Vw. Rd. LS9: Leeds 5B 32
Temple Vw. Ter. LS9: Leeds 6B 32
Temple Vue LS6: Leeds 5B 20
   (off Mansfield Pl.)
Temple Wlk. LS15: Leeds 5B 34
Tenbury Fold BD4: B'frd 4A 36
Tennis Av. BD4: B'frd 6A 36
Tennyson Av. WF3: S'ley 5G 59
Tennyson Cl. LS28: Pud 1H 37
Tennyson St. LS20: Guis 5H 7
   LS27: Morl 5H 49
   LS28: Fars 3F 27
   LS28: Pud 1H 37
Tennyson Ter. LS27: Morl 5H 49
Tenterden Way LS15: Leeds 2F 35
Tenterfields BD10: B'frd 3A 16
Tenterfields Ho. BD10: B'frd 3A 16
Terminus Pde. LS15: Leeds 3C 34
   (off Farm Rd.)
Terrace, The LS28: Pud 3G 37
Tetley Dr. BD11: Birk 5C 46
Texas St. LS27: Morl 1A 56
Thackeray Rd. BD10: B'frd 1A 26
Thackray Ct. LS18: H'fth 3E 19
Thackray Medical Mus. 3B 32
Thackray St. LS27: Morl 6G 49
Thane Way LS15: Leeds 2E 35
The ....
   Names prefixed with 'The' for example
   'The Acres' are indexed under the main
   name such as 'Acres, The'
Theaker La. LS12: Leeds 5H 29
Thealby Cl. LS9: Leeds 5A 32
Thealby Lawn LS9: Leeds 4A 32
Thealby Pl. LS9: Leeds 3H 5 (5A 32)
Theatre Wlk. LS1: Leeds 4E 5
   (off The Core)
Theodore St. LS11: Leeds 6E 41
Third Av. LS12: Leeds 1B 40
   LS26: Rothw 2H 53
Thirlmere Cl. LS11: Leeds 1C 50
Thirlmere Dr. WF3: Ting 3E 57
Thirlmere Gdns. LS11: Leeds 1C 50
Thirsk Gro. LS10: Leeds 6H 51
Thirsk Row LS1: Leeds 5C 4 (6F 31)
Thistle Way LS27: Gil 4D 48
Thistlewood Rd. WF1: Out 6F 59
Thomas Dr. LS20: Guis 3F 7
Thomas St. LS6: Leeds 2E 31
Thoresby Pl. LS1: Leeds 3C 4 (4F 31)
THORNBURY 6A 26
Thornbury Av. BD3: B'frd 5A 26
   LS16: Leeds 4A 20
Thornbury Cres. BD3: B'frd 5A 26
Thornbury Dr. BD3: B'frd 5A 26
Thornbury Gro. BD3: B'frd 6A 26
Thornbury Rd. BD3: B'frd 6A 26
Thornbury St. BD3: B'frd 6A 26
Thorn Cres. LS8: Leeds 2D 32
Thorn Cross LS8: Leeds 1E 33
Thorndene Way BD4: B'frd 2C 46
Thorn Dr. LS8: Leeds 2D 32
Thorne Cl. LS28: Pud 5D 26
Thornefield Cres. WF3: Ting 3B 56
Thorne Gro. LS26: Rothw 3H 53
Thorner La. LS14: T'ner 1E 25
Thornes Farm App. LS9: Leeds 2F 43

Thornes Farm Way LS9: Leeds 2F **43**
Thornfield Av. LS28: Fars 2E **27**
Thornfield Ct. LS15: Leeds 3B **34**
Thornfield Dr. LS15: Leeds 3B **34**
Thornfield M. LS15: Leeds 3B **34**
Thornfield Rd. LS16: Leeds 3H **19**
Thornfield Way LS15: Leeds 3B **34**
Thorn Gro. LS8: Leeds 2D **32**
Thornhill Cl. LS28: Cal 4D **16**
Thornhill Ct. LS12: Leeds 1A **40**
Thornhill Cft. LS12: Leeds 1H **39**
Thornhill Dr. BD10: Cal 3B **16**
  LS28: Cal 3D **16**
Thornhill Gro. LS28: Cal 4D **16**
Thornhill Ho. BD3: B'frd 5A **26**
  (off Thornhill Pl.)
Thornhill Pl. BD3: B'frd 5A **26**
  LS12: Leeds 1H **39**
Thornhill Rd. LS12: Leeds 1H **39**
Thornhill St. LS12: Leeds 6H **29**
  LS28: Cal 4D **16**
Thornhill Ter. BD3: B'frd 5A **26**
Thorn La. LS8: Leeds 4B **22**
Thornlea Cl. LS19: Yead 4B **8**
Thornleigh Gdns. LS9: Leeds 1B **42**
Thornleigh Gro. LS9: Leeds 1B **42**
Thornleigh Mt. LS9: Leeds 1B **42**
Thornleigh St. LS9: Leeds 1B **42**
Thornleigh Vw. LS9: Leeds 1B **42**
Thorn Mt. LS8: Leeds 1E **33**
Thorn Royd Dr. BD4: B'frd 5B **36**
Thorn Ter. LS8: Leeds 1D **32**
Thornton Av. LS12: Leeds 6G **29**
Thornton Cl. WF17: Birs 6H **47**
Thornton Gdns. LS12: Leeds 6G **29**
Thornton Gro. LS12: Leeds 6G **29**
Thornton's Arc. LS1: Leeds 4E **5** (5G **31**)
Thorntons Dale LS18: H'fth 5B **18**
Thorn Vw. LS8: Leeds 2E **33**
Thornville LS27: Chur 2H **49**
Thornville Av. LS6: Leeds 3C **30**
Thornville Ct. LS6: Leeds 3C **30**
  (off Thornville Rd.)
Thornville Cres. LS6: Leeds 2C **30**
Thornville Gro. LS6: Leeds 3C **30**
Thornville Mt. LS6: Leeds 3C **30**
Thornville Pl. LS6: Leeds 3C **30**
Thornville Rd. LS6: Leeds 3C **30**
Thornville St. LS6: Leeds 3C **30**
Thornville Ter. LS6: Leeds 3C **30**
Thornville Vw. LS6: Leeds 3C **30**
Thorn Wlk. LS8: Leeds 2E **33**
Thorpe Cl. LS20: Guis 5D **6**
Thorpe Ct. LS10: Leeds 6G **51**
Thorpe Cres. LS10: Leeds 5G **51**
Thorpe Dr. LS20: Guis 4E **7**
Thorpe Gdns. LS10: Leeds 5G **51**
Thorpe Gth. LS10: Leeds 6F **51**
Thorpe Gro. LS10: Leeds 5G **51**
Thorpe La. LS28: Pud 2D **56**
  LS20: Guis 5C **6**
  WF3: Ting 2D **56**
Thorpe Lodge WF3: Loft 2E **59**
  (off Long Thorpe La.)
Thorpe Lwr. La. WF3: Rothw, Thpe H 1B **58**
Thorpe Mt. LS10: Leeds 6F **51**
THORPE ON THE HILL 1H **57**
Thorpe Pk. LS15: Leeds 6F **35**
Thorpe Rd. LS10: Leeds 4G **51**
  LS28: Pud 5F **27**
  WF3: E Ard 4G **57**
Thorpe Sq. LS10: Leeds 5H **51**
Thorpe St. LS10: Leeds 5G **51**
  LS15: Leeds 5A **34**
Thorpe Vw. LS10: Leeds 6G **51**
Thorverton Dr. BD4: B'frd 1A **46**
Thorverton Gro. BD4: B'frd 1A **46**
Threelands BD11: Birk 3C **46**
Threelands Grange BD11: Birk 3C **46**
Threshfield Cres. BD11: Birk 3C **46**
Throstle Av. LS10: Leeds 6F **51**
Throstle Dr. LS10: Leeds 6E **51**
Throstle Hill LS10: Leeds 6F **51**
Throstle La. LS10: Leeds 6F **51**
Throstle Mt. LS10: Leeds 6F **51**
Throstle Nest 3G **27**
Throstle Nest Vw. LS18: H'fth 4C **18**
Throstle Pde. LS10: Leeds 6F **51**
Throstle Pl. LS10: Leeds 6F **51**
Throstle Rd. LS10: Leeds 6G **51**
Throstle Rd. Nth. LS10: Leeds 4A **52**
Throstle Row LS10: Leeds 6F **51**
Throstle Sq. LS10: Leeds 6H **51**
Throstle St. LS10: Leeds 6F **51**
Throstle Ter. LS10: Leeds 6G **51**
Throstle Vw. LS10: Leeds 6H **51**

Throstle Wlk. LS10: Leeds 6F **51**
Thwaite Ct. LS18: H'fth 3E **19**
THWAITE GATE 4B **42**
Thwaite Ga. LS10: Leeds 4B **42**
Thwaite La. LS10: Leeds 4C **42**
Thwaite Mills Watermill Mus. 4D **42**
Tilbury Av. LS11: Leeds 3D **40**
Tilbury Gro. LS11: Leeds 3D **40**
Tilbury Mt. LS11: Leeds 3D **40**
Tilbury Pde. LS11: Leeds 3D **40**
Tilbury Rd. LS11: Leeds 3D **40**
Tilbury Row LS11: Leeds 3D **40**
Tilbury Ter. LS11: Leeds 3D **40**
Tilbury Vw. LS11: Leeds 3D **40**
Tile La. LS16: Leeds 6B **12**
  (not continuous)
Tingle Vw. LS12: N Far 4G **39**
TINGLEY 2C **56**
Tingley Av. WF3: Ting 2C **56**
Tingley Comn. LS27: Morl 1A **56**
Tingley Cres. WF3: Ting 2A **56**
Tingleyhall Ri. WF3: Ting 2C **56**
TINSHILL 5D **10**
Tinshill Av. LS16: Leeds 6E **11**
Tinshill Cl. LS16: Leeds 6E **11**
Tinshill Cres. LS16: Leeds 5E **11**
Tinshill Dr. LS16: Leeds 4E **11**
Tinshill Gth. LS16: Leeds 5E **11**
Tinshill Grn. LS16: Leeds 5E **11**
Tinshill La. LS16: Leeds 6D **10**
TINSHILL MOOR 4E **11**
Tinshill Mt. LS16: Leeds 5E **11**
Tinshill Rd. LS16: Leeds 6D **10**
Tinshill Vw. LS16: Leeds 5E **11**
Tinshill Wlk. LS16: Leeds 4E **11**
Tiverton Wlk. BD4: B'frd 5A **36**
TOFTSHAW 1A **46**
Toftshaw Fold BD4: B'frd 1A **46**
Toftshaw La. BD4: B'frd 1A **46**
Toftshaw New Rd.
  BD4: B'frd 1A **46**
Tofts Ho. Cl. LS28: Pud 6G **27**
Tofts Rd. LS28: Pud 6F **27**
Toft St. LS12: Leeds 1B **40**
TONG 5F **37**
Tong App. LS12: Leeds 1D **38**
Tong Dr. LS12: Leeds 6D **28**
Tong Ga. LS12: Leeds 6D **28**
Tong Grn. LS12: Leeds 6D **28**
Tong Hall Bus. Pk. BD4: B'frd 5F **37**
Tong La. BD4: B'frd 1E **47**
Tong Rd. LS12: Leeds, N Far 3B **38**
Tong Rd. Bus. Pk.
  LS12: Leeds 6A **30**
TONG STREET 6A **36**
Tong St. BD4: B'frd 6A **36**
Tongue La. LS6: Leeds 3D **20**
Tong Wlk. LS12: Leeds 6D **28**
Tong Way LS12: Leeds 6D **28**
TOPCLIFFE 1A **56**
Topcliffe Av. LS27: Morl 5B **50**
Topcliffe Cl. WF3: Ting 1B **56**
Topcliffe Ct. LS27: Morl 5C **50**
Topcliffe Fold LS27: Morl 1A **56**
Topcliffe Grn. LS27: Morl 5B **50**
Topcliffe Gro. LS27: Morl 5B **50**
Topcliffe La. LS27: Morl 1A **56**
  WF3: Ting 6B **50**
Topcliffe Mead LS27: Morl 5B **50**
Topcliffe M. LS27: Morl 5B **50**
Toplis Way LS10: Leeds 5A **52**
Tordoff Pl. LS5: Leeds 1G **29**
Tordoff Ter. LS5: Leeds 1G **29**
Toronto Pl. LS7: Leeds 5H **21**
Toronto Sq. LS1: Leeds 4D **4**
Toronto St. LS1: Leeds 4D **4** (5F **31**)
  LS6: Leeds 3C **30**
  (off Queen's Rd.)
Torre Cl. LS9: Leeds 5C **32**
Torre Cres. LS9: Leeds 5D **32**
Torre Dr. LS9: Leeds 4C **32**
Torre Gdns. LS9: Leeds 5B **32**
Torre Gro. LS9: Leeds 4C **32**
Torre Hill LS9: Leeds 5D **32**
Torre La. LS9: Leeds 5D **32**
Torre Mt. LS9: Leeds 4C **32**
Torre Pl. LS9: Leeds 5C **32**
Torre Rd. LS9: Leeds 5B **32**
Torre Sq. LS9: Leeds 4D **32**
Torre Vw. LS9: Leeds 4D **32**
Torre Wlk. LS9: Leeds 4D **32**
Tourist Info. Cen.
  Leeds Station 5D **4** (6F **31**)
  Morley 5G **49**

Towcester Av. LS10: Leeds 6H **51**
Tower Ct. LS12: Leeds 5B **30**
Tower Dr. LS13: Leeds 6G **17**
Tower Gro. LS12: Leeds 5G **29**
Tower Ho. St. LS2: Leeds 2F **5** (4G **31**)
Tower La. LS12: Leeds 5F **29**
  (not continuous)
Tower Pl. LS12: Leeds 5F **29**
Towers Sq. LS6: Leeds 3E **21**
Towers Way LS6: Leeds 3E **21**
Tower Works LS11: Leeds 6C **4** (6F **31**)
TOWN END
  LS12 ....2H **39**
  LS13 ....3E **29**
  LS27 ....5G **49**
  WF3 ....2E **59**
Town End LS27: Gil 2D **48**
  LS27: Morl 5H **49**
  (off Middleton Rd.)
Town End Cl. LS13: Leeds 4E **29**
Townend Pl. LS28: Pud 5H **27**
Townend Rd. LS13: Leeds 2H **39**
Town End Yd. LS13: Leeds 4D **28**
Town Ga. LS20: Guis 4G **7**
  LS28: Cal 4D **16**
Town Ga. Cl. LS20: Guis 4G **7**
Town Hall Sq. LS19: Yead 2D **8**
Town Sq. LS18: H'fth 2B **18**
  (off Kerry Gth.)
Town St. BD11: Birk 3C **46**
  LS7: Leeds 4H **21**
  LS10: Leeds 4F **51**
  LS11: Leeds 6C **40**
  LS12: Leeds 5G **29**
  LS13: Leeds 2C **28**
  (Bell La.)
  LS13: Leeds 6G **17**
  (St Andrew's Cl.)
  LS18: H'fth 3B **18**
  LS19: Raw 6F **9**
  LS19: Yead 2D **8**
  LS20: Guis 4G **7**
  LS27: Gil 2C **48**
  LS28: Fars 2F **27**
  LS28: Stan 4G **27**
  WF3: Carl 6F **53**
Town St. M. LS7: Leeds 4H **21**
Town St. Wlk. LS7: Leeds 4H **21**
Town Wells Dr. LS28: Cal 5D **16**
Trafalgar Gdns. LS27: Morl 6G **49**
Trafalgar St. LS2: Leeds 3G **5** (5H **31**)
Trafford Av. LS9: Leeds 3D **32**
Trafford Gro. LS9: Leeds 2C **32**
Trafford Ter. LS9: Leeds 3D **32**
Tramways LS20: Guis 4E **7**
Tranbeck Rd. LS20: Guis 4D **6**
Tranfield Av. LS20: Guis 4E **7**
Tranfield Cl. LS20: Guis 4E **7**
Tranfield Ct. LS20: Guis 4E **7**
Tranfield Gdns. LS20: Guis 4E **7**
Tranmere Ct. LS20: Guis 4E **7**
Tranmere Dr. LS20: Guis 4E **7**
TRANMERE PARK 4E **7**
Tranquility LS15: Leeds 3C **34**
Tranquility Av. LS15: Leeds 3C **34**
Tranquility Ct. LS15: Leeds 3C **34**
  (off Tranquility Av.)
Tranquility Wlk. LS15: Leeds 3C **34**
Tranter Gro. BD4: B'frd 2A **36**
Tranter Pl. LS15: Leeds 5G **33**
Treefield Ind. Est. LS27: Gil 3D **48**
Tree Tops Ct. LS8: Leeds 4E **23**
Trelawn Av. LS6: Leeds 6B **20**
Trelawn Cres. LS6: Leeds 6B **20**
Trelawn Pl. LS6: Leeds 6B **20**
Trelawn St. LS6: Leeds 6B **20**
Trelawn Ter. LS6: Leeds 6B **20**
Tremont Gdns. LS10: Leeds 5A **42**
Trenic Cres. LS6: Leeds 2B **30**
Trenic Dr. LS6: Leeds 2B **30**
Trentham Av. LS11: Leeds 4F **41**
Trentham Gro. LS11: Leeds 4F **41**
Trentham Pl. LS11: Leeds 4F **41**
Trentham Row LS11: Leeds 4F **41**
Trentham St. LS11: Leeds 5F **41**
Trentham Ter. LS11: Leeds 4F **41**
Trent Rd. LS9: Leeds 5B **32**
Trent St. LS11: Leeds 2F **41**
Trescoe Av. LS13: Leeds 4E **29**
Trevelyan Sq. LS1: Leeds 5E **5** (6G **31**)
Trevor Ter. WF2: Carr G 5A **58**
Triangle, The LS3: Leeds 4D **30**
  (off Burley Rd.)
Triangle Bus. Pk. WF17: Birs 6A **48**
Trinity Chapel LS28: Pud 5G **27**
  (off Wesley Sq.)

Trinity Cl. LS18: H'fth 6B 10
Trinity Ct. LS8: Leeds 4A 22
Trinity One LS9: Leeds 6H 5 (6H 31)
Trinity St. LS1: Leeds 4E 5 (5G 31)
Trinity St. Arc. LS1: Leeds 5E 5 (6G 31)
Trinity Vw. LS28: Fars 1F 27
(off Bryan St.)
Tristram Cen., The LS12: Leeds 3C 40
Triumph Cl. LS11: Leeds 1E 41
Trojan Ct. LS27: Morl 4G 49
(off Troy Hill)
Tropical World 2D 22
Troughton St. LS28: Pud 2H 37
TROY 1C 18
TROYDALE 1B 38
Troydale Gdns. LS28: Pud 2B 38
Troydale Gro. LS28: Pud 2B 38
Troydale la. LS12: N Far 1A 38
LS28: Pud 1A 38
Troydale Pk. LS28: Pud 2B 38
TROY HILL 4G 49
Troy Hill LS18: H'fth 1C 18
LS27: Morl 4G 49
Troy Mills LS18: H'fth 1C 18
Troy Ri. LS27: Morl 4H 49
Troy Rd. LS18: H'fth 1C 18
LS27: Morl 4G 49
Truro St. LS12: Leeds 5A 30
Tudor Cl. LS28: Fars 3E 27
Tudor Gdns. LS11: Leeds 5C 40
Tudor Lawns LS8: Leeds 4E 23
WF2: Carr G 6A 58
Tudor Way LS11: Leeds 6C 40
Tulip Retail Pk.
LS10: Leeds 4H 41
Tulip St. LS10: Leeds 4H 41
Tunstall Grn. BD4: B'frd 4A 36
Tunstall Rd. LS11: Leeds 4G 41
Turbary Av. LS28: Fars 3G 27
Turkey Hill LS28: Pud 1H 37
(not continuous)
Turks Head Yd. LS1: Leeds 4E 5
Turlow Ct. LS9: Leeds 6H 5 (6H 31)
Turnberry Av. LS17: Leeds 5F 13
Turnberry Cl. LS17: Leeds 5F 13
WF3: Ting 3B 56
Turnberry Dr. LS17: Leeds 5F 13
WF3: Ting 3B 56
Turnberry Fold LS17: Leeds 5F 13
Turnberry Gdns. WF3: Ting 3B 56
Turnberry Gro. LS17: Leeds 5F 13
Turnberry Pk. Rd. LS27: Gil 5D 48
Turnberry Pl. LS17: Leeds 5F 13
Turnberry Ri. LS17: Leeds 5F 13
Turnberry Vw. LS17: Leeds 5F 13
Turnbull Ct. LS8: Leeds 6F 23
Turner Av. WF3: Ting 3C 56
Turner Dr. WF3: Ting 3C 56
Turner Ho. LS5: Leeds 1F 29
Turner St. LS28: Fars 2F 27
Turner's Yd. LS13: Leeds 3D 28
LS28: Fars 2F 27
Turnpike Cl. BD11: Birk 5C 46
Turnstone Ct. LS10: Leeds 4H 51
Turnways, The LS6: Leeds 1A 30
Turton Grn. LS27: Gil 2D 48
Turton Va. LS27: Gil 3D 48
Twentyman Wlk.
LS10: Leeds 5H 51
Twenty Twenty LS2: Leeds 2H 5 (4H 31)
Tyas Gro. LS9: Leeds 6D 32
TYERSAL 1B 36
Tyersal Av. BD4: B'frd 6B 26
Tyersal Cl. BD4: B'frd 1B 36
Tyersal Ct. BD4: B'frd 1A 36
Tyersal Cres. BD4: B'frd 1B 36
Tyersal Dr. BD4: B'frd 1B 36
Tyersal Gth. BD4: B'frd 1B 36
TYERSAL GATE 3A 36
Tyersal Grn. BD4: B'frd 1B 36
Tyersal Gro. BD4: B'frd 1B 36
Tyersal La. BD4: B'frd 2B 36
BD4: B'frd, Pud 3A 36
LS28: Pud 1E 37
Tyersal M. BD4: B'frd 1B 36
Tyersal Pk. BD4: B'frd 1B 36
Tyersal Rd. BD4: B'frd 1A 36
Tyersal Ter. BD4: B'frd 1A 36
Tyersal Vw. BD4: B'frd 1B 36
Tyersal Wlk. BD4: B'frd 1B 36
Tynedale Ct. LS7: Leeds 5E 21
Tynwald Cl. LS17: Leeds 1E 21
Tynwald Dr. LS17: Leeds 6E 13
Tynwald Gdns. LS17: Leeds 1E 21
Tynwald Grn. LS17: Leeds 6E 13
Tynwald Hill LS17: Leeds 1E 21
Tynwald Mt. LS17: Leeds 6E 13

Tynwald Rd. LS17: Leeds 1E 21
Tynwald Wlk. LS17: Leeds 6E 13

U

Ullswater Cres. LS15: Leeds 6G 33
LS26: Wood 3C 54
Underwood Dr. LS19: Raw 1D 16
Union Bri. Mill LS28: Pud 3B 38
Union Pl. LS11: Leeds 1F 41
Union St. LS2: Leeds 4F 5 (5H 31)
LS27: Chur 1A 50
Union Ter. LS7: Leeds 5G 21
United Bus. Pk. LS12: Leeds 3C 40
Unity Cl. LS6: Leeds 1F 31
Unity Hall Ct. WF3: W Ard 4D 56
Unity St. WF3: Carl 6F 53
University of Leeds
Bodington Hall 1H 19
Cromer Rd. 1B 4 (4E 31)
University Rd. LS2: Leeds 3E 31
Upland Cres. LS8: Leeds 6C 22
Upland Gdns. LS8: Leeds 1C 32
Upland Gro. LS8: Leeds 6C 22
Upland Rd. LS8: Leeds 1C 32
Up. Accommodation Rd.
LS9: Leeds 5A 32
UPPER ARMLEY 4F 29
Upper Armley Tennis Club 4G 29
Up. Basinghall St. LS1: Leeds 3D 4 (5F 31)
UPPER FAGLEY 3A 26
UPPER GREEN 4B 56
Up. Green Av. WF3: W Ard 4B 56
Up. Green Cl. WF3: W Ard 4C 56
Up. Green Dr. WF3: W Ard 4C 56
Up. Green Way WF3: W Ard 4B 56
Up. Lombard St. LS19: Raw 5C 8
Uppermoor LS28: Pud 6E 27
Uppermoor Cl. LS28: Pud 1F 37
UPPER MOOR SIDE 5B 38
Up. Rushton Rd. BD3: B'frd 4A 26
Upper St. WF3: Ting 2D 56
(off Bradford Rd.)
Up. Town St. LS13: Leeds 2C 28
Up. Westlock Av. LS9: Leeds 4C 32
Up. Woodview Pl. LS11: Leeds 5F 41
(off Woodview St.)
UPPER WORTLEY 1H 39
Up. Wortley Cl. LS12: Leeds 6H 29
(off Up. Wortley Dr.)
Up. Wortley Dr. LS12: Leeds 6H 29
Up. Wortley Rd. LS12: Leeds 6H 29
Upton's Yd. LS1: Leeds 4E 5

V

Vale, The LS6: Leeds 6D 20
Vale Av. LS8: Leeds 6C 14
Valentine M. WF3: Loft 3E 59
Valley, The LS17: Leeds 3E 13
Valley Cl. LS17: Leeds 4E 13
LS6: Leeds 1B 30
LS17: Leeds 3H 21
(off Allerton Grange Gdns.)
Valley Dr. LS15: Leeds 4A 34
Valley Farm Rd. LS10: Leeds 6C 42
Valley Farm Way LS10: Leeds 6C 42
Valley Gdns. LS7: Leeds 3G 21
Valley Grn. LS28: Pud 1H 37
Valley Gro. LS28: Pud 1H 37
Valley Mills LS27: Drig 1B 48
Valley Mt. LS13: Leeds 5A 28
Valley Ri. LS13: Leeds 6C 18
Valley Rd. LS13: Leeds 6C 18
LS27: Morl 4H 49
LS28: Pud 1G 37
Valley Sq. LS28: Pud 1H 37
Valley Ter. LS17: Leeds 6B 14
Valley Vw. LS28: Pud 6A 28
Vancouver Pl. LS7: Leeds 5A 22
Varley St. LS28: Stan 3A 28
(not continuous)
Varleys Yd. LS28: Pud 6H 27
Ventnor Cl. BD19: Gom 6D 46
Veritys Pl. LS28: Pud 5H 27
Verity Spur LS9: Leeds 5G 33
Verity St. BD4: E Bier 2B 46
Verity Vw. LS9: Leeds 4G 33
Vermont St. LS13: Leeds 3A 28
Vernon Pl. LS28: Stan 4H 27
Vernon Rd. LS1: Leeds 1C 4 (4F 31)
Vernon St. LS2: Leeds 2D 4 (4F 31)
Vesper Cl. LS5: Leeds 5F 19

Vesper Ct. LS5: Leeds 5E 19
Vesper Ct. Dr. LS5: Leeds 5E 19
Vesper Gdns. LS5: Leeds 6F 19
Vesper Ga. Cres. LS5: Leeds 6F 19
Vesper Ga. Dr. LS5: Leeds 5E 19
Vesper Ga. Mt. LS5: Leeds 5F 19
Vesper Gro. LS5: Leeds 1G 29
Vesper La. LS5: Leeds 6F 19
Vesper Mt. LS5: Leeds 1G 29
Vesper Pl. LS5: Leeds 1G 29
LS27: Morl 6G 49
(off High St.)
Vesper Ri. LS5: Leeds 5E 19
Vesper Rd. LS5: Leeds 5D 18
Vesper Ter. LS5: Leeds 1G 29
Vesper Wlk. LS5: Leeds 6E 19
Vesper Way LS5: Leeds 5E 19
Viaduct Rd. LS4: Leeds 4B 30
Viaduct St. LS28: Stan 4F 27
Vicarage Av. LS5: Leeds 1H 29
LS27: Gil 3C 48
Vicarage Cl. WF1: Out 6D 58
Vicarage Dr. LS28: Pud 6F 27
Vicarage Gdns. BD11: Birk 4C 46
Vicarage M. 1H 29
(off Vicarage Ter.)
Vicarage Pl. LS5: Leeds 1H 29
Vicarage Rd. LS6: Leeds 3D 30
Vicarage Ter. LS5: Leeds 1H 29
Vicarage Vw. LS5: Leeds 1H 29
Vicar La. LS2: Leeds 4F 5 (5G 31)
Vicars Rd. LS8: Leeds 1B 32
Vicars Ter. LS8: Leeds 1B 32
Vickers Av. LS5: Leeds 2F 29
Vickersdale LS28: Stan 3G 27
Vickersdale Ct. LS28: Stan 3G 27
Vickersdale Gro. LS28: Stan 3G 27
(off Arthur St.)
Vickers Pl. LS28: Stan 3G 27
Vickers St. LS27: Morl 6F 49
Victor Dr. LS20: Guis 5G 7
Victoria Av. LS9: Leeds 5C 32
LS18: H'fth 4A 18
LS19: Yead 3F 9
LS26: Rothw 5G 53
LS27: Morl 4G 49
Victoria Cl. LS18: H'fth 4A 18
LS19: Yead 2F 9
Victoria Cl. LS15: Leeds 1D 34
LS27: Morl 4G 49
(off Victoria M.)
Victoria Ct. M. LS6: Leeds 2C 30
Victoria Cres. LS18: H'fth 4A 18
LS28: Pud 6E 27
Victoria Dr. LS18: H'fth 4A 18
LS27: Morl 3H 49
Victoria Gdns. LS18: H'fth 4B 18
LS28: Pud 6E 27
Victoria Grange Dr. LS27: Morl 4G 49
Victoria Grange Way
LS27: Morl 4G 49
Victoria Gro. LS9: Leeds 5D 32
LS18: H'fth 5A 18
LS28: Pud 6E 27
Victoria Ho's. LS5: Leeds 1G 29
(off Church St.)
Victoria Ind. Pk. LS14: Leeds 4B 24
Victoria M. LS18: H'fth 4A 18
LS27: Morl 4G 49
Victoria Mt. LS18: H'fth 3A 18
Victoria Pk. Av. LS13: Leeds 2E 29
Victoria Pk. Gro. LS5: Leeds 2F 29
LS13: Leeds 2E 29
Victoria Pl. LS11: Leeds 1F 41
LS19: Yead 2C 8
Victoria Quarter LS1: Leeds 4F 5 (5G 31)
Victoria Ri. LS28: Pud 6E 27
Victoria Rd. LS5: Leeds 1G 29
LS6: Leeds 2C 30
LS11: Leeds 1F 41
LS14: Leeds 4B 24
LS20: Guis 5F 7
LS26: Rothw 3F 53
LS27: Chur, Morl 4G 49
LS28: Fars 3F 27
LS28: Pud 6E 27
Victoria Sq. LS1: Leeds 3C 4 (5F 31)
Victoria St. LS3: Leeds 2A 4 (4D 30)
LS7: Leeds 4H 21
LS27: Chur 2A 50
LS27: Morl 4F 49
LS28: Cal 5C 16
Victoria Ter. LS3: Leeds 2A 4 (4D 30)
LS5: Leeds 1G 29
LS6: Leeds 5B 20
LS19: Yead 2E 9

Victoria Ter. *LS20: Guis* .4G **7**
         (off Lands La.)
  LS28: Stan 3H **27**
Victoria Vs. LS28: Stan 4G **27**
Victoria Wlk. *LS1: Leeds* 4E **5**
    (within The Core Shop. Cen.)
  LS18: H'fth 4A **18**
Victor St. BD3: B'frd 6A **26**
Vienna Ct. LS27: Chur 1A **50**
View, The LS8: Leeds 3B **22**
  LS17: Leeds 3D **12**
Viewlands Cres. LS29: Men 1F **7**
Viewlands Mt. LS29: Men 1F **7**
Viewlands Ri. LS29: Men 1F **7**
Village Av. LS4: Leeds 3B **30**
Village Gdns. LS15: Leeds 4H **29**
         (not continuous)
Village Hotel & Leisure Club
  Leeds 3A **20**
Village Pl. LS4: Leeds 3B **30**
Village St., The LS4: Leeds 3B **30**
Village Ter. LS4: Leeds 2B **30**
Vine Ct. LS20: Guis 5G **7**
Vinery Av. LS9: Leeds 5C **32**
Vinery Gro. LS9: Leeds 5C **32**
Vinery Mt. LS9: Leeds 6C **32**
Vinery Pl. LS9: Leeds 6C **32**
Vinery Rd. LS4: Leeds 3B **30**
Vinery St. LS9: Leeds 5C **32**
Vinery Ter. LS9: Leeds 6C **32**
Vinery Vw. LS9: Leeds 6C **32**
Violet Rd. WF3: E Ard 3B **58**
Virgin Active
  Leeds, Centaur Ho. 3B **4**
  Leeds, Cardigan Flds. Rd. 4A **30**
Virginia Cl. WF3: Loft 5C **58**
Virginia Ct. WF3: Loft 5C **58**
Virginia Dr. WF3: Loft 5C **58**
Virginia Gdns. WF3: Loft 5C **58**
Vollan's Ct. LS14: Leeds 6A **24**
Vue Cinema
  Leeds, Cardigan Flds. Rd. 4B **30**
  Leeds, The Headrow 3E **5** (5G **31**)
Vulcan St. BD4: B'frd 6A **36**

W

Wade La. LS2: Leeds 3E **5** (5G **31**)
Wade St. LS28: Fars 2F **27**
Wadlands Cl. LS28: Fars 1F **27**
Wadlands Dr. LS28: Fars 2E **27**
Wadlands Gro. LS28: Fars 1E **27**
Wadlands Ri. LS28: Fars 2E **27**
Waggon Rd. LS10: Leeds 5H **51**
Waincliffe Cres. LS11: Leeds 6D **40**
Waincliffe Dr. LS11: Leeds 1D **50**
Waincliffe Gth. LS11: Leeds 6D **40**
Waincliffe Mt. LS11: Leeds 6D **40**
Waincliffe Pl. LS11: Leeds 6D **40**
Waincliffe Sq. LS11: Leeds 6D **40**
Waincliffe Ter. LS11: Leeds 1D **50**
Wainfleet Ho. *BD3: B'frd* 5A **26**
       (off Rushton Rd.)
Wakefield 41 Ind. Pk. WF2: Carr G 6B **58**
        (Telford Way)
  WF2: Carr G .5B **58**
        (Trevor Ter.)
Wakefield Av. LS14: Leeds 4H **33**
Wakefield Rd. BD11: Drig 3H **47**
       (not continuous)
  LS10: Leeds .5B **42**
  LS25: Gar 1E **55**
  LS26: Gar, Swil 1E **55**
  LS26: Leeds, Rothw 4D **52**
  LS26: Oul 6B **54**
  LS27: Gil, Morl 4C **48**
Walesby Ct. LS16: Leeds 1E **19**
Walford Av. LS9: Leeds 5C **32**
Walford Gro. LS9: Leeds 5C **32**
Walford Mt. LS9: Leeds 5C **32**
Walford Rd. LS9: Leeds 5C **32**
Walford Ter. LS9: Leeds 5C **32**
Walk, The LS28: Fars 3E **27**
Walker Ho. LS15: Leeds 1F **29**
Walker Pl. LS27: Chur 2H **49**
Walker Rd. LS18: H'fth 2B **18**
  LS29: Men 1B **6**
Walkers Bldgs. *LS28: Pud* 5G **27**
       (off Clifton Hill)
Walker's Grn. LS12: Leeds 3A **40**
Walker's La. LS12: Leeds 3A **40**
       (not continuous)
Walkers Mt. LS6: Leeds 6D **20**
Walkers Row LS19: Yead 2C **8**
Walker Vw. LS10: Leeds 5H **51**
Wallace Gdns. WF3: Loft 5D **58**

Walmer Gro. LS28: Pud 2H **37**
Walmsley Rd. LS6: Leeds 2C **30**
Walnut Cl. LS14: Leeds 3C **24**
Walsh La. LS12: N Far 5C **38**
Walter Cres. LS9: Leeds 6B **32**
Walter St. LS4: Leeds 4B **30**
Walton Cft. *LS28: Fars* 2F **27**
       (off Water La.)
Walton Dr. BD11: Drig 3H **47**
Walton Gth. BD11: Drig 4H **47**
Walton St. LS10: Leeds 3A **42**
  LS11: Leeds 1F **41**
Wansford Cl. BD4: B'frd 5A **36**
  LS15: Leeds 5E **35**
Ward La. LS10: Leeds 6H **41**
Wareham Cnr. BD4: B'frd 5A **36**
Warehouse, The *LS5: Leeds* 1F **29**
       (off Broad La.)
Warings Bldgs. WF3: W Ard 4B **56**
Warley Vw. LS13: Leeds 1B **28**
Warm La. LS19: Yead 4C **8**
Warnford Gro. BD4: B'frd 4A **36**
Warrel's Av. LS13: Leeds 2C **28**
Warrel's Ct. LS13: Leeds 3C **28**
Warrel's Gro. LS13: Leeds 3C **28**
Warrel's Mt. LS13: Leeds 3C **28**
Warrel's Pl. LS13: Leeds 2C **28**
Warrel's Rd. LS13: Leeds 2C **28**
Warrel's Row LS13: Leeds 3C **28**
Warrel's St. LS13: Leeds 3C **28**
Warrel's Ter. LS13: Leeds 3C **28**
Warren Ho. La. LS19: Yead 1F **9**
Warrens La. BD11: Drig 4G **47**
  WF17: Birs 6F **47**
Warwick Ct. LS18: H'fth 4C **18**
Washington Pl. LS13: Leeds 5A **28**
Washington St. LS3: Leeds 5C **30**
  LS13: Leeds 5A **28**
Washington Ter. LS13: Leeds 5A **28**
Waterfront M. BD10: B'frd 3A **16**
Water Gdns. LS26: Rothw 2F **53**
Water Ho. LS18: H'fth 4B **18**
Waterhouse Ct. *LS10: Leeds* 3H **41**
       (off Joseph St.)
Waterhouse Dr. WF3: E Ard 4F **57**
Watering La. LS27: Morl 6B **50**
  WF3: Ting 6B **50**
Watering Mdw. LS27: Morl 5E **50**
Water La. LS11: Leeds 6E **5** (6G **31**)
       (Bridge End)
  LS11: Leeds 6C **4** (1E **41**)
       (Canal Wharf)
  LS12: Leeds .6D **28**
  LS18: H'fth 2H **17**
  LS28: Fars 2F **27**
Waterloo Apartments LS10: Leeds 6F **5**
Waterloo Cnr. LS26: Oul 6A **54**
Waterloo Cres. BD10: B'frd 3B **16**
  LS13: Leeds 2D **28**
Waterloo Gro. LS28: Pud 6D **26**
Waterloo La. LS13: Leeds 2D **28**
Waterloo Mt. LS28: Pud 5D **26**
Waterloo Rd. LS10: Leeds 3A **42**
  LS28: Pud 5D **26**
Waterloo St. LS10: Leeds 6F **5** (6G **31**)
Waterloo Ter. LS13: Leeds 2D **28**
Waterloo Way LS13: Leeds 2D **28**
Watermans Pl. LS1: Leeds 6D **4**
Waterside Ct. LS13: Leeds 6H **17**
Waterside Ind. Pk. LS10: Leeds 4D **42**
Waterside Rd. LS10: Leeds 5D **42**
Waters Wlk. BD10: B'frd 3A **16**
Waterwood Cl. WF3: W Ard 4D **56**
Watson Rd. LS14: Leeds 4H **33**
Watson St. LS27: Morl 6F **49**
Watt St. BD4: B'frd 1A **36**
Waveney Rd. LS12: Leeds 1A **40**
Waver Grn. LS28: Pud 6G **27**
Waverley Gth. LS11: Leeds 3F **41**
Wayland App. LS16: Leeds 5B **12**
Wayland Cl. LS16: Leeds 5B **12**
Wayland Ct. LS16: Leeds 5B **12**
Wayland Cft. LS16: Leeds 5B **12**
Wayland Dr. LS16: Leeds 5B **12**
Weaver Gdns. LS27: Morl 6B **50**
Weavers Ct. LS12: Leeds 6H **29**
  LS28: Pud 2H **37**
Weavers Cft. LS28: Pud 1H **37**
Weavers Fold *LS19: Raw* 5D **8**
       (off New Rd. Side)
Weavers Grange LS20: Guis 3G **7**
Weavers Ho. LS9: Leeds 6H **5**
Weavers Row LS28: Pud 1H **37**
Weaverthorpe Pk. BD4: B'frd 6A **36**
Weaverthorpe Rd. BD4: B'frd 1A **36**
Webster Row LS12: Leeds 1H **39**

Webton Ct. LS7: Leeds 4H **21**
Wedgewood Ct. LS8: Leeds 2C **22**
Wedgewood Dr. LS8: Leeds 3C **22**
Wedgewood Gro. LS8: Leeds 3C **22**
WEETWOOD 4H **19**
Weetwood Av. LS16: Leeds 4B **20**
Weetwood Ct. LS16: Leeds 3A **20**
Weetwood Cres. LS16: Leeds 3B **20**
Weetwood Grange Gro. LS16: Leeds 3H **19**
Weetwood Ho. Ct. LS16: Leeds 2A **20**
Weetwood La. LS16: Leeds 3H **19**
Weetwood Mnr. LS16: Leeds 3A **20**
Weetwood Mill La. LS16: Leeds 3B **20**
Weetwood Pk. Dr. LS16: Leeds 3H **19**
Weetwood Rd. LS16: Leeds 3H **19**
Weetwood Ter. LS16: Leeds 3B **20**
Weetwood Wlk. LS16: Leeds 3A **20**
Welbeck Rd. LS9: Leeds 6C **32**
  WF17: Birs 6H **47**
Welburn Av. LS16: Leeds 4H **19**
Welburn Dr. LS16: Leeds 4H **19**
Welburn Gro. LS16: Leeds 4H **19**
Weldon Ct. BD4: B'frd 3A **36**
Well Cl. LS19: Raw .6E **9**
Well Cl. Pl. LS2: Leeds 3G **31**
Well Cl. Ri. LS7: Leeds 3G **31**
Wellcroft Gro. WF3: W Ard 4D **56**
Wellfield Pl. *LS6: Leeds* 6B **20**
       (off Chapel St.)
Wellfield Ter. LS27: Gil 2C **48**
Well Gth. LS15: Leeds 3C **34**
Well Gth. Bank LS13: Leeds 1B **28**
Well Gth. Mt. LS15: Leeds 3C **34**
Well Gth. Vw. LS13: Leeds 1C **28**
Well Grn. Ct. BD4: E Bier 2A **46**
Well Hill LS19: Raw 2D **8**
Well Hill Ct. *LS19: Yead* 3D **8**
       (off Well Hill)
Well Holme Mead LS12: N Far 4E **39**
Well Ho. Av. LS8: Leeds 6C **22**
Well Ho. Cl. LS8: Leeds 6B **22**
Well Ho. Cres. LS8: Leeds 6C **22**
Well Ho. Dr. LS8: Leeds 6C **22**
Well Ho. Gdns. LS8: Leeds 6C **22**
Well Ho. Rd. LS8: Leeds 6C **22**
Wellington Bri. St. LS1: Leeds 5A **4** (6D **30**)
  LS3: Leeds 4A **4** (5D **30**)
Wellington Ct. BD11: Birk 3C **46**
Wellington Gdns. LS13: Leeds 2D **28**
Wellington Gth. LS13: Leeds 1D **28**
Wellington Gro. LS13: Leeds 1D **28**
  LS28: Pud 6E **27**
WELLINGTON HILL 3H **23**
Wellington Hill LS17: Leeds 6H **15**
Wellington Mt. LS13: Leeds 1D **28**
Wellington Pl. LS1: Leeds 5A **4** (6E **31**)
Wellington Rd. LS1: Leeds 5A **4** (6D **30**)
  LS12: Leeds 1C **40**
Wellington Rd. Ind. Est. LS12: Leeds 6D **30**
Wellington St. BD4: B'frd 1A **36**
  BD11: Birk 3C **46**
       (off Wellington Ct.)
  LS1: Leeds 4A **4** (5D **30**)
       (not continuous)
  LS27: Morl 5G **49**
Wellington Ter. LS13: Leeds 1D **28**
Well La. LS7: Leeds 4H **21**
  LS19: Raw 6E **9**
  LS19: Yead 3D **8**
  LS20: Guis 4G **7**
Wells Ct. *LS19: Yead* 2D **8**
       (off Well La.)
Wells Cft. LS6: Leeds 4C **20**
Wells Gro. LS20: Guis 4G **7**
Wells Mt. LS20: Guis 4G **7**
Wells Rd. LS20: Guis 4G **7**
Wellstone Av. LS13: Leeds 4B **28**
Wellstone Dr. LS13: Leeds 4B **28**
Wellstone Gdns. LS13: Leeds 5B **28**
Wellstone Gth. LS13: Leeds 5B **28**
Wellstone Grn. LS13: Leeds 4B **28**
Wellstone Ri. LS13: Leeds 5B **28**
Wellstone Rd. LS13: Leeds 5B **28**
Wellstone Way LS13: Leeds 5B **28**
Well St. *LS20: Guis* .4G **7**
       (off Wells Rd.)
  LS28: Fars 2F **27**
Well Ter. LS20: Guis 4G **7**
Well Vw. LS20: Guis 4G **7**
Welton Gro. LS6: Leeds 2C **30**
Welton Mt. LS6: Leeds 2C **30**
Welton Pl. LS6: Leeds 2C **30**
Welton Rd. LS6: Leeds 2C **30**
Wenborough La. BD4: B'frd 4B **36**
Wendover Ct. LS16: Leeds 6B **12**
Wensley Av. LS7: Leeds 4G **21**
Wensley Cres. LS7: Leeds 4G **21**

Wensleydale Av.—Wharfedale Ct.

Wensleydale Av. LS12: Leeds 3F **29**
Wensleydale Cl. LS12: Leeds 3F **29**
Wensleydale Ct. *LS7: Leeds 4G **21***
(off Stainbeck La.)
Wensleydale Cres. LS12: Leeds 3F **29**
Wensleydale Dr. LS12: Leeds 3F **29**
Wensleydale M. LS12: Leeds 3F **29**
Wensleydale Ri. LS12: Leeds 3F **29**
Wensleydale Rd. BD3: B'frd 6A **26**
Wensley Dr. LS7: Leeds 3F **21**
Wensley Gdns. LS7: Leeds 3F **21**
Wensley Grn. LS7: Leeds 4F **21**
Wensley Gro. LS7: Leeds 4G **21**
Wensley Lawn LS10: Leeds 5G **51**
Wensley Rd. LS7: Leeds 3F **21**
Wensley Vw. LS7: Leeds 4G **21**
Wentworth Av. LS17: Leeds 5F **13**
Wentworth Cl. LS29: Men 1C **6**
Wentworth Cres. BD4: B'frd 5B **36**
LS17: Leeds 5G **13**
Wentworth Farm Res. Pk. LS12: N Far 5D **38**
Wentworth Ter. *LS19: Raw 6F **9***
(off Town St.)
Wentworth Way LS17: Leeds 5G **13**
Wepener Mt. LS9: Leeds 4D **32**
Wepener Pl. LS9: Leeds 4D **32**
Wesley App. LS11: Leeds 5D **40**
Wesley Av. LS12: Leeds 6A **30**
Wesley Cl. LS11: Leeds 4D **40**
Wesley Ct. *LS6: Leeds 2E **31***
(off Woodhouse St.)
LS11: Leeds 5D **40**
*LS19: Yead 6H **7***
(off South Vw.)
Wesley Cft. LS11: Leeds 4D **40**
Wesley Gth. LS11: Leeds 4D **40**
Wesley Grn. LS11: Leeds 5D **40**
Wesley Ho. LS11: Leeds 5C **40**
Wesley Pl. LS9: Leeds 6A **32**
LS12: Leeds 6A **30**
Wesley Rd. LS12: Leeds 6A **30**
LS28: Stan 4E **27**
Wesley Row LS28: Pud 5G **27**
Wesley Sq. LS28: Pud 6G **27**
Wesley St. LS11: Leeds 4D **40**
LS13: Leeds 6H **17**
LS27: Morl 5G **49**
LS28: Fars 2F **27**
LS28: Stan 3F **27**
Wesley Ter. *LS9: Leeds 6A **32***
(off Up. Accomodation St.)
LS13: Leeds 2D **28**
(Bellmount Vw.)
LS13: Leeds 6H **17**
(Wesley St.)
LS28: Pud 5G **27**
Wesley Vw. LS13: Leeds 6H **17**
LS28: Pud 6G **27**
WEST ARDSLEY 3C **56**
West Av. LS8: Leeds 3E **23**
Westbourne Av. LS11: Leeds 4F **41**
Westbourne Dr. LS20: Guis 4E **7**
LS29: Men 1C **6**
Westbourne Mt. LS11: Leeds 4F **41**
Westbourne Pl. LS11: Leeds 4F **41**
LS28: Stan 4F **27**
Westbourne St. LS11: Leeds 4F **41**
Westbrook Cl. LS18: H'fth 1B **18**
Westbrook La. LS18: H'fth 1B **18**
Westbury Gro. LS10: Leeds 5B **42**
Westbury Mt. LS10: Leeds 6B **42**
Westbury Pl. Nth. LS10: Leeds 5B **42**
Westbury Pl. Sth. LS10: Leeds 6B **42**
Westbury St. LS10: Leeds 6B **42**
Westbury Ter. LS10: Leeds 6B **42**
W. Chevin Rd. LS29: Men 1F **7**
Westcombe Av. LS8: Leeds 1C **22**
West Ct. LS8: Leeds 3E **23**
LS13: Leeds 4C **28**
Westdale Dr. LS28: Pud 5F **27**
Westdale Gdns. LS28: Pud 5F **27**
Westdale Gro. LS28: Pud 5F **27**
Westdale M. *LS28: Pud 5F **27***
(off Westdale Gro.)
Westdale Ri. LS28: Pud 5F **27**
Westdale Rd. LS28: Pud 5F **27**
West Dene LS17: Leeds 4B **14**
WEST END 2H **17**
West End LS12: N Far 4D **38**
LS27: Gil 2C **48**
West End App. LS27: Morl 6D **48**
West End Cl. LS18: H'fth 2H **17**
West End Dr. LS18: H'fth 2H **17**
West End Gro. LS18: H'fth 2H **17**
West End La. LS18: H'fth 2H **17**
West End Ri. LS18: H'fth 2H **17**
West End Rd. LS28: Cal 5D **16**
West End Ter. LS20: Guis 4E **7**
Westerly Cft. LS12: Leeds 5A **30**
Westerly Ri. *LS12: Leeds 5A **30***
(off Mistresses La.)
Western Gro. LS12: Leeds 2H **39**
Western Mt. LS12: Leeds 2H **39**
Western Rd. LS12: Leeds 2H **39**
Western St. LS12: Leeds 2H **39**
WESTERTON 4D **56**
Westerton Cl. WF3: W Ard 3F **57**
Westerton Rd. WF3: W Ard 4B **56**
Westerton Wlk. WF3: W Ard 3F **57**
W. Farm Av. LS10: Leeds 4F **51**
WESTFIELD 3B **8**
Westfield LS7: Leeds 4G **21**
LS28: Stan 4F **27**
Westfield Av. LS12: Leeds 5F **29**
LS19: Yead 3B **8**
Westfield Bldgs. *LS27: Morl 2A **56***
(off Tingley Comn.)
Westfield Cl. LS19: Yead 3B **8**
LS26: Rothw 5E **53**
Westfield Ct. *LS3: Leeds 4D **30***
(off Westfield Ter.)
LS26: Rothw 5E **53**
Westfield Cres. LS3: Leeds 3D **30**
(Bk. Rosebank Cres.)
LS3: Leeds 4D **30**
(Westfield Rd.)
Westfield Dr. LS19: Yead 3A **8**
Westfield Gro. LS19: Yead 3B **8**
Westfield Ind. Est. LS19: Yead 3C **8**
Westfield Mills *LS12: Leeds 5G **29***
(off Greenock Rd.)
Westfield Mt. LS19: Yead 3B **8**
Westfield Oval LS19: Yead 3A **8**
Westfield Pl. LS27: Morl 5G **49**
Westfield Rd. LS3: Leeds 4D **30**
LS26: Rothw 6E **53**
LS27: Morl 5G **49**
WF3: Carl 6E **53**
Westfield Ter. LS3: Leeds 4D **30**
LS7: Leeds 4G **21**
Westfield Yd. LS12: Leeds 2H **39**
WESTGATE 3E **59**
Westgate LS1: Leeds 4A **4** (5E **31**)
(not continuous)
LS20: Guis 5C **6**
Westgate Cl. WF3: Loft 3E **59**
Westgate Ct. WF3: Loft 3E **59**
Westgate Gro. WF3: Loft 3E **59**
WESTGATE HILL 1C **46**
Westgate Hill St. BD4: B'frd 1B **46**
Westgate Ho. LS28: Pud 5E **27**
Westgate La. WF3: Loft 3D **58**
(not continuous)
Westgate Pl. BD4: B'frd 1C **46**
Westgate Ter. BD4: B'frd 1C **46**
W. Grange Cl. LS10: Leeds 6H **41**
W. Grange Dr. LS10: Leeds 6H **41**
W. Grange Fold LS10: Leeds 6H **41**
W. Grange Gdns. LS10: Leeds 6H **41**
W. Grange Gth. LS10: Leeds 6H **41**
W. Grange Grn. LS10: Leeds 6H **41**
W. Grange Rd. LS10: Leeds 1H **51**
W. Grange Wlk. LS10: Leeds 6H **41**
West Gro. St. LS28: Stan 4F **27**
West Hall LS19: Yead 3E **9**
W. Hill Av. LS7: Leeds 4G **21**
W. Hill Ter. LS7: Leeds 4G **21**
Westland Ct. LS11: Leeds 1F **51**
Westland Rd. LS11: Leeds 6F **41**
Westland Sq. LS11: Leeds 1F **51**
W. Lea Cl. LS17: Leeds 2F **21**
W. Lea Cres. LS19: Yead 3B **8**
WF3: W Ard 4B **56**
W. Lea Dr. LS17: Leeds 2F **21**
WF3: W Ard 4B **56**
W. Lea Gdns. LS17: Leeds 2F **21**
W. Lea Gth. LS17: Leeds 2F **21**
W. Lea Gro. LS19: Yead 3B **8**
Westlock Av. LS9: Leeds 4C **32**
W. Lodge Gdns. LS7: Leeds 5G **21**
Westmead LS28: Stan 4C **26**
Westminster Cl. LS13: Leeds 1H **27**
Westminster Cres. LS15: Leeds 6G **33**
Westminster Cft. LS13: Leeds 1H **27**
Westminster Dr. LS13: Leeds 1H **27**
Westmoor Pl. LS13: Leeds 2B **28**
Westmoor Ri. LS13: Leeds 2B **28**
Westmoor Rd. LS13: Leeds 2B **28**
Westmoor St. LS13: Leeds 2B **28**
Westmoreland Mt. LS13: Leeds 1D **28**
West Mt. St. LS11: Leeds 4E **41**
Westover Av. LS13: Leeds 2C **28**
Westover Cl. LS13: Leeds 2D **28**
Westover Gdns. LS28: Pud 6E **27**
Westover Grn. LS13: Leeds 2C **28**
Westover Gro. LS13: Leeds 2C **28**
Westover Mt. LS13: Leeds 2C **28**
Westover Rd. LS13: Leeds 2C **28**
Westover St. LS13: Leeds 2C **28**
Westover Ter. LS13: Leeds 2C **28**
Westover Vw. LS13: Leeds 2C **28**
West Pde. LS16: Leeds 3G **19**
LS20: Guis 4G **7**
LS26: Rothw 4H **53**
WEST PARK 3G **19**
West Pk. LS20: Guis 3E **7**
LS28: Pud 6F **27**
West Pk. Av. LS8: Leeds 6D **14**
West Pk. Chase LS8: Leeds 6C **14**
West Pk. Cl. LS8: Leeds 6C **14**
West Pk. Ct. LS8: Leeds 6D **14**
West Pk. Cres. LS8: Leeds 1D **22**
West Pk. Dr. LS16: Leeds 3G **19**
West Pk. Dr. E. LS8: Leeds 6C **14**
West Pk. Dr. W. LS8: Leeds 6B **14**
West Pk. Gdns. LS8: Leeds 1D **22**
West Pk. Gro. LS8: Leeds 6C **14**
West Pk. Pl. LS8: Leeds 1D **22**
West Pk. Rd. LS8: Leeds 1D **22**
West Pk. Vs. LS8: Leeds 6D **14**
West Pk. Wlk. *LS16: Leeds 4G **19***
(off Old Oak Dr.)
W. Pasture Cl. LS18: H'fth 2H **17**
West Point LS1: Leeds 5B **4** (6F **31**)
Westray LS12: Leeds 5A **4** (6D **30**)
West Rd. LS9: Leeds 4E **43**
West Rd. Nth. LS9: Leeds 4E **43**
Westroyd LS28: Pud 1E **37**
Westroyd Av. BD19: Hun 6A **46**
LS28: Pud 1E **37**
Westroyd Cres. LS28: Pud 2E **37**
Westroyd Gdns. LS28: Pud 1E **37**
WESTROYD HILL 1F **37**
W. Royd Ho. LS28: Fars 3F **27**
W. Side Retail Pk. LS20: Guis 6H **7**
Westside Vw. *BD11: Drig 3G **47***
(off West St.)
West St. BD11: Drig 4G **47**
LS1: Leeds 4A **4** (5D **30**)
LS20: Guis 4G **7**
LS27: Morl 6H **49**
LS28: Stan 5G **27**
West Ter. St. *LS28: Stan 4F **27***
(off West Gro. St.)
West Vale LS12: Leeds 2C **40**
Westvale M. LS13: Leeds 4E **29**
West Vw. BD11: Birk 5D **46**
LS11: Leeds 4E **41**
LS19: Yead 6H **7**
LS26: Oul 4C **54**
*LS28: Fars 3F **27***
(off New St.)
West Vw. Ct. LS19: Yead 6H **7**
W. Villa Rd. LS20: Guis 4G **7**
West Way LS1: Leeds 4A **4** (5E **31**)
Westway LS20: Guis 5D **6**
LS28: Fars 2E **27**
Westways Dr. LS8: Leeds 4E **23**
West Winds LS29: Men 1A **6**
Westwinn Gth. LS14: Leeds 3C **24**
Westwinn Vw. LS14: Leeds 2C **24**
Westwood Cl. LS27: Morl 3H **49**
West Wood Ct. LS10: Leeds 4E **51**
Westwood Ri. LS27: Morl 3H **49**
West Wood Rd. LS10: Leeds 5D **50**
LS27: Chur 5D **50**
Westwood Side LS27: Morl 2G **49**
W. Yorkshire Ind. Est. BD4: B'frd 1A **46**
West Yorkshire Playhouse, The 4H **5** (5H **31**)
W. Yorkshire Retail Pk. WF17: Birs 5A **48**
Wetherby Gro. LS4: Leeds 3A **30**
Wetherby Pl. LS4: Leeds 3B **30**
Wetherby Rd. LS8: Leeds 5D **22**
LS14: Bard, Leeds, S'cft 4G **23**
LS17: Leeds 2H **23**
Wetherby Ter. LS4: Leeds 3A **30**
Wetton Ct. BD3: B'frd 6A **26**
Whack Ho. *LS19: Yead 3B **8***
(off Westfield Av.)
Whack Ho. Cl. LS19: Yead 3C **8**
Whack Ho. La. LS19: Yead 3C **8**
Wharf App. LS1: Leeds 6C **4**
Wharfdale Av. LS29: Men 3D **6**
Wharfdale Ct. LS29: Men 3C **6**
Wharfdale Cft. LS29: Men 3C **6**
Wharfdale Fold LS29: Men 3C **6**
Wharfe Cl. LS16: Leeds 5B **12**
Wharfedale Av. LS7: Leeds 1F **31**
Wharfedale Bus. Pk. BD4: B'frd 6A **36**
Wharfedale Cl. LS12: Leeds 3F **29**
Wharfedale Ct. LS14: Leeds 6H **23**

A-Z Leeds 109

Wharfedale Gro. LS7: Leeds 1F 31
Wharfedale Mt. LS7: Leeds 1F 31
Wharfedale Pl. LS7: Leeds 1F 31
Wharfedale Ri. WF3: W Ard 4B 56
Wharfedale St. LS7: Leeds 1F 31
Wharfedale Vw. LS7: Leeds 1F 31
   LS29: Men 1C 6
Wharf St. LS2: Leeds 5G 5 (6H 31)
Wharncliffe Cres. BD2: B'frd 1A 26
Wharncliffe Dr. BD2: B'frd 1A 26
Wharncliffe St. BD2: B'frd 1A 26
Wheaters Fold LS28: Stan 4G 27
   (off Woods Row)
Wheatfield Ct. LS28: Pud 1F 37
WHEATFIELDS SUE RYDER HOSPICE 6C 20
Wheatlands LS28: Fars 2E 27
Wheaton Av. LS15: Leeds 5A 34
Wheaton Ct. LS15: Leeds 5A 34
   (off Wheaton Av.)
Wheelwright Av. LS12: Leeds 2G 39
Wheelwright Cl. LS12: Leeds 2G 39
   (not continuous)
Whernside Ct. LS29: Men 2D 6
   (off Jackson Wlk.)
Whimbrel M. LS27: Morl 6A 50
Whinberry Pl. WF17: Birs 6H 47
Whinbrook Cres. LS17: Leeds 2G 21
Whinbrook Gdns. LS17: Leeds 2G 21
Whinbrook Gro. LS17: Leeds 2G 21
Whincover Bank LS12: Leeds 2F 39
Whincover Cl. LS12: Leeds 2F 39
Whincover Cross LS12: Leeds 2F 39
Whincover Dr. LS12: Leeds 2E 39
Whincover Gdns. LS12: Leeds 2F 39
Whincover Grange LS12: Leeds 2F 39
Whincover Gro. LS12: Leeds 2F 39
Whincover Hill LS12: Leeds 2F 39
Whincover Mt. LS12: Leeds 2F 39
Whincover Rd. LS12: Leeds 2E 39
Whincover Vw. LS12: Leeds 2F 39
Whincup Gdns. LS10: Leeds 5A 42
   (off Telford Pl.)
Whinfield LS16: Leeds .5H 11
Whingate LS12: Leeds 5G 29
Whingate Av. LS12: Leeds 6H 29
Whingate Bus. Pk. LS12: Leeds 6H 29
Whingate Cl. LS12: Leeds 6H 29
Whingate Ct. LS12: Leeds 6H 29
Whingate Grn. LS12: Leeds 6G 29
Whingate Gro. LS12: Leeds 6G 29
Whingate Rd. LS12: Leeds 6G 29
WHINMOOR 3B 24
Whinmoor Ct. LS14: Leeds 2A 24
Whinmoor Cres. LS14: Leeds 2A 24
Whinmoor Gdns. LS14: Leeds 2H 23
Whinmoor La. LS17: Leeds, Shad 6G 15
Whinmoor Way LS14: Leeds 6D 24
   (Ash Tree Ct.)
   LS14: Leeds 6C 24
   (Farndale App.)
   LS14: Leeds 4C 24
   (Naburn Cl.)
Whinney Hill BD4: B'frd 2A 36
Whin Wood Grange LS14: Leeds 3B 24
Whisperwood Cl. WF1: Out 6F 59
Whisperwood Rd. WF1: Out 6F 59
Whitaker St. LS28: Fars 4F 27
Whitebeam La. LS10: Leeds 1H 51
Whitebridge Av. LS9: Leeds 5G 33
Whitebridge Cres. LS9: Leeds 4G 33
Whitebridge Spur LS9: Leeds 4G 33
Whitebridge Vw. LS9: Leeds 4G 33
Whitechapel Cl. LS8: Leeds 5D 22
Whitechapel Way LS8: Leeds 5D 22
Whitecliffe Cres. LS26: Swil 5G 45
Whitecliffe Dr. LS26: Swil 5G 45
Whitecliffe La. LS26: Swil 5G 45
Whitecliffe Ri. LS26: Swil 5G 45
WHITECOTE 1C 28
Whitecote Gdns. LS13: Leeds 1B 28
Whitecote Hill LS13: Leeds 1B 28
Whitecote Ho. LS13: Leeds 6B 18
Whitecote La. LS13: Leeds 1B 28
Whitecote Ri. LS13: Leeds 1B 28
WHITE CROSS 3E 7
White Gro. LS8: Leeds 3C 22
Whitehall LS12: Leeds 6A 4 (6E 31)
Whitehall Ct. LS12: N Far 3G 39
Whitehall Cft. LS12: Leeds 3H 39
   (off Whitehall Dr.)
   LS26: Rothw 4H 53
Whitehall Cross LS12: N Far 3F 39
Whitehall Dr. LS12: Leeds 3H 39
Whitehall Grn. LS12: Leeds 3G 39
Whitehall Gro. BD11: Birk 4D 46
   BD11: Drig 3F 47

Whitehall Ind. Est. LS12: N Far 3F 39
Whitehall Pk. LS12: N Far 3F 39
Whitehall Pl. LS12: Leeds 1D 40
Whitehall Quay LS1: Leeds 5C 4 (6F 31)
Whitehall Riverside LS1: Leeds 6B 4 (6E 31)
Whitehall Rd. LS1: Leeds 6A 4 (1D 40)
   LS12: Leeds, N Far 6A 4 (6B 38)
Whitehall Rd. E. BD11: Birk 5C 46
Whitehall Rd. W. BD11: Birk 6A 46
   BD19: Hun 6A 46
Whitehall Waterfront LS1: Leeds 6B 4 (6E 31)
Whitehouse La. LS19: Yead 1G 9
   LS26: Swil 4H 45
Whitehouse St. LS10: Leeds 2H 41
White Laithe App. LS14: Leeds 3B 24
White Laithe Av. LS14: Leeds 3B 24
White Laithe Cl. LS14: Leeds 3B 24
White Laithe Ct. LS14: Leeds 3B 24
White Laithe Cft. LS14: Leeds 3B 24
White Laithe Gdns. LS14: Leeds 3B 24
White Laithe Gth. LS14: Leeds 2B 24
White Laithe Grn. LS14: Leeds 3C 24
White Laithe Gro. LS14: Leeds 3C 24
White Laithe Rd. LS14: Leeds 3B 24
White Laithe Wlk. LS14: Leeds 3C 24
Whitelands LS19: Raw .5C 8
   LS28: Pud 5H 27
Whitelock St. LS7: Leeds 1G 5 (4H 31)
Whitestone Cres. LS19: Yead 2D 8
White St. LS26: Wood .3D 54
Whitfield Av. LS10: Leeds 3A 42
Whitfield Gdns. LS10: Leeds 3A 42
Whitfield Mill BD10: B'frd 3A 16
Whitfield Pl. LS10: Leeds 3A 42
Whitfield Sq. LS10: Leeds 3A 42
Whitfield St. LS8: Leeds 2B 32
Whitfield Way LS10: Leeds 3A 42
WHITKIRK 4C 34
Whitkirk Cl. LS15: Leeds 5E 35
Whitkirk La. LS15: Leeds 5D 34
WHITKIRK LANE END .5D 34
Whitley Gdns. LS8: Leeds 2A 32
   (off Gledhow Rd.)
Whyment Cl. LS27: Chur 6A 40
Wicket, The LS28: Cal .4D 16
Wickets, The LS6: Leeds 4D 20
   LS15: Leeds 6E 35
Wickham St. LS11: Leeds 4E 41
Wide La. LS27: Morl 6H 49
Wigeon App. LS27: Morl 5A 50
Wigton Chase LS17: Leeds 4C 14
Wigton Ga. LS17: Leeds 3A 14
Wigton Grn. LS17: Leeds 3B 14
Wigton Gro. LS17: Leeds 3A 14
Wigton Pk. Cl. LS17: Leeds 3B 14
WIKE 1F 15
Wike Ridge Av. LS17: Leeds 4C 14
Wike Ridge Cl. LS17: Leeds 3D 14
Wike Ridge Ct. LS17: Leeds 3D 14
Wike Ridge Fold LS17: Leeds 3C 14
Wike Ridge Gdns. LS17: Leeds 4D 14
Wike Ridge Gro. LS17: Leeds 4D 14
Wike Ridge La. LS17: Leeds, Wike 4D 14
Wike Ridge Mt. LS17: Leeds 4D 14
Wike Ridge Mt. LS17: Leeds 4D 14
Wike Ridge Vw. LS17: Leeds 4C 14
Wild Gro. LS28: Pud 6C 26
Wilfred Av. LS15: Leeds 5B 34
Wilfred St. LS15: Leeds 5B 34
Wilfred Ter. LS12: Leeds 3G 39
Willans Av. LS26: Rothw 2G 53
William Av. LS15: Leeds 5G 33
William Hey Ct. LS9: Leeds 3D 32
William La. LS28: Pud .6F 27
William Ri. LS15: Leeds 5G 33
Williams Ct. LS28: Fars 2F 27
William St. BD4: B'frd .6A 36
   LS6: Leeds 2C 30
   LS27: Chur 1A 50
   LS28: Stan 3H 27
   (Milestone Ct.)
   LS28: Stan 3H 27
   (Sun Fld.)
William Vw. LS15: Leeds 5G 33
Willis St. LS9: Leeds 6A 32
Willoughby Ter. LS11: Leeds 2D 40
Willow App. LS4: Leeds 4C 30
Willow Av. LS4: Leeds .4C 30
Willow Cl. LS4: Leeds .4C 30
   LS20: Guis 4G 7
Willow Cres. LS15: Leeds 6H 33
Willowdale LS10: Leeds 5A 52
Willow Gdns. LS20: Guis 4G 7

Willow Gth. LS4: Leeds 4C 30
Willow Gth. Av. LS14: Leeds 3B 24
Willow Gth. Cl. LS14: Leeds 3B 24
Willow Ho. LS7: Leeds .4H 21
Willow La. LS20: Bail, Guis 6B 6
Willow Rd. LS4: Leeds .4C 30
   LS28: Fars 3E 27
Willows, The LS10: Leeds 5A 52
   LS17: Leeds 1G 21
   LS26: Wood 3D 54
   (off Aberford Rd.)
Willow Sq. LS26: Oul 4C 54
Willow Ter. LS15: Leeds 1B 4 (4E 31)
Willow Well Rd. LS15: Leeds 5H 33
Wills Gill LS20: Guis 4H 7
Wilmington Gro. LS7: Leeds 3G 31
Wilmington St. LS7: Leeds 3H 31
Wilmington Ter. LS7: Leeds 3G 31
   (off Wilmington Gro.)
Wilsons Yd. LS28: Stan 4F 27
Wilton Gro. LS6: Leeds 5C 20
Winchester Gdns. BD4: B'frd 2A 36
Winchester St. LS12: Leeds 6B 30
Winden Cl. WF3: Loft 6E 59
Winden Gro. WF3: Loft 6D 58
Windermere Dr. LS17: Leeds 3D 12
Winders Dale LS27: Morl 3F 49
Winding Way LS17: Leeds 4F 13
Windmill App. LS10: Leeds 1A 52
Windmill Chase LS26: Rothw 5G 53
Windmill Cl. LS10: Leeds 2A 52
Windmill Cotts. LS15: Leeds 1F 45
Windmill Ct. LS10: Leeds 1G 39
   LS14: Leeds 5B 24
Windmill Fld. Rd. LS26: Rothw 5G 53
Windmill Fold LS19: Yead 2E 9
   (off Windmill La.)
Windmill Gdns. LS15: Leeds 6D 34
Windmill Ga. LS12: Leeds 6G 29
Windmill Grn. LS26: Rothw 5G 53
WINDMILL HILL 1E 37
Windmill Hill LS28: Pud 1E 37
Windmill La. LS19: Yead 3E 9
   LS26: Rothw 3A 52
   LS27: Gil 3D 48
   LS29: Men 1F 7
Windmill Pl. LS19: Yead 3E 9
   (off Windmill La.)
Windmill Ri. LS12: Leeds 1G 39
Windmill Rd. LS10: Leeds 1A 52
Windrush Ct. LS7: Leeds 1H 31
   (off Chapeltown Rd.)
Windsor Av. LS15: Leeds 5B 34
Windsor Ct. LS13: Leeds 3D 28
   LS17: Leeds 1A 22
   LS27: Morl 5G 49
Windsor Cres. LS26: Rothw 3G 53
Windsor Mt. LS15: Leeds 5B 34
Windsor Oval WF3: W Ard 6B 56
Windsor Ter. LS27: Gil .2D 48
Winfield Dr. BD4: E Bier 3A 46
Winfield Gro. LS2: Leeds 3F 31
   (off Devon Rd.)
Winfield Pl. LS2: Leeds 3F 31
Winfield Ter. LS2: Leeds 3F 31
   (off Devon Rd.)
Winker Grn. Lodge LS12: Leeds 5A 30
   (off Eyres Mill Side)
Winker Grn. Mills LS12: Leeds 5H 29
   (off Eyres Mill Side)
Winnipeg Pl. LS7: Leeds 5H 21
Winn Mt. LS7: Leeds 5B 18
Winrose App. LS10: Leeds 2A 52
Winrose Av. LS10: Leeds 1H 51
Winrose Cres. LS10: Leeds 1H 51
Winrose Dr. LS10: Leeds 1H 51
Winrose Gth. LS10: Leeds 1A 52
Winrose Gro. LS10: Leeds 1A 52
Winrose Hill LS10: Leeds 6A 42
Winslow Rd. BD10: B'frd 1A 16
Winstanley Ter. LS6: Leeds 2C 30
   (off Victoria Rd.)
Winston Gdns. LS6: Leeds 6A 20
Winston Mt. LS6: Leeds 6A 20
Winterbourne Av. LS27: Morl 3H 49
Winthorpe Av. WF3: Thpe H 1H 57
Winthorpe Cres. WF3: Thpe H 1H 57
Winthorpe St. LS6: Leeds 5D 20
Winthorpe Vw. WF3: Thpe H 1A 58
Wintoun St. LS7: Leeds 1G 5 (4H 31)
Wira Ho. LS16: Leeds .2F 19
WIRING FIELD 6A 30
Withens Rd. WF17: Birs 6G 47
Wolley Av. LS12: N Far 4D 38
Wolley Ct. LS12: N Far 4D 38
Wolley Dr. LS12: N Far 4D 38
Wolley Gdns. LS12: N Far 4D 38

Wolseley Rd.—Worsted Ho.

Wolseley Rd. LS4: Leeds 4B 30
(not continuous)
Wolston Cl. BD4: B'frd 5A 36
Womersley Ct. *LS28: Pud* *1F 37*
(off Womersley Pl.)
Womersley Pl. LS28: Pud 1F 37
LS28: Stan 4D 26
Woodbine Ter. LS6: Leeds 5C 20
LS13: Leeds 2C 28
LS18: H'fth *4C 18*
(off Wood La.)
WOODBOTTOM 3F 17
Wood Bottom LS19: Raw 3F 17
Woodbourne LS8: Leeds 4E 23
Woodbourne Av. LS17: Leeds 2G 21
Woodbridge Cl. LS6: Leeds 6H 19
Woodbridge Cres. LS6: Leeds 5G 19
Woodbridge Fold LS6: Leeds 6G 19
Woodbridge Gdns. LS6: Leeds 6G 19
Woodbridge Gth. LS6: Leeds 6H 19
Woodbridge Grn. LS6: Leeds 6H 19
Woodbridge Lawn LS6: Leeds 6G 19
Woodbridge Pl. LS6: Leeds 6G 19
Woodbridge Rd. LS6: Leeds 6G 19
Woodbridge Va. LS6: Leeds 6G 19
Wood Cl. LS7: Leeds 4G 21
LS26: Rothw 3F 53
Wood Cres. LS26: Rothw 3F 53
Woodcross LS27: Morl 3G 49
Woodcross End LS27: Morl 2G 49
Woodcross Fold LS27: Morl 3G 49
Woodcross Gdns. LS27: Morl 3G 49
Woodcross Gth. LS27: Morl 2G 49
Wood Dr. LS26: Rothw 3E 53
Woodeson Ct. LS13: Leeds 6H 17
Woodeson Lea LS13: Leeds 6H 17
Woodfield Ter. LS28: Pud 1H 37
Woodgarth Gdns. BD4: B'frd 4B 36
Wood Gro. LS12: Leeds 6D 28
WOODHALL 3C 26
Woodhall Av. BD3: B'frd 4A 26
LS5: Leeds 5E 19
Woodhall Cl. LS28: Stan 3C 26
Woodhall Ct. LS15: Leeds 1D 44
LS28: Cal 6C 16
Woodhall Cft. LS28: Stan 3C 26
Woodhall Dr. LS5: Leeds 5E 19
WOODHALL HILLS 2C 26
Woodhall Hills LS28: Cal 2B 26
Woodhall La. LS28: Cal, Stan 2C 26
WOODHALL PARK 3D 26
Woodhall Pk. Av. LS28: Stan 3C 26
Woodhall Pk. Cres. E. LS28: Stan 4D 26
Woodhall Pk. Cres. W. LS28: Stan 4C 26
Woodhall Pk. Dr. LS28: Stan 4C 26
Woodhall Pk. Gdns. LS28: Stan 4D 26
Woodhall Pk. Gro. LS28: Stan 4C 26
Woodhall Pk. Mt. LS28: Stan 3C 26
Woodhall Pl. BD3: B'frd 4A 26
Woodhall Retail Pk. BD3: B'frd 4A 26
Woodhall Rd. BD3: B'frd 5A 26
BD3: B'frd, Cal 4A 26
LS28: Cal 2A 26
Woodhall Ter. BD3: B'frd 4A 26
Woodhall Vw. BD3: B'frd 4B 26
Woodhead LS29: Burl W, Men 1A 6
Woodhead La. LS27: Gil 2C 48
Woodhead Rd. WF17: Birs 6B 48
Wood Hill LS26: Rothw 3F 53
Wood Hill Ct. LS16: Leeds 5D 10
Wood Hill Cres. LS16: Leeds 6C 10
Wood Hill Gdns. LS16: Leeds 5D 10
Wood Hill Gth. LS16: Leeds 5D 10
Wood Hill Gro. LS16: Leeds 6C 10
Wood Hill Ri. LS16: Leeds 5D 10
Woodhill Ri. BD10: B'frd 3A 16
Wood Hill Rd. LS16: Leeds 6D 10
WOODHOUSE 3F 31
WOODHOUSE CARR 2F 31
WOODHOUSE CLIFF 1E 31
Woodhouse Cliff LS6: Leeds 1E 31
Woodhouse Cl. WF3: E Ard 5F 57
Woodhouse Flats *LS2: Leeds* *2E 31*
(off St Mark's St.)
WOODHOUSE HILL 5A 42
Woodhouse Hill Av. LS10: Leeds 5A 42
Woodhouse Hill Gro. LS10: Leeds 5A 42
Woodhouse Hill Pl. LS10: Leeds 5A 42
Woodhouse Hill Rd. LS10: Leeds 5A 42
(not continuous)
Woodhouse La. LS1: Leeds 1D 4 (4F 31)
LS2: Leeds 1C 4 (2E 31)
WF3: E Ard, Kirk 6F 57
Woodhouse Sq. LS3: Leeds 2B 4 (5E 31)
Woodhouse St. LS6: Leeds 2E 31
WOODKIRK 4B 56
Woodkirk Av. WF3: Ting 3A 56
Woodkirk Gdns. WF12: Dew 5A 56
Woodkirk Gro. WF3: Ting 3B 56
Woodland Av. LS26: Swil 6G 45
Woodland Cl. LS15: Leeds 5C 34
Woodland Ct. LS8: Leeds 6B 22
Woodland Cres. LS26: Rothw 3F 53
LS26: Swil 6G 45
Woodland Cft. LS18: H'fth 1C 18
Woodland Dr. LS7: Leeds 4H 21
LS10: Leeds 5B 52
LS26: Swil 6F 45
Woodland Gro. LS7: Leeds 1A 32
LS26: Swil 6G 45
Woodland Hill LS15: Leeds 5B 34
Woodland La. LS7: Leeds 4H 21
Woodland Mt. LS7: Leeds 1A 32
Woodland Pk. LS26: Oul 4C 54
Woodland Pk. Rd. LS6: Leeds 6C 20
Woodland Ri. LS15: Leeds 5C 34
Woodland Rd. LS15: Leeds 5B 34
Woodlands LS17: Leeds 1A 22
WF3: E Ard 4G 57
Woodlands, The *LS26: Oul* *4C 54*
(off Farrer La.)
Woodlands Av. LS28: Stan 4E 27
Woodlands Cl. BD10: B'frd 2B 16
WF3: E Ard 4G 57
Woodlands Ct. LS16: Leeds 2H 19
LS28: Pud 2F 37
Woodlands Dr. BD10: B'frd 2B 16
LS19: Raw 1C 16
LS27: Morl 3F 49
WF3: E Ard 4F 57
Woodlands Fold BD11: Birk 4D 46
Woodlands Gro. LS28: Stan 4E 27
Woodlands Pk. Gro. LS28: Pud 2F 37
Woodlands Pk. Rd. LS28: Pud 2F 37
Woodland Sq. LS12: Leeds 5F 29
Woodlands Ter. LS28: Stan 4E 27
Woodland Ter. LS7: Leeds 4E 21
Woodland Vw. LS7: Leeds 4H 21
LS28: Cal 4C 16
WF3: W Ard 6B 56
Woodland Vs. LS14: Leeds 1D 34
Wood La. LS6: Leeds 6B 20
LS7: Leeds 4G 21
(not continuous)
LS12: Leeds 5D 28
LS12: N Far 5D 38
LS13: Leeds 1C 28
(Bellmount Pl.)
LS13: Leeds 5D 28
(Ring Rd. Farnley)
LS15: Leeds, Scho 6E 25
LS18: H'fth 4C 18
LS26: Rothw 2D 52
LS28: Cal 4D 16
Wood La. Ct. LS6: Leeds 6C 20
Woodlea App. LS6: Leeds 2D 20
LS19: Yead 3B 8
Woodlea Av. LS6: Leeds 2D 20
Woodlea Chase LS6: Leeds 3D 20
Woodlea Cl. LS19: Yead 4B 8
Woodlea Ct. LS6: Leeds 3D 20
LS17: Leeds 5D 14
Woodlea Cft. LS6: Leeds 2D 20
Woodlea Dr. LS6: Leeds 2D 20
LS19: Yead 4B 8
Woodlea Fold LS6: Leeds 2D 20
Woodlea Gdns. LS6: Leeds 2D 20
Woodlea Gth. LS6: Leeds 2D 20
Woodlea Ga. LS6: Leeds 3D 20
Woodlea Grn. LS6: Leeds 2D 20
Woodlea Gro. LS6: Leeds 3D 20
LS11: Leeds *4D 40*
(off Woodlea Mt.)
LS19: Yead 3B 8
Woodlea Hall LS6: Leeds 2D 20
Woodlea Holt LS6: Leeds 2D 20
Woodlea La. LS6: Leeds 2D 20
Woodlea Lawn LS6: Leeds 2D 20
Woodlea Mt. LS11: Leeds 4D 40
LS19: Yead 3B 8
Woodlea Pk. LS6: Leeds 3D 20
Woodlea Pl. LS6: Leeds 2D 20
LS11: Leeds 4E 41
Woodlea Rd. LS19: Yead 3B 8
Woodlea Sq. LS6: Leeds 3D 20
Woodlea St. LS11: Leeds 4D 40
Woodlea Vw. LS6: Leeds 3D 20
LS19: Yead 4B 8
Woodleigh Hall M. LS19: Raw 2F 17
Woodleigh Hall Vw. LS19: Raw 2G 17
WOODLESFORD 2C 54
Woodlesford Station (Rail) 2D 54
Woodliffe Ct. LS7: Leeds 4G 21
Woodliffe Cres. LS7: Leeds 4G 21
Woodliffe Dr. LS7: Leeds 4G 21
Woodman St. LS15: Leeds 5A 34
Woodman Yd. *LS16: Leeds* *5B 20*
(off Otley Rd.)
Wood Moor Ct. LS17: Leeds 3H 13
Wood Mt. LS26: Rothw 3E 53
Woodnook Cl. LS16: Leeds 1D 18
Woodnook Dr. LS16: Leeds 1D 18
Woodnook Gth. LS16: Leeds 1D 18
Woodnook Rd. LS16: Leeds 6D 10
Wood Nook Ter. LS28: Stan 4E 27
WOOD ROW 6H 55
Wood Row LS26: Meth 6H 55
Woodrow Cres. LS26: Meth 6G 55
Woodside LS26: Meth 6G 55
Woodside Av. LS4: Leeds 3A 30
LS7: Leeds 4D 20
Woodside Cl. LS27: Morl 3G 49
Woodside Ct. LS16: Leeds 2F 19
LS18: H'fth *3E 19*
(off Broadgate La.)
LS18: H'fth 3E 19
(Tanhouse Hill)
Woodside Dr. LS27: Morl 2G 49
Woodside Gdns. LS27: Morl 2G 49
Woodside Hill Cl. LS18: H'fth 3E 19
Woodside La. LS27: Morl 2G 49
Woodside Lawn LS12: Leeds 6D 28
Woodside M. LS7: Leeds 4D 20
Woodside Pk. Av. LS18: H'fth 3D 18
Woodside Pk. Dr. LS18: H'fth 3D 18
Woodside Pl. LS4: Leeds 3A 30
Woodside Ter. LS4: Leeds 3A 30
Woodside Vw. LS4: Leeds 2A 30
LS10: Leeds 5A 52
WF3: Loft 3D 58
Woodsley Grn. LS6: Leeds 3D 30
Woodsley Rd. LS2: Leeds 4C 30
LS3: Leeds 4C 30
LS6: Leeds 4C 30
Woodsley Ter. LS2: Leeds 1A 4 (4E 31)
Woods Row LS28: Stan 4G 27
Woodstock Cl. LS16: Leeds 6B 12
Wood St. LS18: H'fth 1C 18
LS27: Morl 4F 49
WF3: E Ard 3H 57
Woodthorne Cft. LS17: Leeds 5C 14
Woodvale Cl. BD4: B'frd 2A 36
Woodvale Ter. LS18: H'fth 4D 18
Wood Vw. LS27: Chur 1B 50
Woodview BD11: Drig 2F 47
Woodview Cl. LS18: H'fth 1C 18
Woodview Ct. LS14: Leeds 1D 34
Woodview Gro. LS11: Leeds 5F 41
Woodview M. LS14: Leeds 6D 24
Woodview Mt. LS11: Leeds 5F 41
Woodview Pl. LS11: Leeds 5F 41
Woodview Rd. LS11: Leeds 5F 41
Woodview St. LS11: Leeds 5F 41
Wood Vw. Ter. LS27: Chur 1B 50
Woodview Ter. LS11: Leeds 5F 41
Woodville Av. LS18: H'fth 3D 18
Woodville Ct. LS8: Leeds 2D 22
Woodville Cres. LS18: H'fth 2E 19
Woodville Gro. LS10: Leeds 6A 42
LS18: H'fth 3D 18
Woodville Mt. LS10: Leeds 6A 42
Woodville Pl. LS18: H'fth 2E 19
Woodville Sq. LS10: Leeds 6A 42
Woodville St. LS18: H'fth 3E 19
Woodville Ter. LS18: H'fth 2D 18
Wood Vine St. LS28: Stan 4E 27
Woodway LS18: H'fth 4C 18
Woodway Dr. LS18: H'fth 4C 18
Woolcombers Way BD4: B'frd 2A 36
Wooler Av. LS11: Leeds 5E 41
Wooler Dr. LS11: Leeds 5E 41
Wooler Gro. LS11: Leeds 5E 41
Wooler Pl. LS11: Leeds 5D 40
Wooler Rd. LS11: Leeds 5D 40
Wooler St. LS11: Leeds 5D 40
Woolford Way WF3: Loft 5F 59
Woollin Av. WF3: W Ard 6C 56
Woollin Cres. WF3: W Ard 5C 56
Worcester Av. LS10: Leeds 5B 52
Worcester Cl. WF3: E Ard 2G 57
Worcester Dr. LS10: Leeds 5B 52
Wordsworth Ct. LS26: Oul 6C 54
Wordsworth Dr. LS26: Oul 6C 54
Wordsworth Gro. WF3: S'ley 6G 59
Works, The 2H 41
World's End LS19: Yead 2E 9
Wormald Lea *BD4: B'frd* *4A 36*
(off Kirkwall Dr.)
Wormald Row LS2: Leeds 3E 5 (5G 31)
Worrall St. LS27: Morl 6F 49
Worsted Ho. LS9: Leeds 6H 5

A-Z Leeds 111

WORTLEY 1A 40
Wortley Hgts. LS12: Leeds 1B 40
Wortley La. LS11: Leeds 1D 40
    LS12: Leeds 1D 40
Wortley Moor La. LS12: Leeds 1H 39
Wortley Moor La. Trad. Est.
    LS12: Leeds 1H 39
Wortley Moor Pde. LS12: Leeds 6G 29
Wortley Moor Rd. LS12: Leeds 6G 29
Wortley Pk. LS12: Leeds 1B 40
Wortley Rd. LS12: Leeds 6G 29
Wortley Towers LS12: Leeds 1C 40
Wrangthorn Av. LS6: Leeds 2D 30
Wrangthorn Pl. LS6: Leeds 2D 30
Wrangthorn Ter. LS6: Leeds 2D 30
Wrenbury Av. LS16: Leeds 4D 10
Wrenbury Cres. LS16: Leeds 4D 10
Wrenbury Gro. LS16: Leeds 4E 11
Wren Dr. LS27: Morl 6B 50
Wycliffe Cl. LS13: Leeds 6F 17
Wycliffe Dr. LS17: Leeds 1H 21
Wycliffe Rd. LS13: Leeds 6F 17
Wycombe Grn. BD4: B'frd 4A 36
Wykebeck Av. LS9: Leeds 6F 33
Wykebeck Cres. LS9: Leeds 5F 33
Wykebeck Gdns. LS9: Leeds 5F 33
Wykebeck Gro. LS9: Leeds 5F 33
Wykebeck Mt. LS9: Leeds 6F 33
Wykebeck Pl. LS9: Leeds 5G 33
Wykebeck Rd. LS9: Leeds 5F 33
Wykebeck Sq. LS9: Leeds 5F 33
Wykebeck St. LS9: Leeds 5F 33
Wykebeck Ter. LS9: Leeds 5F 33
Wykebeck Valley Rd. LS9: Leeds 3F 33
Wykebeck Vw. LS9: Leeds 5F 33
Wyncliffe Ct. LS17: Leeds 1G 21
Wyncliffe Gdns. LS17: Leeds 1H 21

Wynford Av. LS16: Leeds 2H 19
Wynford Gro. LS16: Leeds 2H 19
Wynford Mt. LS16: Leeds 2G 19
Wynford Ri. LS16: Leeds 2G 19
Wynford Ter. LS16: Leeds 2G 19
Wynyard Dr. LS27: Morl 5F 49
Wyther Av. LS5: Leeds 2F 29
Wyther Dr. LS5: Leeds 2G 29
Wyther Grn. LS5: Leeds 2G 29
Wyther La. LS5: Leeds 2F 29
Wyther La. Ind. Est. LS5: Leeds 2G 29
Wyther Pk. Av. LS12: Leeds 4F 29
Wyther Pk. Cl. LS12: Leeds 4F 29
Wyther Pk. Cres. LS12: Leeds 4F 29
Wyther Pk. Gro. LS12: Leeds 3F 29
Wyther Pk. Hill LS12: Leeds 3F 29
                        (not continuous)
Wyther Pk. Mt. LS12: Leeds 4F 29
                        (not continuous)
Wyther Pk. Pl. LS12: Leeds 3F 29
Wyther Pk. Rd. LS12: Leeds 4E 29
Wyther Pk. Sq. LS12: Leeds 3E 29
Wyther Pk. St. LS12: Leeds 4F 29
Wyther Pk. Ter. LS12: Leeds 4F 29
Wyther Pk. Vw. LS12: Leeds 3F 29

Y

Yarn St. LS10: Leeds 2A 42
Yarra Ct. LS27: Gil 2D 48
YEADON 2D 8
Yeadon Airport Ind. Est. LS19: Yead 1G 9
Yeadon Moor Rd. LS19: Yead 3G 9
                        (Bayton La.)
    LS19: Yead 2A 10
                        (Scotland La.)

Yeadon Row LS18: H'fth 4C 18
                        (off Regent Av.)
Yeadon Stoops LS19: Yead 3F 9
                        (off Bayton La.)
Yewdall Rd. LS13: Leeds 6F 17
Yew Tree Ct. LS17: Leeds 6E 13
Yew Tree Dr. LS26: Wood 3E 55
Yew Tree La. LS15: Leeds 6E 35
York Ga. LS21: Otley 1G 7
York Gate Garden 4B 12
York Ho. LS28: Fars 3F 27
                        (off South Dr.)
York Pl. LS1: Leeds 4C 4 (5F 31)
York Rd. LS9: Leeds 5A 32
                        (not continuous)
    LS14: Leeds 4G 33
    LS15: Leeds, T'ner 3E 25
Yorkshire County Cricket Club 1B 30
Yorkshire Cricket School 1B 30
YORKSHIRE EYE HOSPITAL 4A 16
York St. LS2: Leeds 5G 5 (6H 31)
    LS9: Leeds 5G 5 (6H 31)
York Towers LS9: Leeds 5C 32
York Towers Pde. LS9: Leeds 5C 32
                        (off York Towers)

Z

Zermatt Gro. LS7: Leeds 5G 21
Zermatt Mt. LS7: Leeds 5G 21
Zermatt St. LS7: Leeds 5H 21
Zermatt Ter. LS7: Leeds 5H 21
Zetland Pl. LS8: Leeds 2B 32
Zoar St. LS27: Morl 5G 49

SAFETY CAMERA INFORMATION

Safety camera locations are publicised by the Safer Roads Partnership which operates them in order to encourage drivers to comply with speed limits at these sites. It is the driver's absolute responsibility to be aware of and to adhere to speed limits at all times.

By showing this safety camera information it is the intention of Geographers' A-Z Map Company Ltd., to encourage safe driving and greater awareness of speed limits and vehicle speed. Data accurate at time of printing.

Printed and bound in the United Kingdom by Gemini Press Ltd., Shoreham-by-Sea, West Sussex
Printed on materials from a sustainable source